T0330329

Investor Behavior

Investor Behavior

The Psychology of Financial Planning and Investing

EDITORS

H. KENT BAKER
VICTOR RICCIARDI

WILEY

Library of Congress Cataloging-in-Publication Data:

Baker, H. Kent (Harold Kent), 1944-
  Investor behavior : the psychology of financial planning and investing /
H. Kent Baker and Victor Ricciardi.
     pages cm. — (Kolb series)
  Includes index.
  ISBN 978-1-118-49298-7 (cloth); ISBN 978-1-118-72701-0 (ebk);
  ISBN 978-1-118-72702-7 (ebk)
  1. Investments—Psychological aspects.   2. Finance—Psychological aspects.
 I. Ricciardi, Victor. II. Title.
  HG4515.15.B34 2014
  332.601'9—dc23
                                                          2013027577

Contents

PART THREE

Financial Planning Concepts

CHAPTER 11

Policy-Based Financial Planning: Decision Rules for a Changing World   191
Dave Yeske and Elissa Buie

CHAPTER 12

Financial Counseling and Coaching   209
John E. Grable and Kristy L. Archuleta

CHAPTER 13

Financial Therapy: De-Biasing and Client Behaviors   227
Joseph W. Goetz and Jerry E. Gale

CHAPTER 17
Knowing Your Numbers: A Scorecard Approach to Improved Medical and Financial Outcomes   307
Talya Miron-Shatz and Stephanie Gati

PART FOUR

Investor Psychology

CHAPTER 18
Risk Perception and Risk Tolerance   327
Victor Ricciardi and Douglas Rice

Acknowledgments

Leonard Feather, the British-born jazz pianist, composer, and producer who was best known for his music journalism and other writing, once wrote "Finishing a good book is like leaving a good friend." Whether he was speaking about finishing a book in the sense of reading or writing it is unclear. In either case, his sentiments are correct. As coeditors, we hope that you think *Investor Behavior: The Psychology of Financial Planning and Investing* is a "good book." If so, many people merit credit. Foremost among them are the chapter writers who shared their knowledge and devoted countless hours to writing and revising their work. To them, we owe our special thanks. Also, the professional team at John Wiley & Sons deserves our appreciation for exhibiting a high degree of professionalism from inception through publication. We also want to recognize the support provided by the Kogod School of Business at American University and the Business Management Department at Goucher College. The editors dedicate this book to Linda Baker and Vito and Loretta Ricciardi. In particular, Professor Ricciardi would like to thank his parents for the support, encouragement, and love throughout his lifetime that made this book possible. He also acknowledges and thanks those who mentored him in pursuing a career as a finance professor: Igor Tomic, Anoop Rai, Hank Pruden, Bob Olsen, Hugh Schwartz, David Hua, Hamid Shomali, and Mike Jensen.

Foundations of
Investor Behavior

CHAPTER 1

Investor Behavior: An Overview

H. Kent Baker
University Professor of Finance, Kogod School of Business, American University
Victor Ricciardi
Assistant Professor of Financial Management, Department of
Business Management, Goucher College

INTRODUCTION

In the 1990s, the terms *behavioral finance* and *behavioral economics* started to appear in academic journals for finance professors, practitioner publications for investment professionals, investing magazines for novice investors, and everyday newspapers read by the general public (Ricciardi and Simon 2000). The foundation of behavioral finance and the subtopic of investor behavior, however, can be traced back throughout financial history in events such as the speculative behavior during tulip mania in the 1600s. Books published in the 1800s and early 1900s about psychology and investing marked the beginning of the theoretical basis for today's theories and concepts about investor behavior (Ricciardi 2006). Finance and the role of money are fundamental underpinnings of many important events throughout history (Ferguson 2008) and the development of financial innovations (Goetzmann and Rouwenhorst 2005). For example, Bernstein (1996) provides an extensive time line of risk throughout history and its application in the world of finance. Another important work in this arena is Rubinstein (2006), who depicts a historical anthology of investment theory. In recent times, the Internet stock market bubble of the late 1990s and the financial crisis of 2007 and 2008 demonstrate the importance of understanding investment behavior (Reinhart and Rogoff 2011).

Relevant Books in the History of Finance and Investment Thought

Understanding the history of finance and the development of investment theory is important for all types of investors. Goetzmann and Rouwenhorst (2005), Rubinstein (2006), and Ferguson (2008) offer extensive discussions of books and other publications in financial history and investment theory. The next section provides a discussion of important books in the history of finance and the natural progression of understanding investor theory and behavior. Exhibit 1.1 provides a chronological timeline of a sample of noteworthy books in financial history and investment theory from 1841 to 1978. This list of books is merely illustrative of classic or seminal works.

EXHIBIT 1.1   A Sample of Relevant Books in Financial History and Investment Theory

Original Publication Date	Author(s)/ Editor(s)	Title	Subject Matter
1841	Charles Mackay	*Extraordinary Popular Delusions and the Madness of Crowds*	Crowd psychology, panics, and financial schemes
1895	Gustave Le Bon	*The Crowd: A Study of the Popular Mind*	Group psychology
1903	Edward Meade	*Trust Finance: A Study of the Genesis, Organization, and Management of Industrial Combinations*	The role of trust in finance
1911	Garet Garrett	*Where the Money Grows and Anatomy of the Bubble*	Bubbles
1912	George Selden	*Psychology of the Stock Market*	Investor psychology
1922	William Hamilton	*The Stock Market Barometer*	Dow Jones investment approach
1923	Edwin Lefèvre	*Reminiscences of a Stock Operator*	Trader psychology
1924	Merryle Rukeyser	*The Common Sense of Money and Investments*	Investment and financial issues
1930	Philip Carret	*The Art of Speculation*	Speculative behavior
1931	Frederick Allen	*Only Yesterday: An Informal History of the 1920s*	Historical perspective of the 1920s
1934	Benjamin Graham and David Dodd	*Security Analysis*	Value investing
1935	Gerald M. Loeb	*The Battle for Investment Survival*	Investing in different securities and markets
1938	John B. Williams	*The Theory of Investment Value*	Financial securities valuation
1940	Fred Schwed	*Where Are the Customers' Yachts? or a Good Hard Look at Wall Street*	Financial service issues and practices
1949	Benjamin Graham	*The Intelligent Investor*	Value investing
1951	Donald Cressey	*Other People's Money: A Study in the Social Psychology of Embezzlement*	Violation of financial trust
1954	John Kenneth Galbraith	*The Great Crash of 1929*	Stock market crash of 1929
1954	Humphrey B. Neill	*The Art of Contrary Thinking*	Popular opinion and group behavior

EXHIBIT 1.1 (*Continued*)

Original Publication Date	Author(s)/ Editor(s)	Title	Subject Matter
1957	William Sargeant	*Stock Market Behavior: A Descriptive Guidebook for the New Investor*	Stock market psychology
1958	Philip Fisher	*Common Stocks and Uncommon Profits*	Investing in common stocks
1969	John Brooks	*Once in Golconda: A True Drama of Wall Street 1920–1938*	The investment history of the 1920s
1970	Mark Appleman	*The Winning Habit: How Your Personality Makes You a Winner or a Loser in the Stock Market*	Investor personality and individual behavior
1970	William Scheinman	*Why Most Investors Are Mostly Wrong Most of the Time*	Bad investment decisions by financial advisors
1973	John Brooks	*The Go-Go Years: The Drama and Crashing Finale of Wall Street's Bullish 60s*	The investment history of the 1960s
1973	Burton Malkiel	*A Random Walk Down Wall Street*	Random walk theory of stock prices
1977	David Dreman	*Psychology and the Stock Market Investment Strategy beyond Random Walk*	Investor psychology and group behavior
1978	Charles Kindleberger	*Manias, Panics and Crashes: A History of Financial Crisis*	Historical financial crises

Note: This exhibit provides a chronological timeline of a sample of relevant books in financial history and investment theory from 1841 to 1978. These books cover a wide range of subject matter including: crowd psychology, group behavior, individual behavior panics, bubbles, crashes, speculative behavior, investor psychology, trader psychology, investment strategies and theories, financial mistrust, and investor personality.

Period: 1841 to 1912 Initially published in 1841, *Extraordinary Popular Delusions and the Madness of Crowds* (MacKay 1980) depicts the role of bubbles and panics that is still applicable for investor psychology. Published in the late 1800s, *The Crowd: A Study of the Popular Mind* (Le Bon 1982) describes the role of group behavior in different environments and markets. Published in 1903, *Trust Finance: A Study of the Genesis, Organization, and Management of Industrial Combinations* (Meade 2003) describes the importance of trust in a wide range of areas including corporate finance, financial services, and investments. *Where the Money Grows and Anatomy of the Bubble* (Garrett 1998), published in 1911, presents the role of different stakeholders involved in the investment management process on Wall Street. *The Psychology of the Stock Market* (Selden 1996), published in 1912, represents one of the first books that applied psychology to the decision-making process of investors. Selden's book describes the behavioral and emotional issues that influence traders and investors in the stock market.

Period: 1922 to 1938   Published in 1922, *The Stock Market Barometer* (Hamilton 1998) discloses the approach known as the *Dow Theory*, which is based on stock price movements as a predictive investment tool. Published in 1923, *Reminiscences of a Stock Operator* (Lefèvre 1994) depicts the life of a Wall Street trader and different approaches to trading in the markets. The author interviews traders to build the portrait of the fictional stock trader in the novel. *The Common Sense of Money and Investments* (Rukeyser 1999), published in 1924, provides a discussion of various personal finance and investment topics that are still relevant. Published in 1930, *The Art of Speculation* (Carret 1997) offers a thorough discussion of the speculation process involving financial markets and investment products. *Only Yesterday: An Informal History of the 1920s* (Allen 2010), first published in 1931, provides a general narrative description of life during the 1920s and also examines that decade's bull market, stock market crash, and the early years of the Great Depression.

In 1934, Graham and Dodd (1996) published *Security Analysis* in which they developed the foundation for value investing by identifying undervalued companies based on accounting information and financial statements. *The Battle for Investment Survival* (Loeb 2010), published in 1935, provides an extensive approach for investing in all types of financial securities and markets. Published in 1938, *The Theory of Investment Value* (Williams 1997) describes how to value financial assets based on accounting data such as cash flow and profits. In particular, this approach uses the distribution of dividends as forecasting the stock price of a company known as *stock valuation*.

Period: 1940 to 1958   First published in 1940, *Where Are the Customers' Yachts? or a Good Hard Look at Wall Street* (Schwed 2006) depicts the questionable investment practices of Wall Street firms toward their clients. In 1949, Graham (2005) published *The Intelligent Investor,* which reveals the approach known as *value investing* (i.e., a method for evaluating and identifying stocks that an investor considers underpriced based on different types of accounting or financial information). Today, value investing is one of the most important investing strategies. Published in 1951, *Other People's Money: A Study in the Social Psychology of Embezzlement* (Cressey 1951) uses psychological theories to explain why individuals commit financial crimes and violate the trust of the public. Galbraith's (2009) *The Great Crash 1929*, published in 1954, serves as a reminder even today of how financial history repeats itself in understanding the financial crisis of 2007 and 2008.

Other notable books during this period include *The Art of Contrary Thinking* (Neill 1992), published in 1954, which describes why consensus investor group decision-making is sometimes wrong and how investors can use contrary strategies or trends to profit in the stock market. Published in 1957, *Stock Market Behavior: A Descriptive Guidebook for the New Investor* (Sargeant 1957) provides a perspective of the psychology underlying the stock market for novice investors. In 1958, Fisher (1997) published *Common Stocks and Uncommon Profits*, in which he reveals how to evaluate a firm's business prospects and financial health based on accounting data and financial statement information.

Period: 1969 to 1970   In the book first published in 1969, *Once in Golconda: A True Drama of Wall Street 1920–1938* (Brooks 1999a) describes the time of economic expansion of the 1920s, the crash of 1929, and the aftermath of the 1930s Great Depression. *The Winning Habit: How Your Personality Makes You a Winner or a Loser in the Stock Market* (Appleman 1970) discloses an array of different personality types and connects them to how investors make decisions about stock investing. Published in 1970, *Why Most Investors are Mostly Wrong Most of the Time* (Scheinman 1991) describes the author's perspective of crowd psychology and the role of contrary opinions within the stock market during the 1960s.

Period: 1973 to 1978 In 1973, Brooks (1999b) authored *The Go-Go Years: The Drama and Crashing Finale of Wall Street's Bullish 60s,* in which he describes the speculative behavior during the bull market of the 1960s and the stock market crash in 1970. Malkiel (1973) published his highly popular A *Random Walk Down Wall Street* in which he discloses the importance of the *random walk theory.* Malkiel contends that investors cannot outperform stock market indexes on a regular basis because prices are random. Dreman's (1977) *Psychology and the Stock Market: Investment Strategy beyond Random Walk* depicts the importance of crowd psychology and group behavior within the stock market by highlighting topics such as bubbles, the social psychology of groups, groupthink, and herd behavior. This book also offers a counter argument to the random walk theory and efficient market hypothesis. First published in 1978, *Manias, Panics and Crashes: A History of Financial Crisis* (Kindleberger 1996) provides an extensive financial history of bubbles, frauds, crashes, contagions, and crises.

Investor Behavior

What is investor behavior? The field of investor behavior attempts to understand and explain investor decisions by combining the topics of psychology and investing on a micro level (i.e., the decision process of individuals and groups) and a macro perspective (i.e., the role of financial markets). The decision-making process of investors incorporates both a quantitative (objective) and qualitative (subjective) aspect that is based on the specific features of the investment product or financial service. Investor behavior examines the cognitive factors (mental processes) and affective (emotional) issues that individuals, financial experts, and traders reveal during the financial planning and investment management process. In practice, individuals make judgments and decisions that are based on past events, personal beliefs, and preferences.

Since 1995, an increasing number of books on investor behavior have been published in tandem with the emerging research literature within the overall discipline of behavioral finance. Exhibit 1.2 provides a chronological time line of investor behavior books published between 1995 and 2012. This compilation of books covers different subject matter including: stock market inefficiencies (Haugen 1995; Shleifer 2000), stock market psychology (Warneryd 2001; Schindler 2007), speculative behavior (Shiller 2000), anomalies (Zacks 2011), neuroeconomics and neurofinance (Peterson 2007; Zweig 2007), money behaviors (Furnham and Argyle 1998), money disorders (Klontz and Klontz 2009), investor personality (Pompian 2012), behavioral investment management (De Brouwer 2012; Davies and de Servigny 2012), psychological trading strategies (Lifson and Geist 1999), trader psychology (Oberlechner 2004; Fenton-O'Creevy et al. 2005; Shull 2012), investor emotions (Tuckett and Taffler 2012), and investor behavior or psychology (Belsky and Gilovich 1999; Shefrin 2000; Nofsinger 2002; Geist 2003;

Pompian 2006; Montier 2007; Baker and Nofsinger 2010; Wood 2010; Statman 2011). This collection of books and other academic literature, such as published academic papers, working papers, conference presentations, and dissertations, serves as a reference point for developing the current content in this book in order to identify the most important emerging topics in investor behavior and psychology.

The importance of documenting the past and current research is to assist individual investors and their financial advisors about these biases and improve the decision-making process in selecting investment services, products, and strategies. As a result of the financial crisis of 2007 and 2008, the discipline of psychology began to focus even more on the financial decision-making process of individuals. This renewed interest by the social sciences and business disciplines has spurred new research on investor behavior including financial therapy, money counseling, financial psychology, consumer finance, investor personality, and household finance.

EXHIBIT 1.2   A Sample of Investor Behavior Books Since 1995

Original Publication Date	Author(s)/Editor(s)	Title	Subject Matter
1995	Robert Haugen	*The New Finance: The Case Against Efficient Markets*	Stock market inefficiencies
1998	Adrian Furnham and Michael Argyle	*The Psychology of Money*	Money behaviors
1999	Gary Belsky and Thomas Gilovich	*Why Smart People Make Big Money Mistakes and How to Correct Them: Lessons from the New Science of Behavioral Economics*	Various topics of behavioral finance and investor behavior
1999	Lawrence Lifson and Richard Geist	*The Psychology of Investing*	Psychological trading strategies
2000	Hersh Shefrin	*Beyond Greed and Fear: Understanding Behavioral Finance and the Psychology of Investing*	Investor psychology
2000	Robert Shiller	*Irrational Exuberance*	Investor speculative bubble of the 1990s
2000	Andrei Shleifer	*Inefficient Markets: An Introduction to Behavioral Finance*	Stock market inefficiencies
2001	Karl-Erik Warneryd	*Stock Market Psychology: How People Value and Trade Stocks*	Psychology of stock investors
2002	John Nofsinger	*The Psychology of Investing*	Investment behavior
2003	Richard Geist	*Investor Therapy: A Psychologist and Investing Guru Tells You How to Out-Psych Wall Street*	Investor psychology

EXHIBIT 1.2 *(Continued)*

Original Publication Date	Author(s)/Editor(s)	Title	Subject Matter
2004	Thomas Oberlechner	*The Psychology of the Foreign Exchange Market*	Trader psychology
2005	Mark Fenton-O'Creevy, Nigel Nicholson, Emma Soane, and Paul Willman	*Traders: Risks, Decisions, and Management in Financial Markets*	Trader psychology
2006	Michael Pompian	*Behavioral Finance and Wealth Management: How to Build Optimal Portfolios that Account for Investor Biases*	Individual investor behavior
2007	James Montier	*Behavioral Investing: A Practitioner's Guide to Applying Behavioral Finance*	Investor psychology
2007	Richard Peterson	*Inside the Investor's Brain: The Power of Mind over Money*	Neurofinance and investor decisions
2007	Mark Schindler	*Rumors in Financial Markets: Insights into Behavioral Finance*	Stock market psychology
2007	Jason Zweig	*Your Money and Your Brain: How the New Science of Neuroeconomics Can Help Make You Rich*	Neuroeconomics and investor psychology
2009	Brad Klontz and Ted Klontz	*Mind over Money: Overcoming the Money Disorders That Threaten Our Financial Health*	Financial trauma, money disorders
2010	H. Kent Baker and John Nofsinger	*Behavioral Finance: Investors, Corporations, and Markets*	Psychological concepts, investor biases, investor behavior, and social influences
2010	Arnold Wood	*Behavioral Finance and Investment Management*	Investor psychology
2011	Meir Statman	*What Investors Really Want: Know What Drives Investor Behavior and Make Smarter Financial Decisions*	Individual investor psychology
2011	Leonard Zacks	*The Handbook of Equity Market Anomalies: Translating Market Inefficiences into Effective Investment Strategies*	Investor anomalies

(continued)

EXHIBIT 1.2   (*Continued*)

Original Publication Date	Author(s)/Editor(s)	Title	Subject Matter
2012	Philippe De Brouwer	*Maslowian Portfolio Theory: A Coherent Approach to Strategic Asset Allocation*	Individual psychology and behavioral portfolio decisions
2012	Greg Davies and Arnaud de Servigny	*Behavioral Investment Management: An Efficient Alternative to Modern Portfolio Theory*	Individual investor behavior and decisions
2012	Michael Pompian	*Behavioral Finance and Investor Types: Managing Behavior to Make Better Investment Decisions*	Investor personality
2012	Denise Shull	*Market Mind Games: A Radical Psychology of Investing, Trading and Risk*	Trader psychology
2012	David Tuckett and Richard Taffler	*Fund Management: An Emotional Finance Perspective*	Emotional aspects of investing

Note: This exhibit provides a chronological time line of a sample of investor psychology books for the time period between 1995 and 2012. This collection of books covers different topics including: stock market inefficiencies, investor behavior, speculative behavior, stock market psychology, individual and group psychology, investor personality, money disorders, neurofinance, anomalies, and behavioral investment management.

Purpose of the Book

This book's main purpose is to provide readers with the emerging theoretical trends about investment behavior within the ever-changing and growing financial services and investment management industry. Readers of *Investor Behavior—The Psychology of Financial Planning and Investing* will gain an in-depth understanding of the major types and the latest trends within the field of investor behavior. The book features empirical evidence and current literature about each investment issue. Cited research studies are presented in a straightforward manner focusing on the comprehension of study findings, rather than on the details of mathematical frameworks. Authors contributing chapters consist of a mix of academics and practitioners.

Distinctive Features of the Book

Investor Behavior—The Psychology of Financial Planning and Investing has the following distinctive features.

- The book provides a detailed discussion of investor behavior including empirical evidence and practice within the various topics covered. It attempts not only to blend the conceptual world of scholars with the pragmatic view of practitioners, but also to synthesize relevant research studies including recent developments in a succinct and clear manner.

- The book contains contributions from numerous authors, which assures a variety of perspectives and a rich interplay of ideas.
- When discussing the results of empirical studies that link theory and practice, the objective is to distill them to their essential content so that they are understandable to readers. Theoretical and mathematical derivations are included to the extent that they may be necessary and useful to readers.
- The end of each chapter contains four to six discussion questions that help to reinforce key concepts with guideline answers presented at the end of the book. This feature should be especially important to faculty and students using the book in classes.

Intended Audience

The book should be of interest to various groups including academics, practitioners, investors, and students. Academics can use this book not only in their undergraduate and graduate investment courses but also to understand the various strands of research emerging from this area. The book can help practitioners navigate through the key areas in investor behavior. Individual and institutional investors can use the book to expand their knowledge base. They can also apply the concepts contained within the book to the management of their portfolios. The book can serve as an introduction to students interested in investor behavior. Finally, *Investor Behavior—The Psychology of Financial Planning and Investing* can be of interest to members of such organizations as the Academy of Behavioral Finance & Economics, Financial Therapy Association, Association for Financial Counseling and Planning Education, Financial Planning Association, The CFA Institute, Academy of Financial Services, Society for the Advancement of Behavioral Economics (SABE), American Accounting Association: Accounting, Behavior, and Organizations Section (Behavioral Accounting Group), International Association for Research in Economic Psychology (IAREP), and Society of Judgment and Decision Making.

ORGANIZATION OF THE BOOK

The remaining 29 chapters are organized into six sections. A brief synopsis of each chapter by section follows.

Part I: Foundations of Investor Behavior

Besides this introduction, Part I consists of two other chapters. Chapter 2 focuses on the basic principles of traditional (standard) finance and behavioral finance. Chapter 3 examines behavioral economic approaches to decision-making.

Chapter 2: Traditional and Behavioral Finance (Lucy F. Ackert)   The purpose of this chapter is to compare and contrast traditional and behavioral finance. In traditional finance, which has been the dominant paradigm for several decades, investors make rational choices leading to maximizing expected utility. The fundamental issues of traditional finance are classical decision theory, rationality, risk aversion, model portfolio theory (MPT), the capital asset pricing model (CAPM), and the efficient market hypothesis (EMH). However, evidence shows that many of the assumptions and findings associated with traditional finance are invalid. Thus, behavioral finance researchers turned to observed behaviors to develop models that describe how investors actually reach their decisions. Behavioral finance uses insights from the social sciences to better understand the investor behavior of individuals, groups, and markets. Among the foundation topics in behavioral finance are behavioral decision theory, bounded rationality, prospect theory, framing, heuristics, overconfidence, regret theory, and mental accounting. The emerging areas of research are behavioral portfolio theory, the behavioral asset pricing model (BAPM), and the adaptive markets hypothesis.

Chapter 3: Behavioral Economics, Thinking Processes, Decision-Making, and Investment Behavior (Morris Altman)

This chapter provides a critical review of behavioral economic approaches to decision-making with a focus on the thinking processes of investors. It discusses the bounded rationality approach to decision-making as compared to the errors and biases approach for better understanding decision-making processes and outcomes. The latter focuses on the importance of cognitive illusions and biases whereas the former pays more attention to the optimality of institutional design and the limited information processing capacity of the human brain. Both approaches attempt to make sense of and explain why decision-making outcomes tend to be inconsistent with the predictions of the conventional economics wisdom, especially regarding the efficient market hypothesis. The chapter also extends the analyses of the behavioral understanding of decision-making, especially from the bounded rationality modeling perspective.

Part II: Personal Finance Issues

Part II consists of Chapters 4 through 10. The section explores such important areas as financial literacy and education (Chapter 4) and household investment decisions (Chapter 5). It also examines the role of personality traits (Chapter 6), demographic and socioeconomic factors (Chapter 7), and religion (Chapter 8) on investor behavior. The final two chapters investigate money and happiness (Chapter 9) and motivation and satisfaction (Chapter 10).

Chapter 4: Financial Literacy and Education (Michael S. Finke and Sandra J. Huston)

Financial literacy is a form of human capital that includes knowledge and skills related to personal finances including mathematical ability, knowledge of financial instruments and financial theory, and the ability to apply knowledge effectively. This chapter reviews how financial literacy has been conceptualized and measured in the literature. Financial literacy is related to many positive financial outcomes. Newer studies focus on identifying the pathways between financial literacy and asset accumulation, portfolio selection, and credit choice. Evidence shows that financial education can improve financial literacy and decision quality, but also questions whether financial literacy education is effective or socially efficient. Low levels of financial literacy among consumers suggest a need for increased high school financial literacy education and policies that provide simplified disclosure and high quality defaults.

Chapter 5: Household Investment Decisions (Vicki L. Bogan) Within the area of finance, most basic theoretical models do not fully describe true household investment decision-making behavior. This is due in large part to the fact that most traditional finance models are based on the assumptions that financial markets operate without frictions and that all people make perfectly rational decisions. Yet, when considering how academic models are applied in the real world, these fundamental assumptions do not always hold. This chapter discusses how market frictions and specific behavioral biases actually influence household investment behaviors.

Chapter 6: Personality Traits (Lucia Fung and Robert B. Durand) Personality captures a person's essence. Understanding one's personality helps explain and predict the decisions an individual makes and what a person will do. This chapter focuses on the predominant structural model of personality—the Five-Factor Model—which encapsulates personality using five higher-order traits: Extraversion, Agreeableness, Conscientiousness, Neuroticism, and Openness to Experience/Intellect. The Five-Factor Model is rooted in biology and is genetically based. Personality traits are a major aspect of risk taking and overconfidence behaviors. Understanding personality can improve decision-making if it helps to regulate and override dispositional tendencies leading to suboptimal outcomes.

Chapter 7: Demographic and Socioeconomic Factors of Investors (James Farrell) Examining the demographic and socioeconomic factors in investor behavior is important to understanding how investors choose their portfolios. The extant literature suggests that men invest more aggressively than women and white investors invest more aggressively than African American investors. The reasons for the differences include income, wealth, age, education, risk preference, and background. Although studies try to explain away the differences attributable to gender and race, these differences persist. The chapter includes theories about how psychological differences help to explain losses and intergenerational transfers of wealth. It also examines recent research on the roles of gender and race in investment preferences. The analysis confirms that white males are the most aggressive investors and African American men take a more active approach to their investments. By contrast, white women tend to default into more conservative investments.

Chapter 8: The Effect of Religion on Financial and Investing Decisions (Walid Mansour and Mouna Jlassi) Religion has a major impact on people's daily life and is closely connected with their economic condition. The purpose of this chapter is to discuss the connection between religion and economic factors and to show how religion affects investment and financing decisions. It focuses on this interplay by emphasizing various corporate and personal facets. For instance, the chapter analyzes the effect of religious beliefs on investors' preferences, risk perception, ethical values, and psychological behavior. This aspect is often missing in academic finance including the behavioral paradigm. Furthermore, the chapter discusses how religious beliefs can conflict with financial theory involving making financial and investing decisions.

Chapter 9: Money and Happiness: Implications for Investor Behavior (Jing Jian Xiao) This chapter provides a synthesis of the research literature on the relationship between money and happiness. Money refers to income and income-related factors. Happiness is typically measured by life satisfaction, but also by daily happiness and living a meaningful life. Based on research evidence, personal income increases happiness to a certain degree in a nonlinear fashion. In the range from low to middle income, income has a strong positive relationship with happiness. From middle to high income levels, the positive association between income and happiness diminishes. People living in richer countries are happier. Unhappiness results from seeking materialist goals. Most research studies examine whether income increases happiness. The emerging academic literature examines the reverse causality and explores whether happier people make more money, which is gaining empirical support. The chapter provides a discussion of the implications of these research findings for investor behavior.

Chapter 10: Motivation and Satisfaction (Lewis J. Altfest)   This chapter attempts to answer the question, "What motivates people and can they be helped to achieve life satisfaction?" It transitions from classical economic theory to behavioral economics, which includes the behavioral life cycle hypothesis, and on to humanistic thoughts. Each theory presents differing views of motivation and satisfaction. The centerpiece of the chapter is Maslow's hierarchy of needs, which ranges from basic needs to highly sophisticated aspirations. Maslow's humanistic emphasis places it in conflict with classical economic beliefs. The chapter presents an approach that strives to integrate classical theory and Maslow-influenced humanism within a personal financial planning framework.

Part III: Financial Planning Concepts

This seven-chapter section begins by discussing policy-based financial planning (Chapter 11). Next, it turns to evolving topics such as financial counseling and coaching (Chapter 12), financial therapy (Chapter 13), and transpersonal economics (Chapter 14). The section then focuses on advising the behavioral investor (Chapter 15) and the contributions of behavioral finance and behavioral economics to retirement planning (Chapter 16). The final chapter in this section discusses how to use a scorecard approach to improve medical and financial outcomes.

Chapter 11: Policy-Based Financial Planning: Decision Rules for a Changing World (Dave Yeske and Elissa Buie)   Financial planning policies are compact decision rules that can act as a touchstone for both clients and their advisors and allow for rapid decision-making in the face of a changing environment. Good policies represent the distillation of client goals and values, as well as the relevant financial planning best practices, in a form that can both anchor the client to a consistent course of action and save the advisor from the necessity of "crunching the numbers" every time a question arises. Evidence suggests that the process of developing policies involving the client is largely associated with higher levels of client trust and relationship commitment. Further, trust and commitment are associated with qualities predictive of a successful financial planning engagement, including higher client satisfaction and retention, with a greater propensity to reveal personal and financial information and to implement planning recommendations.

Chapter 12: Financial Counseling and Coaching (John E. Grable and Kristy L. Archuleta)   Financial counseling is generally conceptualized as a short-term process concerned with helping people change their financial behavior through applied education and guidance. Counseling typically involves helping people clarify issues, explore options, assess alternatives, make decisions, develop strategies, and plan courses of action in an effort to change financial attitudes and behavior. Similarly, financial coaching blends aspects of financial counseling, financial planning, and personal coaching to help clients establish and reach long-term financial goals through directed behavioral change. This chapter discusses the history of financial counseling and financial coaching, theoretical approaches commonly used in financial counseling, and the current state and professional directions of counseling and coaching.

Chapter 13: Financial Therapy: De-Biasing and Client Behaviors (Joseph W. Goetz and Jerry E. Gale) This chapter introduces an emerging field of study and practice called financial therapy. Financial therapy has applications in furthering the knowledge base around money psychology and addressing maladaptive financial beliefs and decisions of individuals and families. In contrast to traditional finance, financial therapy assumes individuals and couples often fail to make the rational financial decisions that lead to expected utility maximization. It also assumes that individuals' financial choices are strongly influenced by their financial socialization, cognitive biases, emotional factors, and their past experiences with money within various social systems. Foundational topics in financial therapy covered in this chapter include the concept and history of financial therapy, theoretical and conceptual frameworks that provide a basis for financial therapy practice and research, and the need for evidence-based financial therapy interventions.

Chapter 14: Transpersonal Economics (Renée M. Snow) The need for economic stability has received considerable attention during the past few years as a result of the severity of the global recession. Financial pathology arises from personal, cultural, and transpersonal influences that comprise belief systems. In turn, these belief systems inform thoughts, emotions, and behaviors. Examining the historical roots of Western misidentification with wealth creates awareness and provides space for new choices. The wisdom tradition of Jainism illustrates the ability to be mindful of the ecology while creating economic prosperity. A study of Certified Financial Planners (CFPs) who scored high in transpersonal awareness reveals the same essential practice and soul recognition as Jains employ. These participants experience higher client retention and job satisfaction rates than those who score lower in transpersonal awareness. This research suggests the possibility of improving economic performance through exploring and implementing practices rooted in transpersonal psychology.

Chapter 15: Advising the Behavioral Investor: Lessons from the Real World (Gregg S. Fisher) According to behavioral finance theory, investors are not the rational actors that economic theory describes. Rather, they are human beings whose decision-making can be driven by cognitive and emotional factors. Research evidence shows innumerable examples of investors behaving in ways that are counter to their own best interests. But there is good news about behavioral investors. First, many ways are available in which financial advisors can help their clients stay rational when the markets are not, thus improving their chances of staying with a well devised long-term investment strategy and realizing its ultimate benefits. Second, investment strategies can be constructed that actually profit from the bias-driven decisions of other market participants. Thus, investors can learn and profit from others' mistakes. The purpose of this chapter is to apply the theory in behavioral finance and economics by exploring the practical, observable manifestations of investor behavior and to quantify their impact on investment results.

Chapter 16: Retirement Planning: Contributions from the Field of Behavioral Finance and Economics (James A. Howard and Rasoul Yazdipour) An important challenge facing employees and societies is saving and investing sufficient funds for a comfortable retirement. Research shows that human financial decision-making behavior is not always rational and that public trust in the economy can be lost. Surprisingly, neither better disclosure of financial services and products nor education has had a discernible effect in motivating individuals to effectively plan and save for transitioning out of the workforce. The fields of cognitive psychology and neuroscience identify many behavioral obstacles individuals face in taking the needed steps to save and invest more for the future. A host of behavioral issues influence an individual's decision-making about retirement including biases, heuristics, framing, hyperbolic discounting, self-awareness, and self-control. The emerging works on trust also add to understanding the retirement planning system. Exploring these findings and strategies for mitigating financial decision-making errors can make a substantive contribution to achieving a more secure retirement.

Chapter 17: Knowing Your Numbers: A Scorecard Approach to Improved Medical and Financial Outcomes (Talya Miron-Shatz and Stephanie Gati) Health literacy is the ability to obtain, process, and understand basic health information needed to make appropriate health decisions and follow instructions for treatment. Financial literacy is its equivalent in the financial domain, facilitating decisions on investments, retirement, health insurance, and more. This chapter proposes to overcome the medical and financial consequences of poor health literacy with a short, simple, and motivating digital scorecard for maintaining health and controlling chronic disease such as diabetes. The scorecard aggregates medical and lifestyle indicators that are easily interpretable without mediation by a physician, thereby informing the public of health-promoting behaviors. A pilot study project and surveys done at Carnegie Mellon University demonstrate the competitive strengths of a scorecard approach versus existing tools. Drawing parallels between health and financial literacy, the chapter illustrates the cost of low financial literacy and proposes that it can be improved through this approach, thereby strengthening financial decision-making.

Part IV: Investor Psychology

Part IV consists of seven chapters involving investor psychology. The section begins by examining risk perception and risk tolerance (Chapter 18). Next, it examines the important topics of emotions (Chapter 19), human psychology and market seasonality (Chapter 20), and neurofinance (Chapter 21). The remaining three chapters investigate diversification and asset allocation puzzles (Chapter 22), behavioral portfolio theory and investment management (Chapter 23), and post crisis investor behavior (Chapter 24).

Chapter 18: Risk Perception and Risk Tolerance (Victor Ricciardi and Douglas Rice) This chapter provides an overview of the research literature and the important issues regarding risk perception and risk tolerance. The academic literature reveals that various disciplines provide an assortment of perspectives in terms of how to define, describe, and analyze risk. The behavioral finance perspective encompasses the subjective and objective factors of risk within the domains of risk perception and risk tolerance. *Risk perception* is the subjective decision-making process that an investor uses when evaluating risk and the amount of uncertainty. *Risk tolerance* is the degree of risk that an investor is willing to endure in the pursuit of a financial objective. A major problem within the risk tolerance literature is the lack of general agreement about issues such as a standard definition, a uniform theory or model, measurement discrepancies, and the growing number of questionnaires. Academic researchers and practitioners are only now starting to study and understand the long-term effects of the financial crisis in 2007 and 2008 on investor risk-taking behavior.

Chapter 19: Emotions in the Financial Markets (Richard Fairchild) Standard or traditional finance research is based on the rational choice model that assumes market participants are fully rational, unbiased, emotionless, self-interested maximizers of expected utility. Recent research in behavioral finance recognizes that real-world investors and managers are not fully rational because they are affected by psychological biases and subject to conscious emotions in their decision-making. In a paradigm shift, emotional finance considers the effect of investors' and managers' unconscious emotions and infantile phantasies on market behavior employing a Freudian psychoanalytical framework. This chapter reviews this research and considers a formal modeling framework for emotional finance.

Chapter 20: Human Psychology and Market Seasonality (Lisa A. Kramer) Evidence suggests that human psychology plays a role in individuals' financial decisions, with economically meaningful consequences observed even at the aggregate market level. This chapter considers many instances whereby human mood induced by exogenous factors is associated with economically large, statistically significant effects in financial markets. Some regularities covered by this chapter arise due to environmental factors. For instance, a relationship appears between seasonal length of day and stock returns, working through seasonal changes in depression and risk aversion. This chapter also considers financial market regularities that are consistent with mood changes due to events in the news, such as terrorist attacks, and forms of entertainment such as sporting events. In most cases, authors of the original studies apply extensive robustness checks to explore alternate hypotheses, namely that the phenomenon may arise for non-psychological reasons. The body of research builds a compelling case that human mood can markedly affect markets.

Chapter 21: Neurofinance (Richard L. Peterson) Biology can have both constructive and damaging effects on investment decision-making. Both research and clinical evidence confirm that subtle shifts in neurochemistry affect financial decision-making. These alternations in brain functioning are driven by events as mundane as the weather and as intense as images from a riot. Despite the individual nature of financial decision making, an understanding of neurobiology can also be applied at the group level. Exogenous shocks and the endogenous environment affect both individuals and the crowds of financial decision makers of which they are a small part. The decisions of such crowds shift global asset prices. This chapter explores research into the biology of financial decision-making and demonstrates how many of the most successful financiers have built decision processes that strengthen vulnerabilities identified by neurofinance researchers.

Chapter 22: Diversification and Asset Allocation Puzzles (Dimitris Georgarakos) Asset allocation and portfolio diversification decisions have important welfare and policy implications. This chapter reviews studies that examine three key aspects of financial investing: participation in stock markets, portfolio diversification, and trading behavior. Standard finance theory predicts the optimal investment behavior of rational agents with reference to each of these three aspects. Yet, empirical studies document that observed behavior of investors largely deviates from theory predictions. The chapter also provides a discussion of empirical regularities that point to these deviations such as the limited stock market participation, the poor diversification and preference for domestic securities, and the contrast between excess trading activity of a few wealthy investors and considerable trading inertia exhibited by the majority of the population. These issues become increasingly topical as investors face a richer menu of complex financial instruments and gradually assume higher responsibility for retirement financing.

Chapter 23: Behavioral Portfolio Theory and Investment Management (Erick W. Rengifo, Rossen Trendafilov, and Emanuela Trifan) This chapter focuses on the attitude of investors toward financial gains and losses and their decisions on wealth allocation, and how these changes are subject to behavioral factors. The focal point is the integration of behavioral elements into the classic portfolio optimization. Individual perceptions are modeled according to four separate frameworks that build on each other: prospect theory, safety-first portfolio theory, security-potential/aspiration (SP/A) theory, and behavioral portfolio theory. SP/A theory evolves from safety-first portfolio theory and the introduction of aspiration level. The behavioral portfolio theory integrates the idea of mental accounts from prospect theory with the portfolio optimization framework of the SP/A theory and in this way it creates a unified model. The last part of the discussion addresses the behavioral asset pricing model (BAPM).

Chapter 24: Post-Crisis Investor Behavior: Experience Matters (Joseph V. Rizzi) The historic financial crisis in 2007 and 2008 seriously affected investors. In general, stock market values declined by about 50 percent but largely recovered from pre-crisis levels by the end of 2012 due in part to unprecedented stimulus efforts. Nonetheless, the cumulative return on stocks over the five-year period was close to zero. Investors are likely to learn from this experience and may adjust their investment behavior. Both individual experience and the collective behavior of groups sharing the same historical event influence risk tolerance. Recent studies highlighting a collective memory effect support this notion, which has important implications on investor asset allocation decisions. This chapter illustrates how a lingering generational effect influences the risk appetite and equity allocations of younger investors.

Part V: Trading and Investing Psychology and Strategies

Part V consists of three chapters. The first two chapters deal with various aspects of trading and investing psychology (Chapters 25 and 26) and the third chapter examines strategies (Chapter 27).

Chapter 25: The Psychology of Trading and Investing (Julia Pitters and Thomas Oberlechner)   In contrast to the assumption of standard economic theories, human beings cannot always make rational investment and trading decisions. Thus, psychological explanations are needed to shed light on the complexity of actual decision-making processes. The purpose of this chapter is to provide an overview of relevant psychological perspectives to explain trading and investment decisions. Starting on the individual level, the chapter examines how personality, mood, affect, and cognitive biases shape investment and trading decisions. Next, the chapter moves to the societal level and discusses how herding, social norms, cultural norms, and ethics play a role in financial decisions. Finally, the chapter shows how news, rumors, and market mood influence trading behavior on the macro level.

Chapter 26: The Surprising Real World of Traders' Psychology (Denise K. Shull, Ken Celiano, and Andres Manaker)   Trading psychology offers a unique look at unexpected factors in risk decisions made in uncertain circumstances. Traders, by definition, constantly make judgment calls and face a roller coaster of positive and negative feedback via the authority figure of price. Emanating from the historically dominant theories of efficient markets, human rationality, and the cognitive-behavioral school of psychology, conventional wisdom teaches that success emerges from accurate quantitative analyses. Multidisciplinary research in perception, judgment, and decision-making under uncertainty combined with qualitative evidence from hundreds of client interviews and coaching sessions with traders about investment performance reveal a different story. Unconscious affective contexts stemming from historical and current social milieus and revealed in what today's brain scientists call "embodied cognition" paint a more accurate picture.

Chapter 27: Trading and Investment Strategies in Behavioral Finance (John M. Longo)   The chapter describes investment and trading strategies rooted in behavioral finance that historically have generated superior profits. The failure of traditional finance models, such as those based on purely rational behavior, to explain how markets work has enabled behavioral finance to move into the foreground among practitioners. Most investors are fraught with behavioral biases and their investment performance reflects this unfortunate fact. However, hope exists for those seeking to improve investment performance. Investment analysts will become akin to doctors analyzing the vast complexity of the human genome. An individual may be susceptible to a specific disease based on his or her genetic makeup, but something, such as an environmental trigger, must activate it. Similarly, successful investment analysts should examine not only the fundamental and technical aspects of securities but also the behavioral factors that ultimately influence their market prices.

Part VI: Special Investment Topics

The final section presents a discussion of three diverse but highly relevant topics. The first topic involves an engaging discussion of ethical and socially responsible investing (Chapter 28). The next topic is an examination of behavioral issues involving mutual funds and individual investors (Chapter 29). The final topic deals with psychological biases involving investing in real estate (Chapter 30).

Chapter 28: Ethical and Socially Responsible Investing (Julia M. Puaschunder)   The chapter describes the various forms and emergence of ethical investing and discusses investor motives to engage in socially responsible investment (SRI). Ethical investing and SRI are derived from historical incidents, legislative compulsion, and stakeholder pressure in response to social, environmental, and political deficiencies as well as humanitarian crises in recent decades. Private investors choose socially conscious screenings, shareholder advocacy, community investing, and social venture capital funding for efficiency and long-term competitive considerations coupled with altruistic and personal social responsibility, entrepreneurial endeavors, and self-expression. The chapter also provides a synthesis of research on the performance of SRI funds relative to conventional stock mutual funds. Finally, the chapter provides a discussion of international financial social responsibility practices and standardization attempts throughout the international arena as well as the potential of SRI to avert future financial market downfalls in the aftermath of the global financial crisis.

Chapter 29: Mutual Funds and Individual Investors: Advertising and Behavioral Issues (John A. Haslem)

The chapter reviews important interactions between mutual funds and individual investors in choosing equity mutual funds. An important question is why both sophisticated and unsophisticated investors continue to invest in actively managed funds that generally underperform. Actively managed funds have histories of high levels of spending on advertising because they know it works in increasing assets under management. Fund managers have learned that investors chase past performance in the mistaken belief that the past predicts future performance. Funds further take advantage of investors by increasing advertising when current past performance is high. Advertising encourages individual investors to make fund choices in specific funds because they are generally unsophisticated, uninformed, and have low financial literacy, including a lack of knowledge of both transparent and opaque fund expenses and fees. Any persistence in high fund performance is also much more likely due to luck than portfolio manager skill. The Securities and Exchange Commission (SEC) has also failed to prohibit performance advertising or to require it to be unambiguous.

Chapter 30: Real Estate Investment Decision-Making in Behavioral Finance (Eli Beracha and Hilla Skiba)

The real estate market displays many of the behavioral biases documented in the traditional financial markets. During bull markets, investor overconfidence, optimism, representativeness, and self-attribution bias among others drive prices far above their fundamental values. Conversely, during bear markets, loss aversion, false reference points and anchoring, and familiarity bias drive prices below their fair values. Combining these behavioral biases with severe limits to arbitrage including the illiquid nature of the market, high transaction costs, and short sale constraints can magnify the effect of psychological biases on real estate valuations. As a result, real estate prices in the short and medium time horizon often deviate from their fundamental values and price adjustments are slow. This chapter reviews common psychological biases in the context of real estate and the consequences of these biases to markets.

SUMMARY

Although traditional finance has been the recognized theory of academic finance since the 1960s, the field of behavioral finance offers a new perspective of investment psychology for finance professors, financial practitioners, individual investors, and finance students. In the early to mid-1990s, the academic literature on investor behavior began to emerge that questioned many of the tenets and theories of traditional finance. The foundation for this new body of knowledge has developed over the past 150 years as demonstrated with the publication of books and other academic literature on financial history and investment theory. In the aftermath of the financial crisis of 2007 and 2008, behavioral finance has a wider acceptance among financial practitioners and individual investors. However, a strong level of resistance to behavioral finance still exists within academic finance among those trained in and proponents of traditional finance.

A unique aspect of this book is that many of the emerging topics in the forthcoming chapters focus on the psychologically oriented subject matter of the individual decision maker, also known as *microbehavioral finance*. This perspective is especially important for understanding and improving the client-advisor relationship between individual investors (clients) and investment professionals (advisors). Although financial planners, investors, and others can't change the past, they can learn from it and move forward. This book provides guidance on leaving old, well-trodden paths and venturing forward to follow new ones. Enjoy the journey!

REFERENCES

Allen, Frederick L. 2010. *Only Yesterday: An Informal History of the 1920s.* New York: Harper Perennial Modern Classics.

Appleman, Mark J. 1970. *The Winning Habit: How Your Personality Makes You a Winner or a Loser in the Stock Market.* New York: The McCall Publishing Company.

Baker, H. Kent, and John R. Nofsinger, eds. 2010. *Behavioral Finance: Investors, Corporations, and Markets.* Hoboken, NJ: John Wiley & Sons.

Belsky, Gary, and Thomas Gilovich. 1999. *Why Smart People Make Big Money Mistakes and How to Correct Them: Lessons from the New Science of Behavioral Economics.* New York: Simon & Schuster.

Bernstein, Peter L. 1996. *Against the Gods: The Remarkable Story of Risk.* New York: John Wiley & Sons.

Brooks, John. 1999a. *Once in Golconda: A True Drama of Wall Street 1920–1938.* New York: John Wiley & Sons.

Brooks, John. 1999b. *The Go-Go Years: The Drama and Crashing Finale of Wall Street's Bullish 60s.* New York: John Wiley & Sons.

Carret, Philip L. 1997. *The Art of Speculation.* New York: John Wiley & Sons.

Cressey, Donald R. 1951. *Other People's Money: A Study in the Social Psychology of Embezzlement.* Belmont, CA: Wadsworth Publishing Company.

Davies, Greg B., and Arnaud de Servigny. 2012. *Behavioral Investment Management: An Efficient Alternative to Modern Portfolio Theory.* New York: McGraw-Hill.

De Brouwer, Philippe J. S. 2012. *Maslowian Portfolio Theory: A Coherent Approach to Strategic Asset Allocation.* Brussels: Brussels University Press.

Dreman, David. 1977. *Psychology and the Stock Market: Investment Strategy beyond Random Walk.* New York: AMACOM (A Division of American Management Associations).

Fenton-O'Creevy, Mark, Nigel Nicholson, Emma Soane, and Paul Willman. 2005. *Traders: Risks, Decisions, and Management in Financial Markets.* Oxford, UK: Oxford University Press.

Ferguson, Niall. 2008. *The Ascent of Money: A Financial History of the World.* New York: Penguin Publishing.

Fisher, Philip A. 1997. *Common Stocks and Uncommon Profits*. New York: John Wiley & Sons.

Furnham, Adrian, and Michael Argyle. 1998. *The Psychology of Money*. London: Routledge.

Galbraith, John K. 2009. *The Great Crash of 1929*. New York: Houghton Mifflin Harcourt.

Garrett, Garet. 1998. *Where the Money Grows and Anatomy of the Bubble*. New York: John Wiley & Sons.

Geist, Richard. 2003. *Investor Therapy: A Psychologist and Investing Guru Tells You How to Out-Psych Wall Street*. New York: Crown Business.

Goetzmann, William N., and K. Geert Rouwenhorst, eds. 2005. *The Origins of Value: The Financial Innovations that Created Modern Capital Markets*. New York: Oxford University Press.

Graham, Benjamin, and David Dodd. 1996. *Security Analysis*. New York: McGraw-Hill.

Graham, Benjamin. 2005. *The Intelligent Investor: The Classic Text on Value Investing*. New York: HarperCollins.

Hamilton, William P. 1998. *The Stock Market Barometer*. New York: John Wiley & Sons.

Haugen, Robert A. 1995. *The New Finance: The Case Against Efficient Markets*. Upper Saddle River, NJ: Prentice Hall.

Kindleberger, Charles P. 1996. *Manias, Panics and Crashes: A History of Financial Crisis*. New York: John Wiley & Sons.

Klontz, Brad, and Ted Klontz. 2009. *Mind over Money: Overcoming the Money Disorders That Threaten Our Financial Health*. New York: Broadway Books.

Le Bon, Gustave. 1982. *The Crowd: A Study of the Popular Mind*. Marietta, GA: Cherokee Publishing Company.

Lefèvre, Edwin. 1994. *Reminiscences of a Stock Operator*. New York: John Wiley & Sons.

Lifson, Lawrence E., and Richard A. Geist. 1999. *The Psychology of Investing*. New York: John Wiley & Sons.

Loeb, Gerald M. 2010. *The Battle for Investment Survival*. Blacksburg, VA: Wilder Publications.

Mackay, Charles. 1980. *Extraordinary Popular Delusions and the Madness of Crowds*. New York: Crown Publishing Group.

Malkiel, Burton G. 1973. *A Random Walk Down Wall Street*. New York: W. W. Norton & Company.

Meade, Edward S. 2003. *Trust Finance: A Study of the Genesis, Organization, and Management of Industrial Combinations*. Honolulu: University Press of the Pacific.

Montier, James. 2007. *Behavioral Investing: A Practitioner's Guide to Applying Behavioral Finance*. Chichester, UK: John Wiley & Sons.

Neill, Humphrey B. 1992. *The Art of Contrary Thinking*, Caldwell, Idaho: The Caxton Printers.

Nofsinger, John R. 2002. *The Psychology of Investing*. Upper Saddle River, NJ: Pearson Education.

Oberlechner, Thomas. 2004. *The Psychology of the Foreign Exchange Market*. Chichester, UK: John Wiley & Sons.

Peterson, Richard L. 2007. *Inside the Investor's Brain: The Power of Mind over Money*. Hoboken, NJ: John Wiley & Sons.

Pompian, Michael M. 2006. *Behavioral Finance and Wealth Management: How to Build Optimal Portfolios that Account for Investor Biases*. Hoboken, NJ: John Wiley & Sons.

Pompian, Michael M. 2012. *Behavioral Finance and Investor Types: Managing Behavior to Make Better Investment Decisions*. Hoboken, NJ: John Wiley & Sons.

Reinhart, Carmen M., and Kenneth Rogoff. 2011. *This Time Is Different: Eight Centuries of Financial Folly*. Princeton, NJ: Princeton University Press.

Ricciardi, Victor, and Helen K. Simon. 2000. "What Is Behavioral Finance?" *Business, Education and Technology Journal* 2:2, 1–9. Available at http://ssrn.com/abstract=256754.

Ricciardi, Victor. 2006. "A Research Starting Point for the New Scholar: A Unique Perspective of Behavioral Finance." *ICFAI Journal of Behavioral Finance* 3:3, 6–23. Available at http://ssrn.com/abstract=928251.

Rubinstein, Mark. 2006. *A History of the Theory of Investments: My Annotated Bibliography*. Hoboken, NJ: John Wiley & Sons.

Rukeyser, Merryle S. 1999. *The Common Sense of Money and Investments*. New York: John Wiley & Sons.

Sargeant, William P. 1957. *Stock Market Behavior: A Descriptive Guidebook for the New Investor*. New York: Exposition Press.

Scheinman, William X. 1991. *Why Most Investors Are Mostly Wrong Most of the Time*. Burlington, VT: Fraser Publishing Company.

Schindler, Mark. 2007. *Rumors in Financial Markets: Insights into Behavioral Finance*. West Sussex, UK: John Wiley & Sons.

Schwed, Fred. 2006. *Where Are the Customers' Yachts? or A Good Hard Look at Wall Street*. New York: John Wiley & Sons.

Selden, George C. 1996. *The Psychology of the Stock Market*. Burlington, VT: Fraser Publishing Company.

Shefrin, Hersh. 2000. *Beyond Greed and Fear: Understanding Behavioral Finance and the Psychology of Investing*. Boston MA: Harvard Business School Press.

Shiller, Robert J. 2000. *Irrational Exuberance*. Princeton, NJ: Princeton University Press.

Shleifer, Andrei. 2000. *Inefficient Markets: An Introduction to Behavioral Finance*. New York Oxford University Press.

Shull, Denise. 2012. *Market Mind Games: A Radical Psychology of Investing, Trading and Risk*. New York: McGraw-Hill.

Statman, Meir. 2011. *What Investors Really Want: Know What Drives Investor Behavior and Make Smarter Financial Decisions*. New York: McGraw-Hill.

Tuckett, David, and Richard Taffler. 2012. *Fund Management: An Emotional Finance Perspective*. Charlottesville, VA: CFA Institute Research Foundation.

Warneryd, Karl-Erik. 2001. *Stock Market Psychology: How People Value and Trade Stocks*. Cheltenham, UK: Edward Elgar Publishing.

Williams, John B. 1997. *The Theory of Investment Value*. New York: Fraser Publishing Company.

Wood, Arnold S., ed. 2010. *Behavioral Finance and Investment Management*. Charlottesville, VA: CFA Institute Research Foundation.

Zacks, Leonard. 2011. *The Handbook of Equity Market Anomalies: Translating Market Inefficiencies into Effective Investment Strategies*. Hoboken, NJ: John Wiley & Sons.

Zweig, Jason. 2007. *Your Money and Your Brain: How the New Science of Neuroeconomics Can Help Make You Rich*. New York: Simon & Schuster.

ABOUT THE AUTHORS

H. Kent Baker is a University Professor of Finance in the Kogod School of Business at American University. Professor Baker has authored or edited 20 books of which his most recent with Oxford University Press are *Portfolio Theory and Management* (2013), *International Finance: A Survey* (2013), *and Survey Research in Corporate Finance* (2011). His most current books with John Wiley & Sons are *Market Microstructure in Emerging and Developed Markets* (2013), *Alternative Investments: Instruments, Performance, Benchmarks, and Strategies* (2013), *and Socially Responsible Finance and Investing: Financial Institutions, Corporations, Investors, and Activists* (2012). As one of the most prolific authors among finance academics, he has published more than 150 refereed articles in such journals as the *Journal of Finance, Journal of Financial and Quantitative Analysis, Financial Management, Financial Analysts Journal, Journal of Portfolio Management,* and *Harvard Business*

Review. He has consulting and training experience with more than 100 organizations and serves on six editorial boards. Professor Baker holds a BSBA from Georgetown University; MEd, MBA, and DBA degrees from the University of Maryland; and MA, MS, and two PhDs from American University. He also holds CFA and CMA designations.

Victor Ricciardi is an Assistant Professor of Financial Management at Goucher College. He teaches courses in financial planning, investments, corporate finance, behavioral finance, and the psychology of money. He is the editor of several eJournals distributed by the Social Science Research Network (SSRN) at www.ssrn.com, including behavioral finance, financial history, behavioral economics, and behavioral accounting. He received a BBA in accounting and management from Hofstra University and an MBA in finance and Advanced Professional Certificate (APC) at the graduate level in economics from St. John's University. He also holds a graduate certificate in personal family financial planning from Kansas State University. He can be found on Twitter @victorricciardi.

CHAPTER 2

Traditional and Behavioral Finance

Lucy F. Ackert
Professor of Finance, Coles College of Business, Kennesaw State University

INTRODUCTION

Psychologists and other social scientists have made great strides in understanding how individual and group behavior, as well as brain function, shape the decisions people make. Throughout history, financial commentators and scholars recognized the impact of human psychology on financial decision-making and market outcomes. For example, the prominent economist John Maynard Keynes (1964) notes that people's decisions about the future could not depend only on mathematical expectations because the world is fraught with uncertainty. Instead, Keynes contends that human decisions are often based on whim, sentiment, or simple chance. Despite the recognition that human psychology has an important role in determining economic and financial decisions, traditional finance theory reflects the abrupt and overwhelming movement of economists toward the mathematical modeling tools used in the hard sciences. In hindsight, finance theorists apparently fell prey to "physics envy," the desire to mathematize the study of financial behavior.

Certainly, mathematical paradigms are useful in numerous applications, but empirical evidence contradicting traditional finance models mounted over recent years. Even very simple choices in controlled environments were inconsistent with the theories that dominated just a few decades ago. Thus, behavioral finance theorists moved toward incorporating what has been learned from the social sciences more formally into models of financial behavior.

This chapter provides an overview of how the theory of investment behavior has evolved in recent times. Researchers have accumulated much knowledge relating to the forces shaping investment decisions. The chapter is organized as follows. The first half focuses on the traditional view of how people make investment choices. This section of the chapter reviews classical decision theory, rationality, and utility theory, with particular attention to risk preferences. With this background the section proceeds to review modern portfolio theory, asset pricing models, and a dominant paradigm in finance, the efficient market hypothesis (EMH). The second half of the chapter shifts focus to behavioral finance. This second section begins with a review of behavioral decision theory and prospect theory, the most widely used alternative to the classical theory. Special attention is given to the issues of framing, heuristics, overconfidence, and regret. The next section provides discussion of some important behavioral finance contributions offering new emerging research topics to offer alternatives to traditional finance theory. The final section of the chapter provides concluding remarks.

TRADITIONAL FINANCE

Classical decision theory, which assumes that rational decision makers evaluate all possible outcomes, serves as the basis for developing the traditional view in finance. The optimal choice is determined by finding the highest possible expected utility. Finance theorists then assume that these rational people are averse to risk, so that investors must receive compensation if they are going to take on risk. With this basis, theorists can provide models of important financial decisions including portfolio composition and asset pricing.

Classical Decision Theory

Decision-making requires humans to evaluate choices under conditions of uncertainty. The classical approach takes a normative view of decision-making in that it attempts to identify the best or optimal decision. Classical decision theory assumes that people are rational decision makers who are self-interested and optimize in the presence of constraints. Many conceptualizations are available of what it means to be rational, as is discussed later.

Unfortunately, uncertainty greatly complicates financial decision-making. Assessing the probabilities of outcomes is generally difficult and people may be unaware of all the possible outcomes. In contrast to an uncertain situation, the probabilities of the possible outcomes are known in a risky environment. While the world is best characterized as uncertain, theory is usually developed to describe risk rather than uncertainty.

Classical decision theory models how people make choices when faced with a variety of potential actions. People are able to evaluate their preferences over possible outcomes and are also able to associate probabilities with each potential outcome. These preferences satisfy certain conditions if they are rational. For example, classical decision theory assumes that people know what they like and are consistent in these preferences. If someone prefers Coke to Pepsi, that individual consistently picks Coke when offered the choice between the two.

Rationality and Utility

In classical decision theory, a rational person has consistent preferences, even in complex situations. Deciding on a course of action is not always easy even in conditions of certainty. But when risk is added, how does a rational person choose the best course of action? Von Neumann and Morgenstern (1944) developed expected utility theory (EUT) to describe choices that are made in risky states of the world. Assuming rational preferences and that people prefer more to less, EUT defines rational choices under uncertainty.

A utility function converts alternatives into measurable rankings of preferences. Utility functions assign higher numbers to preferred outcomes and can be used to rank combinations of risky alternatives. Each person's utility function is unique to that person and, while outcomes can be compared for an individual, preferences cannot be compared across people. Exhibit 2.1 illustrates a typical utility function. The horizontal axis represents wealth and utility is mapped on the vertical axis. Notice that utility increases with wealth but at a decreasing rate. In other words, an additional $1 increases an individual's utility less when wealth is high than when wealth is low. Expected utility is computed by evaluating the utility of each outcome and weighting the assigned number by the outcome probability. When choosing among a set of possible outcomes, the rational person picks the outcome with highest expected utility.

Risk Aversion

The trade-off between risk and return is fundamental for investment choices. A basic finance tenet is that an investor's required return will increase with risk. Regarding their wealth, most investors are risk averse. One of the many benefits of the expected utility framework is that it permits establishing what is meant by risk aversion.

Consider again Exhibit 2.1. The shape of this utility function suggests risk aversion. A person with such preferences would rather have the expected value of a gamble than the gamble itself. For a risk averter, the expected utility of an uncertain outcome is less than the utility of the expected value of the possible outcomes.

This framework also allows measuring an individual's risk premium. The *risk premium* is the amount of wealth the investor is willing to give up in order to avoid taking a gamble. Suppose someone is offered a bet on the flip of a fair coin. Suppose further that the person wins $2 if the coin flip results in heads and zero if tails. The expected value of this bet is $1. If the person was offered this bet or $1 with certainty, she would surely take the $1 if she is risk averse. If the person is indifferent between $0.75 and taking the bet, her risk premium is $0.25. She would be willing to give up a quarter to avoid taking this bet.

Modern Portfolio Theory

Finance theory assumes that people are risk averse regarding their wealth. By definition, the future payoff associated with a risky asset is uncertain. A positive risk premium must exist if there is any risk or investors will refuse to hold the asset. In the coin flip example, the risk-averse gambler would not take the bet at a price of $1 or more. The asset price will fall due to supply and demand factors until the asset's price in equilibrium reflects the appropriate risk premium. But how is risk measured?

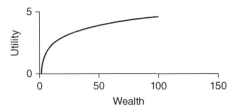

EXHIBIT 2.1 The Traditional Finance Viewpoint: The Utility Function for a Risk Averter

Note: This exhibit illustrates the utility function for a person who is averse to risk.

The asset's return variability provides a first measure of risk. The standard deviation of returns can be easily measured with a sample of historical data. A higher standard deviation suggests greater dispersion and thus greater absolute risk. An investor can evaluate the risk and return trade-offs across assets by comparing means and standard deviations across investment opportunities. History shows that assets with higher risk generally provide higher returns over the long run. For example, stocks generate higher risk and return than corporate bonds and the yield on corporate bonds is higher than on U.S. government bonds.

An investor evaluating assets naturally asks if an optimal way is available to allocate wealth in a portfolio. An important contribution of modern finance is providing direction to investors on how to form optimal portfolios. Harry Markowitz received the Nobel Prize in Economics in 1990 for developing the theory of portfolio choice. The advice is simple based on the adage "Don't put all your eggs in one basket." While the basic idea underlying Markowitz's (1952) work may seem like common advice, it provides the basis for modern finance theory. Markowitz recognizes that while the return for a combination of securities is the average of the return for each asset in the portfolio (properly weighted by its contribution to the portfolio), the risk is not the simple average. Putting securities together in a portfolio can eliminate some variability. Portfolio risk will depend critically on the correlation between the assets' returns. If the assets' returns do not move together, when one asset does poorly, the other does well so that a combination has less variability than either asset alone. If the assets tend to move very closely together, less benefit occurs when combining them in a portfolio. When one asset does well, so will the other asset, and when one performs poorly, so will the other. As long as the securities are not perfectly positively correlated, benefits from diversification occur.

Investors have literally thousands of opportunities to consider. As assets are added to a portfolio, some risk, called *diversifiable* or *unsystematic risk*, is diversified away. The goal is to create a portfolio with the maximum return for a given level of risk. To do so, the investor will evaluate the expected returns and standard deviations for all investment opportunities, as well as the correlation between each investment pair. The efficient set represents the portfolios with the highest return at each value of the portfolio standard deviation. While this process may seem burdensome, with today's easy access to data and fast computing systems, it is now possible but, as is discussed subsequently, may not be necessary.

To choose the best portfolio from the efficient set, add a risk-free asset, often proxied by U.S. Treasury bills. The risk-free asset allows the investor to identify which risky portfolio offers the best return for the risk taken. This is referred to as the *optimal risky portfolio*. All investors should hold this single, optimal portfolio regardless of their preferences. However, their portfolios are different in that those who are more risk averse will put a greater proportion of wealth in the risk-free asset and those who are more tolerant to risk will allocate more to the risky portfolio. This result is referred to as *portfolio separation*, first introduced by Tobin (1958). The investor's portfolio choice can be made after completing two separate tasks. First, the investor (or his or her financial advisor) identifies the optimal risky portfolio using historical returns data. Second, the investor determines his or her level of risk tolerance, which depends on individual preferences and life situation. After following these two steps, the investor can identify his or her optimal portfolio.

The optimal risky portfolio is also the market portfolio. The optimal risky portfolio is identified by combining risky assets into portfolios using estimates of the average and standard deviations of returns, along with return correlations. These estimates could differ across investors, but if no reason exists to expect anyone to have superior information, investors will have similar expectations. This means that all will hold the market portfolio as the best efficient portfolio.

Capital Asset Pricing Model and the Trade-Off between Risk and Return

From the discussion of optimal portfolio selection, investors have learned that the risk of an asset cannot be evaluated in isolation. Instead, the risk of the asset has to be based on its contribution to the risk of the portfolio. Further, the risk of the asset is defined in relation to the market portfolio. As noted previously, some risks are diversifiable. Other risks are not diversifiable because they affect the entire market, that is, they are systematic risks. Risk-averse investors should only take risk if they are appropriately compensated. In response to the advancements made by early finance researchers, theorists searched for a way to quantify the trade-off between risk and return. They understood that investors would not be compensated for risks they could avoid through diversification by adding diversifiable or unsystematic risk.

The result is the capital asset pricing model (CAPM). The CAPM provides a measure of risk of a security called *beta* (β). Beta quantifies the sensitivity of a security's return to the market. Of course, each asset has its own beta. The beta of the market is 1.0 and the beta of the risk-free asset is zero, as it is, by definition, risk free. Operationally, the beta for an asset is computed by dividing the covariance of the security's return and the market by the variance of market returns.

In 1990, William Sharpe received the Nobel Prize in Economics, in part for his work on the trade-off between risk and return. Sharpe (1964) provides a simple, yet powerful model of returns. Equation 2.1 shows the CAPM as:

$$E(R_i) = R_f + \beta_i(E(R_m) - R_f) \tag{2.1}$$

so that the expected return for asset i ($E(R_i)$) varies directly with the measure of risk (β_i). R_f denotes the risk-free interest rate and $E(R_m)$ is the expected return for the market. Note that the market risk premium ($E(R_m) - R_f$) must be positive because, if it were not, no investor would invest in risky assets. According to this model, the expected return of the asset increases with increases in risk.

Although initial tests show that the CAPM appears to work well (Fama, 1991), later evidence suggests that returns depend on other factors in addition to the market. Theorists proposed alternatives to the CAPM and one example is the three-factor model proposed by Fama and French (1996). The idea is that the CAPM does not pick up other risk factors. For example, Fama and French identify two other factors: firm size and the book-to-market ratio. Fama and French model these factors because evidence indicates that the CAPM apparently does not perform well in explaining the cross-section of returns across stocks. Small firms and those with high book values relative to market values have high returns. As the CAPM, a cornerstone of modern finance, was called into question, another fundamental theory based on the efficiency of financial markets was also revealing evidence of flaws in the academic literature. The following section describes the dominant view of the functioning of markets, the efficient market hypothesis (EMH).

Efficient Market Hypothesis

The CAPM and other asset pricing models gave investors models they could use to try to evaluate how stocks and other assets are priced. Even casual market observers would note that investors compete vigorously to identify mispriced assets. Mispricing must be evaluated based on a model of returns. For the CAPM, for example, abnormal return is measured by taking the difference between an asset's actual return and the expected return predicted by the model in Equation 2.1. If the model is descriptive of pricing and investors actively compete to identify mispriced assets, few opportunities should be available to generate abnormal returns.

Before financial economists presented the CAPM, a British statistician named Maurice Kendall provided some startling evidence on stock and commodity prices that received considerable attention from finance academics and professionals (Kendall 1953). Kendall's evidence suggests that past price information is not useful in predicting future prices. According to Kendall (p. 13), "it seems that the change in price from one week to the next is practically independent of the change from that week to the week after. This alone is enough to show that it is impossible to predict the price from week to week from the series itself." This means that prices follow a random walk so that future price changes are unpredictable. This is not welcome news to a profession that devotes time and resources to giving investment advice! Perhaps even more surprising is that in 1900 a French doctoral student named Louis Bachelier made similar arguments. In his study of the properties of option prices, Bachelier (1900) concludes that "the mathematical expectation of the speculator is zero" (Davis, Etheridge, and Samuelson 2006, p. 28). While his work was not fully appreciated at the time, Bachelier is known as the father of mathematical finance.

Suppose that Bachelier and Kendall were wrong and that the price of a share of stock is predictable based on current information. If information is useful in generating profitable trading opportunities, investors would be encouraged to spend more time seeking out information. They would actively compete to gain the advantage. Will this competition lead to market prices that reflect all available information?

This is the essence of the EMH, a dominant paradigm in finance for the last several decades. In competitive markets, prices reflect all available information so that no investor can consistently generate abnormal returns. New information arrives randomly so that price changes in response to new information are unpredictable. As Bachelier (1900) and Kendall (1953) document, price changes follow a random walk.

Fama (1970) distinguishes three versions on the EMH to clarify what he means by "all information." *Weak form efficiency* asserts that prices reflect any information in their history. Thus, technical analysis of past price data will not be fruitful. Under *semi-strong form efficiency*, prices reflect any public information in addition to past price data. This form of the EMH suggests that investors cannot generate abnormal returns using information releases such as earnings statements or media reports. The strictest form of the EMH is the *strong form*, which asserts that prices reflect even private information. Thus, even company insiders cannot devise a strategy to consistently generate abnormal returns.

A flood of academic research tested the EMH with the initial evidence supporting the hypothesis (Fama 1991). Although some studies reject the EMH, researchers correctly recognize the joint hypothesis problem. A test of the EMH requires using a model of expected returns such as the CAPM. If the EMH is rejected, it could be because the market is not efficient or due to the assumed model of expected returns. Despite this recognition of a joint hypothesis problem, evidence against the EMH continued to mount. Researchers report numerous *anomalies*, which are results that are surprising and inconsistent with the EMH. This new tide in research was a driving force in the birth and growth of behavioral finance.

Before leaving the EMH, a few aspects of the theory are important to highlight. In an efficient market, stock analysis provides no benefits because prices already reflect all information. This does not mean that investors should avoid stocks or other assets. Although investors cannot consistently generate abnormal returns in an efficient market, the return should be warranted based on the risk associated with the investment. Furthermore, financial advisors have a role even in a very efficient market. The benefits to diversification do not evaporate in an efficient market nor do the benefits from wise tax and retirement planning. Investors have different risk preferences and goals for the future.

BEHAVIORAL FINANCE

Expected utility theory provides the basis for much of modern finance theory. Underlying assumptions of this theory are that people have complete information about possible outcomes and their likelihoods, and can evaluate their preferences across different expected options. People put these figures together and choose the outcome that maximizes expected utility. Although the traditional approach provides many useful insights, something seemingly is missing. For example, people consistently suffer from particular behavioral biases and the reigning traditional models do not provide satisfactory explanations. In other words, the models cannot describe actual, observed behavior. Of course, these normative models may fail because people are irrational or because the models rest on false assumptions.

Behavioral finance uses insights from other sciences and business disciplines to understand the decisions investors make. Psychologists and other social scientists have been studying human behavior for a long time and have accumulated considerable evidence on how people make decisions. With advanced technologies, neuroscientists now can show how brain functioning can impact financial decisions in the field of neuroeconomics (neurofinance). Instead of focusing on the outcome, scientists in these other disciplines focus on how decision makers reach outcomes. Traditional finance theory is normative because it indicates how investors should make decisions. By contrast, the behavioral finance approach is to understand why investors make the observed decision.

Behavioral Decision Theory and Bounded Rationality

Behavioral decision theory incorporates evidence on how people actually behave into models of decision-making. Nobel laureate Herbert Simon proposed one of the early alternatives to expected utility theory. Simon (1955, p. 99) notes that "the task is to replace the global rationality of economic man with a kind of rational behavior that is compatible with the access to information and the computational capacities that are actually posed by organisms, including man, in the kinds of environments in which organisms lived." Although this was not an easy task, Simon and other decision researchers realized that the traditional paradigm did not describe the behavior of real people. According to Simon, people "satisfice," rather than "optimize," meaning that they choose the course of action that satisfies their most important needs, but the choice may not be optimal. For example, a car buyer may not exhaustively search out every bit of information about all the cars on the market. Instead, this consumer may search until the person identifies the car that fits his or her tastes and preferences.

Decision researchers document a long list of judgment biases and cognitive imperfections, leading to additional calls for alternatives to expected utility theory. For example, Slovic, Fischoff, and Lichtenstein (1977) provide a review of the decision theory literature. Behavioral theorists are not arguing that people are irrational when behavior does not fit expected utility predictions. People want to make rational choices but they are simply limited by constraints on their ability and resources. Simon's (1978) theory of bounded rationality describes the view that optimal decision-making is limited because of cognitive constraints and information availability. People only have so much time to devote to making a decision. Simon's ideas provide the basis for much of the theory of decision-making that followed. Einhorn and Hogarth (1981) provide a review of this literature.

Prospect Theory and Loss Aversion

Prospect theory is the most widely accepted alternative to expected utility theory. Kahneman and Tversky developed this descriptive model of decision-making under risk to describe observed human behavior (Kahneman and Tversky 1979; Tversky and Kahneman 1992). Although prospect theory has some similarities to expected utility theory, it differs in several key ways.

Financial economists developed expected utility theory as a normative model to describe how people should behave, whereas actual behavior provides the basis for prospect theory. According to psychologists and other decision researchers, people often make inconsistent choices. Consider, for example, the following problem from Tversky and Kahneman (1981):

> Problem 1: Imagine that you face the following pair of concurrent decisions. First examine both decisions, and then indicate the options you prefer.
>
> ■ Decision 1. Choose between A, a sure gain of $240, and B, a 25 percent chance to gain $1,000 and 75 percent chance to gain nothing.
> ■ Decision 2. Choose between C, a sure loss of $750, and D, a 75 percent chance to lose $1,000 and a 25 percent chance to lose nothing.

What did you choose? When making decision 1, the majority of Kahneman and Tversky's respondents choose A (84%), whereas when making decision 2, the majority choose D (87%). This choice pattern is inconsistent with expected utility theory because choosing A in decision 1 indicates risk aversion and choosing D in decision 2 indicates risk taking. In decision 1, A has an expected gain of $240 and B's expected gain is larger ($250) but riskier, so choosing A suggests risk aversion. In decision 2, C has a sure expected loss of $750 and D's expected loss is the same but risky. A risk-averse person would pick A and C because he prefers a riskless action to one that is risky and has equal or smaller expected value. Expected utility theory (i.e., the standard finance view) cannot explain why a person would have a shift in preferences like this but prospect theory (i.e., the behavioral finance perspective) includes this behavior as one of its key precepts.

Exhibit 2.2 illustrates a typical prospect theory value function. Instead of maximizing expected utility, prospect theory posits that people maximize value. A critical feature of the theory is that people evaluate outcomes based on changes in wealth, rather than final position. Thus, in Exhibit 2.2 the horizontal axis represents changes in wealth from a reference point and the vertical axis represents value, which is the evaluation of an outcome analogous to utility. The reference point is typically taken to be the person's initial position or starting wealth. Notice that the value function is convex in the loss domain but concave for gains. This reflects the observation that people's choices reflect risk taking when their decision involves losses, but risk aversion for gains, as in problem 1 above.

The value function in Exhibit 2.2 reflects another key aspect of prospect theory. The choices people make reflect a strong aversion to losses, referred to as *loss aversion*. In other words, the pain experienced from a loss of $100 is felt more sharply than the pleasure experienced from a gain of $100. According to Kahneman and Tversky (1979, p. 279), "losses loom larger than gains." In Exhibit 2.2 the value function is steeper for losses than for gains because a negative change in wealth causes a stronger change in value than a positive change of equivalent size.

Taken together, the prospect theory value function reflects three important properties that distinguish it from the traditional utility function. First, value is measured in terms of changes in wealth from a reference point. Second, the value function is convex for losses reflecting risk taking and concave for gains reflecting

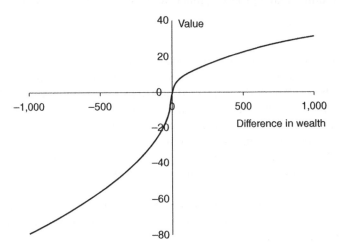

EXHIBIT 2.2 The Behavioral Finance Perspective: The Prospect Theory Value Function for a Loss Averter

Note: This exhibit illustrates prospect theory's value function, which replaces the utility function of expected utility theory.

risk aversion. Third, the value function is steeper for losses than for gains due to loss aversion.

With the value function, people can determine preferred actions by maximizing expected value, similar to the process used when maximizing expected utility. The evaluation is somewhat more complicated with prospect theory, however, in that value weights are not simple probabilities as in expected utility theory. In prospect theory probabilities are transformed into decision weights. A typical weighting function reflects another aspect of behavior reported by Kahneman and Tversky (1979). People tend to overweight low probability events. This can explain why people buy lottery tickets and insurance, both of which have negative expected values. People tend to overestimate the probability that they will win the lottery, which is an extremely low probability event. At the same time, people overestimate the probability of a bad outcome and purchase insurance. Both choices seem at first to be inconsistent with prospect theory, which predicts risk aversion for gains (avoidance of lotteries) and risk seeking for losses (avoidance of insurance), but these choices are consistent with the theory when incorporating the overweighting of low probabilities.

The foregoing discussion notes the important differences between the traditional approach and its most popular alternative. While prospect theory is a powerful approach that can describe many of the decisions people make, the theory cannot rectify some anomalies. One area that is particularly important for financial decision-making is what happens with *path dependence*. Path dependent decisions depend on previous decisions so that the current position results from active choice. Many theories consider one-shot decisions, but the situation gets much more complicated when people make several decisions sequentially. If the decision maker chooses the starting point, will he integrate the results of prior decisions or will he segregate? For example, if the decision maker is evaluating the performance of a stock, what is the starting point? What if the person bought, sold, and later repurchased a stock? While theory has certainly made progress, much work still needs to be done.

Framing

An important observation on which Kahneman and Tversky (1979) relied in developing their theory is that people's choices are inconsistent across different presentations of a choice. Recall that expected utility theory requires that preferences be consistent so that the presentation should be irrelevant. The decision frame refers to how a decision maker views a problem. The perception of a problem depends not only on the presentation but also on the characteristics of the decision maker. Researchers document framing effects across a variety of problems. Here is a well-known example from Tversky and Kahneman (1981).

> Problem 2: Imagine that the United States is preparing for the outbreak of an unusual Asian disease, which is expected to kill 600 people. Two alternative programs to combat the disease have been proposed. Assume that the exact scientific estimate of the consequences of the programs is as follows:
>
> - If Program A is adopted, 200 people will be saved.
> - If Program B is adopted, a 1/3 probability exists that 600 people will be saved, and a 2/3 probability that no people will be saved.

Which of the two programs would you favor?

A second group of people is given the same problem but asked to choose between two different programs, as follows:

- If Program C is adopted, 400 people will die.
- If Program D is adopted, a 1/3 probability exists that nobody will die, and a 2/3 probability that 600 people will die.

Which of the two programs would you favor?

What did you choose this time? When given the choice between programs A and B, the majority of Kahneman and Tversky's respondents choose A (72%), whereas when choosing between C and D, the majority choose D (78%). Based on the behavioral finance perspective, the responses suggest that when a problem is presented in terms of gains, the majority is risk averse but when a problem is presented in terms of losses, the majority is risk taking. According to the traditional finance viewpoint, the two choices are identical and expected utility theory would predict that a rational economic decision maker would consistently choose A and C if risk averse and B and D if risk taking. In terms of the outcomes, A and C are equivalent, as are B and D.

Kahneman and Tversky's (1979) observation that the decision frame depends on how a problem is formulated and the individual characteristics of the decision maker has powerful implications for financial decision-making. An investor's perception of a choice may change by manipulating the presentation of information. Of course, this idea may not seem particularly surprising to anyone involved in designing sales marketing programs, but remember that in the traditional (standard) finance paradigm a rational decision maker should see through the frame.

Heuristics

A rational decision maker should also base decisions on available information. Recall Simon's (1955, 1978) theory of bounded rationality. People face both cognitive and environmental constraints. A *heuristic* is a useful rule-of-thumb that people can use for problem solving. While some view heuristics narrowly as the result of cognitive error, they are more broadly viewed as useful tools for people who make decisions with limits on cognition in complex environments. In some cases, the full evaluation of information and construction of probabilities are overly burdensome or perhaps even impossible because of information overload. The world is full of uncertainty and a person's time is limited. A decision needs to be made and a heuristic can promote appropriate decision-making under certain conditions.

Heuristic-based decision-making can be efficient and optimal depending on the environment. A heuristic can be ecologically rational when is takes advantage of the structure of information in the decision maker's environment (Gigerenzer, Todd, and ABC Research Group 1999). Take, for example, a simple heuristic such as familiarity. When choosing a stock to add to his portfolio, suppose the investor chooses the one from the opportunity set that he knows or thinks he knows. This strategy is wise if he is more likely to be familiar with stocks that will perform well in the future. Although some research concludes that heuristic-based decision-making can lead to suboptimal outcomes (Huberman 2001), others contend that these decisions can lead to good outcomes in particular environments (Todd and Gigerenzer 2003).

Overconfidence

When people are asked about their driving ability, most will say it is above average. People tend to be overconfident about their skills, abilities, and knowledge. In finance, overconfidence has garnered particular attention because researchers show this bias to have an important impact on financial decisions for both investors and managers. For example, researchers report that overconfident traders trade too much and incur inferior returns (Barber and Odean 2000, 2001). Regarding managerial decisions, hubris can lead to excess entry into markets and may explain the high rate of failure among business start-ups (Camerer and Lovallo 1999).

One challenge for researchers is measuring the level of confidence. With market data, researchers use proxies for overconfidence such as gender or trading intensity so that the evidence can only indirectly link overconfidence with poor outcomes (Barber and Odean 2000, 2001). Researchers report that men and those who trade frequently are overconfident. In experimental laboratories, survey techniques provide a more direct way of measuring confidence, but even here different views of what confidence is complicate measuring confidence (Ackert and Deaves 2010). Overconfidence could manifest as a view of superiority, possessing greater skill and knowledge than others, or being better than average. Overconfidence could be revealed by expectations that are overly optimistic. Overconfidence could also result from an illusion of control wherein a decision maker believes she can control chance events. Finally, overconfidence can reveal itself through miscalibration or overestimation of the precision of knowledge. In an uncertain information environment, confident people tend to believe their information is more accurate than that of others.

In laboratory experiments, researchers often use a calibration test to measure overconfidence. For example, a researcher may give respondents a survey with 10 questions with numerical answers. The researcher asks the subjects to provide upper and lower bounds on their estimated answer so that they are, say, 90 percent confident that their bounds contain the correct answer. The researcher will observe that 9 or 10 intervals will contain the correct answer for a calibrated respondent. Miscalibration occurs when many of the intervals fail to contain the true answer. The idea is that a person who understands the precision of his knowledge will set a wide interval to reflect doubt about the quantity.

Financial advisors understand that knowing their clients is important and widely use questionnaires to evaluate various financial and investment behaviors. To determine the basic financial preferences of the individual and also assess who may be prone to bias, a first step is to have a client fill out a survey instrument. This questionnaire can be designed to measure a client's risk tolerance, personal investment history, spending habits, and money personality attributes. With this knowledge, an advisor is better able to provide appropriate counsel to clients.

Regret Theory

A widely documented investor bias is the disposition effect. The *disposition effect* is the tendency to hold onto losing investments too long, while selling winners too soon. With a proprietary database including more than 10,000 discount brokerage accounts and nearly 100,000 transactions, Odean (1998) reports that investors are hesitant to realize losses but quick to realize gains.

Emotion is one possible explanation for the disposition effect. Emotions can be differentiated from other mental states because they are associated with observable features (Elster 1998). For example, *a bad mood* is a general sour feeling, whereas a negative emotion can be associated with a particular person or object, such as a poor-performing stock. Two emotions have received particular attention in behavioral finance: regret and pride. Like people in general, investors dislike wishing they had made a different decision. This dislike is so strong that behavior is actually affected before the emotion is even experienced, in other words, by fear of regret. For example, investors do not want to miss out on "the next big thing," particularly if their friends, colleagues, and neighbors are happily relaying their success. Pride and regret are flip sides of each other, but the negative emotion evokes a stronger reaction, consistent with prospect theory's loss aversion.

Behavioral researchers have developed models that incorporate a role for these important emotions. Loomes and Sugden (1982) propose regret theory as an alternative to prospect theory. This theory rests on the assumptions that people experience pride and regret and also make decisions in conditions of uncertainty that take into account these emotions. Fear of regret may underlie the disposition effect if it leads investors to hold onto losers to avoid having to acknowledge their loss and experience regret, while at the same time selling stocks that have performed well and feeling prideful. Experimental studies of the disposition effect provide support for both prospect theory and regret as important drivers on the decision-making process (Weber and Camerer 1998; Summers and Duxbury 2012)

Advances in Behavioral Finance

Thus far, this section has reviewed the foundations of behavioral finance. Behavioral finance researchers have made great progress in building on this base to provide more satisfactory explanations of observed individual and market behavior. While complete coverage of this burgeoning field requires more than a single chapter, this subsection describes a few important contributions to illustrate the directions taken in the literature. Baker and Nofsinger (2010) provide extensive coverage of behavioral finance.

This chapter previously discussed how the framing of a question can affect decision-making. Behavioral researchers find that in addition to the importance of the frame, people seem to use particular cognitive operations in keeping track of their financial situation. They use certain rules to define how to categorize activities and to monitor the frequency of an activity. *Mental accounting* is the term used to describe this process. Thaler (1999) provides a review of how mental accounting can help us understand a wide variety of financial behaviors. For example, a persistent question in finance is why firms pay dividends. Mental accounting can explain why an investor might prefer cash dividend payments to capital gains even with similar tax treatment. An investor who uses mental accounting might keep dividend payments in a "current income" account and capital gains in a separate account, perhaps labeled "long-term savings." The investor might feel free to spend current income but not savings.

In addition to alternatives to the traditional approach to individual decision-making, researchers have made progress on models to describe pricing in markets. Hirshleifer (2001) provides a review of investor psychology and behavioral asset pricing models. An example of a proposed alternative to the CAPM is Shefrin and Statman's (1994) behavioral capital asset pricing model (BAPM). This model incorporates two types of traders: some who make cognitive errors and others who do not. In their model, information sometimes efficiently drives pricing, but other times pricing may be inefficient because uninformed traders move markets. Shefrin (2008) presents detailed development of behavioral asset pricing with different trader types.

In the CAPM or its three-factor extension, a trade-off occurs between risk and return. The BAPM assumes that beta is not a sufficient measure of risk and that risk is not the only factor that determines returns. Statman, Fisher, and Anginer (2008) recognize that personal evaluations of an asset will affect its price. For example, investors will pay a higher price for stock in a "good" company. In fact, how investors feel about a stock, referred to as *affect*, actually underlies the factors that traditional models employ to measure risk. Statman (2010) posits that other behavioral variables, such as a firm's display of social responsibility or social status derived from an association, affect pricing. In the CAPM, return is a function of risk as measured by beta, as expressed in Equation 2.1, and shown in a modified form here:

$$E(R_i) = f(\text{market risk factor}) \tag{2.2}$$

The three-factor model also models return as a function of risk factors as:

$$E(R_i) = f(\text{market, book-to-market, and size risk factors}) \tag{2.3}$$

The BAPM recognizes that other factors affect pricing and is expressed as:

$$E(R_i) = f(\text{risk factors, affect, social responsibility, status, etc.}) \tag{2.4}$$

Behavioral theorists also contribute practical descriptions of how investors form portfolios. Shefrin and Statman (2000) use mental accounting as a basis for their behavioral portfolio theory (BPT) in which some investors segregate assets into layers, or mental accounts, depending on their investment goals. For example, one investment goal might be to provide for retirement, while another is to try to improve the standard of living (i.e., move to a higher level of wealth). An investor with these two goals is risk averse with the retirement account but risk seeking with the "get rich" account. Traditional models do not allow for such goals, but BPT recognizes that investors have subportfolios with disparate aspirations. More recently, Das, Markowitz, Scheid, and Statman (2010) develop a theory of portfolio optimization with mental accounting that brings together important features of traditional mean-variance portfolio theory and BPT. This model combines the two frameworks to connect investors' goals and portfolio construction.

Behavioral finance researchers also propose alternatives to the widely accepted EMH. In particular, Andrew Lo develops the adaptive markets hypothesis (AMH). Lo (2004, 2005, 2012) maintains that the EMH is not wrong, but simply incomplete because human biology cannot be ignored. Markets reflect changes through evolution, just as human behavior is shaped by evolutionary forces. In this view, market efficiency is not absolute, but measured on a continuum. If market participants are well-adapted to the environment, the market will function more efficiently. In a new market or one with a shift in fundamentals, less efficiency can be expected.

Recent studies examine whether market behavior is consistent with the predictions of the AMH. Markets are prone to cycles of efficiency because natural selection encourages learning as new information arrives and as traders compete over resources and profits. Neely, Weller, and Ulrich (2009) examine profit opportunities in foreign exchange markets and find that the observed patterns are consistent with the AMH. Profit opportunities declined too slowly over time to be consistent with the traditional EMH. Instead, the market behaves adaptively and is subject to evolutionary pressures. Similarly, Kim, Shamsuddin, and Lim (2011) report that changing market conditions drive time-varying predictability in returns for the Dow Jones Industrial Average, which is consistent with the AMH.

SUMMARY

Although policy makers, researchers, investment professionals, and investors may continue to debate whether markets are efficient and investors are rational, behavioral finance has made great strides in understanding observed behavior. Just a few short decades ago, questioning the efficiency of market prices was akin to heresy. Today, many recognize that persistent deviations from the predictions of theory provide useful information about how and why people make decisions. Observation of actual behavior informs the development of good theory.

The theory of investment behavior has evolved in recent times. Starting with research in the social sciences, behavioral researchers have accumulated much knowledge relating to the forces shaping investment decisions. Today, few accept the notion that market outcomes are always efficient or that *homo economicus*, or rational man, is the only financial decision maker of interest.

Moving forward, this direction will benefit both policy makers whose goal is to develop appropriate procedure and investors who strive to maximize wealth with limited time and resources in an increasingly complicated world. Behavioral finance seeks to describe the choices not of rational or irrational man, but of real people. The benefits of these insights are already being observed.

DISCUSSION QUESTIONS

1. Describe the primary differences in the measurement of risk between the utility function used in expected utility theory by traditional finance and the value function posited by prospect theory in behavioral finance.
2. What is the difference between risk aversion and loss aversion?
3. What does modern portfolio theory (i.e., traditional finance) say about how an investor should form an optimal stock portfolio?
4. How does Simon's concept of satisficing differ from the traditional approach in which investors maximize expected utility?
5. Describe a heuristic that can be used in decision-making and whether it is ecologically rational.

REFERENCES

Ackert, Lucy F., and Richard Deaves. 2010. *Behavioral Finance: Psychology, Decision-Making, and Markets.* Independence, KY: South-Western, Cengage Learning.
Bachelier, Louis. 1900. *Theorie de la Speculation.* Paris: Gauthiers-Villars.

Baker, H. Kent, and John R. Nofsinger, eds. 2010. *Behavioral Finance—Investors, Corporations, and Markets*. Hoboken, NJ: John Wiley & Sons.

Barber, Brad, and Terrance Odean. 2000. "Trading is Hazardous to Your Wealth: The Common Stock Investment Performance of Individual Investors." *Journal of Finance* 55:2, 773–806.

Barber, Brad, and Terrance Odean. 2001. "Boys Will Be Boys: Gender, Overconfidence, and Common Stock Investment." *Quarterly Journal of Economics* 116:1, 261–292.

Camerer, Colin, and Dan Lovallo. 1999. "Overconfidence and Excess Entry: An Experimental Approach." *American Economic Review* 89:1, 306–318.

Das, Sajiv, Harry Markowitz, Jonathan Scheid, and Meir Statman. 2010. "Portfolio Optimization with Mental Accounts." *Journal of Financial and Quantitative Analysis* 45:2, 311–344.

Davis, Mark, Alison Etheridge, and Paul A. Samuelson. 2006. *Louis Bachelier's Theory of Speculation: The Origins of Modern Finance*. Princeton, NJ: Princeton University Press.

Einhorn, Hillel J., and Robin M. Hogarth. 1981. "Behavioral Decision Theory: Processed of Judgment and Choice." *Journal of Accounting Research* 19:1, 1–31.

Elster, Jon. 1998. "Emotions and Economic Theory." *Journal of Economic Literature* 36:1, 47–74.

Fama, Eugene F. 1970. "Efficient Capital Markets: A Review of Theory and Empirical Work." *Journal of Finance* 31:1, 383–417.

Fama, Eugene F. 1991. "Efficient Capital Markets: II." *Journal of Finance* 46:5, 1575–1617.

Fama, Eugene F., and Kenneth R. French. 1996. "Multifactor Explanations of Asset Pricing Anomalies." *Journal of Finance* 51:1, 55–84.

Gigerenzer, Gerd, Peter M. Todd, and ABC Research Group, eds. 1999. *Simple Heuristics That Make Us Smart*. Oxford, UK: Oxford University Press.

Hirshleifer, David. 2001. "Investor Psychology and Asset Pricing." *Journal of Finance* 56:4, 1533–1597.

Huberman, Gur. 2001. "Familiarity Breeds Investment." *Review of Financial Studies* 14:3, 659–680.

Kahneman, Daniel, and Amos Tversky. 1979. "Prospect Theory: An Analysis of Decision under Risk." *Econometrica* 47:2, 263–291.

Kendall, Maurice G. 1953. "The Analysis of Economic Time-Series, Part I: Prices." *Journal of the Royal Statistical Society* 116:1, 11–25.

Keynes, John Maynard. 1964. *The General Theory of Employment, Interest, and Money*. New York: Harcourt, Brace, Jovanovich.

Kim, Jae H., Abul Shamsuddin, and Kian-Ping Lim. 2011. "Stock Return Predictability and the Adaptive Markets Hypothesis: Evidence from Century-Long U.S. Data." *Journal of Empirical Finance* 18:5, 868–879.

Lo, Andrew W. 2004. "The Adaptive Markets Hypothesis: Market Efficiency from an Evolutionary Perspective." *Journal of Portfolio Management* 30:5, 15–29.

Lo, Andrew W. 2005. "Reconciling Efficient Markets with Behavioral Finance: The Adaptive Markets Hypothesis." *Journal of Investment Consulting* 7:2, 21–44.

Lo, Andrew W. 2012. "Adaptive Markets and the New World Order." *Financial Analysts Journal* 68:2, 18–28.

Loomes, Graham, and Robert Sugden. 1982. "Regret Theory: An Alternative Theory of Rational Choice under Uncertainty." *Economic Journal* 92:368, 805–824.

Markowitz, Harry. 1952. "Portfolio Selection." *Journal of Finance* 7:1, 77–91.

Neely, Christopher J., Paul A. Weller, and Joshua Ulrich. 2009. "The Adaptive Markets Hypothesis: Evidence from the Foreign Exchange Market." *Journal of Financial and Quantitative Analysis* 42:2, 267–488.

Odean, Terrance. 1998. "Are Investors Reluctant to Realize Their Losses?" *Journal of Finance* 53:5, 1775–1798.

Sharpe, William F. 1964. "Capital Asset Prices: A Theory of Market Equilibrium under Conditions of Risk." *Journal of Finance* 19:3, 425–442.

Shefrin, Hersh. 2008. *A Behavioral Approach to Asset Pricing*, 2nd ed. New York: Academic Press Advanced Finance.

Shefrin, Hersh, and Meir Statman. 1994. "Behavioral Capital Asset Pricing Theory." *Journal of Financial and Quantitative Analysis* 29:3, 323–349.

Shefrin, Hersh, and Meir Statman. 2000. "Behavioral Portfolio Theory." *Journal of Financial and Quantitative Analysis* 35:2, 127–151.

Simon, Herbert A. 1955. "A Behavioral Model of Rational Choice." *Quarterly Journal of Economics* 69:1, 99–118.

Simon, Herbert A. 1978. "Rationality as Process and as Product of Thought." *American Economic Review* 68:2, 1–16.

Slovic, Paul, Baruch Fischoff, and Sarah Lichtenstein. 1977. "Behavioral Decision Theory." *Annual Review of Psychology* 18, 1–39.

Statman, Meir. 2010. "What Is Behavioral Finance?" In Arnold S. Wood, ed., *Behavioral Finance and Investment Management*, 1–12. New York: Research Foundation of CFA Institute.

Statman, Meir, Kenneth L. Fisher, and Deniz Anginer. 2008. "Perspectives: Affect in a Behavioral Asset-Pricing Model." *Financial Analysts Journal* 64:2, 20–29.

Summers, Barbara, and Darren Duxbury. 2012. "Decision-Dependent Emotions and Behavioral Anomalies. *Organizational Behavior and Human Decision Processes* 118:2, 226–238.

Thaler, Richard H. 1999. "Mental Accounting Matters." *Journal of Behavioral Decision Making* 12:3, 183–206.

Tobin, James. 1958. "Liquidity Preference as Behavior towards Risk." *Review of Economic Studies* 25:2, 65–86.

Todd, Peter M., and Gerd Gigerenzer. 2003. "Bounding Rationality to the World." *Journal of Economic Psychology* 24:2, 143–165.

Tversky, Amos, and Daniel Kahneman. 1981. "The Framing of Decisions and the Psychology of Choice." *Science* 211:4481, 453–458.

Tversky, Amos, and Daniel Kahneman. 1992. "Advances in Prospect Theory: Cumulative Representation of Uncertainty." *Journal of Risk and Uncertainty* 5:4, 297–323.

Weber, Martin, and Colin F. Camerer. 1998. "The Disposition Effect in Securities Trading: An Experimental Analysis." *Journal of Economic Behavior and Organization* 33:2, 167–184.

von Neumann, John, and Oskar Morgenstern. 1944. *Theory of Games and Economic Behavior*. Princeton, NJ: Princeton University Press.

ABOUT THE AUTHOR

Lucy F. Ackert is Professor of Finance in the Michael J. Coles College of Business at Kennesaw State University. Her research interests include individuals' use of information and financial market reaction to information. Professor Ackert has published numerous articles in refereed journals including the *American Economic Review*, *Journal of Accounting Research*, and *Journal of Behavioral Finance*. In 1993 she received a Smith Breeden Prize for a distinguished paper in the *Journal of Finance*. Professor Ackert recently coauthored *Behavioral Finance: Psychology, Decision-Making, and Markets* and continues to pursue research that provides insights into the behavior of individuals and markets. She is Associate Editor for the *Journal of Economic Psychology* and *Journal of Banking and Finance* and an editorial board member for the *International Journal of Behavioural Accounting and Finance*. Professor Ackert holds a PhD in financial economics from Emory University.

Behavioral Economics, Thinking Processes, Decision Making, and Investment Behavior

Morris Altman
Professor of Behavioral and Institutional Economics,
School of Economics and Finance, Victoria University of Wellington, New Zealand
and Professor of Economics, University of Saskatchewan, Canada

INTRODUCTION

According to traditional economic theory embodied in the efficient market hypothesis (EMH), investor behavior should be rational in terms of incorporating all relevant information into the decision-making process, as well as being calculating, forward looking, and not subject to regret. Such behavior also is ideally bereft of emotions because emotions are assumed to bias decisions away from calculating, forward-looking, and maximizing outcomes. In other words, traditional economics assumes decisions result in optimal financial outcomes. What it assumes to be rational behavior should generate the highest possible returns compared to less rational or irrational behavior. Moreover, rational investor outcomes should be efficient such that, on average, market prices reflect the fundamentals of investment choices and therefore incorporate all relevant information about investment prospects.

This chapter addresses the empirical reality that investor behavior often does not generate outcomes that are efficient, yielding suboptimal financial returns, and market prices often deviate from their fundamental values (e.g., resulting in bubbles and busts) (Shiller 2000). Moreover, the evidence indicates that the returns of active market traders or investors are typically below those generated by passive (or systematic) investors (Malkiel 1973, 2003). This suggests that active decision-making strategies, using modern knowledge technology, including sophisticated financial data gathering and analyses typically do not beat less calculating behavior that relies on decision-making shortcuts. Thus, what many would deem to be more rational behavior often generates subpar economic and financial outcomes.

This chapter examines the contradictions between empirical reality and traditional economic theory through the lenses of behavioral economics. Behavioral economists and behavioral finance researchers play an important role in identifying these various mismatches between reality and theory. Many behavioral economists contend that individuals are characterized by large and persistent biases when making decisions, often driven by the leading role that emotions and *heuristics* (mental shortcuts or mistakes) play in the decision-making process (Tversky and Kahneman 1974; Kahneman and Tversky 1979, 2000; Kahneman 2003, 2011; Altman 2004, 2010b, 2012b; Shefrin 2007; Thaler and Sustein 2008). These biases result in decisions and outcomes that differ from the predictions of traditional economic wisdom, given its prior assumptions about what constitutes rational choice behavior.

Behavioral economics, rooted in the bounded rationality approach developed by Simon (1955, 1978, 1987) and March (1978), who were early pioneers of behavioral economics, also find that real world decision making generates choices and outcomes that deviate from the predictions of the traditional economic wisdom. But from this perspective, the decision-making heuristics are rational given the decision constraints faced by the individual and often generate superior outcomes than what would arise from adopting traditional economic decision-making norms. Errors in decision making can be corrected by improving the decision-making environment (incorporating informational and incentive variables) and through learning (Smith 2003; Gigerenzer 2007).

BEHAVIORAL ECONOMICS, HEURISTICS, AND DECISION MAKING

From the perspective of behavioral economics, both the limited and unique processing capacity of the human brain and the decision-making environment influence decision makers. People adopt ways to decide and choose that differ from how they would behave under the behavioral and institutional assumptions of traditional economics. For instance, many behavioral economists assume that individuals or organizations adopting non-conventional approaches to decision making, rooted in real world decision-making parameters, make rational or smart decisions. This would be the case for household decision makers, management, and investors (March 1978).

Simon (1978, 1987) developed the concepts of bounded rationality and satisficing to encapsulate smart decision-making processes that smart human decision makers develop, adapt, and adopt. Some view this approach as part of an alternative theoretical decision-making framework to the conventional concepts of pure rationality of narrowly calculating and materially maximizing individuals. A boundedly rational satisficing individual does the best she can, given her physiological, psychological, and institutional decision-making parameters. Simon (1987, p. 267) defines *bounded rationality* as "rational choice that takes into account the cognitive limitations of the decision-maker—limitations of both knowledge and computational capacity. Bounded rationality . . . is deeply concerned with the ways in which the actual decision-making process influences the decisions that are reached."

Boundedly rational individuals can make errors in their decisions, but these are often correctable through learning and experience. Moreover, institutional change can reduce the extent of errors in decision making. This approach does not focus on possible biases or persistent errors in decision making. Following this approach, researchers offer arguments and evidence on boundedly rational behavior that often produce superior results (Smith 2003; Gigerenzer 2007; Altman 2012a, 2012b).

Todd and Gigerenzer (2003) and Gigerenzer (2007) refer to decision-making shortcuts that are satisficing by nature as fast and frugal heuristics. Such heuristics might be largely intuitive or more deliberative in nature. Kahneman (2011) calls the former *fast thinking* and the latter *slow thinking*. A key argument here is that individuals learn through education and experience as well as from others and develop methods of arriving at decisions that are best practice. These decision-making heuristics evolve over time (Hayek 1945). They develop through experience and learned behavior based on knowledge of best-practice decision-making behavior developed in one's family or community. Some refer to such evolved decision-making behavior as *evolutionary rationality* (Smith 2003; Gigerenzer 2007).

Fast and frugal heuristics are similar to the *affect heuristic*. It represents a decision-making shortcut that is quick and relatively easy and is typically predicated on intuition and influenced by emotional considerations. This reduces the cost of search and information processing. Given bounded rationality, efforts to reduce decision-making costs are eminently intelligent. However, the affect heuristic can result in errors in decision making or in superior decisions depending on the circumstance.

Although biases and persistent errors, often called *irrational behavior*, are not the mainstay of the boundedly rational approach, they are critical to the Kahneman-Tversky perspective. Here errors are all too often a product of cognitive biases, which persist over time with little or no substantive *Bayesian updating* taking place (i.e., individuals do not update their mental models with new and relevant information). Emotions, which are part of the human decision-making mechanism, play a vital role in generating errors and biases in decision making (Kahneman and Tversky 1979; Kahneman 2003). In the errors and biases approach, even if no limitations exist to an individual's information gathering and processing capacity, the average individual would not behave in the fashion prescribed and predicted by the conventional wisdom because of the introduction of emotional considerations. Emotions would generate errors and biases in decision making.

Recognizing the importance of emotions to decision making is critical to Kahneman and Tversky's development of prospect theory. It represents an alternative to subjective expected utility theory as a means of better understanding and describing decision making under uncertainty (Altman 2010b). Emotions and intuition inform decision-making heuristics, often resulting in suboptimal results (biases and errors) from an individual's long-term perspective.

INVESTMENT HEURISTICS AND INVESTING IN FINANCIAL ASSETS

Investors use various decision-making shortcuts or heuristics to save time and money in a world of uncertainty. Much of this uncertainty is immeasurable in contrast to risk, where probabilities of future events can be determined and assigned (Knight 1921). Using heuristics yields outcomes that often differ from what conventional wisdom predicts. Key questions are whether these heuristics are smart or rational from an individual and social perspective and whether these heuristics can be improved. To introduce some key decision-making variables most pertinent to investors, a good starting point is to provide a narrative on investor decision making in financial markets.

The manner in which individuals tend to invest in financial assets helps illustrate why and the extent to which individuals do not conform to traditional economics (i.e., neoclassical rational behavior) and how this affects economic outcomes. It also helps clarify the distinction between different approaches to behavioral economics and between such approaches and the traditional economic wisdom. Traditional finance's EMH maintains that not only should asset prices reflect the underlying fundamental values of the assets, incorporating all pertinent information, but also that no individual can predict future movements in asset prices because these prices follow a random walk. This is known as the *random walk hypothesis*, articulated in Malkiel (1973) and developed by Fama (1965). In terms of normative behavior, conventional wisdom holds that individuals should follow neoclassical behavior for market efficiency to prevail.

The EMH has three components. One relates to the notion that one cannot consistently predict short-term movements in asset prices. Another assumes that market prices reflect the fundamental value of assets. The third assumes that neoclassical behavior generates optimal financial results.

The evidence does not support the hypothesis that conventional behavioral norms yield optimal results. For example, passive investment (non-super-calculating) strategies typically yield higher returns than more aggressive calculating active approaches. If public policy succeeds in converting passive to active (super-calculating) traders or in hiring the services of active traders, the evidence suggests that such individuals would be worse off financially. Passive investment being superior in terms of outcomes is consistent with the EMH, but not with the normative behavioral perspective of the traditional economic wisdom or with the errors and biases approach to behavioral economics. All that is required for passive investment to be a superior decision-making heuristic is that one cannot predict day-to-day movements in stock and related prices (Thaler 2009).

Wärneryd (2001) concludes that passive investors are typically more successful than the relatively more neoclassical (super-calculating) oriented sophisticated investors. Passive investors hold on to their financial assets over the long term with only marginal adjustments in the short run. They make no effort to engage in active market analysis in an effort to beat the market. Passive traders apply the decision-making heuristic of buying and holding representative shares in, for example, the Standard & Poor's 500 index. This strategy is referred to as *indexing*. The objective is to replicate the returns of such a target fund. Passive investors do not try to beat the index's rate of return and remain passive when facing market volatility. This riding-the-wave heuristic does significantly better than actively engaging in intensive calculating behavior.

Gigerenzer (2007) finds that passive investing strategies are both rational and efficient. He uses the investment behavior of Harry Markowitz to exemplify his case. Markowitz (1952) developed a mathematical formulation to determine the structure of a rate of return maximizing asset portfolio, given an individual's risk preference. He uses what Gigerenzer refers to as the *1/N rule*, wherein available investment funds are equally dispersed across each of the designated N funds. This is a form of passive investment, which is a type of satisficing behavior. This satisficing approach outperforms, net of investment fees, investment portfolios constructed using the optimal algorithms derived from economic theory, except over very long spans of time. For example, 50 assets distributed using the complex algorithm require 500 years to outperform the 1/N rule asset distribution. Passive-based portfolios typically outperform investment portfolios designed by major investment houses and fund managers using active investment strategies (Malkiel 2003). Although active investment strategies sometimes outperform passive, satisficing strategies, these successes do not persist over time and are largely idiosyncratic and consistent with a random walk. Active strategies might achieve superior returns based on superior heuristics, but the typical individual in a world of asymmetric information would have difficulty distinguishing the active investors whose superior results are idiosyncratic from those who results are time consistent.

Overall, passive investment strategies, exemplified by the 1/N heuristic, is a fast and frugal decision-making heuristic that is consistent with the computational capacities of the human brain working within the realm of imperfect and asymmetric information as well as uncertainty. Passive investment strategies also minimize emotional drivers to decision making, which often motivate and determine individuals' investment decisions and can generate errors in decision making. With passive strategies, individuals will not, for example, engage in herding behavior, which is one cause of severe bubbles and busts in asset prices. The passive investor maintains a default investment strategy irrespective of movements in asset prices.

An important caveat exists to this argument. Many individuals or groups of individuals who invest in active-led investment financial portfolios do so passively. They do not intentionally choose an active strategy. Given imperfect, asymmetric, and even incorrect information, they often follow passive strategies to select who will manage their funds. But they do so without necessarily knowing the details of how their funds will be managed or even the difference between passive and active investment strategies. Nor do they necessarily have true knowledge about the expected present discounted value of the returns of a fund managed using a passive versus an active investment strategy. But using passive heuristics to choose investment funds can be rational given a world of bounded rationality. Nonetheless, investors might end up holding a fund that they would have preferred not owning if they had better information and understood the risk-return differences among various funds.

The passive investment heuristic is not the preferred option of most investors who are intent on beating the market. Owners and managers as investors differ from individuals who are investing their money in financial assets but are not fund owners and managers. These are more akin to consumers of financial assets. These investor-consumers typically adopt passive strategies using fast and frugal heuristics. What the preferred investment strategy is for the consumer-investors is unclear because their choices are not based on whether a fund is managed passively or actively. The passive heuristic does a better job describing the behavior of consumer investors than the choices made by investors in general.

For many behavioral economists and economic psychologists, the passive investment strategy of investing in a relatively diversified asset portfolio (such as is given by the 1/N rule) is the optimal heuristic for investor behavior. This assumes that investors are not privy to insider information. Of critical importance is that the active investing behavioral norm (the neoclassical heuristic) tends to result in suboptimal returns. Many investors adopt neoclassical behavioral norms despite the fact that passive investment strategies achieve superior returns. This raises the question: Why would rational individuals adopt investment strategies that are objectively known to yield inferior returns?

The reality of passive investment strategies outperforming active strategies is consistent with the bounded rationality approach to behavioral economics but it is inconsistent with neoclassical economics decision-making norms. However, the superiority of passive strategies is consistent with the hypothesis put forth by Kahneman (2003,

2011) that choices determined by emotional considerations can be error-prone and result in suboptimal decision making. Overall, behavioral economics helps explain why individuals make investment choices that are inconsistent with neoclassical predictions; why fast and frugal heuristics can generate superior financial results; and why some individuals make choices that produce suboptimal economic returns.

THE TRUST HEURISTIC AND DECISION MAKING

The trust heuristic is a nonconventional tool used by decision makers who might engage in irrational or error prone and biased behavior. This heuristic is part of the fast and frugal heuristic toolbox. Like many such heuristics, emotional and intuitive variables affect the trust heuristic. Trust has been part the human decision-making toolbox for a millennium. In the absence of legal guarantees for enforcing contracts, the trust heuristic becomes a substitute for such legal guarantees. It also lowers the transaction costs of engaging in contractual arrangements and buying goods and services, even when legal guarantees and redress are in place (Greif 1989; Landa 1994; Kohn 2008).

Trust is the high probability expectation that the other party to a transaction will deliver on promises made. The reputation of the other party often serves as the basis for trust. Trust-based transactions are often enforced through the negative reputational effect when reneging on a transaction or a relationship and the positive effect when holding true to a contract or a relationship. The reputational effect carries with it economic consequences. Over time, being trustworthy becomes a social norm and evolves into intuitive forms of behavior. Legal and informal sanctions and economic rewards encourage trust. Investors frequently use the trust heuristic as the most effective and efficient way to execute transactions.

When employing the trust heuristic, decision makers locate proxies for the trustworthiness for detailed, complex, and reliable information that cannot be accessed either at all or only at substantial economic and time costs. Among these proxies are the rating agencies of financial assets, government sanction of financial assets, expert opinion, and ethnic, neighborhood, religious, and racial groupings one identifies with or trusts. For example, if Standard & Poor's assigns a triple-A rating to particular financial asset, individuals and financial organizations are likely to trust that such a rating is reliable.

Individuals will invest with family, friends, and members of their community or religious group because they believe that these individuals can be trusted. This type of trust can be enforced if one believes that if the bonds of trust are broken the party in question will suffer reputational and/or economic costs. Moreover, individuals often follow the leaders whom they trust and engage in herding behavior when they are unsure about what product or financial asset to buy or sell. Herding can result in market inefficiencies called *price cascades* or *asset price bubbles* that can be severe, especially when based on misleading information. Investors often assume that portfolio managers are relatively better informed in a world of complex and often misleading information.

Although the trust heuristic is not part of the traditional economics toolbox, it provides an efficient decision-making tool that appears to achieve economic results that are often superior to those obtained when relying on conventional search and information gathering processing decision-making tools. It is also often more efficient and effective than relying on formal and detailed contracts. Thus, the trust heuristic is a form of rational or boundedly rational or smart behavior. However, the effectiveness and efficiency of the trust heuristic is a function of the extent to which trustworthiness and reciprocity in trust-based transactions have become part of one's community and society's social norms. It is also a function of the extent to which both proxies for trustworthiness can be trusted and decision makers have accurate and reliable information with which to make decisions. If someone makes a decision on the basis of false information that is believed to be true, this decision is not the individual's preferred decision and does not reflect her true preferences (Altman 2010b).

The trust heuristic results in a market failure in a world of false and deceptive information. This would be the case when individuals invest in triple-A rated assets when in fact the assets should be rated A or below. This would also be true when an individual invests in funds that she believe to be legitimate and whose rate of return and risk information are accurate and reliable. The Madoff Ponzi fund is a good example of individuals investing in a fund they falsely believed to be legitimate and subject to government regulatory scrutiny. People decide intuitively given the trust proxies and related signals at hand. Hence, this illustrates the importance of the trustworthiness of trust proxies for the efficiency of the trust heuristic.

Institutional design positively affects the efficiency of the trust heuristic and increases the probability that information to investors is reliable and accurate (i.e., trustworthy). This reduces the chances that consumer-investors and investors make choices on prospects that are inconsistent with their preferences. Although this does not preclude errors in decision making, it does reduce the probability of making errors. Also, enhancing the capacity of decision makers to understand the relevant information and presenting information in a relatively easily understandable format (known as *financial literacy*) also contributes to reducing the extent of decision-making errors. Such institutional design often involves government intervention in certifying and rating financial information, investment funds, and fund managers (Altman 2012a).

OTHER CRITICAL DECISION-MAKING HEURISTICS

Behavioral economists have identified other heuristics important to investor decision making. Some view these as generating errors and biases in decision making. Others arguably produce superior financial results. These heuristics, whether they result in optimal or best possible economic results, characterize the decision-making behavior of real world investors. One important determinant of the heuristics adopted is that immeasurable forms of risk, sometimes referred to as uncertainty, frequently characterize decision-making environments.

Knightian Uncertainty versus Risk

Behavioral economics views uncertainty where outcomes can be projected based on assigned probabilities (expected values) and also when uncertainty is such that expected outcomes cannot easily be predicted. Much of contemporary behavioral economics focuses on how humans would behave when probabilities are easily assigned to outcomes and when expected values can be computed with relative ease. However, the decision-making environment is also of considerable importance where investors cannot easily determine expected values.

Knightian uncertainty is uncertainty that cannot be measured with any precision. Risk can be measured in terms of probabilistic outcomes, based on past parameters and outcomes. Although contemporary economics focuses on risk, Knight (1921) considers uncertainty to be critical to substantive economic analysis. Although risk is important, uncertainty is often more so. Rational individuals can be expected to behave differently when faced with risk as compared to uncertainty.

Animal Spirits

Animal spirits, also called *irrational exuberance*, is an important driver of investment behavior (Shiller 2000; Akerlof and Shiller 2009; Farmer 2010). In traditional economic modeling, animal spirits do not affect investor behavior. But animal spirits are certainly a fast and frugal heuristic that characterizes much investor decision making. They are highly intuitive and involve trusting one's gut instincts, which are often experientially based, as well as the gut instincts of others. In contemporary behavioral economics, animal spirits are often a source of error and bias in decision making, which can result in manias, panics, and eventually crashes in asset markets, with large repercussions for the rest of the economy. For Keynes (1936), animal spirits are much more than this. They characterize much of investor and consumer behavior and need to be integrated into the modeling of the economic decision making.

Keynes (1936) refers to *animal spirits* as behavior that is motivated by emotive factors, as opposed to calculating or hard-core economic rationality demanded by traditional economics. Keynes (pp. 161–162) speculates that decisions "can only be taken as the result of animal spirits—a spontaneous urge to action rather than inaction, and not as the outcome of a weighted average of quantitative benefits multiplied by quantitative probabilities."

Although animal spirits are not calculating behavior, they are based on a sense of what one expects to occur in the near future and a heuristic based on one's expectations in a world of uncertainty. Animal spirits are informed by the information that an individual has at hand and by the behavior of others whom one believes or trusts have a better understanding of market movements and outcomes than oneself. Animal spirits would be most important when uncertainty is Knightian (incalculable), but also when risks are calculable in terms of assigned probabilities to outcomes.

Regarding animal spirits in general, government and central bank pronouncements can affect a person's beliefs about movements in future asset prices, as can the news and statements by preeminent and respected individuals. A key point in favor of introducing animal spirits as a variable in modeling decision making is that price movements such as interest rates and changes in income are not the only important variables determining behavior. Non-economic variables, especially psychological variables, embodied in the concept of animal spirits, are also of overriding importance. Even if interest rates are very low, individuals might not increase spending on financial assets and housing stocks (e.g., if animal spirits are depressed).

Here the elasticity of demand relative to changes in interest rates is at or near zero. Keynes refers to this as the *liquidity trap*. The same elasticity of demand would be expected relative to price changes for a large set of marketed products given a depressed state of animal spirits.

The animal spirits heuristic is consistent with bounded rationality and satisficing. Using this heuristic is smart behavior given the constraints facing the individual. Nevertheless, animal spirits can serve to generate large deviations from economic fundamentals. This is especially true when information is false or misleading and public pronouncements of experts dampen or heighten the state of animal spirits, incentivizing decision makers to make economic choices that help create manias and panics and, hence, avoidable economic crisis. Methods of reducing such deviations involve improving the quality of information and having government recognize the importance of public pronouncements on the economy for decision making in the financial markets and the real economy. Recognizing the importance of animal spirits leads to improved modeling of decision making and to increased efficiency of public policy and institutional design.

Beauty Contest

The concept of a "beauty contest," developed by Keynes (1936), follows from the assumption of Knightian uncertainty. Decision makers do not know what the future might bring. In economics, a *beauty contest* refers to rational individuals estimating what future prices (the beauty) might be by anticipating what other people believe future prices (the most beautiful) will be, as opposed to what the fundamental value (true beauty) of the assets actually is. Such beliefs, if actualized, help determine the direction and movements in future prices (i.e., investor sentiment and momentum).

Assume that how other people behave or how one expects other people to behave in the market motivates animal spirits. In a world of uncertainty, investors use proxies such as rumors or insights from experts to build their expectations. These information flows provide insight on how other investors will behave. Such flows also provide information to the decision maker to make more intelligent investment decisions predicated on gut feeling. This is important to investors who engage in active investment strategies in a world of bounded rationality and Knightian uncertainty. However, such strategies have little to do with the fundamental values underlying the assets.

Herding

Herding occurs when decision makers follow the leader in terms, for example, of investment decisions. Herding is a very common evolved heuristic. It is particularly characteristic of investor behavior and is related to Keynes' model of beauty context behavior. Herding occurs in the face of bounded rationality and Knightian uncertainty. It occurs when investors are unsure how asset prices will move and trust in the wisdom of the crowds or the leader of the crowd. Herding behavior, if persistent, results in price cascades (i.e., when prices increases at an increasing rate) and, therefore, bubbles in asset prices. In other words, such behavior can result in manias, panics, and crashes. Better information about the assets being purchased, especially their true risk and the fundamental value of the asset, can moderate the extent of herding and price cascades. The extent that individuals expect to bear the economic burden of any panics and crashes that invariably follow manias in asset prices is also important. This requires minimizing the extent of *moral hazard* (i.e., when individuals do not bear the full risk of their choices) that characterizes investor behavior.

Loss Aversion

According to Kahneman and Tversky (1979), individuals have a strong aversion to losses (*loss aversion*) when holding risk parameters constant. The authors maintain that people weigh losses about twice as much as gains, so that $100 gained does not neutralize $100 lost, which would be the case based on conventional wisdom. Based on loss aversion, in the previous example, a person's utility would be reduced substantially. An individual characterized by loss aversion would avoid options that might be characterized by losses even when the expected value of such options is positive. Individuals are willing to sacrifice income or wealth to mitigate prospective economic loses. Income and wealth maximization would not be the objective of loss-averse individuals.

Disposition Effect

The *disposition effect* results in individuals selling stocks too quickly that have appreciated in price, but holding on to stocks that have depreciated in price for too long. This is consistent with acknowledging gains but not losses. In this case, individuals will sell high too quickly to avoid possible losses (i.e., a decline in the value of a stock). They will resist selling stocks that are falling in value or a business losing money in an effort to avert losses, hoping that their investment will recover its value in time. Yet, the evidence suggests that in panics many individuals sell stocks that are falling in value too soon, precipitating market crashes.

Illusion of Control

An *illusion of control* occurs when decision makers believe they have some control over outcomes although they do not. These decision makers then proceed to design and adopt strategies that they believe will affect outcomes but which are determined either randomly or are outside of their control. The economic consequence of the illusion of control is that individuals subject to this illusion unnecessarily expend time, money, and mental energy trying to affect outcomes. A classic example of the illusion of control are gamblers who believe that they can consistently win fair bets by devising methods of gambling that objectively have no substantive effect on outcomes. Some contend that this would also be the case of amateur and even professional investors who believe that they can persistently outperform the market.

Overconfidence

Unlike the illusion of control, overconfidence pertains to scenarios in which decision makers can actually affect outcome. Overconfident individuals are those who subjectively believe that they can affect outcomes to a greater extent than they actually can. When this occurs they will invest in projects or overinvest because of *overconfidence bias*. When a person is 100 percent confident of her decision, this decision should be 100 percent correct ex post in terms of outcome (e.g., discounted net present value [NPV]). If a student believes that he will earn a grade of 90 on an exam and objectively can be expected to earn a grade of 60, this is another example of overconfidence bias. An overconfident investor will underestimate the risk of his investment and take greater risk than is wise. Such was the case with Long Term Capital Management, where its PhD-intensive financial management thought they were too smart to make poor and overly risky bets on the market, eventually requiring a $3.6 billion bailout orchestrated by the Federal Reserve. One source of overconfidence is ignoring *sentiment-based risk* (i.e., risk derived from decision makers acting on emotional considerations, which are often informed by the trust heuristic and herding).

Overconfidence bias is not confined to point estimates of prospective outcomes. It also refers to the subjective evaluation of confidence intervals around these point estimates. An individual might predict that he will earn a 30 percent rate of return on a prospect, but an overconfident individual ignores the probability of earning a negative rate of return. In this case, realizing a low probability but highly negative return could have severe economic consequences. This notion is related to what Taleb (2010) refers to as "black swan" events, which are very low probability events that, if they occur, can have major consequences.

Kahneman (2011) maintains that an important factor responsible for overconfidence is the *illusion of validity*. He contends that individuals tend to construct consistent narratives that confirm their prior beliefs. Developing such narratives that provide additional but irrelevant information for predictive purposes also tends to confirm individuals in their prior beliefs. If a narrative is inconsistent, this can motivate individuals to assume that an event is highly improbable when based on objective criteria. One example that follows from Kahneman relates to grades earned by students. One student has a mix of A and B grades (incoherent) and another has straight As (coherent). Some individuals assume that the straight A student is most likely to succeed. But objectively speaking, this is not the case. In the case of an investor, if one can tell a coherent story, for example as done by Bernard Madoff, his profile is that of a successful investor. Thus, consumer-investors assumed that Madoff was a successful investor without consulting more pertinent information. Many investors with coherent narratives are failures as investors including Madoff and Long Term Capital Management. A key supplementary assumption of the illusion of validity is that individuals will systematically ignore contrary evidence given the coherence of a particular narrative. This overlaps with confirmation bias as later discussed. Under the illusion of validity, individuals use inappropriate mental models to engage the decision-making process.

Overoptimism

Overoptimism occurs when an individual believes that he or she is less at risk or more likely to achieve a certain rate of return or outcome than is objectively true. An overly optimistic investor believes that he or she is less likely to fail or is more likely to succeed than another individual, even if no clear and unequivocal objective basis exists for this belief.

Overoptimism can be independent of overconfidence. *Overconfidence* is specific to an individual's subjective and exaggerated perception of his or her capabilities relative to objective standards. Overconfidence and overoptimism are related in that both overoptimistic and overconfident individuals tend to take excessive risks relative to what they would take if their perceptions of risks and reward were more aligned with objective analyses.

Overconfidence and Overoptimism

Both overconfidence and overoptimism characterize many investors. This would be expected in a world of bounded rationality and Knightian uncertainty, assuming a random distribution of preferences for overconfidence and overoptimism. Such individuals may make decisions that may be materially damaging to themselves and others. Determining the extent to which this negative spillover is a function of an incentive environment that facilitates or encourages moral hazard is important to determine. In other words, decision makers can engage in what appears to be overconfident and overoptimistic behavior if they believe that they will not be responsible for the downside of their relatively risky decisions.

Another issue related to both overconfidence and overoptimism is whether such behavioral preferences are necessarily bad for the economy. That is, does some optimal level of overconfidence and overoptimism exist that is good for the individual and the economy? Overconfidence and overoptimism appear to be critical characteristics of entrepreneurship when decision makers cannot predict with any substantial degree of confidence what the outcomes of particular decisions might be. Both entrepreneurs and investors in financial markets take Knightian risks, whereas non-entrepreneurial types have a strong predisposition toward certain outcomes. Individuals characterized by uncertainty avoidance would not be entrepreneurs. Entrepreneurship is crucial to vibrant market economies. Such Knightian decision makers believe that they will succeed where their competitors will fail or not do as well.

Many behavioral economists note that overconfidence and overoptimism are not necessarily suboptimal from a societal perspective but rather that excessive overconfidence and overoptimism tend to produce suboptimal economic results. Moreover, excessive overconfidence and overoptimism are more likely to occur when individuals make decisions independently of others, which facilitate the prevalence of the conformation bias and limit the extent of relevant information available to the decision maker. One method of reducing the extent of excessive overconfidence and overoptimism is for one individual's decisions to be informed by other decision makers or advisors in an open-minded decision-making environment. This would avoid the possible negative spillovers from excessive overconfidence and overoptimism.

In the errors and biases approach, excessive overconfidence and overoptimism are assumed to overwhelm loss avoidance. Another approach is that loss avoidance does not characterize all individuals. Those individuals characterized by excessive overconfidence and overoptimism in the economic domain might be neoclassical in their preferences about losses and gains. This would be particularly true of entrepreneurs.

Overoptimism and overconfidence are related to the *illusion of certainty*, where an individual believes that something is true even though objectively it might not be. It is also related to *hindsight bias*, where individuals believe that given the occurrence of an event, they are responsible for it. This is a form of spurious correlation. The fact that a person's past actions are highly correlated with current positive outcomes does not necessarily mean that the individual's past decisions were responsible for current outcomes. This is synonymous with the *illusion of control*, where a person believes that he has control over outcomes that might occur for random reasons or for reasons unrelated to his behavior. A close connection exists between the illusion of certainty and hindsight bias.

Also related to both overoptimism and overconfidence is *confirmation bias*. Individuals ignore information or other people who challenge their prior hypotheses. Instead, they focus their attention on information and people such as advisors who confirm their prior hypotheses. Such contrary information and people can be dismissed as not being pertinent to their unique situation.

Also pertinent to overoptimism and overconfidence is *representativeness bias*. People believe that past returns or events are indicative or representative of future returns or events, ignoring the probabilistic nature of future outcomes. This is related to the *recency bias* where individuals evaluate economic and financial performance based on the most recent results. In this case, decision makers ignore past events, such as historical market downturns, and assume that the more recent events, such as the upside of asset bubbles, are representative of what one should expect in the future. Although many behavioral economists give the impression that these various biases and illusions are a general human characteristic, they might simply characterize a subset of human decision makers.

Lack of Bayesian Updating

One argument put forth by the errors and biases school in behavioral economics is the persistent lack of updating preferences, decisions, and choices based on new and better information sets. If this were the case, individuals could not and would not learn. Evidence suggests, however, that individuals tend to engage in Bayesian updating. So, in one-shot games, decision makers can make mistakes. But with experience, individuals tend to correct the errors of their ways as long as they have adequate incentives to do so. Bayesian updating over time is consistent with the bounded rationality approach to behavioral economics.

Ambiguity Aversion

Ambiguity aversion occurs when an individual avoids prospects where the outcome is ambiguous (i.e., less information and certainty about ambiguous outcomes exist) and favors more certain outcomes. This is the case even if the expected value of the ambiguous prospect is greater than the present value of the more certain prospect. Some refer to ambiguity aversion as a cognitive bias, although it is actually a by-product of imperfect information and Knightian uncertainty. Given these environmental constraints, the expected value cannot be easily determined and a large band or high variance exists around the point estimate, which is the expected value. The issue is not whether ambiguity-averse individuals do not want to increase their income or wealth. Rather, in any income or wealth maximizing exercise, individuals can be expected to choose the prospect with the less ambiguous outcome. Different individuals can be expected to be characterized by different levels of ambiguity aversion.

Winner's Curse

Some evidence indicates that in auctions and initial stock offerings, investors pay more than the intrinsic value of these options (Thaler 1988; Kagel and Levin 2002). So, if exploration rights to an oil field are auctioned off and this property has an expected present value of $1 billion, the winning bid would be $1.2 billion. The winner is cursed by winning a prospect that either generates financial losses or generates gains that are less than expected. The winner is cursed by overvaluing the intrinsic value of the prospect for which they bid. Although the winner's curse is most prevalent for bidders who are least experienced and poorly informed, it often persists even for experienced investors when faced with many bidders. More competition can result in suboptimal outcomes even for the more experienced and informed investors (a winner's curse). Also, the probability of the being cursed by a winning bid increases with the uncertainty of outcomes. In such situations, experience matters. But individuals continue to bid in auctions even when they know that the winner might be cursed. One way to minimize the probability and extent of a winner's curse is to design auctions such that the second highest bid wins (second-price auction) or introduce Vickrey auctions where the highest bid wins, but the winner only pays the value of the second highest bid.

RATIONAL INVESTOR DECISION MAKING IN A WORLD OF COMPLEX INFORMATION

The errors and biases approach to investor behavior focuses on systematic errors and biases in decision making. In contrast, the bounded rationality approach pays at least as much attention to the decision-making environment, which is assumed to have a critically important effect on decision making. Errors and biases can be a product of this environment as opposed inherent cognitive illusions. Posner (2009) provides an example of this. He contends, as do Lewis (2010) and Roubini and Mihm (2010), that a major cause of the severity of the 2008–2009 financial crisis was the incentive environment that evolved over the prior two decades. This decision-making environment, which was also a by-product of financial market deregulation, reduced the cost to rational individuals and large financial corporations of knowingly engaging in very high-risk behavior. Individuals were protected from downside risks while benefiting from the success of risky bets. This created a classic moral hazard environment that eventually resulted in catastrophic damage to financial markets and to the real economy because markets never internalized the negative externalities. This institutional failure was a product of the belief that individuals will self-regulate, fearing the negative reputational effects of poor decisions. This did not occur. Given, for example, a predisposition toward overconfidence and overoptimism by investors, an appropriately designed decision-making environment could minimize the extent of socially suboptimal economic decisions. Overconfidence and overoptimism need not generate severe booms and consequent busts.

Apart from incentives, the state of information is important to the decision-making environment. Misleading information and information that is difficult to understand or locate can contribute to errors in decision making, given the incentive environment, even in the absence of relevant cognitive biases. For example, informational failures can generate serious and avoidable errors in decision making. Such failures can occur if stocks are inappropriately rated, if individuals falsely believe that funds are properly regulated, if information is framed in a misleading manner, and if managers do not understand the theoretical basis (often scripted in sophisticated mathematical language) for their companies' decisions.

Shiller (2009, 2010) contends that an impartial body, such as a government agency, should be responsible for the provision of quality information. This is akin to the regulation and provision of product labels for foods and certificates of cleanliness earned by restaurants. Without high quality information, rational individuals will most likely make choices that they will regret. This is a form of avoidable market failure. Trustworthy information will increase the probability that individuals will not invest in assets that have higher risks than they can tolerate.

Exhibits 3.1 and 3.2 illustrate some of these arguments. Exhibit 3.1 highlights some main distinctions between the different approaches to behavioral and traditional economics regarding decision making. The errors and biases approach uses the neoclassical benchmark to measure the efficiency of decision-making processes and outcomes. The neoclassical production possibility frontier (PPF) given by (ac) is regarded as optimal, whereas the actual PPF (fg) is assumed to be achieved using heuristics. The gap between (ab) and (fg) is a function of persistent errors and biases in decision making. In the bounded rationality approach, neoclassical decision making yields a PPF of (cd) in Exhibit 3.1, whereas heuristics typically result in a PPF analogous to the thick PPF of (mstn). If the actual outcome is given by PPF (st) or (fg), there might be correctable errors in decision making. The actual outcomes need

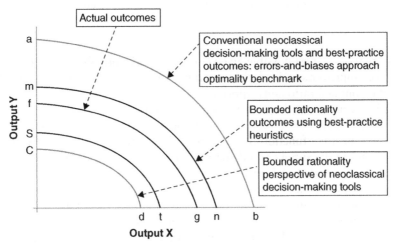

EXHIBIT 3.1 Errors and Biases and Bounded Rationality Perspectives

Note: The errors and biases (EB) and bounded rationality (BR) approaches to behavioral economics use different benchmarks for best-practice decision-making tools and related outcomes. For EB, traditional economic (neoclassical) decision-making tools are the benchmark for optimality, where persistent biases and errors in decision making are common and hardwired into human decision makers. For BR, evolved heuristics are best-practice, although errors and suboptimal outcomes occur for informational, computational, and institutional reasons. Conventional neoclassical decision-making tools often result in seriously suboptimal outcomes.

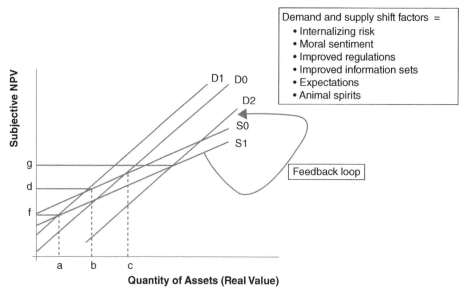

EXHIBIT 3.2   Asset Prices and the Decision-Making Environment

Note: The buying and selling of assets can be modeled as a positive function of the expected net present value of assets. Increases in demand (shifts in the demand curve) can cause manias and bubbles—serious deviations from fundamental values—and, thereafter, severe crashes of asset bubbles. Increases in supply, based on overoptimism and false expectations, can feed back into demand, driving it upward and generating asset bubbles. Internalizing risk, increased moral sentiment, appropriate financial market regulations, improvements to information, and financial education can moderate these movements in demand and supply.

not be optimal or the best possible given constraints. The possibility for error as well as room for improvement in decision-making processes and environment always exists in the bounded rationality approach.

Exhibit 3.2 maps out demand and supply functions for financial or housing assets as these relate to asset prices. A simplifying assumption here is that supply and demand are a positive function of the expected net present value (ENPV) of these assets. Changes in the supply and demand of assets yield changes in price or ENPV of assets. Increases in demand for assets that can cause large manias and bubbles can be moderated by shift factors such as internalizing risk, moral sentiment, improved regulations, improved information sets, and changes to expectations and animal spirits. The same variables affect the supply function. This is an important point because increasing the supply of assets can spark a more than proportionate increase in demand, generating manias and bubbles through feedback loops, illustrated by a shift from S0 to S1 increasing demand from D0 to D2.

SUMMARY

Humans have evolved various decision-making heuristics or fast and frugal shortcuts to cope with a world of bounded rationality. These heuristics might also be optimal given bounded rationality, whereas the neoclassical decision-making alternative might generate suboptimal results. These heuristics can involve both what Kahneman (2011) calls intuitive decision-making processes (fast thinking) or more careful decision-making processes (slow thinking). Sometimes fast thinking processes can generate errors in decision making or decisions that are privately utility maximizing and socially suboptimal, such as the behavior that generated the 2008–2009 stock market and housing market crashes. Much depends on the decision-making environment and the opportunities investors and other decision makers have to learn from their mistakes. Incentives, the quality of information, the ability to understand information, the decision-making process, and moral sentiment all affect the decision-making process, given whatever cognitive shortcomings characterize decision makers.

Behavioral economics recognizes the importance of non-neoclassical decision-making processes as a staple for human decision makers. The errors and biases approach views many of these heuristics as inbred defects in the human decision-making modus operandi, which too often generate errors in decision making and thereby suboptimal outcomes from the perspective of the individual and society at large. Investors are very much party to this defective decision-making apparatus. Moreover, changing error-prone behavior is very difficult. From the perspective of the bounded rationality approach, these heuristics are rational and typically superior in outcomes than what flows from neoclassical decision-making processes. These nonconventional heuristics often make sense given imperfect information, the brain's limited and unique processing capacity, and Knightian uncertainty. From the bounded rationality approach, decision makers can make decision-making errors or make decisions that are suboptimal socially. Changing institutional parameters inclusive of new and improved information sets can seriously and positively affect these decisions.

DISCUSSION QUESTIONS

1. Highlight key differences between the two major approaches to behavioral economics for investment behavior.
2. Identify some issues about financial market outcomes that behavioral economics attempts to address and explain.
3. Compare the errors and biases approach to the origins of financial crises with the bounded rationality approach.
4. Identify the critical differences between conventional risk and Knightian uncertainty and the importance of these differences for understanding investor behavior.
5. Discuss the concept of overconfidence and how this relates to investment failure and possible errors in investor decisions.

REFERENCES

Akerlof, George A., and Robert J. Shiller. 2009. *Animal Spirits: How Human Psychology Drives the Economy, and Why It Matters for Global Capitalism*. Princeton, NJ: Princeton University Press.

Altman, Morris. 2004. "The Nobel Prize in Behavioral and Experimental Economics: A Contextual and Critical Appraisal of the Contributions of Daniel Kahneman and Vernon Smith." *Review of Political Economy* 16:1, 3–41.

Altman, Morris. 2010b. "Prospect Theory and Behavioral Finance." In H. Kent Baker and John R. Nofsinger, eds., *Behavioral Finance*, 191–209. Hoboken, NJ: John Wiley & Sons.

Altman, Morris. 2012a. "Implications of Behavioral Economics for Financial Literacy and Public Policy." *Journal of Socio-Economics* 41:5, 677–690.

Altman, Morris. 2012b. *Behavioral Economics for Dummies*. Mississauga, Canada: John Wiley & Sons.

Fama, Eugene F. 1965. "Random Walks in Stock Market Prices." *Financial Analysts Journal* 21:5, 55–59.

Farmer, Roger E. A. 2010. *How the Economy Works: Confidence, Crashes and Self-fulfilling Prophecies*. New York: Oxford University Press.

Gigerenzer, Gerd. 2007. *Gut Feelings: The Intelligence of the Unconscious*. New York: Viking.

Greif, Avner. 1989. "Reputation and Coalitions in Medieval Trade: Evidence on the Maghribi Traders." *Journal of Economic History* 49:4, 857–882.

Hayek, Friedrich A. 1945. "The Use of Knowledge in Society." *American Economic Review* 35:4, 519–530.

Kagel, John H., and Dan Levin. 2002. *Common Value Auctions and the Winner's Curse*. Princeton, NJ: Princeton University Press.

Kahneman, Daniel. 2003. "Maps of Bounded Rationality: Psychology for Behavioral Economics." *American Economic Review* 93:5, 1449–1475.

Kahneman, Daniel. 2011. *Thinking, Fast and Slow*. New York: Farrar, Straus and Giroux.

Kahneman, Daniel, and Amos Tversky. 1979. "Prospect Theory: An Analysis of Decisions under Risk." *Econometrica* 47:2, 313–327.

Kahneman, Daniel, and Amos Tversky. 2000. *Choices, Values and Frames*. New York: Cambridge University Press and Russell Sage Foundation.

Keynes, John Maynard. 1936. *The General Theory of Employment Interest and Money*. London: Macmillan.

Knight, Frank H. 1921. *Risk, Uncertainty, and Profit*. Boston, MA: Houghton Mifflin.

Kohn, Marek. 2008. *Trust: Self-Interest and the Common Good*. Oxford: Oxford University Press.

Landa, Janet T. 1994. *Trust, Ethnicity, and Identity: The New Institutional Economics of Ethnic Trading Networks, Contract Law, and Gift-Exchange*. Ann Arbor, MI: University of Michigan Press.

Lewis, Michael. 2010. *The Big Short: Inside the Doomsday Machine*. New York: Allen Lane.

Malkiel, Burton G. 1973. *A Random Walk Down Wall Street*, 6th ed. New York: W. W. Norton & Company.

Malkiel, Burton G. 2003. "Passive Investment Strategies and Efficient Markets." *European Financial Management* 9:1, 1–10.

March, James G. 1978. "Bounded Rationality, Ambiguity, and the Engineering of Choice." *Bell Journal of Economics* 9:2, 587–608.

Markowitz, Harry. 1952. "Portfolio Selection." *Journal of Finance* 7:1, 77–91.

Posner, Richard A. 2009. *A Failure of Capitalism: The Crisis of '08 and the Descent into Depression*. Cambridge, MA and London: Harvard University Press.

Roubini, Nouriel, and Stephen Mihm. 2010. *Crisis Economics: A Crash Course in the Future of Finance*. New York: Penguin.

Shefrin, Hersh. 2007. *Behavioral Corporate Finance: Decisions That Create Value*. New York: McGraw-Hill/Irwin.

Shiller, Robert J. 2000. *Irrational Exuberance*. Princeton, NJ: Princeton University Press.

Shiller, Robert J. 2009. "How about a Stimulus for Financial Advice?" *New York Times*, January 17. Available at www.nytimes.com/2009/01/18/business/economy/18view.html?_r=1.

Shiller, Robert J. 2010. "How Nutritious Are Your Investments?" *Project Syndicate*. Available at http://www.project-syndicate.org/commentary/how-nutritious-are-your-investments.

Simon, Herbert A. 1955. "A Behavioral Model of Rational Choice." *Quarterly Journal of Economics* 69:1, 99–188.

Simon, Herbert A. 1978. "Rationality as a Process and as a Product of Thought." *American Economic Review* 70:2, 1–16.

Simon, Herbert A. 1987. "Behavioral Economics." In John Eatwell, Murray Millgate, and Peter Newman, eds., *The New Palgrave: A Dictionary of Economics*, 266–267. London: Macmillan.

Smith, Vernon L. 2003. "Constructivist and Ecological Rationality in Economics." *American Economic Review* 93:3, 465–508.

Taleb, Nassim N. 2010. *The Black Swan*. New York: Penguin.

Thaler, Richard H. 1988. "Anomalies: The Winner's Curse." *Journal of Economic Perspectives* 2:1, 191–202.

Thaler, Richard H. 2009. "Markets Can Be Wrong and the Price Is Not Always Right." *Financial Times*. Available at www.ft.com/intl/cms/s/0/efc0e92e-8121-11de-92e7-00144feabdc0.html#axzz2LsDJHp2e.

Thaler, Richard H., and Cass R. Sustein. 2008. *Nudge: Improving Decisions about Health, Wealth, and Happiness*. New Haven, CT and London: Yale University Press.

Todd, Peter M., and Gerd Gigerenzer. 2003. "Bounding Rationality to the World." *Journal of Economic Psychology* 24:2, 143–165.

Tversky, Amos, and Daniel Kahneman. 1974. "Judgment under Uncertainty: Heuristics and Biases." *Science* 185:4157, 1124–1131.

Wärneryd, Karl-Erik. 2001. *Stock-Market Psychology*.Cheltenham, UK: Edward Elgar.

ABOUT THE AUTHOR

Morris Altman is Head of the School of Economics and Finance at Victoria University of Wellington, where he is also Professor of Behavioral and Institutional Economics. He is also Professor of Economics at the University of Saskatchewan, serving as elected head from 1994 to 2009. Professor Altman was President of the Society for Advancement of Behavioral Economics from 2003 to 2006 and the Association for Social Economics in 2009, and Editor of the *Journal of Socio-Economics* for nine years until 2012. He was selected for the Marquis *Who's Who of the World*. Professor Altman has published 90 refereed papers and six books on behavioral economics, economic history, empirical macroeconomics, and public policy. He has made more than 150 international presentations on these subjects and is actively researching behavioral economics involving choice behavior, institutional frames, and ethical considerations.

Personal Finance Issues

CHAPTER 4

Financial Literacy and Education

Michael S. Finke
Professor and Retirement Planning & Living Director, Department of
Personal Financial Planning, Texas Tech University

Sandra J. Huston
Associate Professor and Personal Financial Literacy Program Director,
Department of Personal Financial Planning, Texas Tech University

INTRODUCTION

Financial literacy is a relatively new term that began appearing in news headlines in the mid-1990s. Since its inception, confusion has surrounded what financial literacy is and how one becomes financially literate. Financial literacy may refer to specific knowledge, specific skill, perceived knowledge, financial behavior, financial experience, financial outcomes, and/or financial education. As a result, researchers have proposed many definitions and methods of measuring financial literacy (Hung, Parker, and Yoong 2009; Huston 2010). In 2008, the President's Advisory Council on Financial Literacy (PACFL) (2008, p. 4) attempted to officially define financial literacy as "the ability to use knowledge and skills to manage resources effectively for a lifetime of financial well-being." However, both the appropriateness and universal adoption of this definition have been questioned (Hung et al. 2009; Huston 2010). The lack of a standard financial literacy measure may be attributed to the relative infancy of the field of study and the confusion surrounding the nature of the construct (Remund 2010; Knoll and Houts 2012).

A new term has emerged in the United States—financial capability. This term originated from work done in Australia and New Zealand. In 2010, the President's Council on Financial Capability replaced the PACFL and defined *financial capability* as "an individual's capacity, based on knowledge, skills, and access, to manage financial resources effectively" (Financial Literacy and Education (FLEC) 2011, p. 8). Although the intent of introducing financial capability was presumably to distinguish it from financial literacy, the definitions from the President's councils do not markedly differ. The issue is not so much about what the construct is called but rather what the construct is and why it is useful in understanding people and their financial situations. For the purposes of this chapter, the term financial literacy is used to describe the knowledge and skills associated with financial behavior. Financial literacy, in this context, is a distinct and different construct than financial education, financial behavior, financial experience, and financial outcome or well-being.

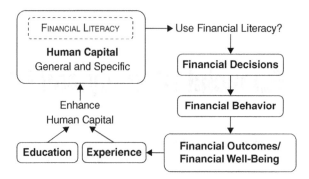

EXHIBIT 4.1   The Nature of Financial Literacy

Note: This exhibit provides the context for defining and measuring financial literacy. Financial literacy is modeled as a specific form of human capital. The exhibit also shows the relationship among financial literacy, financial decisions, financial behavior, financial outcomes/well-being, and financial education.

The Nature of Financial Literacy

Human capital is a term economists use to describe an individual's productive inputs. In other words, human capital is the sum of a person's knowledge, cognitive skills, and physical abilities. Financial literacy is a form of human capital that is specific to the knowledge and skills regarding personal finances (Huston 2010).

Exhibit 4.1 shows how financial literacy is related to financial decisions, behavior, outcomes, education, and experience. Like all human capital, financial literacy may be enhanced or increased through education and/or experience. Delavande, Rohwedder, and Willis (2008) model financial literacy attainment as a human capital investment activity. The idea is that this type of specific capital is an important productive input into producing financial management activities within the household (Hsu 2011).

Individuals who possess relatively high levels of financial literacy will not necessarily use those skills in the financial decision-making process. Similarly, people may not ultimately behave in ways that are consistent with their financial literacy level. Therefore, those who demonstrate poor financial behaviors or exhibit suboptimal financial well-being may not be necessarily financially illiterate. Also, all financially illiterate people may not necessarily have negative financial outcomes because they may have access to another person's human capital or they may be lucky. From a human capital perspective, no theoretically direct connection exists between financial literacy and financial well-being. Yet, the majority of research supports the notion that financially literate people tend to have better financial outcomes than their financially illiterate counterparts.

Most research focuses on the impact of financial literacy on financial behavior or financial outcomes rather than the construct itself. However, a growing body of research examines the conceptualization and measurement of financial literacy (Hung et al. 2009; Huston 2010; Hsu 2011). More researchers are adopting a systematic, human capital approach to understanding financial literacy, although no standard method is currently used to measure this form of human capital specific to personal finances.

Measuring Financial Literacy

Researchers conceptualize financial literacy in different ways and many do not actually define financial literacy (Hung et al. 2009; Huston 2010). For example, in a study reviewing 71 papers related to financial literacy, Huston (2010) reports that the majority (72 percent) fail to define financial literacy. In terms of human capital dimensions, some studies focus on identifying financial concepts (National Council of Economic Education 2005a, 2005b; Lusardi and Mitchell 2007a) or on financial knowledge (FINRA 2003; Hilgert, Hogarth, and Beverly 2003; Moore 2003; Lusardi 2008a, 2008b). Other studies include financial skills (ANZ 2008; Mandell 2008; Lusardi and Tufano 2009) or a combination of knowledge and skills (Servon and Kaestner 2008; Huston 2012).

In addition to identification, knowledge, and skill, some studies include or equate financial literacy to *numeracy*, which is the ability to perform basic mathematical calculations (Lusardi and Mitchell 2007a, 2007b, ANZ 2008; Gustman, Steinmeier, and Tabatabai 2012). Numeracy is a more general form of human capital that may be related to financial literacy, but is a distinct skill from the financial literacy construct (Hung et al. 2009). Financial literacy is more than the ability to perform mathematical calculations. Some studies incorporate perceived or self-reported knowledge and/or skill in lieu of or in addition to objective knowledge and skill measures. Although a self-reported level of financial literacy may be helpful in assessing a person's confidence to use this human capital, it does not provide an accurate indicator of the quality of the human capital stock specific to personal finances.

Definitions of financial literacy that include behavior and/or financial outcome (PACFL 2008; FLEC 2011) fall outside the purview of human capital and are not as useful from a research perspective. Although having an effort to standardize the notion of financial literacy is commendable (Knoll and Houts 2012), Remund (2010) contends that shortcomings exist with this government sanctioned definition, namely its lack of implied measurability and content. Others, including Hung et al. (2009) and Huston (2010), maintain that the greatest shortcoming with the FLEC and related definitions is including financial behavior. The human capital specific to personal finances (i.e., financial literacy) is a distinct and different construct from financial decision-making, financial behavior, financial outcome/well-being, and financial education. If the goal is to understand how human capital specific to personal finance is related to financial behavior and outcome, then the financial literacy concept needs to be limited to the knowledge and skill level of the individual. If the objective is to understand the enhancement process to acquiring or improving a person's financial literacy level, then financial education efforts must be viewed as a separate and distinct activity apart from the stock of human capital itself. Ideally, a financial literacy measure should include an assessment of both knowledge and skills related to personal finances to capture the scope of human capital that may be potentially used when making financial decisions and/or incentivizing financial behavior.

Knowledge and skills pertaining to personal finances encompass a broad array of topics ranging from basic concepts such as compounding and budgeting to more complex aspects such as borrowing, investing, and insurance. Huston (2010) notes three primary management areas pertaining to personal finance: (1) money basics, (2) intertemporal transfers, and (3) resource protection. Money basics include concepts related to the time value of money, purchasing power, transaction accounts, and accounting statements including budgets, cash flow, and balance sheets. Intertemporal transfers include borrowing (moving future anticipated resources into the present) and investing (moving present resources into the future using either lending or equity instruments, or a combination of both). Resource protection involves managing risk and preserving wealth through insurance products, diversification, tax planning, and/or estate planning. In terms of personal finance content, over half of previous studies include either basic, borrowing, or investment content, whereas, one-third include protection content (Huston 2010). About 35 percent of financial literacy studies have measures limited to one content area (e.g., investments or debt), 40 percent have measures with two or three content areas, and the remaining 25 percent have measures that incorporate content from all four areas (basics, borrowing, investing, and protection). If the goal of measuring financial literacy is to get an accurate and complete picture of a person's human capital specific to personal finances, then an assessment in all personal finance content areas seems warranted. However, most research does not incorporate a comprehensive assessment of financial literacy content.

Another source of variation among financial literacy measures is the number of items within the instrument. Among the financial literacy measures reviewed by Huston (2010), items ranged from a minimum of three to a maximum of 68. The mean number of items across all instruments is 16, the median is 13, and the mode is 10 items. Among the comprehensive measures of financial literacy—those including all content areas—the items range from a low of 12 to a high of 36 with a mean of 21 items. Huston (2012) views the *Financial Literacy Assessment Test* (FLAT), which consists of 20 items, as the only comprehensive instrument that is specifically designed to include knowledge and skill human capital dimensions within each of the four content areas.

The majority of financial literacy research does not provide any indication of whether respondents are financially literate. Understandably, research is more concerned with testing whether a positive relationship exists between the quality of human capital specific to personal finances and financial well-being, rather than determining whether a person is financially literate. In practice, establishing a threshold to aid in assessing the quality of a person's human capital specific to personal finances would be helpful. If the hypothesis that financially literate people are more likely to demonstrate optimal financial behavior and experience better financial outcomes than financially illiterate people, then understanding or determining the point at which an individual is considered to be financially literate would also be helpful. In order to design human capital enhancement activities that enable people to become financially literate, an important element is having the ability to determine the point at which a person is deemed to be financially literate.

EXAMPLES OF FINANCIAL LITERACY MEASURES

Although a lack of consensus exists on both the definition and operationalization of the financial literacy construct in financial literacy research, many examples are available in which researchers attempt to measure financial literacy (Hung et al. 2009; Huston 2010). To provide some examples of financial literacy measures used in research, three measures are discussed. The first measure reflects its frequency of use in the literature and the second provides an example of creating a measure based on available financial literacy items. The third measure offers an example of a measure specifically designed to reflect and capture the human capital approach to financial literacy presented in this chapter.

Measure 1—A Widely Used Measure

According to Knoll and Houts (2012), the measures developed by Lusardi and Mitchell (2007b, 2009) dominate the financial literacy research. Although some researchers question the validity of the Lusardi-Mitchell approach (Knoll and Houts 2012; Huston 2010), several national surveys include such questions and are worth examining because of their frequency of use.

The Lusardi-Mitchell approach involves using two measures: One incorporates "basic" financial literacy questions (Lusardi and Mitchell 2007b) and the second adds "sophisticated" financial literacy items (Lusardi and Mitchell 2009). Various national surveys include items from both of these measures such as the Health and Retirement Study (HRS), the American Life Panel (ALP), the National Longitudinal Study of Youth (NSLY97), and the National Survey portion of the 2009 National Financial Capability Study (NS-NFCS). The basic financial literacy assessment includes five questions and all involve using numeracy skills (three items on time value of money and two items on purchasing power calculations). The surveys contain eight items within the sophisticated financial literacy questions and these items all focus on investing (e.g., stocks, bonds, mutual funds, risk, and diversification). Some studies include as few as three basic questions (e.g., HRS 2004) while other studies incorporate all 13 items (e.g., ALP data).

The main drawback of using these measures is that they do not provide a comprehensive measure of financial literacy. The basic questions focus on only one aspect of financial literacy—numeracy—and the sophisticated questions focus on investing. Even used together, these items ignore the areas of borrowing and protection of resources (e.g., risk management and insurance). A second issue is that this measure does not distinguish knowledge from skill in terms of human capital specific to personal finances.

Measure 2—A Composite Measure Based on Available Items

Knoll and Houts (2012) focus on measuring financial knowledge using the item response theory (IRT) technique to create a financial literacy scale based on existing items available in three main data sets: the ALP (waves 5, 21, 50, and 64), the HRS in 2004 and 2008 and NS-NFCS in 2009. From these data, the researchers identify 60 unique items across the three studies. They remove one item because of local dependence issues and analyze the remaining 59 items. Of these, Knoll and Houts select 20 items for inclusion in the financial knowledge scale to provide a broad range of topics and a wide range of difficulty parameters.

The financial literacy knowledge scale includes a combination of nine multiple-choice questions and 11 true/false questions and represents all four areas of personal finance discussed earlier in the chapter. The majority of the items (13 items or 65 percent) relate to investing (stocks, bonds, diversification, and risk). Of the remaining seven questions, three focus on money basics (two on time value of money and one on purchasing power calculations), two are related to borrowing (one on mortgage and one on credit cards), and the remaining two questions involve protection (both on life insurance).

This approach has two main advantages: (1) The IRT method selects the "best" questions to be used and (2) the scale is broad in its content and covers all the personal finance areas. This measure also has some drawbacks. First, the scale focuses on knowledge and does not incorporate the skill dimension of human capital. Second, the items are skewed toward investing, which may be appropriate but no evidence to date suggests this is the case. Finally, the items incorporated in this financial knowledge scale are drawn from a pool of existing questions. Although no evidence suggests these items are the most appropriate measures, this method helps to ensure that they are the most appropriate of those available.

Measure 3—A Measure Designed to Capture Human Capital

The third measure is based on research from the *Financial Literacy Project* at Texas Tech University (Huston et al. 2008). Researchers developed a comprehensive 20-item instrument called the Financial Literacy Assessment Test (FLAT) to measure financial literacy of adults in the United States. In this instrument, the construct of financial literacy consists of the two main human capital elements of knowledge and skill. The instrument also incorporates all four of the personal finance content areas—money basics, borrowing, investing, and protection. Additionally, a scoring grid that aids in interpreting instrument scores accompanies the instrument. Exhibit 4.2 shows some sample questions from the survey.

The instrument consists of 16 objective items: eight knowledge items and eight items that test the respondent's ability to appropriately apply knowledge. Each personal finance area has two items. Each knowledge question relates to a corresponding ability question to enable comparing the pairs to determine the sophistication with which respondents can apply personal finance knowledge. The greater the number of corresponding pairs, the greater is the respondent's sophistication. The remaining four items are subjective and gauge the respondent's confidence about managing and using personal finance concepts and products. The FLAT assessment instructs respondents to rate their level of confidence on a scale from no confidence (0) to a great deal of confidence (10). The combination of ability and confidence items represents skill potential (i.e., the ability and confidence to use personal finance knowledge).

---

1. How confident are you with managing money?
2. Net worth is equal to: (1) total assets, (2) total assets plus liabilities, or (3) total assets minus liabilities.
3. Which bank account is likely to pay the highest interest rate on money saved? (1) Savings account, (2) six-month CD or certificate of deposit, or (3) three-year CD.
4. If your assets increase by $5,000 and your liabilities decrease by $3,000, your net worth would: (1) increase by $2,000, (2) increase by $8,000, or (3) increase by $3,000.
5. Savings accounts and money market accounts are most appropriate for: (1) long-term investments like retirement, (2) emergency funds and short-term goals, or (3) earning a high rate of return.

EXHIBIT 4.2 BASIC Portion of the Financial Literary Assessment Test

Note: This exhibit shows the BASIC portion of the FLAT assessment. The first question asks the respondents to self-report their confidence level on a scale of 0 to 10. The second and third questions are knowledge questions and the remaining questions are designed to assess the respondents' ability to use personal finance knowledge. The FLAT contains three additional portions to assess in the areas of borrowing, investing, and resource protection.

Researchers equally weight the two dimensions (knowledge and application) to determine an individual's overall financial literacy score. To aid with interpretation, they analyze the financial literacy scores in each of the dimensions to segregate respondents into one of three financial literacy zones: target, caution, and danger. The target zone represents high scores in both the knowledge and skill dimensions. The danger zone includes low scores in either knowledge, skill, or both and the caution zone captures the remaining scores (i.e., at least mid-range or higher). Within the danger zone are three sub-categories: overconfidence, paralysis, and unawareness. Financial overconfidence is characterized by respondents with high confidence scores but low knowledge and sophistication. Financial paralysis occurs when the opposite is true (i.e., individuals with high knowledge but low skill and sophistication). Financial unawareness represents those with low scores on both knowledge and skill dimensions.

The main advantage of the FLAT assessment is that it is intentionally designed to capture the human capital specifically related to personal finances. Financial literacy scores, along with the scoring grid, provide useful information for educators who are concerned with designing curriculum to enhance financial literacy capital as it pinpoints particular areas of weakness among those who take the test. Although the Cronbach's Alpha for the FLAT instrument is acceptable (0.86), this method cannot test for the appropriateness of the items to measure knowledge versus skill. *Cronbach's Alpha* is a statistical coefficient used to assess the internal consistency of a scale. Thus, a potential drawback of the FLAT instrument may be in the ability of the items to distinguish knowledge from skill. However, preliminary results from an fMRI analysis of these questions indicate that different parts of the brain are activated when comparing the group of knowledge questions to the group of application questions (Huston and James, 2012). *Functional magnetic resonance imaging* (fMRI) is a procedure used to measure brain activity by detecting changes in blood flow as the respondent is exposed to information on a screen while in the MRI machine. Also, equally weighting both content and human capital dimensions in the scoring process may be inappropriate. More research is needed to identify the most appropriate scoring method.

FINANCIAL LITERACY AND BEHAVIOR

Financial literacy studies show a positive relationship between financial literacy test scores and measures of socioeconomic status such as education, income, and wealth. Evidence by van Rooij, Lusardi, and Alessie (2011) finds that basic financial literacy increases with each level of education and with each quartile of wealth. These results are not entirely surprising because a higher level of education includes coursework in economics or finance and correlates with greater income and wealth.

Lusardi, Mitchell, and Curto (2010) provide evidence that financial literacy is transferred from parents with greater education and investment experience to their children. This transfer of financial knowledge from higher socioeconomic status parents to their children, coupled with higher endowed human capital and increased likelihood of advanced educational attainment, may contribute to a broader gap in knowledge between consumers with and without a college degree.

Peress (2004) creates a model of investment information acquisition where an individual is motivated to invest in costly information when the increase in utility from improved portfolio quality exceeds the time and transaction costs of obtaining financial information. Because the wealthy or those with higher expected lifetime wealth anticipate a larger utility gain from better investment decisions, they are more likely to increase their financial literacy.

Financial literacy gives consumers the tools they need to come closer to maximizing expected lifetime utility by allocating financial resources more effectively. Lifecycle consumption smoothing objectives are easily accomplished by financially literate consumers who are able to calculate optimal savings needed and to select more efficient financial instruments. An example is the understanding of compounding and how much savings would be needed to create an income stream that allows a retiree to maintain his pre-retirement level of consumption. Banks, O'Dea, and Oldfield (2010) find that respondents with higher numeracy are less likely to reduce their consumption after retirement. The unanticipated discontinuity between pre- and post-retirement consumption may be the most significant source of welfare loss from uninformed intertemporal decision-making. All else being equal, one would expect that those with greater financial resources and lower time cost of decision-making (the ability to understand financial concepts) would be more likely to estimate how much they need to save for retirement.

Lusardi and Mitchell (2007a) find that financial literacy, measured by the ability to understand a basic compound interest question, predicts planning for retirement. In a study that attempts to isolate the extent to which greater financial literacy improves retirement wealth, Behrman, Mitchell, Soo, and Bravo (2010) use an instrumental variable to control for common motivations to increase both financial literacy and formal education. The authors find evidence that financial literacy has a positive independent impact on retirement wealth and that the effect of educational attainment alone is minor.

Other sources of welfare loss are inefficient asset allocation, investment selection, and tax efficiency (asset location). The change from defined benefit to defined contribution retirement plans has shifted the burden of investing from more sophisticated money managers to individual investors who have less investment knowledge and experience. One might expect a welfare loss from this shift from professionally directed to individually managed investment portfolios if the individuals have limited financial literacy. According to van Rooij et al. (2011), only 7.5 percent of respondents in the lowest financial literacy quartile own stock compared to 15 percent in the second quartile, 26.5 in the third, and 44.4 percent among those with the highest literacy scores. The authors find that financial literacy predicts stock ownership independent of income, wealth, and education in a multivariate analysis. A person's financial literacy score is also a positive and significant predictor of retirement plan participation (Fornero and Monticone 2011). Household portfolio quality in the United States suffers from insufficient diversification, for example, by investing too much in company stock or in only domestic securities. Evidence by von Gaudecker (2011) finds that numerical ability is significantly related to losses from under-diversified portfolios, but financial knowledge does not predict portfolio quality.

The accumulation of excessive debt may also reflect an inability to make effective life cycle decisions. Those with lower financial literacy may select inappropriate financial products that either transfer rents to a financial institution (e.g., through hidden fees, higher interest rates than expected, or unanticipated product characteristics such as the resetting of adjustable interest rates), or transfer more consumption to the present than a consumer intends. For example, consumers with insufficient financial literacy may not realize how much consumption they are transferring from the future when they use a high interest credit card. This misunderstanding, as opposed to the intentional accumulation of debt by someone with a very high rate of time preference, leads to a welfare loss from a lack of financial literacy.

Soll, Keeney, and Larrick (2013) provide evidence that consumers with lower numerical ability have difficulty understanding the consequences of credit card borrowing. Subjects with lower numeracy skills underestimate the time needed to pay off a loan balance because they have difficulty grasping the implications of interest compounding. Lower levels of debt literacy increase the likelihood of incurring fees for late payment and exceeding borrowing limits and interest charges from revolving card balances and obtaining cash advances (Lusardi and Tufano 2009). Lusardi and Tufano estimate that low debt literacy accounts for as much as a third of the fees and interest expenses paid by borrowers. Stango and Zinman (2011) show that consumers who are less able to estimate compound interest effects are more vulnerable to price discrimination by lenders who are able to shroud borrowing rates.

The selection of complex, inappropriate mortgages by uninformed consumers possibly contributed to the financial crisis of 2008–2009. In reality, demand for these dangerous mortgages seems to have been more a function of geographic home price appreciation than unsophisticated borrowers. More financially literate borrowers obtain lower rates on their mortgage and choose a mortgage product that is more appropriate for their budget (Fornero, Monticone, and Trucchi 2011). More sophisticated borrowers can also better understand the option value of a mortgage requiring a low down payment in an area of high real estate price appreciation.

Amromin et al. (2011) find that those with higher credit scores and incomes more commonly choose complex mortgages that allow a household to postpone loan repayment. Complex mortgage borrowers were also far more likely to default during the financial crisis. These borrowers also walked away from a mortgage when it was in their best interest to do so. In contrast, Duca and Kumar (2011) find an association between lower financial literacy and an increase in borrowing against home equity before the financial crisis. Evidence from the subprime market also suggests a significant correlation between low numeracy and higher default and delinquency rates (Gerardi, Goette, and Meier 2010). The mortgage crisis may be an example of a negative externality caused both by strategic default among overly sophisticated consumers and by consumer financial ignorance.

On average, women have lower levels of financial literacy than men (Fonseca et al. 2010; van Rooij et al. 2011). However, lower literacy scores are only significant for women who are under age 36, college educated, white, earning a higher income, and most significantly those who are currently married. Women who never married are significantly more knowledgeable than men, as are women who are divorced or widowed. Women who have spent more years in a relationship have lower financial literacy scores than men who have been in a long-term relationship. Apparently, when men and women marry, the wife often cedes financial decision-making to the husband in order to more efficiently divide household production activities. Hsu (2011) explains that this incentive to shift decision-making responsibility within a couple can explain lower levels of financial literacy among women. Women who become widows increase their financial literacy scores in order to make effective decisions on their own. Women who are no longer able to delegate financial decisions to their husbands when they become independent either through widowhood or divorce, appear to increase their financial knowledge, reducing the social welfare implications of a gender financial literacy imbalance (Lusardi and Mitchell 2008). These results also suggest the possibility of increasing one's financial literacy scores when incentives are sufficient.

Adults lose some ability to process new information and make accurate complex decisions in old age because financial decisions require information processing skills. Agarwal, Driscoll, Gabaix, and Laibson (2009) investigate whether financial decision-making quality declines with advanced age. They find an inverse U-shaped relationship between age and decision quality within a number of financial domains. For example, interest rates on credit (independent of credit rating) are lowest in the early fifties, and increase with youth and advanced age. In a large sample of respondents age 60 and over, Finke, Howe, and Huston (2011) find a clear negative linear relationship between financial literacy scores and age. Measured financial literacy scores decline in advanced age by about 2 percent per year. The authors also find that confidence in financial decision-making abilities does not decline with advanced age, leading to an increasing disparity between actual and perceived financial abilities that implies substantial vulnerability to financial mistakes in old age.

Higher financial literacy scores and better numerical ability among those with greater cognitive ability suggests that innate ability, and not necessarily attained human capital through education, may explain variation in financial decision-making quality. Lusardi et al. (2010) find that differences in correctly answered numeracy, inflation, and risk diversification questions are greater between groups of high and low cognitive ability young respondents than any other demographic characteristic. Disentangling the effects of innate ability from acquired information requires empirical finesse. Solutions include financial literacy assessment questions that clearly test attained information and financial outcomes variables that are unaffected by differences in preferences between lower- and higher-cognitive ability individuals.

An example is portfolio choice and cognitive ability. Christelis, Japelli, and Padula (2010) find that stock ownership increases with cognitive ability. Because bond ownership is weakly correlated with cognitive ability and is generally less complex to understand, the authors conclude that those with the endowed capacity to better understand more information-intensive financial instruments will favor such instruments. Cole and Shastry (2009) also find that a relationship between higher cognitive ability and stock ownership is independent of years of education. However, the influence of endowed human capital on stock ownership rests on the assumption of similar risk preferences among those with less and more cognitive ability.

According to evidence by Dohmen et al. (2010), respondents with greater measured intelligence have significantly higher levels of risk tolerance and a lower rate of time discounting than those with lower cognitive ability. Hastings and Mitchell (2011), who use a measure of time preference and financial literacy to predict retirement savings, confirm this result. They find that present-biased time orientation has a stronger impact on both likelihood of retirement plan participation and total retirement savings. Low cognitive ability also increases the cost of financial literacy education by increasing the amount of time and effort needed to understand a financial concept. Not surprisingly, a low score on a childhood test of cognitive ability predicts low financial literacy later in life (Herd and Holden 2012).

Although evidence shows that financial literacy and numerical processing ability are related to positive financial outcomes, Gustman et al. (2012) investigate the pathway from numeracy to retirement knowledge and conclude that motivation to learn is more important than mathematical ability. The size of a respondent's pension predicts his understanding of pension characteristics such as knowing the value of his pension income at retirement age and early retirement options. No consistent relationship appears between numeracy and pension knowledge after controlling for other factors such as education and income. Numeracy also does not predict knowledge of Social Security benefits. A more likely explanation for the relationship between cognitive ability and better financial outcomes such as retirement saving or stock ownership is that they may be attributed to other characteristics related to cognitive ability such as risk tolerance, higher income, and a lower rate of time preference. As van Rooij et al. (2011) find, a basic financial literacy test that primarily measures numerical ability is not a consistent predictor of stock ownership while a more direct measure of financial knowledge significantly predicts who will own equities.

FINANCIAL LITERACY EDUCATION

Higher financial literacy is associated with better financial decisions. Thus, financial education to improve literacy can increase social welfare. In theory, subsidized financial education should give people greater access to the tools they need to navigate complex financial markets. Evidence of the effectiveness of financial education, however, is mixed at best. In a review of the financial education literature, Lyons et al. (2006) attribute the variation in estimates of financial education effectiveness to variation in the quality of education programs and the inexact science of measuring improvements in knowledge or decision-making ability. The lack of a standardized, high quality household finance education curriculum is a major barrier to financial education.

Several studies question the effectiveness of financial literacy education. For example, Cole and Shastry (2009) compare financial market participation before and after imposing mandatory financial literacy education in high schools and find no difference. The authors also find no increase in gross state product (GSP) five years after an education mandate. In a review of the financial literacy education literature, Willis (2011) maintains that relying on financial literacy education to improve consumer welfare may be counterproductive. Little empirical evidence indicates that financial education in high school courses or through counseling programs has any impact on increased financial literacy or improved financial decision-making.

The basic lack of skills such as mathematical ability or understanding of financial theory reduces the likelihood that financial education alone will provide consumers with the tools they need to select an optimal portfolio, understand complex mortgage products, or estimate the amount of money they need to save each month to live well in retirement. Even if financial education is improved, producers will respond with even more complex financial products in order to extract rents from the less sophisticated. More efficient solutions might include the following: providing public financial assistance to individuals or subsidizing financial advice as an employee benefit; using defaults to ensure that the less knowledgeable can choose not to invest in financial literacy and still make a good financial choice; prohibiting products that are clearly not in anyone's best interest or establishing suitability thresholds; and regulating sales incentives among those who sell financial products.

Sweden provides the largest laboratory in which to study the impact of widespread financial education on retirement behaviors. In 2000, the Swedish government started a national financial literacy education initiative to help citizens better understand a new pension system. Swedes receive direct information from the government (so-called orange envelopes) intended to improve their ability to make pension decisions. Some information, such as information on mutual fund selection, seems to have resulted in lower portfolio quality because consumers did not have the investment knowledge to use the information effectively (Sunden 2008). Other studies document the ineffectiveness of U.S. mutual fund disclosure information (Choi, Laibson and Madrian 2010). Other informational initiatives that focus on providing more basic and clear information and the judicious use of defaults as well as mandatory contributions have combined to make Swedish citizens more prepared for retirement and invested in higher quality retirement portfolios.

Hsu (2011) finds that financial literacy scores can increase when a greater incentive exists to invest time and effort to improve one's financial knowledge. Clark, Morrill, and Allen (2012) present evidence of the importance of incentives in predicting which employees will respond to financial education. Younger employees, who have more to gain in present value from effective retirement decisions, are far more likely to respond to retirement information initiatives than older employees. If most benefits of improved financial decisions occur in the future, motivation to obtain financial information may be related to the rate of discounting applied to future consumption. Those who place greater value on the future will be more inclined to invest in knowledge that improves future well-being. In an experiment that tested time preference and willingness to receive free financial information, Meier and Sprenger (2007) find that those who value the future less are less likely to participate. This may also explain why more educated, higher-wealth German bank customers are more likely to take advantage of free, high quality financial advice (Hackethal, Haliassos, and Jappelli 2012).

Clark et al. (2012) provide convincing evidence that employer financial education experiments can improve both measured financial literacy and retirement decision-making. The employer provided education to employees during intensive half-day and longer retirement planning programs. Employees were grateful for the financial education, implying that their pre-education level of knowledge was less than optimal. They also scored higher on retirement knowledge questions, even when tested a year after the seminar. Most importantly, workers who held incorrect beliefs about retirement instruments such as Social Security changed their preferences after receiving financial education. A policy change that mandated mortgage counseling to potentially vulnerable consumers applying for a complex mortgage product appears to have led less sophisticated consumers to either abandon their search or to select more competitive mortgage products (Agarwal et al. 2009). These results provide evidence that targeted, high quality information to motivated consumers can improve welfare through improved decision-making quality.

Financial education can be provided either through direct person-to-person education or through indirect information or disclosure. Evidence suggests that information policy that helps people understand tradeoffs of financial choices can be effective. Soll et al. (2013), for example, find that both sophisticated and unsophisticated individuals are better able to estimate the amount of time needed to pay off a loan when presented with a more descriptive credit card statement. A study of information disclosure at the point of sale in a chain of payday lenders finds that information about the fees paid over time reduced demand for payday loans (Bertrand and Morse 2011). An experiment showing participants how compounded savings early in life grows into a much larger amount by retirement increased motivation to increase retirement savings (McKenzie and Liersch 2011). A costly investment in finance-related human capital may not be needed if citizens are able to delegate some complex decision-making to a government entity that then provides disclosure information allowing consumers to better understand financial trade-offs.

If consumers with greater financial literacy are more likely to use financial education services, financial education may have the unintended consequence of increasing gaps in financial literacy. For example, Calcagno and Monticone (2011) find that consumers with lower financial literacy are less likely to seek financial advice. Individuals who are more future-oriented and educated are more likely to benefit from disclosure (Bertrand and Morse 2011). Any information policy that does not mandate exposure to information, such as through required counseling or disclosure, will likely benefit consumers who are most interested in improving their financial literacy. The effectiveness of product disclosure requires substantial oversight and enforcement to ensure that producers do not use biased information to extract rents from less financially literate consumers. For example, Stango and Zinman (2011) find that many lenders attempt to skirt Truth in Lending Act disclosure rules. In markets where enforcement is limited, biased perceptions by less sophisticated consumers lead to market interest rates that are as much as 4 percentage points higher than when disclosure regulation is stronger.

SUMMARY

An important implication of research in financial literacy is recognition that observed variation in household financial decisions cannot necessarily be attributed to variation in individual preferences. If individuals do not have the ability to accurately assess how their financial decisions will affect their welfare, then observed behavior may reflect this ignorance rather than preferences. For example, selecting a mortgage whose rate will likely reset to a much higher rate does not necessarily indicate greater risk tolerance and a higher anticipated future income path. It may simply indicate a lack of awareness of financial product characteristics.

Policy makers interested in improving household financial decision quality may view the correlations between financial literacy and positive outcomes as evidence that public resources should be allocated to financial education. Little evidence, however, suggests that broad financial literacy education initiatives will improve either literacy or decision-making enough to justify the expense. Concise and specific financial education provided to motivated consumers appears to be the most efficient policy solution. Examples include disclosure that easily allows consumers to understand the intertemporal trade-offs of borrowing, or information that allows a consumer to easily select a lower-fee, more diversified mutual fund within a retirement account. This type of policy substitutes preprocessed financial information by a public entity for costly investment in finance-related human capital by the individual. In markets characterized by high welfare loss by individuals because of complexity and transaction amount (e.g., complex mortgages among less sophisticated borrowers or variable annuities among elderly consumers), some type of mandatory third-party counseling may be warranted. Mandatory counseling may be even more important when bad choices resulting from low financial literacy affect social welfare objectives and a present-oriented or low cognitive ability consumer is not motivated or able to effectively use publicly provided financial information.

Financial literacy in the United States is surprisingly low, and certainly too low to expect that consumers can make effective financial decisions with many of the most complex product markets. A basic, high quality standardized financial literacy curriculum provided in high schools would be an important first step. If all Americans are given the ability to understand basic tax laws, the difference between a stock and a mutual fund, and some idea of how retirement savings translates into annual income in retirement, they will be equipped to make some of the most important financial decisions. Beyond high school, financial education is most effective when presented to motivated consumers. As Willis (2011) notes, mandating financial education to consumers who are not interested is a waste of time for consumers and a misuse of resources for educators. With that said, information provided at the point of sale that consumers of below average financial literacy can understand may be the most effective way to efficiently improve financial decision-making quality.

DISCUSSION QUESTIONS

1. Discuss the various facets that the term *financial literacy* has been used to describe and which is most appropriate from a human capital perspective and useful from a research perspective.
2. Discuss the main methods used to measure financial literacy in the academic literature and describe which method is most appropriate.
3. Distinguish between financial literacy and numeracy and discuss the empirical evidence related to the relationship between numerical ability and decision-making quality.
4. Discuss the role of motivation in financial literacy.

REFERENCES

Agarwal, Sumit, Gene Amromin, Itzhak Ben-David, Souphala Chomsisengphet, and Douglas D. Evanoff. 2009. "Do Financial Counseling Mandates Improve Mortgage Choice and Performance? Evidence from a Natural Experiment." Working Paper, Federal Reserve Bank of Chicago.

Agarwal, Sumit, John C. Driscoll, Xavier Gabaix, and David Laibson. 2009. "The Age of Reason: Financial Decisions over the Life Cycle with Implications for Regulation." *Brookings Papers on Economic Activity*, Fall, 51–101.

Amromin, Gene, Jennifer Huang, Clemens Sialm, and Edward Zhong. 2011. "Complex Mortgages." NBER Working Paper No. 17315.

ANZ. 2008. "ANZ Survey of Adult Financial Literacy in Australia." Available at www.anz.com/Documents/AU/Aboutanz/AN_5654_Adult_Fin_Lit_Report_08_Web_Report_full.pdf.

Banks, James, Cormac O'Dea, and Zoe Oldfield. 2010. "Cognitive Function, Numeracy and Retirement Saving Trajectories." *Economic Journal* 120:548, F381–F410.

Behrman, Jere R., Olivia S. Mitchell, Cindy Soo, and David Bravo. 2010. "Financial Literacy, Schooling, and Wealth Accumulation." Population Aging Research Center Working Paper 10–06.

Bertrand, Marianne, and Adair Morse. 2011. "Information Disclosure, Cognitive Biases, and Payday Borrowing." *Journal of Finance* 66:6, 1865–1893.

Calcagno, Riccardo, and Chiara Monticone. 2011. "Financial Literacy and the Demand for Financial Advice." Available at http://ssrn.com/abstract=1884813 or http://dx.doi.org/10.2139/ssrn.1884813.

Choi, James, David Laibson, and Brigitte Madrian. 2010. "Why Does the Law of One Price Fail?" *Review of Financial Studies* 23:4, 1405–1432.

Christelis, Dimitris, Tullio Jappelli, and Mario Padula. 2010. "Cognitive Abilities and Portfolio Choice." *European Economic Review* 54:1, 18–38.

Clark, Robert L., Melinda S. Morrill, and Steven G. Allen. 2012. "The Role of Financial Literacy in Determining Retirement Plans." *Economic Inquiry* 50:4, 851–866.

Cole, Shawn, and Kartini Shastry. 2009. "Smart Money: The Effect of Education, Cognitive Ability, and Financial Literacy on Financial Market Participation." Working Paper No. 09–071, Harvard Business School.

Delavande, Adeline, Susan Rohwedder, and Robert Willis. 2008. "Preparation for Retirement, Financial Literacy and Cognitive Resources." Michigan Retirement Research Center Working Paper WP 2008-190.

Dohmen, Thomas, Armin Falk, David Huffman, and Uwe Sunde. 2010. "Are Risk Aversion and Impatience Related to Cognitive Ability?" *American Economic Review* 100:3, 1238–1260.

Duca, John V., and Anil Kumar. 2011. "Financial Literacy and Mortgage Equity Withdrawals." Working Paper 1110, Federal Reserve Bank of Dallas.

Financial Literacy and Education Commission (FLEC). 2011. "Promoting Financial Success in the United States: National Strategy for Financial Literacy." Available at www.treasury.gov/resource-center/financial-education/Documents/NationalStrategyBook_12310.pdf.

Finke, Michael S., John S. Howe, and Sandra J. Huston. 2011. "Old Age and the Decline in Financial Literacy." Available at http://ssrn.com/abstract=1948627 or http://dx.doi.org/10.2139/ssrn.1948627.

FINRA. 2003. "NASD Investor Literacy Research: Executive Summary." Available at www.finrafoundation.org/surveyexecsum.pdf.

Fonseca, Raquel, Kathleen J. Mullen, Gema Zamarro, and Julie Zissimopoulos. 2010. "What Explains the Gender Gap in Financial Literacy? The Role of Household Decision-Making." RAND Working Paper Series WR-762.

Fornero, Elsa, and Chiara Monticone. 2011. "Financial Literacy and Pension Plan Participation in Italy." *Journal of Pension Economics and Finance* 10:04, 547–564.

Fornero, Elsa, Chiara Monticone, and Serena Trucchi. 2011. "The Effect of Financial Literacy on Mortgage Choices." Working Paper 121/11, Center for Research on Pensions and Welfare Policies.

Gerardi, Kristopher, Lorenz Goette, and Stephen Meier. 2010. "Financial Literacy and Subprime Mortgage Delinquency: Evidence from a Survey Matched to Administrative Data." Working Paper 2010-10, Federal Reserve Bank of Atlanta.

Gustman, Alan L., Thomas L. Steinmeier, and Nahid Tabatabai. 2012. "Financial Knowledge and Financial Literacy at the Household Level." *American Economic Review* 102:3, 309–313.

Hackethal, Andreas, Michael Halissos, and Tullio Jappelli. 2012. "Financial Advisors: A Case of Babysitters?" *Journal of Banking and Finance* 36:2, 509–24.

Hastings, Justine S., and Olivia S. Mitchell. 2011. "How Financial Literacy and Impatience Shape Retirement Wealth and Investment Behaviors." Working Paper 16740, National Bureau of Economic Research.

Herd, Pamela, and Karen Holden. 2012. "The Links between Early-Life Cognition and Schooling and Late-Life Financial Knowledge." *Journal of Consumer Affairs* 46:3, 411–435.

Hilgert, Marianne A., Jeanne M. Hogarth, and Sondra Beverly. 2003. "Household Financial Management: The Connection between Knowledge and Behavior." *Federal Reserve Bulletin* 89:July, 309–322.

Hsu, Joanne. 2011. *Aging and Strategic Learning: The Impact of Spousal Incentives on Financial Literacy.* Dissertation. Ann Arbor: University of Michigan.

Hung, Angela A., Andrew M. Parker, and Joanne K. Yoong. 2009. "Defining and Measuring Financial Literacy." RAND Working Paper WR-708.

Huston, Sandra J. 2010. "Measuring Financial Literacy." *Journal of Consumer Affairs* 44:2, 296–316.

Huston, Sandra J., 2012. "Financial Literacy and the Cost of Borrowing." *International Journal of Consumer Studies* 36:5, 566–572.

Huston, Sandra J., Michael S. Finke, Dorothy Durband, Vickie Hampton, Hyrum Smith, and Sonya Britt. 2008. "Assessing Financial Literacy: From Concept to Measurement." *Academy of Financial Services Proceedings.* Available at www.academyfinancial.org/Proceedings.html.

Huston, Sandra J., and Russell James, III. 2012. "An fMRI Analysis of Financial Literacy." Working Paper, Texas Tech University.

Knoll, Melissa A. Z., and Carrie R. Houts. 2012. "The Financial Knowledge Scale: An Application of Item Response Theory to the Assessment of Financial Literacy." *Journal of Consumer Affairs* 46:3, 381–410.

Lusardi, Annamaria. 2008a. "Household Saving Behavior: The Role of Financial Literacy, Information, and Financial Education Programs." Working Paper 13824, National Bureau of Economic Research.

Lusardi, Annamaria. 2008b. "Financial Literacy: An Essential Tool for Informed Consumer Choice?" Working Paper, Dartmouth College.

Lusardi, Annamaria, and Olivia S. Mitchell. 2007a. "Baby Boomer Retirement Security: The Roles of Planning, Financial Literacy, and Housing Wealth." *Journal of Monetary Economics* 54:1, 205–224.

Lusardi, Annamaria, and Olivia S. Mitchell. 2007b. "Financial Literacy and Retirement Planning: New Evidence from the Rand American Life Panel." Working Paper 2007–157, Michigan Retirement Research Center.

Lusardi, Annamaria, and Olivia S. Mitchell. 2008. "Planning and Financial Literacy: How Do Women Fare?" *American Economic Review* 98:2, 413–417.

Lusardi, Annamaria, and Olivia S. Mitchell. 2009. "How Ordinary Consumers Make Complex Economic Decisions: Financial Literacy and Retirement Readiness." Working Paper, Dartmouth College. Available at www.dartmouth.edu/~alusardi/Papers/LusardiMitchellOrdinaryConsumers.pdf.

Lusardi, Annamaria, Olivia S. Mitchell, and Vilsa Curto. 2010. "Financial Literacy among the Young." *Journal of Consumer Affairs* 44:2, 358–380.

Lusardi, Annamaria, and Peter Tufano. 2009. "Debt Literacy, Financial Experiences, and Overindebtedness." Working Paper No. w14808, National Bureau of Economic Research.

Lyons, Angela C., Lance Palmer, Koralalage S. Jayaratne, and Erik Scherpf. 2006. "Are We Making the Grade? A National Overview of Financial Education and Program Evaluation." *Journal of Consumer Affairs* 40:2, 208–235.

Mandell, Lewis. 2008. "Financial Literacy of High School Students." In Jing Jian Xiao, ed., *Handbook of Consumer Finance Research,* 163–183. New York: Springer.

McKenzie, Craig R. M., and Michael J. Liersch. 2011. "Misunderstanding Savings Growth: Implications for Retirement Savings Behavior." *Journal of Marketing Research* 48 (SPL): S1–S13.

Meier, Stephan, and Charles Sprenger. 2007. "Discounting Financial Literacy: Time Preferences and Participation in Financial Education Programs." Public Policy Discussion Papers, 07–05, Federal Reserve Bank of Boston.

Moore, Danna. 2003. "Survey of Financial Literacy in Washington State: Knowledge, Behavior, Attitudes, and Experiences." Technical Report 03–39, Washington State Department of Financial Institutions. Available www.dfi.wa.gov/news/finlitsurvey.pdf.

National Council on Economic Education. 2005a. "Survey of the States: Economic and Personal Finance Education in Our Nation's Schools in 2004." Available at www.ncee.net/about/survey2004/NCEESurvey2004web.pdf.

National Council on Economic Education. 2005b. "What American Teens and Adults Know about Economics." Available at http://207.124.141.218/WhatAmericansKnowAbout Economics_042605-3.pdf.

Peress, Joel. 2004. "Wealth, Information Acquisition, and Portfolio Choice." *Review of Financial Studies* 17:3, 879–914.

President's Advisory Council on Financial Literacy (PACFL). 2008. "2008 Annual Report to the President." Available at www.treas.gov/offices/domestic-finance/financial-institution/fineducation/council/index.shtml.

Remund, David. L. 2010. "Financial Literacy Explication: The Case for a Clearer Definition in an Increasingly Complex Economy." *Journal of Consumer Affairs* 44:2, 276–295.

Servon, Lisa J., and Robert Kaestner. 2008. "Consumer Financial Literacy and the Impact of Online Banking on the Financial Behavior of Lower-Income Bank Customers." *Journal of Consumer Affairs* 42:2, 271–305.

Soll, Jack B., Ralph L. Keeney, and Richard P. Larrick. 2013. "Consumer Misunderstanding of Credit Card Use, Payments, and Debt: Shortcomings and Solutions." *Journal of Public Policy and Marketing*, 32:1, 66–81.

Stango, Victor, and Jonathan Zinman. 2011. "Fuzzy Math, Disclosure Regulation and Credit Market Outcomes." *Review of Financial Studies* 24:2, 506–534.

Sunden, Annika. 2008. "Learning from the Experience of Sweden: The Role of Information and Education in Pension Reform." In Annamaria Lusardi, ed., *Overcoming the Saving Slump*, 324–390. Chicago: University of Chicago Press.

van Rooij, Maarten, Annamaria Lusardi, and Rob Alessie. 2011. "Financial Literacy and Stock Market Participation." *Journal of Financial Economics* 101:2, 449–472.

von Gaudecker, Hans-Martin. 2011. "How Does Household Portfolio Diversification Vary with Financial Sophistication and Advice?" Discussion Paper 11238, Munich Center for the Economics of Aging.

Willis, Lauren E. 2008. "Against Financial Literacy Education." *Iowa Law Review* 94:1, 197–285.

Willis, Lauren. 2011. "The Financial Education Fallacy." *American Economic Review: Papers and Proceedings* 101:3, 429–434.

ABOUT THE AUTHORS

Michael S. Finke is Professor and Director of Retirement Planning and Living Research and the PhD program in the Department of Personal Financial Planning at Texas Tech University. His research interests include behavioral personal finance, investment advice, financial literacy and aging, financial services regulation, and household asset allocation. He is the author of over 40 refereed journal articles and book chapters, currently serves as Editor of the *Journal of Personal Finance,* and is a contributing editor of the "Finke on Finance" column in *Research Magazine.* Professor Finke holds a PhD in finance from the University of Missouri, a PhD in family resource management from the Ohio State University, and a CFP® designation.

Sandra J. Huston is Associate Professor in the Department of Personal Financial Planning at Texas Tech University. Her research interests focus on human capital specifically related to personal finance and the financial planning process including financial literacy, household use of financial advice, and the impact of financial sophistication on resource allocation within household portfolios. She was the principal investigator of the *Financial Literacy Assessment Project* (2007–2009), is a member of the editorial board for *Journal of Consumer Affairs* and the *Journal of Personal Finance*, and is currently the director of the *Personal Financial Literacy Program* at Texas Tech. She holds a PhD in consumer economics from the University of Missouri-Columbia.

CHAPTER 5

Household Investment Decisions

Vicki L. Bogan
Associate Professor, Cornell University

INTRODUCTION

Household portfolio choices are vital to economic advancement and wealth building, particularly during prosperous economic times. Moreover, recessionary cycles often magnify the economic importance of individual and household financial decision-making. The subprime mortgage crisis of 2008 is a good example of how individual household mortgage decisions had a tremendous effect on financial markets and the economy as a whole. Understanding how household characteristics influence portfolio choice is important to understanding both distributional welfare issues and broader financial market effects (Campbell 2006). Nonetheless, an important limitation of almost any traditional finance model is the imperfect ability to fully reflect actual individual and household financial decision-making behavior.

Traditional (standard) finance theory describes the investment choices that households should make to maximize household welfare—normative household finance models. However, actual and optimal behavior do not always coincide. Thus, the positive study of household financial decision-making behavior is important to better inform tax-related policies, pension-related policies, and regulation of financial markets.

The chapter is organized as follows. The first section discusses financial market participation. The second section presents the effects of market frictions on general individual investment behaviors. The next section focuses on how specific behavioral biases influence household investment behavior. The final section provides a summary and conclusions.

FINANCIAL MARKET PARTICIPATION

The study of participation in financial markets in general and the stock market in particular is a key to understanding the global economy. However, traditional theoretical financial models do not adequately explain participation in financial markets. For example, individual stock market participation is much lower than would be predicted by the consumption capital asset pricing model (CCAPM) and other models, given that the models predict all households should hold some portion of their household portfolio in risky assets or stocks. The Survey of Consumer Finances (SCF) and other reports consistently indicate low rates of U.S. household stock market participation. This is formally referred to as the "stock market participation puzzle."

The United States

With regard to stock market participation in the United States, the Survey of Consumer Finances (2001, 2004, 2010), which is a triennial cross sectional survey of U.S. households administered by the U.S. Federal Reserve Board, provides the following statistics. In 2001, 21.3 percent of American households held stocks, 17.7 percent held pooled investment funds, and 3.0 percent held bonds. These percentages fell after the stock market crash of 2001. In 2004, 20.7 percent of households held stocks, 15.0 percent held pooled investment funds, and 1.8 percent held bonds (Bucks, Kennickell, and Moore 2006). By 2010, 15.1 percent of households held stock, 8.7 percent held pooled investment funds, and 1.6 percent held bonds. In 2001, average stock holdings were 56.0 percent of total financial assets but by 2010 this figure had declined to 47.0 percent (Bricker et al. 2012).

An International Perspective

Low financial market participation rates are not unique to the United States. In terms of Canadian financial market participation, Lipset (1993) observes that Canadians historically have been much less active in the stock market than Americans. Guiso, Haliassos, and Jappelli (2003) compare rates of stock market participation between the United States and countries in Europe and Oceania for which such data are available. They find large variability, with Australia having the highest stock market participation rates and Turkey having the lowest participation rates. Guiso et al. find persistent differences across countries with the United States, the United Kingdom, and Sweden having considerably higher participation than France, Germany, and Italy. The authors demonstrate that differences in stock market participation across these European countries remain large even after controlling for household characteristics. They also find that participation rates are roughly correlated with investor literacy.

Similarly, Asian countries have low stock market participation rates. For example, estimates for 2002 show about 68 million individual stock trading accounts in China, accounting for 5.4 percent of China's 1.28 billion people (Knowledge at Wharton 2007). Cho (2006) estimates that 8.3 percent of Korean households hold corporate stock. Iwaisako (2009) finds that in 1999, 25.2 percent of Japanese households held stock both directly and through mutual funds, while 23.6 percent held stock directly. In terms of share of assets, Iwaisako estimates that 8.5 percent of Japanese household financial assets are held in equity, 2.4 percent in mutual funds, 2.0 percent in trust funds, and 1.9 percent in bonds. He also finds that 28.3 percent of assets in Japan are held in life insurance or pensions. Although studies of participation rates in developing countries are scarce, such rates can be inferred to be extremely low (Ozbilgin 2010).

Determinants of Stock Market Participation

Evidence shows that many factors influence individual investment decisions, particularly stock market participation decisions. Several determinants of household stock market participation are well established. An extensive theoretical finance literature demonstrates that household portfolio decisions depend on factors such as risk aversion (Gollier 2002). Other empirical research shows that household investments strongly increase with wealth and household education, are sensitive to transaction costs (Haliassos and Bertaut 1995; Zhong and Xiao 1995; Bertaut and Haliassos 1997), and are influenced by neighbor, social community, and peer effects (Hong, Kubik, and Stein 2004; Brown et al. 2008; Ng and Wu 2010). Bertaut and Haliassos (1997) show that labor income risk and bequest motives affect stock market participation. Rosen and Wu (2004) find that physical health influences stock-holding behavior. Barber and Odean (2001) identify gender and specific behavioral factors as having an impact on stockholding decisions. Further, Choudhury (2001) finds that minorities in the United States have lower financial market participation rates than white households. Yet, the empirical finance literature on portfolio choice still does not explain much of the cross-sectional variation in household portfolio behavior. Thus, this chapter focuses on the latest advancements in our understanding of the investment behavior of individuals and households.

MARKET FRICTION EFFECTS ON HOUSEHOLD INVESTMENT BEHAVIOR

Although most theoretical finance models assume no market frictions, various market frictions (costs) do affect investor behavior. For example, broker assisted stock purchases can have very large associated fees (Bogan 2008). The primary market frictions that influence household investment behavior are transaction costs, information costs, and taxes. This section discusses how these specific types of market frictions affect household investing decisions.

Transaction Costs

The advent of the Internet provided an important change in how investors could participate in financial markets. Online trading via the Internet mitigated several of the frictions that had previously curtailed household stock market participation: transaction fees, information costs, and limited access. Since the online trading trend emerged in the 1990s, many major U.S. financial service firms developed sizeable online trading practices while other companies focused on providing online stock information and financial analysis tools. By the late 2000s, the majority of individual investors were heavily using online trading and financial investment tools. Overall, firms increased the amount of investment information available, provided easier access to the market, and decreased transaction costs (Bogan 2008).

By studying the advent of online trading, Bogan (2008) finds valuable evidence of the effects of these market frictions on stock market participation. She examines the relationship between the decline in transaction costs due to the availability of online stock trading and stock information and the implications for the stock market participation puzzle. Bogan shows that the decline in transaction fees and information costs associated with online trading significantly increased stock market participation. The results of probit estimations indicate that households that were more comfortable using computers increased participation substantially more than households that were less comfortable using computers.

Bogan (2008) shows that more people started participating in financial markets as a result of the online trading technology reducing transaction and information costs. Further, Choi, Laibson, and Metrick (2002) find that individuals who were already participating in the stock market increased their investment activities due to the availability of online trading. The authors analyze the impact of a web-based trading channel on the trading activity of two corporate 401(k) plans. Over an 18-month period, the inferred online effect was very large. Trading frequency doubled and portfolio turnover rose by more than 50 percent. Choi et al. also find that young, male, wealthy participants are more likely to try online trading. Barber and Odean (2002) find that young men who are active traders with high incomes and a preference for investing in small growth stocks with high market risk are more likely to switch to online trading. They also find that those who switch to online trading experience unusually strong performance before going online. However, after going online, these participants trade more actively, more speculatively, and less profitably than before.

Information Costs

Actual or perceived costly information about the stock market also accounts for individuals who hold portfolios of riskless assets but not stocks. Bertaut (1998) finds that most households persistently invest in riskless assets but not stocks because they estimate information required for market participation to be costly relative to expected benefits. This assertion is supported by her findings that factors such as age and education are significant in explaining the probability of holding stocks. Guiso et al. (2003) also find support for the hypothesis that information-related barriers to entry exist for household stockholding.

Seto and Bogan (2013) analyze the investment behavior of immigrant households to identify the effects of information costs on household investment behavior. They make use of U.S. immigrant heterogeneity with respect to country of origin to better understand the effects of information costs on financial decision-making behavior. The authors find evidence consistent with the *information access hypothesis*, which suggests that immigrants from countries with greater informational exchange and contact with the United States, such as English-speaking countries and those with financial markets highly interlinked with the United States, are more likely to invest in stocks.

Taxes

Several studies investigate the effects of various tax policies on household investment behavior. For example, Brady, Cronin, and Houser (2003) find that 20 percent of the regional differences in the utilization of the U.S. mortgage interest deduction is due to differences in state and local taxes. Poterba (1984) illustrates that tax provisions for mortgage interest deductibility, along with rising inflation rates, could explain most of the 30 percent increase in real estate prices during the 1970s. Barber and Odean (2003) demonstrate that taxes matter for individual investments via brokerage accounts. They find that investors prefer to locate bonds and mutual funds in retirement accounts and to realize losses in their taxable accounts at the end of the tax year. Odean (1998) shows that individual investors realize their profitable stock investments at a much higher rate than their unprofitable ones, except when motivated to realize losses for tax purposes.

Taxes also are an important consideration for households investing in *529 college savings plans*, which are tax-advantaged investment vehicles designed to encourage parental saving for the future higher education expenses of offspring. 529 plan contributions are not deductible on federal tax returns but investments grow tax-deferred and withdrawals for qualified education expenses are exempt from federal income tax. The 529 plans, especially those also with deductibility of contributions from state income, are potentially of great benefit to households with children.

Spitzer and Singh (2001) explore the effects of pre-specified asset allocations on 529 college savings plan participation. They find that participants in higher tax brackets derive greater benefits from investment in 529 plans and that adherence to pre-specified asset allocation for low tax bracket investors often results in return losses that overshadow the tax benefit. Dynarski (2004b) finds that the advantages of 529 plans rise dramatically with income. However, Dynarski (2004a) demonstrates that college savings plans can actually harm certain families on the margin of receiving financial aid when the joint treatment of college savings by the income tax code and financial aid system create tax rates that exceed 100 percent of college savings.

Bogan (2013) analyzes the relationship between investment management firm pricing behavior, state tax benefits, and other plan characteristics. She finds that after accounting for the potential effects of competition, fund portfolio management, administrative structure, fund size, kickbacks, and other state effects, a positive link between state tax rates and 529 plan fees remains. This evidence suggests that government tax benefits designed to make college more affordable could create market frictions that enable investment firms to charge excess fees. Annual asset-based fees can easily usurp any tax benefit households receive from investing in a 529 plan.

THE EFFECTS OF BEHAVIORAL BIASES ON HOUSEHOLD INVESTMENT BEHAVIOR

Most standard theoretical finance models assume that all individuals behave optimally to maximize household welfare. However, researchers have identified many behavioral biases and issues that influence investor behavior. For example, Huberman (2001) illustrates the geographic bias of individual shareholders of Regional Bell Operating Companies (RBOCs). He shows that RBOC's customers tend to hold shares of their local RBOC rather than the shares of other RBOCs that have similar risk and return characteristics. The geographic bias of the RBOC investors is closely related to the general tendency of household portfolios to be concentrated and the home country bias (also known as familiarity bias) with regard to international investments. This provides compelling evidence that people invest in the familiar while often ignoring the principles of portfolio theory.

DeBondt (1998) also provides evidence illustrating that individual investors do not use many of the standard financial analysis principles to construct optimal portfolios. Furthermore, he finds that investors are overly optimistic about the likely performance of their specific equity investments but not about the performance of relevant market indices. This section focuses on several other behavioral factors that influence the investor behavior of specific groups.

Individuals with Mental Health and Cognitive Impairment Issues

Scholars have used mental health problems connected to mood changes to explain fluctuations in capital markets such as stock returns, bond returns, and mutual fund flows. Seasonal affective disorder (SAD) is one example of a behavioral factor affecting the capital market. Some researchers contend that SAD causes emotional fluctuations that affect investor risk aversion, resulting in predictable changes in stock returns (Kamstra, Kramer, and Levi 2003) and bid-ask spreads (DeGennaro, Kamstra, and Kramer 2008). Lo and Repin (2002) demonstrate that emotional reactions, measured by factors such as skin conductance and blood volume pulse, affect trade performance for day traders. Traders who react more emotionally to gains and losses exhibit worse performance. Just as mental health issues affect finance professionals, mental health problems and cognitive impairments also affect individual household investment decision-making behavior.

Individual mental health problems that limit cognitive abilities such as numeracy, verbal fluency, and memory abilities directly contribute to a lack of participation in financial markets. Christelis, Jappelli, and Padula (2010) find that, with other factors held constant, cognitive impairments reduce the propensity to hold stocks and increase the propensity to hold less information intensive assets such as bonds. Additionally, Bogan and Fertig (2013) find that cognitive functioning issues are associated with an increase in financial assets devoted to retirement accounts.

Mental health problems also influence human emotions, which in turn can affect an individual's ability to evaluate investment opportunities. Bogan and Fertig (2013) empirically illustrate that mental health status is an omitted variable that researchers should consider in developing future financial models of household portfolio choice. Using longitudinal data, they use fixed effects logit and Tobit models to study whether changes in mental health exert an independent effect on the probability that a household owns a particular type of asset and on the household share of total financial wealth allocated to particular assets. The authors generally find that households affected by mental illness decrease their investments in risky instruments. Bogan and Fertig also find that single women diagnosed with psychological disorders significantly increase the share of financial assets devoted to safe investments and have an increased probability of holding safe assets. Their findings suggest that various mental issues affect men, women, and couples differently.

With respect to retirement savings and investment vehicles in the United States, the two main types of pensions that households use to supplement Social Security benefits are defined benefit pension plans and defined contribution pension plans. A *defined benefit pension plan* is a type of pension plan in which an employer promises a specified monthly benefit upon retirement that is predetermined by a formula based on the employee's earnings history, tenure of service, and age. For this type of pension plan, benefits are a condition of employment and do not depend on investment returns. A *defined contribution pension plan* is a voluntary contribution type of retirement plan in which the amount of the employer's annual contribution is specified. Participation in these plans is voluntary and only employer contributions to the account are guaranteed, not the future benefits.

Both public and private sector organizations have been shifting away from defined benefit pension plans toward defined contribution pension plans (Poterba, Venti, and Wise 2009). However, Choi, Laibson, and Madrian (2011) demonstrate that individuals do not fully participate in these defined contribution plans even when it represents a significant arbitrage opportunity. Numerous possible reasons could explain this phenomenon. For example, Lusardi, Mitchell, and Curto (2012) show that financial sophistication is deficient in older respondents. Korniotis and Kumar (2011) find that older investors exhibit worse investment skills and are less effective in applying their investment knowledge. Agarwal et al. (2009) show that older adults make more financial mistakes than middle-aged adults.

Traditional economic theories of saving such as the life cycle model or the permanent income hypothesis have embedded assumptions that households have sufficient cognitive ability and willpower to implement the optimal retirement savings plan. Benartzi and Thaler (2007) challenge these assumptions and identify heuristics and biases that influence cognitive ability and thus retirement savings behavior. Bogan and Fertig (2012) show that mental health has a large and significant effect on retirement savings. They find mental health problems substantially decrease the probability of households holding defined contribution pension accounts.

Individuals Who Experience Trauma

With regard to investment decisions, traditional economic theories assume that individuals are endowed with certain risk preferences that are unaffected by experiences. However, recent evidence indicates that experiencing certain types of shocks can alter an individual's financial risk preferences. Evidence by Malmendier and Nagel (2011) shows that experiencing a macroeconomic shock, such as an economic depression or recession, affects an individual's willingness to take financial risks and to invest in certain types of assets. Owen and Wu (2007) find that households that experience adverse financial shocks worry more about the adequacy of their financial resources in retirement, even after controlling for the effects of these shocks on overall wealth.

In the context of investment decisions, Bogan, Just, and Wansink (2013) show that other traumatic life experiences that are not directly connected to the financial sector can affect an individual's risk preferences. Given the extreme psychological impact of combat, they use a sample of veterans to determine whether traumatic experiences (combat experiences) influence the probability of investing in risky financial assets. They find that combat experience is associated with a large decrease in the probability of veterans holding risky assets (stock and mutual funds) and find no significant correlation between combat experience and the probability of veterans holding safe assets. Since the results cannot be explained as a response to a shock that provides increased economic or financial information, Bogan et al. demonstrate that traumatic life experiences can bias financial decision-making behavior.

Marriage and Households with Children

Evidence shows that gender is a key issue within the area of investment behavior. An expanding body of literature documents gender-linked biases that influence investment decision-making (Croson and Gneezy 2009). Jianakoplos and Bernasek (1998) find that single women exhibit relatively more risk aversion in financial decision making than single men. Powell and Ansic (1997) find that women are less risk seeking than men regardless of familiarity, framing, costs, or ambiguity. Their results also indicate that men and women adopt different strategies with respect to financial decisions but that these strategies have no significant impact on performance. Fehr-Duda, DeGennaro, and Schubert (2006) show that the value functions of men and women are not significantly different. However, men and women differ in their probability weighting schemes. In general, the authors find women tend to be less sensitive to probability changes. Women also tend to underestimate large probabilities of gains more strongly than do men. This effect is particularly pronounced when the decisions are framed in investment terms. As a result, women appear to be more risk averse than men when making financial decisions.

As Beyer and Bowden (1997) show, men feel more competent in financial matters than women. Barber and Odean (2001) document that overconfidence affects male trading and investment behavior. Correspondingly, they show that marriage ameliorates some of the behavioral biases that men express with respect to investment decisions.

Researchers have linked many other elements of family structure to aspects of financial decision-making behavior. For example, evidence shows that the number of children a couple has, the average spacing between siblings, and the timing of births within a marriage all affect family savings (Freedman and Coombs 1966; Coombs and Freedman 1970; Keister 2003). This relationship between family size and household savings has long been a popular theme in the demographic and development literature. Researchers view the postulated negative correlation between them as a contributing factor in limiting capital formation and economic growth. Early work involving investigations of U.S. data shows that rapid child-bearing early in marriage inhibits asset growth and that these effects persist over a couple's lifetime (Freedman and Coombs 1966; Coombs and Freedman 1970). Keister (2003) explores the relationship between family size in childhood and adults' wealth accumulation patterns. She shows that siblings reduce the material and nonmaterial resources available for each child in a family and that this diminishment of resources reduces educational attainment and direct intergenerational financial transfers.

Others demonstrate that any savings effects are related primarily to the age of children, not family size (Espenshade 1975). Smith and Ward (1980) find that young children depress savings for young families but increase savings for marriages of duration greater than five years. The main channel through which children act to reduce savings is the decline in female earnings associated with the child-induced withdrawal of wives from the labor force.

Hao (1996) finds that family net wealth varies with family structure along three lines—marriage-remarriage, marriage-cohabitation, and male-female single parenthood—and that marriage is a wealth-enhancing institution. He also shows that wealth accumulation depends on saving behavior, which is a function of income and consumption. Family background and the socioeconomic and demographic characteristics of the parents ultimately determine saving behavior, inheritance, and transfers. Race, sex, age, education of the parents, and community conditions of the residence are measures of these factors. Additionally, he finds that family composition, including the number and ages of children, affects saving and the accumulation of wealth.

Chiteji and Stafford (1999) find that a young family's likelihood of owning transaction accounts and stocks is affected by whether their parents held these financial assets. Love (2010) shows that a family shock with respect to marital status affects household savings and portfolio choice. Further, Chaulk, Johnson, and Bulcroft (2003) find that a child presence in the household is associated with a higher risk tolerance for the highest income households but is generally associated with a lower risk tolerance. Bogan (2013) considers the possibility that children can influence parental portfolio allocation and tests the hypothesis that offspring gender influences stockholding and bondholding decisions. She finds that having only female children increases the probability of holding stock (risky assets) for married respondents and having only male children increases the probability of holding stock for single women.

Under-Represented Ethnic Minorities

Numerous studies document the distinctly different investment patterns between whites and ethnic minorities. These differing patterns are remarkably stable over time and across data sets. For example, Blau and Graham (1990) find that African American families hold a higher proportion of their assets in the form of physical assets such as cars and houses as opposed to income-producing financial assets such as stocks and bonds. Using data from the 1989 SCF and controlling for income and other variables, Zhong and Xiao (1995) find that stock and bondholding levels increase with education and are higher for whites than nonwhites. Badu, Daniels, and Salandro (1999) use 1992 SCF data to demonstrate that whites hold higher asset values than African Americans in every asset category and that white households rely more heavily on higher risk, higher return types of investments such as stocks. Using 1995 SCF data, Gutter, Fox, and Montalto (1999) document that only 23 percent of African American households hold risky assets compared to 46 percent of white households. Plath and Stevenson (2000) analyze 1998 SCF data and find that African Americans have a higher concentration of lower yielding financial assets and a lower concentration of stocks and bonds.

In contrast, using the 1995 and 1998 SCF data, Straight (2002) compares the asset accumulation patterns of different racial groups. He finds that African American families invested three times more in retirement plans than white households and of that amount, African American households had a higher proportion invested in stocks compared to white households. Yet, a subsequent study of 2005 SCF data by DeVaney, Anong, and Yang (2007) reveals that African American families are less likely to own investment accounts and retirement accounts than whites.

Data from the 1998 SCF show that Hispanic households have smaller financial portfolios and that these portfolios grow at a slower rate than those of white households (Plath and Stevenson 2005; Stevenson and Plath 2006). Coleman (2003) also analyzes 1998 SCF data and finds that Hispanic household heads hold a significantly lower percentage of risky assets to net worth. Her results for African American household heads are not significant after controlling for level of household wealth.

Using 1992 Health and Retirement Study (HRS) data, Choudhury (2001) shows that at every income quartile and educational level, both the percentage of African American and Hispanic households that own risky, higher-yielding assets are considerably smaller than the percentage of white households. The differences are largest in the lowest income quartiles, with African American and Hispanic households displaying roughly similar patterns. Even among households that own financial assets, racial and ethnic differences in the share of risky assets are large.

Explanations offered for these low ethnic minority rates of risky asset holdings range from differing levels of risk aversion to discrimination by formal financial institutions. For example, Gutter and Fontes (2006) conclude that the disparity between African American and white risky asset ownership may be attributable to differences in information exposure (information costs) and barriers to investment markets. Using Panel Study of Income Dynamics (PSID) data, Chiteji and Stafford (1999) explore the connection between race and investment choices and find evidence to support the hypothesis that portfolio composition choices of parents carry over to their children. Thus, past discrimination against minority groups could still have an influence on the current financial market participation of minorities.

Immigrant Households

Many studies address differences between immigrants and natives in order to observe the role of immigrant status in financial decision-making behavior. The literature includes studies on immigrant holdings of checking and savings accounts, immigrant relationships with financial institutions, savings rates of immigrants, and immigrant investment behavior.

Osili and Paulson (2006) analyze the financial behavior of U.S. immigrants. They find that immigrants have a lower rate of ownership of financial assets such as checking and savings accounts, which persists even for immigrants who have lived in the United States for many years. Osili and Paulson (2008) also find that immigrants from countries with higher financial institutional quality are more likely than other immigrants to use formal financial markets and to have a relationship with a bank after moving to the United States. Chatterjee (2009) investigates the relationship between immigrant status and ownership of stocks and mutual funds. He finds that U.S. immigrants are less likely to own financial assets such as stocks and mutual funds than are natives.

Other scholars decompose immigrant populations by their country of origin and ethnic background to determine immigrant savings rates. Carroll, Rhee, and Rhee (1994), who study savings rate data from immigrants to Canada, find no support for their hypothesis that ethnic differences affect the savings rates of immigrants. Carroll, Rhee, and Rhee (1999) also conduct the same analysis using U.S. data from the U.S. Census of Population and Housing from 1980 and 1990. Their results show that the savings rates of immigrants do differ across their countries of origin. However, immigrants from countries with historically high savings rates such as Japan, Korea, and Taiwan generally do not have savings rates higher than those of other immigrants. Al-Awad and Elhiraika (2003) examine the savings rates of immigrants to the United Arab Emirates and find that immigrants from Pakistan and India have higher average savings rates than those from Arab countries, despite generally having lower incomes.

Seto and Bogan (2013) show that differences in asset holding rates for various immigrant groups exist even after controlling for a number of immigrant specific characteristics. Their finding that immigrant ethnic concentration has a considerable and significant negative effect on stock and mutual fund holding also provides support for an information access effect (through a peer effects influence) on asset market participation. Immigrants who primarily live around other immigrants would not have the same exposure to U.S.-related information as an immigrant in a community of native U.S. citizens. Thus, one should find that increased ethnic concentration would be negatively related to U.S. asset market participation.

An alternative source of the immigrant participation differences could be that investment behaviors are carried over from an immigrant's country of origin. Seto and Bogan (2013) find little support for this theory. The asset market participation rates of immigrants are not reflective of the rates of their countries of origin. For example, despite the low rate of stock market participation in Hong Kong compared to the United States, immigrants from Hong Kong are significantly more likely to hold stock than Americans. Further, immigrants from Australia, New Zealand, and the United Kingdom, countries shown to have higher rates of stock market participation than the United States, are not significantly more likely to hold stock.

SUMMARY

The understanding of household investment behavior is advancing due to the acknowledgment that many of the standard assumptions in traditional theoretical finance models are not realistic and must be modified. Continued identification of relevant market frictions and behavioral biases is needed to begin to explain more of the empirically identified cross-sectional variation in household portfolio choice. Studies such as Bogan (2008) show that market frictions are an important contributor to the historically low stock market participation rates. Scholars need to continue to search for new, relevant market frictions beyond those previously considered in the literature. Incorporating additional types of market frictions into the standard asset pricing models will facilitate a better understanding of household investment behavior and financial markets. Moreover, finding new technologies and methods to reduce transaction and information costs can increase overall household financial market participation rates. Additionally, lawmakers and regulators should be cognizant of how taxes, policies, and regulations may create market frictions that influence investment behavior. Pension plans and 529 college savings plans in particular are two types of tax-advantaged investment vehicles requiring continued scrutiny and analysis with regard to household investment decision-making.

Despite assumptions to the contrary, people exhibit behavioral biases that influence their investment decisions. Biases associated with mental health issues, family structure, and ethnicity all influence household investment behavior in ways that could have long-term consequences for household wealth building. More positive household finance studies of financial decision-making behavior will lead to an increased understanding of behavioral biases that could challenge the role of the traditional normative finance models. Identifying key investment decision-making related behavioral biases also could facilitate the creation of appropriate default pension investment options and better inform the financial planning industry.

Increasing household access to financial markets, transitioning pension systems, and evolving credit markets require that households take more responsibility for their financial well-being. Individuals are now more directly engaged with financial markets and more actively involved with financial decisions. Furthermore, financial innovation has expanded the set of investment choices available to households. Research repeatedly demonstrates that education is of vital importance to household financial decision-making. Households would be well advised to educate themselves as much as possible about financial management issues including the market frictions and the biases affecting their investment choices. Correspondingly, the long-term financial security and stability of households could improve.

DISCUSSION QUESTIONS

1. Identify two assumptions that traditional financial models make about individual investment behavior and discuss their impact.
2. List three types of market frictions and discuss how they can affect investment behavior.
3. Discuss how family structure influences household investment decision-making behavior.
4. Discuss how mental health issues affect household investment decision-making behavior.

REFERENCES

Agarwal, Sumit, John C. Driscoll, Xavier Gabaix, and David Laibson. 2009. "The Age of Reason: Financial Decisions over the Life-Cycle with Implications for Regulation." *Brookings Papers on Economic Activity* 2, 51–117.

Al-Awad, Mouawiya, and Adam Elhiraika. 2003. "Cultural Effects and Savings: Evidence from Immigrants to the United Arab Emirates." *Journal of Development Studies* 39:5, 139–151.

Badu, Yaw A., Kenneth N. Daniels, and Daniel P. Salandro. 1999. "An Empirical Analysis of Differences in Black and White Asset Liability Combinations." *Financial Services Review* 8:3, 129–147.

Barber, Brad M., and Terrance Odean. 2001. "Boys Will Be Boys: Gender, Overconfidence, and Common Stock Investment." *Quarterly Journal of Economics* 116:1, 261–292.

Barber, Brad M., and Terrance Odean. 2002. "Online Investors: Do the Slow Die First?" *Review of Financial Studies* 15:2, 455–487.

Barber, Brad M., and Terrance Odean. 2003. "Are Individual Investors Tax Savvy? Evidence from Retail and Discount Brokerage Accounts." *Journal of Public Economics*, 88:1–2, 419–442.

Benartzi, Shlomo, and Richard H. Thaler. 2007. "Heuristics and Biases in Retirement Savings Behavior." *Journal of Economic Perspectives* 21:3, 81–104.

Bertaut, Carol C. 1998. "Stockholding Behavior of U.S. Households: Evidence from the 1983–1989 Survey of Consumer Finances." *Review of Economics and Statistics* 80:2, 263–275.

Bertaut, Carol C., and Michael Haliassos. 1997. "Precautionary Portfolio Behavior from a Life-Cycle Perspective." *Journal of Economic Dynamics and Control* 21:8–9, 1511–1542.

Beyer, Sylvia, and Edward M. Bowden. 1997. "Gender Differences in Self-Perceptions: Convergent Evidence from Three Measures of Accuracy and Bias." *Personality and Social Psychology* 23:2, 157–172.

Blau, Francine D., and John W. Graham. 1990. "Black-White Differences in Wealth and Asset Composition." *Quarterly Journal of Economics* 105:2, 321–339.

Bogan, Vicki. 2008. "Stock Market Participation and the Internet." *Journal of Financial and Quantitative Analysis* 43:1, 191–212.

Bogan, Vicki L. 2013. "Savings Incentives and Investment Management Fees: A Study of the 529 College Savings Plan Market." *Contemporary Economic Policy*, forthcoming.

Bogan, Vicki L. 2013. "Household Investment Decisions and Offspring Gender: Parental Accounting." *Applied Economics*, 45:31, 4429–4442.

Bogan, Vicki L., and Angela R. Fertig. 2012. "Mental Health and Retirement Savings: Confounding Issues with Compounding Interest." Working Paper, Social Science Research Network. Available at http://ssrn.com/abstract=2039714.

Bogan, Vicki L., and Angela R. Fertig. 2013. "Portfolio Choice and Mental Health." *Review of Finance*, 17:3, 955–992.

Bogan, Vicki L., David R. Just, and Brian Wansink. 2013. "Do Psychological Shocks Affect Financial Risk Taking Behavior? A Study of U.S. Veterans." *Contemporary Economic Policy*, 31:3, 457–467.

Brady, Peter, Julie-Anne Cronin, and Scott Houser. 2003. "Regional Differences in the Utilization of the Mortgage Interest Deduction." *Public Finance Review* 31:4, 327–366.

Bricker, Jesse, Arthur B. Kennickell, Kevin B. Moore, and John Sabelhaus. 2012. "Changes in U.S. Family Finances from 2007 to 2010: Evidence from the Survey of Consumer Finances." *Federal Reserve Bulletin* 98:2, 1–80.

Brown, Jeffrey R., Zoran Ivkovic, Paul A. Smith, and Scott Weisbenner. 2008. "Neighbors Matter: Causal Community Effects and Stock Market Participation." *Journal of Finance* 63:3, 1509–1532.

Bucks, Brian K., Arthur B. Kennickell, and Kevin B. Moore. 2006. "Recent Changes in U.S. Family Finances: Evidence from the 2001 and 2004 Survey of Consumer Finances." *Federal Reserve Bulletin* 92, A1–A38.

Campbell, John Y. 2006. "Household Finance." *Journal of Finance* 61:4, 1553–1604.

Carroll, Christopher D., Bying-Kim Rhee, and Changyoung Rhee. 1994. "Are There Cultural Effects on Saving? Some Cross-Sectional Evidence." *Quarterly Journal of Economics* 109:3, 685-699.

Carroll, Christopher D., Bying-Kim Rhee, and Changyoung Rhee. 1999. "Does Cultural Origin Affect Saving Behavior? Evidence from Immigrants." *Economic Development and Cultural Change* 48:1, 33–48.

Chatterjee, Swarn. 2009. "Individual Stockownership in the United States: Native-Immigrant Gap and the Role of Risk Tolerance." *International Research Journal of Finance and Economics* 28:June, 160–168.

Chaulk, Barbara, Phyllis J. Johnson, and Richard Bulcroft. 2003. "Effects of Marriage and Children on Financial Risk Tolerance: A Synthesis of Family Development and Prospect Theory." *Journal of Family and Economic Issues* 24:3, 257–279.

Chiteji, Ngina S., and Frank P. Stafford. 1999. "Portfolio Choices of Parents and Their Children as Young Adults: Asset Accumulation by African-American Families." *American Economic Review* 89:2, 377–380.

Cho, Sungwon. 2006. "Evidence of a Stock Market Wealth Effect Using Household Level Data." *Economics Letters* 90:3, 402–406.

Choi, James J., David Laibson, and Brigitte C. Madrian. 2011. "$100 Bills on the Sidewalk: Suboptimal Investment in 401(k) Plans." *Review of Economics and Statistics* 93:3, 748–763.

Choi, James J., David Laibson, and Andrew Metrick. 2002. "Does the Internet Increase Trading? Evidence from Investor Behavior in 401K Plans." *Journal of Financial Economics* 64:3, 397–421.

Choudhury, Sharmila. 2001. "Racial and Ethnic Differences in Wealth and Asset Choices." *Social Security Bulletin* 64:4, 2001–2002.

Christelis, Dimitris, Tullio Jappelli, and Mario Padula. 2010. "Cognitive Abilities and Portfolio Choice." *European Economic Review* 54:1, 18–38.

Coleman, Susan. 2003. "Risk Tolerance and the Investment Behavior of Black and Hispanic Heads of Household." *Financial Counseling and Planning* 14:2, 43–52.

Coombs, Lolagene C., and Ronald Freedman. 1970. "Pre-Marital Pregnancy, Child Spacing, and Later Economic Achievement." *Population Studies* 24:3, 389–412.

Croson, Rachel, and Uri Gneezy. 2009. "Gender Differences in Preferences." *Journal of Economic Literature* 47:2, 448–474.

DeBondt, Werner F. M. 1998. "A Portrait of the Individual Investor." *European Economic Review* 42:3–5, 831–844.

DeGennaro, Ramon P., Mark J. Kamstra, and Lisa A. Kramer. 2008. "Does Risk Aversion Vary During the Year? Evidence from Bid-Ask Spreads." Working Paper, Social Science Research Network. Available at http://ssrn.com/abstract=624901.

DeVaney, Sharon A., Sophia T. Anong, and Yuan Yang. 2007. "Asset Ownership by Black and White Families." *Financial Counseling and Planning* 18:1, 33–45.

Dynarski, Susan. 2004a. "Tax Policy and Education Policy: Collision or Coordination? A Case Study of the 529 and Coverdell Saving Incentives." *Tax Policy and the Economy* 18, 81–116.

Dynarski, Susan. 2004b. "Who Benefits from the Education Saving Incentives? Income, Educational Expectations and the Value of the 529 and Coverdell." *National Tax Journal* 57:2, 359–383.

Espenshade, Thomas J. 1975. "The Impact of Children on Household Saving: Age Effects versus Family Size." *Population Studies* 29:1, 123–125.

Fehr-Duda, Helga, Manuele DeGennaro, and Renate Schubert. 2006. "Gender, Financial Risk, and Probability Weights." *Theory and Decision* 60:2–3, 283–313.

Freedman, Ronald, and Lolagene Coombs. 1966. "Childspacing and Family Economic Position." *American Sociological Review* 31:5, 631–649.

Gollier, Christian. 2002. "What Does Theory Have to Say About Household Portfolios?" In Luigi Guiso, Michael Haliassos, and Tullio Jappelli, eds., *Household Portfolios*, 27–54. Cambridge, MA: MIT Press.

Guiso, Luigi, Michael Haliassos, and Tullio Jappelli. 2003. "Household Stockholding in Europe: Where Do We Stand and Where Do We Go?" *Economic Policy* 18:36, 123–170.

Gutter, Michael S., and Angela Fontes. 2006. "Racial Differences in Risky Asset Ownership: A Two-Stage Model of the Investment Decision Making Process." *Financial Counseling and Planning* 17:2, 64–78.

Gutter, Michael S., Jonathan J. Fox, and Catherine P. Montalto. 1999. "Racial Differences in Investor Decision Making." *Financial Services Review* 8:3, 149–162.

Haliassos, Michael, and Carol C. Bertaut. 1995. "Why Do So Few Hold Stocks?" *Economic Journal* 105:432, 1110–1129.

Hao, Lingxin. 1996. "Family Structure, Private Transfers, and the Economic Well-Being of Families with Children." *Social Forces* 75:1, 269–292.

Hong, Harrison, Jeffrey D. Kubik, and Jeremy Stein. 2004. "Social Interaction and Stock Market Participation." *Journal of Finance* 59:1, 137–163.

Huberman, Gur. 2001. "Familiarity Breeds Investment." *Review of Financial Studies* 14:3, 659–680.

Iwaisako, Tokuo. 2009. "Household Portfolios in Japan." *Japan and the World Economy* 21:4, 373–382.

Jianakoplos, Nancy A., and Alexandra Bernasek. 1998. "Are Women More Risk Averse?" *Economic Inquiry* 36:4, 620–630.

Kamstra, Mark J., Lisa A. Kramer, and Maurice D. Levi. 2003. "Winter Blues: A SAD Stock Market Cycle." *American Economic Review* 93:1, 324–343.

Keister, Lisa A. 2003. "Sharing the Wealth: The Effect of Siblings on Adults' Wealth Ownership." *Demography* 40:3, 521–542.

Knowledge at Wharton. 2007. "Why Some Chinese Invest in the Stock Market and Others Don't." Philadelphia, PA: Wharton School of Business, University of Pennsylvania.

Korniotis, George M., and Alok Kumar. 2011. "Do Older Investors Make Better Investment Decisions?" *Review of Economics and Statistics* 93:1, 244–265.

Lipset, Martin S. 1993. "Culture and Economic Behavior: A Commentary." *Journal of Labor Economics* 11:1, 330–347.

Lo, Andrew W., and Dmitry V. Repin. 2002. "The Psychophysiology of Real-Time Financial Risk Processing." *Journal of Cognitive Neuroscience* 14:3, 323–339.

Love, David A. 2010. "The Effect of Marital Status and Children on Savings and Portfolio Choice." *Review of Financial Studies* 23:1, 385–432.

Lusardi, Annamaria, Olivia S. Mitchell, and Vilsa Curto. 2012. "Financial Sophistication in the Older Population." Working Paper 17863, National Bureau of Economic Research.

Malmendier, Ulrike, and Stefan Nagel. 2011. "Depression Babies: Do Macroeconomic Experiences Affect Risk Taking?" *Quarterly Journal of Economics* 126:1, 373–416.

Ng, Lilian, and Fei Wu. 2010. "Peer Effects in the Trading Decisions of Individual Investors." *Financial Management* 39:2, 807–831.

Odean, Terrance. 1998. "Are Investors Reluctant to Realize Their Losses?" *Journal of Finance* 53:5, 1775–1798.

Osili, Una, and Anna Paulson. 2006. "Immigrant-Native Differences in Financial Market Participation." Working Paper 2004, Federal Reserve Bank of Chicago.

Osili, Una, and Anna Paulson, A. 2008. "What Can We Learn about Financial Access from U.S. Immigrants? The Role of Country of Origin Institutions and Immigrant Beliefs." *World Bank Economic Review* 22:3, 431–455.

Owen, Ann L., and Stephen Wu. 2007. "Financial Shocks and Worry about the Future." *Empirical Economics* 33:3, 515–530.

Ozbilgin, Murat H. 2010. "Financial Market Participation and the Developing Country Business Cycle." *Journal of Development Economics* 92:2, 125–137.

Plath, D. Anthony, and Thomas H. Stevenson. 2000. "Financial Services and the African American Market: What Every Financial Planner Should Know." *Financial Services Review* 9:4, 343–359.

Plath, D. Anthony, and Thomas H. Stevenson. 2005. "Financial Services Consumption Behavior across Hispanic American Consumers." *Journal of Business Research* 58:8, 1089–1099.

Poterba, James M. 1984. "Tax Subsidies to Owner-Occupied Housing: An Asset-Market Approach." *Quarterly Journal of Economics* 99:4, 729–752.

Poterba, James, Steven Venti, and David A. Wise. 2009. "The Decline of Defined Benefit Retirement Plans and Asset Flows." In Jeffrey R. Brown, Jeffrey B. Liebman, and David A. Wise, eds., *Social Security Policy in a Changing Environment*, 333–379. Chicago: University of Chicago Press.

Powell, Melanie, and David Ansic. 1997. "Gender Differences in Risk Behavior in Financial Decision-Making: An Experimental Analysis." *Journal of Economics Psychology* 18:6, 605–628.

Rosen, Harvey S., and Stephen Wu. 2004. "Portfolio Choice and Health Status." *Journal of Financial Economics* 72:3, 457–484.

Seto, Sayako, and Vicki L. Bogan. 2013. "Immigrant Household Investment Behavior and Country of Origin: A Study of Immigrants to the United States." *International Journal of Finance and Economics*, 18:2, 128–158.

Smith, James P., and Michael P. Ward. 1980. "Asset Accumulation and Family Size." *Demography* 17:3, 243–260.

Spitzer, John J., and Sandeep Singh. 2001. "The Fallacy of Cookie Cutter Asset Allocation: Some Evidence from New York's College Savings Program." *Financial Services Review* 10:1–4, 101–116.

Stevenson, Thomas H., and D. Anthony Plath. 2006. "Marketing Financial Services to Hispanic American Consumers: A Portfolio-Centric Analysis." *Journal of Services Marketing* 20:1, 37–50.

Straight, Ronald L. 2002. "Wealth: Asset Accumulation Differences by Race: SCF Data 1995 and 1998." *American Economic Review* 92:2, 330–334.

Survey of Consumer Finances. 2001, 2004, 2010. Washington, DC: Board of Governors of the Federal Reserve System.

Zhong, Lucy X., and Jing J. Xiao. 1995. "Determinants of Family Bond and Stock Holdings." *Financial Counseling and Planning* 6, 107–114.

ABOUT THE AUTHOR

Vicki L. Bogan is an Associate Professor of Finance in the Charles H. Dyson School of Applied Economics and Management at Cornell University. Her research areas are financial economics, behavioral finance, and applied economics. She has published research in both finance and economics journals including the *Journal of Financial and Quantitative Analysis, Review of Economics and Statistics, Review of Finance,* and *Journal of Economic Behavior and Organization.* The media including the *Wall Street Journal* and *Forbes* have covered her research. She holds a BS in applied mathematics and economics from Brown University, an MBA in finance and strategic management from the Wharton School of the University of Pennsylvania, and a PhD in economics from Brown University.

CHAPTER 6

Personality Traits

Lucia Fung
Lecturer in Management, Department of Management, Hong Kong Baptist University
Robert B. Durand
Professor of Finance, School of Economics and Finance, Curtin University

INTRODUCTION

Personality helps to identify who a person is and what motivates him or her (Allport 1966; Hogan and Hogan 1989; Dollinger and Orf 1991; Buss 1992; Langston and Skyes 1997; Soane and Chmiel 2005). Being aware of one's personality and motivation might enable a person to overcome emotions and biases when confronted with a choice. Self-knowledge might also help an individual to use information more effectively to improve decision-making.

Statman and Wood (2004) and Pan and Statman (2012) contend that knowing investors' personalities can help advisors build better portfolios. Pompian (2012, p. 11) maintains that "if you can identify what basic type of investor you are, and then diagnose your unique irrational behaviors, you will be in a much better position to overcome these behaviors and, ultimately, reach your financial goals." For all these authors, personality is a guide to what a person should do.

Some theorists believe that human beings are rational entities. A rational evaluation of their options in each specific situation guides their behavior in each situation. Traditional or standard finance typically bases its analyses on this assumption. Other theorists such as Langston and Sykes (1997) argue against this situation-specific approach by asserting that human rationality alone cannot explain behavior. People's mental processes often operate outside conscious awareness. They regularly fall into lazy patterns of thought and use default assumptions and overpracticed patterns of action. In contrast to traditional finance, behavioral finance is based on assumptions about how people actually think and act.

Behavioral finance has modeled financial phenomena using a range of ideas taken from psychology although it has not considered the role of personality traits to any great extent. For instance, an analyst will use behavioral explanation a for financial phenomenon x. For financial phenomenon y, the analyst will use behavioral explanation b. The question is "Why?" No overarching framework is available to link the many behavioral explanations used in finance. Understanding personality traits might help to fill this gap. Using the Five-Factor Model of personality traits as well as other metrics capturing personality, Durand, Newby, and Sanghani (2008) find that personality traits are associated with a wide range of investment decisions and outcomes. Durand, Newby, Peggs, and Siekierka (2013) claim that prices in financial markets are auctionlike and disparate strands of behavioral finance might be brought together by understanding the personality traits of the marginal price setter (i.e., the investor left holding the asset at the end of the price-setting process). The authors demonstrate that their subjects' conformance with the disposition effect (i.e., holding losers too long and selling winners too soon) (Kaustia 2010), and reliance on the availability heuristic (i.e., relying on information which comes more readily to mind) are functions of their personality traits. Durand, Newby, Tant, and Treepongkaruna (2013) find that overconfidence and overreaction to unexpected news items are associated with personality traits.

To date, behavioral finance has not made full use of the rigorous analysis of personality traits provided by psychology. Consequently, this chapter presents an introduction to the study of personality traits to guide academics in their research and practitioners in their deliberations. The chapter focuses on risk taking and over-confidence to highlight how thinking about personality traits can lead to a deeper understanding of financial phenomena. The chapter is organized as follows. It begins by providing an overview of theoretical models of personality followed by a discussion of the biological basis of personality traits. Next, the chapter considers personality, risk taking, and overconfidence. It also reviews the relationships among gender, personality, and decision-making.

The chapter conveys two important messages. First, personality matters when choosing portfolios and is something investors and their advisors should consider. Second, whether investors have self-awareness or not, they seek portfolios that do not create emotional discomfort. Investors construct portfolios that are congruent with their personalities. Therefore, besides suggesting what investors should do, an understanding of personality will help explain what investors actually do.

A STRUCTURAL MODEL OF PERSONALITY

This chapter bases its discussion on the Five-Factor Model of personality traits (the "Big Five"), which is the dominant paradigm in personality research (McCrae 2009). This structural model of personality provides a hierarchical structure that identifies a small number of higher-order personality factors as an economized representation of a large number of correlated constituent traits (De Raad 2009). The "lexical hypothesis" contends that personality traits are so socially relevant and useful that common words will encode all kinds of personality traits (Goldberg 1993; John and Srivastava 1999). A search of an unabridged dictionary would therefore provide an exhaustive list of personality traits and a hierarchical structure of personality could then be developed by identifying a reduced number of higher-order factors representing the underlying sample of lower-order correlated facet traits (Saucier and Goldberg 1996).

The Five-Factor Model summarizes personality using five higher-order personality factors: Extraversion, Agreeableness, Conscientiousness, Neuroticism, and Openness to Experience /Intellect, representing the more specific lower level constituent traits. Other studies identify structures with six factors (Ashton et al. 2004), seven factors (Almagor, Tellegen, and Waller 1995), or eight factors (De Raad and Barelds 2008). The Five-Factor Model accounts for the co-variation of most personality traits. For example, research shows that the extraversion, intuition, feeling, and judging preferences of the Myers-Briggs Indicators correspond to Extraversion, Openness to Experience, Agreeableness, and Conscientiousness, respectively (McCrae and Costa 1989). Its universality is also validated in cross-cultural research (McCrae, Terracciano, and Members of the Personality Profiles of Cultures Project 2005). Furthermore, the recently released fifth edition of the *Diagnostic and Statistical Manual of Mental Disorders (DSM-5)* (American Psychiatric Association 2013) is also beginning to shift toward a Five-Factor Model conceptualization of personality disorders (American Psychiatric Association 2011; Widiger and Costa, Jr. 2013).

Extraversion refers to the degree of activity level, preferred interaction, need for stimulation, and capacity for joy of the person. A person high in Extraversion tends to be more sociable, active, optimistic, fun-loving, and talkative while someone low in Extraversion tends to be reserved, aloof, and quiet. Similar to Extraversion, Agreeableness is also an interpersonal dimension. An individual high in Agreeableness tends to be trusting, altruistic, good-natured, empathic, and helpful. Yet, someone low in Agreeableness tends to be cynical, rude, suspicious, uncooperative, irritable, and even manipulative, vengeful, and ruthless. Conscientiousness refers to the degree of organization, control, persistence, and motivation to goal-directed behavior. A person high in Conscientiousness tends to be diligent and has a high level of self-control. Someone low in Conscientiousness tends to be lazy, aimless, hedonistic, lax, and careless. Neuroticism refers to a person's level of emotional stability. Individuals high in Neuroticism are more prone to psychological distress, including negative affectivity such as anger, hostility, depression, and anxiety. Openness to Experience refers to the active seeking and appreciation of experiences for their own sake. People high in Openness are imaginative, curious, and open to unconventional ideas and values. On the other hand, those low in Openness tend to be conventional and dogmatic in beliefs and attitudes, set in their ways, and emotionally unresponsive.

The Biological Basis of the Five-Factor Model

Both genes and environment play a role in the development of personality traits, and heritability estimates for personality generally range from 40 to 50 percent, or even 80 percent, depending on the trait being measured (Loehlin 1992; Bouchard 1994; Riemann, Angleitner, and Strelau 1997). Extraversion and Neuroticism are the most commonly studied Big Five traits in neuropsychological research. Durand, Newby, Tant, et al. (2013), who present a meta-analysis of Durand (2008) and Durand, Newby, Peggs, et al. (2013) report that Extraversion and Neuroticism play very important roles in the analyses presented in these three papers.

Genes help explain investors' decisions. Using data from the Swedish twins database and taking advantage of the natural experiment afforded by Swedish pension reform, Cesarini et al. (2010) compare monozygotic (identical) and dizygotic (fraternal) twins (where the degree of relatedness is no different from siblings born at different times). They find that genetic variation explains around a quarter of the variation in exposure to risk. The genetic basis for personality as well as evidence that variance in financial decision-making might have a genetic basis suggest an association between personality traits and financial decision-making.

As the most widely used taxonomy of personality, the Big Five Model offers a useful categorization scheme for personality neuroscience by providing a common language to ensure the results are comparable across studies (DeYoung and Gray 2009). Research findings show that the Five-Factor Model is rooted in biology and genetically based. Evidence shows that the Five-Factor structure of the lower order constituent traits matches the structure of their underlying genes (Yamagata et al. 2006). For example, two facets of Extraversion, warmth and assertiveness, are influenced by some of the same genes. The following sections will introduce the neurobiological basis of each of the Big Five personality factors.

Extraversion is related to the dopamine pathways in the brain, the mesolimbic pathways, which govern "approach" behavior such as attention, motivation, pursuit, positive emotions, and sensitivity to rewards. Dopamine is a neurotransmitter associated with rewards and pleasure. Dopamine can bring about joyous feelings that can reinforce behavior. Evidence shows that dopamine plays a role in approach behaviors toward achieving goals, positive incentives, and rewards (Depue and Collins 1999). Activities at brain regions responding to positive and rewarding stimuli and those associated with approach behavior are positively related to Extraversion (Cohen et al. 2005). According to Depue and Collins (1999), the dopaminergic system affects aspects of Extraversion related to drive and assertiveness. The endogenous opioid systems (i.e., those related to positive emotions after attaining and consuming a reward) more strongly affect the affiliative aspect of Extraversion. Therefore, Extraversion could be associated with risk-taking behavior due to the influence of dopamine on sensation seeking and attaining rewards/gains by taking risks. In economic experiments, Carpenter, Garcia, and Lum (2011) find that the allele of the gene that regulates dopamine uptake predicts risk-taking and time preferences. Apart from the dopamine system, testosterone is positively related to the assertiveness and dominance aspects of Extraversion (Apicella et al. 2008). It may increase the tendencies of individuals high on Extraversion to take risks to obtain personal gains. More discussion of the role of testosterone occurs later in this chapter.

Due to its significance in psychopathology, research on the neurobiological aspects of Neuroticism is particularly extensive. Neuroticism is associated with brain activities related to withdrawal behavior, risk aversion, and negative affect. It is also associated with higher activation of the right frontal lobe relative to the left. The right hemisphere is related to emotions connected to withdrawal whereas the left hemisphere is related to approach behavior (Davidson 2002). The brain's anterior insula governs experiences of disgust, pain, and loss (Wright, He, Shapira, Goodman, and Liu 2004) and the anticipation of aversive affective and noxious physical stimuli (Simmons, Matthews, Stein, and Paulus 2004). Evidence shows insula activation to be positively related to Neuroticism and risk-averse decision-making (Paulus et al. 2003). Neuroticism is associated with bloodstream hormone and neurotransmitter release. Lower functioning of the neurotransmitter serotonin is related to the vulnerability to negative emotion (Arnold, Zai, and Richter 2004). Neuroticism is also associated with higher levels of norepinephrine (adrenaline) (Hennig 2004; Zuckerman 2005) and a higher baseline level of the stress hormone cortisol (Netter 2004). Both norepinephrine and cortisol prepare the body for fight-or-flight response to danger. Coates and Herbert (2008) find a positive relationship between the cortisol levels of traders and both the volatility of their profits and the expected variation in the price of the assets they are trading.

The subtraits of Agreeableness, such as altruism and empathy, are related to brain systems involved in social information processing. For example, self-reported measures of altruism are related to individual differences in brain activities while observing another agent perform a task, in contrast to performing the task themselves (Tankersley, Stowe, and Huettel 2007). Evidence also shows a positive association of empathy with brain activities during observation and imitation of others' action (Gazzola, Aziz-Zadeh, and Keysers 2006). The viewing of different emotional expression of others will activate the brain regions functionally relevant to the emotion in question (Singer et al. 2004; Chakrabarti, Bullmore, and Baron-Cohen 2006).

Conscientiousness appears to reflect an individual's motivational stability, ability to make and carry out plans in an organized and industrious manner, and capability to delay immediate gratification in favor of long-term goals (DeYoung and Gray 2009). Evidence shows that Conscientiousness is associated with serotonin, which is involved in control and restraint (Rosenberg et al. 2006).Conscientiousness could also be associated with glucose metabolism. Individuals whose metabolism provides their brains with an ample supply of glucose (an energy source) are likely to be higher in Conscientiousness because acts of self-control are energy consuming, particularly in the prefrontal cortex, which is involved in the planning and voluntary control of behavior (Gailliot and Baumeister 2007; Gailliot et al. 2007). Neuroimaging studies show that brain activity in the ventral prefrontal cortex during a response inhibition task is strongly negatively correlated with Conscientiousness (Whiteside and Lynam 2011). Conscientiousness may therefore be associated with careful and deliberate decision-making, as well as restraint from impulsive risk taking.

Openness to Experience/Intellect is the least studied Big Five factor in neuropsychological research. It is the trait, however, most strongly and consistently associated with intelligence (Helson 1985; McCrae and Costa 1985; DeYoung, Peterson, and Higgins 2005; DeYoung and Gray 2009). Elevated confidence of people high in Openness is associated with actual knowledge and performance (Schaefer, Williams, Goodie, and Campbell 2004). Openness is positively correlated with performance in working memory and cognitive control tests (DeYoung et al. 2005). Due to the tendencies of the individuals high in Openness to Experience to engage in reflective and intellectual activities and to seek out opportunities to learn in diverse domains, finding that this Big Five personality factor is positively associated with intelligence is not surprising. Neuroticism also shows consistent (negative) correlations with intelligence (Ackerman and Heggestad 1997). This negative correlation is possibly contributed by the impact of anxiety, stress, and negative affect experienced by individuals high in Neuroticism on task performance and decision-making (Moutafi, Furnham, and Tsaousis 2006). Grinblatt, Keloharju, and Linnainmaa (2011) find that higher IQ is associated with a greater propensity to participate in the stock market. Grinblatt, Keloharju and Linnainmaa (2012) find an association with higher IQ and better investment outcomes including lower trading costs.

RISK-TAKING BEHAVIOR

Soane and Chmiel (2005) contend that personality effects on risk-taking behavior can be understood in terms of individual differences in dispositional motivations. People will take or avoid risks to achieve goals consistent with their personality traits. For example, extraverts may take risks due to their needs to seek excitement; people high in Conscientiousness may be more cautious in taking risks due to their need for control, order, and self-discipline; people high in Neuroticism may avoid risks due to fear of negative consequences. Nicholson, Soane, Fenton-O'Creevy, and Willman (2005) report overall risk taking in six decision domains, including recreation, health, career, finance, safety, and social, to be positively associated with Extraversion and Openness to Experience, and negatively associated with Neuroticism, Agreeableness, and Conscientiousness.

Risk is a central concern of finance. Durand, Newby, Peggs, et al. (2013) find that Neuroticism is associated with portfolio diversification and systematic risk. Filbeck, Hatfield, and Horvath (2005) analyze subjects' tolerance for variance and skewness and find that these features are related to Myers-Briggs preferences for extraversion, intuition, thinking, and perceiving.

Grinblatt and Keloharju (2009) capture individuals' sensation seeking and find a positive association between trading activity and sensation seeking. Sensation seeking is likely to be associated with Extraversion due to the need for excitement and stimulation of extraverts, and Openness to Experience due to the active seeking of experiences of open individuals. Evidence shows that high sensation seekers appraise risk as lower and anticipate less anxiety for potentially risky activities (Horvath and Zuckerman 1993). In experimental settings, high sensation seekers bet more and at higher odds in tasks in which they have to decide between alternatives with different degrees of probability and expected return (Wong and Carducci 1991).

Lauriola and Levin (2001) distinguish the personality effects on risk taking to achieve gains and risk taking to avoid loss. Participants perform a series of forced choice trials to select between pairs of alternative choices matched in expected values. The risky option offers a potential gain with the probability $1 - P$. The sure option offers either a sure gain or a sure loss. Their evidence shows that Openness to Experience is associated with risk taking only in achieving a higher gain than the sure option. As Openness to Experience involves the active seeking of experiences for their own sake, finding that it is positively associated with risk-taking behavior to achieve a higher gain is not surprising. Neuroticism is negatively associated with risk taking to achieve higher gain, but positively related to risk taking to avoid loss. Individuals high in Neuroticism are more prone to psychological distress and negative affectivity such as sadness and anxiety, and their behavior may be strongly motivated by loss avoidance. In the domain of achieving gain, these individuals are likely to be more concerned about the possibility of gaining less, rather than the possibility of achieving higher gain, by choosing the risky option. They will therefore become risk averse and secure the gain by choosing the sure gain option. In the domain of loss, these individuals are likely to be more concerned about the negative consequences of the sure loss and hence are willing to choose the risky option to avoid the sure loss.

OVERCONFIDENCE

Overconfidence is a judgmental error in which people overestimate their accuracy or inflate the subjective probability of a particular outcome occurring (Campbell, Goodie, and Foster 2004; Glaser and Weber 2010). People are generally more confident than accurate (Budescu, Wallsten, and Au 1997). Taylor and Brown (1988) maintain that unrealistic optimism is a form of illusory self-enhancing bias that is important to good adjustment and positive affect. Overconfidence can have serious consequences, such as entrepreneurial failures (Malmendier and Tate 2005).

Schaefer et al. (2004) study the associations between the Big Five personality factors and overconfidence. They find that Extraversion is positively correlated with confidence, but not with accuracy on the tests. Therefore, extraverts are significantly more overconfident. This evidence is consistent with findings that Extraversion is linked to dispositional optimism (Williams 1992) and narcissism, which is positively correlated with overconfidence (Paulhus and Williams 2002). Openness to Experience is positively correlated to both confidence and accuracy, and hence uncorrelated with overconfidence. Evidence also shows that the elevated confidence of individuals with higher levels of Openness to Experience is substantiated by their actual knowledge and performance. This may reflect the notion that individuals high in Openness to Experience are more motivated to seek out opportunities to learn in diverse domains (Schaefer et al. 2004). Further, researchers often find Openness to Experience to be related to both intelligence and academic achievement (Helson 1985; McCrae and Costa 1985), which are in turn related to good confidence calibration (Hacker et al. 2000). In the study, Neuroticism, Agreeableness, and Conscientiousness do not significantly predict confidence, accuracy, or overconfidence.

Using data from the Finnish Armed Forces psychological profile, which provides an objective measure of self-confidence that has a low correlation with their measure of sensation seeking, Grinblatt and Keloharju (2009) find a positive association of confidence with trading activity. Alternatively, overconfidence must be inferred from observable characteristics of the participants being studied (e.g., gender, which is discussed in the following section).

Narcissism is a personality trait consistently associated with overconfidence. The two elements defining narcissism are an inflated positive view of oneself and a self-regulatory strategy to maintain and enhance this self-view (Morf and Rhodewalt 2001). Narcissists tend to think of themselves as special and unique (Emmons, 1984) and more intelligent and physically attractive than they actually are (Gabriel, Critelli, and Ee 1994). This strong drive of enhancing and maintaining their elated self-views may preclude them from having an accurate appraisal of their ability and likelihood of success (Campbell et al. 2004). Aktas et al. (2012) analyze takeovers and find that narcissistic chief executive officers (CEOs) are more likely to initiate takeovers but that narcissistic CEOs of their targets can hold out for a better deal.

PERSONALITY AND GENDER

Various studies provide evidence of gender differences in decision-making. In doing so, however, a tendency seems to imply a general personality trait difference between males and females (referred to as "gender trait difference"), which manifests in the differences in their decision-making styles. In finance, Barber and Odean (2001) present the seminal analysis of behavior and gender differences. Using a large data base of individual investors, they use biological gender to proxy for overconfidence. They find that men take bigger risks, trade more, and have lower returns than women. Besides Barber and Odean, other studies of financial decision-making, which are perhaps better known in psychology, also reveal gender difference

(Stinerock, Stern, and Solomon 1991; Powell and Ansic 1997; Dwyer, Gilkeson, and List 2002). Huang and Kisgen (2013), who compare male and female CEOs and chief financial officers (CFOs), find that females have a lower propensity to make acquisitions and issue debt.

Studies examining gender differences, however, simply reinforce the stereotypical view of general personality trait differences between males and females across situations and different domains of decisions. The stereotype is that women are more cautious, less confident, and less aggressive. Other studies challenge this view and find more similarities than differences in personality traits and decision-making styles between males and females (Johnson and Powell 1994; Powell and Ansic 1997). Durand (2008), Durand, Newby, Peggs, et al. (2013), and Durand, Newby, Tant, et al. (2013) consider gender issues by using measures capturing psychological sex roles (Bem 1977; 1994). They contend that Barber and Odean's (2001) findings for gender do not hold when considering psychological traits. Indeed, the evidence in Durand (2008), Durand, Newby, Peggs, et al. (2013), and Durand, Newby, Tant, et al. (2013) for the psychological construct of masculinity is very different from the conclusions drawn on the basis of biological masculinity.

Finance is not alone in finding gender differences in risk preferences. Studies show differences across situations, contexts, populations, and decision-making domains (Byrnes, Miller, and Schafer 1999). Examples include controlled laboratory studies such as computerized military games (Hudgens and Fatkin 1985) and gambling experiments (Levin, Snyder, and Chapman 1988; Johnson and Powell 1994). These studies consistently show that females have a lower preference for risk than males. Adopting the gender trait difference interpretation, males' higher risk preferences can be explained by a naturally lower level of arousal in men (Zuckerman 1991). A lower natural level of arousal implies that men need greater external stimulation to reach their optimal level of arousal and hence higher preference for risks. However, those with a higher natural level of arousal may be overwhelmed by additional external stimulation as they are naturally sensitive and chronically aroused. Wilson and Daly's (1985, p. 66) sociobiological model suggests that risk taking is an "attribute of the masculine psychology" evolved in response to the competitive demands of primitive society.

The question is whether the observed gender difference on overt risk taking behavior should be simply attributed to an underlying personality trait difference between male and female. Gender differences in decision-making styles and values should not, however, be interpreted as general trait differences if they are context specific (Powell and Ansic 1997). Males may take more risks than women in most situations but the gender gap is sensitive to contexts and behavioral domains (Arnett 1992; Byrnes et al. 1999). Gender differences in overt risk taking behavior may reflect gender trait differences to a certain extent, but they may also reflect how the same trait between male and female is expressed in different manners in different contexts, due to the social expectations and constraints imposed on them.

Chemistry plays an important role in explaining differences in risk taking. Evidence shows that testosterone, a steroid hormone mainly produced by the testes, is associated with risk preferences in men, as well as other behaviors including increased aggression (Archer 2006), sensation seeking (Roberti 2004), and dominance (Mazur and Booth 1998). Dreber and Hoffman (2007) find that financial risk aversion is positively associated with the 2D:4D ratio, which is the ratio between the length of the second finger and the fourth ring finger, which is negatively correlated with prenatal testosterone exposure (Hönekopp et al. 2007). Coates, Gurnell, and Rustichini (2009) find that traders' profit and their ability to survive in the market are associated with the 2D:4D ratio (that is, the surrogate of the exposure to prenatal testosterone). Apicella et al. (2008) also find that men with higher levels of circulating testosterone and those with more masculine facial features (as a proxy for testosterone exposure during puberty) are more likely to make risky financial decisions. Coates and Herbert (2008) measure the testosterone levels of London traders and find that higher levels of testosterone in the morning are associated with greater profits during that day, even after accounting for risk. Therefore, biochemistry may provide greater explanatory power for the observed difference in risk-taking behavior than the crude and stereotypical view of dichotomous gender differences in personality.

Personality traits provide a consistent and satisfying framework to discuss overconfidence and risk taking. Personality, as is the case with gender, has a genetic basis. Testosterone plays a critical role in risk taking. What, then, is the role for gender in understanding individuals' financial behavior? Clearly differences exist in the financial behavior of men and women. Yet, biological gender, in itself, is difficult to validly interpret; it does not do justice to the underlying psychological and neurological processes driving individuals' decisions.

PERSONALITY AS A GUIDE FOR INVESTORS

Thus far, this chapter has concentrated on the role of personality traits in influencing what investors do in financial markets. Can personality also serve as a guide to what investors should do? *Personality traits* are defined as dispositions relatively enduring over time and across situations. Personality traits are arguably stable as they are rooted in the neurobiological system (Gray 1987; Depue and Collins 1999; Nigg 2000; Depue and Morrone-Strupinsky 2005). However, personality traits may still change over time, particularly during the volatile period of transition from childhood to adolescence, but they become increasingly stable after the age of 30 and reach a plateau between the ages of 50 and 70 (Roberts and DelVecchio 2000).

If personality traits are relatively stable and only change over a long period of time, are people doomed to be passive victims of the dysfunctional patterns of thought and behavior to which they are predisposed? What happens if the portfolios that investors are predisposed to choose are, in some way, suboptimal?

Personality traits may not change easily, but research shows that they are not the sole determinants of behavior. This is clearly reflected in the person-situation debate in personality psychology. Advocates of the trait approach maintain that personality traits are the primary determinants of behavior. Advocates at the other extreme contend that situation almost exclusively determines how people act. Evidence for cross-situational behavioral consistency is lower than proponents of the trait approach would have expected (Hartshorne and May 1928; Asendorpf 2009). Mischel (1968) points out that personality traits do not strongly predict behavior across situations and rarely correlate with behavior above the 0.30 or 0.40 level. Although personality has some influence on behavior, other factors such as situations can explain a considerable amount of behavior.

While believing that personality traits have little influence on behavior would be illogical, an equally unrealistic belief is that personality completely determines behavior and people cannot adjust their behavior according to the situation. Dispositional tendencies to behave in a certain manner reflect personality traits. Yet, people often consciously override these tendencies and adjust their behavior when they are aware that their most natural reactions are inappropriate or unacceptable in certain contexts. If people become aware of how their dispositional tendencies (traits) may bias decisions, they may make the effort to avoid being the victims of their own flaws.

Promoting self-understanding of one's personality is an important first step to avoid potential pitfalls in decision-making. Self-awareness and self-regulation are two of the five major skills of Goleman's (1995) model of emotional intelligence. Self-awareness is the cornerstone of emotional intelligence (Goleman 1995; Bar-On 1997). As Goleman (1998) notes, *self-awareness* refers to the ability to know one's emotions, strengths, weaknesses, drives, and values. Having a better understanding of one's personality and any predisposition to dysfunctional patterns of thoughts is likely to improve one's self-regulation ability, the ability to control and redirect disruptive impulses and moods, and to think before acting (Goleman 1998). Raising the automatic thinking and behavioral patterns associated with personality to the realm of conscious awareness enables taking conscious effort to regulate and override dispositional tendencies to serve one's best interests.

SUMMARY

The Five-Factor Model of personality is the dominant paradigm in personality research (McCrae 2009). It encapsulates individuals' personalities using five traits, the "Big Five" of Extraversion, Agreeableness, Conscientiousness, Neuroticism, and Openness to Experience/Intellect. These personality traits are strongly rooted in biology and are genetically based. Neuroscience uses the traits to provide a common structure to map the structure of the brain onto certain behaviors. The traits are stable (Roberts and DelVecchio 2000).

Personality is a guide to what investors decide and do and this has far-reaching implications for behavioral finance. Behavioral finance provides interesting and persuasive models for many, if not most, areas of finance. In doing so, it makes great use of a wide range of ideas from psychology, but choosing which idea to take from psychology can appear arbitrary. Behavioral finance is silent on this choice as no overarching framework links all the explanations currently used. Personality is at the core of decision-making and understanding how the traits of investors relate to investment decisions and outcomes may provide this overarching framework.

This chapter focused on two important features of finance—risk taking and overconfidence—and discussed how personality traits explain these phenomena. This is what a good theory of behavioral finance should look like. Such a theory would use the same underlying building blocks to explain different phenomena. An understanding of personality traits has important implications for investors. Self-knowledge might lead investors to articulate and understand the type of decisions they make. From this understanding, investors might be able to modify their behavior.

DISCUSSION QUESTIONS

1. Describe the characteristics of each of the Big Five personality traits.
2. What personality traits are associated with risk taking? How do these traits relate to risk-taking propensities?
3. What is the biological basis of the gender differences in decision-making and risk taking?
4. Discuss how understanding a person's personality could help improve decision-making quality.

REFERENCES

Ackerman Phillip L., and Eric D. Heggestad. 1997. "Intelligence, Personality, and Interests: Evidence for Overlapping Traits." *Psychological Bulletin* 121:2, 219–245.

Aktas, Nihat, Eric de Bodt, Helen Bollaert, and Richard Roll. 2012. "CEO Narcissism and the Takeover Process: From Private Initiation to Deal Completion." AFA 2012 Chicago Meetings Paper. Available at http://ssrn.com/abstract=1784322.

Allport, Gordon W. 1966. "Traits Revisited." *American Psychologists* 21:1, 1–10.

Almagor, Moshe, Auke Tellegen, and Niels G. Waller. 1995. "The Big-Seven Model: A Cross-Cultural Replication and Further Exploration of the Basic Dimensions of Natural Language Trait Descriptors." *Journal of Personality and Social Psychology* 69:2, 300–307.

American Psychiatric Association. 2011. *Personality and Personality Disorders.* Available at www.dsm5.org/PROPOSEDREVISIONS/Pages/PersonalityandPersonalityDisorders.aspx.

American Psychiatric Association. 2013. *Diagnostic and Statistical Manual of Mental Disorders. DSM-5,* 5th ed. Washington D.C., American Psychiatric Publishing.

Apicella, Coren L., Anna Dreber, Benjamin Campbell, Peter B. Gray, Moshe Hoffman, and Anthony C. Little. 2008. "Testosterone and Financial Risk Preferences." *Evolution and Human Behavior* 29:6, 384–390.

Archer, John. 2006. "Testosterone and Human Aggression: An Evaluation of the Challenge Hypothesis." *Neuroscience and Biobehavioral Reviews* 30:3, 319–345.

Arnett, Jeffrey. 1992. "Reckless Behavior in Adolescence: A Developmental Perspective." *Developmental Review* 12:4, 339–373.

Arnold, Paul D., Gwyneth Zai, and Margaret A. Richter. 2004. "Genetics and Anxiety Disorders." *Current Psychiatry Reports* 6:4, 243–254.

Asendorpf, Jens B. 2009. "Personality: Traits and Situations." In Philip J. Corr and Gerald Matthews, eds., *The Cambridge Handbook of Personality Psychology,* 43–53. New York: Cambridge University Press.

Ashton, Michael C., Kibeom Lee, Marco Perugini, Piotr Szarota, Reinout de Vries, Lisa Di Blas, Kathleen Boies, and Boele De Raad. 2004. "A Six-Factor Structure of Personality-Descriptive Adjectives: Solutions from Psycholexical Studies in Seven Languages." *Journal of Personality and Social Psychology* 86:2, 356–366.

Barber, Brad M., and Terence Odean. 2001. "Boys Will Be Boys: Gender, Overconfidence, and Common Stock Investment." *Quarterly Journal of Economics* 116:1, 261–292.

Bar-On, Reuven. 1997. *Emotional Quotient Inventory: Technical Manual.* Toronto: Multi-Health Systems.

Bem, Sandra L. 1977. "Bem Sex-Role Inventory (BRSI)". In John E. Jones and J. William Pfeiffer, eds., *The 1977 Annual Handbook for Group Facilitators*, 83–97. San Diego, CA: University Associates.

Bem, Sandra L. 1994. *Short-Form Bem Sex-Role Inventory (BSRI)*. Palo Alto, CA: Consulting Psychologists Press.

Bouchard, Thomas J., Jr. 1994. "Genes, Environment, and Personality." *Science* 264:5166, 1700–1701,

Byrnes, James P., David C. Miller, and William D. Schafer. 1999. "Gender Differences in Risk Taking: A Meta-Analysis." *Psychological Bulletin* 125:3, 367–383.

Budescu, David V., Thomas S. Wallsten, and Wing Tung Au. 1997. "On the Importance of Random Error in the Study of Probability Judgment. Part II: Applying the Stochastic Judgment Model to Detect Systematic Trends." *Behavioral Decision Making* 10:3, 173–188.

Buss, David M. 1992. "Manipulation in Close Relationships: Five Personality Factors in Interactional Context." *Journal of Personality* 60:2, 477–499.

Campbell, W. Keith, Adam S. Goodie, and Joshua D. Foster. 2004. "Narcissism, Confidence, and Risk Attitude." *Behavioral Decision Making* 17:4, 297–311.

Carpenter, Jeffrey P., Justin R. Garcia, and J. Koji Lum. 2011. "Dopamine Receptor Genes Predict Risk Preferences, Time Preferences, and Related Economic Choices." *Journal of Risk and Uncertainty* 42:3, 233–261.

Cesarini, David, Magnus Johannesson, Paul Lichtenstein, Örjan Sandewall, and Björn Wallace. 2010. "Genetic Variation in Financial Decision Making." *Journal of Finance* 65:5, 1725–1754.

Chakrabarti, Bhismadev, Edward Bullmore, and Simon Baron-Cohen. 2006. "Empathizing with Basic Emotions: Common and Discrete Neural Substrates." *Social Neuroscience* 1:3–4, 364–384.

Coates, John M., Mark Gurnell, and Aldo Rustichini. 2009. "Second-to-Fourth Digit Ratio Predicts Success among High-Frequency Financial Traders." *Proceedings of the National Academy of Sciences of the United States of America* 106:2, 623–628.

Coates, John M., and Joe Herbert. 2008. "Endogenous Steroids and Financial Risk Taking on a London Trading Floor." *Proceedings of the National Academy of Sciences of United States of America* 105:16, 6167–6172

Cohen, Michael X., Jennifer Young, Jong-Min Baek, Christopher Kessler, and Charan Ranganath. 2005. "Individual Differences in Extraversion and Dopamine Genetics Predict Neural Reward Responses." *Cognitive Brain Research* 25:3, 851–861.

Davidson, Richard J. 2002. "Anxiety and Affective Style: Role of Prefrontal Cortex and Amygdala." *Biological Psychiatry* 51:1, 68–80.

Depue, Richard A., and Paul F. Collins. 1999. "Neurobiological of the Structure of Personality: Dopamine, Facilitation of Incentive Motivation, and Extraversion." *Behavioral and Brain Sciences* 22:3, 491–517.

Depue, Richard A., and Jeannine V. Morrone-Strupinsky. 2005. "A Neurobehavioral Model of Affiliative Bonding: Implications for Conceptualizing a Human Trait of Affiliation." *Behavioral and Brain Science* 28:3, 313–350.

De Raad, Boele. 2009. "Structural Models of Personality." In Philip J. Corr and Gerald Matthews, eds., *The Cambridge Handbook of Personality Psychology*, 323–346. New York: Cambridge University Press.

De Raad, Boele, and Dick P. H. Barelds. 2008. "A New Taxonomy of Dutch Personality Traits Based on a Comprehensive and Unrestricted List of Descriptors." *Journal of Personality and Social Psychology* 94:2, 347–364.

DeYoung, Colin G., and Jeremy R. Gray. 2009. "Personality Neuroscience: Explaining Individual Differences in Affect, Behaviour and Cognition." In Philip J. Corr and Gerald Matthews, eds., *The Cambridge Handbook of Personality Psychology*, 148–161. New York: Cambridge University Press.

DeYoung, Colin G., Jordan B. Peterson, and Daniel M. Higgins. 2005. "Sources of Openness/Intellect: Cognitive and Neuropsychological Correlates of the Fifth Factor of Personality." *Journal of Personality* 73:4, 825–858.

Dollinger, Stephen J., and Lisa A. Orf. 1991. "Personality and Performance in 'Personality': Conscientiousness and Openness." *Journal of Research in Personality* 25:3, 276–284.

Dreber, Anna, and Moshe Hoffman. 2007. *Risk Preferences Are Partly Pre-Determined*. Working Paper, Stockholm School of Economics.

Durand, Robert B., Rick Newby, and Jay P. Sanghani. 2008. "An Intimate Portrait of the Individual Investor." *Journal of Behavioral Finance* 9:4, 193–208.

Durand, Robert B., Rick Newby, Leila Peggs, and Michelle Siekierka. 2013. "Personality." *Journal of Behavioral Finance* 14:2, 116–133.

Durand, Robert B., Rick Newby, Kevin Tant, and Sirimon Treepongkaruna. 2013. "Overconfidence, Overreaction and Personality." *Review of Behavioral Finance*, forthcoming.

Dwyer, Peggy D., James H. Gilkeson, and John A. List. 2002. "Gender Differences in Revealed Risk Taking: Evidence from Mutual Fund Investors." *Economic Letters* 76:2, 151–158.

Emmons, Robert A. 1984. "Factor Analysis and Construct Validity of the Narcissistic Personality Inventory." *Journal of Personality Assessment* 48:3, 291–300.

Filbeck, Greg, Patricia Hatfield, and Philip Horvath. 2005. "Risk Aversion and Personality Type." *Journal of Behavioral Finance* 6:4, 170–180.

Gabriel, Marsha T., Joseph W. Critelli, and Jullana S. Ee. 1994. "Narcissistic Illusions in Self-Evaluations of Intelligence and Attractiveness." *Journal of Personality* 62:1, 143–155.

Gailliot, Matthew T., and Roy F. Baumeister. 2007. "The Physiology of Willpower: Linking Blood Glucose to Self-Control." *Personality and Social Psychology Review* 11:4, 303–327.

Gailliot, Matthew T., Roy F. Baumeister, C. Nathan DeWall, Jon K. Maner, E. Ashby Plant, Dianne M. Tice, Lauren E. Brewer, and Brandon J. Schmeichel. 2007. "Self-Control Relies on Glucose as a Limited Energy Source: Willpower Is More Than a Metaphor." *Journal of Personality and Social Psychology* 92:2, 325–336.

Gazzola, Valeria, Lisa Aziz-Zadeh, and Christian Keysers. 2006. "Empathy and the Somatotopic Auditory Mirror System in Humans." *Current Biology* 16:18, 1824–1829.

Glaser, Markus, and Martin Weber. 2010. "Overconfidence." In H. Kent Baker and John R. Nofsinger, eds., *Behavioral Finance—Investors, Corporations, and Markets*, 241–258. Hoboken, NJ: John Wiley & Sons.

Goldberg, Lewis R. 1993. "The Structure of Personality Traits: Vertical and Horizontal Aspects." In David C. Funder, Ross D. Parke, Carol Ann Tomlinson-Keasey, and Keith Widaman, eds., *Studying Lives Through Time: Personality and Development*, 169–188. Washington, DC: American Psychological Association.

Goleman, Daniel. 1995. *Emotional Intelligence: Why It Can Matter More Than IQ*. New York: Bantam Books.

Goleman, Daniel. 1998. "What Makes a Leader?" *Harvard Business Review* 76:6, 93–102.

Gray, Jeffery A. 1987. *The Psychobiology of Fear and Stress*. London: Cambridge University Press.

Grinblatt, Mark, and Matti Keloharju, 2009. "Sensation Seeking, Overconfidence and Trading Activity." *Journal of Finance* 64:2, 549–578.

Grinblatt, Mark, Matti Keloharju, and Juhani T. Linnainmaa. 2011. "IQ and Stock Market Participation." *Journal of Financial Economics* 66:6, 2121–2164.

Grinblatt, Mark, Matti Keloharju, and Juhani T. Linnainmaa. 2012. "IQ, Trading Behavior, and Performance." *Journal of Financial Economics* 104:2, 339–362.

Hacker, Douglas J., Linda Bol, Dianne D. Horgan, and Ernest A. Rakow. 2000. "Test Prediction and Performance in a Classroom Context." *Journal of Educational Psychology* 92:1, 160–170.

Hartshorne, Hugh, and Mark A. May. 1928. *Studies of the Nature of Character (Vol. 1) Studies in Deceit*. New York: MacMillan.

Helson, Ravenna. 1985. "Which of Those Young Women with Creative Potential Became Productive? Personality in College and Characteristics of Parents." In Robert Hogan and Warren H. Jones, eds., *Perspectives in Personality Theory, Measurement, and Interpersonal Dynamics Volume 1*, 49–80. Greenwich, CT: JAI Press.

Hennig, Juergen. 2004. "Personality, Serotonin, and Noradrenaline." In Robert M. Stelmack, ed., *On the Psychobiology of Personality: Essays in Honor of Marvin Zuckerman*, 379–395. New York: Elsevier.

Hogan, Joyce, and Robert Hogan. 1989. "How to Measure Employee Reliability." *Journal of Applied Psychology* 74:2, 273–279.

Hōnekopp, Johannes, Luise Bartholdt, Lothar Beier, and Andreas Liebert. 2007. "Second to Fourth Digit Length Ratio (2D:4D) and Adult Sex Hormone Levels: New Data and a Meta-Analytic Review." *Psychoneuroendocrinology* 32:4, 313–321.

Horvath, Paula, and Marvin Zuckerman. 1993. "Sensation Seeking, Risk Appraisal, and Risky Behavior." *Personality and Individual Difference* 14:1, 41–52.

Huang, Jieken, and Darren J. Kisgen. 2013. "Gender and Corporate Finance: Are Male Executives Overconfident Relative to Female Executives?" *Journal of Financial Economics* 108:3, 822–839.

Hudgens, Gerald, and Linda T. Fatkin. 1985. "Sex Differences in Risk Taking: Repeated Sessions on a Computer-Simulated Task." *Journal of Psychology: Interdisciplinary and Applied* 119:3, 197–206.

John, Oliver P., and Sanjay Srivastava. 1999. "The Big Five Trait Taxonomy: History, Measurement, and Theoretical Perspective." In Lawrence A. Pervin and Oliver P. John, eds., *Handbook of Personality: Theory and Research*, 2nd ed., 102–139. New York: Guilford Press.

Johnson, Johnnie E. V., and Philip L. Powell. 1994. "Decision Making, Risk and Gender: Are Managers Different?" *British Journal of Management* 5:2, 123–138.

Kaustia, Markku. 2010. "Disposition Effect." In H. Kent Baker and John R. Nofsinger, eds., *Behavioral Finance—Investors, Corporations, and Markets*, 241–258. Hoboken, NJ: John Wiley & Sons.

Langston, Christopher A., and W. Eric Sykes. 1997. "Beliefs and the Big Five: Cognitive Bases of Broad Individual Differences in Personality." *Journal of Research in Personality* 31:2, 141–165.

Lauriola, Marco, and Irwin P. Levin. 2001. "Personality Traits and Risky Decision-Making in a Controlled Experimental Task: An Exploratory Study." *Personality and Individual Differences* 31:2, 215–226.

Levin, Irwin P., Mary A. Snyder, and Daniel P. Chapman. 1988. "The Interaction of Experimental and Situational Factors and Gender in a Simulated Risky Decision-Making Task." *Journal of Psychology* 122:2, 173–181.

Loehlin, John C. 1992. *Genes and Environment in Personality Development*. Newbury Park, CA: Sage.

Malmendier, Ulrike, and Geoffrey Tate. 2005. "CEO Overconfidence and Corporate Investment." *Journal of Finance* 60:6, 2661–2700.

Mazur, Allan, and Alan Booth. 1998. "Testosterone and Dominance in Men." *Behavioral and Brain Science* 21:3, 353–363.

McCrae, Robert R. 2009. "The Five-Factor Model of Personality Traits: Consensus and Controversy." In Philip J. Corr and Gerald Matthews, eds., *The Cambridge Handbook of Personality Psychology*, 148–161. New York: Cambridge University Press.

McCrae, Robert R., and Paul T. Costa Jr. 1985. "Updating Norman's Adequate Taxonomy: Intelligence and Personality Dimensions in Natural Language and in Questionnaires." *Journal of Personality and Social Psychology* 49:3, 710–721.

McCrae, Robert R., and Paul T. Costa Jr. 1989. "Reinterpreting the Myers-Briggs Type Indicator from the Perspective of the Five-Factor Model of Personality." *Journal of Personality* 57:1, 17–40.

McCrae, Robert R., Antonio Terracciano, and Members of the Personality Profiles of Cultures Project. 2005. "Universal Features of Personality Traits from the Observer's Perspective: Data from 50 Cultures." *Journal of Personality and Social Psychology*, 88:3, 547–561.

Mischel, Walter. 1968. *Personality and Assessment*. New York: John Wiley & Sons, Inc.

Morf, Carlyn C., and Frederick Rhodewalt. 2001. "Unraveling the Paradoxes of Narcissism: A Dynamic Self-Regulatory Processing Model." *Psychological Inquiry* 12:4, 177–196.

Moutafi, Joanna, Adrian Furnham, and Ioannis Tsaousis. 2006. "Is the Relationship between Intelligence and Trait Neuroticism Mediated by Test Anxiety." *Personality and Individual Differences* 40:3, 587–597.

Netter, Petra. 2004. "Personality and Hormones." In Robert M. Stelmack, ed., *On the Psychobiology of Personality*, 353–377. New York: Elsevier.

Nicholson, Nigel, Emma Soane, Mark Fenton-O'Creevy, and Paul Willman. 2005. "Personality and Domain-Specific Risk Taking." *Journal of Risk Research* 8:2, 157–176.

Nigg, Joel T. 2000. "On Inhibition/Disinhibition in Developmental Psychopathology: Views from Cognitive and Personality Psychology and a Working Inhibition Taxonomy." *Psychological Bulletin* 126:2, 220–246.

Pan, Carrie H., and Meir Statman. 2012. "Investor Personality in Investor Questionnaires." Available at http://ssrn.com/abstract=2022339 or http://dx.doi.org/10.2139/ssrn.2022339.

Paulhus, Delroy L., and Kevin M. Williams. 2002. "The Dark Triad of Personality: Narcissism, Machiavellianism, and Psychopathy." *Journal of Research in Personality* 36:6, 556–563.

Paulus, Martin P., Corianne Rogalsky, Alan Simmons, Justin S. Feinstein, and Murray B. Stein. 2003. "Increased Activation in the Right Insula During Risk-Taking Decision Making Is Related to Harm Avoidance and Neuroticism." *NeuroImage* 19:4, 1439–1448.

Pompian, Michael M. 2012. *Behavioral Finance and Investor Types. Managing Behavior to Make Better Investment Decisions*. Hoboken, NJ: John Wiley & Sons.

Powell, Melanie, and David Ansic. 1997. "Gender Differences in Risk Behavior in Financial Decision-Making: An Experimental Analysis." *Journal of Economic Psychology* 18:6, 605–628.

Riemann, Rainer, Alois Angleitner, and Jan Strelau. 1997. "Genetic and Environmental Influences on Personality: A Study of Twins Reared Together Using the Self-and Peer Report NEO-FFI Scales." *Journal of Personality* 65:3, 449–475.

Roberti, Jonathan W. 2004. "A Review of Behavioral and Biological Correlates of Sensation Seeking." *Journal of Research in Personality* 38:3, 256–279.

Roberts, Brent W., and Wendy F. DelVecchio. 2000. "The Rank-Order Consistency of Personality Traits from Childhood to Old Age: A Quantitative Review of Longitudinal Studies." *Psychological Bulletin* 126:1, 3–25.

Rosenberg, Shai, Alan R. Templeton, Paul D. Feigin, Doron Lancet, Jacques S. Beckmann, Sara Selig, Dean H. Hamer, and Karl Skorecki. 2006. "The Association of DNA Sequence Variation at the MAOA Genetic Locus with Quantitative Behavioural Traits in Normal Males." *Human Genetics* 120:4, 447–459.

Saucier, G., and Lewis R. Goldberg. 1996. "Evidence for the Big Five in Analyses of Familiar English Personality Adjectives." *European Journal of Personality* 10:1, 61–77.

Schaefer, Peter S., Cristina C. Williams, Adam S. Goodie, and W. Keith Campbell. 2004. "Overconfidence and the Big Five." *Journal of Research in Personality* 38:5, 473–480.

Simmons, Alan, Scott C. Matthews, Murray Stein, and Martin Paulus. 2004. "Anticipation of Emotionally Aversive Visual Stimuli Activates Right Insula." *NeuroReport* 15:14, 2261–2265.

Singer, Tania, Ben Seymour, John O'Doherty, Holger Kaube, Raymond J. Dolan, and Chris D. Frith. 2004. "Empathy for Pain Involves the Affective But Not Sensory Components of Pain." *Science* 303:5661, 1157–1162.

Soane, Emma, and Nik Chmiel. 2005. "Are Risk Preferences Consistent?: The Influence of Decision Domain and Personality." *Personality and Individual Differences* 38:8, 1781–1791.

Statman, Meir, and Vincent Wood. 2004. "Investment Temperament." *Journal of Investment Consulting* 7:1, 55–66.

Stinerock, Robert N., Barbara B. Stern, and Michael R. Solomon. 1991. "Gender Differences in the Use of Surrogate Consumers for Financial Decision-Making." *Journal of Professional Services Marketing* 7:2, 167–182.

Tankersley, Dharol, C. Jill Stowe, and Scott A. Huettel. 2007. "Altruism Is Associated with an Increased Neural Response to Agency." *Nature Neuroscience* 10:2, 150–151.

Taylor, Shelley E., and Jonathon D. Brown. 1988. "Illusion and Well-Being: A Social Psychological Perspective on Mental Health." *Psychological Bulletin* 103:2, 193–210.

Whiteside, Stephen P., and Donald R. Lynam. 2011. "The Five-Factor Model and Impulsivity: Using a Structural Model of Personality to Understand Impulsivity." *Personality and Individual Differences* 30:4, 669–689.

Widiger, Thomas A., and Paul T. Costa, Jr. 2013. "Personality Disorders and the Five-Factor Model of Personality: Rationale for the Third Edition." In Thomas A. Widiger and Paul T. Costa, Jr., eds., *Personality Disorders and the Five-Factor Model of Personality*, 3–11. Washington, DC: American Psychological Association.

Williams, D. Gareth. 1992. "Dispositional Optimism, Neuroticism, and Extraversion." *Personality and Individual Differences* 13:4, 475–477.

Wilson, Margo, and Martin Daly. 1985. "Competitiveness, Risk Taking, and Violence: The Young Male Syndrome." *Ethology and Sociology* 6:1, 59–73.

Wong, A., and Bernardo J. Carducci. 1991. "Sensation Seeking and Financial Risk Taking in Everyday Money Matters." *Journal of Business and Psychology* 5:4, 525–530.

Wright, Paul, Guojun He, Nathan A. Shapira, Wayne K. Goodman, and Yijun Liu. 2004. "Disgust and the Insula: fMRI Responses to Pictures of Mutilation and Contamination." *Neuroreport* 15:15, 2347–2351.

Yamagata, Shinji, Atsunobu Suzuki, Juko Ando, Yutaka Ono, Nobuhiko Kijima, Kimio Yoshimura, Fritz Ostendorf, Alois Angleitner, Rainer Riemann, Frank M. Spinath, W. John Livesley, and Kerry L. Jang. 2006. "Is the Genetic Structure of Human Personality Universal? A Cross-Cultural Twin Study from North America, Europe, and Asia." *Journal of Personality and Social Psychology* 90:6, 987–998.

Zuckerman, Marvin. 1991. *Psychology of Personality*. Cambridge, UK: Cambridge University Press.

Zuckerman, Marvin. 2005. *Psychobiology of Personality*, 2nd ed. New York: Cambridge University Press.

ABOUT THE AUTHORS

Lucia Fung is a Lecturer in Management at Hong Kong Baptist University. She has a research background in psychology with expertise in cognitive biases associated with emotion. More specifically, her research focuses on the relationship between anxiety vulnerability and cognitive biases in interpreting ambiguous information in threatening manners. Her current research interests focus on behavioral finance, learning and knowledge management in organizations, and organizational leadership. Her recent work involves the examination of herding behavior of sell-side analysts when making earnings forecasts and the investigation of the influence of personality traits on the tendency to exhibit myopic loss aversion. She holds a BSSc (Honors) from the University of Hong Kong and a PhD in psychology from the University of Western Australia.

Robert B. Durand is Professor of Finance at Curtin University in Western Australia. Professor Durand's experience with the Crash of 1987 stimulated his interest in finance and his research has helped him understand this traumatic event. His work focuses on asset pricing models and behavioral finance. He has published more than 30 articles in scholarly journals including the *Journal of Behavioral Finance, Journal of Empirical Finance, Financial Management, Pacific-Basin Finance Journal*, and *European Journal of Finance*. He holds a BA (Honors) from the University of Sydney, an MBA from the University of Edinburgh, and a PhD from Murdoch University.

CHAPTER 7

Demographic and Socioeconomic Factors of Investors

James Farrell
Assistant Professor of Finance and Economics, Florida Southern College

INTRODUCTION

Differences in investor behavior are largely due to the heterogeneity of the individual investors. This heterogeneity leads to differences in savings rates, investment decisions, and variations in asset prices. Investors base their decisions on many factors, including their expectations about the future and their risk preferences. This chapter focuses on the relationship between investment outcomes and risk preference as well as investor sociodemographic characteristics.

Researchers have studied many sociodemographic characteristics such as race, gender, marital status, age, education, and wealth to help explain differences in investor behavior. This chapter focuses on explaining the roles of race and gender in investor behavior with the goal of understanding the persistence of the differences even after accounting for characteristics such as wealth, income (both the level and security), and age.

The effects of gender and race on investment preferences have been a focus of economic research. The goal has been to identify what demographic factors affect participants' investment choices regarding risk. Although limited research is available on race as a contributing factor, evidence suggests that it plays an important role and merits further study. Research on the topic typically suggests that men have a higher preference for risk than women and white investors have a higher preference for risk than African American and Hispanic investors. Generally, white males invest at the far end of the risk spectrum, white females and African American males occupy the middle, and African American females invest at the conservative end. Evidence also indicates a correlation between higher levels of financial education and education in general and higher preference for financial risk. Additional major factors that contribute to risk preference are age and wealth.

LITERATURE REVIEW

This section discusses the research into how demographic and socioeconomic factors affect investment outcomes and risk.

Studies on Gender Effects

The literature on gender differences in investor behavior typically indicates a significant difference in the way men and women invest, with women investing more conservatively than men. The research differs in the causes and conclusions reached on why these differences persist. Bajtelsmit and Bernasek (1996) summarize the literature that explores risk-taking differences between men and women and attempt to reach a consensus on why men and women invest differently. They find that the differences in outcomes are primarily attributable to a few key underlying factors: differences in wealth, income, employment, discrimination, human capital choices, and preferences. An issue surrounding research is the difficulty of properly controlling for the other contributing factors in order to isolate the gender effect.

This discussion has two sides: One is that men take on too much risk and the other is that women invest too conservatively. Barber and Odean (2001) examine the overconfidence of men to explain the phenomenon. Examining trading data from a discount brokerage firm, they show that men trade 45 percent more than women and that the trading reduces net returns by 2.65 percent for men compared with 1.72 percent for women. Taking a behavioral approach, they maintain that stock trading is an area that would be susceptible to overconfidence based on the low predictability and noisy feedback of trading. Overconfidence in the market would spur trading because individuals would value their own opinion more than others' opinions and would reach differing valuations, thus providing a trading opportunity. The potential for overconfidence in the valuation of securities may cause men to choose riskier strategies or make them more likely to rebalance away from default investments (e.g., underinvest in assets such as bond and real estate mutual funds).

Agnew (2006) studies the role of gender and income in participant investment decisions based on a 401(k) plan, focusing on using a 1/n diversification strategy, investment in company stock, and plan participation. A *1/n diversification* strategy is one in which an investor allocates his or her assets among all available investment options equally so that the allocation weight of each is 1/n where n is the number of available investments. The study finds that men are more likely to own a higher percentage of company stock, which is generally considered a riskier strategy because of the lack of diversification with wage variability, and that women are more likely to participate in the 401(k) plan but that gender plays no role in using a 1/n strategy. The acknowledged drawback of these results is that Agnew does not control for race and financial literacy/education.

To address the issue of education, Lusardi and Mitchell (2007a, 2007b, 2008) use the 2004 Health and Retirement Survey (HRS) to evaluate the responses of men and women to gauge the relationship among financial literacy, financial planning, and gender. Their study shows that women are less likely than men to be able to answer financial knowledge questions correctly and that a propensity to plan for retirement correlated with their ability to answer those questions. These results suggest that some measure of education is needed when trying to isolate the role of gender in investor behavior.

On the other side of the gender argument, Croson and Gneezy (2009) summarize the research covering gender differences in investments and contend that women's level of risk aversion pushes them to choose less risky portfolios. Drawing from psychology, the authors note that women report a more severe reaction to negative outcomes, leading to greater risk aversion, than men. By contrast, men are more likely to feel anger while women feel fear, making women less likely to take risky gambles. The authors also point to research that agrees with Barber and Odean's (2001) hypothesis that men are more overconfident than women. That difference disappears when restricting occupations to managers and entrepreneurs. This evidence suggests that risk taking may be learned but the effect would need to be disentangled from the selection bias of choosing the occupation. Hinz, McCarthy, and Turner (1997) also find that women invest more conservatively than men and a larger percentage of women invest in the minimum-risk portfolio. Although some of the difference is attributable to income, the results persist after economic and demographic controls. The authors are unable to control for education and race.

Measuring the effect of risk preference is difficult because of the lack of available data. Although surveys, such as the Survey of Consumer Finances (SCF), ask a few questions to gauge the level of risk aversion, respondents may not reveal the actual level risk aversion. Sunden and Surette (1998) use the SCF data from 1992 and 1995 to study gender differences in investment allocation decisions, controlling for household assets, marital status, and a risk aversion measure. They find that single men are more likely than single and married women to choose mostly stocks. Marital status has mixed results. When using gender/marital status interaction terms, married men are more risk-averse but when not using the interaction term, marriage does not have a significant effect. Marriage apparently affects men and women differently, pushing men to be more conservative, but potential selection issues need to be considered.

Papke (1998) also addresses the issue of marriage on the gender effect. He examines investment choices using the 1992 National Longitudinal Study (NLS) of Mature Women, which provides detailed household information, but self-reported financial information with a limited choice of investments. This is one of the few studies suggesting no significant gender effect on the choice of stock allocation. The study, however, suffers from several limitations. The sample size is small and the male participants are restricted to married (by default, as they are the husbands of the women in the study). The male restriction introduces selection bias into marriage with their sample counterparty. The results that they invest similarly as reported by their wives have limited applicability to a more generalized population. When compared with Sunden and Surette (1998), the evidence suggests that extrapolating conclusions about the male-female difference from only men and women married to each other is inappropriate.

Studies on Race Effects

The literature specifically focusing on racial differences in investment preferences is limited. Yet, an extensive literature highlights the differences in savings rates and wealth allocation. Blau and Graham (1990) study the accumulated wealth differences across race. Using the 1976 and 1978 National Longitudinal Survey of young men and young women, they compare single and married black investors to single and married white investors. They find that measurable characteristics, including income, left more than 75 percent of the difference in accumulated wealth unexplained. Blau and Graham speculate that intergenerational transfers of financial knowledge and income uncertainty may best explain the difference in accumulated wealth. *Intergenerational transfers* refer to the passing down of knowledge and habits from one generation to the next. In this situation, *income uncertainty* refers to the proportion of income that is transitory rather than permanent. A higher level of income uncertainty provides an incentive for African American investors to invest more conservatively and save at higher rates than white investors.

Hurst, Luoh, and Stafford (1998) study asset ownership by race and show several important differences between African Americans and all others. First, accounting for income and age, African Americans are less likely to hold a transactions account (checking or savings) and stock. Using the data from the Michigan Panel Study of Income Dynamics (PSID), a national household survey in the United States, for 1984, 1989, and 1994, the authors show that African Americans are 19.3 percent less likely to own stock, controlling for marriage, family size, income, age, gender, and years of education. Hurst et al.'s analysis supports the argument that African Americans are differentially involved and tend to take less financial risk.

Chiteji and Stafford (1999) examine the intergenerational effects of stock allocation. They find that parents holding stocks are more likely to have children who hold stocks as young adults. Using the PSID for 1984 and 1994 and matching the parental data in 1984 with young adult data in 1994, Chiteji and Stafford show that whether their parents held stocks in 1984 significantly affects the likelihood of a young adult holding stock in 1994. This effect diminishes those attributed to race, as fewer African American parents hold stocks than non-African American parents. This evidence is important for understanding how culture affects risk and investment preferences. It suggests that increasing financial education may help close the gaps present in investment preferences because such preference may result from a lack of financial education at home.

Gittleman and Wolff (2004) explore this topic further, also using the PSID from 1984, 1989, and 1994 to study the racial differences in wealth accumulation. They report that both higher incomes and higher inheritances contribute to the gap between races. As Gittleman and Wolff note, African Americans have a higher average rate of capital return but attribute this to poor market returns of the sample period and expect the returns to reverse with the stronger market in the late 1990s. The racial differences literature shows many potential factors for differences in investment risk preferences including parental influence, income uncertainty, inheritance, and wealth.

Studies on the White-Male Effect

To further study gender and racial differences, researchers also examine the "white-male effect" to explore the socioeconomic differences between white males and all other groups. Flynn, Slovic, and Mertz (1994) find that factors such as trust, status, and power affect an individual's perception of risk. Their evidence also shows that white males tend to differ from females and nonwhite males in their degree of risk perception and that this may be attributable to these sociopolitical factors. Finucane et al. (2000) further the argument that sociopolitical factors rather than biological ones separate the white male attitude toward risk from the rest of the population. However, they attribute the overall difference to the 30 percent of white males who perceive risks to be extremely low. Kahan et al. (2007) contend that motivated cognition drives individuals to accept or dismiss particular risks in order to protect their cultural identities. *Motivated cognition* refers to a process by which someone makes a decision in order to reach a particular conclusion or goal. In this case, investors are selecting risk attitudes toward sociopolitical issues in order to support their view of themselves in the world.

When looking at the white-male effect beyond world issues, Palmer (2003) finds little connection between the white-male effect found in risk attitudes toward health, technology, and worldviews and risk attitudes toward investing. Her results show no persistent difference in attitudes toward risky investing strategies between white males and all other investors but some difference in attitudes appear toward blue-chip stocks. Rivers, Arvai, and Slovic (2010) try to extend the white-male effect beyond white males and into the African American community. They examine the intraracial heterogeneity to see if the demographic and worldview characteristics found more predominantly among white males (i.e., higher than average education and household income, politically conservative and hierarchal and individualist worldviews), would lead African American males to the same risk perceptions. African American males with demographic and worldview characteristics similar to white males do not have risk perceptions that differ from those with dissimilar characteristics with few exceptions. While the white-male effect literature can identify characteristics and worldviews that correlate with differing risk perceptions, the question still remains as to the underlying cause of the differences and why the differences in characteristics do not translate into differences in risk preferences across race.

Studies on the Role of Education

Many studies focusing on gender and race acknowledge the importance of including a measure of investor education. Based on a university survey from 1997 including both faculty and staff, Grable and Lytton (1999) examine whether demographic factors are good predictors of financial risk tolerance. After separating participants into above and below average risk based on the survey answers, they find that higher risk tolerance is associated with increases in education, personal financial knowledge, income, and professional occupation status. Gender, economic expectations, age, and marital status explain less of the variation. Grable and Lytton highlight the role of financial education in determining risk taking, with the more financially educated participants more likely to take risk.

Lusardi and Mitchell's (2007a, 2007b, 2008) studies using the 2004 HRS reveal racial differences in financial education, with African Americans and Hispanics being less able to answer the financial education questions than their white counterparts. Based on Grable and Lytton (1999), the lack of financial education is likely to lead to a lower preference for risk and participation.

Mitchell et al. (2006) study the lack of attention that investors pay to their investments. The authors examine rebalancing behavior across demographic groups, finding that most participants are inattentive in the oversight of their accounts (i.e., they suffer from inertia or status quo bias) and that men are more likely to be paying attention and trading. This reinforces Barber and Odean's (2001) findings but raises the question whether simple inertia or a lack of knowledge about the benefits of rebalancing causes individuals to avoid rebalancing.

The Role of Wealth and Income

Some studies control for the effects of income on investor behavior. For example, Agnew (2006) finds that higher income leads to fewer behavioral biases, with higher income participants holding lower shares of company stock, as well as being less likely to follow a 1/n diversification strategy and more likely to participate in retirement plans. Hinz et al. (1997) find that income could explain some of the allocation differences found across gender, with higher income investors taking on more risk. Agnew notes, however, that human capital can and should play a role in investment decisions, especially when considering company stock as an option.

According to *life cycle theory*, investors should make decisions based not only on their investable wealth but also their expected income stream. This theory suggests that remaining working years, income (both the level and risk), and the level of wealth all play an important role in determining investment risk. Jagannathan and Kocherlakota (1996) suggest that, as the number of remaining working years diminishes, the expected value of the future income stream also diminishes and that rational investors would reduce the risk level of their investments. Yet, some contend that as the expected risk of income and the proportion of income to wealth vary, rational investors should adjust their investment risk, with higher levels of income, all else being equal, leading to higher levels of investment risk.

A shortcoming of accounting for wealth of many studies is that they have limited information on investor wealth outside of the sample. This is not expected to be detrimental, however. According to Poterba, Venti, and Wise (1998), individuals typically have very limited investable wealth outside of their retirement accounts. Examining portfolio assets separated by earnings levels to show the similarities and differences across assets, the authors are able to confirm the limited size of nonretirement assets for the majority of the population. About 80 percent of households in the 1992 HRS have nonretirement wealth between $100,000 and $200,000 inclusive of home equity.

CASE STUDY: THE FLORIDA DEPARTMENT OF EDUCATION EMPLOYEES

A major challenge of the research into investor behavior by demographic and socioeconomic characteristics has been the lack of data sets available containing both sufficient demographic characteristics and an accurate measure of investor behavior or risk preference. Often, studies must sacrifice at least a key variable or two, or rely on survey responses of financial holdings to assess the behavior. The literature suggests that white males are likely to take greater investment risk than their nonwhite and female counterparts. To study the gender, race, and education effects in combination with the age and wealth effects, Farrell (2011) combines two data sets, the Florida Department of Education's Employee Survey and the Florida State Board of Administration's Investment Plan administrative data. These combined data sets contain both key demographic variables and the investors' actual investment allocations for about 34,000 investors during the third quarter of 2008.

Florida Department of Education's Employee Survey

The Florida Department of Education (FLDOE) data set is based on an annual survey that the FLDOE collects from school districts about their employees. This data set provides detailed demographic information on the FLDOE employees. The major benefit of using this data set is the overlap of individuals who are in both data sets. While the matched data set limits the number of participants and creates a potential selection bias, it provides the key demographic variables needed for a thorough analysis. The FLDOE collects detailed demographic information, including race, gender, income, length of service, education, and age (Florida Department of Education 2009).

Florida State Board of Administration's Investment Plan Administrative Data

The Florida Retirement System (FRS) is one of the largest pension funds in the Unites States, with assets totaling more than $134 billion as of November 30, 2012. Of the total, $127 billion resides in the defined benefit portion of the fund, while $7 billion resides in the defined contribution portion of the fund (State Board of Administration, 2012a). Although the defined benefit portion of the FRS is professionally managed on behalf of its participants, individual participants manage the defined contribution portion for their own benefit (State Board of Administration 2012b).

This study focuses on the risk level of the FLDOE employees who participate in the FRS Investment Plan. Currently, participants have 20 investment choices, but they formerly had as many as 40 choices. Investors are defaulted into a moderate balanced fund (MBF), which consists of a diversified and managed allocation to several of the funds already available to participants. According to plan documentation and the financial planning information available to the employees, this fund provides the level of risk appropriate for the average investor (State Board of Administration, 2012c). Two other balanced funds are available to the participants: a conservative balanced fund and an aggressive balanced fund.

Measuring Investor Behavior

The key variables of risk and return are calculated based on the participants' contribution allocations and historical fund performance. The level of detail found in the FRS data set allows using expected portfolio standard deviation and return, equity allocation, and allocation to the default investment to measure the participants' risk-taking behavior.

Expected portfolio standard deviation measures the actual level of risk that participants expect to take in a given period based on prior results. The risk and return optimization prescribed by Markowitz (1959) was based on using expected portfolio standard deviation. Similarly, expected portfolio return measures the actual expected return based on prior results. Expected portfolio standard deviation and return are calculated based on the contribution allocation during the quarter and historical fund performance over the prior five-year period.

Expected portfolio standard deviation is calculated for each participant based on five-year monthly fund returns. The expected portfolio standard deviations are annualized for scale purposes and to make them more comparable to other studies. This measure may provide a greater understanding of the level of risk that a participant takes than asset allocations because it accounts for the correlations and diversification benefits of the investments. As with the expected portfolio standard deviations, the expected portfolio returns are based on five-year monthly returns and are annualized to make interpretation and comparison easier.

Finally, the allocation includes the default investment (i.e., the MBF). The MBF is a managed fund consisting of other available funds with the goal of providing a diversified investment vehicle at an average level of risk. Most importantly it acts as the default investment.

Key Summary Statistics

Exhibit 7.1 highlights the key demographic statistics by gender of the investor sample. In this sample, male investors have a higher portfolio value and salary but are older. In terms of education, men are more likely to be listed as "not applicable," which implies that their employment does not require a degree, so it is not collected.

Exhibit 7.2 highlights the key demographic statistics by race. The notable differences here are in the length of service and portfolio value, with African American investors having much longer lengths of service (95.4 months as compared

EXHIBIT 7.1   Summary Statistics for the FLDOE Study by Gender

Key Variables	Male	Female
Portfolio value	$26,451	$18,693
Service (months)	67.6	63.9
Age (years)	48.2	43.6
Salary	$37,953	$34,150
Associate degree	0.1%	0.1%
Bachelor degree	32.4%	37.4%
Masters degree	20.9%	23.5%
Specialist	1.5%	1.4%
Doctorate	1.9%	1.0%
Not applicable	43.2%	36.6%

Note: This exhibit provides the means of the key variables used in the FLDOE study by gender. The sample size is 34,409.

EXHIBIT 7.2 Summary Statistics for the FLDOE Study by Race

Key Variables	White	Black	Hispanic
Male	25.4%	27.8%	25.1%
Portfolio value	$17,956	$35,717	$20,174
Salary	$35,861	$33,855	$31,691
Service (months)	59.0	95.4	65.8
Age	44.6	46.1	44.5
Associate degree	0.1%	0.2%	0.1%
Bachelor degree	39.1%	26.3%	29.3%
Masters degree	24.3%	18.9%	17.4%
Specialist	1.3%	1.8%	1.5%
Doctorate	1.2%	1.3%	1.1%
Not applicable	34.0%	51.5%	50.6%

Note: This exhibit provides the means of the key variables used in the FLDOE study by race. The sample size is 34,409.

to 59.0 and 65.8 for white and Hispanic investors, respectively) and portfolio values (99 percent higher than white investors and 77 percent higher than Hispanic investors). In terms of education, white investors are more likely to hold bachelor and masters degrees and less likely to have a position where education in "not applicable" than African American and Hispanic investors. The difference in service given the relationship between contributions and length of service largely explains the difference in portfolio values across race.

Exhibit 7.3 highlights the risk and return statistics by gender and race. Slight differences are evident between genders and races for the risk and return characteristics, with men having a slightly larger expected standard deviation, return, and risky asset allocation and a lower allocation to the default investment than women. African American investors have a lower expected standard deviation, return, and

EXHIBIT 7.3 Risk and Return Measures for the FLDOE Study by Race and Gender

Key Variables	Expected Portfolio Standard Deviation (%)	Expected Portfolio Return (%)	Risky Allocation (%)	Moderate Balanced Fund Allocation (%)
Female	7.6	6.7	56.4	54.2
Male	7.8	6.8	58.2	46.2
White	7.8	6.7	57.5	53.2
African American	7.3	6.6	53.5	47.8
Hispanic	7.7	6.8	56.9	50.9

Note: This exhibit provides the means of the risk and return variables by gender and race. The sample size is 34,409.

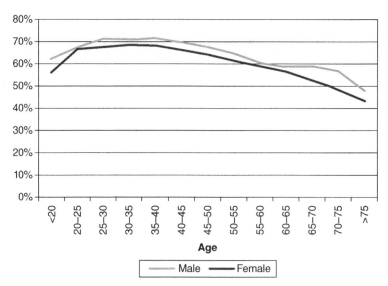

EXHIBIT 7.4 Risky Asset Allocation by Age

Note: This exhibit shows the age profile by gender of the investors' allocation to the risky asset class.

risky asset allocation than white investors, but they also have a lower allocation to the default investment.

Exhibit 7.4 shows the risky asset allocation across age by gender. The differences in behavior persist across age categories with a fairly steady gap between the risky asset allocations. Both male and female investors decrease their risky asset allocation with age as prescribed by many investing rules of thumb.

Empirical Estimation Results

Regression analysis is used to control for key factors that may affect a participant's risk preferences. Equation 7.1 shows the general structure of the model,

$$r_i = f(\text{financials}_i, \text{demographics}_i, \text{employment}_i, \text{school}_i, e_i) \tag{7.1}$$

where r is an appropriate risk and return measure; financials is a vector of financially based characteristics (salary, portfolio value, and accumulated benefit obligation (ABO)); demographics is a vector of demographic characteristics (race/gender combinations, education, and age); employment is a vector of employment-specific characteristics (months of service, current job status, job type); school is a vector of school-specific characteristics (school grade, percent of free and reduced lunch, school district dummies), and e is the error term.

The expected standard deviation and expected return measures use an ordinary least squares (OLS) framework with linear independent variables as follows:

$$r_i = \alpha + \beta_1 \text{financials}_i + \beta_2 \text{demographics}_i + \beta_3 \text{employment}_i + \beta_4 \text{school}_i + e_i \tag{7.2}$$

with the variables as described in the preceding paragraph.

In contrast to the standard deviation and return measures, participants are likely to invest on the corners of the available range of [0,1] for both the risky asset allocation and moderate balanced fund. To acknowledge the potential censoring of the investments, a censored Tobit model is used. Using 0 as a lower limit and 1 as an upper limit, the following model is estimated for risky and MBF asset allocations:

$$r_i^* = \alpha + \beta_1 \text{ financials}_i + \beta_2 \text{ demographics}_i + \beta_3 \text{ employment}_i + \beta_4 \text{ school}_i + e_i$$

$$r_i = \begin{cases} 0 \text{ if } r_i^* < 0 \\ 1 \text{ if } r_i^* > 1 \end{cases} \tag{7.3}$$

where r_i^* is the latent (unobserved) risk preference and r_i is the observed risk preference. This construct allows for a large portion of participants at the corners, rather than imposing a linear relationship throughout.

Exhibit 7.5 shows the results of the regressions including the standard errors. The results are consistent with previous literature showing female investors are more conservative than male investors and African American investors are more conservative than white investors. White females have a 5.2 percent (0.4 percentage point (pp)) lower expected standard deviation, 2.4 percent (0.2 pp) lower expected return, and 5.8 percent (3.4 pp) lower risky asset allocation when compared to white males but have a 101 percent (47.0 pp) higher allocation to the MBF. African American females have 12.2 percent (1.0 pp) lower expected standard deviation, 5.0 percent (0.4 pp) lower expected return and 14.4 percent

EXHIBIT 7.5 Regression Analysis Estimation Results of Demographic and Socioeconomic Factors on Investor Risk Behavior

Variables	Expected Standard Deviation	Expected Return	Risky Asset Allocation	Moderate Balanced Fund Allocation
African American male	−0.004246 ***	−0.001651 ***	−0.034516 ***	0.157706 **
	(0.000720)	(0.000349)	(0.006772)	(0.078644)
Hispanic male	−0.001190	−0.000285	−0.012245	0.101469
	(0.000892)	(0.000432)	(0.008394)	(0.096836)
White female	−0.004047 ***	−0.001841 ***	−0.033985 ***	0.469802 ***
	(0.000354)	(0.000172)	(0.003331)	(0.038286)
African American female	−0.009550 ***	−0.003862 ***	−0.083507 ***	0.635388 ***
	(0.000523)	(0.000254)	(0.004925)	(0.057263)
Hispanic female	−0.004507 ***	−0.001740 ***	−0.037966 ***	0.473574 ***
	(0.000590)	(0.000286)	(0.005548)	(0.064055)
Age	−0.000333 ***	−0.000142 ***	−0.003085 ***	0.016967 ***
	(0.000011)	(0.000005)	(0.000105)	(0.001219)

(*continued*)

EXHIBIT 7.5   (*Continued*)

Variables	Expected Standard Deviation	Expected Return	Risky Asset Allocation	Moderate Balanced Fund Allocation
Associate degree	0.004237	0.000005	0.046021	−0.516787
	(0.004557)	(0.002209)	(0.042752)	(0.499529)
Bachelor degree	0.001724 ***	0.000761***	0.017096 ***	−0.140233 ***
	(0.000464)	(0.000225)	(0.004365)	(0.050150)
Masters degree	0.001935 ***	0.000755***	0.021008 ***	−0.123307 **
	(0.000488)	(0.000237)	(0.004598)	(0.052886)
Specialist	0.006146 ***	0.002597***	0.055209 ***	−0.116543
	(0.001148)	(0.000556)	(0.010801)	(0.124128)
Doctorate	0.002019	0.000632	0.008724	−0.101805
	(0.001256)	(0.000609)	(0.011819)	(0.133796)
Portfolio value ($10K)	−0.001177 ***	−0.000611***	−0.011815 ***	−0.053486 ***
	(0.000098)	(0.000048)	(0.000934)	(0.011340)
Salary ($10K)	0.000394 ***	0.000231***	0.003654 ***	−0.046247 ***
	(0.000108)	(0.000052)	(0.001020)	(0.011894)
Service (Years)	0.000569 ***	0.000339***	0.005852 ***	−0.155810 ***
	(0.000035)	(0.000017)	(0.000335)	(0.004280)
Adjusted R^2	0.062	0.052	1.164	0.055
Number of observations	33,957	33,957	33,957	33,957
Lower-censored observations	—	—	1,286	12,696
Upper-censored observations	—	—	561	15,483
χ^2	—	—	2,213	3,823

Note: ***$p < 0.01$, **$p < 0.05$, *$p < 0.10$.

The district fixed effects, school characteristics, ABO, Asian/Pacific Islander, and American Indian results are suppressed.

This exhibit shows the results of the OLS and Tobit regression analysis with investor risk preference measures as the dependent variables.

(8.4 pp) lower risky asset allocation when compared to white males but have a 137 percent (63.5 pp) higher allocation to the MBF. African American males have 5.4 percent (0.4 pp) lower expected standard deviation, 2.1 percent (0.2 pp) lower expected return, and 5.9 percent (3.4 pp) lower risky asset allocation when compared to white males but have a 34 percent (15.8 pp) higher allocation to the MBF.

Comparing white males to the other demographic groups shows significant differences across all measures of risk outcomes. They hold larger portions of equity and smaller portions of the default investment than all but Hispanic males, who invest similarly. White females and African American males invest similarly in terms of equity allocation and expected risk but they are significantly different in terms of using the default investment.

White females hold much larger portions of the MBF, while African American males have reallocated investment funds from it. African American females are the most risk averse, compounding the differences found among African American males, white females, and white males. The estimations using the MBF show a strong inclination for women to use the MBF but race shows fewer differences. When combining that information with the results using the risky asset allocation, in which race and gender are both factors, their roles become more apparent. The role of gender appears to be one of financial participation. All participants default into the MBF once they choose to participate in the defined contribution plan so reallocation depends on the desire to actively choose investments along with the risk and return objectives. The evidence provided by the MBF regressions indicate that women are more likely than men not to reallocate their portfolios, opting for a larger portion of the default investment, while African Americans are not significantly less likely to reallocate than whites.

With respect to education, higher levels of general education have a significant impact on investor behavior. Bachelor and masters degree holders have significantly higher levels of expected standard deviation, expected return, and risky asset allocation while having lower allocations to the default investment when compared to investors with degree not applicable. Education, which is often unavailable in similar studies, sheds some light on its role in risk preferences. Using "not applicable" degree as a baseline, participants with bachelor, masters, and specialist degrees have a significantly higher standard deviation. Participants with associate degrees do not have a significant standard deviation. Participants with doctoral degrees have a larger coefficient than those with bachelor and masters degrees but they are not significantly different than the baseline. While connections exist between financial education and risk preference, this supports the argument that general education may also play a role. Evidence suggests that African American and Hispanic investors may invest more conservatively, based on their responses to financial education questions (Croson and Gneezy 2009).

Exhibit 7.2 suggests a higher level of risk aversion through the length of service credit for African American investors. With a service credit that is 60 percent higher than the average of the other FLDOE defined contribution plan participants (the others average 59.6 months). The tendency toward staying with an employer longer, rather than switching jobs, implies an inclination toward more risk-averse decisions involving work and retirement.

With respect to wealth and income, increasing portfolio value is related to decreasing levels of investment risk while increasing salary is related to higher levels of investment risk. This evidence supports the life cycle theory of balancing human capital risk with investment risk. For example, for two participants whose only difference is salary, the participant with the larger salary would have a larger human capital value and therefore the portfolio value would account for a smaller portion of overall wealth and more risk could be taken. Although outside wealth is unknown, the previous literature shows outside, investable wealth is limited for most people.

The Long-Run Financial Impact of the Gender and Race Differences

Using impact of the noted difference in investing over time is important to gauge its potential effect on retirement. Assuming investors have a contribution rate of 9 percent on their average salary of about $34,000 for the period, they would have $255 contributed monthly to their defined contribution account. If the expected return for white men is 7.7 percent, then the expected return for similarly positioned African American women would be 7.3 percent (95 percent of the 7.7 percent based on the estimated difference in expected returns). Subtracting out 3 percent for inflation leaves white men with a 4.7 percent expected return and African American women with a 4.3 percent expected return. Over a 30-year investment period, assuming wages do not increase in real terms, white males would expect to have $200,833 while African American females would expect to have $186,761, a difference of $14,072 or 93 percent of the white male's expected wealth in today's dollars.

This difference could have important implications for retirement. Assuming that each person would need to draw down 50 percent of their preretirement income (in this case $17,000) and their investment allocations persist, white males are expected to have 17.6 years of income while African American females are only expected to have 15.2 years of income.

In general, if real contributions are steady over time, the ratio of expected future values (G), is dependent on the number of periods (N), the expected rate of return of the base case (R), the expected rate of inflation (i), and the factor of difference (A), as follows:

$$G = \frac{\sum_{n=1}^{N}\left(1 + AR - i\right)^{N-n}}{\sum_{n=1}^{N}\left(1 + R - i\right)^{N-n}} \tag{7.4}$$

The ratio decreases as both the expected returns and time period increase. For short investment horizons, the impact of the difference in expected returns on retirement wealth is minimal, but for longer periods with reasonable expected long-run returns, the impact may be substantial. The impact on retirement wealth is even greater if contributions cease, but the investment strategy remains, as new contributions are unavailable to dampen the compounding effect. This approach does not account for the variability of the returns, which may increase or decrease the likelihood of outliving one's money. Yet, understanding the magnitude of the expected shortfall from investing too conservatively is important.

Caveats

A few caveats exist using these data. First, some selection issues limit the generalizability of the data set to the population. Investors first select to work in the public sector and more specifically for the FLDOE. They next select to join the investment plan rather than the defined benefit plan. The impact of these selection issues may work against each other as public workers tend to be more risk averse. However, selecting the investment plan tends to be more associated with risk seeking. Second, the data set also lacks information on marital status, family size, and outside financial information. Based on the previous literature, marital status has mixed effects on an individual's investment choices. For example, Hinz et al. (1997) show that married individuals take less risk and that both married men and married women take less risk than their unmarried counterparts. Sunden and Surette (1998), however, show that marriage may not have an effect unless interacted with gender, and that married women are more likely than single women to hold riskier portfolios. The FLDOE employees are a relatively narrow group with respect to education and perhaps studying a more diverse group would allow for greater distinction across educational attainment.

SUMMARY

This chapter provided a background on the roles of both demographic and socio-economic factors in investor behavior. It also provided the results of a newer study that estimates the effects of the roles of race and gender on investment preferences while controlling for income, wealth, and education.

The literature suggests that demographics and socioeconomic factors play an important role in determining investor behavior. In virtually every study, men invest more aggressively than women, even after accounting for the differences in income and wealth. Major behavioral differences also exist across race with respect to financial participation (i.e., having checking accounts and investing in stocks). The justifications for the gender differences beyond economic ones suggest that men and women have different attitudes toward risk and their ability to judge it. Men appear to be more overconfident than women and women tend to react to potential losses with fear rather than anger. The justifications for the racial differences generally point to cultural issues, namely intergenerational transfer of financial knowledge and the overall level of financial education.

This chapter also presented the results of whether the gender and racial differences persist after adding job-specific information and educational level to the usual controls of wealth, age, and income. Using multiple risk and return measures, the evidence indicates significant effects involving both race and gender after the available controls. Estimations using direct measures for standard deviation and return yield a decrease in expected standard deviation of about 5.4 percent for African American men from white men and a corresponding decrease in expected return of 2.1 percent. White women typically take less risk than men, with a 5.2 percent decrease in expected risk, and a corresponding decrease in expected return of 2.4 percent. The largest difference occurs in African American women. They experience a decrease in expected risk of 12.2 percent with a corresponding decrease in expected return of about 5.0 percent.

Despite similar risk and return coefficients when using expected standard deviation and expected return, African American men and white women achieve their risk aversion through different means. African American men appear to actively choose their level of risk, participating in the decision-making process and simply opting for a more conservative portfolio. This is supported by their lower expected standard deviation, expected return, and risky asset allocation, but a relatively similar allocation to the default investment relative to white men. Women, however, seem to default into a more conservative portfolio rather than actively choose it. This is supported by risk and return characteristics quite similar to African American men, except for the allocation to the MBF, which is significantly higher. The higher allocation suggests that women may be opting out of the reallocation process at a higher rate and may not be actively choosing their risk level. The MBF has a lower expected standard deviation and lower expected return than the average portfolio chosen by investors in this sample, both inclusive and exclusive of participants that have the MBF.

The differences in approaches to investing and the persistence of the racial differences after the controls suggest that improving financial education may have long-run implications for investors. The scope of this chapter is not to identify the appropriate portfolios for participants and whether one group is investing more successfully than another group. However, highlighting the investing differences between the demographic groups is important so that education can be targeted properly. The evidence suggests that men, both African American and white, take an active role in their portfolio allocations, with white men choosing riskier portfolios. Providing men, for example, with financial guidance on the implications of their chosen risk level and helping them understand the relevant risks to consider when making those decisions may help in determining whether they have chosen the appropriate risk level for their situation. Women, however, may need assistance with the reallocation process and its benefits. Although women in the sample may have chosen to remain in the MBF as part of their reallocation process, the evidence suggests that women have a tendency not to reallocate. Targeted education may focus on ensuring that women understand the reallocation process and feel comfortable making those decisions before the focus can be placed on the appropriate risk and return level.

Over a participant's working and contributing life, the investment differences can make substantial differences in retirement wealth. The question still remains whether the differences are justifiable by still unmeasured employment or other wealth risk or whether they are driven by differences in financial education and expectations. For example, the relationship between race and unobserved variables is a potential cause of the difference in risk preferences. Future researchers may seek to identify more information about outside wealth/risks, spousal information and marital status, and household size. Adding these controls may attribute the apparent gender and racial differences to other measurable factors.

DISCUSSION QUESTIONS

1. What do Barber and Odean (2001) theorize is a key factor in explaining the difference in investor behavior across gender? What evidence do they provide to support their argument?
2. Discuss the importance of marital status in determining how aggressively men invest. What are some of the outstanding issues with this research?
3. With respect to intergeneration transfers of financial knowledge, what evidence shows differences across racial groups?
4. Discuss the role of income on investor behavior. How does it match up against the life cycle theory?

REFERENCES

Agnew, Julie. 2006. "Do Behavioral Biases Vary Across Individuals?: Evidence from Individual Level 401(k) Data." *Journal of Financial and Quantitative Analysis* 41:4, 938–962.

Bajtelsmit, Vickie, and Alexandra Bernasek. 1996. "Why Do Women Invest Differently Than Men?" *Financial Counseling and Planning* 7, 1–10.

Barber, Brad, and Terrance Odean. 2001. "Boys will be Boys: Gender, Overconfidence, and Common Stock Investment." *Quarterly Journal of Economics* 116:1, 261–292.

Blau, Francine, and John Graham. 1990. "Black-White Differences in Wealth and Asset Composition." *Quarterly Journal of Economics* 105:2, 321–339.

Chiteji, Ngina, and Frank Stafford. 1999. "Portfolio Choices of Parents and Their Children as Young Adults: Asset Accumulation by African-American Families." *American Economic Review* 89:2, 377–380.

Croson, Rachel, and Uri Gneezy. (2009). "Gender Differences in Preferences." *Journal of Economic Literature* 47:2, 448–474.

Farrell, James. 2011. "Demographics of Risky Investing." *Research in Business and Economics Journal*, Special Edition—Florida Economic Symposium.

Finucane, Melissa, Paul Slovic, Chris Mertz, James Flynn, and Theresa Satterfield. 2000. "Gender, Race, and Perceived Risk: The 'White Male' Effect." *Health, Risk and Society* 2:2, 159–172.

Florida Department of Education. 2009. "Information Database Requirements." Available at www.fldoe.org/eias/dataweb/staff_0809.asp#REPORTING%20FORMATS.

Flynn, James, Paul Slovic, and Chris Mertz. 1994. "Gender, Race, and Perception of Environmental Health Risks." *Risk Analysis* 14:6, 1101–1108.

Gittleman, Maury, and Edward Wolff. 2004. "Racial Differences in Patterns of Wealth Accumulation." *Journal of Human Resources* 39:1, 93–227.

Grable, John, and Ruth Lytton. 1999. "Assessing Financial Risk Tolerance: Do Demographic Socioeconomic and Attitudinal Factors Work?" *Family Relations and Human Development/Family Economics and Resource Management Biennial* 3, 80–88.

Hinz, Richard, David McCarthy, and John Turner. 1997. "Are Women Conservative Investors? Gender Differences in Participant-Directed Pension Investments." In Mitchell Gordon, Olivia Mitchell, and Marc Twinney, *Positioning Pensions for the Twenty-First Century*, 91–103. Philadelphia, PA: University of Pennsylvania Press.

Hurst, Erik, Ming Ching Luoh, and Frank Stafford. 1998. "The Wealth Dynamics of American Families, 1984–94." *Brookings Papers on Economic Activity* 1998:1, 267–337.

Jagannathan, Ravi, and Narayana Kocherlakota. 1996. "Why Should Older People Invest Less in Stocks than Younger People." *Federal Reserve Bank of Minneapolis Quarterly Review* 20:3, 11–20.

Kahan, Dan, Donald Braman, John Gastil, Paul Slovic, and Chris Mertz. 2007. "Culture and Identity-Protective Cognitiion: Explaining the White-Male Effect in Risk Perception." *Journal of Empirical Legal Studies* 4:3, 465–505.

Lusardi, Annamaria, and Olivia Mitchell. 2007a. "Baby Boomer Retirement Security: The Roles of Planning, Financial Literacy, and Housing Wealth." *Journal of Monetary Economics* 54:1, 205–224.

Lusardi, Annamaria, and Olivia Mitchell. 2007b. "Financial Literacy and Retirement Preparedness: Evidence and Implications for Financial Education." *Business Economics* 42:1, 35–44.

Lusardi, Annamaria, and Olivia Mitchell. 2008. "Planning and Financial Literacy: How Do Women Fare?" *American Economic Review* 98:2, 1–24.

Markowitz, Harry. 1959. *Portfolio Selection: Efficient Diversification of Investments.* New York: John Wiley & Sons, Inc.

Mitchell, Olivia, Gary Mottola, Stephen Utkus, and Takeshi Yamaguchi. 2006. "The Inattentive Participant: Portfolio Trading Behavior in 401(k) Plans." Working Paper, Michigan Retirement Research Center.

Palmer, Christina. 2003. "Risk Perception: Another Look at the 'White Male' Effect." *Health, Risk and Society* 5:1, 71–83.

Papke, Leslie. 1998. "How are Participants Investing Their Accounts in Participant Directed Individual Account Pension Plans?" *American Economic Review* 88:2, 212–216.

Poterba, James, Stephen Venti, and David Wise. 1998. "401(k) Plans and Future Patterns of Retirement Saving." *American Economic Review* 88:2, 179–184.

Rivers, Louie, Joseph Arvai, and Paul Slovic. 2010. "Beyond a Simple Case of Black and White: Searching for the White Male Effect in the African-American Community." *Risk Analysis* 30:1, 65–77.

State Board of Administration. 2012a. "State Board of Administration Monthly Performance Report to the Trustees: Performance Through November 30, 2012." Tallahassee, FL: State Board of Administrion. Available at www.sbafla.com.

State Board of Administration. 2012b. "Your Money Your Choice: Welcome to the Florida Retirment System." Tallahassee, FL: State Board of Administration. Available at www.myfrs.com.

State Board of Administration. 20012c. "A Quick Guide to the Investment Funds You Can Choose." Tallahassee, FL: State Board of Administration. Available at www.myfrs.com.

Sunden, Annika, and Brian Surette. 1998. "Gender Differences in the Allocation of Assets in Retirement Savings Plans." *American Economic Review* 88:2, 207–211.

ABOUT THE AUTHOR

James Farrell is an Assistant Professor of Finance and Economics at Florida Southern College (FSC). Before joining FSC, he held positions at Merrill Lynch, TD Ameritrade, and the Florida State Board of Administration. His research interests include behavioral economics, behavioral investing, pensions, labor, and industrial organization. He has published in such journals as the *Research in Business and Economics Journal* and the *Journal of Business and Finance Research*. His current work includes research on the design and structure of defined benefit and defined contribution pension plans and how that may affect participant outcomes. He holds MA and PhD degrees from Florida State University as well as the CFA designation.

CHAPTER 8

The Effect of Religion on Financial and Investing Decisions

Walid Mansour
Research Affiliate, Islamic Economics Institute,
King Abdulaziz University, Saudi Arabia

Mouna Jlassi
PhD Student, Ecole Supérieure de Commerce de Tunis,
University of La Manouba in Tunisia

INTRODUCTION

This chapter discusses the relationship between religion and economic factors. It examines the extent to which religion can either influence or be influenced by economic variables, which in turn could affect financing and investment decisions. Religion has always been highly crucial in people's daily lives. The interest of economists in religion stems from the study of the variables driving production. Besides culture, social relationships, and institutional factors, religion is also an important determinant of individual and institutional financial behaviors and investing choices. Although Innoccone (1998) claims that Adam Smith was the first to stress the economic significance of religion, others regard Weber (1905) as the first author to establish a clear link between religion and economics.

To better understand the political economy, economists consider religion as an important variable. McCleary and Barro (2006, p. 760) claim that "successful explanations of economic performance must go beyond narrow measures of economic variables to encompass political social forces." The economic literature contains a rich body of studies that examines the link between religion and economic variables (Guiso, Sapienza, and Zingales 2006; McCleary and Barro 2006; Eum 2011). For instance, Guiso et al. use an empirical design showing that religious beliefs positively affect income and income growth. They also show that the Christian religions are typically more positively correlated with economic growth than others.

Religion is also a determinant at the firm's level of the interplay between financial and investing decisions. Several authors such as Iqbal and Mirakhor (2011) and Schoon and Nuri (2012) claim that religion interferes with the design of the financial instruments that firms trade with their residual and non residual claimants. For instance, the three monotheistic religions—Judaism, Christianity, and Islam—together with Buddhism and Hinduism, forbid the use of interest. Furthermore, religion spurs individuals who claim to be religious to behave differently from those who do not. Porter and Steen (2003) claim that 79 percent of American investors describe themselves as religious or spiritual and 62 percent of them keep in mind their faith when they make financial and investing decisions. The nonreligious and agnostic investors amount to about 33 percent and use personal values in their decisions.

Religion also affects personal financial choices. For example, Renneboog and Spaenjers (2012) survey a sample of Dutch households to study the differences between religious and nonreligious households in terms of financial decisions. The authors show that religious households consider themselves as more trusting, have a longer planning horizon, and have a higher propensity to save.

The purpose of this chapter is to study the relationship between religion and the political economy from the perspective of financial and investing decisions. The chapter adopts a reflexive approach to cover such a relationship and shows how deep religion is rooted in determining economic factors. Although the extant literature sometimes distinguishes among the terms religion, religiosity, and spirituality, this chapter uses the terms interchangeably.

The remainder of the chapter is organized as follows. The first section examines whether a bifurcation or dependence exists between religion and economic factors. The second section discusses how religion's influence on individual personal traits and behavior triggers particular emotions and social behavior that distort investors' investment decisions. The final section provides a summary and conclusions.

RELIGIONS AND ECONOMIC FACTORS: DEPENDENCE OR BIFURCATION?

The literature on the institutional impact on economic growth adds a supplementary dimension related to culture, religion, and social activities. Despite limited empirical evidence, the role of religion is important when studying economic growth. For example, some authors such as El Ghoul et al. (2012) study whether religion affects a firm's financing and investment decisions. This section begins by discussing whether dependence or bifurcation exists between religion and economic factors.

Does Religion Matter?

According to McCleary and Barro (2006), two approaches are available for dealing with the interaction of religion and political economy. The first considers religion as a dependent variable in which decisions by government and other entities affect religion. The second approach views religion as an independent variable. Here, religion influences societal behavior related to work, ethics, and productivity, which, in turn, could influence economic performance.

The seminal study of Weber (1905) spurred a large body of literature on the impact of religion on both macroeconomic aggregates and firm-level indicators. Weber contends that religion has a positive impact on economic growth. He concludes that Protestantism, not Catholicism, has a great impact on economic growth because of the Protestant work ethic. According to Arrunada (2010), the behavior of Protestants is closer to the social ethic hypothesis by increasing the role of social control and ethics. McCleary and Barro (2006, p. 51) state:

> *A key point about the Weberian framework is that religious beliefs are what matter for economic outcomes. This approach contrasts with a social-capital /cultural perspective, in which the networking associated with attendance at formal religious services could be what promotes growth. This alternative perspective trivializes religion by viewing participation in formal religion as just one of many ways to build social clubs.*

McCleary and Barro (2006) emphasize how religion matters to economic and other outcomes. From a religious perspective, some motivators influence human behavior such as salvation, damnation, and nirvana. These compensators spur individuals to behave in a given manner to promote growth.

Various studies examine the issue of dependence or bifurcation of religion and economic variables at the empirical level. For example, Kogut and Singh (1988) investigate the link between countries' cultural distance (religious distance) and their foreign direct investment (FDI). Their results reveal that large cultural distances impede the growth of FDI. Similarly, Guiso Sapienza, and Zingales (2008) find a positive correlation between religion similarity and trading volumes between countries located in Europe. In contrast, Guo (2004) provides empirical evidence that religious dissimilarity plays an important role in delaying foreign trade and as a strong barrier impeding the trade between the United States and China. As Helble (2007) shows, a common religion may increase the FDI but the presence of different religions engenders severe competition and triggers favorable growth because a liberal society in which the religion is diversified attracts foreign investors. Stein and Daude (2001) find that the deterioration of a host country's formal institutions impairs its FDI prospects.

Interplay between Religion and Political Economy

Several cross-country studies examine the connection between religion and the political economy. McCleary and Barro (2006) use survey information, aggregated to the country level, on religious beliefs related to afterlife and on participation in formal religious services and personal prayer. Their evidence shows a close dependence of economic growth in gross domestic product (GDP) on religious beliefs and the attendance of religious services. In contrast, Eum (2011) shows that McCleary and Barro's evidence does not hold true for different time periods. He suggests that religious variables do not have a significant, constant influence on economic growth.

McCleary and Barro (2006) show that economic development and government institutions influence religiosity. They also find that religious beliefs and participation in rituals affect economic growth. These two main results mean that religiosity is simultaneously a dependent and independent variable, which is their baseline focus.

Eum (2011) uses an augmented version of Solow's neoclassical growth model for which an economy converges toward a constant growth rate that only depends on the rates of labor force and technology. Eum adds to Solow's model two variables measuring religious diversity—fragmentation and polarization. *Fragmentation* refers to the probability that two randomly selected individuals in a country belong to different religious groups. Fragmentation increases when the number of religious groups in a society increases. *Polarization* reflects the number of separate groups. The highest value it could take is unity, which is the case of two religious groups of equal size. In other words, both religious groups have the same influence on people. Eum finds that fragmentation and polarization are not strongly correlated with economic growth. Regressing GDP growth with either variable does not show a significant correlation. Eum also shows that monthly church attendance and the belief in heaven are generally statistically significant, which is not fully consistent with the findings of McCleary and Barro (2006).

Rupasingha and Chilton (2009) use religious adherence data from the American Religious Data Archive to study the effect of church adherence rates on U.S. economic growth. The authors use three religious groups: evangelical Protestants, mainline Protestants, and Catholics. The results support the view that religious adherent rates affect U.S. economic growth.

In summary, these studies indicate that religion is simultaneously a significant determinant at the aggregate and firm levels. Although most evidence is based on U.S. data, a clear connection exists between religion and political economy. The next section expands the analysis to cover the link between religion and investment and financing decisions at the corporate level.

RELIGION AND INDIVIDUAL INVESTING BEHAVIOR

Historically, the financial literature ignored discussing how spiritual and religious norms affect decision-making behavior. Yet, the traditional finance theory of capital markets asserts that fundamental variables such as stock prices, profitability, and volatility affect financial decisions. Additionally, behavioral finance contends that human psychology and emotion influences investment choices. Few authors outline the role that religion plays in determining investor emotions and behavioral preferences.

The remainder of this section is organized as follows. First, it shows that individual personal traits (i.e., gender, age, and education level) find their roots in religious adherence. Second, the section focuses on how religion promotes the individual prosocial behavior (e.g., trust, honesty, loyalty, and ethical attitude) to act ethically. Specifically, the section examines how religion dictates investor risk-taking behavior and influences the investment decision. Third, the section highlights the influence of religion on social interaction and investor mood. Religion helps to describe the subtle, complex ways that feelings and opinions are spread among investors in the society. Fourth, it examines the relevant role of religion in expanding the social investing. Finally, the last section includes a discussion of religion's influence on some corporate variables.

Personal Traits

A recent economic perspective holds that cultural and religious norms as well as the environment in which people are raised help to shape personal traits and preferences. Specifically, the literature advances the notion that religion is a determinant of individual personal character. A discussion of how religion affects individual differences related to gender, age, education level, and their implication involving economic behavior follows.

Gender For at least 30 years, the gender-religion link has been central to social and scientific debates. The dilemma is not restricted to being more or less religious but rather to investigating the social, psychological, and behavioral implications. Previous studies about the gender-religion relationship reveal consistently strong agreement that women are more religious than men, which is partly due to the superiority of differential gender socialization (Miller and Hoffmann 1995; Miller and Stark 2002). Heelas and Woodhead (2005), who examine religion practice in the United Kingdom, find that 80 percent of those involved in the religious regions are females. Their evidence shows that females organize their time according to church schedules.

Miller and Hoffmann (1995) realize the influencing role of holding a lower religious degree on males' behavior and report that males with a low religiosity commitment often exhibit behavior that is irresponsible, short-sighted, and seeks excessive risk taking. The authors suggest that individual differences in risk preferences are almost dictated by gender differences in religiosity (Forthun et al. 1999). Several papers highlight that females are often more risk averse than males. For example, Jianakoplos, Ammon, and Bernasek (1998) report that women become more risk averse as they age. Albaity's (2012) study tackles the effect of the gender-religion relationship on risk perception and overconfidence among Malaysian Muslims, Christians, Buddhists, and Hindus. The regression results show that Malaysian Muslim males are more overconfident and more risk taking than Malaysian Muslim females but exhibit similar trust levels. However, Christian males seem to exhibit a lower level of trust than Christian females and a lower degree of risk aversion. Moreover, Buddhist males and females exhibit different scales of overconfidence and risk aversion. Buddhist males exhibit less trust than females. The regression results also show that Hindu males and females display no difference regarding their overconfidence and risk aversion.

Age Parents influence individuals' behavior and choice because they seek to convey their preferences and personal traits to their children by attending particular religious education and church attendance. Therefore, parents help to define the children's religious beliefs and behavior (Benhabib, Bisin, and Jackson 2011). For instance, Heelas and Woodhead (2005) find that older individuals have a high tendency to attend church, which means they are more religious. Fehr et al. (2003) report that retired individuals above the age of 65 tend to be more trustworthy than those below the age of 35. Thus, as individuals get older, their degree of religiosity increases, which improves their ethical behavior (e.g., trustworthiness).

Education Basic financial knowledge is crucial in investment decision-making (Lusardi and Mitchell 2009). Heightened levels of education are relevant to increased economic income. Religious affiliation in childhood and adulthood specifies particular education attainment, family processes, marriage behavior, work behavior, and other behaviors that influence wealth ownership and asset ownership (Keister 2003). According to Chiswick (1995), American Jews earn higher wages and have greater financial outcomes relative to the non Jews. This difference is mainly due to the

Jews' higher education level. Guiso et al. (2006) find that individuals who receive a religious education express a higher level of trust. According to Iannaccone (1998), individuals with a higher educational level exhibit a lower degree of religiosity. Similarly, Fehr et al. (2003) find that professionals or highly educated individuals express lower social behavior (e.g., trust behavior).

Religion and Social Behavior

The underpinnings of religious prosociality go back to the pioneering works of Durkheim (1915). Prosocial behavior reflects all actions, religious norms, and moral values. A wave of psychologists and sociologists emerged who attempt to clarify the connection of religiosity with moral systems and social behavior. However, only recently evolutionist economists document how people frame social and religious adherences, which affects their risk perceptions and decision process. Religiosity is an important driver of individual investment decisions (e.g., cooperation), prosocial behavior (e.g., trust, honesty, loyalty, ethical attitude, and fairness), individual risk perception, and gambling attitude. Religious organizations promote more prosocial behavior than secular (agonistic) ones (Paciotti et al. 2011).

Trust   Religiosity is the most important driver of personal trust (Altman 2012). Both economists and sociologists agree that religiosity promotes trust among individuals (Arrunada 2010). Paciotti et al. (2011) find that religious individuals exhibit a higher trust level compared to secular (i.e., nonreligious) people. The authors add that both religious and agonstic individuals trust religious people. Johansson-Stenman, Mahmud, and Martinsson (2009) examine whether religious differences affect trust among Hindus and Muslims in rural Bangladesh. The results of their questionnaire show that the trust level of participants from different religions is similar to the trust level with their peers from their own religion. This suggests that trust appears to be stable across religions.

    La Portaet et al. (1997) provide evidence that Catholicism hierarchies, contrarily to Protestantism norms, negatively affect trust, which has a negative impact on GDP growth. Other studies, such as Cook, Hardin, and Levi (2005), highlight the relevance of trust in maintaining financial organization contacts and managing employee relations. At the firm level, El Ghoul et al. (2012) advance that a religiosity-trust relationship contributes to decreasing equity financing costs.

Cooperation   Folk sociology is a research route stating that religion influences much of the prosocial behavior. It suggests that religious beliefs favor cooperation and social morals (Iannaccone and Berman 2006; Ruffle and Sosis 2007). However, Dawkins (2006) considers religion as a source of discrimination and conflict. The main trend of research suggests that religious individuals are more likely than secular ones to behave cooperatively. As Sosis and Ruffle (2003) note, participation in collective religious prayers and rituals triggers a higher degree of cooperation. O'Rourke's (2002) study shows that Danish Protestant farmers exhibit more cooperative behavior than Irish Catholic farmers. Based on cooperative games, Paciotti et al. (2011) find that religious individuals compared to agnostic ones are more cooperative and more generous, and often communicate information about the rules on game playing and share their private information with other groups of players.

Loyalty   Game theorists point out that religiosity also stimulates trustworthiness (Paciotti et al. 2011). Few scholars realize the influential role of religious beliefs in cementing investors' loyalty or what Simmel (1950) terms faithfulness. Peifer (2013) finds that investors who invest in both socially responsible (SR) funds and in conventional funds are more loyal to SR funds than to conventional ones. He asserts that the religion stimulates investors' loyalty by increasing the willingness to maintain a religious asset (e.g., religious mutual fund), irrespective of the asset's past low performance. Simmel adds that trust is a relevant ingredient reinforcing investor loyalty. From the perspective of financial organization, Peifer (2013, p. 7) states "loyalty is regarded as the refusal to exit a transaction relationship with a firm." Fairness mitigates agency problems, influences venture capital contracting, and enhances firm performance (Fairchild 2010).

Risk Perception   Although behavioral finance highlights the importance of risk perception to investment decision-making, few studies examine the relationship between investors' religious beliefs and risk perception. Some studies highlight that an individual's risk perception is a function of additional social factors (Renn 2004). According to Olsen (2011), groups with a higher degree of trust have a lower risk perception.

The financial literature broadly categorizes individual risk attitudes into two main types: pure risk and speculative risk. Pure risk, for example, may take the form of diseases and car accidents. Speculative risk corresponds to the case facing both positive and negative chances to realize gains or losses (Shu, Sulaeman, and Yeung 2012). Protestants and Catholics exhibit a similar average score of aversion toward pure risk, but express an opposite attitude toward speculative risk (Benjamin, Choi, and Fisher 2010).

Risk Aversion   Because individual religiosity fosters personal trust, the relationship between religion and perceived risk is expected to reverse. Keister (2003) finds that Jews exhibit a higher degree of risk-taking behavior and earn a high return on financial assets in comparison to non Jews. Hilary and Hui (2009) claim that firms headquartered in highly religious regions exhibit a higher degree of risk aversion and a lower investment rate. Using an experimental survey covering a German sample, Noussairet al. (2012) show that the risk aversion of individuals increases with their degree of religiosity. More particularly, experimental evidence shows that Protestants exhibit a greater risk aversion relative to Catholics. Similarly, Osoba (2003) indicates that the correlation between risk avoidance and church attendance is increasingly positive.

Gambling   Gambling activities exemplify the aforementioned speculative risk. Empirical research asserts that gambling is entangled in religious rituals (Grunfeld, Zangeneh, and Diakoloukas 2008). Economists contend that the involvement in lotteries in a region is dictated by the dominant local religion. Kumar, Page, and Spalt (2011, p. 671) "use religion as a proxy for gambling and investigate whether geographical variation in religion-induced gambling norms affects aggregate market outcomes." Their main hypothesis is that gambling propensity is higher in regions with a higher concentration of Catholics relative to Protestants. Their empirical results show that investors located in regions with a higher Catholic-Protestant ratio exhibit a higher propensity to engage in gambling by holding stocks with lottery features. They also report that Catholics are more inclined to engage in gambling than Protestants, who perceive gambling as a sinful activity.

Shari'a (Islamic law) condemns gambling and considers it as a *Haram* (prohibited) activity, a highly risky activity, and an immoral behavior. Ayub (2007, p. 76) claims that "all instruments like prize bonds or lotteries in which coupons or tabs are given and inducement or incentives are provided by an uncertain or unknown event depending on chance, or disproportionate prizes are distributed by drawing of lots of where the participating persons intend to avail themselves of chances at prizes are repugnant to the injunctions of Islam." *Shari'a*'s jargon uses the moniker *Gharar* to identify uncertainty, which is a very close concept to gambling. According to Schoon (2008, p. 630), *Gharar* (or uncertainty) "is defined as to knowingly expose oneself or one's property to jeopardy, or the sale of a probable item whose existence or characteristics are not certain."

As Ariss (2010, p. 102) notes, "under the precepts of Islamic legal code know as *Shari'a*, a commercial transaction is permissible as long as it is free from *Riba* (interest), *gharar* (uncertainty), *maisir* (gambling), and *non-halal* (prohibited) activities. Because of its socially responsible and ethical underpinnings, the new class of Islamic investments is appealing to both Muslims and non-Muslims who seek to invest in socially responsible products."

Gambling is also forbidden in Judaism. Indeed, gambling is restricted by the rabbinic authorities. The Talmud considers gambling for money as a form of robbery because the loser will never make peace with the winner who took his money. Landman (1967) maintains that professional gamblers are forbidden from being witnesses in Jewish courts and are not allowed to get married in the synagogue because their games of chance do not benefit society.

Religion and Investor Psychological Behavior

Prevailing models of financial theory have limited forms of social interaction and behavior contagion among investors. Understanding the process of contagion among investors' beliefs on investment decisions requires explaining the relevance of religion in conveying individuals' beliefs and emotions.

As Kumar et al. (2011) note, the finance literature omits the salient factor of religion, which is responsibility for influencing and spreading the social behavior of individuals. Religion is an important feature that underlies social communication (Bisin and Verdier 2011), which is known in behavioral finance as the social network process. Such a network encompasses religious activities and practices that spread common values and beliefs among individuals (McGuire, Newton, Omer, and Sharp 2012).

Social norms theory asserts that individuals act in accordance with social norms of their peers (Kohlberg 1984). Individuals choose to work and live in the region where the local culture and religious beliefs are most suitable for them (Cialdini and Goldstein 2004). Individual beliefs tend to be aligned with the average collective local culture and religion trends (Schneider 1987). The deviation from common social and religious norms brings on a cognitive and emotional discomfort bias (Sunstein 1996). Scherer and Cho (2003) find that agents with stronger social and religious linkages tend to exhibit homogenous risk perception. Shu et al. (2012) point out that the religious effect on risk-taking attitudes at the local individual level affects the risk-taking behavior at the organization level.

Others often influence investors in almost every activity, e.g., religious activities. Such an influence can occur through social networks based on neighbors' conversation, observation of actions, sport activity, verbal communication, commentators, and media (Hirshleifer and Teoh 2009), as well as on religious practices (Benhabib et al. 2011). This social interaction conveys psychological, emotional, and religious beliefs among individuals that may bring forth a psychological phenomenon observed in financial markets. Such a phenomenon is labeled a "meme." Distin (2005, p. 238) defines a meme as a mental representation such as "thought to be socially transmissible beliefs, desires, values, and mental representations of tunes, stories, myths, rituals, ways of doing (or saying, or thinking about) things, etc." It may cause stock mispricing. In this context, Kumar et al. (2011) run regression patterns and show that religious characteristics spread among local neighborhoods affect portfolio characteristics of institutional investors.

Norenzayan and Shariff (2008) suggest that religion, as a cultural by-product, induces in human psychology a high sensitivity toward the prosocial reputation within the community group. That is, individuals who venerate moral deities exhibit a high concern for their prosocial reputation. They try to adapt to the business practices that could satisfy their religious tenets. Kennedy and Lawton (1998) assert that an individual's religiosity exerts a substantial influence on the choices of corporate managers. Religion influences the entrepreneurial psychological state and the motivation to start a new business (Papageorgiou 2012).

Nofsinger (2005) recognizes the influence of social mood on financial decision makers. He contends that a high social mood triggers psychological pitfalls (e.g., overconfidence and optimism) that induce an abnormal increase in stock prices and disturb the investing decision. Nofsinger compares the increase in social mood to emotions such as optimism, happiness, and hope. Individuals with high levels of religious affiliation tend to be friendlier, happier, cooperative, and more satisfied in their lives than the others. Hence, they tend to exhibit a high social mood. Thus, social mood may find its root in religious values.

Behavioral economists trivialize the importance of religion in shaping investors' mood and few scholars examine the effect of religiosity-social mood on financial activity. However, Al-Hajieh, Redhead, and Rodgers (2011) discuss the role of religious practices in distorting stock returns distribution. In behavioral finance, this refers to calendar event anomalies. The authors examine an important calendar effect in Muslim countries, labeled the "Ramadan effect," which is a period associated with great social emotion influencing investors' moods. Similarly, a Ramadan period promotes solidarity and social identity among Muslims. This generates a good mood, a positive psychology, and stimulates the tendency to invest.

Religion and Social Investing

The recent meltdown of the financial system highlights the consequences of neglecting ethical values, ignoring investors' psychological biases, and allowing free rein of inadequate regulation. Social investing corresponds to an investment process translating the investment decision from a pure classical structure, based on financial needs, to a framework linking this financial objective to take account of the social, moral, and environmental effects and governance issues (Eurosif 2010).

Although once considered as a fringe activity, socially responsible investment (SRI) has now become mainstream (Sparkes and Cowton 2004). According to Eurosif (2010),

SRI amounted to about $3.07 trillion in early 2010, which is 12.2 percent of the managed assets in the U.S. economy. As Peifer (2013) notes, social norms, moral values, and ethical behavior find their roots in religion. Thus, religion plays an important role in spurring SRI growth.

During the past two decades, empirical studies show that religion and faith help to explain the correlation between SRI and the improvement of financial systems. Forte and Miglietta (2007) report that institutional investors such as pension funds, charitable organizations, and churches hold more than 92 percent of social investments. Kurtz (2008, p. 253) states that "religious belief was the first rationale for socially responsible investment, and remains an important force today."

The main ethical condition for SRI stemming from religious norms maintains that individuals and institutions should apply ethical and moral values within the investment decision-making process. Such a condition indicates that investors should avoid "sin stocks," which may potentially hinder them from maximizing their returns. Satisfying both financial and moral objectives can be a challenging task for the investors. Avoiding investments in sin stocks may lead to portfolio under-diversification. Hence, investing in socially responsible stocks or funds could be less profitable relative to investing in conventional funds. About a third of SRI funds in the United States (71 of out 250 funds) have religious affiliations, with a substantial proportion belonging to Muslim mutual funds (Peifer 2013).

Religious forces orient the investor behavior from being fully profit-maximizing to prioritizing ethical goals. Peifer (2013) reports that U.S. investors continue to invest in religious funds and pay less attention to the past return performance of these funds. McGuire et al. (2012) study the influence of religiosity on corporate social responsibility (CSR). Their results show that the local religion enhances stakeholders' incentive to get involved in CSR activities. Further, firms headquartered in highly religious areas achieve better return performance.

Judaism spurs believers to be active in alleviating social discrepancies in terms of wealth distribution and justice. Indeed, Lifshitz (2004, p. 34) claims that "Judaism is concerned with caring for the needy, it is said. Therefore, it looks to remedy or eliminate the differences in income that are the true cause of poverty." Although some misinterpret Judaism as playing the same role as socialism, Lifshitz asserts that differences exist between them. Although the Torah and the rabbinic tradition instruct the social role of people in alleviating poverty and helping the needy, this does not restrict them from their property rights and does not expropriate their wealth to be redistributed. In a comparative survey of U.K. churches, Kreander, McPhail, and Molyneaux (2004) examine the impact of Judeo-Christian churches on the development of ethical investment. The authors show that both churches employ ethical criteria in their investment process. More particularly, the Methodist church has a higher commitment in its practice to invest ethically.

Religion and Corporate Investment Decisions

Religion can also affect corporate investment decisions (McCleary and Barro 2006; Hilary and Hui 2009). Some examples of how religion interacts with corporate finance follow.

Cost of Funds and Financial Instruments The cost of funds is a primary issue that is central to the interaction of the firm's financial and investment decisions. Can religion interfere with the financial choices of the firm? The answer is an unambiguous yes. As Schoon and Nuri (2012) show, religion interferes with the cost of financial instruments. The authors discuss the prohibition of interest by the three major monotheistic religions in the world—Judaism, Christianity, and Islam. Ample evidence also indicates that Hinduism and Buddhism forbid charging interest (Visser and McIntosh 1998). The legal ban or the restriction of the interest rate to a maximum limit aims at protecting the poor and needy by allowing them to have access at an appropriate interest rate. Consequently, various financial instruments stem from religion. Such instruments are different from the classic debt contract. Forbidding the financial practice of charging interest in excess of the loan has sizeable consequences on the capital structure and firm value.

Schoon and Nuri (2012, p. 24) maintain that "the *'isqa*, which is described in the Talmud as having characteristics of both a loan and a trust became one of the important financial instruments to finance trade and business. The *'isqa* is a type of joint venture in which an investor provides funds or merchandise to a borrower. The borrower applies the funds to investments or trade as he sees fit, and the profits are shared between the parties based on the proportionate liability of the partners." Christian beliefs do not allow paying back in excess of what was borrowed and consider it to be a sin. *Shari'ah* (the jurisprudence in Islam) does not only forbid interest, but also suggests alternative financial instruments. Those instruments should be compliant with *Shari'ah*. The *Moudaraba* contract is a typical example of the financial instruments that do not encompass interest. It consists of a partnership in which an economic agent having an excess of capital develops a partnership with another one that has expertise in deploying capital into business activities, with an agreement to share profits (Iqbal and Mirakhor 2011). Al-Suwailem (2005, p. 146), who compares a sharing contract, as proclaimed by *Shari'ah*, to a standard debt contract, shows that "aggregate expected profits from sharing exceed those of debt, under both symmetric and asymmetric information." The parties are both better off signing a contract instead of a debt agreement. When they move to a debt agreement only one of them may be better off while the other must be worse off.

Schoon and Nuri (2012), among others, show that religion interferes with the interaction between financial and investment decisions. Indeed, Judaism, Christianity, and Islam forbid interest, which has a direct impact on the cost of loanable funds as well as on the design of the financial instruments that firms offer.

Managerial Behavior Managers in areas with high religious adherence tend to be highly risk averse (Hilary and Hui 2009). Further, managers manifesting a higher risk aversion tend to avoid violating the law (Lerner and Yahya 2007). For example, managers are less likely to be the target of class action securities lawsuits and litigation (Lisowsky 2010; McGuire et al. 2012). Grullon, Kanatas, and Weston (2010) study the impact of religious norms on corporate misbehavior. Specifically, they examine the role of religious adherence in mitigating unethical managerial behavior such as aggressive earnings manipulation. Their empirical results suggest that firms headquartered in a highly religious community exhibit a lower likelihood of such managerial misbehavior. Nicolosi (2010) asserts that young chief executive officers holding Christian beliefs might exhibit more pessimistic firm forecasts.

Investment Decisions   The effect of religion on firm's investment decisions can be seen through various perspectives. For instance, Hilary and Hui (2009) study how religious norms that affect investment decisions influence a firm's risk exposure. The authors survey managers of U.S. firms located in highly religious regions and find that these managers exhibit low degrees of risk exposures, which indicate a low level of risky investments and hence lower long-term growth.

Kumar et al. (2011) focus on the corporate attitude toward excessive speculative risk based on gambling activities. They show that local religious beliefs influence corporate decisions. The authors use employee stock option plans as a proxy of gambling preferences for non-executive employees in firms located in high Catholic areas. Studies such as Hodge, Rajgopal, and Shevlin (2010) confirm that employees recognize stock options as lottery tickets. Hence, stock options are a seductive source of wealth for employees with strong gambling preferences. Their results reveal that the magnitude of the negative lottery-stock premium is stronger in regions with high Catholic beliefs. Consequently, this result suggests that high Catholic regions are associated with participating in gambling activities.

Religion is a double-edged sword for firm performance. Following moral religious beliefs can increase firm performance and profitability (Forte and Miglietta 2007). However, incorporating ethical attributes in corporate policies can be very costly, especially when social management goes beyond stakeholders' expectations (Baron 2009). As Peifer (2013) shows, moral religious orientations foster the managers' commitment to religious SRI funds, despite such funds having a lower return performance.

Dyreng, Mayew, and Williams (2012) examine the influence of local religious affiliations on managers' voluntary disclosure. The authors report that divulging bad news in the press is higher for firms located in areas in which the religious adherence is low. Religious social norms such as honesty encourage announcing genuine information. Keister (2003) asserts that Jewish investors tend to invest in human capital and transportable capital rather fixed capital and they are less likely to own houses.

Corporate Governance   As a source of moral values and ethical attitudes, religion may present a key incentive to improve corporate governance. Welch, Tittle, and Petee (1991) maintain that the religion substantially decreases the individual tendency to avoid taxes. Further, religion eliminates the managerial opportunism to realize personal gains. Dyreng et al. (2012) confirm this finding and suggest that firms located in highly religious regions enjoy greater accruals quality and a lower likelihood of fraudulent accounting. As Grullon et al. (2010) show, religion can serve as an alternative regulatory process for corporate misbehavior.

Firms involving managers with strong religious beliefs tend to pay dividends more regularly. Religion presents a prevalent monitoring instrumental tool mechanism (Dyreng et al. 2012). El Ghoul et al. (2012), who assume that equity financing costs decline with better corporate governance, show that firms headquartered in highly religious areas exhibit a low equity financing cost and enhanced corporate governance. Their empirical results suggest that the monitoring role of religiosity is more relevant when the firm's governance structure is too fragile to protect investor interests.

SUMMARY

The extant literature helps to explain economic performance and factors affecting economic growth. One of these factors is religion. Research corroborates the positive relationship between religion and economic factors. However, few studies deal with the financing and investing decisions that have a direct impact on the corporate level. Studies show that religion has corporate implications in terms of risk perception, psychological behavior of investors, and governance. Such implications influence not only financing and investment decisions but also firm performance. Highly religious investors do not behave in the same manner as secular ones do. Religion not only affects the level of risk that investors are willing to undertake, but also influences the nature of the investment that they choose. The decision to avoid investing in sin stocks illustrates this point.

Religion plays an important role in designing some financial instruments. Indeed, the three monotheistic religions in the world (Judaism, Christianity, and Islam), together with Buddhism and Hinduism, do not allow financial instruments to use interest. Religion affects financial and investing decisions, which can have reverberations on the firm's capital structure and value.

DISCUSSION QUESTIONS

1. Discuss whether empirical studies show dependence between religion and the political economy.
2. Explain why economists sometimes use religion to explain financial and investment decisions.
3. Discuss the impact of religion on individual behavior.
4. Discuss the role of religion in influencing personal financial attitudes.
5. Explain how religious attitudes affect firm behavior.
6. Discuss how religion interferes with the interplay between financial and investing decisions.

REFERENCES

Albaity, Mohamed S. 2012. "Gender, Ethnicity, and Religion and Investment Decisions: Malaysian Evidence." *Journal of Sociological Research* 3:2, 502–519.

Al-Hajieh, Heitham, Keith Redhead, and Timothy Rodgers. 2011. "Investor Sentiment and Calendar Anomaly Effects: A Case Study of the Impact of Ramadan on Islamic Middle Eastern Markets." *Research in International Business and Finance* 25:3, 345–356.

Al-Suwailem, Sami. 2005. "Optimal Sharing Contracts: Properties and Evolution." In Munawar Iqbal and Tarikullah Khan, eds., *Financial Engineering and Islamic Contracts*, 146–196. Hoboken, NJ: John Wiley & Sons.

Altman, Morris. 2012. "Implications of Behavioral Economics for Financial Literacy and Public Policy." *Journal of Socio-Economics* 41:4, 677–690.

Ariss, Rima T. 2010. "Competitive Conditions in Islamic and Conventional Banking: A Global Perspective." *Review of Financial Economics* 19:3, 101–108.

Arrunada, Benito. 2010. "Protestants and Catholics: Similar Work Ethic, Different Social Ethic." *Economic Journal* 120:547, 890–918.

Ayub, Muhammad. 2007. *Understanding Islamic Finance*. Hoboken, NJ: John Wiley & Sons.

Baron, David P. 2009. "A Positive Theory of Moral Management, Social Pressure, and Corporate Social Performance." *Journal of Economics & Management Strategy* 18:1, 7–43.

Benhabib, Jess, Alberto Bisin, and Matthew O. Jackson. 2011. *Handbook of Social Economics*. Amsterdam: Elsevier Science.

Benjamin, Daniel J., James J. Choi, and Geoffrey Fisher. 2010. "Religious Identity and Economic Behavior." Working Paper No. 15925, National Bureau of Economic Research.

Bisin, Alberto, and Thierry Verdier. 2011. "The Economics of Cultural Transmission and Socialization." In Jess Benhabib, Alberto Bisin, and Matthew O. Jackson, eds., *Handbook of Social Economics*, 339–416. Amsterdam: Elsevier Science.

Chiswick, Carmel U. 1995. "The Economics of American Judaism." *Shofar* 13:4, 1–19.

Cialdini, Robert B., and Noah J. Goldstein. 2004. "Social Influence: Compliance and Conformity." *Annual Review of Psychology* 55, 591–621.

Cook, Karen S., Russell Hardin, and Margaret Levi. 2005. *Cooperation without Trust?* New York: Russell Sage Foundation.

Dawkins, Richard. 2006. *The God Delusion*. Boston: Houghton Mifflin.

Distin, Kate. 2005. *The Selfish Meme: A Critical Reassessment*. Cambridge: Cambridge University Press.

Durkheim, Emile. 1915. *The Elementary Forms of the Religious Life*. London: Cambridge University Press.

Dyreng, Scott, William J. Mayew, and Christopher D. Williams. 2012. "Religious Social Norms and Corporate Financial Reporting." *Journal of Business Finance & Accounting* 39:7–8, 845–875.

El Ghoul, Sadok, Omrane Guedhami, Yang Ni, Jeffrey Pittman, and Samir Saadi. 2012. "Does Religion Matter to Equity Pricing?" *Journal of Business Ethics* 111:4, 491–518.

Eum, Wonsub. 2011. *Religion and Economic Development—A Study on Religious Variables Influencing GDP Growth over Countries*. Berkeley: University of California.

Eurosif. 2010. "European SRI Study, 2010." Available at www.eurosif.org.

Fairchild, Richard J. 2010. "Fairness Norms and Self-Interest in Venture Capital/Entrepreneur Contracting and Performance." Working Paper, University of Bath.

Fehr, Ernst, Urs Fischbacher, Bernhard von Rosenbladt, Jürgen Schupp, and Gert G. Wagner. 2003. "A Nation-Wide Laboratory: Examining Trust and Trustworthiness by Integrating Behavioral Experiments into Representative Surveys." Working Paper, Institute for Empirical Research in Economics, University of Zurich.

Forte, Gianfranco, and Federica Miglietta. 2007. "Islamic Mutual Funds as Faith-Based Funds in a Socially Responsible Context." Working Paper, Bocconi University.

Forthun, Larry F., Nancy J. Bell, Charles W. Peek, and Sheh-Wei Sun. 1999. "Religiosity, Sensation Seeking, and Alcohol/Drug Use in Denominational and Gender Contexts." *Journal of Drug Issues* 29:1, 75–90.

Grullon, Gustavo, George Kanatas, and James Weston. 2010. "Religion and Corporate (Mis) behavior." Working Paper, Jesse H. Jones Graduate School of Business, Rice University.

Grunfeld, Robert, Masood Zangeneh, and Lea Diakoloukas. 2008. "Religiosity and Gambling Rituals." In Masood Zangeneh, Alex Blaszczynski, and Nigel E. Turner, eds., *In the Pursuit of Winning: Problem Gambling Theory, Research and Treatment*, 155–165. New York: Springer.

Guiso, Luigi, Paola Sapienza, and Luigi Zingales. 2006. "Does Culture Affect Economic Outcomes?" *Journal of Economic Perspectives* 20:2, 23–48.

Guiso, Luigi, Paola Sapienza, and Luigi Zingales. 2008. "Trusting the Stock Market." *Journal of Finance* 63:6, 2557–2600.

Guo, Rongxing. 2004. "How Culture Influences Foreign Trade: Evidence from the U.S. and China." *Journal of Socio-Economics* 33:6, 785–812.

Heelas, Paul, and Linda Woodhead. 2005. *The Spiritual Revolution: Why Religion Is Giving Way to Spirituality*. Oxford: Blackwell.

Helble, Matthias. 2007. "Is God Good for Trade?" Working Paper, Graduate Institute of International Studies, University of Geneva.

Hilary, Gilles, and Kai Wai Hui. 2009. "Does Religion Matter in Corporate Decision-Making in America?" *Journal of Financial Economics* 93:3, 455–473.

Hirshleifer, David, and Siew Hong Teoh. 2009. "Thought and Behavior Contagion in Capital Markets." In Klaus Reiner Schenk-Hoppé and Thorsten Hens, eds., *Handbook of Financial Markets: Dynamics and Evolution*, 1–56. Amsterdam: Elsevier.

Hodge, Frank D., Shiva Rajgopal, and Terry Shevlin. 2010. "Do Managers Value Stock Options and Restricted Stock Consistent with Economic Theory?" *Contemporary Accounting Research* 26:3, 899–932.

Iannaccone, Laurence R. 1998. "Introduction to the Economics of Religion." *Journal of Economic Literature* 36:3, 1465–1495.

Iannaccone, Laurence R., and Eli Berman. 2006. "Religious Extremism: The Good, the Bad, and the Deadly." *Public Choice* 128:1, 109–129.

Iqbal, Zamir, and Aabbas Mirakhor. 2011. *An Introduction to Islamic Finance: Theory and Practice*. Hoboken, NJ: John Wiley & Sons.

Jianakoplos, Nancy Ammon, and Alexandra Bernasek. 1998. "Are Women More Risk Averse?" *Economic Inquiry* 36:4, 620–630.

Johansson-Stenman, Olof, Minhaj Mahmud, and Peter Martinsson. 2009. "Trust and Religion: Experimental Evidence from Rural Bangladesh." *Economica* 76:303, 462–485.

Keister, Lisa A. 2003. "Religion and Wealth: The Role of Religious Affiliation and Participation in Early Adult Asset Accumulation." *Social Forces* 82:1, 173–205.

Kennedy, Ellen J., and Leigh Lawton. 1998. "Religiousness and Business Ethics." *Journal of Business Ethics* 17:2, 163–175.

Kogut, Bruce, and Harbir Singh. 1988. "The Effect of National Culture on the Choice of Entry Mode." *Journal of International Business Studies* 19:3, 411–432.

Kohlberg, Lawrence. 1984. *The Psychology of Moral Development: The Nature and Validity of Moral Stages. Essays on Moral Development*. San Francisco: Harper & Row.

Kreader, Niklas, Ken McPhail, and David Molyneaux. 2004. "God's Fund Managers: A Critical Study of Stock Market Investment Practices of the Church of England and UK Methodists." *Accounting, Auditing and Accountability Journal* 17:3, 408–441.

Kumar, Alok, Jeremy K. Page, and Oliver G. Spalt. 2011. "Religious Beliefs, Gambling Attitudes, and Financial Market Outcomes." *Journal of Financial Economics* 102:3, 671–708.

Kurtz, Lloyd. 2008. "Socially Responsible Investment and Shareholder Activism." In Andrew Crane, Abagail McWilliams, Dirk Matten, Jeremy Moon, and Donald S. Siegel, eds., *The Oxford Handbook of Corporate Social Responsibility*, 249–280. Oxford: Oxford University Press.

Landman, Leo. 1967. "Jewish Attitudes toward Gambling: The Professional and Compulsive Gambler." *Jewish Quarterly Review* 57:4, 298–318.

La Porta, Rafael, Florencio Lopez-de-Silanes, Andrei Shleifer, and Robert W. Vishny. 1997. "Trust in Large Organizations." *American Economic Review* 87:2, 333–338.

Lerner, Craig S., and Moin A. Yahya. 2007. "'Left Behind' After Sarbanes Oxley." *American Criminal Law Review* 44:4, 1383–1416.

Lifshitz, Yosef Y. 2004. "*Foundation of Jewish Economic Theory*." Available at www.azure .org.il.

Lisowsky, Petro. 2010. "Seeking Shelter: Empirically Modeling Tax Shelters Using Financial Statement Information." *Accounting Review* 85:5, 1693–1720.

Lusardi, Annamaria, and Olivia S. Mitchell. 2009. "How Ordinary Consumers Make Complex Economic Decisions: Financial Literacy and Retirement Readiness." Working Paper, National Bureau of Economic Research, Cambridge University.

McCleary, Rachel M., and Robert J. Barro. 2006. "Religion and Economy." *Journal of Economic Perspectives* 20:2, 49–72.

McGuire, Sean T., Nathan J. Newton, Thomas C. Omer, and Nathan Y. Sharp. 2012. "Does Local Religiosity Impact Corporate Social Responsibility?" Working Paper, Texas A&M University.

Miller, Alan S., and John P. Hoffmann. 1995. "Risk and Religion: An Explanation of Gender Differences in Religiosity." *Journal for the Scientific Study of Religion* 48:2, 232–240.

Miller, Alan S., and Rodney Stark. 2002. "Gender and Religiousness: Can Socialization Explanations Be Saved?" *American Journal of Sociology* 107:6, 1399–1423.

Nicolosi, Gina. 2010. "Convertible Debt Demographics." Paper Presentation, Annual Meeting of the Academy of Behavioral Finance and Economics, September 15–17, Chicago.

Nofsinger, John R. 2005. "Social Mood and Financial Economics." *Journal of Behavioral Finance* 6:3, 144–160.

Norenzayan, Ara, and Azim F. Shariff. 2008. "The Origin and Evolution of Religious Prosociality." *Science* 322:5898, 58–62.

Noussair, Charles N., Stefan Trautmann, Gijs van de Kuilen, and Nathanael Vellekoop. 2012. "Risk Aversion and Religion." Working Paper, Tilburg University.

Olsen, Robert A. 2011. "Financial Risk Perceptions: A Behavioral Perspective." In Rassoul Yazdipour, ed., *Advances in Entrepreneurial Finance with Applications from Behavioral Finance and Economics*, 45–68. New York: Springer.

O'Rourke, Kevin H. 2002. "Culture, Politics and Innovation: Evidence from the Creameries." CEPR Working Paper No. 3235, London.

Osoba, Brian J. 2003. "Risk Preferences and the Practice of Religion: Evidence from Panel Data." Working Paper, West Virginia University.

Paciotti, Brian, Peter Richerson, Billy Baum, Mark Lubell, Tim Waring, Richard McElreath, Charles Efferson, and Ed Edsten. 2011. "Are Religious Individuals More Generous, Trusting, and Cooperative? An Experimental Test of the Effect of Religion on Prosociality." In Lionel Obadia and Donald C. Wood, eds., *The Economics of Religion: Anthropological Approaches (Research in Economic Anthropology)*, 267–305. London: Emerald Group Publishing Limited.

Papageorgiou, Maria. 2012. "Religion and Entrepreneurship: The Case of Muslim Minority in Thrace." Working Paper, Democritus University of Thrace.

Peifer, Jared L. 2013. "Fund Loyalty among Socially Responsible Investors." *Journal of Business Ethics*, forthcoming.

Porter, Brian E., and Todd P. Steen. 2003. "Investing in Stocks: Three Models of Faith Integration." Working Paper, Hope College.

Renn, Ortwin. 2004. "Perception of Risks." *Toxicology Letters* 149:1–3, 405–413.

Renneboog, Luc, and Christophe Spaenjers. 2012. "Religion, Economic Attitudes, and Household Finance." *Oxford Economic Papers* 64:1, 103–127.

Ruffle, Bradley J., and Richard Sosis. 2007. "Does It Pay to Pray? Costly Ritual and Cooperation." *The B.E. Journal of Economic Analysis & Policy* 7:1, 1–35.

Rupasingha, Anil, and John B. Chilton. 2009. "Religious Adherence and Country Economic Growth in the US." *Journal of Economic Behavior and Organization* 72:1, 438–445.

Scherer, Clifford W., and Hichang Cho. 2003. "A Social Network Contagion Theory of Risk Perception." *Risk Analysis* 23:2, 261–267.

Schoon, Natalie. 2008. "Islamic Finance—An Overview." *European Business Organization Law Review* 9:4, 621–635.

Schoon, Natalie, and Julinda Nuri. 2012. "Comparative Financial Systems in Judaism, Christianity and Islam: The Case of Interest." Working Paper, University of Surrey, United Kingdom.

Schneider, Benjamin. 1987. "The People Make the Place." *Personnel Psychology* 40:3, 437–453.

Shu, Tao, Johan Sulaeman, and Eric P. Yeung. 2012. "Local Religious Beliefs and Mutual Fund Risk-Taking Behaviors." *Journal of Management Science* 58:10, 1779–1796.

Simmel, Georg. 1950. "Faithfulness and Gratitude." In Kurt H. Wolff, ed., *The Sociology of Georg Simmel*, 379–395. New York: The Free Press.

Sosis, Richard, and Bradley J. Ruffle. 2003. "Religious Ritual and Cooperation: Testing for a Relationship on Israeli Religious and Secular Kibbutzim." *Current Anthropology* 44:5, 713–722.

Sparkes, Russell, and Christopher J. Cowton. 2004. "The Maturing of Socially Responsible Investment: A Review of the Developing Link with Corporate Social Responsibility." *Journal of Business Ethics* 52:1, 45–57.

Stein, Ernesto, and Christian Daude. 2001. "Institutions, Integration, and the Location of Foreign Direct Investment." Washington, DC: Inter-American Development Bank.

Sunstein, Cass R. 1996. "Social Norms and Social Rules." *Columbia Law Review* 96:4, 903–968.

Visser, Wayne A. M., and Alastair McIntosh. 1998. "A Short Review of the Historical Critique of Usury." *Accounting, Business & Financial History* 8:2, 175–189.

Weber, Max. 1905. The Protestant Ethic and the Spirit of Capitalism. London: Unwin Hyman.

Welch, Michael R., Charles R. Tittle, and Thomas Petee. 1991. "Religion and Deviance among Adult Catholics: A Test of the 'Moral Communities' Hypothesis." *Journal for the Scientific Study of Religion* 30:2, 159–173.

ABOUT THE AUTHORS

Walid Mansour is a Research Affiliate at the Islamic Economics Institute, King Abdulaziz University. He has taught courses and has presented seminars at several universities including the University of Monastir, University of Sousse, College of Mount Saint Vincent, and California State University at Fresno. He was a postdoctoral research and teaching affiliate at the University of Kansas. Dr. Mansour was also a Fulbright scholar. He holds a BA in finance (University of Sousse in Tunisia), a BA in English (University of Tunis El-Manar), an MSc in finance (University of La Manouba in Tunisia), an MSc in risk management (University of Paris X, France), a PhD in finance (University of La Manouba in Tunisia), and a postdoctoral diploma (Kansas University).

Mouna Jlassi is a PhD student at the University of La Manouba in Tunisia. She was awarded the Erasmus-AVERROES fellowship by The European Committee. Her research interests include behavioral finance, animal spirit, market bubbles, and banking regulation. She holds a BA in quality management from IAE Business School (University of Montpellier, France) and HEC Institute (University of Sousse in Tunisia), and an MS in Finance from the University of Monastir.

CHAPTER 9

Money and Happiness: Implications for Investor Behavior

Jing Jian Xiao
Professor, University of Rhode Island

INTRODUCTION

Can money buy happiness? A clear definition of these terms is necessary before researchers can answer this question. *Money* refers to income and related economic factors such as work, spending, and money attitudes. Besides micro level measurements, money can also be related to macroeconomic factors such as per capita gross domestic product (GDP), unemployment rate, inflation, income inequality, economic growth, and economic policies. Happiness is measured in various ways. One common measure of happiness is life satisfaction and others include having a positive mood on a daily basis and living a meaningful life.

The research literature on money and happiness suggests that money is important for achieving happiness. Specifically, a strong association exists between personal income and life satisfaction, especially when the income level increases from the low to middle level (Diener and Biswas-Diener 2002). This positive association diminishes when the income level continues to increase from the middle to high level. Country comparisons also show that money makes people happier. People in richer countries are generally happier than those in poorer countries. However, pursuing a materialist goal decreases happiness. Living a meaningful life and maintaining good social relationships with family members, friends, and colleagues increase happiness (Seligman 2002; Lyubomirsky 2008; Diener and Biswas-Diener 2008).

Macroeconomic factors affect people's happiness. Income inequality causes unhappiness and differences exist among countries. Although both unemployment and inflation decrease happiness, the negative impact of unemployment on people is more painful than that of inflation (Di Tella, MacCulloch, and Oswald 2001). Perceptions of unfair public policies decrease people's happiness level (Sun and Xiao 2012).

Economic growth does not increase happiness, which is called the *Easterlin Paradox* (Easterlin 1974). During the past 40 years, Easterlin and other researchers use data from various countries to repeatedly confirm this puzzling finding. Although some researchers contend that they have solved the puzzle, others disagree (Diener, Helliwell, and Kahneman 2010).

Most research studies treat money as an independent variable and examine whether money is associated with happiness. In recent years, researchers started to investigate the possible reverse causality and examine whether happier people make more money. The evidence provides support for reverse causality, suggesting that money and happiness may interact to improve subjective well-being (De Neve and Oswald 2012).

Research findings on the association between money and happiness may have implications for investor behavior. Because of the limited research on the association between investor behavior and happiness, the following discussion represents hypotheses that need further research to verify them. Based on the literature of happiness research, professionals in the investment industry may have lower levels of daily happiness because of their highly demanding jobs. Their life satisfaction level may also be lower than average because of the nature of their jobs. If they want to live a meaningful life while still working in the investment industry, they should pay more attention to socially responsible investing. Some evidence shows that socially responsible investing may result in higher company valuations (Hill et al. 2007), which might have spillover effects that benefit workers in these companies. The implication about living a meaningful life may also apply to individuals who are interested in investing but not in the investment industry.

The rest of this chapter is organized as follows. The first section reviews key research findings on effects of money-related factors on happiness. Next, the subject of reverse causality (i.e., whether happiness increases income) is examined, followed by a section discussing implications of these research findings on investor behavior. The final section draws conclusions.

CAN MONEY BUY HAPPINESS?

This section begins with a discussion of various measurements of happiness. Next, it describes research findings on the effects of microeconomic factors such as income, work, spending, and materialism on happiness. Finally, the section examines the effects of macroeconomic factors such as economic growth, inflation, unemployment, and income inequality on happiness.

Measurements of Happiness

In the literature of happiness research, happiness refers to subjective well-being (SWB), which can be defined in different ways. According to Diener et al. (1999, p. 277), *subjective well-being* is "a broad category of phenomena that includes people's emotional responses, domain satisfactions, and global judgments of life satisfaction." This definition casts SWB as representing a broad area of research activity and interest, rather than as a specific construct (Sirgy et al. 2006).

The measure of SWB has three components: positive affect, negative affect, and life satisfaction. The labels "life satisfaction" or "satisfaction with life" are usually associated with a very broad conceptual level, involving summary judgments of one's life as a whole (Pavot and Diener 1993). Multimethod longitudinal research demonstrates that all three components are separable constructs (Lucas, Diener, and Suh 1996).

Diener (1984) identifies several characteristics of SWB. First, SWB is subjective, residing within the individual, and is based on an individual's unique experience of the world. Second, SWB includes positive experience, rather than just the absence of negative factors. Third, researchers usually consider SWB from a broad level, as an overall assessment, rather than according to specific experiences or aspects of an individual's life.

As psychologist William Paviot explains, SWB is not psychological well-being because this type of well-being refers to caring for others (Sirgy et al. 2006). SWB has the philosophical origins of ancient Greece (Ryan and Deci 2001). The "hedonic view" follows from the philosophy of Aristippus who advocated maximizing pleasure as the goal of life and the source of happiness. The "eudaimonic view" stems from the Aristotelian perspective. For Aristotle, the degree of virtue in one's life is the critical standard of evaluation. As Ryan and Deci note, living a life of virtue, rather than a life of pleasure, is the key to reaching the desirable state of eudaimonia.

Researchers use various measures of happiness or SWB. For example, Dolan, Layard, and Metcalfe (2011) divide measures of SWB into three broad categories: evaluation, experience, and eudaimonic. The evaluation measure refers to life satisfaction and domain satisfactions. The experience measurement equates to happiness yesterday and positive or negative affect (worried, energetic, or relaxed yesterday). The eudaimonic measure refers to purpose in life. It asks people to identify purpose in life in general and purposes and meanings of specific activities. Most empirical studies on money and happiness use life satisfaction and domain satisfactions to measure happiness. Debate exists over which definition should be used to help policy makers when they use happiness data for policy-making purposes (Graham 2011). To help better understand investor behavior, three types of definitions are relevant and considered in this chapter.

Income and Happiness

Researchers use micro and macro data as well as cross-sectional and longitudinal data to study the relationship between income and happiness. This relationship is complicated when measuring happiness using individual data. Researchers usually measure income using either micro data such as personal income or macro data such as per capita GDP. The association between the two variables becomes more complicated when making international comparisons (Diener et al. 2010).

Research based on micro data shows that personal income increases happiness but the relationship is not perfectly linear. Among low to middle income groups, the association is strong but becomes weaker from middle income to high income groups (Diener and Biswas-Diener 2002). Based on data from the United States and the United Kingdom, Blanchflower and Oswald (2004) find that money buys happiness and people also care about relative income.

Income effects may vary when using different measures of happiness. Kahneman and Deaton (2010) examine the effect of income on SWB. They measure SWB using two sets of variables: emotional well-being and life evaluation. *Emotional well-being* or daily happiness refers to the emotional quality of an individual's everyday experience (i.e., the frequency and intensity of experiences of joy, stress, sadness, anger, and affection) that make a person's life pleasant or unpleasant. *Life evaluation* or *life satisfaction* refers to the thoughts that people have about their life when they think about it. Kahneman and Deaton raise the question of whether money buys happiness and happiness refers to these two aspects of well-being separately. Their analysis of more than 450,000 responses to a daily survey of 1,000 U.S. residents conducted by the Gallup Organization shows that emotional well-being (measured by questions about emotional experiences yesterday) and life evaluation (measured by Cantril's Self-Anchoring Scale) have different correlates. Income and education are more closely related to life evaluation, but health, caregiving, loneliness, and smoking are relatively stronger predictors of daily emotions. When plotted against log income, life evaluation rises steadily. Emotional well-being also rises with log income, but does not progress beyond an annual income of $75,000.

Happiness researchers also observe the *adaptation effect*, which is the positive effect of personal income on happiness lasting over time. People are happy when their incomes increase. The effect decreases over time but lasts for several years. Using panel data from Germany, researchers find that German homeowners who are presumably wealthier than tenants adapt fully to the effects of higher levels of the income (in log form) after around seven years. With panel data from Europe, they find that in wealthy European countries, full adaptation may take at least five years (Di Tella and MacCulloch 2010).

In another study with a panel of German data, Di Tella, Haisken-De New, and MacCulloch (2010) examine happiness adaptation to income and to status. Specifically, they estimate a "happiness equation" defined over several lags of income and status and compare the long-run effects. They reject the hypothesis of no adaptation to income during the four years following an income change. In the short run, a one standard deviation increase in status and 52 percent of one standard deviation in income are associated with similar increases in happiness. However, 65 percent of the current year's impact of income on happiness is lost over the following four years whereas the impact of status remains intact.

Aspiration may play an important role in the relationship between income and happiness. Easterlin (2001) finds that material aspiration is initially fairly similar among income groups; consequently, more income brings greater happiness. Over the life cycle, however, aspirations grow along with income and undercut the favorable effect of income growth on happiness but the cross-sectional happiness-income difference persists.

Work and Happiness

Most people make money by working. Job satisfaction and career satisfaction are closely related to happiness. Work characteristics such as work hours and job fit may affect happiness. Using data from the 2006 wave of the Gallup World Poll, Harter and Arora (2010) examine the relationship between hours worked and job fit and their impact on well-being. They measure SWB using the Cantril striving scale that asks respondents to rate their lives on the Ladder of Life: "If the top step is 10 and the bottom step is 0, on which step of the ladder do you feel you personally stand at the present time?" High perceived job fit explains about 1.5 steps on the ladder of life satisfaction after controlling for demographic differences and other subjective life domains. Number of hours worked per week explains about 1.5 steps on the ladder of life satisfaction. Optimum well-being measured by life evaluation is observed for those working between 35 and 44 hours per week with high perceived job fit.

Working status affects happiness. Clark (2010) analyzes repeated cross-sectional data from several Organization for Economic Cooperation and Development (OECD) countries to examine relationships between work and happiness. He finds a wide gap in well-being between employment and unemployment and no evidence that individuals adapt to unemployment. He also finds that three to four times as many people say they would prefer to be self-employed than are actually self-employed. The self-employed are more satisfied about their jobs than employees.

Working status may also have spillover effects on happiness. Tadic et al. (2012) examine the role of work status (i.e., working versus not working) in the relationship between time-use and momentary happiness. They employ a longitudinal research design using monthly assessments via the day reconstruction method over three years among 579 older adults. Overall, the results reveal that working older individuals are not happier than nonworking individuals, but involvement in work as a daily activity coincides with higher levels of momentary happiness.

Worker characteristics affect job satisfaction. Clark (1996) examines factors associated with job satisfaction with data from 5,000 British employees. He finds that men, workers in their thirties, the well-educated, those working longer hours, and workers in larger establishments have lower levels of job satisfaction. Using a large sample of British employees, Clark, Oswald, and Warr (1996) study the association between age and job satisfaction. They observe a strongly significant U-shape for overall job satisfaction, satisfaction with pay, and satisfaction with the work itself. Despite including 80 control variables, significant coefficients persist for the age and age-squared variables.

Job satisfaction and happiness may interact. Bowling, Eschleman, and Wang (2010) conduct a meta-analysis and examine the relationship between job satisfaction and SWB. Consistent with *the spillover hypothesis* stating that the experiences from one life domain have corresponding influences on the experiences in other life domains, they find positive relationships between job satisfaction and a set of subjective well-being factors (i.e., life satisfaction, happiness, positive affect, and the absence of negative affect). Additionally, an examination of longitudinal studies suggests that the causal relationship from SWB to job satisfaction is stronger than the causal relationship from job satisfaction to SWB.

Some researchers consider career satisfaction as a measure of job satisfaction in the longer term. Career satisfaction as a whole is stable in the long term but one of its components (e.g., income) may be a factor that causes dissatisfaction. Using panel data, Spurk, Abele, and Volmer (2011) examine the validity of a career satisfaction measurement. They find that as a group, career satisfaction is stable during the study period except for the income component. The career satisfaction component regarding meeting income goals shows a U-shape in the five-year study period.

To better understand the association between job and happiness, Warr (2011) proposes an approach combining environment-centered and person-centered frameworks. An environment-centered perspective examines job characteristics on worker happiness and identifies 12 major characteristics of a job that are related to happiness or unhappiness. A person-centered perspective examines worker mental process and happiness. A combined perspective is to consider happiness as a function of both job and personal characteristics. Based on the research review, Warr concludes that environmental features are associated with happiness or unhappiness to different degrees and in various ways according to a worker's characteristics.

Spending and Happiness

Consumer financial behavior may affect happiness. Lyubomirsky, Sheldon, and Schkade (2005) review the literature of happiness research and summarize three broad factors that influence happiness: set points (50 percent), circumstances (10 percent), and intentional activity (40 percent). They stress the importance of intentional activity and contend that to develop effective interventions to improve the happiness level, intentional activity or behavior is an important factor to consider. Their own research provides supporting evidence for this argument. Other research on behavior and happiness also supports this argument. For example, using data from a sample of college students, Xiao, Tang, and Shim (2009) find that positive financial behaviors contribute to both financial satisfaction and life satisfaction.

Spending is a major consumer financial behavior that may bring happiness. Using data from the United Kingdom and Hungary, Headey, Muffels, and Wooden (2008) find nondurable consumption to be as important as income to life satisfaction. Using data from Peru, Guillen-Royo (2008) finds that consumption has a meaning beyond merely satisfying basic needs. Other factors significantly predicting happiness include status concerns, the reference group, and the pleasure of consuming.

Spending for others may also increase happiness. Dunn, Aknin, and Norton (2008), who examine the relationship between prosocial spending behavior and life satisfaction, find that spending on others contributes to life satisfaction. The authors base their study on a common finding in the SWB literature showing a positive association between social relationship and SWB.

If the notion is true that prosocial spending behavior generates life satisfaction, it should be shown in other prosocial behaviors such as environment friendly behavior. In studying ecological sustainability, Jacob, Jovic, and Brinkerhoff (2009) find that ecologically sustainable behavior independently explains statistically significant amounts of variance in SWB. Brown and Kasser (2005), who study both an adolescent and an adult sample, find that individuals higher in SWB report more ecologically responsible behavior. Using data collected from consumers in 14 cities China, Xiao and Li (2011) find that consumers who report green purchase intention and behavior have higher scores in life satisfaction compared to individuals that make non-environmentally related consumer purchases.

Materialism and Happiness

Materialism refers to the tendency of seeking material goods as the life goal. Richins and Dawson (1992) view materialism as a consumer value. They describe a values-oriented materialism scale with three components: acquisition centrality, acquisition as the pursuit of happiness, and possession-defined success. In validation tests, high scorers desire a higher level of income, place greater emphasis on financial security and less on interpersonal relationships, prefer to spend more on themselves and less on others, engage in fewer voluntary simplicity behaviors, and are less satisfied with their lives.

Seeking materialism may result in a low level of happiness. Kasser and Ryan (1993) examine associations between values/expectancies for wealth/money and personal well-being and find negative associations between the two sets of factors. Their results show that the relative centrality of money-related values and expectancies is negatively related to college students' well-being and mental health.

Other researchers confirm this finding in a setting of situational materialism. Bauer et al. (2012) find that situational materialism undermines personal and social well-being. Specifically, situational cuing can trigger materialistic mindsets, with similarly negative personal and social consequences. The authors conclude that signs of materialism are not localized only in particularly materialistic people, but also are present in individuals who are exposed to environmental cues that are commonplace in contemporary society. Other factors such as time affluence may moderate the negative association between materialism and well-being (Manolis and Roberts 2012).

Materialism may increase life satisfaction indirectly through luxury consumption. Hudders and Pandelaere (2012) conduct a large scale survey in Dutch-speaking Belgium and find that materialistic consumers are more inclined to consume luxury goods than less materialistic consumers. Luxury consumption leads to enhanced positive mood, diminished negative mood, and increased life satisfaction. Furthermore, the impact of luxury consumption on life satisfaction is more pronounced for materialistic consumers than for less materialistic consumers. These results suggest that the key to reducing luxury consumptions that have adverse effects on individual and societal well-being is to educate consumers to be less materialistic.

Materialism may also reduce work-related well-being. A field study by Deckop, Jurkiewicz, and Giacalone (2010) finds a negative association between materialistic values and a range of indicators of work-related personal well-being, including intrinsic and extrinsic reward satisfaction, job satisfaction, and career satisfaction.

Researchers attempt to understand factors associated with materialism. For example, Sirgy (1998) tries to establish a theory of materialism and quality of life. The theory posits that satisfaction with one's standard of living partly determines overall life satisfaction. In turn, evaluations of one's actual standard of living compared to a set goal determine satisfaction with standard of living. Materialists experience greater dissatisfaction with their standard of living than nonmaterialists, which spills over to overall life causing dissatisfaction with life in general. Materialism may be related to different motives for making money (Srivastava, Locke, and Barton 2001). Karabati and Cemalcilar's (2010) research suggests a positive association between self-enhancement motives and materialism.

Macroeconomic Factors and Happiness

Consumer well-being is jointly determined by the economic environment. Many macroeconomic factors such as unemployment, inflation, income inequality, economic growth, and economic policy may affect happiness. Happiness data can be informative in macroeconomic research. Di Tella and MacCulloch (2006) contend that using happiness data in economic research is natural because many questions in economics are fundamentally about happiness. Using happiness data, economists simply compare measures of welfare, and what causes changes in welfare, under different scenarios. Di Tella and MacCulloch present evidence showing how happiness data can be used in macroeconomic analyses.

Based on research using data from a quarter of a million randomly sampled Europeans and Americans from the 1970s to 1990s, Di Tella, MacCulloch, and Oswald (2003) show that macroeconomic movements have strong effects on the happiness of nations. Their results indicate a correlation between movements in reported well-being and changes in macroeconomic variables such as GDP. Recessions create large psychic losses that extend beyond the fall in GDP and rise in unemployment. The welfare state appears to be a compensating force: Higher unemployment benefits are associated with higher national well-being.

Undesirable macroeconomic indicators may have differential negative effects on happiness. Di Tella et al. (2001) find that people appear to be happier when inflation and unemployment are low. They also examine marginal effects of happiness on the two factors. At the margin, unemployment depresses reported well-being more than does inflation. Their estimates suggest that people would trade off a 1 percentage point increase in the unemployment rate for a 1.7 percentage point increase in the inflation rate. In other words, unemployment seems more painful than inflation for consumers.

Inequality may decrease happiness but differences exist between countries. Alesina, Di Tella, and MacCulloch (2004) find that individuals have a lower tendency to report being happy when inequality is high. The effect, however, appears to be stronger in Europe than in the United States. Decreased happiness associated with inequality may be related to perceived fairness and trust. Oishi, Kesebir, and Diener (2011), using General Social Survey data from 1972 to 2008, find that Americans are, on average, happier in the years with less national income inequality than in the years with more national income inequality. The authors demonstrate that perceived fairness and general trust explain this inverse relationship between income inequality and happiness.

Economic Growth and Happiness

The Easterlin Paradox is the most controversial part of income and happiness research. Easterlin (1974) shows no association between life satisfaction and economic growth. In the past 40 decades, Easterlin and many other researchers repeatedly confirm this fact with data from both developed and developing countries and using both cross-sectional and longitudinal data (Easterlin and Sawangfa 2010). Some researchers even document a negative association between per capita income growth rate and life satisfaction, which is labeled the *paradox of unhappy growth* (Graham, Chattopadhyay, and Picon 2010). Other researchers also provide evidence to support this paradox. For example, Blanchflower and Oswald (2004) find that reported levels of well-being have declined over the last quarter of a century in the United States and life satisfaction has run approximately flat through time in the United Kingdom. The happiness of African Americans, however, has risen. White women in the United States have been the biggest losers since the 1970s. These findings are consistent with the Easterlin hypothesis.

Some researchers claim that their evidence does not support the Easterlin Paradox (Deaton, 2008; Stevenson and Wolfers 2008). However, several major researchers believe the evidence is not strong enough to solve the paradox (Easterlin and Sawangfa, 2010; Layard, Mayraz, and Nickell 2010). The general consensus now is that the relationship between economic growth and happiness is complicated and requires more systematic data collection in a broader scale and longer time frame to clarify the issue (Diener et al. 2010).

Many researchers attempt to explain the paradox. For example, Di Tella and MacCulloch (2008) try to explain the Easterlin Paradox using data from almost 400,000 people living in the OECD countries during 1975 and 1997. After controlling for country and year dummy variables, they find a positive correlation of the happiness responses with absolute income, generosity of the welfare state, and life expectancy but a negative correlation with the average number of hours worked, measures of environmental degradation, crime, openness to trade, inflation and unemployment. Di Tella and MacCulloch claim that the unexplained trend in happiness is even bigger than would be predicted if income is the only argument in the utility function. In other words, introducing omitted variables worsens the income-without-happiness paradox. Using data from the Gallup international study of happiness, Di Tella and MacCulloch (2010) find that the economic growth rate increases life satisfaction among poorer countries but not among richer countries. They attribute the difference to the *adaptation effect* (i.e., happiness fades after several years of income increase).

Based on a comprehensive review of happiness research, Clark, Frijters, and Shields (2008) emphasize the importance of social comparison and self comparison under the framework of a utility function. Graham et al. (2010) review studies on this topic and propose several explanations. They speculate that several factors such as the choice of micro or macro data, framing of happiness questions, countries included in the sample, and possible mediating factors affect the relationship between economic growth measured by per capital income growth and happiness.

Economic Policy and Happiness

Researchers in economics and psychology consider plans to use happiness data for economic policy making. They propose a National Time Accounting approach using a U-index to introduce happiness data into the economic policy-making process (Kahneman and Krueger 2006; Krueger 2009). They believe that both National Income Account and National Time Account represent the true welfare of people in an economy. The authors propose a summary measure of SWB called the U-index, or percentage of time that an individual or group of individuals spends in an unpleasant emotional state. An *unpleasant emotional state* is an interval in which the strongest negative emotion is coded as 1 under the economic utility framework.

Public perceptions of social policies contribute to SWB (Wong, Wong, and Mok 2006). Progressive policy makers also need to hear people's perceptions and evaluations of existent and new social policies in addition to information from objective measures (Veenhoven 2002). Using data from Hong Kong, Wong et al. examine perceptions and evaluations of social programs on SWB and find positive associations. Veenhoven suggests including subjective indicators in social policy indicators to provide more comprehensive and accurate information for policy makers. Consumer perceptions of different economic policies may have different effects on happiness. Using data from a random telephone survey conducted in Beijing, China, Sun and

Xiao (2012) find that perceived fairness of social security and income distribution policies are positively associated with SWB. After controlling for income, age, and education, the effect of income distribution fairness on work satisfaction is positive and significant but has decreased in intensity, while the effect on life satisfaction is almost unchanged. Effects of social security fairness on both life and work satisfaction are significant but have changed in different directions after adding demographic variables, in which the effect on life satisfaction has increased, while the effect on work satisfaction has decreased.

CAN HAPPINESS BUY MONEY?

Many happiness research studies attempt to examine whether higher income contributes to happiness. However, some researchers explore whether happiness would increase one's income. If they find causality, SWB may be a factor to be promoted to increase productivity for society. Oishi (2012) considers happiness as psychological wealth and contends that a nation's psychological wealth is important for a good society.

Researchers document the causal relationship between happiness and positive life outcomes, including economic outcomes. Happiness may result in positive life outcomes. Lyubomirsky, King, and Diener (2005) suggest a conceptual model arguing that the happiness–success link exists not only because success makes people happy, but also because positive affect engenders success. Their results reveal that happiness is associated with and precedes numerous successful outcomes, as well as behaviors paralleling success.

Happiness may raise productivity. Oswald, Proto, and Sgroi (2009) examine whether happiness raises productivity in research experiments and find supporting evidence. In Experiment 1, treated subjects have 12 percent greater productivity compared to subjects in the control group. To check the robustness and lasting nature of this kind of effect, the authors conduct Experiment 2, in which they study major real-world unhappiness shocks—bereavement and family illness. The findings in the real-life setting match those in the laboratory setting.

Happiness may contribute to job satisfaction and high income. Diener et al. (2002) examine the relationship between dispositional affect and job outcomes. They assess the influence of *dispositional affect*, defined as self-rated cheerfulness at college entry on three job outcomes (i.e., current income, job satisfaction, and unemployment history) assessed about 19 years later. The results show that individuals with a higher cheerfulness rating at college entry have a higher current income and a higher job satisfaction rating and are less likely ever to have been unemployed than individuals with a lower cheerfulness rating. Although cheerfulness generally has a positive effect on current income, this effect is curvilinear, with current income increasing more rapidly at lower than at higher cheerfulness ratings. Graham, Eggers, and Sukhtankar (2004) use panel data from Russia to assess the reverse causation—that happiness itself affects income, health, and other factors. They find that people who had higher "residual happiness" in 1995 (i.e., people who were happier after correcting for the usual determinants of well-being) make more money and are in better health in a survey five years later.

Using data from a large U.S. representative panel of more than 10,000 individuals, De Neve and Oswald (2012) show that adolescents and young adults who report higher life satisfaction or positive affect grow up to earn significantly higher levels of income later in life. The study's results are robust to the inclusion of controls such as education, intelligence quotient, physical health, height, self-esteem, and later happiness. To explore how psychological well-being may influence income, the authors identify several mediating factors: Being happy may be associated with a higher probability of obtaining a college degree, getting hired and promoted, and having higher degrees of optimism and extroversion and less neuroticism. De Neve and Oswald contend that the relationship between income and happiness is dynamic and the effects may run in both directions. The literature of happiness research shows that happiness has various correlates such as health (Frey 2011), social networks (Fowler and Christakis 2009), and self-esteem (Lyubomirsky, Tkach, and Di-Matteo 2006) that, in turn, are known to positively influence labor market outcomes and may thus play a mediating role. More recent neuroscientific research provides clues that greater SWB is associated with particular neurological variation, which, in turn, is associated with improved cognitive skills and economic outcomes (De Neve and Oswald 2012).

Happier people make more money but the association may be nonlinear, especially in the high end of the happiness spectrum. Different life outcomes may occur between moderately and extremely happy people. Oshi, Diener, and Lucas (2007) examine happiness and life outcomes including income. They find that people who experience the highest levels of happiness are the most successful in terms of close relationships and volunteer work, but that those who experience slightly lower levels of happiness are the most successful in terms of income, education, and political participation. Once people are moderately happy, the most effective level of happiness appears to depend on the specific outcomes used to define success as well as the available resources.

Happiness contributes to consumption and saving behavior. Guven (2009) examines the impact of happiness on consumption and savings behavior using data from Netherlands and Germany. He finds that happier people save more, spend less, and have a lower marginal propensity to consume. Happier people take more time for making decisions and have more control over expenditures; they expect a longer life and seem more concerned about the future than the present; they also expect less inflation in the future.

Happiness and life outcomes may interact with each other. Binder and Coad (2010) examine the coevolution of changes in happiness and changes in income, health, marital status as well as employment status with the British Household Panel Survey (BHPS) data set. They find that increases in happiness are associated with subsequent increases in income, marriage, employment, and health variables, while increases in these life-domain variables (except health) tend to be followed by decreases in happiness in subsequent periods, suggesting adaptation dynamics in all domains.

If happiness is a resource for a better life, people should mobilize and use it. Based on his research of college students at Harvard, Achor (2010) develops principles to fully take the "happiness advantage" such as to retrain the brain to capture positivity and to adjust the mindset in a way to gain power to be more fulfilled and successful.

IMPLICATIONS FOR INVESTOR BEHAVIOR

Research findings on the association between money and happiness have implications for investor behavior. Because of the limited direct research on money and happiness pertinent to investor behavior, the following is speculation. The discussion focuses on how investors gain happiness when they engage in investment activities. Individual investors can be categorized in two broad categories: professional investors and nonexpert individual investors including novice and sophisticated investors. According to Dolan et al. (2011), the research literature often measures happiness in three ways: daily happiness, life satisfaction, and living a meaningful life. These measures are relevant to investors' job satisfaction, career satisfaction, and socially responsible investing (SRI). For professionals, their daily happiness level may be lower than that of people who are not in the investment industry because they have to work longer hours and have more pressure. Professionals may also have a lower level of life satisfaction because they have limited time to spend with their family and friends due to highly demanding work. Job fit may alleviate the lower than the average happiness level. If they are highly motivated to work hard in the industry, they may consider long hours and high pressure as necessities to be successful at work.

The professional investors could live a meaningful life if they make a strong commitment to socially responsible investing and sacrifice monetary benefits when they face moral dilemmas at work. To live a happier life when they prefer staying in the investment industry, they may consider adjusting their working hours to allow more quality time to be with their family and friends. They also could be more selective in investment options and make positive contributions to the economy. From a human resource perspective, selecting the right workers for investment companies may involve considering not only conventional recruiting criteria used in the industry but also whether a person's job fit is consistent with his work-life values and worldviews on sustainable developments. Positive psychological characteristics such as cheerfulness and optimism may also be competitive advantages for these individuals. Investment professionals when advising clients apply a comprehensive financial planning process and experts should use the same approach to themselves in establishing their career goals. Self-employed financial planners can extend this method by defining and determining the overall size and scope of their firms (e.g., a company objective could be to establish a maximum number of clients and assets under management) to specific levels of happiness, satisfaction, and motivation.

Some researchers examine SRI from a corporate perspective. For example, SRI may increase corporation values in a long term. Hill et al. (2007) analyze the relationship between corporate social responsibility (CSR) and company stock valuation across three regions of the world. They find that in the short run (three years), only the European portfolios outperform the larger equity market. However, in the long term (10 years), both the United States and European portfolios outperform their comparison markets. The Asian portfolio is close to being statistically significant in this same period, suggesting possible movement in the direction of western counterparts.

Soppe (2009) discusses a concept of sustainable finance as a connection between CSR and socially responsible investment (SRI). Limited research is available on SRI and happiness among individual professional investors. This line of research should be encouraged to enrich the literature of money and happiness research.

For amateur investors (i.e., nonexpert individual investors) to enjoy a happier life, they may need to limit their time investing so that they have adequate time to spend with their family and friends. They may also keep learning investment skills and methods to successfully achieve their investment goals. Making a profit is a minimum requirement for investment but being too greedy may result in unhappiness. To be happy in a long term, investors may want to participate in SRI to make their spare time investing more meaningful. Individual investors should also meet with investment professionals on a yearly basis on various issues such as financial planning advice, financial counseling assistance, and life planning needs to achieve the proper balance of happiness. The research literature on investor behavior is extensive but little research relates investor behavior with happiness.

SUMMARY

This chapter reviewed the research literature on the relationship between money and happiness. Research findings suggest that income is important for happiness, especially when the income grows from the low to middle level. When income reaches the middle level, its marginal positive effect on happiness decreases. For an individual, emphasizing social relationships is more important than focusing on materialist goals. To live a happy life in the long run, one strategy is to seek a meaningful life. Spending for others or meaningful social causes may bring more happiness than spending on oneself. Research also suggests that happier people may do better financially. Implications of these research findings for individual investors are suggestive because of limited direct research. If research findings of the association between money and happiness are true, people should avoid entering a career with high time demands and pressure such as jobs in professional investments if they want to live a life with a higher level of daily happiness and life satisfaction. Many anecdotal examples show that employees within the financial services industry enjoy high pay but also must tolerate long hours and high pressure at work. Those working in this industry may still have ways to increase the chance of living a happy life by skillfully keeping a work-life balance. For example, they could adjust their working hours and forgo some monetary benefits to spend more time with their family and friends. Engaging in SRI could result in happiness because they would be proud of their work by making positive contributions to society through their hard work. Some of these implications also apply to nonexpert individual investors.

DISCUSSION QUESTIONS

1. Discuss whether money can buy happiness.
2. What is the Easterlin Paradox?
3. Identify the similarities and differences of the effects of inflation and unemployment on happiness.
4. Discuss whether happier people make more money.
5. What can practitioners in the investment industry learn from research findings on money and happiness?

REFERENCES

Achor, Shawn. 2010. *The Happiness Advantage*. New York: Random House.

Alesina, Alberto, Rafael Di Tella, and Robert MacCulloch. 2004. "Inequality and Happiness: Are Europeans and Americans Different?" *Journal of Public Economics* 88:9, 2009–2042.

Bauer, Monika A., James E. B. Wilkie, Jung K. Kim, and Galen V. Bodenhausen. 2012. "Cuing Consumerism Situational Materialism Undermines Personal and Social Well-Being." *Psychological Science* 23:5, 517–523.

Binder, Martin, and Alex Coad. 2010. "An Examination of the Dynamics of Well-Being and Life Events Using Vector Autoregressions." *Journal of Economic Behavior & Organization* 76:2, 352–371.

Blanchflower, David G., and Andrew J. Oswald. 2004. "Well-Being over Time in Britain and the USA." *Journal of Public Economics*, 88:7, 1359–1386.

Bowling, Nathan A., Kevin J. Eschleman, and Qiang Wang. 2010. "A Meta-analytic Examination of the Relationship between Job Satisfaction and Subjective Well-Being." *Journal of Occupational and Organizational Psychology* 83:4, 915–934.

Brown, Kirk Warren, and Tim Kasser. 2005. "Are Psychological and Ecological Well-Being Compatible? The Role of Values, Mindfulness, and Lifestyle." *Social Indicators Research* 74:2, 349–368.

Clark, Andrew E. 1996. "Job Satisfaction in Britain." *British Journal of Industrial Relations* 34:2, 189–217.

Clark, Andrew E. 2010. "Work, Jobs, and Well-Being across the Millennium." In Ed Diener, John F. Helliwell, and Daniel Kahneman, eds., *International Differences in Well-Being*, 436–468. Oxford: Oxford University Press.

Clark, Andrew, Andrew Oswald, and Peter Warr. 1996. "Is Job Satisfaction U-Shaped in Age?" *Journal of Occupational and Organizational Psychology* 69:1, 57–81.

Clark, Andrew E., Paul Frijters, and Michael A. Shields. 2008. "Relative Income, Happiness, and Utility: An Explanation for the Easterlin Paradox and Other Puzzles." *Journal of Economic Literature* 46:1, 95–144.

De Neve, Jan-Emmanuel, and Andrew J. Oswald. 2012. "Estimating the Influence of Life Satisfaction and Positive Affect on Later Income Using Sibling Fixed Effects." *Proceedings of the National Academy of Sciences* 109:49, 19953–19958.

Deaton, Angus. 2008. "Income, Health and Well-Being around the World: Evidence from the Gallup World Poll." *Journal of Economic Perspectives* 22:2, 53–72.

Deckop, John R., Carole L. Jurkiewicz, and Robert A. Giacalone. 2010. "Effects of Materialism on Work-Related Personal Well-Being." *Human Relations* 63:7, 1007–1030.

Di Tella, Rafael, John Haisken-De New, and Robert MacCulloch. 2010. "Happiness Adaptation to Income and to Status in an Individual Panel." *Journal of Economic Behavior & Organization*, 76:3, 834–852.

Di Tella, Rafael, and Robert MacCulloch. 2006. "Some Uses of Happiness Data in Economics." *Journal of Economic Perspectives* 20:1, 25–46.

Di Tella, Rafael, and Robert J. MacCulloch. 2008. "Gross National Happiness as an Answer to the Easterlin Paradox?" *Journal of Development Economics* 86:1, 22–42.

Di Tella, Rafael, and Robert J. MacCulloch. 2010. "Happiness Adaptation to Income beyond 'Basic Needs'." In Ed Diener, John F. Helliwell, and Daniel Kahneman, eds., *International Differences in Well-Being*, 139–165. Oxford: Oxford University Press.

Di Tella, Rafael, Robert J. MacCulloch, and Andrew J. Oswald. 2001. "Preferences over Inflation and Unemployment: Evidence from Surveys of Happiness." *American Economic Review* 91:1, 335–341.

Di Tella, Rafael, Robert J. MacCulloch, and Andrew J. Oswald. 2003. "The Macroeconomics of Happiness." *Review of Economics and Statistics* 85:4, 809–827.

Diener, Ed. 1984. "Subjective Well-Being." *Psychological Bulletin* 95:3, 542–575.

Diener, Ed, and Robert Biswas-Diener. 2002. "Will Money Increase Subjective Well-Being?" *Social Indicators Research* 57:2, 119–169.

Diener, Ed, and Robert Biswas-Diener. 2008. *Happiness: Unlocking the Mysteries of Psychological Wealth*. Malden, MA: Blackwell.

Diener, Ed., John F. Helliwell, and Daniel Kahneman. 2010. *International Differences in Well-Being*. Oxford: Oxford University Press.

Diener, Ed., Carol Nickerson, Richard E. Lucas, and Ed Sandvik. 2002. "Dispositional Affect and Job Outcomes." *Social Indicators Research* 59:3, 229–259.

Diener, Ed, Eunkook M. Suh, Richard E. Lucas, and Heidi L. Smith. 1999. "Subjective Well-Being: Three Decades of Progress." *Psychological Bulletin* 125:2, 276–302.

Dolan, Paul, Richard Layard, and Robert Metcalfe. 2011. "Measuring Subjective Well-Being for Public Policy." Available at http://eprints.lse.ac.uk/35420/1/measuring-subjective-wellbeing-for-public-policy.pdf.

Dunn, Elizabeth W., Lara B. Aknin, and Michael I. Norton. 2008. "Spending Money on Others Promotes Happiness." *Science* 319:5870, 1687–1688.

Easterlin, Richard A. 1974. "Does Economic Growth Improve the Human Lot?" In Paul A. David and Melvin W. Reder, eds., *Nations and Households in Economic Growth: Essays in Honor of Moses Abramovitz*, 89–125. New York: Academic Press.

Easterlin, Richard A. 2001. "Income and Happiness: Towards a Unified Theory." *Economic Journal* 111:473, 465–484.

Easterlin, Richard A., and Onnicha Sawangfa. 2010. "Happiness and Economic Growth: Does the Cross Section Predict Time Trends? Evidence from Developing Countries." In Ed Diener, John F. Helliwell, and Daniel Kahneman, eds., *International Differences in Well-Being*, 166–216. Oxford: Oxford University Press.

Fowler, James H., and Nicholas A. Christakis. 2009. "Dynamic Spread of Happiness in a Large Social Network: Longitudinal Analysis over 20 Years in the Framingham Heart Study." *British Medical Journal* 338:7685, 23–27.

Frey, Bruno S. 2011. "Happy People Live Longer." *Science* 331:6017, 542–543.

Graham, Carol. 2011. *The Pursuit of Happiness: An Economy of Well-Being*. Washington, DC: Brookings Institution Press.

Graham, Carol, Soumya Chattopadhyay, and Mario Picon. 2010. "The Easterlin and Other Paradoxes: Why Both Sides of the Debate May be Correct." In Ed Diener, John F. Helliwell, and Daniel Kahneman, eds., *International Differences in Well-Being*, 247–288. Oxford: Oxford University Press.

Graham, Carol, Andrew Eggers, and Sandip Sukhtankar. 2004. "Does Happiness Pay? An Exploration Based on Panel Data from Russia." *Journal of Economic Behavior & Organization* 55:3, 319–342.

Guillen-Royo, Monica. 2008. "Consumption and Subjective Well-being: Exploring Basic Needs, Social Comparison, Social Integration and Hedonism in Peru." *Social Indicators Research* 89:3, 535–555.

Guven, Cahit. 2009. "Reversing the Question: Does Happiness Affect Consumption and Savings Behavior?" German Socio-Economic Panel, Berlin, SOEP Papers on Multidisciplinary Panel Data Research No 219.

Harter, James K., and Raksha Arora. 2010. "The Impact of Time Spent Working and Job Fit on Well-Being around the World." In Ed Diener, John F. Helliwell, and Daniel Kahneman, eds., *International Differences in Well-Being*, 398–435. Oxford: Oxford University Press.

Headey, Bruce, Ruud Muffels, and Mark Wooden. 2008. "Money Does Not Buy Happiness: Or Does It? A Reassessment Based on the Combined Effects of Wealth, Income and Consumption." *Social Indicators Research* 87:1, 65–82.

Hill, Ronald Paul, Thomas Ainscough, Todd Shank, and Daryl Manullang. 2007. "Corporate Social Responsibility and Socially Responsible Investing: A Global Perspective." *Journal of Business Ethics* 70:2, 165–174.

Hudders, Liselot, and Mario Pandelaere. 2012. "The Silver Lining of Materialism: the Impact of Luxury Consumption on Subjective Well-Being." *Journal of Happiness Studies* 13:3, 1–27.

Jacob, Jeffery, Emily Jovic, and Merlin B. Brinkerhoff. 2009. "Personal and Planetary Well-Being: Mindfulness Meditation, Pro-environmental Behavior and Personal Quality of Life in a Survey from the Social Justice and Ecological Sustainability Movement." *Social Indicators Research* 93:2, 275–294.

Kahneman, Daniel, and Angus Deaton. 2010. "High Income Improves Evaluation of Life But Not Emotional Well-Being." *Proceedings of the National Academy of Sciences* 107:38, 16489–16493.

Kahneman, Daniel, and Alan B. Krueger. 2006. "Developments in the Measurement of Subjective Well-Being." *Journal of Economic Perspectives* 20:1, 3–24.

Karabati, Serdar, and Zeynep Cemalcilar. 2010. "Values, Materialism, and Well-Being: A Study with Turkish University Students." *Journal of Economic Psychology* 31:4, 624–633.

Kasser, Tim, and Richard M. Ryan. 1993. "A Dark Side of the American Dream: Correlates of Financial Success as a Central Life Aspiration." *Journal of Personality and Social Psychology* 65:2, 410–422.

Krueger, Alan B., ed. 2009. *Measuring the Subjective Well-Being of Nations: National Accounts of Time Use and Well-Being.* Chicago: University of Chicago Press.

Layard, Richard, Guy Mayraz, and Stephen Nickell. 2010. "Does Relative Income Matter? Are the Critics Right?" In Ed Diener, John F. Helliwell, and Daniel Kahneman, eds., *International Differences in Well-Being*, 139–165. Oxford: Oxford University Press.

Lucas, Richard E., Ed Diener, and Eunkook Suh. 1996. "Discriminant Validity of Well-Being Measures." *Journal of Personality and Social Psychology* 71: 3, 616–628.

Lyubomirsky, Sonja. 2008. *The How of Happiness: A Scientific Approach to Getting the Life You Want.* London: Penguin Books.

Lyubomirsky, Sonja, Laura L. King, and Ed Diener. 2005. "The Benefits of Frequent Positive Affect: Does Happiness Lead to Success?" *Psychological Bulletin* 131:6, 803–855.

Lyubomirsky, Sonja, Kennon M. Sheldon, and David Schkade. 2005. "Pursuing Happiness: The Architecture of Sustainable Change." *Review of General Psychology* 9:2, 111–131.

Lyubomirsky, Sonja, Chris Tkach, and M. Robin DiMatteo. 2006. "What Are the Differences between Happiness and Self-Esteem?" *Social Indicators Research* 78:3, 363–404.

Manolis, Chris, and James A. Roberts. 2012. "Subjective Well-Being among Adolescent Consumers: The Effects of Materialism, Compulsive Buying, and Time Affluence." *Applied Research in Quality of Life* 7:2, 117–135.

Oishi, Shigehiro. 2011. *The Psychological Wealth of Nations: Do Happy People Make a Happy Society.* West Sussex, UK: John Wiley & Sons.

Oishi, Shigehiro, Ed Diener, and R. Lucas. 2007. The Optimum Level of Well-Being: Can People Be Too Happy?" *Perspectives on Psychological Science* 2:4, 346–360.

Oishi, Shigehiro, Selin Kesebir, and Ed Diener. 2012. "Income Inequality and Happiness." *Psychological Science* 22:9, 1095–1100.

Oswald, Andrew J., Eugenio Proto, and Daniel Sgroi. 2009. "Happiness and Productivity." *IZA Discussion* Paper No 4645, Institute for the Study of Labor, Bonn.

Pavot, William, and Ed Diener. 1993. "Review of the Satisfaction with Life Scale." *Psychological Assessment* 5:2, 164–172.

Richins, Marsha L., and Scoot Dawson. 1992. "A Consumer Values Orientation for Materialism and Its Measurement: Scale Development and Validation." *Journal of Consumer Research* 19:3, 303–316.

Ryan, Richard M., and Edward L. Deci. 2001. "On Happiness and Human Potentials: A Review of Research on Hedonic and Eudaimonic Well-Being." *Annual Review of Psychology* 52:1, 141–166.

Seligman, Martin. 2002. *Authentic Happiness: Using the New Positive Psychology to Realize Your Potential for Lasting Fulfillment.* New York: Free Press.

Sirgy, M. Joseph. 1998. "Materialism and Quality of Life." *Social Indicators Research* 43:3, 227–260.

Sirgy, M. Joseph, Alex C. Michalos, Abbott L. Ferriss, Richard A. Easterlin, Donald Patrick, and William Pavot. 2006. "The Quality-of-Life (QOL) Research Movement: Past, Present, and Future." *Social Indicators Research* 76:3, 343–466.

Soppe, Aloy. 2009. "Sustainable Finance as a Connection between Corporate Social Responsibility and Social Responsible Investing." *Indian School of Business WP Indian Management Research Journal* 1:3, 13–23.

Spurk, Daniel, Andrea E. Abele, and Judith Volmer. 2011. "The Career Satisfaction Scale: Longitudinal Measurement Invariance and Latent Growth Analysis." *Journal of Occupational and Organizational Psychology* 84:2, 315–326.

Srivastava, Abhishek, Edwin A. Locke, and Kathryn M. Bartol. 2001. "Money and Subjective WellBeing: It's Not the Money, It's the Motives." *Journal of Personality and Social Psychology* 80:6, 959–971.

Stevenson, Betsey, and Justin Wolfers. 2008. "Economic Growth and Subjective Well-Being: Reassessing the Easterlin Paradox." *Brookings Papers on Economic Activity* 2008:1, 1–87.

Sun, Feng, and Jing Jian Xiao. 2012. "Perceived Social Policy Fairness and Subjective Wellbeing: Evidence from China." *Social Indicators Research* 107:1, 171–186.

Tadic, Maja, Wido G. M. Oerlemans, Arnold B. Bakker, and Ruut Veenhoven. 2012. "Daily Activities and Happiness in Later Life: The Role of Work Status." *Journal of Happiness Studies*. Available at www.beanmanaged.com/doc/pdf/arnoldbakker/articles/in_press_arnold_bakker_310.pdf.

Veenhoven, Ruut. 2002. "Why Social Policy Needs Subjective Indicators." *Assessing Quality of Life and Living Conditions to Guide National Policy* 58:1–3, 33–45.

Warr, Peter. 2011. "Jobs and Job-Holders: Two Sources of Happiness and Unhappiness." In Susan David, Ilona Boniwell, and Amanda Conley Ayers, eds., *Oxford Handbook of Happiness*, 733–750. Oxford: Oxford University Press.

Wong, Chack Kie, Ka Ying Wong, and Bong Ho Mok. 2006. "Subjective Well-Being, Societal Condition and Social Policy—The Case Study of a Rich Chinese Society." *Social Indicators Research* 78:3, 405–428.

Xiao, Jing Jian, and Haifeng Li. 2011. "Sustainable Consumption and Life Satisfaction." *Social Indicators Research* 104:2, 323–329.

Xiao, Jing Jian, Chuanyi Tang, and Soyeon Shim. 2009. "Acting for Happiness: Financial Behavior and Life Satisfaction of College Students." *Social Indicators Research* 92:1, 53–68.

ABOUT THE AUTHOR

Jing Jian Xiao is Professor in the Department of Human Development and Family Studies at the University of Rhode Island who teaches courses and conducts research in consumer economics and personal finance. He edited and contributed to several books including the *Handbook of Consumer Finance Research* and *Mathematics of Personal Finance*. He has been the editor-in-chief of the *International Series on Consumer Science* since 2008 and was the editor-in-chief of *Journal of Family and Economic Issues* from 2001 to 2011. He serves on editorial boards of the *International Journal of Bank Marketing, Journal of Consumer Affairs, Journal of Consumer Education, Journal of Family and Economic Issues, Journal of Financial Counseling and Planning*, and *Journal of Personal Finance*. He became the editor-in-chief of *Journal of Financial Counseling and Planning* in 2014. Professor Xiao received a BS and MS in economics from Zhongnan University of Economics and Law and a PhD in consumer economics from Oregon State University.

CHAPTER 10

Motivation and Satisfaction

Lewis J. Altfest
Associate Professor of Finance, Pace University

INTRODUCTION

This chapter focuses on the linkages among motivation, satisfaction, and personal finance. Motivation provides the incentive to take certain actions. For many, the actions often coalesce around establishing certain goals. Satisfaction can be viewed as the feelings of pleasure surrounding the movement toward and the achievement of those objectives. Personal finance has traditionally made those goals tangible by attempting to measure them using objective values such as money. Financial planning is fundamentally concerned with the process that directs people to efficient progress toward reaching their goals or objectives.

Financial planning in practice includes the realm of behavioral economics and behavioral finance. It deals with how people really think and act as opposed to the classical economics rational man theory that indicates how they should act. The behavioral approach takes its cues from psychology as well as economics and finance.

The chapter has the following organization. It begins by examining the roots of economic theory, particularly Modigliani's Life Cycle Theory, which serves as a basis for personal financial planning. This chapter then covers behavioral finance. This is followed by a detailed discussion of what motivates people beyond money. This part of the chapter is an empirical analysis based on the seminal work by the psychologist Abraham Maslow and his hierarchy of needs theory of motivation. Next, the chapter brings this psychological theory into the financial realm. The chapter ends with a summary and conclusions.

CLASSICAL ECONOMIC MOTIVATION

Classical economic theory (i.e., the foundation of standard or traditional finance) provides a broad beginning framework for understanding what motivates people. Its most basic form is the economic theory of consumer choice. The theory of consumer choice indicates that people are motivated by the goal of achieving the highest level of satisfaction they can. They do so by purchasing the greatest amount of goods and services they can afford.

In a one-period model in which the consumer spends all money available in the current year, the consumer selects only the most satisfying bundle of goods. The particular bundle of goods selected depends on the preferences of the individual. For example, one person may spend more on clothing and an expensive car while another may enjoy eating out often and buying costly electronic leisure equipment. Each, of course, is limited by the money he or she earns, which is called the *budget constraint*. The amount of satisfaction received cannot be measured exactly but preferences are obtained by rank ordering each alternative bundle.

People may not spend all their money in the period they receive it. They have the option of consuming it over a longer period of time, which is called *intertemporal choice*. In other words, they can save and invest part of their income for use later. Investing money not only postpones the consumption outlay but also increases the amount available as given by the return on the amount invested. Others may borrow money temporarily to spend more than their current income.

Some assumptions in the model are that consumers get additional satisfaction from buying more goods and that they act rationally. Rationality can mean they perform logically in value-oriented quantitative terms. As discussed later, people do not always act in a logical way that is fully consistent with achieving their goals. They also may need help in becoming more efficient consumers. Another problem can be the treatment of families. While individuals may have their own preferences, they are often assumed to act as if they have the same preferences as those for the household taken as a whole.

Modigliani (1980) made famous an applied version of the multiperiod model called the Life Cycle Theory. Before his works, economics placed more stress on single-period income received and spent. According to Modigliani, human beings are motivated to become planners. That is, they project their cash inflows from salaries, investment income, and other sources and determine the amount of expenditures they can afford. Underlying the theory is the goal of maximization of resources during one's life cycle. This implies dying with no savings. Modigliani assumes that people attempt to equalize their expenditures each year over their life cycle. To support these expenditures in retirement when no income is earned, individuals have to save money earlier.

Modigliani's model has weaknesses. For example, the model does not include risk: No one can predict with certainty such things as their job-related or investment income, costs, or longevity. Instead, they must use estimates. Additionally, financing a level standard of living over time is difficult if not impossible because banks will not lend to fund lifestyles early in careers when income is low. As part of their estate planning, some people want to leave money to their children or others instead of dying broke. Not all people save money but use government support, such as Social Security, to fund retirement living closer to the one-period model.

Nonetheless, when taken as a whole, Modigliani's approach has become the most popular economic model of rational human household behavior. Financial planners and others still find value in this approach even with many of the model's weaknesses. From a personal finance standpoint, his model with its emphasis on forward thinking can be viewed as the forerunner of the field of personal financial planning.

BEHAVIORAL ECONOMIC MOTIVATION

A strictly orthodox rational approach to planning and investing has limitations. Compared to man as machine behavior, which is often called "economic man" or "homo economicus," people make mistakes in such areas as having correct recall of previous occurrences or reacting emotionally when it is not in their long-term interests to do so. Instead of maximizing as called for in economic theory, they may come up short, preferring a less rigorous satisficing approach based on bounded rationality (Simon 1955). That is, an individual may receive more satisfaction from a less intensive, less than optimal decision process, in which that person acts as a "human being" and selects the satisfactory option. Tversky and Kahneman (1981), who are noted behavioral psychologists, popularized human inconsistencies through their heuristics (i.e., mental shortcuts or mistakes) and biases. The differences between economic man as he should be according to standard finance theory and the way people actually act led to behavioral economics and finance.

Behavioral economics has given rise to a modification of Modigliani's Life Cycle Theory, which can be called the behavioral life cycle hypothesis. Instead of one choice as in classical theory, some researchers view the individual as having many selves. Multiple selves, in essence inner voices exposing conflict in selection, create a less concrete form of motivation. On the other hand, multiple selves allow insight into *self-control bias*, which is decision-making involving restraint or judgment that is distorted or inconsistently applied according to classical economic thought. *Bias* is an inclination of temperament outlook to present or hold a partial perspective at the expense of (possibly equally valid) alternatives in reference to objects, people, or groups. For example, if classical economics theory is right about individuals having one fixed preference, why does the need exist for exercising control, which implies inner conflict? Also, people make different choices at different times. Overweight people sometimes avoid high caloric deserts and at other times they indulge. Which self wins may come about through cyclical changes in willpower at different times, a change in circumstances, or both.

An application of motivation and self-control about which people are concerned is in the realm of personal financial planning. Thaler and Shefrin (1981) make a prominent adjustment to established economic theory by assuming that people have two preference systems that are independent and can conflict at a point in time. They call this a two self economic man. According to Thaler and Shefrin, people have conflicts between short- and long-run motivations. The authors hypothesize that individuals have planner and doer sides. The planner is farsighted and motivated by lifetime satisfaction. The doer is concerned about current satisfaction and is completely selfish and myopic.

The approaches taken to control the doer's lure can be: (1) to save the amount needed automatically, which can overcome the superior short-term pleasure that certain people get from spending today; (2) to monitor savings periodically using budgets; (3) to reduce the amount of pleasure for outlays by establishing other restrictions; or (4) to increase rewards for good behavior. At an extreme, an entire set of doer actions can be eliminated through, for instance, keeping credit cards and large sums of cash at home.

Thaler and Shefrin's (1981) approach modifies the standard rational model. Classical theory might say intention and knowledge of what is needed and outcome are the same, while individuals know the temptation to have pleasure today can affect lifetime goals. Thaler and Shefrin (p. 32) say that in their modification "people will rationally choose to impose constraints."

Thaler and Shefrin's (1981) model deviates markedly from Modigliani's (1980) model. It more closely highlights those characteristics of individuals that can weaken the singular goal and undercut the money wealth maximization hypothesis of neoclassical theory. It indicates that people respond favorably to help control their short-term temptations. Using behavioral techniques including financial advisors can help Modigliani's life cycle hypothesis come to fruition.

Later, Shefrin and Thaler (1988) specifically analyze Modigliani's life cycle theory and modify it for what they view as realistic human conditions. Their tests of the hypothesis show mixed results. For example, some tests do not support the notion that people plan in the life cycle manner. Improved outcomes could occur by incorporating behavioral characteristics, specifically self-control, mental accounting and framing, which are typically left out when using a classical economic approach. These modifications are similar to those of Fisher (1930), who had five variables entering into personal savings decisions: self-control, foresight, habits, expectations of mortality, and love for posterity.

Shefrin and Thaler (1988) elaborate on self-control and distinguish between self-control and ordinary choice. Self-control requires a "feeling of effort," which refers to mental rather than physical effort. Self-control involves three elements: internal conflict, temptation, and willpower. In effect, self-control involves a choice between pleasure today and higher benefits in the future. The conflict is one of an emotional choice for gratification now (called the *short-run doer*) versus (economically) rational choice for the individual's future (called the *long-range planner*). People need to exert willpower to resist temptation.

Mental accounting can be viewed as compartmentalizing inputs mentally that an economically rational person would view as equivalent to one another but in practice individuals treat as deserving of differing actions. People attempt to develop limitations on their actions (impulses) in the most painless way possible. They try to find rules that can evolve into habits, specifically habits that require minimum conscious thinking in an area in which thinking about that subject is typically painful.

Shefrin and Thaler (1988) separate individual wealth into mental accounts of current spendable income, current assets, and future income. Placing money in different accounts results in different outcomes. For example, given a desire to spend a withdrawal from an available current income account today will result in different spending or saving decisions compared with placing the cash in a pension account. That is true even if no tax penalty exists on a pension withdrawal. Because withdrawal from a pension may represent a more serious incursion, the pension serves as an impulse control device.

Mental accounting is a subset of Tversky and Kahneman's (1981) *framing*. This final characteristic indicates how an individual communicates something that can affect the subsequent decision made. For example, if a financial planner tells a client that he made an ill-advised financial decision, the planner is less likely to get the client to make the correct decision in the future. The authors conclude that people do not act with machinelike logic but employ imperfect rules of thumb. Following heuristics or rules of thumb results in actual behavior that is not economically rational behavior as to how people should act.

Shefrin and Thaler (1988) suggest that analysis and testing should go forward using actual, not assumed, behavior. The broader understanding of human behavior, which would be applied to behavioral economics, could help people operate more efficiently according to their goals. For instance, financial professionals could expand their use of mental accounting techniques to help people save more money, which is often in their best interest to do.

MASLOW'S HIERARCHY OF NEEDS

Behavioral economics questions the assumption of a fully rational, emotionless, profit-maximizing individual. It often leaves in place the particular individual's desire to maximize satisfaction with materialism as a key part. Humanists extend the scope to emphasize higher forms of satisfaction that have little or even no concentration on materialism. One of the most creative humanists is Abraham Maslow. Maslow is best known for his hierarchy of needs theory of human motivation (Maslow 1943; Maslow and Frager 1987). In developing this theory, Maslow interviewed others and incorporated believed characteristics of leaders in society from their biographies and generalized from the data received.

Maslow thought of individual makeup in a holistic fashion, something that is practiced in personal financial planning today. In other words, he regarded the individual as fully integrated because the whole individual is motivated, not one part at a time. For example, if people have insufficient social interaction, it affects many or all of their functions, not just their need for human discourse.

According to Maslow, many motivations that people have are not so important in themselves but serve as paths to ultimate goals, desires, or needs. Individuals are unaware of all of their motivations because some are unconscious. Yet, they universally share the same ultimate goals or objectives despite having differing short-term wishes. Maslow differs from many psychologists who focus on the factors that make individuals unique and enable them to satisfy their goals. At the same time, motivations for striving to attain a goal may have various underlying reasons. For example, someone may want to get an advanced degree in business to impress, to be intellectually more sophisticated, to advance in business, or to earn more money.

Motivation, according to Maslow, is an underlying force that is always present, with many dimensions. After satisfying one goal, the individual moves on to another. Isolating drivers is difficult because they are multifaceted in their impact and overlap with other drivers.

In contrast to isolating drivers, Maslow indicates that people should generalize about fundamental goals and needs. He believes that environment influences their behavior but does not displace their own underlying motivations. While people can usually be thought of as an integrated whole, they do not always act that way. Not all the things that people do are motivated by their needs.

Maslow's hierarchy of needs is a compendium of needs starting from the most fundamental and moving up to higher needs once each is satisfied. That is, higher needs emerge after achieving more basic goals. If individuals have not satisfied higher needs, they focus their attention on doing so. Maslow begins with the basic needs hierarchy. The preconditions for the basic needs include the freedom to speak, defend, express, and seek information. Exhibit 10.1 provides a diagram of the entire process. A brief description of each need follows.

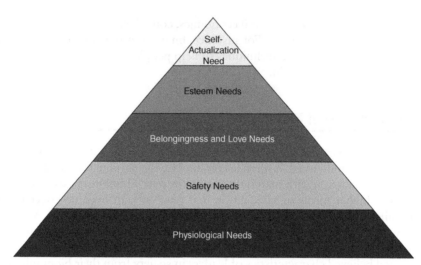

EXHIBIT 10.1   Maslow's Hierarchy of Needs

Note: This exhibit illustrates Maslow's hierarchy of needs, which begins with satisfying psychological needs and progress to fulfilling the need of self-actualization.

Physiological Needs

Individuals must satisfy the underlying paramount need for food. They also must be able to drink water, sleep, feel safe, and perform bodily functions. If physiological needs are unsatisfied, they become dominant and the other needs are dormant. If one is hungry, nirvana can be a full stomach.

Safety Needs

The next higher step after meeting physiological needs is safety. Safety encompasses many different items including protection from bodily harm, security, stability, lack of fear and anxiety about such items as health, and the ability to finance the most basic economic needs. More broadly, safety needs include possessing a secure job, having insurance against potential losses, and an emergency fund. Maslow views religion as partly a safety need that helps people integrate the world around them.

Belongingness and Love Needs

Maslow presents belongingness and love immediately above safety needs. Here, people place their needs for love, affection, and sense of closeness with others. Thus, they may include friends, mates, children, and more broadly belonging to groups as well as giving and getting affection.

Esteem Needs

Esteem needs refer to having a good opinion of oneself and being viewed favorably by others. Such factors include achievement, competency, strength, confidence, and independence in formulating one's opinion. Other esteem needs include reputation, status, and appreciation. When a person is satisfied with his self-esteem, he feels confident, strong, and capable. These factors can be hard to achieve and therefore some people can feel weak, insecure, and neurotic. Maslow pays respect to other thinkers, warning of dependency on the views of others, and emphasizes earning respect from others instead of gaining fame and celebrity for little justification. In a survey of psychology in relation to economics, Earl (1990) indicates that conspicuous consumption in relation to Maslow's esteem needs varies by individual. Those who are insecure may lean on conspicuous consumption, as is stereotypically assumed for the nouveau riche.

Self-Actualization

Self-actualization is the highest level need. At this point a person has satisfied all the other needs including having achieved self-respect and recognition. However, people desire more—a cause to which they can dedicate themselves or something that helps them realize their potential. The items that people focus on to achieve this varies considerably and examples include athleticism, artistic ability, raising a family, and religious devotion. Progressing through these states generally requires independent thinking and is challenging.

Maslow discusses two other needs. One is a cognitive need to know, understand, and be curious. People also have an aesthetic need to seek out beauty. Some of Maslow's followers add these as separate needs that may be conscious or unconscious. Across cultures, basic needs are more common than higher level ones. This is understandable because people in less developed countries do not progress far up enough in the hierarchy to reach higher level needs.

CRITICISM OF MASLOW'S HIERARCHY OF NEEDS

Critics of Maslow's hierarchy of needs theory voice many objections including the following.

Hierarchical Values Vary by Country Maslow's hierarchy is expressed using U.S. values. In the United States, people place great emphasis on the individual, material success, individual expression, and reaching for personal goals. In Japan, however, a greater emphasis focuses on group goals and risk aversion, while deemphasizing individual opinions and creative lifestyles. Other countries may have a more doctrinaire religious approach or view work as a necessary evil compared to the United States, where people seek partial fulfillment through work.

Hierarchical Values Vary by Interest Beliefs in rigid hierarchies of uniform values within the United States are invalid. Instead, values within our country can vary considerably. Materialistic preferences can range from working almost all the time and being able to afford material possessions and expensive vacations to selecting the minimum salary needed to allow for funding life's pleasures. For example, an artist may have a very low standard of living to allow for creative expression. People may engage in altruistic acts, a higher level need, even though they have not satisfied their love needs.

Hierarchical Values Vary by Income Strata Drive, intelligence, values, luck, and background are all among the factors that enter into the positioning of people within social classes. A survey of values by Gratton (1980) by class strata shows the following needs/priorities:

Class	Needs
Middle class	Esteem and self-actualization
Working class	Esteem and belonging
Lower class	Physiological and belonging

Needs Are Not Fully Satisfied Separately With the exception of physiology, needs are not like glasses of water that get filled up, with individuals then moving on to the next need. Even if they were, events can intervene such as sickness and divorce that bring people back to previously satisfied factors. Instead, needs should be grouped together in seeking satisfaction.

Testing Standards Are Not Strong Much scientific testing occurs under tight methodological standards. Maslow presents an all-encompassing theory with a relatively weak methodology. Generally, he uses his own observations and beliefs to personally interview or study the biographies of leading past and then-resent dignitaries. Maslow's own perceptions may have tainted the conclusions.

Criticism of Self-Actualization

Self-actualization, which involves making ongoing moves toward or reaching an individual's potential, has its own list of criticisms.

Testability Self-actualization exists principally in the minds of those engaged in that activity. Unlike other hierarchical levels, it does not have clearly definable characteristics. Outcomes do not necessarily lead to an ultimate end, just more searching and satisfaction in performing the search. Further, no criteria are available for distinguishing between satisfaction and frustration. Consequently, testability may be difficult or impossible.

Too Stringent The theory suggests that people who do not self-actualize are not truly satisfied. Yet, the vast majority of people may not have self-actualization as a priority or even engage in this step. These people upon retirement participate in discretionary activities they find fruitful and describe themselves as happy. Furthermore, the theory is based on an analysis of especially gifted people who exhibit great achievement and psychological health. This may not reflect a standard that most individuals can achieve in the real world.

Overall Summary and Appraisal

Maslow applies a step-by-step approach to progress toward fulfillment of personal goals. He describes how individuals satisfy their needs in motivational terms.

The process begins with physiological needs that people require to keep alive. The next step involves safety goals in which people try to achieve freedom from harm and feelings of insecurity. They then seek belongingness and love based on social needs. The penultimate step involves achieving self-esteem and the esteem of others.

All steps are expressed as deficiency needs and each must be fully satisfied to be able to move to the next step upward. The final need, self-actualization, is the one that is not a deficiency but a goal to develop the capacity to maximize and achieve potential.

On balance, Maslow has created a highly powerful theory. The fact that it may have limitations in regard to its hierarchical nature or its perceived uniformity of values throughout the world may not be that important. Evidence exists that Maslow himself knew of these weaknesses, for example in selection of subjects (Maslow 1968). Theories seldom fully comply with reality.

Maslow provides a simple structure that resonates with many people. Individuals move up in interests and goals once they satisfy more basic needs. People can aspire to higher level self-actualization goals once they meet their basic needs. The fact that the general public and many professionals in psychology, management, economics, and finance support this theory attests to its popularity.

HIGHER LEVEL MOTIVATION

Maslow's hierarchy of needs is appealing to many people, especially in the United States, because it is consistent with the goal of climbing the ladder of success. The highest part of its hierarchy, self actualization, may be attractive but may be less clearly defined as to what it comprises and whether most people require it for long-term satisfaction. The following discussion begins with life satisfaction and proceeds to further analyze Maslow's higher level needs and his belief in dual selves with its relationship to higher level needs. This section sets the stage for a discussion on humanism.

Satisfaction

Satisfaction is closely attached to motivation. It emerges when something that people want to have happen does so. Satisfaction is the utility part of all motivational approaches already discussed. It can be used, for example, to express pleasure at eating a good meal when someone is very hungry. In that application, satisfaction applies to a basic need in Maslow's hierarchy. After exploring the term satisfaction, its meaning, and how to distinguish it from other related terms, the discussion then turns to identifying the items that bring about life satisfaction.

Satisfaction refers to the fulfillment of one's wishes, expectations, or needs or the pleasure derived from this. In an economic sense, satisfaction represents the pleasure arising from achieving part or all of a goal. Further discussion focuses on broader goals that result in the term "life satisfaction." *Life satisfaction* is an integration of the positive and negative occurrences leading to an overall personal assessment of life's experiences resulting in relative degrees of fulfillment.

Life satisfaction differs from well-being, which includes both cognitive (mental) and emotional terms (Lucas, Diener, and Shu 1996). Some areas overlap in that mental processes can influence emotional ones and vice versa. However, life satisfaction tends to be principally a mental process. This suggests that the term fits an economic and finance orientation more closely and is less influenced by people's momentary moods. Life satisfaction can provide both a more consistent and objective opinion of people's perception of their long-term status.

Self-esteem is highly correlated with life satisfaction while happiness and mood as more emotional transitory terms are less so. For example, a person can be happy at a moment in time but be far away from achieving life satisfaction. On balance, life satisfaction best fits the terms of this chapter overall and Maslow's higher level needs in particular.

Self-Actualization

Self-actualization is the ultimate step in Maslow's hierarchy of needs. At this level people are seeking personal growth and fulfillment. *Personal growth* is striving to become a better person. *Fulfillment* is an inner satisfaction not intended principally for external recognition. Maslow (1968) received his insights by viewing exceptional people and many others do not rise to this level. However, if fulfillment comes from some basic desires such as charitable pursuits or helping to raise well-adjusted children, this level may include more people. Depending on the goals, the areas may require further material discretionary expenditures, not just time and effort, which in strict financial terms are not costly.

Maslow and the Dual Self

After the hierarchy of needs became popular, Maslow wrote about multiple selves and indicated that individuals have higher and lower inclinations. He differentiated between their potential (i.e., what they strove for) and what they were presently (i.e., their current reality). He said people have deficiency motives and personal growth motives. Their higher self consists of pure principals such as integrity, truth, and love. The lower self, which is more consistent with the standard finance approach, is attracted to pleasure and self-interest. Maslow, by appealing to higher needs, promoting fairness, and engaging in satisfying work, was challenging traditional economic thought of selfish pleasures and emphasizing altruistic behavior.

Characteristics of the Self-Actualized

According to Boeree (1998) and Mcleod (2007), Maslow established certain characteristics of people who are candidates for self-actualization. Some of these characteristics include:

- Seeing things as they are, including uncertainties
- Accepting one's own and other peoples' personalities
- Being spontaneous
- Not focusing on oneself but dealing with real issues
- Being comfortable alone
- Having deep personal relationships
- Thinking independently and having independence from social pressures

- Being humorous, not hostile
- Having humility and respect for others
- Incorporating strong ethics and morals
- Being creative
- Engaging in many peak experiences
- Focusing on concern for others
- Enjoying life experiences
- Having democratic attitudes

HUMANISM

The humanists provide an even broader perspective than the behaviorists. As least in part, behavioral economists retain the economic discipline's emphasis on material values. Humanistic economics in contrast employs behavioral characteristics but generally moves beyond largely materialistic goals. Humanists indicate that some objective values such as morality, human rights, and concern for others focus on individual potential. For these believers, life satisfaction comes from achieving purer goals.

As one of the most famous humanists, Maslow's research influenced many people. His work consists of two major parts: (1) deficiency goals, which are set up through hierarchical levels, and (2) higher level, more humanistic goals on which people concentrate after achieving the deficiency goals. For the most part, these have been discussed already.

Lutz (1999), another prominent humanist, provides a perspective based on Maslow. He indicates that humans have conflicting desires: Some are more basic (deficiency motivation) and others involve personal growth including love, truth, and integrity. Lutz, who emphasizes altruistic behavior, indicates that pleasure maximization and selfish behavior can inhibit growth of personality. Lutz (p. 318) states, "Psychologically a preoccupation with materialism can be explained in Maslowian terms as the result of stunted growth brought about by a blocked security need."

Lutz (1999, p. 318) indicates that for people it "is not so much the optimal satisfaction of our desires to consume but the development of a meaningful life embedded in human community and the natural environment." Maslow stresses that the higher human needs of social esteem and self-respect cannot be satisfied through purchases. Lutz's point of view as a humanist is that too much focus on consumption could restrict the climb for self-esteem. Consumerism retards the progress of humanity. Lutz believes that passing Maslow's security need stage in particular would allow concentrating on higher social and moral needs.

Heylighen (1992) indicates that the person who is a self-actualizer needs to be receptive to new ideas, have a realistic perception of reality, be enthusiastic, and want to learn more about unknowable items. Self-actualizing represents a particular type of maximally healthy personality. This suggests that many or most people will not achieve this state. Each individual has much hidden potential. If they have not met the highest needs, people will not really be happy. This negative occurrence takes place even if they receive respect from peers, enjoy an inner sense of personal achievement, and have a loving family. Such individuals will still experience a feeling of boredom and meaninglessness because they have not achieved all their desires. Heylighen maintains that people must be made aware of their need for self-actualization.

According to Heylighen (1992), self-actualizers are not afraid of being wrong when presented with problems. Many may be unconventional in their thinking or creativity. They accept others, have a sense of morality, are patient, and can focus on a problem. Self-actualizers can make decisions themselves, engage in value detachment, feel for others, be sincere, and relate only to a selected group of people. Heylighen views Maslow's theory as not well structuredand maintains that theory and observations are not always the same. Self-actualization could come from solving a frustration as well as seeking future gratification. Humanists moved even farther away from orthodox economics in their promotion of unselfish behavior, such as concern for others and doing what is ethically correct.

MASLOW AND INVESTMENT MANAGEMENT

Before moving on to integration of motivation, humanism, and personal finance, discussing Maslow's hierarchy of needs and its relationship to investment management could be useful. Shefrin and Statman (1994) already had presented behavioral portfolio theory that extended finance theory and investor motivation beyond the established risk-return model. De Brouwer (2010, 2012) drew parallels between each of Maslow's levels of human needs and appropriate investments for that level. For the most basic physiological needs given the high cost of falling short, Maslow indicates that people should probably hold money in cash or a money market account. For safety needs, they should place at least a portion in low risk investments. For social needs, at least for close personal relationships, individuals may move beyond self-interest to those of the family. They should be separated and base their investments on each specific family goal including such factors as time horizon and relative importance. More risk is called for than in previous levels.

For esteem needs the investor's risk tolerance is considered as in traditional theory. Where esteem incorporates separate goals each may have a different investment vehicle, with mutual funds perhaps having a role. Humanistic influenced self actualization may take the approach of forming a tailored portfolio, thereby adding an element of self exploration and development of a successful portfolio. Increased levels of risk are considered as one moves to higher risk.

De Brouwer (2010) calls the result Maslowian portfolio theory. His purpose is to show that another dimension exists beyond risk and return and that psychology and behavioral finance help satisfy individual needs as manifested by Maslow's hierarchy. Hoffman (2007) supports this approach by stating that people have many alternative reasons for selecting stocks to meet their needs with substantial differences by sex, age, knowledge, and experience. Aspara and Tikkanen (2012) add a specific behavioral component to expected risk and return indicating that people have further motivation to invest in a specific company based on their affinity for that company.

One segment of personal finance is investments. De Brouwer's emphasis on providing advice indicating how to construct individualized behavioral influenced investment portfolios is a basic precursor to a more broad-based discussion of personal finance and motivation.

PERSONAL FINANCE INTEGRATION

The discussion on investment management from a Maslowian behavioral standpoint makes this chapter's thought process more practical. It can be differentiated from the previous humanistic section, which is more idealistic. The idealistic humanist appraisal has a problem. It not only expands the framework for motivation and satisfaction from the pure economic approach but also may conflict with it. People may have higher needs than money, such as self respect, truth, justice, self-actualization, and self-transcendence. On the other hand, Belk (1999) notes that money has material impact and influence on how individuals view themselves, including feelings of self-esteem, control, security, and indebtedness. Howell, Kurai, and Tam (2012) indicate that money purchases financial security and satisfaction of financial needs.

Some formal integration of the two approaches is needed. Maslow, perhaps inadvertently, provides a framework for doing so. The deficiency motives in his hierarchy have as a key factor the need for material financial income to rise to be able to move beyond these motives. However, if one is in the self-actualization stage, money is much less of a factor. Still, money through continuing income and/or achieved wealth can support higher level personal growth.

Even in people who Maslow admired such as higher level public citizens, both forms of motivation—"selfish" material and higher level characteristics—would appear to coexist. For example, presidents of the country may enjoy the pomp, travel, gifts, and respect generated by the position in addition to the altruistic potential to help raise citizens' standard of living.

Finance requires that an important component of any analysis be material satisfaction. Under business systems such as in the United States, people highly value making economic progress. Unlike certain other countries, such as France, where work and leisure may be strictly divided, in the United States fundamental goals can bring self-expression, which is a pleasurable goal, into the workplace environment. Many view the United States as having more materialistic goals than other developed societies. The stress on materialism and workplace achievement can easily be reflected in the average number of hours devoted to work in the United States, which exceeds most of economically advanced European countries.

Life Planning and Satisfaction

Until this point, the chapter has avoided discussing the role of personal finance in higher level goals. Now, the chapter introduces *life planning*, which is a system that combines the traditional financial planner's role of providing financial insight to clients with their desire to receive help to move beyond materialism.

Life planning by financial advisors is somewhat controversial. Many planners believe that their advice to clients should be limited to financial aspects of their well-being because they are unqualified to extend their role to areas established by psychologists, coaches, career counselors, and others. Furthermore, some financial planners may not have the patience or interest in listening to the nuances of a discussion that will include the specialized motivations of each individual.

Advocates of life planning note that while they do not rule out training in this area, what is needed is common sense. Many do not provide tangible recommendations, but merely a platform for individuals to uncover their own preferences. Financial advisors may be qualified because they are among their clients' closest advisors and many life decisions involve financial considerations. Clients may bring up the subject and planners offer assistance despite not viewing themselves as life planners.

According to Anthes and Lee (2001), life planning is the practical embodiment of uncovering what motivates people and how they can derive satisfaction from their efforts. By combining both financial and nonfinancial factors, life planning places human behavior alongside strict money factors in financial planning. Financial planners in this context extend beyond growing assets to helping people live happier, more productive lives.

Financial planning incorporates financial objectives such as the amount of money needed to meet a family's cost of living. Unlike the hierarchy of needs that focuses on the individual, financial planning emphasizes costs and focuses on the needs of the individual's family. The cost figures should be adjusted for risk so that a probabilistic framework can be created to conduct "what if" scenarios. For example, projected cost figures for the family could be set out for three inflationary scenarios: the current modest 2 percent framework, a rise to the 3 percent level, and one at 5 percent. The financial planner could give a probability to each scenario such as 40 percent, 40 percent, and 20 percent, respectively.

According to Anthes and Lee (2001), the prerequisite for decision-making and changeover to life planning should be:

- Motivation—an intense desire for the change
- All the required information necessary for the decision
- The ability to focus on the changes necessary (today)
- Preparations for problems and upside that can come
- An ability to make changes as circumstances change
- A keen understanding of your own policy
- Preparation of some people for unselfish behavior

Life planning can be broader in scope than self-actualization. Some people do not have the intensity of feeling and desire to do things that are both noble and altruistic. For them satisfaction comes from a simple and enjoyable retirement. Instead of realizing one's destiny, they talk in terms of a busy leisure time. Consequently, basic leisure time activities will be explored in more detail.

According to Moore (1998), two standards are needed to experience leisure: freedom to choose the activity and intrinsic motivation. *Intrinsic motivation* means interest that comes from within and not from how others view a person. Caring about how others see someone can make a person more materialistic and status-oriented. From this perspective, people who continue to work because they like what they do and not because they need to do it can be viewed as partaking in a leisure time pursuit.

Csikszentmihalyi's (1999) flow approach indicates that an individual's strongly positive leisure time involves active total absorption and intense concentration. Thus, an individual can lose perspective of time and the notion of being in control of his or her time. In contrast, passive activities, such as watching television, are like leisure's empty calories. Such activities provide relaxation but not great enjoyment because they involve no goals, challenges, and skills. Hence, the more someone watches television at one time, the worse his mood becomes. Planners can encourage their clients to develop interests in more hands-on leisure pursuits.

The other extreme could be what some would consider a more intricate, idealistic life-planning framework. Financial advisors could use such a framework to help their clients reach their full potential. The advisor's goal could be to help reveal or highlight those items that their clients are not aware of. One approach would be for life planners to teach people to:

- Be genuine—understand yourself
- Reach beyond your own culture
- Discover your calling in life
- Recognize that life is precious
- Accept people as they are
- Make sure basic needs have been reached
- Appreciate beauty
- Be in control as much as possible
- Focus on really important problems in life
- Select good choices among those presented

In sum, life planning helps people find what genuinely motivates them and helps them identify their goals and the necessary steps to reach them. The life planner may help guide that process by providing a structure and ongoing review. Finance is at the core of the planner's activity because clients may be unable to reach their goals without sufficient resources. However, the exact proportion of money and nonfinancial objectives is dependent on the wants and needs of clients.

SUMMARY

This chapter has examined motivation and satisfaction. It started by discussing classical economic theory with its emphasis on preferences revealed through purchases in the marketplace. In this context, consumer satisfaction comes through fulfilled spending decisions. The classical lifecycle theory of consumption and saving indicates that people are motivated to save for such reasons as accumulating financial resources for retirement. This lifecycle approach is one of the key components of personal financial planning in its quest for lifetime satisfaction.

In recognizing that consumers are motivated by many items such as the desire for relationships and mental challenges, the concreteness and objectivity of the classical model may be exchanged for the more judgmental behavioral model. This model can be more practical because it attempts to mirror how people act as opposed to how they should act. Put simply, the work on the behavioral life cycle theory and on control reflects this line of thinking.

Behavioral economics and behavioral finance have moved in a different direction. Instead of emphasizing man as machine, they focus on the particular wants and shortcomings of people. For example, people have conflicting goals and do not always react the same way in similar circumstances. In fact, they are motivated by more than money. Understanding what motivates them requires going beyond a single factor model as represented by the classical model.

Maslow's hierarchy of needs presents a fundamental approach to human motivation with a kind of ladder propelling people to higher needs as they achieve success with lower ones. Once someone meets the lower deficiency goals, they can move on to the higher level self-actualization. While the rigid hierarchical levels and what some may regard as the idealistic self-actualization level have been contentious, it has had a strong impact in a number of fields including finance.

Maslow was a humanist. Humanists further moved the field of economics away from the classical model. They indicated that people have motivations that are broader than the goal of maximization of their own interests. Many behavioral economists still seek a link to classical theory, whereas humanists have altruistic objectives and may even be thought to have a duty to be concerned about others and to act in an ethical manner. They may focus more attention on those people who are educated and have achieved esteem in their lives. Money has less to do with humanistic goals and may even serve as an obstruction to achievement of those higher level aspirations. Their goals may be appealing to some but may not resonate with others who have not reached the top rung and can be satisfied by retiring with more simple leisure time and less far-reaching personal goals.

Where does that place personal finance? People need money to climb Maslow's hierarchy and, for many, to help achieve life satisfaction. However mistaken or immature humanists may call having money as a goal, it can motivate many people. Such people achieve satisfaction from buying goods and services. Such individuals also derive satisfaction from other activities, however, and have other values with the preferential breakdown dependent on the values of each individual. Perhaps the multiple selves conflict between the planner and the doer should be extended to concern about one's self versus the desire to help others.

Personal finance should form a middle ground between too-rigid classical economics and too-idealistic humanism. It should retain its focus on money but encompass the flexibility and practicality of behavioral elements. Within this context, some personal financial planners may seek to help clients with their life planning goals. Most planners will feel comfortable giving advice in the financial realm concerning money issues and many will use at least basic behavioral techniques to help motivate and advance their clients' interest in life satisfaction.

DISCUSSION QUESTIONS

1. What are the strengths and weaknesses of the classical economic approach?
2. Explain the advantages and disadvantages of Maslow's hierarchy of needs approach.
3. Discuss Thaler and Shefrin's major contributions to behavioral finance.
4. Discuss whether self-actualization should be everyone's goal.
5. Discuss whether life planning is a legitimate area for financial planners to offer clients.
6. Identify and discuss the contributions of motivation and satisfaction within behavioral and personal finance.

REFERENCES

Anthes, William, and Shelley Lee. 2001. "Experts Examine Emerging Concept of Life Planning." *Journal of Financial Planning* 14:6, 90–101.

Aspara, Jakko, and Henrikki Tikkanen. 2012. "Individuals' Affect Based Motivations to Invest in Stocks: Beyond Expected Financial Returns and Risk." *Journal of Behavioral Finance* 12:2, 78–89.

Belk, Russell W. 1999. "Money." In Peter E. Earl and Simon Kemp, eds., *The Elgar Companion to Consumer Research and Economic Psychology*, 383–388. Cheltenham, UK: Edward Elgar.

Boeree, C. George. 1998. *Personality Theories*. Shippensburg University. Available at www.ship.edu%7Ecgboeree/persocontents.html.

Csikszentmihalyi, Mihaly. 1999. In Peter E. Earl and Simon Kemp, eds., *The Elgar Companion to Consumer Research and Economic Psychology*, 364–365. Cheltenham, UK: Edward Elgar.

De Brouwer, Philippe J. S. 2010. "Maslowian Portfolio Theory: An Alternative Formulation of the Behavioral Portfolio Theory." *Journal of Asset Management* 9:2, 359–365.

De Brouwer, Philippe J. S. 2012. *Maslowian Portfolio Theory: A Coherent Approach to Strategic Asset Allocation*. Brussels: Brussels University Press.

Earl, E. Peter. 1990. "Economics and Psychology: A Survey." *Economics Journal* 100:402, 718–755.

Fisher, Irving. 1930. *The Theory of Interest*. London: Macmillan.

Gratton, Lynda C. 1980. "Analysis of Maslow's Need Hierarchy with Three Social Class Groups." *Social Indicators Research* 7:1–4, 463–476.

Heylighen, Francis. 1992. "A Cognitive-Systemic Reconstruction of Maslow's Theory of Self-Actualization." *Behavioral Science* 37:1, 39–58.

Hoffmann, Arvid O. I. 2007. "Individual Investors' Needs and the Investment Professional: Lessons from Marketing." *Journal of Investment Consulting* 8:2, 80–91.

Howell, Ryan T., Mark Kurai, and Wing Yin Leona Tam. 2012. "Money Buys Financial Security and Psychological Need Satisfaction: Testing Need Theory in Affluence." *Social Indicators Research* 110 (1), 17–29. Available at http://ro.uow.edu.au/cgi/viewcontent.cgi?article=3557&context=commpapers.

Lucas, E. Richard, Ed Diener, and Eunkook Suh. 1996. "Discriminant Validity of Well-Being Measures." *Journal of Personality and Social Psychology* 71:3, 616–628.

Lutz, Mark. 1999. "Humanistic Perspective." In Peter E. Earl and Simon Kemp, eds., *The Elgar Companion to Consumer Research and Economic Psychology*, 314–319. Cheltenham, UK: Edward Elgar.

Maslow, Abraham H. 1943. "A Theory of Human Motivation." *Psychological Review* 50:4, 370–396.

Maslow, Abraham H. 1968. *Toward a Psychology of Being*, 2nd ed. New York: D. Van Nostrand Company.

Maslow, Abraham H., and Robert Frager. 1987. *Motivation and Personality*, 3rd ed. New York: Addison Wesley Longman.

Mcleod, Saul. 2007. "Simply Psychology; Maslow's Hierarchy of Needs." Available at www.simlypsychology.org/maslow.html.

Modigliani, Franco. 1980. "The Life Cycle Hypothesis of Saving." *The Collected Papers of Franco Modigliani*, Vol. 2. Cambridge, MA: MIT Press.

Moore, Kevin. 1998. "Psychology of Leisure." In Peter E. Earl and Simon Kemp, eds., *The Elgar Companion to Consumer Research and Economic Psychology*, 363–367. Cheltenham, UK: Edward Elgar.

Shefrin, Hersh, and Meir Statman. 1994. "Behavioral Capital Asset Pricing Theory." *Journal of Financial and Quantitative Analysis* 29:3, 323–349.

Shefrin, Hersh, and Richard Thaler. 1988. "The Behavioral Life-Cycle Hypothesis." *Economic Inquiry* 26:4, 609–643.

Simon, Herbert. 1955. "A Behavioral Model of Rational Choice." *Quarterly Journal of Economics* 69:1, 99–118.

Thaler, Richard H., and Hersh M. Shefrin. 1981. "An Economic Theory of Self-Control." *Journal of Political Economy* 89:2, 392–406.

Tversky, Amos, and Daniel Kahneman.1981. "The Framing of Decisions and Psychology of Choice" *Science* 211:4481, 453–458.

ABOUT THE AUTHOR

Lewis J. Altfest is Associate Professor of Finance at the Lubin School of Business at Pace University. He is also President of Altfest Personal Wealth Management, a fee-only financial planning and investment firm located in New York City with about two dozen employees. His research interests include personal financial planning, investments, and behavioral finance. He has published in both academic and professional journals such as the *American Economist*, *Journal of Financial Planning*, and *Journal of Accountancy*. He has also published a textbook, *Personal Financial Planning*. His Total Portfolio Management (TPM™) system of integrating personal financial planning and investment management is currently being practiced and further developed at his firm. He has a BBA from City College New York (Baruch College), an MBA from New York University, and a PhD from City University of New York, and holds the CFP, CFA, CPA, and PFS designations.

Financial Planning Concepts

Policy-Based Financial Planning: Decision Rules for a Changing World

Dave Yeske, CFP®
Managing Director, Yeske Buie, and Distinguished Adjunct Professor,
Golden Gate University
Elissa Buie, CFP®
CEO, Yeske Buie, and Adjunct Professor, Golden Gate University

INTRODUCTION

Although the field of behavioral finance helps to provide a deeper understanding of the cognitive biases present when individuals make financial decisions, practitioners need not only understanding but also practical tools. Policy-based financial planning is one such tool, offering a framework and approach that allows practitioners to craft decision rules that can keep clients committed to a consistent course of action in a seemingly chaotic and unpredictable world. Hallman and Rosenbloom (1975, p. 4), who first articulated the concept of policy-based financial planning, describe personal financial policies as follows:

> *Also involved in the planning process is the development of personal financial policies to help guide a person's financial operations. An example of such policies in investments would be deciding what percentage of an investment portfolio is to go into bonds (or other fixed-dollar securities) and what percentage into common stocks (or other equity-type investments). Another example, involving life insurance, is that a consumer may want to purchase mainly cash-value life insurance or decide to buy mostly term life insurance and place the savings dollars elsewhere. Unfortunately, many people do not follow consistent policies in making these decisions.*

Three decades later, Yeske and Buie (2006) expand and operationalize the notion of personal financial policies into "policy-based financial planning," offering both a fuller definition of policies as decision rules and a process for their development. This process combines client goals, values, and circumstances with financial planning best practices to create concise decision rules. These comprehensive yet compact decision rules serve as a touchstone for both client and advisor, providing clear guidance in the face of rapidly changing external circumstances. In their ideal form, financial planning policies are both broad enough to encompass virtually any external change and specific enough to return clear answers as to appropriate action. As such, they are similar to or encompass investment policies (Boone and Lubitz 1992, 2003), safe-withdrawal policies (Guyton 2004; Guyton and Klinger 2006), and opportunistic rebalancing rules (Daryanani 2008), all of which provide clear guidance to clients and practitioners even in the face of unanticipated or rapidly changing events.

Before delving more deeply into the development and application of financial planning policies, stating what policies are not might be helpful. Policies are not beliefs or values, action items, implementation steps, observations, or goals, although all of these are present in the financial planning process and can be antecedents to or flow from the actual policies themselves. Instead, as previously noted, a policy is a decision rule that embodies client goals and values, with financial planning best practices in a form that allows for rapid decision-making in the face of changing external circumstances. An example of the connection among beliefs, goals, policies, and action items follows.

- **Client's belief:** Too much inheritance blunts ambition, reduces motivation, and creates inertia among certain heirs.
- **Client's goal:** To provide for a surviving spouse without leaving too much money to our grown children.
- **Policy:** We will own life insurance for survivor needs only, establishing charities as contingent beneficiaries on our life insurance.
- **Action item:** Buy term insurance based on capital needs analysis (i.e., the technique for determining how much life insurance a person needs to have proper coverage); coordinate insurance beneficiary designations, monitor survivor needs regularly. Using term insurance is consistent with the client's desire not to leave a legacy, only to bridge the financial gap that exists before accumulating adequate capital to meet the client's retirement income needs.

In this simple example, a belief gives rise to a goal, which leads to the formulation of a policy, which in turn dictates an action or implementation step based on current circumstances. As long as the beliefs and goals remain unchanged, the policy returns unambiguous answers as external circumstances change or new questions arise. In the preceding example, such changing circumstances might include changing capital needs due to market fluctuations, investment growth, or changes in spending pattern. For example, if the client accumulates sufficient capital to meet projected spending needs, the policy will dictate canceling the life insurance policies.

Another example relates to charitable giving, an area that can be stressful for clients to manage in the face of frequent appeals. A truism is that a check written to a charitable organization is but the first of two gifts—the second being made when the charity sells the donor's name to a mailing list. Thus, those who donate regularly must often manage a large number of appeals from organizations with wide-ranging missions.

- **Client's belief:** Preschool enrichment programs are one of the greatest predictors of lifetime educational success.

- **Client's goal:** To devote a sustainable portion of annual income to supporting preschool enrichment programs.
- **Policy:** I will focus my charitable giving exclusively on preschool enrichment programs and will annually donate to such organizations an amount not to exceed 10 percent of the annual safe-withdrawal spending target for my portfolio.

This policy yields clear and unambiguous answers to any appeal from a charitable organization. Either the organization's mission satisfies the first part of the policy or it does not. If it does, the donor has either expended 10 percent of her safe-withdrawal spending target in the current year or she has not. The donor need not return to first principles with every appeal after articulating and adopting such a policy.

When developing financial planning policies, the policy must pass a two-part test: (1) it should actually be a policy and (2) it should be a good policy. In order to be deemed an actual policy, a given formulation must deliver new answers as external circumstances change. If the answer is always the same, then the financial planner is most likely dealing with a belief, observation, value, or goal. If the policy passes the first filter, the financial planner should apply a two-part quality test by determining whether the policy is broad enough to encompass any changing circumstances and whether it returns a clear, unambiguous answer. Furthermore, the answers must be specific enough so that the financial planner is not in doubt as to the next steps to take. If the answer is unclear or lacks specificity, the financial planner is dealing with something other than a policy or with an inadequately developed policy.

Policies are almost always implicitly present in financial planning recommendations. However, financial planners often omit the extra step of articulating and memorializing the underlying policy and then sharing it with clients. In the more common approach to developing financial planning recommendations, financial planners collect and analyze information about client goals, values, and resources, which lead to specific recommendations and action items. Either at a periodic update or in response to some change in external circumstances, the financial planner will gather fresh data, update the analysis, and offer a new set of recommendations. Well-crafted policies, by contrast, can act as a bridge between client values and goals and the changing external environment in a way that results in rapid decision-making without the need to crunch the numbers anew. Put another way, financial planning policies transcend the current situation by expressing in general terms what clients plan to do and how they plan to do it in terms that are not limited to the current situation.

Before proceeding to a discussion of the process of how to develop effective policies, another example is offered involving a multipart policy that addresses spending and the use of debt:

- We will use credit cards for convenience and only for those purchases that are part of our monthly budget.
- For purchases equal to 10 percent or less of our annual after-tax earnings, we will set aside funds monthly until the needed sum is accumulated.
- For purchases equal to more than 10 percent of our annual after-tax earnings, we will use amortized debt, such that total monthly debt service is not to exceed 30 percent of our after-tax earnings.

This example illustrates a policy that satisfies the dual requirement that it be broad enough to encompass any circumstance while also being specific enough to leave no doubt as to the appropriate action. This policy accommodates all types of purchases and clearly articulates whether or when to use debt financing. Also implicit are both the client's value system and the relevant financial planning best practices.

MANAGING BEHAVIORAL BIASES IN THE FINANCIAL PLANNING ENGAGEMENT

Financial planning clients are as prone to behavioral biases as anyone and advisors must work to mitigate these tendencies. A brief tour of some of these biases and heuristics (i.e., mental shortcuts) helps to illustrate the powerful role that financial planning policies can play in keeping clients committed to a consistent course of action.

An important mental shortcut that financial planners can use is known as the availability heuristic. Ricciardi (2008, p. 96) describes the availability heuristic as "... in various experiments in psychology ... individuals tend to be biased by information that is easier to recall, influenced by information that is vivid, well-publicized, or recent." The availability of personal examples of long- or short-lived relatives often influences a client's willingness to save aggressively to support a long retirement. This availability heuristic (Tversky and Kahneman 1973) also affects the likelihood that a client acts on recommendations for more life or disability insurance, depending on whether she knows of someone who became disabled or died prematurely. Financial planners can use policies to reframe financial planning decisions in terms not related to the availability of personal examples. A policy related to life insurance, for instance, might frame the decision in terms of the important goals that the client has set for her family and the time and savings required to meet those goals without invoking the actual probability of premature death.

As a consequence of the "representativeness heuristic" (Tversky and Kahneman 1973), clients often see or anticipate patterns that do not exist and make suboptimal choices based on their misperception. For example, they may assume that a given political party winning the presidency will have a predictable impact on financial markets and seek to "trade" the expected pattern, notwithstanding the lack of evidence for such a relationship (Siegel 2007). Clients will also often assume that bad news in general must always be bad for the stock market. For example, assume that a retired nuclear engineer insisted that the financial planner liquidate his entire portfolio after the 2011 earthquake and tsunami in Japan. In his expert opinion as a nuclear engineer, the damage to the Fukushima nuclear power plant was much worse than early reports indicated—an assessment that ultimately proved correct. Unfortunately for the client, bad news did not automatically equal a downturn in the stock market. While the Dow Jones Industrial Average (DJIA) fell 400 points in the first five days after the disaster, it was 1,200 points higher a mere six weeks later. Investment policies and safe-withdrawal policies can be an effective counter to these propensities by offering framing and decision rules that transcend the particulars of any moment in time.

Kahneman and Tversky (1984) show that individuals are subject to *loss aversion,* which describes feeling an emotional loss such as regret or the prospect of a loss more keenly than the pleasure (or pride) from a gain or the prospect of a gain.

Among other things, loss aversion causes clients to underinvest or disinvest in reaction to negative news or declines in the stock market.

According Fischhoff, Slovic, and Lichtenstein (1977), optimism and overconfidence are another set of biases that can lead clients into suboptimal or even financially hazardous paths. In the financial planning context, clients often insist on holding large, undiversified positions in the stock of their employer based on both excessive optimism and overconfidence in the value of their insider's perspective. For example, Shefrin and Statman (1986) note that a client working for a technology company during a boom period may override the financial planner's recommendation to liquidate and diversify employer stock and options due to overconfidence. Yet, the client continues to hold the stock as it falls due to risk aversion and the hope of getting back to even.

In the preceding examples, financial planning policies serve to reframe the issue or circumstance in a way that either draws the client's attention to a different aspect of the situation, one that transcends the present moment, or enlists client heuristics to nudge them into a healthy direction (Thaler and Sustein 2008). Many people are also subject to mental accounting. Such people tend to locate funds for particular purposes in specific earmarked accounts, even though cash and securities are fungible and they could manage these funds in a single account. Cash flow and spending policies can harness this propensity to help clients make good decisions in the face of unexpected windfalls such as a bonus, tax refund, or inheritance. Such policies would incorporate a series of spending and saving "buckets" arranged in a cascading series based on priorities, with the emergency fund and retirement fund filling first, followed by a college fund, a vacation fund, and other "play" funds. As Thaler and Sunstein note, people tend to underestimate the impact of arousal on decision-making. Thus, a helpful approach is to direct any windfall into a simple series of buckets. This avoids the temptation to spend the entire windfall on play or fun activities.

A PROCESS FOR DEVELOPING FINANCIAL PLANNING POLICIES

Morgan and Hunt (1994) first suggested the constructs of trust and commitment in the context of relationship marketing. Since then, researchers in financial planning have widely used these constructs (Christiansen and DeVaney 1998; Sharma and Patterson 1999, 2000; Kirchmajer and Patterson 2004; Sharpe et al. 2007; Anderson and Sharpe 2008). Importantly, trust and commitment are associated with client behaviors that are highly predictive of a successful financial planning engagement in general and the successful deployment of financial planning policies in particular. Among other things, higher levels of trust and relationship commitment are associated with higher client satisfaction and retention as well as a greater propensity to reveal personal and financial information, implement planning recommendations, and resolve conflicts effectively (Anderson and Sharpe 2008).

As Sharma and Patterson (1999) point out, another reason client engagement in the process is so important is that financial planning has high credence properties. That is, clients have difficulty assessing the quality of the service even after it has been delivered. Sharma and Patterson (p. 3) observe:

After all, if clients have trouble evaluating outcomes, then it seems reasonable that interactions ("how" the service is delivered) and all forms of communications will take on added significance as clients seek to minimize dissonance and uncertainty about the adviser they have chosen.

While testing a model of the strategy-making activities of financial planners, Yeske (2010) finds that of five proposed modes of strategy making, the policy-driven mode is the only one that provides a statistically significant predictor of client trust and relationship commitment. Yeske's Financial Planning Strategy Modes model posits five modes of planning based on the degree of client engagement in the process. In the order of increasing client engagement, these modes are: Planner-Driven, Data-Driven, Policy-Driven, Relationship-Driven, and Client Driven.

Client engagement is nearly absent altogether in the Planner-Driven mode, while the advisor's role in the Client-Driven mode, which focuses on validation only, is minimized. One explanation that Yeske offers for the Policy-Driven mode's high association with client trust and relationship commitment is that this mode represents an almost equal balance between client and planner engagement in the planning process. This explanation is consistent with other research related to planner-client engagement (Christiansen and DeVaney 1998; Sharma and Patterson 1999, 2000; Kirchmajer and Patterson 2004; Sharpe and Anderson 2008). Hence, the degree of client engagement in the policy development process may be highly predictive of trust and relationship commitment as well as clients' propensity to embrace the resultant policies as an enduring touchstone and guide. The process of working with clients to develop financial planning policies is as important as the policies themselves in keeping clients committed to a consistent planning path even as they sometimes face a chaotic financial and economic environment. This is because the process of developing policies involves the active participation of clients and, if done correctly, can lead to higher levels of client trust and relationship commitment.

The process for developing financial planning policies involves six major steps. The following section describes each of those steps.

Step One—Engage in the Discovery Process

The development of financial planning policies begins with a thorough discovery process in which the financial planner learns about the client's personal history, values, beliefs, goals, and resources. Financial planners often employ an unstructured and intuitive approach to this step and some delve no deeper than the articulation of goals. However, Anderson and Sharpe (2008) find that clients rate the use of a "structured process" for uncovering goals, values, and beliefs as "very important." The authors also find that such an approach is associated with greater client trust and relationship commitment.

Engaging in such deep discovery is important for at least three reasons. First, beyond the explicit goals that may be served by a given policy, the planner must understand enough about the client's history, beliefs, and values to know what he is willing and unwilling to do in pursuit of those goals. Second, in proposing a particular policy, the planner must not only employ the relevant financial planning best practices, but also consider the strategies that will be most suited to what Heller and Surrenda (1995) call the client's "bureaucracy of habits." As Heller and Surrenda (p. 57) note, "our habits of perception limit and shape our ability to respond." This "bureaucracy" is the equivalent of Thaler and Sunstein's (2008) "Automatic System," the bundle of heuristics, or mental shortcuts, for making most daily decisions. Only in understanding the client's prior history, belief system, and behavioral biases can the planner propose effective policies. As previously discussed, if a client is particularly prone to "mental accounting" (Thaler 1999), one might propose a policy that creates specific buckets or "mental accounts" for managing debt, savings, or cash flow. An extended example of a policy using this approach is offered later. Third, a deep discovery process helps to ensure that clients see their personal goals and values reflected in the policies. This is a necessary condition if clients are to truly embrace and act on them.

Step Two—Identify Planning Areas and Best Practices

The second step in the policy-development process is to identify the relevant planning areas and associated best practices. Although the importance of the client seeing his goals and values implicitly and explicitly present in the policies has been emphasized, the policies will not be effective unless they also incorporate the best of the financial planning perspective. Relevant planning areas may include, though not be limited to, the following: (1) cash flow planning, (2) debt management, (3) risk management and using insurance, (4) legacy goals, (5) charitable giving, and (6) saving and investing.

Having identified the relevant areas, the planner must determine which of the profession's best practices offers a technically feasible solution and is most suited to the client's values, goals, and behavioral biases. Although no unanimity exists among financial planners as to what constitutes the one best practice for each situation, Buie and Yeske (2011) suggest planners should first seek out and adopt only those best practices that have been empirically validated through formal research and testing, whenever such are available. As Buie and Yeske (p. 39) note:

> *Our trouble as a profession is that most of our best practices stop at the formation of a belief (the case study presented below, for example, was a best practice for decades before eventually being empirically-tested). And we're quite comfortable stopping there because our personal experience and the experience of colleagues will often seem to confirm and reinforce those beliefs (an example of the phenomenon known as "confirmation bias" in the literature of behavioral finance). However, such informal "evidence" is properly termed anecdotal and cannot be the foundation of a truly learned profession's best practices. Instead, we must take the next step: We must form our beliefs into hypotheses, then gather appropriate data and formally test those hypotheses. Only then can we say with confidence that our "best" practices are founded upon the "best" evidence.*

Yeske and Buie (2011) propose an eight question approach to evaluating research-based literature when considering the adoption of new tools and techniques.

1. What is the problem or question?
2. How was the problem/question conceptualized?
3. What are the key findings from prior research?
4. What methodology did the research use to test the question?
5. What were the results of the testing?

6. Were the results compelling?
7. What are the practical applications of the results?
8. Will this change current practice and if so, how?

Regardless of the source and level of support, advisors typically form beliefs about the best practices related to each relevant planning area and these must be reflected in the policy.

Step Three—Combines Goals and Values with Best Practices

The next step of the process combines client goals and values with financial planning best practices. This is where the planner first drafts a proposed policy, focusing on integrating financial planning best practices and the client's goals, values, and circumstances. If the planner does not phrase and frame the policy to enable the client to see her goals and values reflected therein, the client is unlikely to embrace the policy. In pursuit of this, the planner should think carefully about what was learned during the discovery process and attempt, whenever practicable, to incorporate the client's own words into the policy's formulation.

Step Four—Test the Policy

During this step, the financial planner should answer two questions: Is this a policy and is it a good policy? To answer the first question, the planner must determine whether changing external circumstances causes the policy to return new and actionable answers. If this is not the case (e.g., if the proposed formulation returns the same answer), then it is more likely a goal or action item than a policy. To determine whether the policy is a good one, the financial planner should engage in scenario planning by feeding a changing array of circumstances into the policy to determine whether it satisfies the following dual criteria: (1) The policy must be broad enough to encompass any novel event that might arise and (2) the policy must be specific enough to return a clear, actionable answer.

For example, a policy related to risk management and using insurance would be expected to return fresh answers when the client's income, assets, retirement goals, or family composition change. Assume that a client's family increases from two to three children. A policy that incorporates the desire to finance children's college education, even in the case of the wage earner's premature death, might dictate an increase in life insurance coverage equal to the discounted present value of future higher education expenses, assuming all current savings are already earmarked for other goals. A policy that is ambiguous with respect to the impact on insurance fails the second part of this test, while one that returns the same answer when assuming additional children is more likely an action item.

Step Five—Test Draft Policies with Clients

The fifth step concerns testing draft policies with clients. This is probably the most important step in the entire process because it enables refining the policy and ensuring that clients take ownership and fully embrace it. At this stage, the planner can do much to enhance client trust and relationship commitment. The deep discovery of step one, combined with the client review and editing of step five, ensure that the client has as much involvement in the process as the planner. From the standpoint of client trust and relationship commitment, Anderson and Sharpe (2008) find the planner-client activities that clients value most highly and act as the best predictors of trust and commitment include the following:

- The planner and client mutually define the scope of the financial planning engagement before the planner provides any analysis or advice to the client.
- The planner helps the client identify meaningful personal and financial goals and objectives.
- The planner uses a systematic process to help the client clarify values and priorities.
- The planner endeavors to explore and learn about the client's cultural expectations/biases, personality type/traits, money attitudes/beliefs, and family history/values.
- The planner explains how financial advice aligns with and supports the client's values, goals, needs, and priorities.

The first four activities are part of a good discovery process, while the last activity is the focus of the fifth step in the policy development process. Beyond explaining how the policies align with and support the client's values, goals, needs, and priorities, the planner at this stage can invite the client to participate in crafting the policy's wording. Some planners take the approach of proposing several variations on a proposed policy and asking the client to choose the one they most prefer. In this way, the planner draws the client into the process in order to generate greater ownership of the policies that are ultimately adopted.

Step Six—Conduct Periodic Reviews and Updates

As with all aspects of the financial planning process, policies are subject to periodic review and update. Because financial planning policies are meant to act as a touchstone and enduring guide in the face of changing circumstances, they change when a fundamental or structural shift occurs, not because of cyclical triggers. For example, a change in the tax code represents a structural shift that might affect financial planning best practices. Likewise, a fundamental change in a client's beliefs or values may require modifying the policy. For instance, a client who had previously held the belief that too much inheritance blunts ambition might alter his view and decide that providing a legacy to children and grandchildren is desirable. In such a case, the planner would need to update any policies focusing on legacy planning. However, a cyclical fluctuation such as a substantial decline in stock prices or an economic recession would not change the policy itself but might well trigger new recommended actions as the changed circumstances are fed through the policy.

APPLICABILITY OF FINANCIAL PLANNING POLICIES

Although financial planning policies are useful in financial planning engagements, they could be particularly powerful in several situations. One of these is where the financial advisor conducts financial planning on an hourly, on-demand basis, with no ongoing advice or supervision. In this situation, a client armed with clear, well-crafted policies is better prepared to update his strategies in the face of a changing external environment. Another situation where policies are particularly helpful is when people are beginning their careers. These individuals generally have little income and few assets, and their family situation is likely to change dramatically because their most important decisions are in the future. They may also find themselves struggling to manage their cash flow as they begin to develop an independent life. For these individuals, simple, easy-to-follow policies that help them prioritize important needs in the face of limited cash flow can be very important. The following is an example of just such a series of cash flow and investment policies:

1. I will save 10 percent of every paycheck.
2. My savings will go first to my emergency fund until such time as this fund is equal to three months living expenses.
3. Thereafter, my savings will go into a retirement savings vehicle up to the applicable contribution limit and according to the following priorities:
   a. If my employer offers a retirement plan, I will direct savings in this account, at least up to the amount of the employer match, if applicable.
      i. If my marginal federal tax rate is 25 percent or less, I will direct retirement savings above the employer match into a Roth IRA or Roth 401(k), if available.
      ii. If my marginal tax rate is greater than 25 percent, I will direct retirement savings above the employer match into the employer-sponsored plan.
   b. If my employer does not offer a retirement plan, I will direct savings as follows:
      i. If my marginal federal tax rate is 25 percent or less, I will direct retirement savings into a Roth IRA.
      ii. If my marginal tax rate is greater than 25 percent, I will direct retirement savings into a traditional IRA.
4. Any remaining savings will be directed to an after-tax "opportunity fund" or supplemental retirement account.
5. With respect to investments:
   a. The emergency fund will always be maintained in a money market or similarly liquid account.
   b. All retirement savings will be invested in a diversified mix of index mutual funds or, if unavailable, low-cost actively managed mutual funds, including in equal proportion as many as possible of the following categories:
      i. U.S. large company stocks
      ii. U.S. small company stocks
      iii. Non-U.S. large company stocks
      iv. Non-U.S. small company stocks
      v. High-quality, short-to-intermediate duration bonds

The foregoing saving and investing policies are comprehensive and complete and satisfy all the criteria for a good financial planning policy. Even in the face of changes in earnings, living expenses, tax status, or investment options, the policies continue to return clear, unambiguous answers as to what the individual should do.

Also, financial planning best practices are implicitly and explicitly present in these policies, including the following:

- In the absence of additional factors, such as a longer or shorter elimination period for disability insurance, size of other insurance deductibles, and stability of employment, a minimum emergency reserve should be equal to three months living expenses.
- Starting young and saving 10 percent of all earnings, if properly invested, is likely to result in an adequate retirement fund over the course of a normal working lifetime.
- The trade-off between pre-tax investing and investing after-tax dollars in a Roth favors the Roth when marginal tax rates are 25 percent or less.
- Markets are fundamentally efficient and low-cost index funds are the best building blocks with which to assemble a portfolio.
- In order to mitigate risk and capture the benefits of diversification, allocating both across distinct asset classes (e.g., U.S. large company stocks and non-U.S. small company stocks) and within asset classes (the reason to choose mutual funds, especially index funds) is important.

Although some of the foregoing best practices are based on a particular reading of the evidence and may vary from advisor to advisor, a grounded best practice underlies each policy.

POLICY-BASED FINANCIAL PLANNING: THE STRATEGIC PERSPECTIVE

Much of financial planning involves identifying and analyzing a client's current or expected resources in relation to one or more specific future goals. The analysis invariably incorporates various assumptions about stochastic economic variables, such as inflation rates and investment returns. The planner structures policies to be enduring guides even as external circumstances change. For example, the policies described in the foregoing section would automatically adapt to changing inflation rates. This occurs by adjusting the size of the emergency fund as living expenses shift due to inflation and by expressing the emergency fund in terms of a fixed temporal framework (three months living expenses) rather than a fixed dollar amount, and also by adjusting the amount being saved because the savings target is a fixed proportion of income (10 percent) and not a fixed dollar amount. Of course, this latter assumes that income will shift in response to changing inflation rates. Similarly, rebalancing policies will automatically adjust to changes in the relative returns of different asset classes within the portfolio. Again, these policies provide clear guidance with respect to changing external conditions.

Besides the unknowns associated with the external economic and regulatory environment, some uncertainties are unique to each client for which policies may prove to be a powerful tool. For example, in addition to existing and future resources that may be projected with some confidence (e.g., ongoing contributions to an employer-sponsored retirement plan), the planner and client may identify contingent resources for which the value, timing, and probability of occurrence are highly uncertain. Contingent resources may include such things as the possibility of receiving an inheritance, selling a business, exercising stock options, or receiving a bonus. Because the probability of occurrence and the value of the resource are sometimes difficult or impossible to state, the planner cannot incorporate them into the formal analysis relating current and projected resources to future needs and goals. In such instances, the planner can use policies to formally incorporate those contingent resources into the plan and to establish in advance the appropriate actions to take if contingent resources ultimately materialize. As in prior examples, such policies can express, among other things, the prioritization by which contingent resources will be deployed toward various competing goals.

Here is an example that might apply to a client who holds currently worthless options that could become valuable if a product in development at her company became commercially successful. Assume further that she requires all currently identifiable resources to meet her retirement goal but wants to help pay for her granddaughter's education, make a gift to her alma mater, and remodel her kitchen. Her policy might look something like this:

> Any financial windfall from stock option exercise or other sources will be allocated as follows:
> - First, toward my granddaughter's college fund up to an amount equal to one half of the then projected cost for four years of tuition and housing.
> - Next, to my alma mater up to an amount equal to 10 percent of my then annual earned income.
> - Next, toward a kitchen remodel not to exceed 5 percent of the appraised value of my home.
> - Any remaining funds will be added to my supplementary retirement savings account.

Without knowing whether or when her options might become valuable, or their ultimate value, this policy explicitly incorporates into the plan client goals that based on conventional analysis would be deemed unattainable and often left out altogether. It also allows incorporating into the plan the client's personal values and desires with respect to those possibly unattainable goals.

EXAMPLE OF POLICIES DERIVED THROUGH STOCHASTIC MODELING

A *stochastic model* is one that is designed to estimate the probability of various outcomes arising from a system or process that involves random variables. A good example of a financial planning policy derived through a process of stochastic modeling is the safe withdrawal rate policies developed by Guyton and Klinger (2006). The authors used a Monte Carlo simulation that incorporates their proposed decision rules for maximizing the initial sustainable withdrawal rate from a given portfolio over a projected 40-year retirement. Monte Carlo simulations are generated by assigning a probability distribution to the random variables contained within a model—in this case inflation and stock market returns—and running multiple simulations in which, year-by-year, a rate of return is randomly selected from the specified distribution and applied to the portfolio and an inflation rate is likewise randomly selected from the specified distribution and applied to projected spending.

After several thousand runs, one can begin to make probabilistic statements about the range of outcomes one might expect.

Using two datasets for stocks, bonds, and inflation, namely, multi-equity for the 1973 to 2004 period and single equity (S&P 500) for the period 1928 to 2004, Guyton and Klinger (2006) run 14,000 40-year Monte Carlo simulations for each portfolio tested. They find that using dynamic decision rules raises the initial sustainable withdrawal rate from the 3.0 percent to 3.6 percent reported in prior studies using a static approach (Bengen 1994, 1996, 1997; Cooley, Hubbard, and Walz 1998) to as high as 5.5 to 6.0 percent. The Guyton and Klinger safe-withdrawal policies, which are applied annually on a fixed anniversary, are as follows:

- **Inflation rule:** Target spending will be increased by the change in the Consumer Price Index (CPI) for the preceding 12 months, except when the portfolio has had a negative return over that same 12 months and the current withdrawal rate is greater than the initial withdrawal rate.
- **Capital preservation rule:** If current spending as a percentage of the portfolio is more than 20 percent larger than the initial withdrawal rate, target spending is reduced by 10 percent.
- **Prosperity rule:** If current spending as a percentage of the portfolio is more than 20 percent smaller than the initial withdrawal rate, target spending is increased by 10 percent.

The foregoing clearly satisfies the dual criteria for a good policy. It is broad enough to encompass any possible change in the environment, while providing clear, unambiguous answers. From their simulations, Guyton and Klinger (2006) find that the prosperity rule is generally triggered about twice as often as the capital preservation rule and that about 99 percent of purchasing power is maintained over a 40-year retirement.

SAMPLE CASE APPLICATIONS

The following case studies illustrate the process of developing and applying financial planning policies. These cases indicate how the policies are matched to a client's particular set of goals and objectives in a way that takes into account personal history, values, and behavioral biases.

Case One: The Retirement Dream House

Otto and Sara Bittner finished constructing their retirement home when Otto retired at age 65. Their financial planner projects that their living expenses in the new home will be fully covered by their available financial assets. The couple made a supplementary withdrawal from their portfolio in order to help their daughter and son-in-law purchase property. As time passed, the Bittners made more supplementary withdrawals from their portfolio in order to subsidize their daughter and son-in-law's living expenses, as they had insufficient disposable income to support their new household. Updated projections prepared by their financial planner suggest that they would exhaust their portfolio in less than 10 years. Faced with this, the Bittners ceased subsidizing their daughter's monthly household expenses. This resulted in their daughter and son-in-law running up large credit card balances that they could not pay, which the Bittners repeatedly paid off to prevent the debt from going to collections. Their financial planner would have likely uncovered their desire to help their children if he had engaged them in deep discovery as part of the policy development process.

What kind of financial planning policies might have prevented this situation? Here is one set of possibilities relating to the Bittners.

- We will spend each year from our portfolio a sum not to exceed the spending targets specified by our safe withdrawal rate (SWR) policies.
- We will not facilitate the purchase of assets by our children that they cannot afford to maintain with their own earnings.
- We will provide financial education and counseling to our children and other family members, but we will not provide direct financial support.

The Bittners' SWR policies, if adopted along the lines proposed by Guyton and Klinger (2006), would have provided continuous and evolving feedback. Without requiring updated projections, the SWR policies would have likely triggered the capital preservation rule, perhaps on every anniversary. The Bittners would not only see that they were exceeding their target spending but they would also have the additional feedback that their target spending was getting smaller each year. The second policy would have hopefully caused them to inquire more closely as to their daughter and son-in-law's ability to maintain the mortgage and property taxes on the home for which the Bittners were about to make the down payment. Finally, when their children became financially burdened, the third policy would have resulted in paying for their daughter and son-in-law to see a credit counselor or bankruptcy attorney, but they would not have repeatedly paid off the credit cards.

Case Two: Unable to Shift from Saving to Spending

Karen Chen had just retired from San Francisco State University. She was anticipating spending her retirement years traveling extensively with her husband Jon, including frequent trips to Switzerland to see their son, who is an investment banker. Karen had retired with a state pension equal to 85 percent of her pre-retirement earnings. The Chens also had a portfolio worth $1,000,000, the result of a lifetime of saving and investing, including wise stewardship of the inheritance Jon received when his parents passed away. Jon, meanwhile, has managed the household since their son was three, including looking after the family finances. He has spent the past 24 years diligently managing the household budget, ensuring that they saved regularly and invested with discipline. Shortly after Karen's retirement, she was surprised when Jon informed her that "we're going to have to tighten our belts, I'm afraid, since your pension is only equal to 85 percent of your regular earnings." What was the point of all that saving and investing, Karen asked herself, if we cannot use those funds to support our lifestyle in retirement? Karen suggested that they visit their financial planner, Kyla Jennings, to discuss post-retirement cash flow management.

Kyla was not entirely surprised to hear of the difficulty the Chens, especially Jon, were having with the transition into retirement. From her experience she realized that the families who were most prepared financially were often the least prepared psychologically, finding that a lifetime of virtuous saving habits was hard to change when the spending phase of life arrived. During two decades of working with the Chens, Kyla observed that Jon seemed to be particularly prone to a behavioral bias known as "mental accounting." Every time Kyla managed to consolidate investment accounts in order to achieve greater trading efficiencies and lower costs, Jon would start finding excuses to create new accounts, each with its own purpose or goal associated with it. Kyla decided that she could harness this propensity as a way of overcoming Jon's reluctance to use the Chens' savings to support their lifestyle in retirement. What policies might Kyla suggest to the Chens to get them through this impasse? Here is one possible set of policies.

- An amount equal to the sustainable-withdrawal-rate target will be transferred quarterly to a separate "play" account, which is to be used for travel, dining, and other leisure activities.
- The play account will be kept liquid.
- All travel, vacations, and other discretionary expenditures will be made from the play account.
- Transfers will be suspended when the play account exceeds 150 percent of the annual target.

These policies simultaneously ensure that any expanded spending is bounded by a set of SWR policies, that the target spending is transferred to an account specifically earmarked for play, and that a mechanism is in place to trigger a review if it seems the Chens are not using the funds as intended and to ensure that the portfolio is not systematically liquidated for no reason. This scenario is based on a real client situation and the proposed policies proved effective in creating an environment where the client couple could responsibly use their available resources in a way that satisfied both of them.

SUMMARY

Financial planning policies are structured decision rules that can act as a touchstone for both clients and their advisors and allow for rapid decision-making in the face of a changing environment. Although policies are implicit in most financial plans and financial planning recommendations, articulating those policies in a concise and effective way is time-consuming. The additional effort offers several benefits. For example, good policies represent the distillation of client goals and values, as well as the relevant financial planning best practices, in a form that can both anchor the client to a consistent course of action and save the advisor from the necessity of crunching the numbers each time a question arises. Furthermore, Yeske (2010) shows that the process of developing policies with high client involvement is associated with higher levels of client trust and relationship commitment. Anderson and Sharpe (2008) find an association between trust and commitment and characteristics predictive of a successful financial planning engagement. These characteristics include a higher level of client satisfaction and retention and a greater propensity to reveal personal and financial information. Such an association can help in effectively implementing planning recommendations and resolving conflicts.

The field of behavioral finance has reached a point where the presence of biases, emotions, and systematic cognitive errors when individuals are making decisions is beyond dispute within the financial planning profession. What is called for now are better tools for keeping individuals committed to a consistent course of action in the face of all the environmental "noise" that can trigger inherent biases. Policy-based financial planning is one such tool that not only can improve client trust and relationship commitment but also can lessen the impact of cognitive errors.

DISCUSSION QUESTIONS

1. In the context of financial planning, define the term "policy" and identify the characteristics of good policy.
2. A client says, "I believe education is critically important to a successful life so I would like to pay for my grandson's college education." This statement encompasses a belief and a goal. Write an example of a policy for this client.
3. Explain how financial planning policies incorporate a client's values and beliefs.
4. Discuss how the process of developing financial planning policies helps lead to a client embracing the ongoing and changing recommended action items.

REFERENCES

Anderson, Carol, and Deanna L. Sharpe. 2008. "The Efficacy of Life Planning Communication Tasks in Developing Successful Planner-Client Relationships." *Journal of Financial Planning* 21:6, 66–77.

Bengen, William P. 1994. "Determining Withdrawal Rates Using Historical Data." *Journal of Financial* 7:4, 171–180.

Bengen, William P. 1996. "Asset Allocation for a Lifetime." *Journal of Financial Planning* 9:4, 58–67.

Bengen, William P. 1997. "Conserving Client Portfolios during Retirement, Part III." *Journal of Financial Planning* 10:6, 84–97.

Boone, Norman M., and Linda S. Lubitz. 1992. "Developing an Investment Policy Statement for the Qualified Plan." *Journal of Financial Planning* 5:2, 58–70.

Boone, Norman M., and Linda S. Lubitz. 2003. "A Review of Difficult Investment Policy Issues." *Journal of Financial Planning* 16:5, 56–63.

Buie, Elissa, and Dave Yeske. 2011. "Evidence-Based Financial Planning: To Learn . . . Like a CFP®." *Journal of Financial Planning* 24:11, 38–43.

Christiansen, Tim, and Sharon A. DeVaney. 1998. "Antecedents of Trust and Commitment in the Financial Planner-Client Relationship." *Financial Counseling and Planning* 9:2, 1–10.

Cooley, Philip L., Carl M. Hubbard, and Daniel T. Walz. 1998. "Retirement Savings: Choosing a Withdrawal Rate That Is Sustainable." 1998. *American Association of Independent Investors Journal* 20:February, 16–21.

Daryanani, Gobind. 2008. "Opportunistic Rebalancing: A New Paradigm for Wealth Managers." *Journal of Financial Planning* 21:1, 48–61.

Fischhoff, Baruch, Paul Slovic, and Sarah Lichtenstein. 1977. "Knowing with Certainty the Appropriateness of Extreme Confidence." *Journal of Experimental Psychology: Human Perception and Performance* 3:4, 552–564.

Guyton, Jonathan T. 2004. "Decision Rules and Portfolio Management for Retirees: Is the 'Safe' Initial Withdrawal Rate Too Safe?" *Journal of Financial Planning* 17:10, 54–62.

Guyton, Jonathan, and William Klinger. 2006. "Decision Rules and Maximum Initial Withdrawal Rates." *Journal of Financial Planning* 19:3, 48–58.

Hallman, Victor G., and Jerry S. Rosenbloom. 1975. *Personal Financial Planning: How to Plan for Your Financial Freedom.* New York: McGraw-Hill.

Heller, Stuart, and David Sheppard Surrenda. 1995. *Retooling on the Run: Real Change for Leaders with No Time.* Berkeley, CA: North Atlantic Books.

Kahneman, Daniel, and Amos Tversky. 1984. "Choices, Values, and Frames." *American Psychologist* 39:4, 341–350.

Kirchmajer, Les, and Paul Patterson. 2004. "The Role of Interpersonal Communication in the Development of Client Trust and Closeness in a SME Professional Services Context." *Small Enterprise Research* 12:1, 46–56.

Morgan, Robert M., and Shelby D. Hunt. 1994. "The Commitment Trust Theory of Relationship Marketing." *Journal of Marketing* 58:3, 20–38.

Ricciardi, Victor. 2008. "The Psychology of Risk: The Behavioral Finance Perspective." In Frank J. Fabozzi, ed., *The Handbook of Finance, Volume 2: Investment Management and Financial Management*, 85–111. Hoboken, NJ: John Wiley & Sons.

Sharma, Neeru, and Paul G. Patterson. 1999. "The Impact of Communication Effectiveness and Service Quality on Relationship Commitment in Consumer Professional Services." *Journal of Services Marketing* 13:2, 151–170.

Sharma, Neeru, and Paul G. Patterson. 2000. "Switching Costs, Alternative Attractiveness and Experience as Moderators of Relationship Commitment in Professional Consumer Services." *International Journal of Service Industry Management* 11:5, 470–490.

Sharpe, Deanna, Carol Anderson, Andrea White, Susan Galvan, and Martin Siesta. 2007. "Specific Elements of Communication That Affect Trust and Commitment in the Financial Planning Process." *Financial Counseling and Planning* 18:1, 2–17.

Shefrin, Hersh M., and Meir Statman. 1986. "How Not to Make Money in the Stock Market." *Psychology Today* 20:2, 52–54.

Siegel, Jeremy. 2007. *Stocks for the Long Run*, 4th ed. New York: McGraw-Hill.

Thaler, Richard H. 1999. "Mental Accounting Matters." *Journal of Behavioral Decision Making* 12:3, 183–206.

Thaler, Richard H., and Cass R. Sunstein. Nudge: Improving Decisions About Health, Wealth, and Happiness. New York: Penguin Group.

Tversky, Amos, and Daniel Kahneman. 1973. "A Heuristic for Judging Frequency and Probability." *Cognitive Psychology* 5:2, 207–232.

Yeske, David B., and Elissa Buie. 2006. "Policy-Based Financial Planning Provides Touchstone in a Turbulent World." *Journal of Financial Planning* 19:7, 50–58.

Yeske, David B. 2010. "Finding the Planning in Financial Planning." *Journal of Financial Planning* 23:9, 40–51.

ABOUT THE AUTHORS

Dave Yeske, CFP® is Managing Director at Yeske Buie and holds an appointment as Distinguished Adjunct Professor in Golden Gate University's Ageno School of Business. He is a past chair of the Financial Planning Association, where he has also chaired the political action committee, Research Center Team, and Academic Advisory Council. Professor Yeske has published in the *Journal of Financial Planning* and contributed 13 chapters to the CFP Board's *Financial Planning Competency Handbook*. He holds a BS in applied economics, an MA in economics from the University of San Francisco, and a DBA from Golden Gate University.

Elissa Buie, CFP® is CEO of Yeske Buie and an Adjunct Professor in Golden Gate University's Ageno School of Business. She is a past chair of the Financial Planning Association (FPA) and the 2013 Chair of the Foundation for Financial Planning, a nonprofit devoted to fostering and supporting the delivery of pro bono financial planning services to those in need. In 2013, she received the P. Kemp Fain, Jr. Award, the highest honor granted by the Financial Planning Association, in recognition of her contributions to the profession, society, and academia. She has published in the *Journal of Financial Planning* and contributed 17 chapters to the CFP Board's *Financial Planning Competency Handbook*. She holds a BS in commerce from the University of Virginia's McIntire School and an MBA from the University of Maryland.

CHAPTER 12

Financial Counseling and Coaching

John E. Grable
Professor and Athletic Association Endowed Professor of Family Financial Planning,
University of Georgia
Kristy L. Archuleta
Associate Professor, Personal Financial Planning, Kansas State University

INTRODUCTION

We were headed for bankruptcy. We had an immense amount of debt. We were fighting and I felt depressed. I couldn't sleep and it became difficult to make decisions, even if they were minor ones. We didn't know what to do. Then, we learned about financial counseling. . . .

A financial counseling client

The term financial counseling, and by extension, activities performed by financial counselors, has evolved over the past century. In the early- to mid-twentieth century, financial counseling was a phrase most closely associated with investment guidance. Those working as a financial counselor were essentially performing what today might be described as investment advisory functions. Financial counselors were primarily interested in helping clientele increase their wealth through the design and implementation of investment strategies. By the 1960s, the names used by investment professionals to describe their business activities grew to such an extent that few advisors referred to their work as financial counseling. Instead, they adopted titles such as broker, investment representative, investment advisor, financial planner, and money manager to help consumers better understand the services being provided by a firm. Today, financial counseling is generally considered to be descriptive of a reactive, supportive, holistic, and remedial process that focuses on evaluating a client's past and current financial behavior, with an emphasis on current concerns and problems (e.g., overindebtedness, lack of cash flow, and access to public and community support). The ultimate goal associated with both financial counseling and financial coaching involves changing client financial behavior in order to meet financial goals.

The learning outcomes associated with this chapter are threefold. The chapter begins by providing a historical context for financial counseling and coaching. Next, it presents conceptual and theoretical approaches that are commonly used by financial counselors when working with clients. The chapter concludes with a discussion of professional directions in financial counseling in the twenty-first century. Specifically, the chapter describes extensions of financial counseling—coaching, financial therapy, and life planning.

FINANCIAL COUNSELING: A HISTORICAL PERSPECTIVE

Financial counseling has been defined numerous ways. For example, Pulvino and Lee (1979) describe counseling as a process of orderly, systematic steps whereby counselors help clients understand and act on their concerns and of helping others understand who they are and what skills and abilities they have. The authors note that remedial counseling helps clients arrive at some solution and that productive counseling can help clients develop or expand existing resources. Pulvino and Lee comment that preventive counseling can help a client to meet immediate crises that may cause the person undue anxieties through wise money management and planning; preventative counseling can develop the attitude that the client is responsible and capable of controlling the future in a positive, purposeful way.

Williams (1991) views financial counseling as the professional field of assisting clients to obtain economic well-being and security. According to Williams, financial counseling is conceived in a broad sense. It uses skills and information to assist clients in changing behavior in financial management, consumption, lifestyle, and the use of all types of resources in order to obtain and maintain economic security.

By definition, financial counseling shares many of the features associated with psychotherapeutic and family counseling approaches (Williams 1991). For instance, financial counseling is premised on the following notions: (1) Counseling, as a process, is relationship oriented; (2) counseling is cooperative, with both client and counselor contributing to solutions; and (3) counselors ought to be both objective observers and active participants. Pulvino and Lee (1979, p. 5) summarize the client-counselor relationship as follows: "The counselor's responsibility revolves around structure, the client's around content."

Although similar in many ways to other forms of interpersonal psychotherapy treatment, financial counseling differs from services provided by clinical social workers, psychologists, marriage and family therapists, and others in one significant way; namely, financial counselors do not treat clinical disorders and the focal point of advice and guidance is directed at a client's household or family financial situation. Williams (1991) contends that financial counseling's unique contribution is using economic theory as a guiding principle to improve the well-being of clients by improving standards of living and economic security. This is an important theoretical perspective that helps differentiate financial counseling from other forms of interpersonal therapy.

Often those unfamiliar with the financial services marketplace confuse financial counseling and investment/financial planning. Financial counseling is similar to, but different from, investment advisory work. In the case of investment planning, the goal of the investment management process is to increase wealth in pursuit of long-term financial goals. Financial counseling also differs from financial planning. Financial planners generally review a wide variety of topics related to a client's financial affairs (e.g., insurance, tax, retirement, estate, investments, and special needs). However, few planners get involved with helping clients create a spending plan (i.e., budget), negotiate with creditors, or change spending behaviors. An implicit assumption held by practicing financial planners in the mainstream is that a client's financial situation, as measured by factors such as cash flow and net worth position, should already be healthy enough to implement savings recommendations. That is, the role of a financial planner is to help clients manage their cash flow and net worth position in such a way that wealth is created over the life span as a way to fund tangible financial goals. Financial counselors, on the other hand, tend to provide guidance in ways that will achieve baseline levels of financial health without regard to wealth accumulation.

The market for financial counseling services is potentially quite large. The distressing reality is that few households in the United States can be described as financially healthy enough to value the services of either an investment advisor or financial planner. As of 2012, for example, Americans saved approximately 4 percent of their household income (U.S. Department of Commerce 2012). Financial planners typically recommend a household saving rate closer to 10 percent (Grable, Klock, and Lytton 2012). Based on aggregate figures in the United States, Americans owed over $2.5 trillion in consumer debt (Federal Reserve 2012). Of this amount, consumers held over $800 billion in open-ended revolving debt (i.e., credit card debt). Additionally, the average default rate on home mortgages was close to 10 percent in the period of 2009 to 2012, which represented a 50 percent increase over historical nonpayment rates (U.S. Census Bureau 2010).

These figures alone are not necessarily indicative of financial stress at the household level. If employment rates in a country are high, income is increasing at a rate faster than inflation, and asset values are rising, the ability of households to carry debt is less problematic, making the market demand for financial counseling relatively minor. What makes the statistics just described problematic is that the conditions necessary for aggregate financial health, particularly during the first decades of the twenty-first century, were missing. The situation facing Americans at this writing was not radically different from other distressed periods in American history when Americans faced decreases in wealth and restrictions on credit (e.g., bank run of 1907, deflation and high unemployment of the 1930s, and stagflation and severe household financial stress of the 1970s). In general, describing the average consumer as being in a position of financial health in the twenty-first century or at any sustained period of time during the twentieth century would be difficult.

The preceding discussion highlights the role financial counselors can play in the consumer finance marketplace. Many Americans face financial stress and worry on a daily basis. These consumers are not in a position to save and invest immediately. Rather, they face challenges associated with mismanagement of household financial resources that result in daily financial hardship and hassles. With the lack of assistance and services provided by traditional investment and financial planning professionals, consumers historically could turn to few help providers for expert advice. This has been true for well over a century in the United States (Churaman 1977). Financial counselors have been among the few providers of basic financial education, guidance, and assistance.

Home Economics' Influence on Financial Counseling

Financial counseling has its historical roots in the home economics movement that began in the mid- to late 1800s. The term home economics is a fair description of the early studies conducted to determine how households manage their resources (e.g., time, money, talent, and labor). Although "home economics" has come to be associated with training young women in household tasks such as sewing and cooking, the original basis of this offshoot of economics was to study how consumers and families make decisions when faced with limited resources and nearly unlimited wants. Considering the substantial impact household consumption has on gross domestic product (GDP), determining why the field of home economics failed to gain traction as an academic pursuit is somewhat puzzling.

Today, divisions of home economics in colleges and universities have generally been renamed; departments such as Family and Consumer Sciences, Human Sciences, or Human Ecology Now exist. Traditional economists who study household resource management sometimes refer to their work as "New Home Economics." These economists apply principles of economics to study consumer and household consumption and decision-making in relation to the allocation of scarce resources, labor, household composition, transportation, fertility, and health (Grossbard-Shechtman 2001).

At nearly the same time, researchers and land-grant university extension specialists were taking steps to organize studies and training dedicated to the establishment of financial counseling as a field of study and practice. Family and consumer economists have traditionally maintained an interest in applying economic principles to develop normative strategies to help people function within the broader economic environment. Yet, the establishment of family resource management, within the context of family economic theory, gave financial counseling a true academic home (Williams 1991). Although some social workers, psychologists, marriage and family therapists, and other help providers (e.g., clergy) were active in providing financial counseling from a non-economic perspective, the financial aspects of literacy and advice was almost always secondary to the help provider's primary calling. Linking family resource management with financial counseling enabled new professionals to describe their primary client interaction activity as financial, rather than relational or psychotherapeutic.

Williams (1991) was among the first researchers to argue for a linkage between family resource management and financial counseling. She maintained that what makes financial counseling unique is the manner in which economic theory is blended with management processes. Specifically, as Williams (p. 7) notes, the basic tasks of financial counseling, as an offshoot of resource management, "are to reconcile expenses with income, provide a balance among needs and wants, maintain a life style in light of hazards against economic security, provide stability while promoting growth, and to distribute resources in a just way (which depends on one's philosophy of justice) equally, efficiently, and effectively."

Financial Counseling as a Profession

The study of household decision-making is grounded in home, family, and consumer economics. Although financial counseling emerged from these studies in the 1960s (Churaman 1977), people have been providing financial counseling services from a multitude of professional perspectives for well over a century. According to Bagarozzi and Bagarozzi (1980), social workers, the clergy, and other paraprofessionals typically provided financial counseling before the 1960s. Rarely, however, was financial counseling offered as a primary service, but rather as a reaction to a client crisis in conjunction with another presenting issue.

Feldman (1976) categorized financial problems typically encountered by social workers and other help providers into four interrelated domains: (1) learned behavior; (2) behavior brought on through external stimuli, such as economic recession, deflation, and unemployment; (3) family crisis; and (4) financial behavior that is a symptom of emotional and/or personality characteristics. What makes this list unique from behavioral problems studied by family and consumer economists is the inclusion of family dynamic and psychosocial causal factors.

This list also indicates the chasm that existed among help providers who were interested in helping individuals and families deal with financial stress through the 1970s. On one side of the divide were those trained in traditional economics (also known today as standard or traditional finance) who viewed financial behavior from a perspective of normative resource allocation choice, in which decisions were based on quantitative or statistical attributes. On the other side were help providers who viewed financial behavior as a function of other underlying personal and family issues (e.g., overspending as an outcome of child deprivation). Their perspective tended to be more qualitative, with much looser theoretical assumptions related to utility maximization at the household level. The result was a mixed approach to the delivery of financial counseling services. The type of services provided, the materials presented, and the resources gained by a consumer would vary dramatically based on who was providing the counseling service and how the counselor was trained. Bagarozzi and Bagarozzi (1980) reasoned that, in many ways, this haphazard approach to financial counseling process development slowed the training and outcome effectiveness research needed to ground financial counseling as a professional field of endeavor.

Although social workers and the clergy continued to provide financial counseling services throughout the 1970s and still do, the field of financial counseling began to crystallize with the work of family economists and resource management specialists who began to study how traditional economic theory could be blended with organizational behavior, counseling, and household management concepts. Bagarozzi and Bagarozzi (1980) document three ways (i.e., remedial, preventative, and productive) in which financial counseling that originated from a resource management perspective was most often provided during the mid- to late 1970s.

During that time, credit unions were very active in providing financial counseling services to members. Credit unions required their members (i.e., depositors) who applied for a loan typically to receive a form of financial counseling. They provided remedial counseling in cases where a loan was rejected. The purpose of this form of counseling was to help members improve their financial situation so that they could receive loans in the future. Credit unions provided preventative counseling to members who were interested in learning strategies to avoid future financial difficulties. They offered productive counseling to credit union members who needed some form of long-term financial planning—investment, retirement, college savings, and other forms of proactive planning advice.

At the same time, many of the largest U.S. for-profit firms instituted corporate financial counseling programs. According to Bagarozzi and Bagarozzi (1980), some companies required all junior executives to receive financial counseling. This approach to human resource management is almost unheard of today. In general, however, the primary purpose of corporate financial counseling was to provide a competitive working environment by improving the human capital of the workforce by including financial counseling services among other human resource offerings.

The third, and largest, providers of financial counseling services were consumer credit counseling firms of which almost all were operating as 501(c)(3) nonprofit corporations. An active debate still exists as to whether consumer credit counseling firms were truly engaged in a core purpose of financial counseling—behavioral change. Bagarozzi and Bagarozzi (1980, p. 398) contend that many firms, both for profit and nonprofit operations, relegated clients "to the role of passive recipient of a weekly allowance while he/she temporarily surrenders his/her financial responsibilities to the consumer credit counselor." To understand their concern requires recognizing how these firms typically operated.

Generally, consumer credit counseling companies marketed their expertise (e.g., firms widely advertised these services in radio and television commercials) to the most financially distressed consumers in the marketplace. In almost all cases, these consumers were on the brink of declaring bankruptcy. Knowing that bankruptcy can have a devastating impact on future credit acquisition, these consumers turned to "financial counselors" for immediate help in eliminating their debt while avoiding asset liquidation. On the whole, these firms did as advertised but little more. The financial counselor would meet with the client. During the initial meeting the client would assign responsibility for negotiating with creditors to the financial counseling firm. The financial counselor would work out a debt repayment plan with the client's creditors. Once the plan was established, the client would send a check once a month to the counselor who would distribute payments to each creditor. In most situations, the client and counselor would never meet again. The client's creditors directly paid the counseling firm. Credit card companies, for example, believed that a better approach was to negotiate repayments from a consumer and pay a financial counselor a percent of each payment rather than losing the entire debt through a bankruptcy filing.

This system of financial counseling was the dominant form of help for most resource constrained consumers throughout the century. As a result, financial counseling came to be most associated with debt restructuring and bankruptcy avoidance. In 2005, Congress passed the Uniform Debt Management Services Act. This law effectively altered the functional aspects of the credit counseling industry. For example, the law mandated additional consumer disclosures and prohibited certain practices, such as paying referral fees. Additionally, the act forced the Internal Revenue Service to more heavily scrutinize credit counseling firms. Consumer advocates argued for passage of the act on the basis that few credit counseling firms were truly acting for the public benefit and that nearly all such firms were in-fact for-profit enterprises.

The 2005 act prompted creditors, such as the major credit card companies, to substantially reduce the amount paid to credit counselors. As such, many counseling firms either went out of business or began charging fees for service. The act did promote some positive financial counseling changes, however. Today, for example, anyone who files for bankruptcy is required to receive debt and credit counseling from an approved organization within 180 days of filing for bankruptcy protection. Counseling organizations that want to provide this service must be approved through the U.S. Department of Justice's Trustee Program. Alabama and North Carolina have a separate counselor registration system.

As this discussion highlights, financial counseling has been burdened with two conceptual handicaps. As previously noted, financial counseling has its process roots in the early home economics movement. For whatever reason, many view home economics as a "soft" discipline. Although little evidence supports this perception, many people, both within and outside of the academy, hold a disparaging view of fields associated with the old and new home economics. Second, financial counseling has become most associated with credit counseling. In some respects, this is appropriate. Until the 1990s the majority of firms and organizations providing widespread counseling services were those whose primary role focused on restructuring consumer debt, especially revolving credit (e.g., credit card debt). Although an important and useful outcome associated with financial counseling, debt management is just one of many financial counseling goals, at least when defining financial counseling holistically. Even so, the general assessment of financial counseling in the early twenty-first century does not match well with the aspirations of those who envisioned a professional activity devoted to "assisting clients in the development and creative use of all their resources to achieve economic security or well-being generating alternatives" (Williams 1991, p. 1).

THEORETICAL APPROACHES: A FINANCIAL COUNSELING PERSPECTIVE

Financial counseling might have been founded with the academic study of economics of the home, but it had its coming of age during a time when strategic management was the dominant planning and decision-making framework used in government and corporate organizations (Overton 2008). Strategic management is not, and never was, a theoretical practice model or theoretical approach per se. Rather, strategic management was developed as an applied process approach to thinking focused on documenting how problems should be addressed. This explains how financial counseling practice models—distinct ways in which a practitioner approaches each financial counseling situation, excluding the economic approach—have emerged in an almost atheoretical manner. By contrast, other fields of study have developed practice models only after identifying theoretical perspectives. The pioneers of the modern financial counseling movement were interested in applying concepts from business management, economics, social work, and psychology. They were less interested in explaining behavioral phenomena; this led to the practice of borrowing theoretical concepts and conceptualizing financial counseling as a process akin to widely used strategic management processes being proposed in the 1960s and 1970s.

Consider the financial counseling process model first introduced by Pulvino and Lee (1979). Their model describes the steps involved in the counseling process, beginning with building a counselor-client relationship and ending with recommendation evaluation. The process is not a practice model, but rather a best-practices procedure. When viewed contextually, the process is quite similar to the traditional financial planning method of client engagement advocated by nearly all certification and designation boards (Grable et al. 2012). The process model assumes constant feedback from one element to another. For example, recommendation evaluation involves monitoring each client's progress. As information is obtained, the financial counselor can use new data to help strengthen the client-counselor relationship, diagnose additional needs, generate new counseling alternatives, provide additional core recommendation strategies, and work toward enhanced plan implementation.

One obvious limitation associated with the financial counseling process model is that it is not unique to the financial counseling profession. Financial planners, for instance, use a similar process approach when working with their clientele. Additionally, the process model does not adequately define or explain how financial counselors do or should interact with clients. The process approach only describes the steps that should be taken—in specific order—when working with clients. The exact theoretical approach to be applied (i.e., practice model) is left undefined. For example, a financial counselor whose training is in psychology will approach the process of client interaction differently than someone trained using an economic perspective. Little empirical evidence exists within the literature to suggest that one practice approach is more effective than another. The unfortunate outcome associated with the lack of evidence-based evaluation is that beyond studying the process of counseling, few practitioners have been trained to use clinically adapted practice models.

Wall (2002) maintains that the practice of financial counseling can be classified into one of three approaches: (1) psychological, (2) behavioral, and (3) pragmatic. In essence, the categories used in this section incorporate Wall's segmentation more broadly. As Exhibit 12.1 shows, financial counselors tend to use one of four broadly encompassing theoretical perspectives when working with clients. While nearly all counselors may apply a similar client engagement process, each practitioner's preferences, training, and core technical competencies tend to drive the choice of theoretical perspective when working with clients. The remainder of this section describes each theoretical perspective in greater detail.

EXHIBIT 12.1   Financial Counseling Perspectives

Family Resource Management Perspective

For many decades, Flora Williams, Professor Emeritus at Purdue University, was the leading spokesperson for the development of financial counseling as an academic field of study and practice. One of her foremost contributions to the field was integrating family economic theory with resource management and psychological concepts. She conceptualized her work in the following economic security model (Williams 1991, p. 5), which shows economic security to be a function of a variety of financial, psychosocial, and sociological concepts:

$$E\$ = f(\$Mo, Fa, Pa, CR, D, At, Mg, Ct, VS, I) A \qquad (12.1)$$

where   E\$ = economic security, which is conceptualized to be the result "of income in the total concept through developing, acquiring, and maintaining personal, household, and community resources"

  \$Mo = money income, transfer payments, and in-kind income
  Fa = financial assets
  Pa = personal and human assets
  Cr = community resources
   D = durable goods
  At = attitude toward money
  Mg = management abilities
  Ct = control over financial affairs and resources
  VS = value of simplicity
   I = insurance; and
   A = ability to adjust.

As conceptualized, the resource management approach is premised on several key assumptions. First, household resources are limited. For instance, income, assets, and access to help providers are restricted for most individuals and families. Second, household demands for additional resources are nearly limitless. Third, the inherent conflict between limited resources and unlimited needs results in unmet needs. Fourth, households act in a rational manner by identifying and ranking resources and resource demands when making decisions related to which needs will remain unmet. That is, households make cost-benefit choices in a rational manner by considering financial and opportunity costs, weighing alternatives, and choosing among preferences to reach predetermined financial objectives. Underlying theoretical approaches associated with the resource management approach include the permanent income hypothesis, the relative income hypothesis, and the theory of consumption.

Williams (1991) maintains that those who rely on a resource management perspective as a practice model share a common perspective that includes: (1) helping clients balance income and expenses, (2) developing procedures to help clients balance needs and wants, (3) providing rules to help maintain current living standards while maintaining economic security, (4) promoting financial growth and stability, and (5) teaching clients to distribute resources justly. The way in which these outcomes are accomplished involves combining aspects of economic theory (see key assumptions previously shown) with strategic management processes. Financial counselors who follow a resource management perspective tend to focus efforts on identifying and expanding concepts of income, time usage, social resources, household labor usage, household leadership, and knowledge enhancement related to consumer protection and choice, financial institution information, and public policy. The core underlying purpose driving nearly all financial counselors who employ a resource management perspective involves behavioral change at the individual and household level.

Resource Acquisition Perspective

Financial counselors whose practice model focuses on helping clients acquire resources often work from a social justice theoretical perspective. Broadly defined, social justice combines aspects of progressive economic thinking with social policy activism. Although social justice is a theoretical perspective that is still actively debated, common linkages underlying a social justice perspective include: (1) recognizing the inherent dignity and equality of all individuals, (2) creating opportunities for economic equality, and (3) redistributing income and wealth to produce economic equality.

Garasky, Nielsen, and Fletcher (2008) provide a broad summary of the issues facing low- and moderate-income families in the United States. They show that between 10 and 20 percent of households in the United Stated do not have a bank account. Fewer have adequate savings or asset accumulation strategies to meet an emergency. When viewed holistically, this helps financial acquisition counselors explain why many households engage in credit abuse and borrowing from predatory lenders. In general, financial counselors who use a resource acquisition approach when working with clients focus on helping their clientele increase access to resources, such as income, assets, and insurance. Often, the focus is on helping clients obtain publicly available—either governmental or private donation based—resources. These counselors tend to be less fixated on the behavioral change aspects of financial counseling primarily because they believe the free-market financial marketplace is fundamentally unfair, and this unfairness limits choice and creates uncertainty for vulnerable households. Focusing on behavioral change, at least in relation to resource allocation choices, would be, for a resource acquisition counselor, of modest value compared to improving a client's access to income, asset, and insurance resources.

Psychological Perspectives

Nearly all the discussion up until this point has focused on the economic aspects of financial counseling. In some respects, this is logical. An easy assumption to make is that financial issues should be of primary importance when someone seeks financial counseling services. Consider the resource management and resource acquisition practice models. While these seem at odds with each other, both share a common economic foundation—just different core assumptions. Yet, not all financial counselors view their interactions with clients from a core economic or resource development viewpoint. Some financial counselors incorporate psychologically based approaches in their work with clients. Psychology is the study of normal and abnormal functioning of individuals, in which physiological and psychological aspects are considered and the applied goal is to help individuals with cognitive, behavioral, and emotional problems.

One psychological approach used by financial counselors is the practice of psychoanalysis, which Sigmund Freud developed to help explain how unconscious thought, primarily developed in youth, creates historical precursors of current behavior (Burke 1989; Klontz and Klontz 2009). Multiple philosophical approaches fall under the psychotherapy umbrella. Examples include Gestalt models (i.e., methods that assume self-actualization occurs by focusing on analyzing the present rather than the past), existential frameworks (i.e., approaches that encompass an evaluation of the entire human condition), Adlerian models (i.e., methods that focus on each person's self-centeredness, vulnerability, and powerlessness), and trait-factor counseling (i.e., a general approach designed to help clients value their unique motivations, skills, and abilities) (Williams 1991).

Cognitive/Behavioral Approaches Cognitive/behavioral counseling is a common psychological approach typically applied to financial counseling. Although conceptualized distinctly when originated in the 1940s and 1950s, many theorists now consider cognitive and behavioral perspectives to be closely linked. As Williams (1991) notes, a practitioner's philosophical approach has a direct influence on the type of recommendations made to help a client deal with financial stress. Cognitive theory suggests that humans make behavioral decisions based on factors such as perceptions, attitudes, and beliefs (Burke 1989; Williams 1991). Those working from a cognitive perspective assert that any behavior can be changed by restructuring how an action or behavioral outcome is contextualized. Behaviorists contend that human activity is a function of stimuli response. That is, some people react to positive stimuli; others respond to negative inducements. Control of stimuli and reinforcement of positive behavior and punishment of negative behavior are characteristics of a behavioral perspective.

During the formative years when the two theoretical perspectives were being intellectualized, a common tendency was to choose one practice approach, rather than both. Today, practitioners more commonly combine elements of the two into a practice framework. Common assumptions held by cognitive/behavioral practitioners include the following: (1) Individuals can control their own environment, (2) human behavior can be changed, (3) people prefer to be in control of their own thoughts and actions, and (4) humans are constantly learning. What differentiates this practice approach from, say, a resource management perspective, is a counseling focus on helping clients gain control over their financial situation rather than a focus on maximizing a client's financial satisfaction, although this can be an outcome associated with the cognitive/behavioral approach.

Techniques that might be used by a cognitive/behavioral counseling practitioner include helping clients redefine what appropriate behavior is and then reinforcing the new definition with rewards and/or punishments. For example, assume a client falls prey to high pressure salespeople when shopping at the mall. The outcome is impulse purchasing, high credit card debt, and financial stress. In contrast, a practitioner employing a psychoanalytic approach might first focus on tracing the client's buying behavior to childhood trauma; a cognitive/behavior practitioner might begin by helping the client redefine what the purpose of shopping means for the client. This might be supplemented with assertiveness training to empower the client to "say no" when feeling pressured to purchase an expensive unneeded item. Depending on the client's preferences, a form of reward or punishment would then be instituted to support behavioral change. For example, each time the client leaves the mall without an impulse purchase, the client may reward his effort by having a milkshake or going to a movie. But when the impulse is too great and the client "fails," the client might punish his own effort by making a donation to a charitable organization that supports a cause counter to the client's core belief. In this way, the client has cognitively changed his behavioral pattern and reinforced the change through conditioned stimuli.

Systems Perspective

Thus far, financial counseling has been discussed as a personal endeavor, focusing solely on an individual from economic and psychological perspectives. Thinking about finances as an individual concern is easy. However, what happens when more than one person is involved in the financial counseling process? Family systems theory is a perspective that is increasingly being applied when working with individuals and with groups in a financial counseling setting. Family systems theory grew out of psychological processes by addressing similar issues related to cognition, behavior, and emotion. Systems theory also encompasses issues associated with relational aspects of a client's life. Family systems theory has its roots in Bertalanffy's general systems theory and cybernetics, which views an individual as being part of larger family and social systems. Nichols and Schwartz (2001, p. 104) describes a *system* as "an organic whole whose parts function in a way that transcends their (i.e., individuals) separate characteristics." In short, this means that individuals are still individuals, but understanding a person's behavior without considering her social or family context is impossible. Like the psychological approaches mentioned, many psychotherapy approaches are rooted in systems theory, including solution-focused grief therapy, Bowen family therapy, and structural therapy, to name a few. Psychological perspectives that primarily address individual needs such as psychoanalysis and cognitive-behavioral approaches can be practiced with a systemic twist. In these cases, the individual's family and social contexts are considered as a way to help understand a client's behavior.

Consider, for example, solution-focused financial counseling. This is a pragmatic, person-centered, and present- and future-oriented counseling approach that helps clients understand their strengths in such a way that client skills are used to meet current and future financial constraints. Sometimes strengths, when defined by solution-focused practitioners, include resources such as income and assets. Often, however, strengths represent forms of human capital (e.g., knowledge and experience) and family and community support systems. Unlike other psychotherapy approaches, a solution-focused financial counselor is not likely to dwell on a client's past actions or mistakes. Instead, the solution-focused counselor will take a stance of curiosity and ask questions to help the client search for exceptions to the disruptive financial behavior, identify what is working well for the client—and encourage the client to do more of it—and help the client take small steps in order to reach established financial goals.

Examples of other systems theory approaches include both Bowen family (intergenerational) systems counseling and structural therapy approaches. These practice models use interventions tailored to change family dynamics. According to Nichols and Schwartz (2001, p. 153), Bowen family systems counseling aims to lower anxiety and increase "the ability to see and regulate one's own role in an interpersonal process" as mechanisms to change behavior. Structural therapy approaches aim to change behavior and the experience of family members to change family functioning patterns by using altering boundaries and realigning subsystems. What separates each of the psychotherapy (i.e., psychological and systemic) practice models mentioned here from more traditional financial counseling approaches is a philosophical perspective that focuses primarily on human attitudes and behavior and less on an assumption of economic rationality or utility maximization.

FINANCIAL COUNSELING IN THE TWENTY-FIRST CENTURY

The following discussion highlights three fields of practice that have their roots in traditional financial counseling: (1) financial coaching, (2) financial therapy, and (3) life planning. What makes these three approaches of interest is that each relies on a unique theoretical perspective that helps shape the way in which client issues and concerns are addressed.

Financial Coaching

Wall (2002, p. 17) defines financial counseling in the following way:

> *Financial counseling is a short-term educative process concerned with helping people to help themselves through the application of financial information, education, and guidance to specific situations. It typically involves helping people clarify issues, explore options, assess alternatives, make decisions, develop strategies, and plan courses of action.*

Williams (1991) would argue that what this definition lacks is a focus on behavioral change and would not be alone in offering this critique. Many practitioners and policy makers have expressed concern that financial counseling, as generally practiced, tends to be too short-term oriented. This helps explain the growing interest in exploring new models and approaches that blend the best aspects of financial counseling with other interpersonal behavioral change techniques. One relatively new practice approach is known as *financial coaching*. Financial coaching is a subset of something known as personal coaching, which has been practiced since the 1970s. Financial coaching combines aspects of financial counseling, financial planning, and personal coaching.

Consider a report funded by the Annie E. Casey Foundation (Collins, Baker, and Gorey 2007). The authors contend that financial coaching is increasingly being applied as an intervention technique that can be used effectively with high-, moderate-, and low-income households. Rather than directing efforts at helping clients solve short-term financial emergencies, financial coaches tend to focus on helping their clientele establish and reach long-term financial goals through directed behavioral change. Financial coaching is premised on five key assumptions: (1) Long-term, rather than short-term goals are of most importance; (2) helping clients achieve long-term financial goals is a collaborative process between client and coach; (3) the coach's primary role is to provide support to clients; (d) each client has unique skills and abilities and the coach's task is to help each client discover and use these resources; and (5) clients have the capacity to change behavior.

According to Collins et al. (2007), those delivering financial coaching are typically volunteer coaches, staff working for a nonprofit organization, and for-profit financial advisors. Yet, financial planners are increasingly incorporating aspects of coaching into their practices (Dubofsky and Sussman 2009). Clients who seek the help of a financial coach often find the term coach to be attractive because the idiom is most often associated with athletic success. Coaches are known to help others set goals, develop strengths to meet and surpass goals, and provide ongoing feedback and guidance. In some ways, financial coaching combines aspects of resource management and cognitive/behavioral frameworks associated with financial counseling. Because of the relative newness of the financial coaching movement, no generally established and monitored ethical guidelines, practice models, or training requirements are available to become a financial coach. However, two organizations provide a professional home for financial coaches: Association for Financial Counseling and Planning (AFPCE) and the International Coach Federation (ICF). Collins et al. conclude that financial coaching may, in fact, provide some individuals and households with meaningful help. Ideal candidates for behavioral coaching are those whose (1) financial situation is relatively simple, (2) financial and personal situation is stable, and (3) ability to engage in behavior change is high. Clientele who need more fundamental resource acquisition help and/or therapy to delve into deep emotional issues typically do not find financial coaching to be quite as valuable.

Financial Therapy

Financial therapy is an emerging area of study and practice that has its roots in the financial counseling, financial planning, and mental health fields. Financial therapy is conceptualized as the integration of cognitive, emotional, behavioral, relational, and economic aspects that promote financial health (Financial Therapy Association 2012). Financial therapy is often practiced when a professional has training in both personal finance and mental health or when a financial professional (e.g., advisor, planner, counselor, or coach) and a mental health clinician (e.g., marriage and family therapist, psychologist, or social worker) collaborate (Archuleta et al. 2011). Financial therapists typically engage in a process to help clients improve their overall quality of life by helping clients improve their financial well-being (Archuleta et al. 2012). The process typically consists of (1) developing a relationship between the client and practitioner, (2) addressing presenting issues and goals, and (3) creating an intervention or introducing tools as a mechanism to meet clients' expected outcomes and goals (e.g., changing one's relationship with money). As financial therapy continues to grow, and as the field transforms into a credible profession, researchers are studying the mechanisms of financial therapy and approaches that are effective in helping clients not only change behavior but also increase overall quality of life, financial well-being, and health. The *Journal of Financial Therapy* is publishing much of this work.

Life Planning

Life planning, while similar to both financial coaching and financial therapy, has a longer history of development and use. Life planning emerged as an alternative practice approach for financial planners who were less interested in following the systematic financial planning process, which, by definition, tends to be focused heavily on financial problem analyses and solutions. Those advocating the life planning method, such as Carol Anderson, Mitch Anthony, Roy Diliberto, George Kinder, Ross Levin, and Richard Wagner, contend that helping clients achieve financial objectives is essentially ineffectual unless other elements in the client's life are also addressed and improved. This is the core perspective of life planners; namely, the advisor must first help clients establish a general life, rather than financial goals, and objectives. This is the starting point in the client-advisor relationship.

Many definitions of financial life planning are available. For example, Sharpe et al. (2007, p. 2) state that life planning is "a holistic, values-based, client-centered approach to financial planning." Anthes and Lee (2001, p. 90) define life planning as follows:

> *A process of helping people focus on the true values and motivations in their lives, determining the goals and objectives they have as they see their lives develop, and using these values, motivations, goals, and objectives to guide the planning process and provide a framework for making choices and decisions in life that have financial and non-financial implications or consequences.*

These two definitional frameworks highlight the following core assumptions underlying life planning: (1) Clients are viewed holistically rather than financially; (2) planner advice must be multidimensional, looking at financial and non-financial aspects of each client's situation; (3) financial recommendations and solutions create interactions in other areas of a client's life; and (4) attitudes, feelings, and interactions with others influence a client's behavior. Life planners also describe their work as client-centered planning or counseling, values-based planning or counseling, and as interior-finance (Kinder 2000; Wagner 2000).

The unique contribution of life planning, as it relates to the historical development of financial counseling, is the recurring requirement to continually focus on each client as an individual interacting in a complex world. Rather than separating client goals and objectives into financial and other, life planners attempt to provide counsel that addresses multiple life outcomes simultaneously. To date, however, little empirical evidence suggests that life planning provides better overall outcomes for clients compared to other forms of financial therapy and/or counseling. Sharpe et al. (2007) note that life planners can use effective communication strategies to improve client outcomes by enhancing trust and commitment, but this insight applies to nearly all forms of financial planning, coaching, therapy, and counseling. Whether and how financial life planning will grow in the future is unknown. Given the high financial, emotional, and time commitments necessary to be an effective life planner, the life planning process may become a niche approach used with high net worth clientele who can afford the costs of such specialized care.

SUMMARY

This chapter has highlighted several important factors associated with the manner in which financial counseling and financial coaching is currently practiced. First, nearly all financial counseling practitioners agree that the counseling process as illustrated in Exhibit 12.1 is an appropriate framework to guide client-advisor interactions. Although little empirical evidence supports this assertion, experience among financial counselors suggests the assertion is correct.

Second, no consistent or correct practice model is currently being taught in colleges and universities. As currently practiced, each financial counselor is responsible for selecting a philosophical approach to guide his practice. The approach selected has a direct impact on the type of counseling services provided to clients. Because of this inconsistency, few empirical studies exist to document the effectiveness of financial counseling in general or the usefulness of specific practice management models specifically.

Third, unlike the fields of psychology or marriage and family therapy, those interested in learning the art and craft of financial counseling and financial coaching are forced to choose, sometimes without enough information, a philosophical practice approach before entering school rather than learning multiple approaches and later choosing a framework that matches the student's skills and abilities. This occurs because few academic programs offer more than one philosophical approach when training students. Nearly all students must select between the four philosophical approaches described in the chapter when choosing an academic degree program. This leaves consumers facing a quandary. Few financial counselors and financial coaches advertise their theoretical approach. Some might argue that even fewer counselors and coaches could articulate their practice model approach well enough to create such an advertisement. This means, for better or worse, those seeking financial counseling and financial coaching services receive services that tend to be inconsistent from one counselor/coach to the next with no evidence to support that the approach the counselor/coach is using actually works any better than another approach in any context.

Finally, behavioral change is a common, hoped-for outcome associated with counseling and coaching processes. Yet, the road to change and the empirical evidence to support such change continue to hinder the potential growth and impact of financial counseling and financial coaching as helping professions.

DISCUSSION QUESTIONS

1. When and where did financial counseling develop as a field of study and practice?
2. Identify and briefly explain the four approaches that financial counselors commonly use when engaging with clients.
3. Describe the differences among financial counseling, financial coaching, financial therapy, financial planning, and life planning.
4. Go to www.youtube.com/watch?v=wEfQ4nOz6s8&feature=youtube and watch the video in order answer the following questions:
   - What kind of help did this couple receive from Housing and Credit Counseling, Inc. as it relates to this chapter?
   - How was the help the couple received from HCCI beneficial?
   - If financial counseling services were unavailable for this couple, where could they have sought help?
5. How can the fields of financial counseling and coaching increase their credibility and quality of services?

REFERENCES

Anthes, William, and Shelley A. Lee. 2001. "Experts Examine Emerging Concept of Life Planning." *Journal of Financial Planning* 14:6, 90–101. Available at www.fpanet.org/journal/articles/2001_Issues/jfp0601-art11.cfm.

Archuleta, Kristy L., Emily A. Burr, Anita K. Dale, Anthony Canale, Dan Danford, Erika Rasure, Jeff Nelson, Kelley Williams, Kurt Schindler, and Brett Coffman. 2012. "What Is Financial Therapy? Discovering the Mechanisms and Aspects of an Emerging Field." *Journal of Financial Therapy* 3:2, 57–78.

Archuleta, Kristy L., Anita K. Dale, Dan Danford, Kelley Williams, Erika Rasure, Emily Burr, Kurt Schindler, and Brett Coffman. 2011. "An Initial Membership Profile of the Financial Therapy Association." *Journal of Financial Therapy* 2:2, 1–19.

Bagarozzi, Judith I., and Denis A. Bagarozzi. 1980. "Financial Counseling: A Self Control Model for the Family." *Family Relations* 29:3, 396–403.

Burke, Joseph F. 1989. *Contemporary Approach to Psychotherapy and Counseling: The Self-Regulation and Maturity Model.* Pacific Grove, CA: Brooks-Cole.

Churaman, Charlotte. 1977. "Home Economists at Work: A Roundup of Experiences." *Journal of Home Economics* 19:1, 18–21.

Collins, J. Michael, Christi Baker, and Rochelle Gorey. 2007. "Financial Coaching: A New Approach for Asset Building." A Report for the Annie E. Casey Foundation. Available at http://fyi.uwex.edu/financialcoaching/files/2010/07/Financial_Coaching_Policy_Lab_Paper.pdf.

Dubofsky, David, and Lyle Sussman. 2009. "The Changing Role of the Financial Planner Part 1: From Financial Analytics to Coaching and Life Planning." *Journal of Financial Planning* 22:8, 48–57.

Federal Reserve. 2012. "Consumer Credit—G.19." Available at www.federalreserve.gov/releases/g19/current/default.htm.

Feldman, Frances L. 1976. *The Family in Today's Money World.* New York: Family Service Association of America.

Financial Therapy Association. 2012. Available at http://financialtherapyassociation.org/About_the_FTA.html.

Garasky, Steven, Robert B. Nielsen, and Cynthia Needles Fletcher. 2008. "Consumer Finances of Low-Income Families." In Jing Jian Xiao, ed., *Handbook of Consumer Finance Research,* 223–237. New York: Springer.

Grable, John E., Derek Klock, and Ruth H. Lytton. 2012. *A Case Approach to Financial Planning,* 2nd ed. Cincinnati, OH: National Underwriter.

Grossbard-Shechtman, Shoshana. 2001. "The New Home Economics at Colombia and Chicago." *Feminist Economics* 7:3, 103–130.

Kinder, George. 2000. *The Seven States of Money Maturity.* New York: Dell.

Klontz, Brad, and Ted Klontz. 2009. *Mind over Money: Overcoming the Money Disorders That Threaten Our Financial Health.* New York: Crown Business.

Nichols, Michael P., and Richard C. Schwartz. 2001. *Family Therapy: Concepts and Methods,* 5th ed. Needham Heights, MA: Pearson.

Overton, Rosalyn. 2008. "Theories of the Financial Planning Profession." *Journal of Personal Finance* 7:1, 13–41.

Pulvino Charles J., and James L. Lee. 1979. *Financial Counseling: Interviewing Skills.* Dubuque, IA: Kendall/Hunt.

Sharpe, Deanna L., Carol Anderson, Andrea White, Susan Galvan, and Martin Siesta. 2007. "Specific Elements of Communication that Affect Trust and Commitment in the Financial Planning Process." *Journal of Financial Counseling and Planning* 18:1, 2–17.

U.S. Census Bureau. 2010. "Banking, Finance, and Insurance." Available at www.census.gov/prod/2011pubs/11statab/banking.pdf.

U.S. Department of Commerce. 2012. "Personal Income and Outlays, October 2012." Available at www.bea.gov/newsreleases/national/pi/pinewsrelease.htm.

Wagner, Richard. 2000. "The Soul of Money." *Journal of Financial Planning* 13:8, 50–54.

Wall, Ronald W. 2002. *Financial Counseling in Practice: A Practical Guide for Leading Others to Financial Wellness.* Honolulu, HI: Financial Wellness Associates.

Williams, Flora L. 1991. *Theories and Techniques in Financial Counseling and Planning: A Premier Text and Handbook for Assisting Middle and Low Income Clients.* West Lafayette, IN: Purdue Research Foundation.

ABOUT THE AUTHORS

John E. Grable is Professor and Athletic Association Endowed Professor of Family Financial Planning at the University of Georgia. He teaches and conducts research in the Certified Financial Planner™ Board of Standards Inc. undergraduate and graduate program at the University of Georgia where he holds an Athletic Association Endowed Professorship. Professor Grable served as the founding editor for the *Journal of Personal Finance* and coeditor of the *Journal of Financial Therapy*. His research interests include financial risk tolerance assessment, psycho-physiological economics, and financial planning help-seeking behavior. He has been the recipient of several research and publication awards and grants. Professor Grable is active in promoting the link between research and financial planning practice where he has published numerous refereed papers, coauthored two financial planning textbooks, and coedited a financial planning and counseling book of scales. Professor Grable currently writes a quarterly column for a leading financial services journal. He received his undergraduate degree in business/economics from the University of Nevada, an MBA from Clarkson University, and a PhD in resource management at Virginia Tech.

Kristy L. Archuleta is an Associate Professor in the Personal Financial Planning program in the School of Family Studies and Human Services at Kansas State University and a licensed marriage and family therapist in the state of Kansas. Her research integrates interpersonal and relational factors with financial counseling and planning. She is cofounder and co-director of the Institute of Personal Financial Planning Clinic where she conducts research and practices in the area of financial therapy. Professor Archuleta is a cofounder and currently serves as a board member for the Financial Therapy Association and is coeditor of the *Journal of Financial Therapy*. She teaches undergraduate and doctoral level financial counseling courses. Professor Archuleta obtained a BS in family relations and child development with a minor in business management from Oklahoma State University, and an MS and PhD in marriage and family therapy with an emphasis in personal financial planning from Kansas State University.

CHAPTER 13

Financial Therapy: De-Biasing and Client Behaviors

Joseph W. Goetz
Associate Professor of Financial Planning, University of Georgia
Jerry E. Gale
Associate Professor of Marriage and Family Therapy, University of Georgia

INTRODUCTION

The research fields of behavioral finance/economics and neuroeconomics have made great progress in explaining individuals' financial behavior as well as the factors that shape financial decision-making. Behavioral finance researchers clearly show that individuals are subject to cognitive and emotional biases that may lead to suboptimal financial decisions. Similarly, as documented in medicine, patients do not always follow best medical practices, which have led to the merging of medicine with the behavioral sciences (McDaniel, Hepworth, and Doherty 1992; Marmot 2005; Gale, Goetz, and Britt 2012). The field of neuroeconomics further explains these biases affecting financial behaviors from a physiological perspective and presents clear implications for financial planners (Goetz and James 2008). Therefore, the integration of multiple disciplines is a foundation for the new field of *financial therapy*. Financial therapy blends knowledge from the fields of financial planning and mental health services to better understand financial behavior and implement interventions to improve financial and relational well-being.

Despite much empirical data corroborating the fact that cognitive biases and emotions have an integral role in financial decisions and behaviors, few professionals in the financial planning field address their own biases or those of their clients. Similarly, few psychologists or therapists directly address the issue of money or money biases within their service models. The development of the concept of financial therapy reflects the strong acknowledgment from a subset of practitioners and researchers that money affects relationships and overall well-being. Additionally, psychological and relational well-being influence one's financial management. For example, Stolz (2009) notes that more financial planners are seeking training to acquire skills and knowledge on how to prevent or decrease marital discord from causing a financial plan to fail.

An individual's level of financial failure or success may affect that person's sense of identity. The level of income may also influence the power dynamics in relationships. Gender dynamics, cultural background, and family financial socialization all influence an individual's relationship with money and a family's relational dynamics about finances. Some contend that licensed therapists and counselors should learn basic skills in addressing money issues and establishing relationships with financial planners for purposes of referral or collaboration to best serve their clientele. This may be particularly important during challenging economic periods when many more families are in financial distress. The economy clearly affects family dynamics, such as more adult children returning home (or failing to leave) during tough economic times, sudden losses of income due to layoffs, and higher divorce rates.

Research indicates a strong link between financial stress and physical health. For example, researchers have examined the effects of weekly changes in financial stressors on physical and mental health with individuals coping with existing health conditions (Skinner, Zautra, and Reich 2004). The findings indicate that fluctuations in financial stress are associated with increased complaints about health. Additionally, they report an interaction between increased financial and interpersonal stress with increased pain and health problems. Thus, financial stress contributes to both physical and mental health.

The American Psychological Association conducts an annual national survey called *Stress in America: Our Health at Risk* to identify the leading causes of stress and the impact of these stressors on health and well-being. Respondents consistently report money as the top source for stress among adults in the United States, with 75 percent of people attributing their stress to money issues. More than a third (37 percent) of the respondents indicate a goal to pay off debts and the majority (52 percent) report the goal to increase their savings behavior. Yet, more than a quarter of the respondents (27 percent) state that lack of willpower prevents them from making positive changes in their financial behavior. Children also appear to be adversely affected when families are under financial stress with almost a third of youth (30 percent) reporting being worried about whether their family would have enough money. Studies show that stress and the unhealthy ways people manage it contribute to serious health problems (e.g., heart disease, diabetes, and obesity) in the United States (Baum and Posluszny 1999). Thus, implementing strategies for people to address financial stress and increase their overall financial well-being is imperative.

A strong connection exists between relationship well-being and financial well-being. Empirical evidence finds a reciprocal relationship wherein financial stress can increase couple and family stress and difficulties within relationships can negatively affect financial decisions and stability (Elder, Nguyen, and Caspi 1985; Aniol and Synder 1997; Kerkmann, Lee, Lown, and Allgood 2000; Gudmunson et al. 2007; Dew and Dakin 2011). Even absent financial challenges, money conflicts are often reported as a major issue in relationships (Papp, Cummings, and Goeke-Morey 2009). Research literature substantiates this strong association between relational and financial stress. In fact, evidence shows that financial stress negatively affects marital satisfaction (Locke and Wallace 1959; Spanier 1976; Blumstein and Schwartz 1983) and that couples who engage in marriage therapy commonly indicate financial challenges and stress as a primary concern (Aniol and Snyder 1997; Miller, Yorgason, Sandberg, and White 2003). Newlyweds are particularly vulnerable to the negative impact of financial factors on their relationship satisfaction given the debt that is often brought into a marriage coupled with the lack of understanding on how best to manage debt (Skogrand et al. 2005).

Economic hardship in families can have adverse effects for multiple generations (Scaramella et al. 2008). Research indicates that long periods of economic adversity can send families into a downward spiral in that parents often withdraw or become more irritable with their children. With less parental support, the academic performance of children decreases, potentially leading to less economic stability in adulthood (Conger and Donnellan 2007). In 2009, the U.S. Department of Treasury hosted a Relationship Finance Summit to address the need for financial literacy work to occur within a family and relational context. Advocates of financial therapy recognize that financial education in itself may not always be enough to yield behavioral changes and much value exists in addressing financial issues within a psychological and relational context.

This chapter provides an overview of the emerging field of financial therapy research and practice. It also presents examples of how theoretical perspectives and conceptual frameworks born in the mental health fields (e.g., family therapy and psychology) are beginning to be used to understand and develop interventions to influence financial thinking and behavior. The chapter is structured in the following manner. The first section provides an introduction to the history and concept of financial therapy. The next section provides an overview of theoretical perspectives that can be applied to financial therapy practice and research. The penultimate section provides discussion on research areas needed to support the development of tools that financial planners, counselors, and educators need in order to be more therapeutic and effective in their work with clients. The final section provides a summary and discussion questions.

WHAT IS FINANCIAL THERAPY?

The terms *financial planning, financial counseling,* and more recently *financial therapy* are becoming increasingly more common in U.S. culture. In 2012, the Financial Planning Association (FPA) announced plans for joint initiatives with the Association for Financial Counseling and Planning Education (AFCPE). The primary purpose of this strategic partnership was to facilitate the development of financial counseling and financial planning as complementary specialties for financial service professionals. Implicit in this message is a distinct difference in the meaning of financial planning and financial counseling. Financial planners typically work with high-income or high-net-worth individuals and families, and financial counselors generally work with low and middle-income individuals and families. Financial planners commonly have more in-depth knowledge in areas such as investment management, tax planning, and retirement planning. Financial counselors usually have more in-depth knowledge in areas such as budgeting, student loan management, bankruptcy strategies, increasing creditworthiness, and housing issues. In general, financial therapists have more in-depth knowledge on how to help people understand why they make financial decisions, how to change financial behavior, and how to effectively communicate about money, as well as dealing with some topics addressed by financial planners and counselors. Maton, Maton, and Martin (2010) describe financial therapists as having an empathic and strong understanding of a client's needs and goals to ensure implementing optimal strategies needed to meet those objectives.

Because this emerging field of financial therapy is still in its infancy, some inconsistency or disagreement on the definition and conceptual understanding of the term *financial therapy* is understandable. The meaning of financial therapy is likely to evolve over time as the field develops a broader and deeper body of research literature. Some still debate the meaning of the term *financial planning* within this more established field. The widely applied word *therapy* refers to a treatment, especially of bodily, mental, or behavioral disorder. Financial therapy takes place when financial conversations or financial interventions are therapeutic to a client, particularly in terms of treating or improving an individual's or couple's suboptimal way of thinking around money or negative financial behaviors. The Financial Therapy Association (FTA) (Grable, McGill, and Britt 2010, p. 1) defines financial therapy within its purpose statement:

- *To share a vision of financial therapy—i.e., the integration of cognitive, emotional, behavioral, relational, and economic aspects that promote financial health.*
- *To provide a forum for researchers, practitioners, the media, and policy makers to share research and practice methods and models of financial therapy.*
- *To promote methods of training for those involved in financial therapy.*
- *To inform public policy and practice management standards as these relate to financial therapy.*
- *To stimulate and disseminate clinical, experimental, and survey research on financial therapy.*

FTA's definition of financial therapy is designed to be as inclusive as possible given its hopes to appeal to professionals and researchers from varying disciplines. The definition also emphasizes the interdisciplinary nature of the practice of financial therapy with the goal of increasing the financial health of individuals, couples, and families. Pairing *financial* with *therapy* reflects the need for therapeutic interventions and strategies to address suboptimal financial decision-making and maladaptive financial behavior. Professionals who work with individuals and families on personal finance issues understand the strong connections among money, emotions, and relationships. Financial therapy takes place when financial planners and mental health professionals implement therapeutic interventions that increase rational thinking around money or improve financial behaviors.

A professional financial planner or therapist engaging in financial therapy may focus on improving a person's money scripts or maladaptive beliefs and feelings toward money (Klontz, Kahler, and Klontz 2008). This may mean empowering individuals and couples to understand their conscious and unconscious emotional connection with money, money's effect on their lives, and the need to develop a financial plan for both short-term and long-term needs and goals. Financial therapy interventions may involve exploration into an individual's family financial socialization and the messages about money they received from their parents.

Unfortunately, most financial and mental health professionals do not receive education and training specific to the other's field of study (Dubofsky and Sussman 2009; Durband, Britt, and Grable 2010). Thus, either professional may have difficulty assisting clients with financial challenges that have an emotional or complex relational component, as described by Kim, Gale, Goetz, and Bermudez (2011, p. 230):

> *Couple and family therapists have expertise in helping clients with relationship issues while financial planners are experts in helping clients improve their financial literacy and money management. However, both service providers share challenges when client's relationship and financial needs are intertwined and knotted. Couple and family therapists are not trained to address client's specific financial difficulties, which can lead to missed opportunities for positive, relational change. Financial planners are not trained to attend to emotional, relational difficulties and dysfunctional communication patterns, which, in turn, can limit their success with clients.*

Aniol and Snyder (1997) posit that financial and mental health professionals should both develop expertise in the basics of the other's profession to more effectively assist clients presenting with concomitant financial and relational challenges. As previously stated, a professional practicing financial therapy is one who is intentional in addressing the cognitive, emotional, and relational factors in a way that increases a client's overall financial well-being.

BRIEF HISTORY OF FINANCIAL THERAPY

In 1970, the first professional association reflecting financial planning was formed. In contrast, the formation of the Financial Therapy Association (FTA) (FinanicalTherapyAssociation.org), the first professional association representing the field of financial therapy, occurred in 2009. Thus, only a few years have passed since a more structured system has been in place to encourage research, education, and practice in financial therapy. Grable, McGill, and Britt (2010) provide a brief history of the FTA.

Gale et al. (2012) outline the following 10 considerations for this new field to be successful:

1. Defining financial therapy and successful outcomes of financial therapy services.
2. Developing theoretical model(s) to explain and predict how people change behavior, cognition, and relationships within the context of financial therapy.
3. Identifying of the unit of service or treatment (e.g., individual, couple, family, or broader) in financial therapy.
4. Defining relationship dynamics and boundaries between professionals from different professions of practice, and between the professional and client when providing financial therapy services.
5. Developing a set of skills required to provide financial therapy services.
6. Developing assessment tools to determine when good work is achieved.
7. Ensuring knowledge expertise required to provide financial therapy services (e.g., credentialing or continuing education).
8. Acknowledging the responsibilities of the professional and client and developing a sensitivity to power dynamics.
9. Addressing cultural and spiritual diversity.
10. Adhering to a code of ethical behavior, professional standards, and best practices.

The FTA is currently involved in addressing each of these 10 considerations. Neither the FTA nor any other entity serves as a self-regulatory organization for the practice of financial therapy. No professional credentials or designations are specific to financial therapy. Although no regulation of the term *financial therapist* exists, an opportunity is available to create a type of credentialing process and designation for the practice of financial therapy in the future. Currently, professionals adhere to the legal and ethical requirements specific to their home disciplines when providing therapy services (e.g., requirements associated with the practice of financial planning, family therapy, counseling, social work, psychology, or coaching).

THEORETICAL FOUNDATIONS FOR FINANCIAL THERAPY

Establishing common theoretical underpinnings is integral to the development of a new field of study and practice. Archuleta and Grable (2010) emphasize the lack of a discipline-specific theoretical basis for financial planning-counseling-therapy, and provide summary descriptions of various potentially applicable approaches from other fields. This section provides a summary of specific frameworks and theories from the mental health fields that have either already been applied within a financial planning context or have potential future applications.

Theoretical orientations and approaches to work with clients mostly fall in one of three intrapsychic domains (i.e., cognition, affect, and behavior) or a systems domain (i.e., relational and family dynamics) (Meier and Davis 2013). *Cognitions* refer to the thoughts or patterns of thought that people have (e.g., "I'll start saving a few years from now, when I make more money" or "I'm terrible at managing my finances"). The concept of one's *affect* refers to emotion and how one's feelings and emotional states can influence perceptions and cognitions (e.g., hopelessness, frustration, and optimism). Actions people carry out refer to *behaviors,* such as setting up an automatic savings plan, tracking one's spending, or borrowing money. From an intrapsychic perspective, a person's internal cognitions and emotional states (as well as biological and neurological factors) determine behavior. *Systems* theory, while not denying that a person's biological and internal dynamics play a part, also attends to multiple environmental contexts (e.g., social, culture, family, historical, and economic) of the person, and how these contexts inform an individual's choices in making decisions.

Within the therapy and counseling professions, much disagreement exists over which domain should be the focus when working with clients. The financial planning profession traditionally focuses on the individual behavior domain. Yet, many financial planners would also likely acknowledge the importance of the other domains in terms of fully understanding their clients' goals and relationship with money. Although financial planners sometimes employ strategies based in the domains of affect, cognition, or family systems, they traditionally have not based their approaches within the context of more formalized and established theoretical perspectives. The emerging field of financial therapy is attempting to implement research and interventions based in theoretical perspectives from the field of family therapy and psychology. Financial planners and other financial service professionals who work directly with clients may benefit from developing familiarity with basic theory and the skills associated with multiple approaches. Within a financial planning context, many recognize effective communication as leading to greater client trust and commitment (Sharpe et al. 2007). Having a theory or conceptual framework provides a basis for structuring financial planners' communication, processes, and services.

The following section describes some common frameworks and theories that have been applied to the practice and research of financial therapy interventions. Given the broad and inclusive definition of financial therapy, a multitude of theories from varying fields could be applied to developing financially therapeutic interventions. Varying helping professions focus differently on aspects of individuals' behaviors, cognitions, emotions, relationships, and financial factors. For example, social workers applying financial therapy interventions may focus on cultural and social dynamics, whereas psychologists may concentrate on an individual's cognitions. As another example, a financial planner may focus on a client's financial needs less systemically than a family therapist. Compared to mental health professionals, financial planners may be more likely to use knowledge from the relatively new fields of behavioral economics and neuroeconomics (Goetz and James 2008). Each profession that engages in the study or practice of financial therapy has different theoretical foundations specific to its field. For this reason, a transtheoretical, integrative, or eclectic approach may make sense to some researchers and practitioners.

Integrative Therapy

Smith et al. (2012) suggest integration theory as a foundation for financial therapy practice. Integrative therapy is a client-centered approach that pulls from various theories and their associated therapeutic interventions depending on the presenting issues of the client (Scaturo 2005). Integrative theory recognizes that hundreds of theoretical orientations and therapies are available, and the optimal intervention may vary based on the presenting context and issues of a client.

Client-Centered Therapy

The client-centered theoretical perspective is based on the work of Carl Rogers (1990). Those practicing this approach communicate with their clients using warm, unconditional positive regard, genuineness, and empathy to help clients fully experience and understand their affect. The focus is centered on the individual and values the clients' ability to identify the most important issues affecting them and their ability to find solutions to successfully address those issues. Practitioners using a client-centered approach assume all clients are working to attain self-actualization, and therefore view their clients very positively. Using a client-centered approach may involve giving clients as much space and time as they need before addressing challenging issues, thereby maintaining a comfortable environment and sense of control for the client (Kinder and Galvin 2007).

Behavioral Therapy

The behavioral perspective assumes that if the client wants or needs to change behavior, then behavior should be the focus of the work (Wolpe 1990). Some therapists assume that clients' problems result from inappropriate learning and reinforcement for their problematic behaviors. For example, clients may have learned to mistrust banks, that credit cards allow them to buy whatever they want whenever they want, or that spending now is better because saving money is ineffective. The focus concerns modifying behaviors through behavioral contracts, positive and sometimes aversive reward systems, and rehearsing new behaviors, with less emphasis on cognitive processes. Financial therapy interventions based in the behavioral orientation might include the goals of changing spending or saving behaviors as well as investing behaviors. Another example of a behavioral goal is a couple meeting and discussing household finances once a week with a reward system in place to encourage that behavior.

Cognitive Therapy

The cognitive perspective assumes that a client's negative thoughts or schemas are a result of painful emotions from past experiences, which often lead to maladaptive behavior. For example, illogical reasoning, over-magnification of problems, overly selective attention to certain information, and irrational beliefs can lead to suboptimal behaviors and emotional states. The cognitive therapy approach is one of the most effective therapies for anxiety and obsessive-compulsive disorders (Sexton 1997). Thus, a financial therapy intervention based in a cognitive theoretical orientation may be particularly effective for client issues such as problem gambling or spending disorders. A combined cognitive and behavioral based financial therapy intervention may involve changing the negative belief a client has about his ability to manage his finances or calibrating a client's expectations when carrying out certain behaviors.

Family Systems Therapy

Unlike other approaches that focus either exclusively or predominantly on the processes within the individual as the core mechanism for change, the family systems perspective assumes the social systems influence on clients should be the focus of client work (Becvar and Becvar 2009). Financial therapy interventions based in family systems theory focus on the relational dynamics and elements of communication between family members. How the family interacts and communicates within its environmental context affects the behavior, thoughts, and feelings of each person within that system. Family systems theoretical perspective applies well to the practice of financial therapy for a family business or dealing with the complexities of intergenerational planning for a family with multiple generations who may have different values and goals. Varying family therapy models provide a different emphasis on such issues as family history, family structure, emotions, and narratives.

Solution-Focused Therapy

Solution-focused therapy is practice with an emphasis on a client's strengths and goals, and a belief that a client already has the resources he or she needs to change (O'Connell 2005). The focus on current and future goals coincides well with the traditional goals-based financial planning process, and thus may feel more natural to financial planning practitioners implementing financial therapy interventions. Rather than focusing on clients' problems, common solution-focused interventions involve a client increasing behaviors that are already working and doing less of what is not working. The therapist tries to clearly and descriptively identify small goals and client motivation, and reinforces hope through incrementally achieving these objectives. Rather than focusing on the past issues or problems, a financial therapist using a solution-focused perspective might ask a client to clearly articulate his intended outcomes through the financial therapy process, and then use that information in co-developing each step necessary to achieve those goals.

Behavioral Finance-Based Cognitive-Behavioral Therapy

A cognitive-behavioral approach based in knowledge from the field of behavioral finance assumes clients can make more rational choices and improve their financial well-being through increasing awareness of their own cognitive and emotional money biases and implementing behaviors that compensate for these biases. For example, having a client respond to questions used in behavioral economic experiments can illustrate to clients their natural tendencies toward using heuristics (i.e., mental shortcuts) and mental accounting. Once clients have an increased awareness of their biases such as mental accounting, overconfidence bias, and sunk cost fallacy, leading to potentially suboptimal decisions, the financial therapist can begin implementing financial planning strategies with client buy-in to limit the effect of these biases.

For example, a therapist or planner might develop multiple savings accounts associated with different goals to yield positive effects from mental accounting (i.e., individuals tend to consider their accounts separately rather than jointly). A therapist or planner may work with a client to set up an automated or auto-escalating savings plan through his employer, online savings account, or discount brokerage company. In response to an overconfidence bias (i.e., tendency of individuals to be more confident than is objectively reasonable given their skills or abilities) and using a behavioral perspective, a planner might implement a financial therapy intervention wherein a client agrees to carefully record each of his investment decisions and continues to review the performance of not only the new security held but also of the security sold that led to the new position. This approach also assumes the behavioral change can occur when a client is able to intellectualize his tendencies toward cognitive biases. In other words, helping a client understand the time value of money and power of compounding interest may increase savings behavior or a client who is aware of the sunk cost fallacy might think twice before spending more money on car repairs (or a particular investment) simply because he previously invested money on repairs for that same car.

The *sunk cost fallacy* refers to situations wherein individuals irrationally consider sunk costs (i.e., past expenditures that cannot be recovered) when making decisions, rather than using a purely rational economic perspective and considering only the future variable costs. By helping a client understand the sunk cost fallacy, the sunk cost should have no (or at least less) effect on the more rational client's best choice. This approach assumes a process of de-biasing (i.e., the process or methods for overcoming bias or behaviors) can take place through cognitive-behavioral interventions that allow clients to make better financial decisions.

Although in-depth description of the myriad theoretical perspectives that may be applied to financial therapy practice is beyond the scope of this chapter, many resources exist that elaborate on these theories (Ivey 2002; Hutchinson 2011; Smith et al. 2012). Theories and conceptual models are valuable in that they inform financial therapy practice and the research process. Different models can provide varying perspectives on individual and relational change. For example, some theories and models are attentive to how others (e.g., friends, partner, and parents) influence an individual's perceptions and actions while other models focus predominantly on an individual's cognitions, behaviors, and mental health. Since financial therapy stems from multidisciplinary perspectives, practitioners may use theories and models specific to different disciplinary frameworks in developing and applying financial therapy interventions.

The new field of financial therapy should consider adopting theories and models that examine how an individual's financial behaviors are shaped and changed. Taking the following actions could be useful in identifying appropriate theoretical underpinnings for financial therapy: (1) identifying theories or models that inform the professional practice of financial planners and mental health professionals, (2) exploring theories applied to collaborative professions, (3) considering theories that focus on change, and (4) investigating the potential for new or integrated theory. Broad theoretical perspectives may also prove informative, such as social constructivist theory, the biopsychosocial perspective (Engel 1977), social learning theory, or ecosystems theory (Auerswald 1968, 1972). Gale et al. (2012, p. 7) suggest the following:

> To obtain a better understanding of the processes and outcomes of financial therapy, it may be helpful to examine the commonalities (rather than potential differences) across the multiple disciplines and areas of practice already informing this relatively new interdisciplinary area of interest. For example, the concept of a service provider-client working alliance, or the strength of the bond and level of agreement between tasks and goals by the service provider and client, is recognized across many professions and would also likely be a core concept to the practice of financial therapy. The importance of factors associated with one's family socialization, such as gender scripts or money scripts, is also recognized across multiple disciplines and areas of practice. Additional factors relevant in informing practitioners in what they attend to in their practice that have potential to be agreed upon across multiple professions include: (a) issues of resiliency and a strengths-based model of human behavior versus a psychopathology-based approach; (b) sensitivity and attention towards the influence of race, culture, ethnicity, gender, and relational power dynamics; and (c) an appreciation of relational patterns (generational and interpersonal) that influence individual behaviors.

Researchers consistently find that a positive working alliance is one of the most powerful predictors of achieving a client's goals (Horvath and Symonds 1991; Martin, Garske, and Davis 2000). Thus, a focus on the factors associated with building a strong working alliance with clients within the context of financial therapy may be extremely helpful to the development of this new field.

Archuleta et al. (2012) conduct a qualitative analysis involving 18 professionals engaged in some form of financial therapy in one of the first attempts to generate a theoretical framework for financial therapy. The authors find that integration, or the intersection of personal, relational, and money issues, is central to the framework.

The importance of the service provider-client relationship, process of assessment, and process of reaching a goal is also central to their conceptual model. Archuleta et al. (p. 73) present the following nine hypotheses that may inform the development of best practices in financial therapy:

1. Integration of cognition, behavior, emotion, relationship, and finances is central to the mechanisms and aspects of financial therapy.
2. Money and intrapersonal and interpersonal aspects of one's life are inseparable.
3. Within the financial therapy process, the help seeker and helper relationship is positively associated with help-seeker outcomes.
4. Financial therapy is complex.
5. Helpers must maintain appropriate boundaries and clear expectations and roles with help seekers, collaborators, and themselves.
6. Cross-discipline integration and collaboration is positively associated with help-seeker outcomes.
7. Multiple implementation methods, approaches, and tools are associated with positive help-seeker outcomes.
8. Assessment of help-seeker readiness is positively associated with help-seeker outcomes.
9. Specialized training, education, and understanding of professional roles and boundaries are necessary to implement a financial therapy.

THE PRACTICE OF FINANCIAL THERAPY

Financial therapy assumes that while childhood experiences around money can have powerful effects on financial thinking and behavior, financial cognitions and behaviors can be changed. Financial therapy is also based in the assumption that emotional and cognitive biases, emotional triggers from previous experiences, and relational factors can negatively impact financial decisions and that financial decisions can negatively affect relationships. Financial therapy interventions may be designed to empower individuals or couples to overcome financial challenges and effectively communicate about finances with their partners or other members of their family (Ford, Baptist, and Archuleta 2011). Financial planners and therapists can facilitate clients' understanding their conscious and unconscious feelings and behaviors around money. When working with couples, a financial planner can facilitate the development of empathy between each member of a couple regarding the feelings and behaviors around money. Financial therapy interventions that increase understanding and empathy may include examining an individual's or couple's personal finance patterns, such as tracking spending behavior and the emotions being experienced when spending money. Organizing financial documents and developing written, prioritized financial goals can be therapeutic. Only a few resources currently exist specific to integrating financial decisions and the psychological (emotional, cognitive, and neurological) elements affecting those decisions (Klontz et al. 2008, Klontz and Klontz 2009, Smith et al. 2012).

Financial therapy in practice occurs most often with either low-income families or very high-income families. For example, a financial planner, when working with an ultra-high net-worth family, may ask a family therapist or financial psychologist to assist with determining the optimal methods of intergenerational transfer of wealth such that this transfer does not negatively affect the development of younger members of the family. Individuals and families currently struggling to cover the cost of even basic needs such as housing and food may also need help. A professional providing financial therapy services might address relational issues while also addressing financial strategies for survival (e.g., government assistance programs and community food banks).

Only two studies specifically examine the effectiveness of financial therapy (Kim et al. 2011; Klontz et al. 2008). Both indicated positive outcomes, but further research needs to be conducted to establish the various potential outcomes of financial therapy. For example, possible outcomes of financial therapy may include increased economic stability, decreased financial stress, having a financial plan, reduced debt, increased financial self-confidence, increased relational stability in the family, and increased overall well-being. Financial health does not necessarily increase with additional resources. However, two important objective assessments specific to overall financial well-being are increases in savings and investments or decreases in high-interest debt. Numerous psychometrically validated scales exist to assess changes in financial attitudes, behaviors, stress, and overall well-being (Grable, Archuleta, and Nazarinia 2010).

The required skill sets and knowledge base to be qualified to practice financial therapy have not been well defined. Traditional financial planning programs and family therapy programs foster knowledge and skill sets that are quite different. Given that some professionals have completed training in both the areas of personal finance and psychology, these individuals may be particularly skilled in financial therapy applications and evaluations. As the field of financial therapy develops, the skill sets required to carry out financial therapy interventions will likely become more defined. As the University of Georgia and Kansas State University develop evidence-based models for this interdisciplinary work and financial therapy interventions, other family therapy and financial planning training programs may integrate components of financial therapy training into their curricula.

Currently, the various professionals who are implementing financial therapy into their client work are following different ethical frameworks. For example, mental health professions adhere to definitive rules against dual roles, while most financial planners encourage dual relationships with clients. Further discussion will need to take place about professional boundaries as well as ethical guidelines and standards of practice for financial therapy. Gale et al. (2012, p. 9) emphasize this issue:

The inherent intricacy of relationship dynamics and boundaries is compounded when two professionals from different disciplines or practice areas are working in tandem with a client. For example, a financial planner and therapist providing co-counseling to a couple in financial distress may wonder if each professional needs only to adhere to their own respective professional standards or whether issues of confidentiality and dual roles should rise to the highest common denominator (i.e., to whichever profession has the highest, most conservative, professional standards). There may be unintended consequences to more conservative standards imposed on certain types of service providers. Perhaps there are multiple strategies equally effective for the client when it comes to professional boundaries, with the only common denominator being full disclosure of those boundaries to the client.

Although financial planners may be skilled at investment management and retirement planning, they often lack the knowledge and skills to optimally address the emotional side of money, such as when family conflict occurs when discussing finances. While family therapists, psychologists, and professional counselors are skilled at assisting clients with communication and relationship issues, these professionals typically lack the knowledge and skills required to address financial difficulties that individuals, couples, and families may be facing. A therapist who fully addresses issues of financial well-being with her clients is an exception to the rule. Relatively few examples are available in which family therapists address financial challenges or collaborate with financial planners. However, the opportunities for collaborative practice of financial therapy are clear given the different skill sets of traditional financial planners and family therapists or psychotherapists. Considering the following four distinct models of collaboration between a financial and mental health professional is important: (1) referral, (2) parallel, (3) consultative, and (4) integrative.

- **Referral framework.** The professional referral framework involves identifying when a client could benefit from the other service and facilitating or encouraging that engagement. Many consider this approach to be the least collaborative framework between the mental health and financial professional. Based on a relatively simple assessment, each professional can evaluate whether his client could benefit from the other's services and integrate a referral mechanism into the standard process.
- **Parallel framework.** The parallel framework for collaboration between professionals involves the financial planner and therapist both working with the same client at different times but communicating about interventions and the client's progress toward common goals. This approach requires a shared paradigm of when and how to intervene.
- **Consultative framework.** The consultative framework involves either the therapist or planner inviting the other practitioner to join occasional meetings to help address a specific concern or issue. The consultation occurs on an as-needed approach and can address important issues on a one-time basis. Parallel services may arise out of this approach. This collaboration model also requires a shared paradigm of when and how to intervene, good communication, and common goals to work toward.
- **Integrative framework.** The integrative framework involves the client and two practitioners working together in the same room. This planner-therapist collaboration includes aspects of parallel and consultative collaboration as it provides an integrative and systemic collaboration. This model may have efficiencies as both in-depth financial and relational issues can be addressed in the same meeting, but does require strong agreement between the financial planner and therapist on the tasks and goals of each session.

As just described, financial planners can collaborate with family therapists using different strategic models. Therapists and planners could simply create a cross-referral network or serve in a consultative role but not meeting at the same with the client (Falconier and Epstein 2011) or by participating in a client session only when the need arises. Kahler (2005) suggests the most beneficial model is two professionals from the different disciplines working side-by-side to assist clients with both relational and financial problems. Due to different regulatory requirements, professionals across disciplines may disagree on the optimal delivery model for therapeutic work regarding an individual's or couple's financial well-being. To date, only one study examines the effectiveness of experts from the financial planning and family therapy field working collaboratively to extend financial therapy services (Gale, Goetz, and Bermudez 2009; Kim et al. 2011). A subset of individual financial planners and therapists has developed skills and knowledge in the other's field to make financial therapy a focus of their practice. However, this model involves high training and education costs.

FUTURE RESEARCH AND PRACTICE

Practitioners and researchers of financial therapy should consider how cultural and historical contexts as well as religion affect the financial well-being of individuals, couples, and families. Individuals within the same family form and influence each other's values, perceptions, and behaviors. Both a person's family and culture of origin affect an individual's values. Skills in financial management are, for the most part, learned behaviors that are strongly influenced by an individual's values and attitudes toward money that may be formed early in life from within various systems. Future research is needed to understand how attitudes toward money and maladaptive money behaviors are formed.

Some consider money the last taboo, referring to the personal nature of openly discussing one's income and expenses. Given the high amount of concurrent financial and relational dysfunction within families, a need exists for practitioners to develop financial therapy interventions and for researchers to conduct clinical and experimental research to test the effectiveness of interventions. The financial planning and mental health professions require more evidence-based financial therapy interventions to support their work with clients. Models of collaboration also need to be further tested. The development of assessment tools and techniques based in theory as well as empirical results from clinical research can support an important evolution of the financial planning, counseling, and therapy fields.

SUMMARY

Financial therapy, as compared to classical economics or the traditional practice of financial planning, takes a more psychological and relational perspective in understanding financial behavior and in providing financial recommendations and education. Over the past decade, the interest in financial planning, literacy, and behavior has increased and emphasized the need to educate and serve individuals across their life span to be financially capable and secure. Defining financial therapy as an interdisciplinary field of study means that research and practice can be conducted from multiple discipline perspectives to best determine how to increase the financial capabilities and security of individuals and families. Empirically supported research that informs practice and policy is a prerequisite for the advancement of the emerging field of financial therapy.

A person's financial, personal, and relational well-being are all interconnected. Therefore, changes in financial position can affect a person's cognitive and emotional state of being. Also, one's emotional and cognitive state of being can influence financial behavior and decision-making. All this is embedded within social and cultural contexts. Financial therapy is a recent development to address the complexity of human behavior to help individuals, couples, and families make optimal financial choices in their lives.

DISCUSSION QUESTIONS

1. Describe the primary differences among the concepts and practice of financial planning, financial counseling, and financial therapy.
2. Explain the need for a new field of financial therapy.
3. Describe the four models of professional collaboration in providing financial therapy services.
4. Discuss whether clear evidence exists as to which theoretical or conceptual approach to financial therapy is likely to be most effective.
5. Describe two opportunities for future research in the field of financial therapy.

REFERENCES

Aniol, Julie C., and Douglas K. Synder. 1997. "Differential Assessment of Financial and Relationship Distress: Implications for Couples Therapy." *Journal of Marital and Family Therapy* 23:3, 347–352.

Archuleta, Kristy L., Emily A. Burr, Anita K. Dale, Anthony Canale, Dan Danford, Erika Rasure, Jeff Nelson, Kelley Williams, Kurt Schindler, Brett Coffman, and Ed Horwitz. 2012. "What Is Financial Therapy? Discovering Mechanisms and Aspects of an Emerging Field." *Journal of Financial Therapy* 3:2, 57–77.

Archuleta, Kristy L., and John E. Grable. 2010. "The Future of Financial Planning and Counseling: An Introduction to Financial Therapy." In John E. Grable, Kristy L. Archuleta, and R. Roudi Nazarinia, eds., *Financial Planning and Counseling Scales*, 33–59. New York: Springer.

Auerswald, Edgar H. 1968. "Interdisciplinary versus Ecological Approach." *Family Process* 68:7, 202–215.

Auerswald, Edgar H. 1972. "Families, Change, and the Ecological Perspective." *Family Process* 10:3, 263–280.

Baum, Andrew, and Donna M. Posluszny. 1999. "Health Psychology: Mapping Biobehavioral Contributions to Health and Illness." *Annual Review of Psychology* 50:1, 137–163.

Becvar, Dorothy S., and Raphael. J. Becvar. 2009. *Family Therapy: A Systemic Integration*, 7th ed. Boston, MA: Allyn & Bacon.

Blumstein, Philip, and Pepper Schwartz. 1983. *American Couples: Money, Work, Sex*. New York: Morrow.

Conger, Rand D., and M. Brent Donnellan. 2007. "An Interactionist Perspective on the Socioeconomic Context of Human Development." *Annual Review of Psychology* 58, 175–199.

Dew, Jeffrey, and John Dakin. 2011. "Financial Disagreements and Marital Conflict Tactics. *Journal of Financial Therapy* 2:1, 23–42.

Dubofsky, David, and Lyle Sussman. 2009. "The Changing Role of the Financial Planner Part 1: From Financial Analytics to Coaching and Life Planning." *Journal of Financial Planning* 22:8, 48–57.

Durband, Dorothy B., Sonya L. Britt, and John E. Grable. 2010. "Personal and Family Finance in the Marriage and Family Therapy Domain." *Journal of Financial Therapy* 1:1, 7–22.

Elder, Glen H. Jr., Tri Van Nguyen, and Avshalom Caspi. 1985. "Linking Family Hardship to Children's Lives." *Child Development* 56:2, 361–375.

Engel, George L. 1977. "The Need for a New Medical Model: A Challenge for Biomedicine. *Science* 196:4286, 129–136.

Falconier, Mariana K., and Norman B. Epstein. 2011. "Couples Experiencing Financial Strain: What We Know and What We Can Do." *Family Relations* 60:3, 303–317.

Ford, Megan R., Joyce A. Baptist, and Kristy L. Archuleta. 2011. "A Theoretical Approach to Financial Therapy: The Development of the Ford Financial Empowerment Model." *Journal of Financial Therapy* 2:2, 20–40.

Gale, Jerry E., Joseph Goetz, and Maria Bermudez. 2009. "Relational Financial Therapy." *Family Therapy Magazine* 8:5, 25–30.

Gale, Jerry E., Joseph Goetz, and Sonya Britt. 2012. "Ten Considerations in the Development of the Financial Therapy Profession." *Journal of Financial Therapy* 3:2, 1–13.

Goetz, Joseph, and Russell James. 2008. "Human Choice and the Emerging Field of Neuroeconomics: A Review of Brain Science for the Financial Planner." *Journal of Personal Finance* 6:2, 13–36.

Grable, John E., Kristy L. Archuleta, and R. Roudi Nazarinia. 2010. *Financial Planning and Counseling Scales*. New York: Springer.

Grable, John, Samantha McGill, and Sonya Britt. 2010. "The Financial Therapy Association: A Brief History." *Journal of Financial Therapy* 1:1, 1–6.

Gudmunson, Clinton G., Ivan F. Beutler, Craig L. Israelsen, J. Kelly McCoy, and E. Jeffrey Hill. 2007. "Linking Financial Strain to Marital Instability: Examining the Roles of Emotional Distress and Marital Interaction." *Journal of Family and Economic Issues* 28:3, 357–376.

Horvath, Adam O., and B. Dianne Symonds. 1991. "Relation between Working Alliance and Outcome in Psychotherapy: A Meta-Analysis." *Journal of Counseling Psychology* 38:2, 139–149.

Hutchinson, David. 2011. *The Essential Counselor: Process, Skills, and Techniques*. Boston, MA: Houghton Mifflin.

Ivey, Allen. 2002. *Intentional Interviewing and Counseling*, 4th ed. Pacific Grove, CA: Brooks/ Cole.

Kahler, Rick S. 2005. "Financial Integration: Connecting the Client's Past, Present, and Future." *Journal of Financial Planning* 18:5, 62–71.

Kerkmann, Barbara C., Thomas R. Lee, Jean M. Lown, and Scot M. Allgood. 2000. "Financial Management, Financial Problems and Marital Satisfaction among Recently Married University Students." *Financial Counseling and Planning* 11:2, 55–65.

Kim, Ji-Hyun, Jerry Gale, Joseph Goetz, and Maria Bermudez. 2011. "Relational Financial Therapy: An Innovative and Collaborative Treatment Approach." *Contemporary Family Therapy* 33:3, 229–241.

Kinder, George, and Susan Galvan. 2007. "Psychology and Life Planning." *Journal of Financial Planning* 20:3, 58–66.

Klontz, Bradley T., Alex Bivens, Paul T. Klontz, Joni Wada, and Richard Kahler. 2008. "The Treatment of Disordered Money Behaviors: Results of an Open Clinical Trial." *Psychological Services* 5:3, 295–308.

Klontz, Bradley T., Rick Kahler, and Paul T. Klontz. 2008. *Facilitating Financial Health: Tools for Financial Planners, Coaches, and Therapists*. Erlanger, KY: National Underwriter Company.

Klontz, Bradley T., and Paul T. Klontz. 2009. *Mind Over Money: Overcoming the Money Disorders That Threaten Our Financial Health*. New York: Crown Business.

Locke, Harvey J., and Karl M. Wallace. 1959. "Short Marital-Adjustment and Prediction Tests: Their Reliability and Validity." *Marriage and Family Living* 21:3, 251–255.

Marmot, Michael. 2005. "Social Determinants of Health Inequalities." *Lancet* 365:9464, 1099–1104.

Martin, Daniel J., John P. Garske, and M. Katherine Davis. 2000. "Relation of the Therapeutic Alliance with Outcome and Other Variables: A Meta-Analytic Review." *Journal of Consulting and Clinical Psychology* 68:3, 438–450.

Maton, Cicily Carson, Michelle Maton, and William Marty Martin. 2010. "Collaborating with a Financial Therapist: The Why, Who, What and How." *Journal of Financial Planning* 23:2, 62–70.

McDaniel, Susan H., Jeri Hepworth, and William J. Doherty. 1992. *Medical Family Therapy: A Biopsychosocial Approach to Families with Health Problems*. New York: Basic Books.

Meier, Scott T., and Susan R. Davis. 2013. *The Elements of Counseling*. Independence, KY: Cengage Learning.

Miller, Richard B., Jeremy B. Yorgason, Jonathan G. Sandberg, and Mark B. White. 2003. "Problems that Couples Bring to Therapy: A View Across the Family Life Cycle." *American Journal of Family Therapy* 31:5, 395–407.

O'Connell, Bill. 2005. *Solution-Focused Therapy*, 3rd ed. London: Sage.

Papp, Lauren M., E. Mark Cummings, and Marcie C. Goeke-Morey. 2009. "For Richer, For Poorer: Money as a Topic of Marital Conflict in the Home." *Family Relations* 58:1, 91–103.

Rogers, Carl. 1990. *Client-Centered Therapy*. Boston, MA: Houghton Mifflin.

Scaramella, Laura V., Tricia K. Neppl, Lenna L. Ontai, and Rand D. Conger. 2008. "Consequences of Socioeconomic Disadvantage Across Three Generations: Parenting Behavior and Child Externalizing Problems." *Journal of Family Psychology* 22:5, 725–733.

Scaturo, Douglas J. 2005. *Clinical Dilemmas in Psychotherapy: A Transtheoretical Approach to Psychotherapy Integration*. Washington, DC: American Psychological Association.

Sexton, Thomas L. 1997. *Integrating Outcome Research into Counseling Practice and Training*. Alexandria, VA: American Counseling Association.

Sharpe, Deanna L., Carol Anderson, Andrea White, Susan Galvan, and Martin Siesta. 2007. "Specific Elements of Communication That Affect Trust and Commitment in the Financial Planning Process." *Financial Counseling and Planning* 18:1, 2–17.

Skinner, Michelle A., Alex J. Zautra, and John W. Reich. 2004. "Financial Stress Predictors and the Emotional and Physical Health of Chronic Pain Patients." *Cognitive Therapy and Research* 28:5, 695–713.

Skogrand, Linda M., David G. Schramm, James P. Marshall, and Thomas R. Lee. 2005. "The Effects of Debt on Newlyweds and Implications for Education." *Journal of Extension* 43:3, 1–8.

Smith, Thomas M., Rebekah J. Nelson, Kristin V. Richards, and Victoria M. Shelton. 2012. *Financial Therapy: 5 Steps toward Financial Freedom*. Tallahassee, FL: Southeastern Professional Books.

Spanier, Graham B. 1976. "Measuring Dyadic Adjustment: New Scales for Assessing the Quality of Marriage and Similar Dyads." *Journal of Marriage and the Family* 38:1, 15–28.

Stolz, Richard F. 2009. "When Couples Clash over Finances." *Journal of Financial Planning,* 22:7, 20–25.

Wolpe, Joseph. 1990. *The Practice of Behavior Therapy*, 4th ed. New York: Pergamon Press.

ABOUT THE AUTHORS

Joseph W. Goetz is an Associate Professor of Financial Planning in the CFP Board-registered degree programs at the University of Georgia where he cofounded the ASPIRE Clinic. His research interests include financial planning, financial therapy, and the fiduciary standard. He serves on the editorial boards of the *Journal of Financial*

Therapy, Journal of Financial Counseling and Planning, Journal of Personal Finance, and *Journal of Financial Planning.* He is the 2013 president of the Financial Therapy Association. He was the recipient of the 2007 Robert O. Herrmann PhD Dissertation Award from the American Council on Consumer Interests and 2012 Richard B. Russell Excellence in Teaching Award. He is a founding principal at Elwood & Goetz Wealth Advisory Group, a fee-only financial planning and investment management firm. Professor Goetz received his undergraduate degree in psychology from the University of Missouri-Columbia and a master's degree in counseling and a PhD in financial planning from Texas Tech University.

Jerry E. Gale is Associate Professor of Marriage and Family Therapy in the Department of Human Development and Family Science at The University of Georgia. He is the director of the Accredited Family Therapy Doctoral Program. He has written three books and has more than 75 publications. Professor Gale has presented nationally and internationally and received the American Family Therapy Academy Outstanding Research Contribution Award. He is on the editorial board of the *Journal of Financial Therapy* and cochaired the 2nd Annual Financial Therapy Conference in 2011. He is cofounder of the ASPIRE Clinic. His research interests include financial therapy, discourse analysis of clinical talk, and using meditation with couples and families. Professor Gale received his undergraduate degree in psychology from the University of Michigan, a master's degree in counseling from University of Arizona, and a PhD in marriage and family therapy from Texas Tech University.

CHAPTER 14

Transpersonal Economics

Renée M. Snow CFP®
Adjunct Professor, Sofia University

INTRODUCTION

Today the world is struggling to emerge from the worst recession since the Great Depression. The global economic crisis began in the United States after authorities relaxed banking regulations and a new industry based on a culture of achieving wealth quickly became the norm. This new financial culture affected many people including homeowners who began to view their primary residences as investments and mortgage bankers who offered complicated loans to unsophisticated borrowers. The aspiration led investment bankers to bundle these loans and offer them to investors. This culture of getting rich quickly also moved investors, including those abroad, to believe these mortgage pools would make them a fortune. Blinded by avarice and ignoring the economic truth that securities, like planets, move in cycles, those involved depended on a continuous rise in real estate prices. This is also the typical behavior people exhibit in times of market bubbles and manias. When the natural law reasserted itself, some of the largest, most established investment companies and banks, as well as millions of homeowners, experienced financial ruin. The carnage spread to industries and people not directly involved including manufacturing industries in countries outside the United States dependent on Americans' consumerism and materialism.

Globalization brought by improvements in technology and transportation calls extreme individualism into question. As with other types of disasters, some people are reassessing what is truly important in their lives. Viewed from another perspective, the financial crisis may represent an opportunity for Westerners to learn interdependence and to examine their long-held wealth paradigms. Individuals and businesses currently face some of the greatest challenges in decades that largely resulted from irrational, emotion-based choices rather than ignorance. People made these choices in spite of increased access to financial information, education, and counseling. The downturn was not a market failure of equal access to information; instead, it was caused by emotions, beliefs, and false self-identification with wealth.

Techniques and skills unique to transpersonal psychology are especially suited to examine the spiritual, cultural, and personal worldviews that contributed to the economic downturn. The term *transpersonal* comes from the Latin words trans and personal (Braud and Anderson 1998). *Trans* means beyond or through and *personal* refers to the mask or façade presented to the world. Transpersonal psychology questions the sense of self, the Freudian ego, with the intent of transcending this limiting concept to give a broader sense of life meaning and purpose. Given transpersonal psychology's objective, for purposes of this chapter, *transpersonal economics* refers to the identification, meaning, and purpose underlying resource management in an economic setting. As ancient philosophers have understood, issues pertaining to identity, life meaning, and purpose are necessarily spiritual. Due mostly to the advent of modernity, evoking the notion of spirituality as a construct directly relevant to the nature of economics holds the potential to become a stumbling block. People often view spirituality and religion as inseparable. However, while spirituality may well be what all religions have in common, spirituality is not dependent on religion. According to Maslow (1971), there is no way to avoid such concepts as soul, heart, intuition, instincts, a calling, or spirituality when discussing the full actualization of human potential. His ideas apply equally to the actualization of our economic potential. For example, Maslow's ideas on meta-motivation can be applied by investors and consumers to help identify investing and spending opportunities that align with their highest goals.

Instead, current American business practices support the claim made by Austrian psychiatrist Frankl (1959), a founder of transpersonal psychology, that without a transcendent life purpose humans will grasp for pleasure and avoid pain. Like existentialists before him, Frankl thought that to live is to suffer. The key to survival is to find meaning in the suffering. In fact, as opposed to the Freudian view that humankind's primary motivation is to seek pleasure or avoid pain, Frankl's Logotherapy, a precursor to transpersonal therapy, rests on the premise that a person's primary motivation is the "will to meaning" (Frankl 1959, p. 113). As Frankl (p. 104) states:

> *That is why I speak of a will to meaning in contrast to the pleasure principle (or, as we could also term it, the will to pleasure) on which Freudian psychoanalysis is centered, as well as in contrast to the will to power on which Adlerian psychology, using the term "striving for superiority," is focused.*

In short, transpersonal psychology is unique in its ability to explore life's meaning, purpose, and self-identity. While the Freudian belief that humankind's primary motivation to seek pleasure and avoid pain supports the neoclassical economic model of utility maximization and incentive rewards, Frankl and other transpersonal thinkers hold the hope that humanity can move beyond these short-term urges to deeper ontological space.

People form their beliefs about money through personal interaction with the world, cultural norms, and transpersonal paradigms that provide identity and life meaning. These beliefs can be both unconscious and conscious. The personal, cultural, and transpersonal domains give rise to belief systems, or what psychologists call *construct systems*. In turn, beliefs lead to thoughts, thoughts to emotions, and emotions to behavior.

As an illustration, assume a Western-based financial planner personally views money as a symbol of power and finds evidence to support this view both within the industry culture and society at large. Furthermore, the Adlerian view is substantiated transpersonally, as the planner also identifies with wealth, "I am my net worth," and achieving wealth becomes the planner's life purpose. The three domains—personal,

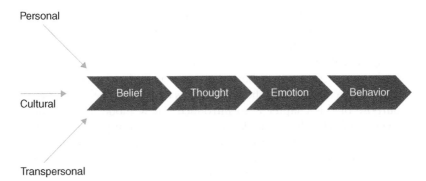

EXHIBIT 14.1 Transpersonal Realm to Behavior Diagram

Note: This diagram shows how personal, cultural, and transpersonal realms comprise beliefs that generate thoughts leading to emotions that provoke behavior.

cultural, and transpersonal—flow into the planner's belief system. Suppose suddenly, the S&P 500 drops by 30 percent and the planner makes a cognitive appraisal of the decline by thinking, "The S&P 500 has fallen by 30 percent and I am ruined." The thought about being ruined leads to emotions of panic and despair that guide the ultimate behavior of selling near the bottom of a market correction. This illustration reveals the power of transpersonal economics.

The planner's transpersonal paradigm that aligned life purpose and identity to wealth partially created a belief system that resulted in irrational behavior. The goal of transpersonal economics would be to uncover and reassess the paradigm at the root of the behavior. Instead, most psychological treatments aimed at treating money pathology are cognitive-behavioral in orientation and stop short of addressing transpersonal issues (Klontz and Britt 2012). Exhibit 14.1 displays a common path for financial decision-making and shows how the personal, cultural, and transpersonal realms relate to behavior.

Recently, neuroscience has supported the position of transpersonal psychologists that personal identity affects behavior. Standard (traditional) finance constructed systematic and rigorous frameworks around the fallacious notion that humans behave rationally (Hausman 2008). Later, behavioral economics studied what some believed to be "anomalous departures" from rationality and arrived at a long list of emotionally based judgments that do not lend themselves to the classical model of financial decision-making (Damasio 1994; Camerer and Loewenstein 2004). Given the brain studies that reveal humans have evolved a triune brain, these anomalous departures may actually be predictable and normal responses to a threat to self or identity. The studies show that rationality arises from the most recent portion of the brain, called the frontal cortex (Kolb and Whishaw 1990). The frontal cortex, which is not very developed at birth, is open to being shaped by life experience (Siegel 2007). This plasticity accounts for the wide variation in humans' ability to plan, display mindfulness, and behave rationally. As Siegel notes, the limbic region of the human brain, which all mammals share, evolved before the frontal cortex and is involved in creating attachment, affect, and inner sensations of emotion.

For example, research in neuroscience reveals when the self is threatened, the limbic system reacts automatically for self-preservation. When the self is defined by a status function such as money, the limbic system, sensing a threat to life, overrides the system, drowning out calls for mindfulness from the frontal cortex. Thus, supporting the transpersonal claim, neuroscience shows how false identification and attachment to wealth contributes to the irrational behavior that is the focus of behavioral economics.

The purpose of this chapter is to introduce a new model for examining economic management. The chapter makes explicit the Western personal, cultural, and transpersonal construct systems that comprise common beliefs. From this standpoint, the chapter offers an alternative paradigm for wealth creation based on the notion of transpersonal economics to mitigate the ecological damage brought by unrestrained capitalism. A corporate example from the alternative paradigm displays how revenue and transpersonal awareness can coexist. Finally, elements of this alternative paradigm are incorporated into the financial planning process to reveal a conscious method for interacting in the financial services industry.

The remainder of the chapter is organized into four main sections. The first section provides a historical and spiritual overview of money, introduces a model for understanding the relationship between the economy and ecology, and explores economic imbalances and time dimensions. The second section reveals the major components of the Western wealth paradigm. The third section offers an alternative perspective for wealth creation from the Jain community and shows how a transnational corporation currently employs this method. The final section illustrates how elements from the alternative perspective translate into financial planning.

HISTORICAL AND SPIRITUAL OVERVIEW OF MONEY

An initial step to uncover the purpose and meaning of money is to provide a historical account of the origins of money and wealth across several cultures, revealing the units of exchange and their significance. Human beings form concepts of reality through history. Those most ignorant of history are most controlled by it as they are the least likely to understand the sources of their beliefs. They are most likely to confuse their inherited prejudices with ultimate truth (Allison 1995). Therefore, understanding money's history and cultural context is necessary to appreciate the current financial situation and question predominant beliefs.

World History of Money

The origin of money stems from satisfying several non-economic needs. The first form of money was most likely the family meal (Desmonde 1962). In this exchange, food and community were the rewards for fulfilling familial duties. Failures to fulfill these obligations often meant the community would ostracize the useless member and thereby cause death by starvation. Between 9,000 and 6,000 BCE, people used livestock, particularly cattle, as money in many different societies (Davies and Davies 1996). The domestication of animals preceded agriculture; using cattle as a medium of exchange was already in place by the time crops were cultivated. Using cattle as money was so pervasive that several modern terms pertaining to monetary matters originate from using cattle as a unit of value. For example, the term *fee* is derived from the Gothic failhi, which means cattle. The Indian rupee stems from the Sanskrit word for cattle. The word *capital* and the legal word *chattel* also stem from capitale, which originally denoted cattle counted by the head (Desmonde 1962). To this day, cows are sacred animals in India due to their work utility, milk production, and status in Hindu mythology, while capital and money hold sacred value for many people in the West.

Between 6,000 and 3,100 BCE, writing was invented in Mesopotamia, born out of the necessity to keep accounts (Davies and Davies 1996). Much later, around 1,200 BCE, the Chinese invented the first money minted to serve as a medium of exchange (Crawford 1994). Interestingly, this money took the shape of miniatures of commonly used tools rather than cattle or other animals. This is an important departure because a tool is a device that facilitates work or the expenditure of energy. By shaping their money in the form of a tool, the Chinese implied that the miniature represented a store of effort or work. Thus, currency, another term for money, also denotes the flow of energy (Butterworth 2001).

The Eco Model

Having established money as a representation or store of energy, the need arose to examine its role within the economy. Interestingly, economy and ecology share the common prefix, *Eco*. Eco comes from the Latin word *oeco* and means household (*Merriam-Webster's Collegiate Dictionary* 1993). The words economy and ecology came into being almost simultaneously (McCaslin and Snow 2010). Economics concerns itself with household management, while ecology refers to household relationships. Therefore, ecology originally enlisted the environmental aspect of Eco while economics took on a managerial aspect. Economics' original definition as household management later broadened into the management of resources and as a social science concerned chiefly with description and analysis of the production, distribution, and consumption of goods and services. Simultaneously, ecology, which originally meant house habitation, became known as the science or study of the interrelationships between organisms and their environment. Therefore, human ecology represents the interrelationship between human beings and their environment.

Exhibit 14.2 illustrates the harmonious balance of ecology and economics or relationships and management. Unfortunately, the post-Enlightenment Western model is out of balance and heavily weighted on the economics side. The current model even attempts to measure the sacred, thereby degrading the ecology. Those who attempt to add weight to the ecology side often do so by managing relationships or forcing ecology into economy.

In this model, the ecological interrelationship is exemplified by the philosopher Martin Buber, who differentiated relationships into two types: I-You (Thou) and I-It (Buber 1970). I-You encounters occur when beings exchange holistic reverence for one another. In contrast, I-It meetings entail objectification of the other. Buber believed this objectification of another or the self, while necessary to live in the world, should never exist on its own. As Buber (p. 68) notes:

> *You must become an It in our world. However exclusively present it may have been in the direct relationship—as soon as the relationship has run its course or is permeated by means, the You becomes an object among objects, possibly the noblest one and yet one of them, assigned its measure and boundary.*

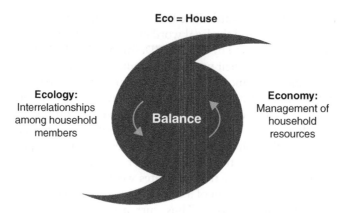

EXHIBIT 14.2   The Eco Model

Note: The Eco Model reveals the relationship between ecology and the economy. The Western paradigm emphasizes the economy over ecology and has led to imbalance.

The I-You establishes the world of relation that forms the ecological container of life. The most important question to ask when considering the Eco is, "Who is in the household?" or in Buber's terminology, "Who is a You (Thou)?" One of the consequences of capitalism is the commoditization of beings where most relationships are permeated by means, or profit at the expense of strong interrelationship. Michael Sandel, an American political philosopher and Harvard professor, has written extensively about this phenomenon and the intrusion of the markets into sectors formerly allocated as social goods (Sandel 2012a).

In one study, Sandel (2012b) cites that parents who were late picking up their children from a day-care center felt guilty about inconveniencing the day-care workers until the center imposed a fine. Contrary to expectations, implementation of the fine increased the number of tardy parents and interviews revealed that these parents abandoned their guilt. The imposition of the fine transitioned the day-care workers from the ecology where they enjoyed an interrelationship with parents to the economy where the workers became consumable.

Sandel expresses two main concerns about the market's overreach: increasing inequality and amorality. Inequality rises as markets invade areas formerly prohibited by social constraint. The selling of prison cell upgrades is an example of this occurrence (Sandel 2012a). Correlational evidence supports Sandel's claim of rising inequality as America's Gini coefficient, a measure of income inequality where zero indicates perfect income equality and one means all the income is earned by one person, increased from 0.34 in the 1980s to 0.38 in the mid-2000s (*The Economist* 2011). Coinciding with the rise in inequality is the rise of amorality. Economics has termed itself a value-neutral discipline but monetizing goods such as term papers, apologies, and best-man speeches corrupts their significance (Sandel 2012b). Rather than passively allowing the economy to overtake the ecology, society must consciously decide which goods belong in the markets and which are invaluable (i.e., which goods belong in the economy and which in the ecology). The rules of energy balance govern items that belong in the economy, while the depth of the ecology determines how soon this energy must be repaid.

Economic Imbalances

The deeper the ecology, the longer energy imbalances can persist in the economy. Large outstanding loans between family members may carry on for years while small loans between acquaintances require immediate repayment. When a person obtains money in ways other than by work, such as by inheritance, gifts, or luck, an energy imbalance exists. Psychologists have termed the phenomenon of receiving windfalls the *sudden money syndrome*, characterized by feelings of disorientation, paranoia, and guilt (Phelan 2001).

The reality of the dream of unlimited wealth turns out less promising than imagined. A 2009 study by Scherer and Bloomgarden-Smoke (2012) reveals winning the Mega Millions Lottery merely serves to postpone bankruptcy for three to five years for lottery winners in dire straits before winning. Other studies such as O'Connor (2010) reveal divorce as a consequence of winning the lottery. Similarly, as Phillips (1974) notes, those who inherit money often have difficulty trusting others for fear of being used for their money. He also notes that they may also struggle with feelings of guilt for having received money without effort and are overwhelmed by the responsibility to help those in need. Studies of beneficiaries show that inheritors have a lower internal locus of control than non-beneficiaries (Freeman 2004). Moreover, often when money is given, the donor has some implicit expectations of the beneficiary. The inability to fulfill these expectations causes 70 percent of wealth to evaporate by the second generation and 90 percent to dissipate by the third (Anderson 2003).

Energy imbalance also plays an important role in gambling addiction and crime. Gambling addicts often describe obsessive and materialistic thought patterns that take over their minds (Lin et al. 2010). Research on how gambling affects individuals reveals a multitude of problems arising from this addiction. As Barnes et al. (1999) and Shaffer and Korn (2002) note, these troubles include impairment of physical and mental health; reduction in study performance and work efficiency; commitment of crime to support gambling; financial hardship via debts and asset/money losses; and psychological disturbance such as depression, guilt, anxiety, suicide attempts, and drug and alcohol addiction. Interpersonal problems between gamblers and their intimate relationships include relationship breakdown, family neglect, domestic violence, and deterioration of the physical and mental health of family members (Lorenz and Yaffee 1988).

The Economic Time Dimension

Money not only represents a store of energy but also contains a time element. In September 1958, Bank of America mass-mailed to every resident of Fresno, California the first credit card, called BankAmericard, and the era of credit card debt began (May 2008). By the second quarter of 2008, revolving debt in the United States had reached $969.9 billion. As May (2008) notes, in 2007, just before the collapse of the world economy, Americans spent $1.22 for every dollar they earned. No longer limited by cash on hand or in the bank, the financial realities of consumers' lives stand in the distance. Returning to the definition of money as a store of energy, Americans' negative savings rate represents an energy drain on the population. Part of mindfulness practice, a component of transpersonal therapy, requires a full and focused awareness to the present moment (Kasser and Sheldon 2009). As applied to transpersonal economics, most energy should be expended to satisfy present needs with smaller portions to diminish debts and save for the future.

Just as future concerns over outliving wealth create anxiety, debt oppresses mindfulness as it directs the flow of energy backward, to the past, when people purchased goods based on future energy expenditure. When the consumer debt reaches a high enough level, most work-related efforts go to meet past debt rather than current lifestyle needs. Similar to rehashing painful childhood memories, this financial living in the past can lead to depression. On the other end of the spectrum, anxiety, worry, or fear about future events commonly leads to hoarding. The *Diagnostic and Statistical Manual* of the American Psychiatric Association (2000) reveals comorbidity of major depression and anxiety. While no studies show the correlation of debt to hoarding, financial planners report that the two syndromes often appear in the same individual (Dubofsky and Sussman 2009). Anxiety often propels people to seek out financial planners to provide reassurance, while depression diminishes the desire to take action and thereby contributes to the downward economic spiral. Exploring the main ingredients of the West's philosophy of wealth assists in understanding how the United States fell so heavily into the trap of overconsumption where today consumer spending comprises over 70 percent of gross domestic product (GDP) (*The Economist* 2012).

THE WESTERN ECO/HOUSE

Two major forces help to explain the foundation of the narrow entryway into the Western house: Aristotle and the Bible. These forces limited household members to men, usually white men. Aristotle granted all living organisms souls and divided these among nutritive (vegetative) pertaining to plants, perceptive (sensitive) pertaining to animals, and intellectual (rational) pertaining to human beings (Del Rio and White 2012). The telos of the rational soul was to seek the divine. Because humans were the only organisms with a rational soul, they were the only organisms with a link to the divine. To further narrow the doorway into the Western house, Aristotle (1946, p. 16) said "the male is by nature superior, and the female inferior; and the one rules and the other is ruled." According to Armstrong (2006), Aristotle believed that although women had rational souls, they were primarily governed by their emotions and thereby unable to access their rationality.

The Abrahamic traditions, Judaism, Christianity, and Islam, the primary religions of the West, stem from the Old Testament of the Bible. The book of Genesis directs humankind to:

> Be fruitful, and multiply, and replenish the earth, and subdue it: and have dominion over the fish of the sea, and over the fowl of the air, and over every living thing that moveth upon the earth. (The Holy Bible: King James Version, Genesis, 1973, 1:28).

This directive established a fissure between human beings and other living creatures that persists to this day, where humans consider themselves to have been made in the image of God and the rest of creation placed on earth for their use.

St. Thomas Aquinas brought together the divergent streams of Aristotelian logic and Biblical faith into a unified theory called the Medieval Synthesis (Armstrong 1993). Under the hierarchy of the Medieval Synthesis human beings straddled between the angelic realm and the animalistic realm. Of the beings on earth, humans alone possessed divine powers of reason, imagination, and spiritual essence (Lovejoy 1964). As with Aristotle and the Bible, humans were set in a position at the apex of earth's triangle rather than enmeshed in the web of life. Although the Copernican and Darwinian revolutions of the Enlightenment scientifically proved humanity and earth were not the focal points of the universe, the beliefs about the unique specialness of humankind remain culturally entrenched. The conviction that only human beings possess a spiritual essence limits the number of creatures allowed into the Western Eco. Without reverence, organisms outside of the Eco are fair game for exploitation. With so many creatures to serve as means to economic ends, Western capitalism was successful in generating great wealth. As Weber (1992) illustrated, humanity's religious paradigms play a large role in the economy.

Weber's work is relevant to the Western Eco in two main respects. First, it demonstrates the power of religion in the economy, and second, it reveals how the Western identity of the individual self was shaped. In 1904, Weber published his famous book, *The Protestant Ethic and the Spirit of Capitalism* (Weber 1992). In this work, Weber put forward the thesis that Calvinist ethic and ideas influenced the development of capitalism. Weber relied heavily on the statistics from the era, which indicated a predominance of Protestants among the wealthy, industrial, and technical classes relative to Catholics. Weber demonstrated that the capitalistic spirit arose from psychological tensions that Calvinist theological commitments tended to trigger in the minds of followers, most notably tensions caused by rationalism and predestination (Novak 2005). Questioning the fate of their individual souls led many followers into spiritual isolation where the faithful are first and foremost concerned with their own salvation. This concern formed the paradigm of Western individualism.

Originally, those operating under the Protestant Work Ethic were ascetic and saved most of what they earned. Later, when the masses of Protestants lost touch with their Calvinistic roots, wealth shifted from being a natural byproduct to being an end in itself. Marx (1983) predicted this shift when he claimed that capitalism would eventually grow into hedonism as the capitalistic machine creates artificial desires to keep demand high. Capitalism, according to Marx, demands that a consumer society be created and enlarged. Although Marx wrote most of his works as a reaction to the Industrial Revolution, themes such as alienation and exportation of desire are equally apropos today as Americans report increasing levels of depression (American Psychological Association 2011), while witnessing the emergence of capitalism in formerly communist nations such as China. However, what Marx failed to predict was how insatiable consumers would become. Instead, Marx believed that once capitalism had run its course, and the populace was awakened to "objective reality," humans would return to a life of work and leisure balance. So far, this balance has not returned and American's over-consumptive patterns that led to physical comforts are now turning around to harm through conditions such as obesity, overwhelming personal debt, and global warming.

AN ALTERNATIVE PERSPECTIVE

After this thorough exploration of the Western Eco, with its economic prosperity leading to ecologic poverty, this section investigates an alternative perspective of wealth that may offer a solution to rein in the adverse consequences of unbridled capitalism. The wisdom tradition of Jainism predates the Abrahamic traditions and arose in India thousands of years ago as referenced in the Vedic Scriptures (Dundas 1992). This tradition holds a vastly different approach to the Eco due to the doctrines of karma and interconnection of all beings—concepts foreign to individualistic Western economic philosophy. It differs from religions that regard humankind to have been created by God in his divine image by its focus on life rather than the human person. Jainism gives reverence to all life, irrespective of its place in the biological hierarchy. In other words, in Jainism the pathway to the Eco's ecology is wider than the West's and allows veneration of all types of living organisms.

Jainism

Unlike Buddhism, Jainism has not spread much beyond India, its country of origin, for several reasons. First, Jainism is decidedly ascetic; the discipline required for householders is the equivalent of that required for renunciants in other traditions (Carrithers and Humphrey 1991). Second, the Jain philosophy that knocks down the door of the Eco by granting sentience, the defining characteristic of the soul, even to microscopic beings creates an ethical dilemma to human reproduction (Tatia 1994). Jainism asserts that existing in the world without exploiting other souls is impossible. Thus, the belief "to live is to harm" limits householder reproduction. Jains have one of the lowest birthrates of any religious tradition in India, as systems must be in place to minimize injury before bringing new life into the world (Sangave 2001). Third, the central philosophy of Jainism is *ahimsa*, which means nonharming, limits the mobility of adherents. Traditionally, Jains abstained from travel during the rainy season in order to protect the lives of creatures, such as worms, that may be inadvertently stepped on in walking (Dundas 1992). Today, this restriction has been relaxed but still Jains take extraordinary measures to prevent harming other organisms.

Jainism is one of the world's oldest shramanic, or ascetic, religions. Both ascetics and lay people practice the same five vows, only to different degrees. The five vows practiced stringently by ascetics are known as the great vows and the five vows practiced by householders with leniency are known as the lesser vows. The five vows, in order of importance, are abstinence from violence (ahimsa), falsehood, stealing, carnality, and possessiveness (Tatia 1994). The final vow to abstain from possessiveness necessitates that Jain monks and nuns renounce all worldly possessions. However, the Jains correctly realize that no religious institution can survive without the laity being involved in an active way.

Jain monks and nuns believe they have a duty to teach the laity; simply working on personal enlightenment is unacceptable. Jain ascetics insist that teaching the laity is a central part of their dharma (life path), a form of religious study, and thus, one of the internal forms of asceticism. Renouncers receive everything they use in the form of a gift from lay supporters: clothes, books, medicine, and furniture (Laidlaw 1995). In exchange, the laity receive teaching, ascetic example, and spiritual uplift. Reciprocity between renouncers and laity balances the energy flow within the Eco even though no money has been exchanged. By supporting the monks and nuns engaged in religious work, Jain laity consider their commercial success a holy duty (Nevaskar 1971). Another reason Jain householders regard financial wealth as a necessity is the belief that the five vows are easier to follow in times of abundance. Finally, as Laidlaw notes, Jains prefer to run an economic surplus, to be net givers to society, rather than drains on society's resources. Still, the force for generating wealth often runs counter to the mandate of harmlessness and creates occupational constraints.

Jains are strongly encouraged to follow professions with the least potential for violence. Therefore, the practice of ahimsa has led to the exclusion of the Jains from all industrial trades endangering life: trades that use fire, involve work with sharp instruments, masonry, the majority of industrial and agricultural occupations, as well as the entire military industry (Nevaskar 1971). Furthermore, the vow to abstain from falsehood requires Jains to practice absolute honesty in business. All maya (illusion) is prohibited, including dishonest gain through smuggling, bribery, and any sort of disreputable financial practice. Therefore, Nevaskar notes that Jains have stayed away from government jobs in India, where bribery is commonplace. With all these occupational restrictions, Jains have concentrated in the merchant, banking, and money-lending businesses. They have flocked to the cities where they can engage in these commercial activities without compromising the doctrine of ahimsa. As a result of their honesty in business, they have also attracted the trade of non-Jains.

Like the ascetics, Jain laymen hope someday to achieve liberation. The lesser vows taken by Jain householders either partially eliminate or attract beneficial karma. As a result of their preoccupation with enlightenment, Jains give generously to charitable causes in hopes of receiving spiritual merit. In India, they are responsible for a disproportionate share of charitable hospitals, rest houses, educational institutions, and homes for aged and disabled animals (Nevaskar 1971). Their ascetic, nonviolent approach has served the Jains well financially. Today, while the Jains account for about 0.5 percent of India's population, they account for nearly a quarter of India's tax revenue (Nadu 2007).

The most famous Jain manual that focuses solely on business ethics, Ratnasekhara Suri's *Light on Purity of Business Activity*, composed in the early fifteenth century, provides Jains with clear instruction on proper business activities.

The omniscient Jina states that purity of business activity is the basis of dharma. Purity of money in worldly existence comes about from pure business activity; through pure money there comes pure food; through pure food comes purity of body in worldly existence; with a pure body one becomes suitable for dharma. Whatever action he performs yields fruit in worldly existence. (Chapple 2002, p. 104)

A present day example of Ratnasekhara Suri's instruction is Jain Irrigation Systems Limited (JISL), a transnational, publicly traded corporation located in Jalgaon, Maharashtra, India. Founded in 1986, JISL's mission statement is "Leave this world better than you found it" (Jain Irrigation Systems Ltd. 2009b). The Corporation is the second largest micro-irrigation company in the world, offering drip irrigation systems to rural India that promise "more crop per drop" (Jain Irrigation Systems Ltd. 2007). In 2009, the International Finance Corporation (IFC), a member of the World Bank, whose mission is to create opportunity for people to escape poverty and to foster sustainable economic growth in developing countries, invested nearly $60 million in JISL (Banik 2009). Echoing the Jain vows of ahimsa and non-possession, JISL's chairman's statement (Jain Irrigation Systems Ltd. 2009a, p. 5) reads:

> *We do not believe in building a corporation on the weaknesses and frailties of humans or by venturing into businesses that produce harmful or intoxicating substances, or providing services that are unworthy of enlightened human endeavor. We work toward reduction, recycling and reuse of process wastes at every stage; towards conservation of natural resources, whether water, soil, forest, or energy. We model our processes to source from nature only that which is minimal and which is absolutely essential for sustenance.*

JISL's non-exploitive ventures are also profitable. In their 2009–2010 annual report, JISL's 2009 financial statements show a 29 percent increase in sales from the previous year despite the global economic meltdown and subdued growth environment (Jain Irrigation Systems Ltd. 2009b). Anil Jain, the chief executive officer (CEO), attributes this increase to the company's credo of sustainability. In keeping with the Jain practice of charity, JISL gives 5 percent of profits to charities that support society through education via the Gandhi Research Foundation, as well as through health care and village development. The popular financial press is taking note of Jain Irrigation's commitment to service but interestingly has not made the link between the company's good works and Jainism. In December 2012, *Forbes India* magazine awarded the company with a philanthropy award (Paul 2012). Paul notes that the CEO mentions the fifth main vow of nonpossession as a driving factor of his business model but attributes the philosophy of nonpossession to the CEO rather than Jainism. This omission both showcases the gap in understanding between transpersonal and business realms and reveals the strength transpersonal ideals hold over resource management.

With its high level of personal responsibility and severe asceticism, the fact that Jainism has been unable to flourish like less stringent traditions is not surprising. However, for those able to adhere to the standards of self-discipline, the ideals Jainism espouses create power in the world as witnessed by Mahatma Gandhi, who listed a Jain, Rajchandra, as one of his three primary influences (Gandhi 1957). Jainism shares the West's philosophy of free will and capital accumulation yet does so through a sustainable and compassionate lens. The next section translates the open ecology and several Jain principles of resource management to the financial planning industry.

THE OPEN ECO IN FINANCIAL PLANNING

Beginning in 2008, the decline in client portfolios due to the financial crisis affected virtually all levels of the financial advisory community by damaging relationships and eroding trust. Clients became enraged and fearful as their futures became uncertain. With institutional failures, scandals, and bursting economic bubbles, investors turned into irrational clients unwilling to show patience and hope for a future market upturn. These dire circumstances and emotional, limbic system reactions required financial planners who had the appropriate skills to manage the situation. Planners needed to reestablish trust and confidence in the face of uncertainty.

A set of transpersonal practices provides the framework for an advisor to work through emotionally challenging issues. The framework also enables clients to reevaluate their roles and responsibilities in the current situation. Optimal client engagement and progress are achieved when elements of transpersonal psychology and supplemental coaching skills are a part of the advisor's approach. This includes understanding how client identification with wealth leads to emotional reactions and developing enhanced listening skills. Other skills consist of: avoiding defensiveness when the client seeks to place blame; generating a sense of greater control in the client's mind; encouraging positivity and hope during challenging periods; facilitating a redefinition or reframe of the situation; establishing more frequent communication either in person or electronically; focusing on building or rebuilding trust; and adapting a communication style similar to the client's (Gounaris and Prout 2009).

Snow (2009) provides evidence supporting the effectiveness of transpersonal practices in a financial advisory setting. Her study involves conducting interviews with a group of Certified Financial Planners (CFPs) who scored exceptionally high on an assessment called the Spirituality Assessment Scale. This scale, which has no correlation to religiosity, tests four dimensions of spirituality prevalent in the Jain community: unifying connectedness, inner resourcefulness, life purpose, and transcendence. The interviews attempt to identify the theoretical best practices of transpersonal CFPs that promote greater awareness.

The interviews also include four subquestions designed to uncover how transpersonal practices impact distinct facets of the financial planning career. The four questions that provide structure for the open and reflective coding sequences in order to reveal the emergent theory are: (1) How do transpersonal practices help achieve professional goals? (2) How do transpersonal practices assist in gaining autonomy and flexibility? (3) How do transpersonal practices influence professional organizations? and (4) How do transpersonal practices impact relationships with clients?

The central properties revealed by the CFPs through these interviews are: integrity, a holistic client approach, open-mindedness, and inner spiritual guidance. As Exhibit 14.3 shows, the matrix indicates the processes that create the properties and displays how the properties reveal themselves through the work practices of the CFPs in the dimensional range. The matrix also shows the context for uncovering the properties: professional goals, autonomy, professional organizations, and client relationships.

The four common transpersonal practices revealed through these interviews recognize the essence or soul value of the client, which is the central tenet of Jainism. This recognition lies in stark contrast to the typical investment industry mode of operation that objectifies or creates an I/It relationship in which the client serves as a source of income for the planner. The shortsighted practice of viewing clients as revenue sources for planners stifles personal growth and development. This was not the case for the participants in Snow's (2009) study, who display self-awareness and continuous growth in consciousness. Ironically, even though income was not the primary motivation for the transpersonal CFPs, the quantitative portion of the study reveals a statistically significant positive correlation between scores on the Spirituality Assessment Scale and job satisfaction and client retention. The participants in the study uncover the upward spiral available to those who thoroughly integrate transpersonal awareness. This awareness begins to define the nature of conscious financial planning.

Practicing the elements of transpersonal psychology as shown in Exhibit 14.3 facilitates a cooperative alliance toward greater financial well-being for clients and job satisfaction for planners. Transpersonal financial planning, through its depth, has the power to loosen the grip money has over self-identity. By creating a mindful distance between wealth and life purpose, it also has the ability to engage the frontal cortex where rationality naturally optimizes financial outcomes. Within this context, individuals will be better equipped to handle economic problems and

EXHIBIT 14.3 Transpersonal Financial Planner Matrix

Core Category		Transcendent Life Purpose		
Properties	Integrity	Holistic Client Approach	Open-Minded and Tolerant	Inner Spiritual Guidance
Processes	Flowing from their spiritual practices	Viewing money as a device used to manifest their clients' dreams	Having an inclusive attitude of acceptance	Meeting clients at their level of consciousness
	Engaging in self-reflection	Awakening possibilities for clients	Presenting an opportunity to further consciousness and uplifting approaches for both the client and practitioner at once	Discovering internal truths
	Living it; not being a hypocrite	Looking for a whole life and comprehensive answers for clients	Being there for clients at a higher level of consciousness	Relying heavily on intuition when working with clients
	Providing a continuous process of self-awareness	Providing customized solutions for clients based on spiritual beliefs	Honoring clients' unique spiritual approach	Knowing room for doubt still exists
	Being willing to turn away potentially high revenue clients who are unwilling to accept personal responsibility in the investment process	Determining what has value and what is most important to the client	Maintaining openness and a willingness to listen	Quieting the ego intentionally
	Viewing economic conditions from a spiritual perspective	Offering personalized support in service to clients' greatest potential	Being open to learning	Arriving at conclusions through a deep soul-searching effort

EXHIBIT 14.3 (*Continued*)

Core Category Properties	Transcendent Life Purpose			
	Integrity	Holistic Client Approach	Open-Minded and Tolerant	Inner Spiritual Guidance
		Having deep and meaningful conversations		Focusing attention on staying present in the moment
Dimensional range	Providing service and a commitment to the right action	Resisting external pressures to perform	Embracing an organization of CFPs devoted to holistic full life planning	Embracing a conviction to spiritual and relationship values
	Shifting priorities from earning money to helping humanity	Constructing purpose-driven, meaningful lives	Possessing the wisdom to avoid dangerous products and practices	Offering transpersonal practices to enhance client relationships in a positive and meaningful way
	Viewing personal income as a byproduct of engaged service	Helping people live the life of their dreams	Building a sense of community through professional organizations	Expressing concern for clients
	Providing consciousness raising to a higher level or a higher frequency	Being less vulnerable to group think	Viewing the economic crisis as an opportunity to raise consciousness	Being sensitive
	Surviving challenges as a function of spirituality	Being willing to take responsibility	Building new levels of consciousness within professional organizations	Having a commitment to self-care
	Helping people and valuing client relationships	Facilitating clients' capacity to learn to think on their own	Honoring clients' spiritual values even though they may differ from ours	Providing energy management
	Embracing a strict ethical code	Assisting clients to avoid materialistic traps	Being reluctant to assign blame for outer circumstances	Being centered and grounded
	Avoiding abuses that violate an internal sense of justice	Being true to the clients' needs, feelings, and values		Providing a growing self-awareness

(*continued*)

EXHIBIT 14.3 (*Continued*)

Core Category Properties	Integrity	Transcendent Life Purpose		
		Holistic Client Approach	Open-Minded and Tolerant	Inner Spiritual Guidance
		Offering a people relationship orientation		Possessing the faith that the process will work
				Having a divine connection guiding all aspects of life
Contexts	Professional goals	Autonomy	Professional organizations	Client relationships
Outcomes of emerging theories	The four common transpersonal practices—integrity, holistic client approach, open-minded tolerance, and inner spiritual guidance—revealed through these participants, recognize the essence or soul value of the client.			

Note: This exhibit displays the common traits found in CFPs® who scored exceptionally high on the Spirituality Assessment Scale and shows how they create and use these qualities in their work practices.

make choices aligned with consciously created core values. The current and limited behavioral emphasis of treating money pathology merely provides a surface layer of healing and is limited by the shallowness of the behavioral approach. By uncovering the personal, cultural, and transpersonal paradigms that flow into client belief systems, transpersonal economics has the strength to eradicate irrational money behaviors.

SUMMARY

Short-sighted Western financial practices maintain Freud's pleasure principle by rewarding profits at any cost. Unfortunately, policy makers in charge of rekindling the market have counted on consumer spending to lead the recovery (Rugaber 2009). While comforting in the short term, this level of consumption is not environmentally sustainable. Within the financial industry, the generalized objectification of clients parallels the objectification of nature. Participants in Snow's (2009) study are an exception to the common mode of operation. Possessing a transcendent life purpose cleared the thoughts of these CFPs from obsessions with unsatisfying material gain and superficial competition. Freed from ego-centered demands, these practitioners express greater interest in building synergistic relationships as revealed through the core properties: integrity, holistic client approach, open-minded tolerance, and inner spiritual knowing. The participants used their economic awareness and expertise and applied it to the ecology of the financial industry. Without knowing it, these CFPs incorporate the wisdom Jains have successfully and consistently implemented for centuries.

More broadly, using nature as a mirror of our treatment of one another, if the West continues to treat the environment as a resource to be consumed without conscience or foresight, human relationships will also be built on aggression and domination (Rankin 2006). This exploitation is the result of objectifying or economizing other life forms; of turning I/Thou relationships into I/It. Jains understand the interconnection among humankind, animals, and nature. That is, they allow other beings into the Eco and grasp the importance of ecological sensitivity. The tradition also provides substantial guidance on how to incorporate this ecological awareness into the economy by balancing the energy of money.

The idea that each individual has value and is endowed with inalienable rights is central to Jain dharma; the rights in question are balanced by responsibilities (Rankin 2006). Today's Western economic model supports the rights without the accompanying responsibility. The recent worldwide banking and mortgage crisis that grew out of materialism and corruption in a deregulated financial services industry would never have been allowed under Jain business doctrines that disallow falsehood and greed. With a transcendent life purpose and vow against possessiveness, this ancient religion offers a business model that could lead to a more equitable distribution of worldwide wealth.

DISCUSSION QUESTIONS

1. What influence does Freud's pleasure principle exert over the U.S. economy?
2. How does mindfulness practice assist in rational decision-making?
3. Discuss the costs and benefits of allowing other life forms into the Eco.
4. Despite occupational constraints brought by an open Eco, Jains are exceptionally prosperous. What are some possible reasons for this prosperity?
5. Identify the four emergent qualities of transpersonal CFPs and discuss how they affect their practices.

REFERENCES

Allison, Clinton B. 1995. *Past and Present: Essays for Teachers in the History of Education*. New York: Peter Lang.

American Psychiatric Association. 2000. *Diagnostic and Statistical Manual of Mental Disorders*, 4th ed. Washington, DC: American Psychiatric Association.

American Psychological Association. 2011. *Stress in America: Our Health at Risk*. Washington, DC: American Psychological Association.

Anderson, Brett. 2003. "100 Year Plan Introduction: Making Meaning of Wealth across Generations." *Worth* December 1, 47–50.

Aristotle. 1946. *The Politics, Book 1, Chapter 5*. New York: Oxford University Press.

Armstrong, Karen. 1993. *A History of God: The 4,000-Year Quest of Judaism, Christianity and Islam*. New York: Random House.

Armstrong, Karen. 2006. *The Great Transformation: The Beginning of Our Religious Traditions*. New York: Random House.

Banik, Abanti. 2009. "IFC, Jain Irrigation Launch Footprint Initiative in India to Conserve Water." *India PR Wire*. Available at www.indiaprwire.com/pressrelease/financial-services/ 2009110436897.htm.

Barnes, Grace, John Welte, Joseph Hoffman, and Barbara Dintcheff. 1999. "Gambling and Alcohol Use among Youth: Influences of Demographic, Socialization, and Individual Factors." *Addictive Behaviors* 24:6, 749–767.

Braud, William, and Rosemarie Anderson. 1998. *Transpersonal Research Methods for the Social Sciences: Honoring Human Experience*. Thousand Oaks, CA: Sage.

Buber, Martin. 1970. *I and Thou*. New York: Simon & Schuster.

Butterworth, Eric. 2001. *Spiritual Economics*. Unity Village, MO: Unity House.

Camerer, Colin, and George Loewenstein. 2004. "Behavioral Economics: Past, Present, Future." In Colin Camerer, George Loewenstein, and Matthew Rabin, eds., *Advances in Behavioral Economics*, 3–51. Princeton, NJ: Princeton University Press.

Carrithers, Michael, and Caroline Humphrey. 1991. *The Assembly of Listeners: Jains in Society*. New York: Cambridge University Press.

Chapple, Christopher, ed. 2002. *Jainism and Ecology: Nonviolence in the Web of Life*. Cambridge, MA: Harvard University Press.

Crawford, Tad. 1994. *The Secret Life of Money: Teaching Tales of Spending, Receiving, Saving, and Owing*. New York: Putnam.

Damasio, Antonio. 1994. *Descartes' Error: Emotion, Reason, and the Human Brain*. New York: Putnam.

Davies, Glyn, and Roy Davies. 1996. *A History of Money, From Ancient Times to the Present Day*. Cardiff: University of Wales Press.

Del Rio, Carlos, and Lyle White. 2012. "Separating Spirituality from Religiosity: A Hylomorphic Attitudinal Perspective." *Psychology of Religion and Spirituality* 4:2, 123–142.

Desmonde, William. 1962. *Magic, Myth, and Money: The Origin of Money in Religious Ritual*. New York: Free Press of Gencoe.

Dubofsky, David, and Lyle Sussman. 2009. "The Changing Role of the Financial Planner Part 1: From Financial Analytics to Coaching and Life Planning." *Journal of Financial Planning* 22:8, 48–57.

Dundas, Paul. 1992. *The Jains*. New York: Routledge.

Frankl, Victor. 1959. *Man's Search for Meaning*. Boston, MA: Beacon Press.

Freeman, Michael. 2004. *The Impact of Inherited Wealth: A Psychological and Spiritual Inquiry*. Unpublished Doctoral Dissertation, Institute of Transpersonal Psychology, Palo Alto, CA.

Gandhi, Mohandas. 1957. *Gandhi an Autobiography: The Story of My Experiments with Truth*. Boston, MA: Beacon Press.

Gounaris, Kathleen M., and Maurice F. Prout. 2009. "Repairing Relationships and Restoring Trust: Behavioral Finance and the Economic Crisis." *Journal of Financial Service Professionals* 63:4, 75–83.

Hausman, Daniel. 2008. *The Philosophy of Economics: An Anthology*. New York: Cambridge University Press.

Jain Irrigation Systems Ltd. 2007. *Diary: Small Ideas, Big Evolutions*. Jalgaon, India: Jain Irrigation Systems, Ltd.

Jain Irrigation Systems Ltd. 2009a. *Prosperity for Posterity; Sustainability Report*. Jalgaon, India: Jain Irrigation Systems, Ltd.

Jain Irrigation Systems Ltd. 2009b. *23rd Annual Report*. Jalgaon, India: Jain Irrigation Systems, Ltd.

Kasser, Tim, and Kennon M. Sheldon. 2009. "Time Affluence as a Path toward Personal Happiness and Ethical Business Practice: Empirical Evidence from Four Studies." *Journal of Business Ethics* 84:2, 243–255.

Klontz, Bradley, and Sonya Britt. 2012. "How Clients' Money Scripts Predict Their Financial Behaviors." *Journal of Financial Planning* 25:11, 33–41.

Kolb, Bryan, and Ian Whishaw. 1990. *Fundamentals of Human Neuropsychology*. New York: W. H. Freeman and Co.

Laidlaw, James. 1995. *Riches and Renunciation: Religion, Economy, and Society among the Jains*. New York: Oxford University Press.

Lin, Judy, Sally Casswell, Brian Easton, Taisia Huckle, Lanuola Asiasiga, and Ru Quan You. 2010. "Time and Money Spent Gambling and the Relationship with Quality-of-

Life Measures: A National Study of New Zealanders." *Journal of Gambling Issues* 24: July, 33–53.

Lorenz, Valerie C., and Robert A. Yaffee. 1988. "Pathological Gambling: Psychosomatic, Emotional and Marital Difficulties as Reported by the Spouse." *Journal of Gambling Behavior* 4:1, 13–26.

Lovejoy, Arthur. 1964. *The Great Chain of Being: A Study of the History of an Idea.* Cambridge, MA: Harvard University Press.

Marx, Karl. 1983. "Capital." In Eugene Kamenka, ed., *The Portable Karl Marx Vol. 1*, 432–493. New York: Penguin Group.

Maslow, Abraham H. 1971. *The Farther Reaches of Human Nature.* New York: Viking Press.

May, Patrick. 2008. "50 Years of Credit Cards: How 'A Piece of Plastic' Helped Put Consumers Nearly $1 Trillion In Debt." *San Jose Mercury News,* September 14. Available at www.pressdisplay.com/pressdisplay/mobile/articleview.aspx?articleId=74c68229-7937-4f68-81e9-7e6f7fc3b169.

McCaslin, Mark, and Renée Snow. 2010. "The Human Art of Leading: A Foreshadow to the Potentiating Movement of Leadership Studies." *Integral Leadership Review* X:5. Available at www.archive-ilr.com/archives-2010/2010-10/ilr1010mccaslinsnow.pdf.

Merriam-Webster's Collegiate Dictionary, 10th ed. 1993. Springfield, MA: Merriam-Webster.

Nadu, Tamil. 2007. "Jains' Contribution to Exchequer 'Astounding.'" *The Hindu,* August 20. Available at www.hindu.com/2007/08/20/stories/2007082057190800.htm.

Nevaskar, Balwant. 1971. *Capitalists without Capitalism: The Jains of India and the Quakers of the West.* Westport, CT: Greenwood.

Novak, Michael. 2005. "Max Weber Goes Global." *First Things* 1:150, 26–29.

O'Connor, Brian. 2010. "When Winners Lose: Think a Lucky Lottery Ticket Will Solve All Your Problems? Maybe Not." *Detroit News* D.1, November 15. Available at http://search.proquest.com/docview/773630007?accountid=25304.

Paul, Cuckoo. 2012. "Playing for the Long Term." *Forbes India*, 60–64.

Phelan, Sarah. 2001. "Dealing with the Sudden Money Syndrome." *The Planner* 16:2, 7–8.

Phillips, Michael. 1974. *The Seven Laws of Money.* New York: Random House.

Rankin, Adrian. 2006. *The Jain Path: Ancient Wisdom for the West.* Seattle, WA: O Books.

Rugaber, Christopher. 2009. "Jobless Claims Rise for Second Straight Week." *The San Jose Mercury News* E3, August 21.

Sandel, Michael. 2012a. "What Isn't for Sale?" *Atlantic* 309:3, 62–66.

Sandel, Michael. 2012b. *What Money Can't Buy: The Moral Limits of Markets* [MP3 recording]. London: The London School of Economics.

Sangave, Vilas Adinath. 2001. *Facets of Jainology: Selected Research Papers on Jain Society, Religion and Culture.* New Delhi: Popular Prakashan.

Scherer, Ron, and Kara Bloomgarden-Smoke. 2012. "Note to Mega Millions Lottery Winner: Beware!" *The Christian Science Monitor* 10: March 30. Available at http://search.proquest.com/docview/962425988?accountid=25304.

Shaffer, Howard, and David Korn. 2002. "Gambling and Related Mental Disorders: A Public Health Analysis." *Annual Review of Public Health* 23, 171–212.

Siegel, Daniel. 2007. *The Mindful Brain: Reflection and Attunement in the Cultivation of Well-Being.* New York: W. W. Norton & Company.

Snow, Renée. 2009. *Transpersonal Practices for Certified Financial Planners.* Unpublished Doctoral Dissertation. Palo Alto, CA: Institute of Transpersonal Psychology.

Tatia, Nathmal. 1994. *Tattvartha Sutra: That Which Is.* San Francisco, CA: HarperCollins.

The Economist. 2011. January 21. "The Rise and Rise of the Cognitive Elite: Brains Bring Ever Larger Rewards" 398:8717, 7.

The Economist. 2012. July 14. "America's Economy" 404:8793, 21–24.

The Holy Bible: King James Version. 1973. Iowa Falls, IA: World Bible Publishers.

Weber, Max. 1992. *The Protestant Ethic and the Spirit of Capitalism.* New York: Routledge.

ABOUT THE AUTHOR

Renée M. Snow is an Adjunct Professor at Sofia University (formerly the Institute of Transpersonal Psychology) and Chair of the Financial Planning program at the University of California (UC), Santa Cruz extension. At Sofia University she teaches advanced and quantitative research methods. At UC Professor Snow grounds students in the philosophy of economics while giving them the practical tools to work with in the financial services industry. She also manages her own firm and specializes in tax planning, asset management, and the psychological aspects of wealth management. Her research focuses on how the ancient texts of Buddhism, Hinduism, and Jainism apply to financial management. She has published works in the areas of leadership and behavioral finance. Professor Snow received an MS in accountancy from San Jose State University, an MA in spiritual psychology from the University of Santa Monica, and a PhD in psychology from the Institute of Transpersonal Psychology. She holds the Enrolled Agent and Certified Financial Planner® designations.

CHAPTER 15

Advising the Behavioral Investor: Lessons from the Real World

Gregg S. Fisher, CFA
Chief Investment Officer, Gerstein Fisher

INTRODUCTION

U.S. President Franklin Delano Roosevelt, during his first inaugural address in 1933, stated that "The only thing we have to fear is fear itself." He made this statement when the country was in the throes of the Great Depression. More than 80 years later, academic research in the field of behavioral finance demonstrates that this celebrated line applies equally to investing. Investors are often their own worst enemies because they are susceptible to mental mistakes and emotional responses. These biases often lead to poor decision-making and, ultimately, inferior financial outcomes.

One of the greatest services a financial advisor can provide to clients is helping to ensure that in times of market turbulence, reason, discipline, and objectivity triumph over emotions such as fear, greed, and regret. This chapter explores some reasons for which overcoming emotional and cognitive biases in investing is both vital to individuals' long-term wealth creation and also a perennial challenge for financial advisors. It explains common emotional biases and how these impact the development of investment strategy and, ultimately, investment results. Additionally, this chapter draws on both academic theories in the area of behavioral finance and the real-life manifestations of behavioral and cognitive biases on investors' long-term wealth.

The chapter is organized as follows: The first section examines the complex relationship among risk, return, and the investor. Next, the chapter outlines several common emotional biases that can jeopardize an investor's prospects for long-term wealth creation. The next section discusses the impact of investor behavior on portfolios, including why investors tend to underperform the asset classes and funds in which they invest. The chapter then details approaches financial advisors can use to help investors avoid emotionally driven decision-making and stay on track to meet their long-term goals. Finally, the chapter explores strategies that seek to turn predictable, common investor behavioral biases into profit opportunities.

RISK, RETURN, AND THE INVESTOR: A COMPLEX RELATIONSHIP

Consistent opportunities for excess returns with zero extra risk relative to a market index simply do not exist because market participants arbitrage them away. In other words, there is no free lunch in investing because investors must incur risk in order to earn return. The fact that equities have historically outperformed fixed income stems largely from the fact that equities are inherently riskier. That is, investors must be compensated for that additional risk in the form of additional return. Otherwise, why would they incur it?

A Premium for Stock Risk

Normally, investors are compensated for the additional risk that equities entail over so-called riskless assets such as short-term Treasuries in the form of the equity risk premium (ERP). Equation 15.1 shows a simple calculation of the ERP:

$$MKT - RFR = ERP \qquad\qquad (15.1)$$

where MKT is the equity market return and RFR is the risk-free rate, commonly measured as the one-month Treasury bill.

The ERP is not supposed to be negative (recall that it is referred to as a premium). Yet, investors have actually been penalized instead of rewarded for taking on risk during some multiyear periods. During the Great Depression between 1930 and 1939, the ERP averaged –0.60 percent a year, using the S&P 500 Index to measure MKT and the one-month U.S. Treasury bill to represent RFR. For the decade starting in January 2000 and ending in December 2009, the ERP was –3.7 percent a year. Over the long term, however, the ERP has been positive: more than 6 percent annualized over the period between January 1926 and December 2012, which makes intuitive sense given the "normal" relationship between risk and return.

Investors will not realize the longer-term ERP if they panic and sell their equity holdings based on short-term, negative market events. In fact, weakening prices can represent buying opportunities from which long-term investments have the potential to gain great value. When price volatility or an increase in uncertainty about the future value of assets occurs, opportunities are available for investors to be rewarded for placing or keeping assets in the stock market.

The Sentiment Roller Coaster

Unfortunately, even prudent risks that investors objectively know should pay off are often psychologically difficult to incur. Hence, the advisor's challenge is to keep clients who are nervous and fearful in the market after a protracted downturn. While most investors understand the concept of market cycles, when the economy has been stuck in a trough for an extended period they often have difficulty believing that stock markets will eventually recover. This is when investors should be reminded that one of the greatest long-term wealth hazards they face is having no or minimal ownership in stocks when the cycle turns up because they panicked, sold their equity holdings, and moved into cash when stocks were in a severe downturn.

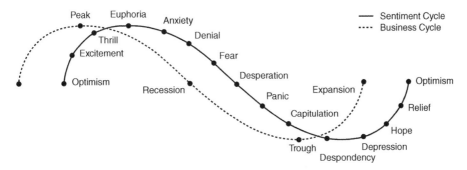

EXHIBIT 15.1 Investor Sentiment and the Business Cycle

Note: This exhibit depicts the relationship between investor sentiment and the business cycle. The points on the investor sentiment curve (solid line) correspond to the various stages of the business cycle, with a certain lag time.

The scariest times to invest have often proven to be the best times to invest. Warren Buffett famously advised investors to "be fearful when others are greedy and greedy when others are fearful" (Buffett 2008). Yet, market participants often tend to do just the opposite. Exhibit 15.1 depicts how investor sentiment relates to the business cycle. The points on the investor sentiment curve generally correspond to the various stages of the business cycle (as indicated by the dotted line).

Even a cursory look at Exhibit 15.1 reveals how emotions such as fear, regret, optimism, and pride can have a detrimental effect on the size of an investor's overall portfolio. For instance, if one invested at the first point of the graph, while being optimistic about the market, would adding even more money at that point have been a good idea? The answer is probably not. However, based on historical fund flows as shown in Exhibit 15.2, that is what many people do. Similarly, being depressed about recent underperformance often leads investors to exit the market just when opportunity is actually highest.

For example, as Exhibit 15.2 shows, in 1990 average cash allocations were as high as 50 percent just as the S&P 500 was poised to take off on a 10-year run. In other words, many investors had withdrawn their money from stocks for emotional reasons when their growth potential was at its highest.

Poor Timing

Historically, groups of individuals exhibit herd behavior that results in stock market bubbles because long-term investors start to act like short-term traders. People have a tendency to chase returns; to overinvest money in sectors and asset classes that have exhibited strong recent outperformance in the hopes that their superior performance persists into the future. For example, in the late 1990s and early 2000s, approximately $18 billion of new assets flowed into domestic growth equity funds, fueled by investor enthusiasm for the growth-dominated tech industry. In the three years before their peak level of net inflows, U.S. large cap growth stocks had returned more than 14 percent annualized and had outperformed the global equity markets by almost 4 percentage points a year. Investors also suffered from representativeness bias during this time period because they overweighted their portfolios in

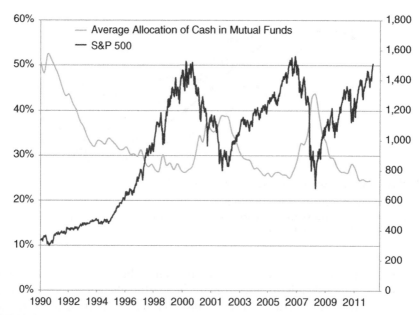

EXHIBIT 15.2 Average Cash Allocations of U.S. Mutual Fund Owners versus S&P 500 Price Return: 1990–2012

Note: This graph demonstrates the historic relationship between S&P 500 movements and the cash allocations of investors. When the stock market level is high, as in 2000 and 2007, investors are heavily invested in stocks and their cash holdings are relatively low. By contrast, investors exit stocks and build cash allocations after markets fall, as in 2002 and 2008.

Sources: Standard & Poor's Index Services, Investment Company Institute.

growth stocks and underinvested in value stocks. The *representativeness bias* states that individuals have a tendency to project past and current investment returns into the future. Investors were expecting growth stocks to continue to outperform other assets classes for several more years. However, shortly thereafter the dot-com bubble burst, wiping out trillions of dollars in market value over the ensuing two years.

When investors examine past returns to determine their investment strategy going forward, they often find themselves on the wrong side of the old adage, "buy low and sell high." Indeed, Morningstar reports that the mutual fund categories with the greatest inflows tend to underperform those with the greatest outflows over the following three- and five-year periods (Morningstar 2009). Exhibit 15.3 illustrates this phenomenon by showing the performance in the three years leading up to and the one year following peak mutual fund flows into U.S. large cap growth funds. The peak flows occurred in February 2000.

Too often, when perceived risk increases, investors become risk averse at the wrong time and lower their equity allocations within their overall portfolios. As such, they are reducing their chances for long-term wealth creation. A recent example involves the euro zone debt crisis. At Gerstein Fisher, an independent investment management and advisory firm, the volume of calls to client advisors spiked as nervous clients called to ask why the firm continued to own European equities. Some wanted to sell their European equity holdings. Yet, research conducted by

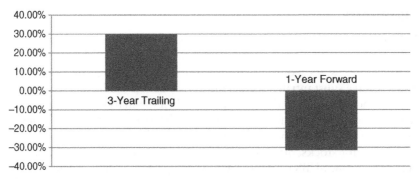

EXHIBIT 15.3   Three-Year Trailing Returns from Peak Fund Flows and One-Year Forward Returns from Peak Fund Flows (Annualized)

Note: This bar chart shows how investors tend to base their investment strategy on past market returns. Peak flows into U.S. large-cap growth funds in February 2000 occurred after three years of strong performance and were followed by a year of very poor performance.

Sources: Morningstar, Bloomberg.

the firm illustrated that between 1970 and 2011, the cost of capital (or the returns investors demand for holding companies' equity shares) for the United States, euro zone countries, and Japan was nearly equal. Short-term differences such as those witnessed in 2011 and 2012 do occur. However, such changes usually are triggered by systemic events such as the Greek/euro zone debt crisis and effectively make access to global companies that happened to be based in one region of the world available to investors at a substantial discount.

Over the long run, markets are a good mechanism for pricing (known) risk. While markets are reasonably efficient, pricing in all known information, they are not perfectly efficient due largely to investor behavior. As individual theories, the efficient market theory and behavioral finance theory do not sufficiently explain how security prices work in the marketplace. Rather, the interplay between efficient markets and behavioral finance helps to explain the complex reality of market performance.

Part of this reality is the fact that the emotions of fear and regret often overcome the power of facts and logic. Although investors may objectively understand the relationship between risk and return, they often are resistant to embrace the concept in practice. This is one of the myriad ways in which financial advisors can help improve their clients' investment success, as is discussed later in the chapter.

INVESTMENTS WITH PEOPLE PROBLEMS

All too often, investors jeopardize their long-term portfolio returns and financial goals through cognitive and emotional biases. Many financial advisors can likely relate to the saying, "We don't have people with investment problems; we have investments with people problems." The following examples illustrate some common investor lapses that stem largely from heuristics (i.e., cognitive or mental mistakes) or emotional tendencies.

Failing to Rebalance

Rebalancing is a simple yet important investment principle that entails systematically selling winners (i.e., securities whose prices increase to the point that their portfolio weight now exceeds their strategic target) and buying losers (i.e., securities whose prices have substantially declined in value) on a periodic basis. Yet too often, investors instinctively seek to do the opposite when the market is rising or falling.

Rebalancing is an important form of portfolio risk management. Consider an example where an investor has set strategic asset allocations at 60 percent in the S&P 500 Index for stocks, 30 percent in five-year Treasuries for bonds, and 10 percent in the Dow Jones-UBS Commodity Index as part of an investment policy statement that reflects not only his desired exposure to certain asset classes but also the risk and return goals of his portfolio. If he allows allocations to drift as asset prices fluctuate over time, however, the more volatile asset classes will tend to become a larger share of the total and increase overall portfolio risk. Hence, the investor needs to periodically rebalance his portfolio. For example, comparing the performance of a quarterly rebalanced 60/30/10 portfolio from January 1992 to December 2012 with a portfolio never rebalanced, the rebalanced one achieved an annualized return of 7.78 percent (compared to 7.36 percent for the portfolio never adjusted), with a standard deviation of 9.37 percent versus 10.67 percent.

An equally large problem is the tendency for workers to ignore the allocations in their defined contribution retirement plans, such as a 401(k). In managing their own defined contribution accounts, investors seem prone to *status quo bias*, perhaps out of sheer inertia. That is, employees tend to adopt a "set it and forget it" approach with their retirement portfolios, with the result that initial asset allocations and portfolio risk migrate to levels that are inappropriate for the investor's long-term goals and risk tolerance.

Overlooking Human Capital

Many workers also compound investment risk by failing to consider their human capital (i.e., the present value of a worker's expected future labor income during her working lifetime) when investing. Perhaps due to *overconfidence* and *familiarity bias*, employers and employees very often overestimate their investment skills and overweight familiar assets within their retirement funds. This results in a lack of diversification within their overall portfolio and raises the odds of both human and financial capital being simultaneously devastated.

Instead, as a worker allocates personal assets, she may be better off underweighting investments that are closely correlated with her employment and instead allocating more money toward better diversifiers. For example, if she works for a brokerage firm, which is vulnerable to volatile stock market cycles, then she might consider a higher weighting in bonds and a below-market-weight allocation to financial sector stocks. If she is in the real estate business, she could consider underweighting property stocks. Consider the wealthy client of an advisor whose entire human capital is tied up in ownership of stores that sell a major consumer brand. The bulk of his investable assets are also tied up in the same brand's stock. The advisor might recommend that the client sell a large portion of the stock in his tax-deferred account, where the realized capital gains are not subject to taxes.

Reaching for Yield

Particularly in very low interest rate environments, generating portfolio income can be a challenge for investors—one that may push them to display greed and cognitive bias. Investors who overweight their portfolios in high yield bonds and preferred stocks can be employing a risky strategy. Some fail to recognize, for instance, that high yield bonds are highly correlated with stocks; and that preferred stocks are highly concentrated in one sector (financials), tend to move with common shares and are potentially more vulnerable to inflation. Investors nearing or in retirement are often those who reach for yield most consistently, ignoring the fact that an income-dominated portfolio is particularly vulnerable to the long-term effects of inflation.

Underestimating the Impact of Inflation

Inflation presents a special challenge for all investors, one that is detrimental and unforgiving to an investment portfolio. In fact, for some investors, "risk" is not so much the risk of investment loss in the near term as it is the risk of outliving their assets (referred to as *longevity risk*). Because people are living longer, retirees often underestimate the need to preserve purchasing power during decades of retirement and also might be overly risk averse. Investors who reduce their exposure to equities in favor of bonds are basically making a trade: acquiring higher current income in exchange for a higher risk to their future income. A more balanced and prudent approach is one that includes income-generating investments within the framework of a well-diversified, total return-oriented portfolio that includes equities and other assets with the potential for capital appreciation.

Thinking Too Much or Too Little about Taxes

Regarding taxes, behavioral biases reduce investor returns. Due to *loss aversion*, people own losing stocks longer than they logically should. Instead, they should sell the losers and deploy tax-loss harvesting techniques to realize a tax loss that can be used to offset capital gains. This approach could effectively add money to a portfolio and improve after-tax cash flow. By contrast, people with large, concentrated stock positions and substantial embedded capital gains resist selling positions because they dislike realizing taxable gains. In doing so, however, they are increasing systemic risk in their portfolios.

Another area in which investors make detrimental judgments as related to taxes is compartmentalizing their financial lives—separating their tax returns from their investment portfolios in an example of *mental accounting,* a cognitive bias in which people treat a sum of money differently from another equal-sized amount depending on the mental "account" to which they assign the money. Investors may lose an annualized percentage or more of their total return to taxes but often do not fully comprehend this because the information appears on two different documents. Investors should focus much more on after-tax returns. For investors in taxable accounts, how much return an investment earns matters less than how much of that return the investor actually keeps after taxes. Adept tax management can add a full percentage point each year (Arnott, Berkin, and Ye 2001) to an investor's after-tax return, which is substantial when compounding returns over a long investing career.

Indeed, taxes and sound tax management should be key considerations when formulating and executing an investment strategy.

THE IMPACT OF INVESTOR BEHAVIOR ON PORTFOLIOS

Investors who are subject to emotions such as fear, greed, and regret often act against their own best interests when investing. But how, in practice, do these biases manifest themselves in portfolios and ultimately in investor returns? This section examines this question and offers both qualitative and quantitative answers.

Suboptimal Strategies

Perhaps the best place to begin this discussion is how financial advisors should build emotions and behavior into portfolio construction. A basic assumption of modern portfolio theory (MPT) is investor rationality (Markowitz 1952). With the emergence of behavioral finance, the paradigm shifted to include psychological variables that can influence and distort investors' decision-making. Instead of debating which school is more accurate, an investment advisor should borrow from both. The result will be an investment portfolio and strategy that may be suboptimal from an MPT standpoint, but may be the right approach for the investor. In other words, sometimes "the right portfolio isn't the right portfolio" as prescribed by traditional finance.

Dollar-Cost Averaging Dollar-cost averaging (DCA) is a popular investment strategy among some individual investors and investment professionals. In dollar-cost averaging, individuals gradually invest money in the market by setting aside an amount at a certain frequency, such as monthly. Nonetheless, Gerstein Fisher Research (2011) finds that a lump-sum investment strategy produced superior results over 20-year rolling periods from January 1926 to December 2010. This evidence is consistent with the findings of Constantinides (1979), Rozeff (1994), and Leggio and Lien (2001).

Yet, despite studies that point to the superiority of a lump-sum approach, risk-averse investors find the structured and disciplined approach of DCA strategies emotionally comforting and satisfying. In practice, people typically use DCA when markets are down and they are fearful, which is frequently a time when they would be better off investing lump sums. By contrast, they demonstrate a greater willingness to invest lump sums when markets are rising and they are overconfident. Indeed, DCA's greatest (behavioral) value may be as a good exercise for people to become comfortable with investing, particularly in volatile markets.

Variable Annuities Before investing a client's money, an advisor should attempt to identify that client's risk tolerance. During bull market cycles, however, getting individuals to conceptualize how they will behave when turbulence occurs is difficult. For example, assume an investor is in his late fifties and eagerly planning for retirement when the market suddenly drops. The logical side of his brain knows that, long-term, stocks are generally a good investment that should maintain or increase purchasing power during retirement. But his emotional side simply cannot handle the volatility. In this scenario, a variable annuity invested in a diversified equity portfolio may be a good compromise for the behavioral investor.

From an MPT perspective, a variable annuity, which provides downside protection in the form of a guaranteed income stream regardless of stock market performance, is suboptimal. Contract fees tend to be very high, reducing equity investment returns. But if the alternative is for an anxious investor to liquidate stocks and exit the market completely, then an annuity with an aggressive allocation to equities may be preferable to an "uninsured" portfolio. This scenario exemplifies the late economist Herbert Simon's concept of *satisfice*, which combines "satisfy" and "suffice" to describe decisions or solutions that are acceptable and adequate but not optimal (Simon 1955).

A typical case illustrates the dilemma. In the fall of 2002, suppose an investor in her late fifties, unnerved by the 40–50 percent stock market collapse, says she wants to sell $400,000 of stocks (nearly 10 percent of her portfolio) and buy $400,000 of bonds. Based on her financial profile (she already had an adequate amount in cash, bonds, and other liquid instruments to meet 10 to 15 years of expenses), she has no logical reason to make the sudden change in her portfolio. Typical of the behavioral investor, she was extrapolating recent events into the future and feared that the market would fall yet another 40 to 50 percent. Despite valiant effort, Gerstein Fisher could not keep her in the equity market and thus introduced her to the idea of a variable annuity invested 100 percent in stocks. This allowed her to keep the $400,000 invested in the market, but within a variable annuity structure. The insurance costs her 1.5 percentage points per year more than not having it, reducing her expected annual stock return by that amount. Yet, this was still preferable to liquidating equities to buy bonds on the heels of a major stock market downturn. As it turns out, she had sought to exit stocks right near the bottom of the market, and by October 2007, five years later, the value of her annuity account had nearly doubled (i.e., a 100 percent cumulative return). If she had instead put the money into five-year Treasuries in the fall of 2002, the money five years later would have been worth only about 16 percent more.

When Suboptimal Is Better Another real-life example will help to illustrate the trade-offs between optimality from an MPT standpoint and what may be optimal for a given investor's circumstances. Take the case of an investor with two children who is in her forties when her husband passes away, leaving her with the payout from a $2 million life insurance policy. She earns a decent salary and has a mortgage and some student loans. An MPT-based portfolio optimizer might advise her to invest the entire insurance proceeds aggressively, perhaps 100 percent in stocks, and simply accept the volatile cycles in the markets for the next 30 years. But this is probably the wrong advice for her. What if the market falls 50 percent and she still has that mortgage on her house? Based on information about this individual, as well as experience with other clients in similar situations, an advisor might conclude that she would panic and sell equities at a major loss at the market bottom.

As a financial advisor, the best advice may be to recommend that this investor pay off the mortgage and student loans with the insurance money before investing in risky assets. Again, no standard finance optimizer will recommend this strategy, but the advisor's role is to keep the client invested so that she can earn the equity risk premium, which she would not do if she sold stocks in a moment of panic.

Reducing or eliminating leverage will provide her with some peace of mind and increase the chances that she will stay the course and remain rational in a turbulent stock market. In short, doing certain "boring" things during peaceful times, such as properly diversifying the portfolio, building up adequate emergency funds, purchasing insurance, and reducing leverage, may be irrational under MPT but will feel very rational in times of crisis and should help to improve long-term equity returns for the client.

Paying for Bad Behavior: Why Investors Underperform Investments

The data show that investments consistently outperform investors. Using Morningstar data, Maymin and Fisher (2011a) examine the average investor's actual return in mutual funds from January 1996 to December 2010. Their evidence shows that fully one percentage point of the investor's annual underperformance relative to the funds can be attributed to trading activity.

Dalbar, a financial services market research firm, studied the average equity investor's returns during the 20 years ending in December 2011 as compared to the annualized returns of the corresponding benchmarks (Dalbar 2012). The findings show that investors lagged their benchmarks by a stunning 4.23 percentage points per year. In other words, investors who attempt to time the market are unsuccessful. Too often investors depart from a well-designed long-term strategy to pursue short-term approaches that entail excessive trading, higher costs and taxes, and ultimately result in subpar long-term returns. No wonder investment sage Warren Buffett, in a play on Sir Isaac Newton's laws of motion, has said, "For investors as a whole, returns decrease as motion increases" (Buffett 2005).

For many investors, the hardest decision is to invest in equities when the market is down. When confronted with the kind of fight-or-flight scenario that down markets present, one's reflexive system comes into play. The same system motivates people to satisfy their basic needs and to avoid harmful situations quickly. For instance, advisors often heard such statements from clients in the wake of the market crash in 2008 as: "I want out of the market until it starts doing better—put my money in cash" and "I would like to stop investing until the markets go back up, then I will start again."

Investors also tend to chase returns by allocating more to "hot" funds or asset classes. Incessant media noise and aggressive advertising and marketing by mutual fund companies exacerbate this tendency for investors to make emotionally charged decisions. Evidence by Barber, Odean, and Zheng (2005) shows that mutual fund investors are attracted to funds through current high performance, marketing, or advertising. For instance, in the second half of 2011, a turbulent period in the stock market, an investor observes that gold is surging. Bombarded by negative news headlines that create high levels of anxiety, he is convinced that gold is going to $3,000 an ounce and he does not want to miss the ride. Despite the fact that he has a well-diversified portfolio that is appropriate for his long-term objectives, he calls his advisor to say that he wants to liquidate the entire portfolio and put everything into gold.

Maymin and Fisher (2011b) study the relationship between gyrations in the equity market and the volume of Gerstein Fisher client inquiries and attempts to alter portfolios from 1993 to mid-2010. Perhaps unsurprisingly, the volume of client inquiries was highest right after the sharpest rises and falls in the market (excluding the high volume of client contact right after opening an account). The data show that clients waited until the period of greatest volatility had passed and then wanted to do exactly what any advisor would tell them not to do: sell at the bottom or buy at the top of the cycle.

Consider the example of a chronic market timer whose risk tolerance is inconsistent. When markets are buoyant, he calls to increase his allocation to stocks; when stocks are plummeting, he seeks to reduce his exposure to equities and buy bonds. Intellectually, he knows his diversified portfolio, designed expressly for his situation, is rational. Yet, due to *recency bias*—placing undue weight on recent ob-servations—and other emotions, he obsesses about short-term risks. As Nobel Lau-reate Daniel Kahneman notes, investors frequently hurt themselves by exaggerating the importance of and focusing on recent news. Kahneman (2011, pp. 286–287) de-scribes the investor's dilemma as follows: "Humans are . . . guided by the immediate emotional impact of gains and losses, not by long-term prospects of wealth."

The next section discusses some ways in which financial advisors can help inves-tors increase their returns by adhering to their strategy and maintaining discipline even during turbulent market conditions.

HOW ADVISORS CAN HELP THE BEHAVIORAL INVESTOR

Being an effective financial advisor requires an understanding of investor psychology. Every day, advisors face the challenge of recommending rational investment strate-gies to behavioral investors. As long as investors are human, this challenge will re-main. Sometimes facts and figures are no match for the emotions of individuals who have experienced a large decline in wealth in a market downturn. Advisors can add value to the client relationship by factoring the investor behavioral component into their thinking and actions as it relates to working with their clients in both calm and turbulent times in the market. Following are key strategies and tactics for doing so.

Know Clients' Investing and Risk-Taking History

An investor whose first experience in the market was the dot-com bust will likely have a different attitude toward risk and investing than one who has never had a substantial loss of wealth over such a short period. Investors' histories often inform the decisions they make in the present and in the future. Such histories sometimes cause them to be inherently more risk-averse than they need to be given their goals and time horizon, or in some instances overly aggressive based on past successes. Understanding a client's past experiences up to the point at which he meets with the advisor helps to frame discussions and decisions in a way that will increase the likelihood that the client will act objectively in his own best interests as it relates to his investments.

However, drawing conclusions or making assumptions about risk-taking behav-ior based solely on past experiences also entails risks. The reality is that neither advisor nor investor really knows how the investor will react to a situation until that situation presents itself. One way to try to preview this is by talking through scenarios with clients. For example: "How would you feel if your daughter's 529 savings plan for college was down 30 percent next year?" By using specific, plausible scenarios and engaging in honest dialogue with clients about how they would likely react, advisors can gain additional insight into the level of risk the investor is able to bear (as opposed to what he tells the advisor he can bear). When that risk materializes, both advisor and client are better equipped to handle it.

Lay the Groundwork during Calm Times

The time to question an individual's investing strategy is not when it is being tested by volatile markets. Perhaps the best defense against behavioral biases is a disciplined investment strategy based on sound portfolio structure and managed in an equally disciplined manner. Advisors should work with investors to develop a clear road map and plan based on their near-, medium- and longer-term objectives and constraints, and build downside protection for unexpected negative events. Although building portfolios entirely around low-probability negative events is inadvisable, the advisor and client should account for the fact that rare events may occur and position portfolios to weather events such as a 40 percent market correction or a loss of employment without the need to sell securities to meet liquidity needs when stock prices may be significantly down. As discussed earlier, the only way an investor can realize the long-term equity risk premium is by staying invested for the long term and not selling during hard times.

Show, Don't Tell: Conduct Research for Clients

Instead of stating their opinions and beliefs, advisors are likely to have greater success with clients when advisors support what they are recommending with facts and evidence. Rather than behaving as though they can predict the future, advisors can conduct relevant historical studies that often help to convince clients to maintain the preselected portfolio choice. For instance, when clients were impatient with underperforming international markets in 2012, Gerstein Fisher conducted research demonstrating that, from January 1997 to September 2012, a global equity portfolio had outperformed a U.S.-only portfolio during all 10-year rolling periods (Fisher 2012). Likewise, during turbulent times, an advisor can show clients a convincing piece of research evidence, such as Exhibit 15.4, to remind them that, while 1-year returns can fluctuate substantially, 20-year rolling returns are much more tightly clustered in the 6 to 14 percent (annualized) range. This may temper investors' emotions and keep them focused on the long-term time horizon.

Share Experiences

When logic and facts fail to prevail over investor emotions, drawing on past experiences gained from working with other investors with similar fact patterns is often useful. Individuals typically relate better to others and their experiences than they can to financial data or a research study. By saying to a client, "We worked with a person last year with a similar financial profile as yours who unexpectedly lost a spouse, and here is what her experience was and what we did," an advisor is framing the discussion and connecting with the client on a human and emotional level. Additionally, when advisors have worked with investors to help them navigate through financial and life events, they can add real value to the client relationship.

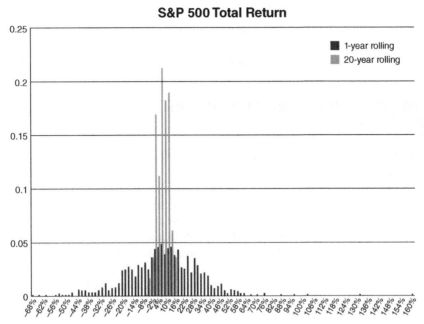

EXHIBIT 15.4   Distribution of S&P 500 Returns, 1926–2012: 1-Year Rolling versus 20-Year Rolling

Note: This graph depicts the stark difference between stock market returns during 1-year and 20-year rolling periods. During single-year periods, stock returns vary dramatically from large negative to large positive numbers. Over rolling 20-year periods, annualized returns are clustered more tightly in the 6 to 14 percent range.

Source: Standard & Poor's Index Services.

While knowing how every client scenario will play out is impossible, past experience with similar scenarios can provide a useful guide.

Obtain Discretion

If a financial advisor has been given discretion over a personal account, that advisor is able to make investment decisions on behalf of the client, and the risk of a client being harmed by emotionally driven actions can be mitigated. For advisors, having discretion over client accounts enables them to act in their clients' best interests and presumably make sound, healthy, and timely decisions. When advisors must first discuss portfolio changes with their clients before implementing them, the risk increases that the client will prevent the change from happening for behavioral reasons (e.g., not wanting to sell a position at a loss even when harvesting that loss will lower her overall tax bill). Such discussions may also prolong the time needed to implement the change due to additional discussions and coaching that may be required to help the client feel comfortable with the decision. Building trust and periodic communication between the financial advisor and the client are also required to ensure that this type of relationship agreement is successful for both parties.

Maymin and Fisher (2011b) conclude that an important way an advisor adds value to the client relationship is by restraining clients from their own tendencies to aggressively trade based on emotions such as fear, regret, and greed. The best conceived investment strategy is useless if the investor cannot maintain discipline due to emotional issues.

TURNING BIAS INTO BENEFIT: HOW TO PROFIT FROM INVESTOR BEHAVIOR

The possibility exists to harness and turn to an advantage predictable investor behavior during various parts of the economic cycle. Understanding the sentiment of market participants can help inform decisions on when to adjust market exposures. Because small (individual) investors are often an accurate contrarian indicator in the markets, a profitable strategy may be to implement an approach that is the opposite of this investor group (i.e., buy (sell) when small investors are selling (buying)).

Investors may also create long-term investment strategies by studying investor behavior. Substantial volatility in stock prices over any given year does not reflect the actual change in the relatively stable values of the underlying businesses. Exhibit 15.5 shows the wide historical discrepancy between stable dividend yields and movements in stock prices of the same businesses.

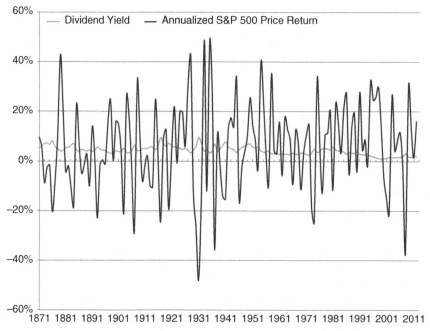

EXHIBIT 15.5   The Market Fluctuates Much More Than the Fundamentals: Dividend Yield versus Annualized S&P 500 Price Return: 1871–2012

Note: This graph demonstrates the wide historical discrepancy between volatile stock prices and the relatively stable values of the underlying businesses listed on the market, as captured by the dividend yield.

Sources: Robert Shiller, Gerstein Fisher Research.

Gauging Sentiment

Mutual fund flows are a good indicator with which to measure investor sentiment. As previously discussed, investors tend to buy stocks when the market has risen and they are feeling confident about investing. History shows this is generally not a good predictor of future returns. For example, in 2007 net inflows into equity funds were $75 billion (Investment Company Institute 2008). In 2008, the S&P 500 Index plunged 37 percent.

By contrast, past periods in which investors have been fearful and avoided risk have often portended strong market returns. In 2008, the worst year of the global financial crisis, investors withdrew $228 billion (net) from stock funds, only to witness a market increase of 27 percent the following year. Similarly, in 2011, a year punctuated by the euro zone sovereign debt and U.S. debt ceiling crises and high volatility, investors sold a net $98 billion of equity funds. In 2012 the S&P 500 Index jumped 16 percent (S&P Index Services 2012).

The VIX index is another gauge of investor sentiment. Often called the "fear index," VIX measures implied volatility in the stock market. VIX typically spikes when investors are nervous about markets and perhaps the economy, as depicted in Exhibit 15.6. Importantly, the VIX index generally rises **after** stocks have fallen sharply, not before. In other words, bearish markets lead to high volatility (e.g., in the summer of 2011) and bullish markets lead to lower volatility (e.g., during most of 2012). Most often, individuals are panicking and selling when the bad news is already priced into the market and the VIX is soaring. Therefore, an investor could

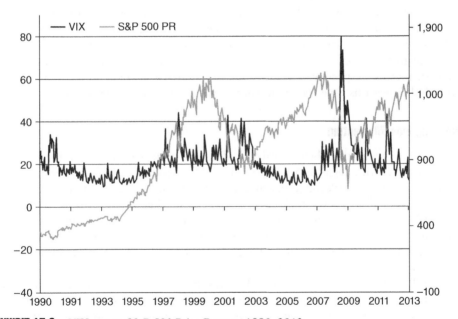

EXHIBIT 15.6 VIX versus S&P 500 Price Return: 1990–2012

Note: The VIX index, also called the "fear index," is a measure of implied volatility in the stock market. This graph demonstrates how VIX spikes, as in 2008, when investors are nervous and anxious about the market. The VIX index generally rises after stocks fall sharply, not before.

Sources: Standard & Poor's Index Services, Bloomberg.

create a strategy to increase equity exposure when the VIX, a good contrarian indicator, has risen to a certain level.

Embracing the Risks Others Won't

Because investors are so consistently illogical, this behavior can be predicted. Therefore, studying other investors' recurring patterns of irrational behavior can enable the development of long-term investment strategies that profit from the lack of perfect efficiency in markets driven by cognitive lapses and emotional biases. If markets provide an accurate assessment, on average, of pricing risk and if a riskier investment provides a higher rate of return, then the riskier the asset, the greater is the expected return. But the riskier the asset (i.e., perhaps it is more volatile, less liquid or not as well understood), the less willing investors will be to allocate to it.

As a result and as first formalized by Fama and French (1993) as a factor-based model, investors who are willing to take risks by overweighting portfolios toward small-company and value stocks historically have been rewarded with superior risk premia. From January 1926 through December 2012, the smallest 20 percent of stocks returned 12.02 percent annualized, compared to just 9.32 percent annualized for the largest 20 percent of listed companies (Center for Research in Security Prices 2012). Owing to the power of compounding over those 87 years, a $1,000 investment in small-cap stocks increased to $19.4 million, or more than eight times more than an identical investment in large companies over the same time frame. However, this higher return was associated with higher volatility because the annual standard deviation for small caps was 32.6 percent, or 80 percent higher than for large stocks.

In a similar vein, from July 1926 to December 2012 domestic large-company value stocks returned an annualized 11.67 percent, compared to just 9.34 percent for large growth stocks based on the Fama/French Large Cap Value and Large Cap Growth indices, respectively. Value stocks generated 6.2 times more wealth than growth did over this time frame but came with 35 percent more volatility.

Profiting from Momentum

Momentum is another behavioral-linked factor that can be used to enhance investment returns. Jegadeesh and Titman (1993) first identified momentum as a systematic source of risk for equity investors. Their research reveals that momentum investing provides excess stock returns over a market index. Although finance academics widely acknowledge the notion that momentum exists in the market, no agreement prevails as to why it exists. One common theory is that some of the momentum premium can be understood in the framework of investor behavioral biases.

Momentum is the tendency of stock market winners to keep winning and losers to keep losing relative to their peers. This results from the fact that people tend to take pleasure and pride in holding onto their winners, often longer than they should. Investors also tend to hold losing stocks longer than they should because they do not want to realize losses by selling (i.e., *loss aversion*) and experience an emotional loss such as regret. Just like Newton's first law of motion, which posits that objects in motion will stay in motion, stocks on a winning streak often tend to stay on a winning streak until they reach highs well above their fundamental values. Likewise, stocks on losing streaks tend to fall lower than an unemotional assessment of their inherent values would indicate they should. The pattern occurs so frequently that Jegadeesh and Titman (1993) find that by applying an investment strategy to the momentum phenomenon, investors could earn returns of about 1 percent per month, which is a substantial premium to the standard market results.

Investors can potentially profit from momentum investing by making it a component of a comprehensive investment strategy. As discussed earlier, history shows that over the long term, investors tend to be compensated with returns in excess of the market's average in exchange for assuming certain types of excess risk. Along with small cap and value stocks, momentum stocks are characterized by both higher volatility and higher long-term returns than the market as a whole.

SUMMARY

Investors are not the rational actors that traditional finance theory would make them out to be, which has considerable implications for both their investing experience and other market participants. Investors' cognitive and emotional tendencies such as heuristics, overconfidence, fear, greed, or regret often drive them to trade excessively, which results in lower investment returns than they would otherwise earn.

Historical fund flows and other data demonstrate that individual investors tend to exit or enter the market at the wrong times. That is, they enter the market (buy) right after a dramatic increase in market values at the peak or cash out (sell) just after a substantial decrease in prices at the bottom. Although risk and return are inextricably linked (investors need to incur risk in order to earn return), investors find that being greedy when others are fearful or vice versa is psychologically difficult no matter how logically compelling the data are.

The environment in which investors and their advisors operate today is complex and imperfect. While the reality of markets cannot be explained solely by the tenets of standard or traditional finance, behavioral finance by itself also is insufficient to fully explain security prices. Rather, understanding the interaction between the two is essential to comprehending the entire decision-making process experienced by investors. As discussed in this chapter, an investment strategy or portfolio structure that may be suboptimal from an MPT standpoint may be the most appropriate solution for a specific individual given the circumstances or how the person is likely to act in different market scenarios.

Against this backdrop, individual investors are likely to value financial advisors who can manage the emotional and behavioral aspects of the client relationship. By educating their clients on an ongoing basis and helping them to maintain perspective and to stay focused during times of market stress, advisors should be able to help them make better decisions and ultimately experience improved investment results. Additionally, by designing investment strategies that capitalize on common investor behavioral biases, advisors can help their clients actually profit from these phenomena.

DISCUSSION QUESTIONS

1. Provide several examples of ways in which investors are their own worst enemies.

2. Explain why investors underperform the actual funds and asset classes in which they are invested.
3. Discuss the meaning of suboptimal investing, provide some examples of suboptimal strategies, and explain why suboptimal may actually be right for some investors.
4. Discuss how investment advisors can help their "behavioral" clients.
5. Indicate some strategies that investors could employ to profit from investor behavior.

REFERENCES

Arnott, Robert D., Andrew L. Berkin, and Jia Ye. 2001. "Loss Harvesting: What's It Worth to the Taxable Investor?" *Journal of Wealth Management* 3:4, 10–18.

Barber, Brad R., Terrance Odean, and Lu Zheng. 2005. "Out of Sight, Out of Mind: The Effects of Expenses on Mutual Fund Flows." *Journal of Business* 78:6, 2095–2119.

Buffett, Warren E. 2005. "Berkshire Hathaway 2005 Chairman's Letter." Available at www.berkshirehathaway.com/letters/2005ltr.pdf.

Buffett, Warren E. 2008. "Buy American. I Am." *New York Times*, October 17, A33.

Center for Research in Security Prices. 2012. University of Chicago. Available at www.crsp.com/.

Constantinides, George M. 1979. "A Note on the Suboptimality of Dollar-Cost Averaging as an Investment Policy." *Journal of Financial and Quantitative Analysis* 14:2, 443–450.

Dalbar. 2012. "Quantitative Analysis of Investor Behavior 2012." Available at www.dalbar.com/ProductsServices/AdvisorSolutions/QAIB/tabid/214/Default.aspx.

Fama, Eugene, and Kenneth French. 1993. "Common Risk Factors in the Returns on Stocks and Bonds." *Journal of Financial Economics* 33:1, 3–56.

Gerstein Fisher Research. 2011. "Does Dollar Cost Averaging Make Sense for Investors? *DCA's Benefits and Drawbacks Examined*," 1–8. Available at www.gersteinfisher.com/assets/files/research/GF_Research_Dollar_Cost_Averaging_Oct_2011.

Fisher, Gregg S. 2012. "Don't Give Up on the Global Portfolio." *Forbes.com*, November 7. Available at www.forbes.com/sites/greggfisher/2012/11/07/dont-give-up-on-the-global-portfolio/.

Investment Company Institute. 2008. *2008 Investment Company Fact Book*, 48th ed. Available at www.ici.org/pdf/2008_factbook.pdf.

Jegadeesh, Narsimhan, and Sheridan Titman. 1993. "Returns to Buying Winners and Selling Losers: Implications for Stock Market Efficiency." *Journal of Finance* 48:1, 65–91.

Kahneman, Daniel. 2011. *Thinking, Fast and Slow*. New York: Farrar, Straus and Giroux.

Leggio, Karyl B., and Donald Lien. 2001. "Does Loss Aversion Explain Dollar-Cost Averaging?" *Financial Services Review* 10:1–4, 117–127.

Markowitz, Harry. 1952. "Portfolio Selection." *Journal of Finance* 7:1, 77–91.

Maymin, Philip Z., and Gregg S. Fisher. 2011a. "Past Performance Is Indicative of Future Beliefs." *Risk and Decision Analysis* 2:3, 145–147.

Maymin, Philip Z., and Gregg S. Fisher. 2011b. "Preventing Emotional Investing: An Added Value of an Investment Advisor." *Journal of Wealth Management* 13:4, 34–43.

Morningstar. 2009. *Morningstar Fund Flows and Investment Trends. Annual Report 2009*. Available at www.morningstardirect.morningstar.com/clientcomm/2009.pdf.

Rozeff, Michael S. 1994. "Lump-Sum Investing versus Dollar-Averaging." *Journal of Portfolio Management* 20:2, 45–50.

Simon, Herbert A. 1955. "A Behavioral Model of Rational Choice." *Quarterly Journal of Economics* 69:1, 99–118.

S&P Index Services. 2012. Available at www.standardandpoors.com/indices/main/en/us.

DISCLOSURE

Different types of investments involve varying degrees of risk. Therefore, readers should not assume that future performance of any specific investment, investment product, or investment strategy (including the investments and/or investment strategies referenced in this chapter, or any of the chapter's non-investment related content), will be profitable, prove successful, or be applicable to any individual's specific situation. Readers should not assume that this chapter serves as the receipt of, or a substitute for, personalized advice from Gerstein Fisher, GFA Securities, LLC, or from any other investment professional. Should readers have any questions regarding the applicability of any portion of the chapter's content to their individual situations, they are encouraged to consult with the professional advisors of their choosing.

ABOUT THE AUTHOR

Gregg S. Fisher, CFA founded independent investment management and advisory firm Gerstein Fisher in 1993. Gerstein Fisher was one of the first organizations to integrate investment management, financial planning, and tax management within a single firm. Today, Gerstein Fisher manages investments on behalf of individuals, families, other financial advisors and institutions using a quantitative, research-based investment approach that incorporates both risk and investor behavioral factors. As Chair of the firm's Investment Strategy Group, Mr. Fisher is responsible for the management and oversight of Gerstein Fisher's investment strategies. He also spearheads research projects on areas of study that have included momentum and valuation models and tax-efficient investment strategies. Through the Gerstein Fisher Research Center, which he established in 2009, Mr. Fisher partners with leading academics in the areas of finance, risk engineering, and economics to conduct research that has immediate, real-world applicability to the practice of investing. Some of the Center's studies have been published in leading industry journals including *Journal of Wealth Management*. Mr. Fisher holds a degree in finance from the State University of New York at Buffalo.

Retirement Planning: Contributions from the Field of Behavioral Finance and Economics

James A. Howard
Professor of Finance, University of Maryland, University College

Rassoul Yazdipour
Professor of Finance, California State University and
Academy of Behavioral Finance and Economics

INTRODUCTION

Retirement involves withdrawal from one's position or occupation or from active working life. Often people less than 50 years old have difficulty imagining themselves in a retirement state. Planning for the future takes effort, especially when considering the generally unpleasant thought of aging and eventual mortality. Kahneman (2011) discusses this propensity for people to fail to deal with issues such as planning. He characterizes the mind as composed of two systems: system 1 represents intuition and system 2 represents cognition. System 1 functions rapidly in considering a course of action, while system 2 is slower, requires effort, and is naturally "lazy." When faced with a decision-making challenge, system 1 has the initial option of deciding whether to deal with the situation using intuition or heuristics or to defer to system 2. An individual needs discipline, effort, and the right incentives to employ system 2 and engage in financial/wealth planning when many uncertainties exist and the perceived need for immediate action is low.

Other obstacles exist in the way the human brain has evolved over time. Humans appear to have acquired ingrained behaviors that motivate them to overemphasize the present, which makes initiating actions with future well-being in mind difficult. When considering all the biases, heuristics, and framing effects that individuals face, major obstacles exist in planning for retirement.

The majority of writings dealing with retirement planning tend to focus on examining various types of products and identifying future income needed to replace a certain percentage of working income. This approach provides useful information. Yet, without a planning framework and context, people have difficulty sorting through the recommendations and aligning them with their own personal situation based on their own degree of wants, needs, motivation, and satisfaction.

The purpose of this chapter is to help readers incorporate knowledge gained from behavioral finance and economics into their planning for a secure and comfortable retirement. The chapter begins with a review of a life cycle financial planning and wealth management model as an example of a useful framework for developing a path to wealth accumulation and a secure retirement. Next, it presents an overview of the economic and demographic context needed to provide a clear picture of evolving macro trends as a basis for realistic planning. Instead of building the analysis around selected special situations, the chapter addresses more generic or common issues across age groups and economic brackets. Major life events and the aging process drive investment, saving, and consumption requirements at different points in the life cycle model. Within this context, the relevant findings from cognitive psychology and neuroscience and how such findings affect financial decision-making behaviors are reviewed. Next, the role of trust in the financial markets and products marketed by financial services companies is analyzed and discussed. The final section provides a summary and conclusions.

A LIFE CYCLE FINANCIAL PLANNING AND WEALTH MANAGEMENT MODEL

Retirement/wealth management planning can be facilitated by considering financial requirements over a person's life cycle. The Life Cycle of Financial Planning (Mainstreet Wealth Group 2012) provides a good example of life cycle

EXHIBIT 16.1   Life Cycle Needs by Age Group

Young Adult: Ages 18–24	Adult with or without Children: Ages 25–34
<ul><li>Establishing a household</li><li>Establishing credit</li><li>Training for career</li><li>Establishing savings</li><li>Earning financial independence</li><li>Creating a spending plan</li><li>Determining insurance needs</li><li>Developing a personal financial identity</li></ul>	<ul><li>Engaging in child-bearing</li><li>Managing increased need for credit</li><li>Engaging in child-raising</li><li>Discussing and managing additional insurance needs</li><li>Starting an education fund for children</li><li>Creating a will</li><li>Expanding career goals</li></ul>
Working Parent or Adult: Ages 35–44	**Midlife: Ages 45–54**
<ul><li>Upgrading career training</li><li>Building on children's education fund</li><li>Developing protection needs for head-of-household</li><li>Arising requirement for greater income due to expanding needs</li><li>Establishing retirement goals</li></ul>	<ul><li>Assisting with higher education for children</li><li>Investing</li><li>Updating retirement plans</li><li>Developing estate plans</li></ul>

EXHIBIT 16.1   (*Continued*)

Pre-Retirement: Ages 55–64	Retired: Ages 65 and over
• Consolidating assets • Planning future security • Reevaluating property transfer (estate) • Investigating retirement part-time income or volunteer work • Evaluating expenses for retirement and current housing • Meeting responsibilities of aging parents	• Reevaluating and adjusting living conditions and spending as related to health and income • Acquiring assistance in management of personal and financial affairs • Adjusting insurance programs for increasing risks • Finalizing estate plans • Finalizing a will or letter of last instructions

Note: The exhibit provides a model for wealth and retirement planning divided into six age groups and shows characteristics for each group.

Source: Modified from http://mainstreetwealthgroup.com/wp/wp-content/uploads/2011/12/Life_Events_of_Financial_Planning.pdf.

planning. This model helps individuals become familiar with how important events over a life span largely drive their saving, spending, investment, and retirement needs. Starting at the young adult stage, Exhibit 16.1 shows what a typical individual can use as a basis for budgeting in the near term and planning in the longer term.

While this model is not optimal for everyone, it is a good starting point for determining the requirements for satisfying spending, investing, and retirement needs as one gets older. Using a similar framework provides a sound basis for aligning planning with the competing needs for resources over time. To effectively manage their wealth over their lifetime, both the young and old should adopt a similar structure as a vehicle for near-term budgeting and long-term planning. Although many do not develop a detailed plan too far into the future, they should at least think about the goals along a time line and reconcile near-term planning and financial actions with these goals.

DEMOGRAPHIC AND MACROECONOMIC CONTEXT

The purpose of this section is to recognize the overwhelming external challenges to developing a good retirement financial plan. According to the Federal Reserve (2012), median net worth fell 38.8 percent for U.S. households between 2007 and 2010 while mean net worth fell 14.7 percent for the same period. The major cause of losses in net worth is attributed to the collapse of housing prices beginning in 2007 and continuing through 2012. According to a press release from S&P Dow Jones Indices (2012), the S&P 500 companies with defined contribution plans were underfunded by about 30 percent or $355 billion at the end of 2011. Combined with the continuing trend of moving from defined benefit to defined contribution plans, many employees will need to save more in preparation for retirement.

A recent *Financial Finesse Reports* (2012) poll of a sample of workers shows that despite all the educational materials available urging workers to save more for retirement, a substantial proportion of workers confirm they are not taking the necessary actions to secure their retirement. The recent bursting of the technology and real estate bubbles and volatility in the stock market have intensified the obstacles to saving more for retirement. Although everyone hopes for a vibrant economy to return soon, demographics pose a problem. A housing recovery may take a generation or so because the baby boomer generation is in the early stages of entering retirement and downsizing to smaller homes. This would not necessarily be a problem if the following generation (popularly termed generation X, born from the early 1960s through the early 1980s) contained sufficient numbers in their cohort to absorb the oversupply of housing. Yet, generation X is much smaller than the baby boomer generation. Consequently, the effect could be a long, drawn-out recession in housing and a recovery in market values that may take decades.

BIASES, HEURISTICS, AND FRAMING EFFECTS ON RETIREMENT PLANNING

Beginning in the late 1940s, finance was entering its golden age of financial theory. The important aspect of these theories is the set of assumptions of classical decision theory related to *homo-economicus*, or the rational man. Neumann and Morgenstern (1944) formalized this concept of the rational man in the form of expected utility theory. In this theory, they assumed man acted rationally in making economic decisions according to the following axioms:

- *Completeness.* People can rank order all choices/alternatives (revealed preferences).
- *Transitivity.* If a person prefers B to A and C to B, then this individual prefers C to A.
- *Continuity.* When an individual prefers A to B and B to C, then there should be a feasible combination of A and C in which the individual is then indifferent between this combination and B.

Financial theory was met by great enthusiasm and continued to build momentum through the 1960s but it had its critics. Both researchers and practitioners identified numerous exceptions to theories, especially to the efficient markets hypothesis (EMH) and the capital asset pricing model (CAPM). Given the strong assumptions required by the theories, criticisms could be expected, but the volume and degree of deviations from how individuals were supposed to make financial decisions and how asset prices were supposed to act grew to a crescendo by 1970. A new paradigm, behavioral finance, was emerging in the early 1970s to address the documented deficiencies associated with the theory of finance.

In experiments, Kahneman and Tversky (1972) observed how people behaved when offered various choices/gambles. They identified situations where people systematically deviated from classical decision theory and the rational models of economic/financial theory. This research resonated with both academics and practitioners and stimulated the development of prospect theory (Tversky and Kahneman 1974; Kahneman and Tversky 1979; Kahneman, Slovic, and Tversky 1982) and behavioral finance/economics. Behavioral inconsistencies, with contributions from many researchers, can be sorted into three broad categories: biases, heuristics, and framing effects.

Biases

Biases are the predispositions to commit specific types of errors. Research shows that people typically exhibit biases on a systematic basis, even when they are shown to be acting irrationally and not in their own best interests (Agarwal et al. 2006; Knoll 2010). A heightened awareness of irrational behavior increases the potential for developing mitigating strategies that recognize impulses to act in a biased fashion and to make corrections in real time. This is not an easy accomplishment and the ability to achieve it varies widely across different categories of investors.

All the biases shown in Exhibit 16.2 adversely affect financial planning and wealth management. For instance, status quo encourages one to delay. Overconfidence, confirmation, excessive optimism, and illusion of control feed into procrastination by creating more reasons for deferring planning until later. Biases also facilitate unwise management of investments, lowering the potential return through poor selection strategies or by allowing emotion to play too prominent a role. Hindsight bias makes the past seem easier to explain and therefore acts to feed overconfidence in the ability to use acquired knowledge to forecast the future. Conservatism affects the timeliness of the wealth management plan and intermediate objectives by blinding individuals to new information affecting current financial plans.

EXHIBIT 16.2 Biases Affecting Financial Planning and Wealth Management

Description
When people procrastinate or have a preference for the current state of affairs.
When people overestimate how frequently they will experience favorable outcomes and underestimate how frequently they will experience unfavorable outcomes.
When people make mistakes more frequently than they believe and view themselves as better than average.
When people attach too much importance to information that supports their views relative to information that runs counter to their view.
When people overestimate the extent to which they can control outcomes.
When people, after learning the eventual outcome, give a much higher estimate for the predictability of that outcome than subjects who predict the outcome without advance knowledge.
When people demonstrate an attachment to past analyses, practices, beliefs, and commitments even when they start to prove erroneous, counterproductive, even unsustainable.

Note: The exhibit lists and describes various predispositions for committing financial decision-making mistakes.

Heuristics

When uncertainty characterizes the decision-making context, limited availability of information, or urgency, simplifying shortcuts or heuristics can lead to financial planning errors. Exhibit 16.3 describes four heuristics categories: representativeness, availability, anchoring, and affect heuristic. Being a function of the fast thinking system 1, heuristic-driven decisions are made quickly and are frequently accompanied by relatively high emotions (or affect) and serious financial decision-making errors (Slovic, Peters, Finucane, and McGregor 2005, 2007).

Mercier and Sperber (2011) contend that what researchers label as biases and heuristics may be more accurately captured as a general unconscious confirmation bias. They rely on psychological research showing that people consistently fail in arguing logically (Evans 2002), exhibit biased reasoning (Kahneman et al. 1982), and make serious mistakes in estimating probabilities (Kahneman and Tversky 1972; Tversky and Kahneman 1983). Mercier and Sperber conclude that something innate exists in humans at the unconscious level that serves as the source of this innate bias behavior. A general confirmation bias is portrayed as an evolutionary human adaptation for communicating effectively in a group environment. This is consistent with anthropological conclusions about human brain development.

Early humans were primarily motivated to develop survival strategies. Gaining access to resources and avoiding danger were high priorities for survival, and being able to reason effectively was critical to being a successful member of the group. This has obvious connections with neuroscience and cognitive psychology research, providing support for a more comprehensive approach to financial decision-making. The implication that humans come prewired to view the world with a strong confirmation bias is consistent with the observed persistence in using of biases and

EXHIBIT 16.3   Heuristics Categories

Heuristic	Description
Representativeness	When people try to determine the probability that a data set A was generated by a model B, or that an object A belongs to class B (i.e., they evaluate the probability by the degree to which A reflects the essential characteristics of B).
Availability	When people rely on information that is readily available and intuitive relative to information that is less salient and more abstract.
Anchoring	When people form an estimate by beginning with an initial number and adjusting to reflect new information or circumstances but they tend to make insufficient adjustments relative to that number, thereby leading to anchoring bias.
Affect heuristic	When people base their decisions primarily on intuition, instinct, and gut feeling.

Note: The exhibit lists and describes how mental shortcuts contribute to financial decision-making mistakes.

EXHIBIT 16.4   Framing Effects

Framing Effect	Description
Glass half empty/half full	Preference for an option depends on whether choices are couched in terms of probabilities of success or failure.
Aversion to a sure loss	When subjected to a loss from a starting endowment, a tendency exists to hold the investment/project until break even, irrespective of whether the outlook is positive or negative for future performance.
Mental accounting	The mental account associated with the decision to accept a gamble includes money won or lost in that gamble and excludes other assets or the outcome of previous bets.

Note: The exhibit lists and describes how framing effects influence financial decision-making.

heuristics in financial decision-making, even among investment experts with high levels of education and experience.

Framing Effects

Framing affects investment and saving choices for all types of investors. Exhibit 16.4 lists several examples of framing. For example, how employers disclose defined contribution options to employees affects their saving choices through this vehicle. If the employer gives an employee a match of a certain percentage of pay based on the employee's contribution, then not matching the potential maximum employer contribution is an inferior choice. When employees must choose the percentage of pay to contribute, many contribute nothing or something well below the match (Choi, Laibson, and Metrick 2002).

Thaler and Sunstein (2003) introduce the concept of "libertarian paternalism" (also known as nudging) in recommending "nudges" to save and invest more. In the example of a worker contributing to a defined contribution or 401(k) plan, the employee would be automatically enrolled to contribute the required amount to receive the maximum employer match. The employee could opt out by selecting an alternative contribution or by withdrawing from the plan. As Choi et al. (2002) and Benartzi and Thaler (2007) note, automatic enrollment with the ability to opt out results in higher savings rates by employees. While evidence shows that this increases savings rates, it relies on the passivity of the individual (i.e., status quo bias or inertia), rather than a proactive component in the employee's financial and wealth management plan (Benartzi, Previtero, and Thaler 2011).

HYPERBOLIC DISCOUNTING

In the theory of finance, comparing alternative choices requires discounting expected future benefits back to the present at the required rate of return (or the return required to delay consumption to a future date) so that decision makers make choices on a common discounted basis (Samuelson 1937). For example, savers may require a return on their money in a savings account of 3 percent annually as a requirement to save for future consumption and not spend now. A key finding from cognitive psychology is that humans deviate from theory. The rate of time preference or discount rate is not constant through time. Instead, people appear to employ hyperbolic discounting in deciding whether to take rewards sooner rather than later (i.e., based on the underlying assumption that people suffer from self-control bias, in which individuals prefer to spend money today at the cost of investing for a future goal such as retirement savings). Thus, people tend to overweight the preference for immediate consumption. Exhibit 16.5 shows this human tendency, where the solid line represents a constant time discount and the dotted line represents hyperbolic discounting.

Frederick, Loewenstein, and O'Donoghue (2002) cite a large number of studies implying that most people apply hyperbolic discounting when choosing between taking a reward now and waiting for a larger reward. In experiments, if an individual were offered $100 right now or $110 a week from now, which would they choose? Most subjects choose to take $100 now because they do not view waiting a week for only $10 more as a sufficient trade-off. However, if the individual were offered $100 a year from now or $110 a year and one week from now, most would wait the extra week for the $110. These are equivalent choices in economic/finance theory, but people usually reverse their preferences and choose to wait an extra week for an extra $10 if the reward is delayed for a year. As Exhibit 16.5 shows, the farther an event lies in the future, the less people care about it and the

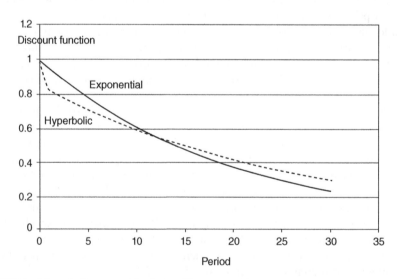

EXHIBIT 16.5   Hyperbolic versus Traditional/Exponential Discount Function

Note: The exhibit illustrates how reward timing affects financial decision-making. For decisions in the near term, an overweighted preference occurs for the more immediate reward beyond that described by a traditional discount function. In the longer term, a reversal takes place and the preference for the more immediate reward is under weighted compared to a traditional discount function.

Source: Ackert and Deaves (2010).

less hyperbolic discounting affects the choice. For choices in the very near term, an individual exhibits an overweighted preference for consumption now. As the time horizon lengthens, this overweighting of the nearer reward declines and eventually reverses to underweighting a preference for the shorter-term option. This propensity that people have for consumption now rather than waiting, which relates to the issue of self-control bias, can prove catastrophic for saving toward long-term goals and retirement.

THE ROLE OF THE BRAIN IN FINANCIAL DECISION-MAKING

Neuroscience, also known as neurofinance, has had a substantive impact on the study of financial decision-making behavior since the mid-1980s. In describing the following changes in the brain when exposed to various decision-making situations and their emotional content, some liberty has been taken to simplify very complex processes that are still not completely understood. Based on current knowledge, the human brain and its functions can be described in terms of three major components.

In Exhibit 16.6, the base of the brain, known as the *midbrain*, is the most ancient component (equivalent to lizards and snakes) and is located right above the

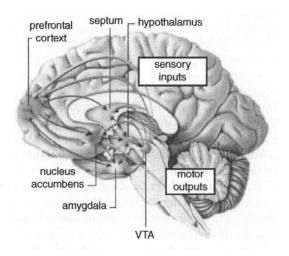

EXHIBIT 16.6   Brain Loss-Avoidance and Reward Systems

Note: The exhibit shows the brain structure. The most ancient part is the midbrain, primarily responsible for the regulation of body functions, at the top of the brain stem and including the portion is labeled "motor outputs" in the exhibit. The limbic system is the center of human emotions (gains/approach and loss/avoidance circuits) and lies above the midbrain, including the amygdala, ventral tagmental area (VTA), nucleus accumbens, hypothalamus, and septum areas in the exhibit. The most modern part of the brain is the cerebrum, lying above the limbic system and including the areas labeled sensory inputs and prefrontal cortex in the exhibit. The prefrontal cortex is the center of human cognition and decision-making.

Source: Wikipedia.

brain stem. The midbrain, which is the area labeled motor outputs, the cerebellum, in Exhibit 16.6, is part of the central nervous system and is involved with hearing, motor control, vision, and body temperature regulation. As life on Earth evolved, the limbic system developed. Located above the midbrain, the limbic system is the center of emotions. The limbic system is the area including the hypothalamus, nucleus accumbens, amygdala, and ventral tagmental area (VTA) in Exhibit 16.6. As a higher-level component of brain physiology, emotions are necessary to initiate action. The third part of the brain, the center of cognition, is the prefrontal lobe/cortex of the cerebrum lying around and on top of the limbic system. As the most modern part of the brain, some estimate it to be millions of years old, although modern human behaviors, such as tool making, are not evident until around 80,000 years ago.

With functional magnetic resonance imaging (fMRI) equipment, researchers can observe what happens in the brain as emotions signal that action is needed. The scanner uses radio waves and a strong magnetic field to make images of the brain showing brain activity. Neural activity causes changes in the need for oxygen, which causes changes in blood flow. Differences in the magnetic properties arising from hemoglobin in the blood when the brain is oxygenated, compared to when it is depleted of oxygen, result in magnetic fluctuations that are recorded by the fMRI. Through many experiments using the fMRI with subjects, researchers have identified a *gains circuit* (anticipating gains and pleasure) that connects the nucleus accumbens in the limbic system (emotional brain) to the prefrontal lobes/cortex (cognitive brain). Similarly, a loss circuit (anticipating and experiencing losses) begins in the amygdala (emotional brain) of the limbic system and travels to the prefrontal lobes. Gains and losses emotions generate messages along these circuits calling for action by the prefrontal cortex (lobes) or thinking part of the brain. The messages are interpreted and acted (or not acted) on by either system 1 or system 2.

Human behavior in the forms of biases, heuristics, framing effects, and hyperbolic discounting can now be placed into a physiological context of how decisions are initiated and made in the brain. Emotions play an important role in this judgment process. Errors in handling and interpreting these emotions can result in serious decision-making mistakes. Good decisions require a balance between emotions and using cognitive skills to interpret and act on these emotions. As Kahneman (2011) explains, people are predisposed to make the quick decision based on emotion and intuition (system 1, thinking fast). The ability to balance emotions and cognition and make the best financial decisions is termed *emotional intelligence*. It can be acquired through learning and self-awareness, but takes considerable effort and conditioning or practice and a willingness to be accountable for lapses when poor decisions have been made.

Trust is an important variable in decisions related to purchasing financial products and services. Oxytocin, a mammalian hormone that acts primarily as a neuromodulator in the brain, has an important role in establishing feelings of trust in humans. In trust games, Zak (2011) shows that subjects treated with oxytocin exhibit a higher level of trust in the amounts of money they were willing to distribute to others in the expectation of receiving reciprocity from the other party. This is because oxytocin, which is released by the pituitary gland, stimulates feelings of contentment, reductions in anxiety, and feelings of calmness and security. Other studies show that oxytocin has a correlation with human bonding, that it increases trust and decreases fear (Marazziti et al. 2006).

Marketers of financial services are effective consumers of research into how human decision-making behavior motivates a person to purchase financial products and services. While marketing can contribute valuable information to consumers about the availability, features, and quality of competitive offerings, it has a dark side that is especially harmful to the financial security of individuals. Products and services are designed and promoted by approaches that are intended to stimulate the release of oxytocin and misguided feelings of trust in potential customers. Such marketing programs are primarily meant to separate potential customers from their money, rather than help them make sound financial decisions. For example, financial services commercials such as those involving annuities that present a retired family in a secure and happy context go beyond informing and rely upon stimulating warm fuzzy feelings to affect financial decisions.

Also, consider the predictable ads that appear when an asset class is experiencing gains, such as trading currencies in a $1 million margin account for $100,000 cash or that involve buying software to trade trends. The impression communicated by the ads is that this is easy money, where bad gambles would be a better representation. Individuals vary in their receptiveness to these marketing efforts. Aware individuals who understand ad characteristics meant to instill an unjustified state of trust can be protected from reacting in ways that are not in their best interests. Segments of the population who are less aware and sophisticated are more prone to purchasing inferior products and services, simply because they have been primed or conditioned to feel they are dealing with trustworthy financial providers.

FINANCIAL DECISION-MAKING QUALITY AND AGE

Agarwal, Driscoll, Gabaix, and Laibson (2009) report on recent research that documents the effects of aging on our decision-making capability. One component of decision-making quality is the cognitive or analytic capability or potential in the brain. The analytic potential of the brain develops quickly after birth, increases to its maximum at around the age of 20, and then begins to decline at the rate of an average of about 1 percent per year through the age of 90. The decline in analytic potential after the age of 20 is offset by the positive effects of experience on decision-making quality. Exhibit 16.7 reflects the interaction of these influences.

According to Agarwal et al. (2009), neurological research indicates that the net quality of decision-making reaches a maximum in the mid-fifties (see Exhibit 16.7), with the risk of dementia beginning to increase markedly in the early seventies. By the time the average senior is 85, approximately 30 percent will suffer serious dementia. Besides making the individual more prone to financial decision-making mistakes as they age (i.e., a decline in financial literacy as a person ages), declining capability increases the susceptibility to schemes and scams. This has important implications for wealth management and retirement planning. A financial plan should incorporate some proactive strategy to cope with the inevitable decline in financial decision-making quality as a person ages. For example, this could include a

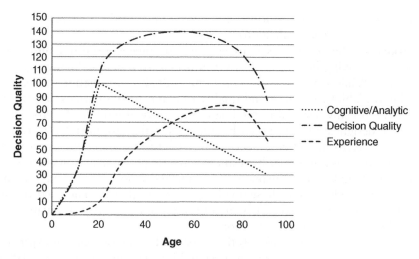

EXHIBIT 16.7 Financial Decision-Making Quality and Age

Note: The exhibit illustrates how brain aging and experience interact to affect decision quality. It shows that decision-making quality is a combination of the potential for cognitive ability based on development and aging of the physical brain and life experiences. Cognitive/analytical capability reaches its maximum potential at around the age of 20 and declines at the rate of approximately 1 percent per year. As a human ages and gains experience, this positive affects decision-making quality. As the individual ages, the positive effect of experience is greater than the decline due to aging of the brain, allowing decision-making quality to increase until the mid-fifties. At that point, the marginal increase from experience is less than the decline due to an aging brain, causing an overall decline in decision-making quality. This decline typically quickens when individuals enter their eighties.

Source: Modified from Agarwal et al. (2009).

procedure for progressively delegating some decision-making to a trusted party over time. The government plays a possible role that goes beyond the behavioral nudges described earlier. Regulations about better disclosure of financial products and fees and aligning policies with age cohorts and the testing of cognitive abilities are public policy options worth considering.

THE ROLE OF SELF-AWARENESS AND SELF-CONTROL

Perhaps the most important conclusion from cognitive psychology and neuroscience research is that individuals need to become more self-aware of their emotions and ingrained biases. Understanding the source of these predispositions to make mistakes is a necessary step toward improved decision-making and retirement planning. Given how the brain functions, individuals have a greater propensity to act in a specified manner if they experience or practice desired behaviors. In terms of brain function, positive experiences and training strengthen the connections between the neurons in the brain forming memories. This increases the probability of being able to override ingrained biases and poor performing heuristics in planning for retirement.

One way of achieving this objective is through the use of aged–progressed renderings of the future self (Hershfield et al. 2011). A recent facial picture is processed using software showing how the individual will look in his or her mid-sixties. The authors conduct four studies where the subjects are exposed to pictures showing how they currently appear compared to how they will look at the age of 65. Researchers then place subjects in experimental situations where they have to decide on the attractiveness of immediate rewards (see the discussion on hyperbolic discounting). In all cases, individuals who are exposed to the age renderings of themselves at retirement age give a greater weight to deferred rewards than before the experiment. Consistent with neuroscience findings, seeing a future self appears to spark a strong emotional reaction and lessens the tendency to overweight immediate rewards.

Another approach is through a pre-commitment strategy (Ariely and Wertenbroch 2002). The authors find that if people self-impose deadlines to overcome procrastination (status quo bias), this would improve performance. According to Choi et al. (2006) and Thaler and Benartzi (2004), some companies have been successful in structuring retirement programs employing pre-commitment saving strategies. For example, employees may agree, through a signed commitment, to save X percent of their salary via their 401(k), which would be reapplied as the employees received pay increases.

A third approach would be to administer a questionnaire assessing impulsiveness, or the degree to which emotions affect decisions. Taking this assessment, scoring it, and reflecting on decision-making behavior during a time span (e.g., five years) makes one more aware of how impulses or emotions affect decision-making quality.

TRUST AND RETIREMENT SAVING AND PLANNING: THE BASICS

Trust and confidence in the working of a financial system are critical to a well-functioning economic system. Trust is powerful enough to effectively discourage people from even considering planning for their retirement. For example, establishing trust between an expert (e.g., a financial planner) and a new client (e.g., an individual investor) is a very important aspect within the retirement planning process.

Trust is the product of both cognitive and affective or emotional attributes. This follows from what is known about the brain and how humans make decisions. Trust is also needed in situations where risk and uncertainty are present. Trust is not needed with complete foresight and knowledge. Trust is at its lowest possible level in an environment where absolutely nothing is known. However, an individual can have almost perfect trust in totally transparent and familiar environments and situations. Looking at trust this way, trust has many similarities with risk. Risk and trust can be considered to be the two sides of the same coin. When trust is at its highest level, the related perceived risk is very low or even nonexistent. In the same fashion, when no trust exists, the perceived risk would most probably be at its highest possible level.

According to Olsen (2008, p. 2190), "trust is primarily sociological since it would not be needed if only one person existed or if all persons where fully knowledgeable in a deterministic universe." He also notes that trust is a man-made device designed to reduce complexity in social relationships and the uncertainty of the natural world.

Moreover, according to Slovic and as reported in Olsen (2008),

- Trust tends to be fragile and easily broken.
- Trust takes much more time to create than to lose.
- Trust-destroying events usually are more salient than trust-building events.
- Distrust, once initiated, tends to reinforce and perpetuate additional distrust.
- Trust tends to disproportionately increase with the perceived benefit of the decision outcome especially when the truster's expertise is low.

Das and Teng (2004) discuss a risk-based view of trust by bringing probability into their discussion and relating perceived risk to subjective trust. As Das and Teng (2004, p. 98) note, "Having trust in someone does not imply 100 percent confidence in that person for any task and under any circumstance. Rather, subjective trust refers to the assessment of probability that the person will perform as expected." The authors break down the notion of subjective trust into its two components: goodwill and competence, with competence being a probability-based construct. Their probability-based approach to trust allows for more rigorous model building around the notion of trust. In this chapter, wherever the term confidence is used, it refers to the probability-based version of that construct.

Becerra, Heard, and Kremer (2005) offer four discovery methods, which effectively are devices to measure trust. Those factors are:

1. *Intuition.* "Any computation" that a truster can perform on a trustee including game theoretic approaches.
2. *Experience.* A trustee's integrity and competence as observed by the truster or others in the past.
3. *Hearsay.* A trustee's reputation and influence in the past.
4. *Records.* Any information on the trustee that could be obtained from an institution or authority.

By stating that no economic agent can possess information that is 100 percent accurate or correct about any product, Caldwell (2010) develops a model to explore the nature of the beliefs held by economic agents about the flow of information and the effect of such information on asset prices. A trust or belief variable is then part of such a model. Agents, goods, and exchange rates are other elements of the model.

TRUST AND RETIREMENT SAVING AND PLANNING: THE DECISION

Standard (traditional) finance largely ignores the role of trust in financial decision-making, despite trust playing a central role in the evaluation stage of the decision-making process. Accordingly, trust can be considered the glue holding together the different pieces of the financial systems and markets that serve the needs of all future retirees.

Trust affects the decision-making process for retirement at three stages: (1) the saving stage, (2) the investment stage, and (3) the spending or withdrawal stage.

More specifically, trust influences the decision-making process at the following key points:

- Stage 1: Decision to save and plan for retirement regardless of the available options; whether a company-sponsored plan (e.g., a 401(k) plan) or a personal retirement plan (e.g., a Roth IRA).
- Stage 2: Decision to invest in specific asset classes: financial and non-financial assets.
- Stage 3: Decision to spend or withdraw at the retirement age from any retirement account that one might have built over the working years.

The level of trust (confidence) that an individual has in the financial institutions, markets, industries, and companies in a given country affects these four decisions. The lack of trust or distrust over the past decade or so in the United States can largely explain the low participation rates by employees in company-sponsored plans such as 401(k). As Nofsinger (2008, p. 1) notes "Most employees know little about their retirement plan. They may know even less about the stock market. Under these circumstances, it takes much trust to lock up a portion of your salary for many years or even decades."

Alesina and La Ferrera (2002) show that while an average of 40 percent of survey respondents report that they trust other people, the percentage drops dramatically when they are asked about their confidence in other institutions. Specifically, an average of only 27 percent of people report having confidence in financial institutions. Since the authors conducted this survey long before the 2008 global financial crisis, the percentage reporting trust is likely to be much lower today.

According to a recent study on existing 401(k) plans, Munnell (2012) reports that about 20 percent of employees do not join the plans, more than 90 percent do not contribute the maximum amount, and about 40 percent cash out of the plans when they change jobs.

Regarding cashing out plans, the hefty penalties for such early withdrawals can deduct 20 to 30 percent from the accumulated sum withdrawn. The displayed national data get even worse for some of the largest states in the United States. As an example, according to a UC-Berkeley Research Brief (2012):

- Based on data from the three-year period 2008 to 2010, only 45 percent of private sector workers age 25 to 64 in California work for an employer who sponsors a retirement plan—even less than the U.S. average of 53 percent.
- Only 37 percent of employed private sector workers in California actually participate in an employer-sponsored retirement plan.
- A downward trend in workplace retirement plan coverage has occurred in California since 1998–2000, when 50 percent of private sector workers had access.

TRUST-BASED IMPLICATIONS FOR RETIREMENT SAVING AND PLANNING

This section summarizes what is already known about the role of trust in retirement planning efforts. This is needed before discussing specific solutions and strategies for increasing participation in available retirement plans.

A Summary of Knowledge about Trust

Following is a summary of material covered about trust and confidence to this point.

- Trust has both cognitive and affective attributes. The cognitive attribute allows for quantification of trust and consequently added rigor to any model-building effort and analysis.
- Trust is primarily a sociological phenomenon. That is, trust would not be needed if only one person existed or if all people where fully knowledgeable in a deterministic universe.
- Trust tends to be fragile and easily broken.
- Trust takes more time to create than to lose.
- Trust-destroying events usually are more salient than trust-building events.
- Distrust, once initiated, tends to reinforce and perpetuate additional distrust.
- Trust tends to disproportionately increase with the perceived benefit of the decision outcome, especially when a truster's expertise is low.
- Goodwill and competence are two major elements of trust. By the same token, competence, being a probability-based construct, allows for more rigorous model building around the notion of trust.
- Trust and perceived risk have an indirect relationship with each other.
- Trust reduces risk and uncertainty; and consequently, transaction costs.

Trust-Induced Regulatory Solutions

If distrust of the financial system and its institutions and actors impedes joining or staying in the available retirement plans such as 401(k)s, then removing or at least minimizing such mistrust should have an opposite effect on all actions related to retirement planning. Thus, a relevant question is: How can the public trust and confidence in the relatively complex and interlocking subsystems that make up the financial system serve as an incubator for individual and company-sponsored retirement accounts be restored?

An important lesson from the horrible experiences of the 2008 financial market collapse is that a lack of sound regulations and full enforcement powers to keep rule breakers away and out of the system account for the loss of trust and many of the problems experienced. A truly competitive, highly transparent, and efficient regulatory system with fully funded enforcement power would help restore trust. Under such a system, agents in the financial system would think twice about breaking the public's trust in the system. Although a discussion on the types of regulations needed is beyond the scope of this chapter, governmental systems at the federal, state, and municipal levels are assumed to be functional and able to work effectively in regulating, funding, and enforcing them. However, if the experiences over the past 30 years or so are any indicators, such assumptions may just be wishful thinking. The well-intended Dodd-Frank Act and the way special interest groups resisted it provide an example of the obstacles faced in establishing an effective and efficient financial regulatory system.

"Community-Based Trusts" Solutions

Genuinely trustworthy and stable regulatory systems are necessary for increased individual participation in available retirement plans in any society. However, trust alone is not enough to attain such an objective because the need also exists to build and put in place complementary apparatuses that further nudge individuals toward saving and planning for their retirement. The following discussion introduces a new device with such a goal in mind.

The Community-Based Trust (CBT) construct serves both as a financial and risk mitigation strategy to all parties involved in retirement planning. Such a strategy rests on intuition and knowledge, as discussed earlier in this chapter. Trust among the participating individuals, once attained and maintained over some period of time, reduces complexity and consequently reduces risk and uncertainty among all involved. Reduced levels of risk and uncertainty, and the associated reduced transactional costs, should encourage elevated levels of participation in retirement saving and planning. More importantly, the CBT construct requires no government involvement except for support at the initial stage of rulemaking and future enforcement.

The CBT possesses the power of intuition and common sense, as well as the logic and the accumulated knowledge of psychology, neuroscience, and Multi-Agent Systems (MAS). According to Wooldridge (2002, p. 366), a MAS is "a system composed of multiple interacting intelligent agents within an environment. Multi-agent systems can be used to solve problems that are difficult or impossible for an individual agent or a monolithic system to solve." He also notes that the agents in a multi-agent system have several important characteristics:

- *Autonomy*. The agents are at least partially autonomous.
- *Local views*. No agent has a full global view of the system, or the system is too complex for an agent to make practical use of such knowledge.
- *Decentralization*. No controlling agent is designated or the system is effectively reduced to a monolithic system.

Professional associations and groups such as the local and regional chambers of commerce or the local and regional National Federation of Independent Businesses (NFIB) provide examples of MAS. The American Association of Retired Persons (AARP), the local and regional American Federation of Labor and Congress of Industrial Organizations (AFL-CIO), and any other trade, industrial, or technology group where employees work in the same environment with possibly similar goals and concerns can also be considered MAS.

For example, ISB 1234 in California, which the state's governor signed into law, permits the formation of the statewide "California Secure Choice Retirement Savings Trust." ISB 1234 directs automatic enrollment in a plan that withholds 3 percent of the wages of the employees with no 401(k) plan and invests the funds in a personal retirement account for them. Employees can decide not to join the plan but to do so they must act or opt out. Although the spirit of this plan is compatible with the proposed CBT, plans such as this one are governmental mandates and placed under the power of the state. The proposed CBT is community-based and privately owned throughout its operation.

To recap, the CBT strategy could work best when individuals belong to a trade or social association similar to those listed. If people can manage their retirement saving and planning at the individual level, that would be ideal as far as trust is concerned because at the individual level, trust is infinite. This case is similar to principal-agent theory in standard (traditional) finance where for an owner-manager the agency cost would be zero.

The CBT proposal outlined in this chapter should be familiar because of its similarity to a defined benefit plan, with one major exception. The responsible parties in a CBT are the locally/regionally-managed trusts and not the employers. Furthermore, the real power of a CBT structure lies in the fact that it can also bring back the badly needed public trust to the entire financial system because it has to do with the lives of all people.

Summary Empirical data do not support the hypothesis that education, planning tools, and improved disclosure make a major impact on saving behaviors. Nudges (also known as the process of nudging), such as automatic enrollment in defined contribution plans, increase savings rates, but the low contribution rates considered feasible using this vehicle only marginally lessens savings deficiencies. Informed individuals become more proactive and motivated to make sure they have a safe and yet adequate "nest egg" to rely upon when they enter retirement.

Given that regardless of how intelligent and careful individuals are and how they remain at the mercy of the prevailing financial system, two sets of solutions or strategies are offered. One strategy is based on adopting a life-cycle financial planning and wealth management framework that considers the challenges posed by macroeconomic and demographic factors. Understanding the systematic behavioral mistakes in decision-making and how the human brain functions in facilitating such mistakes should improve the quality of this plan. Another strategy is to simply help build, manage, and grow the retirement fund as if no one else in the world cares about one's financial health during retirement. Such a strategy involves direct involvement and participation in a CBT, where trust in CBT has nothing to do with omnipresent marketing and sales strategies and has everything to do with "we are in the same boat." CBT reduces complexity and thus increases employee participation.

Behavioral finance, cognitive psychology, neuroscience, and the trust construct provide excellent insights into human financial decision-making behaviors and how prone individuals are to act in ways that can damage their own interests. Making sound long-term financial decisions is difficult due to the natural proclivity to default to the easy way out by relying on emotions, biases, heuristics, framing effects, and hyperbolic discounting. Even more difficult work is regaining trust in the prevailing financial system. Creating and managing your own financial system to safeguard your nest egg avoids relying on the untrustworthy elements in the financial system. The post-2008 era demonstrates that individuals must become more active in the development, implementation, and supervision of retirement planning issues over their lifetime. The good news is that some solutions discussed in this chapter allow one to turn "you are on your own" into "we all are in the same boat" and use that as the foundation for taking control of retirement savings.

DISCUSSION QUESTIONS

1. List and explain some challenges and risks that are unique to the retirement problem.
2. Referring to the Life Cycle Needs by Age Group Model in Exhibit 16.1, identify where you are on the life cycle and the major life events that you

should be planning for in the next five years. Indicate whether you are on track to be able to fund these requirements to the desired level and simultaneously meet your saving objectives for your anticipated retirement date.

3. Identify several ways to make better decisions about retirement.
4. Discuss how considering several aspects of trust may help in making better decisions about retirement.

REFERENCES

Ackert, Lucy F., and Richard Deaves. 2010. *Behavioral Finance: Psychology, Decision-Making, and Markets*. Mason, OH: South-Western Cengage Learning.

Agarwal, Sumit, John C. Driscoll, Xavier Gabaix, and David Laibson. 2006. "Financial Mistakes over the Life Cycle." Available at www.leland.stanford.edu/group/SITE/archive/SITE_2006/Web%20Session%207/Gabaix_mistakes_aging.pdf.

Agarwal, Sumit, John C. Driscoll, Xavier Gabaix, and David Laibson. 2009. "The Age of Reason: Financial Decisions over the Life-Cycle with Implications for Regulation." *Brookings Papers on Economic Activity*. Available at www.brookings.edu/~/media/Files/Programs/ES/BPEA/2009_fall_bpea_papers/2009b_bpea_agarwal.pdf.

Alesina, Alberto, and Eliana La Ferrara. 2002. "Who Trusts Others?" *Journal of Public Economics* 85:2, 207–234.

Ariely, Dan, and Klaus Wertenbroch. 2002. "Procrastination, Deadlines, and Performance: Self-Control by Precommitment." *Psychological Science* 13:3, 219–224.

Becerra, Gabriel, Jason Heard, and Rob Kremer. 2005. "Trust Attributes, Methods, and Uses." Working Paper, University of Calgary. Available at http://pages.cpsc.ucalgary.ca/~kremer/papers/aamas07.pdf.

Benartzi, Shlomo, Alessandro Previtero, and Richard H. Thaler. 2011. "Annuitization Puzzles." *Journal of Economic Perspectives* 25:4, 143–164. Available at www.aeaweb.org/articles.php?doi=10.1257/jep.25.4.143.

Benartzi, Shlomo, and Richard H. Thaler. 2007. "Heuristics and Biases in Retirement Savings Behavior." *Journal of Economic Perspectives* 21:3, 81–104.

Caldwell, Leigh. 2010. "Trust, News and the Efficient Markets Hypothesis." Working Paper, Inon Behavioral Economics Consulting, London.

Choi, James, David Laibson, Brigitte Madrian, and Andrew Metrick. 2006. "Saving for Retirement on the Path of Least Resistance." In Ed McCaffrey and Joel Slemrod, eds., *Behavioral Public Finance: Toward a New Agenda*, 304–351. New York: Russell Sage Foundation.

Choi, James J., David Laibson, and Andrew Metrick. 2002. "Defined Contribution Pensions: Plan Rules, Participant Decisions, and the Path of Least Resistance." In James Poterba, ed., *Tax Policy and the Economy*, 16th ed., 67–113. Cambridge, MA: MIT Press.

Das, T. K., and Bing-Sheng Teng. 2004. "The Risk-Based View of Trust: A Conceptual Framework." *Journal of Business and Psychology* 19:1, 85–116.

Evans, Jonathan St. B. T. 2002. "Logic and Human Reasoning: An Assessment of the Deduction Paradigm." *Psychological Bulletin* 128:6, 978–996.

Federal Reserve. 2012. "Changes in U.S. Family Finances from 2007 to 2010: Evidence from the Survey of Consumer Finances." *Federal Reserve Bulletin*. Available at www.federalreserve.gov/pubs/bulletin/2012/pdf/scf12.pdf.

Financial Finesse Reports. 2012. "Trends in Employee Financial Issues Q1 2012." Available at www.financialfinesse.com/wp-content/uploads/2012/05/Q1_2012_Full_Report.pdf.

Frederick, Shane, George Loewenstein, and Ted O'Donoghue. 2002. "Time Discounting and Time Preference: A Critical Review." *Journal of Economic Literature* 40:2, 351–401.

Hershfield, Hal G., Daniel F. Goldstein, William F. Sharpe, Jesse Fox, Leo Yeykelis, Laura L. Carstensen, and Jeremy N. Baoilenson. 2011. "Increasing Saving Behavior through Age-Progressed Renderings of the Future Self." *Journal of Marketing Research* 48:S23–S37, 23–27.

Kahneman, Daniel. 2011. *Thinking, Fast and Slow*. New York: Farrar, Straus, and Giroux.

Kahneman, Daniel, Paul Slovic, and Amos Tversky. 1982. *Judgment under Uncertainty: Heuristics and Biases*. New York: Cambridge University Press.

Kahneman, Daniel, and Amos Tversky. 1972. "Subjective Probability: A Judgment of Representativeness." *Cognitive Psychology* 3:3, 430–454.

Kahneman, Daniel, and Amos Tversky. 1979. "Prospect Theory: An Analysis of Decisions under Risk." *Econometrica* 47:2, 263–291.

Knoll, Melissa A. Z. 2010. "The Role of Behavioral Economics and Behavioral Decision Making in Americans' Retirement Savings Decisions." *Social Security Bulletin* 70:4, 1–23. Available at www.ssa.gov/policy/docs/ssb/v70n4/v70n4p1.html.

Mainstreet Wealth Group. 2012. "The Life Cycle of Financial Planning." Available at http://mainstreetwealthgroup.com/wp/wp-content/uploads/2011/12/Life_Events_of_Financial_Planning.pdf/.

Marazziti, Donatella, Bernardo Dell'Osso, Stefano Baroni, Francesco Mungai, Mario Catena, Paola Rucci, Francesco Albanese, Gino Giannaccini, Laura Betti, Laura Fabbrini, Paola Italiani, Alessandro Del Debbio, Antonio Lucacchini, and Liliana Dell'Ossoet. 2006. "A Relationship between Oxytocin and Anxiety of Romantic Attachment." Available at http://www.cpementalhealth.com/content/2/1/28.

Mercier, Hugo, and Dan Sperber. 2011. "Why Do Humans Reason? Arguments for an Argumentative Theory." *Behavioral and Brain Sciences* 34:2, 57–111.

Munnell, Alicia. 2012. "Are Americans Really Able to Manage Their 401k Plans?" Available at www.nextavenue.org/article/2012-05/are-americans-really-able-manage-their-401k-plans.

Neumann, John von, and Oskar Morgenstern. 1944. *Theory of Games and Economic Behavior*. Princeton, NJ: Princeton University Press.

Nofsinger, John. 2008. "Can You Trust the Stock Market?" *Mind over Money*. December 26. Available at www.psychologytoday.com/blog/mind-my-money/200812/can-you-trust-the-stock-market.

Olsen, Robert A. 2008. "Trust as Risk and the Foundation of Investment Value." *Journal of Socio-Economics* 37:6, 2189–2200.

S&P Dow Jones Indices. 2102. "S&P 500 Companies Post Record Level of Pension & OPEB Underfunding: Might Be Too Late for Baby Boomers to Safely Build-Up Assets." Press Release, July 17. Available at http://www.prnewswire.com/news-releases/sp-500-companies-post-record-level-of-pension--opeb-underfunding-might-be-too-late-for-baby-boomers-to-safely-build-up-assets-162754796.html.

Samuelson, Paul. 1937. "A Note on Measurement of Utility." *Review of Economic Studies* 4:2, 155–161.

Slovic, Paul, Ellen Peters, Melissa L. Finucane, and Donald G. McGregor. 2005. "Affect, Risk, and Decision Making." *Health Psychology* 24:4, 35–40.

Slovic, Paul, Ellen Peters, Melissa L. Finucane, and Donald G. McGregor. 2007. "The Affect, Heuristic." *European Journal of Operational Research* 177:3, 1333–1352.

Thaler, Richard H., and Shlomo Benartzi. 2004. "Save More Tomorrow (TM): Using Behavioral Economics to Increase Employee Saving." *Journal of Political Economy* 112:1, 164–187.

Thaler, Richard H., and Cass Sunstein. 2003. "Libertarian Paternalism." *American Economic Review* 93:2, 175–179.

Tversky, Amos, and Daniel Kahneman. 1974. "Judgment under Uncertainty: Heuristics and Biases." *Science* 185:4157, 11241–131.

Tversky, Amos, and Daniel Kahneman. 1983. "Extensional Versus Intuitive Reasoning: The Conjunction Fallacy in Probability Judgment." *Psychological Review* 90:4, 293–315.

UC-Berkeley Research Brief. 2012. "6.3 Million Private Sector Workers in California Lack Access to a Retirement Plan on the Job." Available at http://laborcenter.berkeley.edu/research/ca_private_pension_gap.shtml.

Wooldridge, Michael. 2002. *An Introduction to MultiAgent Systems.* Chichester: John Wiley & Sons.

Zak, Paul. 2011. "Trust, Morality and Oxytocin." Video file available at www.ted.com/talks/paul_zak_trust_morality_and_oxytocin.html.

ABOUT THE AUTHORS

James A. Howard is Program Director and Professor of Financial Management at the University College Graduate School, University of Maryland and co-director of the Academy of Behavioral Finance and Economics. He is a University of Maryland System Regents Award winner for mentoring and innovation in accounting and finance program development. Professor Howard's graduate finance program was one of the first in the United States to incorporate a strong emphasis on behavioral finance. He has published in such journals as the *Journal of Organizational Psychology* and *Issues in Accounting Education.* He received a BA in mathematics from the University of Nebraska, an MBA from Syracuse University, and a PhD in finance from the George Washington University.

Rassoul Yazdipour is Professor of Finance at the Craig School of Business, California State University, where he has taught and worked for more than 20 years. He is the founder of the Academy of Behavioral Finance and Economics. His interest in behavioral finance followed his early attraction to entrepreneurial finance. Professor Yazdipour has also advised various businesses from startup ventures to mid-market companies both as a board member and as consultant. His latest academic work includes *Advances in Entrepreneurial Finance: With Applications from Behavioral Finance and Economics.* He received a BBA from Tehran Business School, an MBA from Indiana University, and a PhD in business administration from The Ohio State University.

Knowing Your Numbers: A Scorecard Approach to Improved Medical and Financial Outcomes

Talya Miron-Shatz
Founding Director, Center for Medical Decision Making,
Ono Academic College; Senior Fellow, Center for
Medicine in the Public Interest

Stephanie Gati
Global Health Intern, Johnson and Johnson

INTRODUCTION

Health literacy and chronic diseases are inextricably linked. In order to make healthy lifestyle choices to prevent chronic disease, such as exercising or limiting alcohol intake, a person must first be aware of the impact these kinds of decisions have on health, wealth, and well-being. This is not unlike the way financial literacy is associated with one's wealth, leading to decision-making that may be suboptimal. Health literacy and financial literacy are further connected because of the effect of health literacy on decisions that involve health, but have financial consequences, such as insurance and health care. This chapter proposes a short, clear, and actionable approach to overcoming health literacy barriers, thereby potentially preventing or curbing chronic disease. References to financial literacy are woven through the chapter based on the belief that a similar approach might be beneficial for improving financial decision-making and ultimately outcomes.

Health literacy is a person's ability to understand information about health and to incorporate this information into a healthy lifestyle. Key components of definitions converge, such as the degree to which individuals have the capacity to obtain, process, and understand basic health information and services needed to make appropriate health decisions. This is linked to action through the competence to use health information and services to enhance and maintain health (Ratzan and Parker 2000) and to make appropriate health decisions and follow instructions for treatment (White 2008). Health literacy is also essential for accomplishing shared decision-making by offering the patient an active role. By comparison, a financial consumer is always required to take an active role in decision-making. Therefore, financial literacy includes a similar aspect of knowledge as a prerequisite for informed and smart financial choices.

Despite the need for comprehension, people often misunderstand medical information (Miron-Shatz et al. 2009), especially when confronted with multiple choices, as in the case of Medicare Part D, where failing to choose the most suitable medication insurance program may result in considerable financial loss (Hanoch et al. 2010). Yet, as documented in a report by the American Medical Association (White 2008), over 89 million American adults have limited health literacy skills. Given these limitations, conveying important medical and financial information in ways that are easily intelligible to the population is advisable, even at the risk of being considered simplistic. Further, while health and financial literacy belong to the individual, they can be enhanced by providing suitable materials that take into account the level of ability in the population.

Similar considerations of a population's literacy level are taken into account in the financial planning world. Financial planners and others use simple tools to assess financial literacy by asking basic questions to measure understanding of concepts. Almost one third of college graduates answer some of these questions incorrectly, signifying a high proportion of financial illiteracy across the board. According to Lusardi and Mitchell (2005), those who understand financial concepts including inflation, compound interest, risk diversification, or stock risk, make better choices, such as effective investment choices. Additionally, those with higher financial literacy have greater wealth accumulation, even when controlling for other determinants of wealth, such as income, age, education, family composition, risk tolerance patience, and saving behavior. Van Rooij, et al. (2011) believe this occurs because heightened financial knowledge reduces the barriers to gathering and processing information and increases involvement in the stock market. This connection between financial literacy and financial behavior highlights the importance of promoting knowledge and motivation in order to encourage better health- or money-related decisions.

Health literacy directly affects health outcomes, some of which bear financial consequences, both on patients and on the health care and welfare systems. Even when adjusting the analyses for socioeconomic status, health status, and health behaviors, Medicare enrollees with low health literacy had higher hospitalization rates (Baker et al. 2007). The American Medical Association (AMA) estimates that individuals with limited health literacy incur medical expenses that are up to four times greater than patients with adequate literacy skills, costing the health care system billions of dollars every year in unnecessary doctor visits and hospital stays (White 2008). Vernon, Trujillo, Rosenbaum, and DeBuono (2007) estimate that limited health literacy will cost the nation between $100 and $200 billion a year.

Improving health literacy would result in higher levels of efficiency, reduced collection costs, and consequently, improved bottom lines for medical institutions. As an analogy, financial literacy programs are fast becoming a key ingredient in financial policy reform worldwide (Xu and Bilal 2012). Similarly, the promotion of health literacy is in the best interest of both individuals and institutions.

The remainder of this chapter has the following organization. The next section provides a brief discussion of the need for better control of chronic diseases. Next the chapter explains the relevance using a scorecard approach followed by a discussion of its advantages. Attention then focuses on the Take Care scorecard before introducing considerations for developing health and financial literacy scorecards and discussing their limitations. The penultimate section sets forth implications for financial literacy. The final section provides a summary and conclusions.

THE NEED FOR BETTER CONTROL OF CHRONIC DISEASES

This chapter proposes a digital health scorecard to help prevent chronic disease (e.g., diabetes, cardiovascular diseases, and cancer). These are among the most prevalent, costly, and preventable of all health problems (Clark 2003). The Sixty-sixth United Nations General Assembly (September 19, 2011) proclaimed the spread of non-communicable diseases (i.e., chronic, noncontagious) as a socioeconomic and development challenge of epidemic proportions. Preventing diseases before they start is one of the most commonsense ways to keep people healthy at relatively low costs. The Robert Wood Johnson Foundation president and chief executive officer (CEO) maintains that instead of focusing on treating disease, people should be kept out of the doctor's office in the first place by investing in proven, community-based prevention efforts (Lavizzo-Mourey 2012). Most pertinent to this chapter is the fact that chronic diseases are increasingly self-managed by the patient, resulting in reduced hospitalizations, emergency department use, and overall managed care costs (Coleman, Thoesen, and Newton 2005).

A growing body of evidence supports the advantages of self-management and patient participation approaches in terms of knowledge, performance of self-management behaviors, monitoring, self-efficacy, health care use, and aspects of health status (Lorig et al. 1999). Patient participation has been recognized as a crucial element in chronic disease prevention (Institute of Medicine 2001), and interventions incorporating self-management had the most positive outcomes (Barlow et al. 2010). Still, patients are often reluctant to take part in decision-making processes, perhaps because they feel ill-equipped to deal with medical information. Yet, this can be countered by presenting information in a clear and understandable way, and interventions such as using decision aids to inform patients of decision options lead to a dramatic increase in participation (Van Tol-Geerdink et al. 2006).

Similar to patient participation, which occurs more often when patients feel knowledgeable about their health and the impact of the choices they make, connections exist between financial literacy and financial planning. Lusardi and Mitchell (2005) find that financially literate populations (assessed through ability to answer three questions on compound interest, inflation, and stock risk) have much higher rates of retirement planning. Retirement planning also requires using tools such as financial calculators. The authors also note that people with higher financial literacy are more likely to use these tools and plan efficiently. Further, financial instruction should include not only focus on subject matter-related material, but also links to implementation (Hill, Meszaros, and Yetter 2012). All this supports the need for a simple tool to make health knowledge widely accessible and actionable and a financial literacy tool to follow.

THE SCORECARD APPROACH

To better address the need for a brief, easily comprehensible and widely accessible self-management tool for prevention and monitoring of chronic disease, a general-purpose digital health scorecard is proposed. This user-friendly, efficient tool focuses on key indicators to help consumers understand how to optimize health behaviors in terms of medical testing and lifestyle. Alongside promoting disease prevention and management, the scorecard is an education tool. Users learn what healthy behaviors are and what their numbers for indicators such as blood pressure should be based on the values presented on the scorecard. Additionally, users discover their problem areas and the choices they can make to positively affect their health.

Yates and Ward (2012) propose a similar approach for financial literacy, rating it, interestingly, from being in "excellent health" to "moderately healthy" to "unhealthy." The authors find that while most people are knowledgeable about credit cards and mortgages, knowledge varies substantially across topics. For example, people often mishandle estate planning and emergency funds. Individuals appear to be aware of what they do not know, and many point to the latter topics as ones about which they would like to become more knowledgeable.

Mandell and Schmid Klein (2009) study individuals from one school district, who either did or did not choose to take a course in personal financial management when they were in high school. Of the 79 respondents, about half took the course, with college-bound students no more likely to take it than other students. In their follow-up study, the authors find that those who took the course did not consider themselves to be more savings-oriented than those who did not take the course, nor did they report better financial behavior than those who did not take the course. While Mandell and Schmid Klein find positive financial behavior associated with respondents who were full-time college students or graduates, their results are driven by paying credit cards in full and the belief that their savings and investments are adequate for their needs. This might suggest that minimal training, in several basic aspects of prudent financial behavior, would suffice, as more elaborate training did not have meaningful outcomes. Such minimal training is in line with the scorecard approach and could be more beneficial when administered to adults, who are already managing their own finances, than to high school students.

Studies show that a majority of patients prefer to receive numerical information as part of their care (Wallsten et al. 1993). Such major organizations as the Mayo Clinic staff have developed paper-based health scorecards designed to address this need. Even more promising are scorecards that use Interactive Health Communication Applications (IHCAs) for the user to access or transmit health information or receive guidance and support on a health-related issue (Adler et al. 1998). IHCAs have a significant positive effect on knowledge, perceived social support, health behaviors, and clinical outcomes, and may have a positive effect on self-efficacy (Murray, Burns, See Tai, Lai, and Nazareth 2005). Still, most (73 percent) technology-based interventions require therapist involvement (Rosser et al. 2009). Because the proposed digital scorecard would not require a comprehensive medical assessment, the consumer can see which behaviors and biochemical markers contribute to a better score and are thus linked to improved health status.

TARGET POPULATION AND ADVANTAGES

Besides promoting action in patients with chronic disease, the scorecard can be used to promote disease prevention among healthy people who want to assess or maintain their health status. A report by the Pew Internet and American Life Project reveals that in 2009, 61 percent of American adults looked online for health information, with more than 90 percent of them seeking material related to illnesses (Fox and Jones 2009). However, a need still exists for online material to motivate action or nudge individuals toward healing and prevention.

Preliminary surveys taken by Carnegie Mellon University students, faculty, and staff show that even educated populations are unaware of what is considered healthy behavior and numbers, and should also be targeted by this intervention (Bhavnani et al. 2011). A later section addresses the full results of this study. By harnessing technology, a digital scorecard has the potential to control chronic illness and provide health information to people all over the world. Even a single use of the tool is important in teaching the consumer how to live a healthier lifestyle, which may lead to changes, even if they are relatively minor. The surveys from Carnegie Mellon reveal that the simplicity of the scorecard would appeal to a variety of populations.

Because the scorecard has a greater ability to be a learning tool than other similar tools currently on the market, it is more likely to inspire change (Bhavnani et al. 2011). The most prominent feature of the proposed digital Take Care scorecard is its ability to capture an individual's overall health (or preventable disease risk) with a single, easily comprehensible number and a guideline for interpretation with clear implications. Thus, the scorecard focuses on the major determinants of health and is easily comprehensible rather than encumbered by medical jargon.

CONTENT OF THE TAKE CARE SCORECARD

A digital scorecard can display a person's ratings on several basic health measures associated with preventable disease. As Exhibit 17.1 shows, the Take Care scorecard includes body mass index (BMI), blood sugar, blood pressure, and cholesterol levels, as well as behavioral factors such as smoking and exercise. The scorecard provides recommended actions on each health measure, allowing users to keep track of their health and monitor risk factors. The inclusion of the recommending sources suggests a convergence of recommendations.

Converging evidence for the seven health indicators included in the Take Care scorecard comes from research suggesting that glucose control (individualized for type 2 diabetic patients), smoking cessation, aspirin use, blood pressure, and LDL control are an effective multi-factorial therapy for reducing diabetes complications (Cleary et al. 2006). As Miron-Shatz and Ratzan (2011) point out, as few as five lifestyle factors—smoking, alcohol use, diet, body mass index, and physical activity—account for a 58 percent reduction in risk of developing pancreatic cancer and are related to diabetes incidence in 90 percent of new cases. These same factors are also related to recommended interventions for other diseases such as cardiovascular illness (Mayo Clinic Staff 2011). Because the health indicators included in the proposed scorecard are key variables for many chronic diseases, the scorecard use may result in better control of a variety of chronic conditions. A key determinant for including an

EXHIBIT 17.1 Recommendations for Preventing Chronic Disease

Recommended Action	NIH (2011)	AHA (2011)	Mayo (2011)	ACC (2011a, 2011b)	HMS (2010)	Mozaffarian et al. (2009)	Cleary et al. (2006)
Maintain blood pressure within normal range	X	Goal is 120/80 mmHg	Goal is 120/80 mmHg	X	Under 120/80 mmHg		X
Keep proper weight	X	X	Keep BMI below 25	X	Keep BMI below 25	X	
Exercise more	X	150 min/week or more	150 min/week or more		150 min/week or more	X	
Quit smoking	X	X	X	X	X	X	X
Eat a healthy diet	X	X	X	X	X	X	
Reduce blood cholesterol	X	Less than 300 mg/day		Lower intake of saturated fats; Reduce LDL Increase HDL	Less than 200 mg/dl		X Control LDL
Manage diabetes		X			Keep fasting blood sugar under 100 mg/dl		X
Reduce stress		X					
Limit alcohol to moderate amounts		X	X			X	
Learn about major risk factors that cannot be changed		X		Find out about health of relatives			
Get regular health screenings			X				

Note: NIH = National Institutes of Health; AHA = American Heart Association; Mayo = Mayo Clinic; ACC = American College of Cardiology; HMS = Harvard Medical School.

The exhibit lists recommended health actions alongside their sources. This suggests a convergence of recommendations, which facilitates the creation of the 'Take Care' scorecard.

indicator in the scorecard is simple measurability and comprehensibility. Although a healthy diet is a key variable (Mayo Clinic Staff 2011), it was not included because a healthy diet is complex to explain, varies across people, and is difficult to measure (Canoy and Buchan 2007).

CONSIDERATIONS FOR HEALTH AND FINANCIAL LITERACY SCORECARDS

An overall health score is computed that is well-suited for evaluation, surveillance, and comparison across multiple locations and populations. As Exhibit 17.2 shows, the score is computed as the total number of health indicators within the healthy (goal) range provided alongside each indicator. The proposed digital scorecard includes a continuous composite overall health score along with score ranges and a brief action-oriented interpretation of this score (0–4, "Take care!"; 5–6, "Getting there"; and 7, "Excellent"). Using a composite score that integrates multiple measurements has key advantages, including increased validity by providing a more representative sample of information about the underlying concept and increased precision by decreasing score variability (Stewart, Hays, and Ware 1992). These same considerations can serve when creating a scorecard for financial literacy.

The scorecard embodies knowledge translation, an emerging concept in medical practice and interventional epidemiology (Davis et al. 2003). Translational medicine aims to optimize patient care by entering the realm of lifestyle practices. The proposed

Get a √ for each indicator in recommended range

Key Health Indicators	Goal	2012	2013	2014
Body Mass Index	19–25	☐	☐	☐
Blood Pressure	120/80	☐	☐	☐
Cholesterol	Under 200 mg/dl	☐	☐	☐
Fasting Blood Sugar	Under 100	☐	☐	☐
Smoking/Tobacco Use	No smoking/using	☐	☐	☐
Exercise	30 minutes five times a week	☐	☐	☐
Alcohol	No more than two drinks a day	☐	☐	☐
		☐	☐	☐

Overall Health Score (how many √s)

7 Excellent   Successful attainment of all indicators; continue to monitor.
5–6 Getting there   A few key indicators need to be attained.
0–4 Take care!   Immediate attention required to reach attainment for better health.

EXHIBIT 17.2   The Proposed Health Scorecard: "Take Care—7 Steps for Better Health"

Note: The Take Care scorecard allows users to evaluate their health in a simple way and to learn the targets they should be aiming for to improve health.

scorecard is designed to improve health by promoting healthy behaviors in consumers' daily routines. Further, consumers may share their scorecard information with physicians, enabling them to better monitor progress and develop an optimal treatment plan.

To help overcome barriers to health literacy and create motivation for health improvement, the Take Care scorecard is designed according to recommendations for health literacy enhancement interventions, including provision of simplified (Miron-Shatz et al. 2011) and more attractive written materials (Apfel et al. 2010). Recommended formats are those with more white space, friendlier layout, short sentences, simple words, and large fonts (Apfel et al. 2010). Also recommended is text that is action- and goal-oriented, with a clear explanation of its purpose.

Both the scorecard and the lowest of the score ranges are named Take Care as an affective cue to spur the consumer to action. Taking care of oneself implies cautious and responsible action, and the phrase is commonly used to wish others well. Researchers document the importance of affect in information processing and decision-making (Zajonc 1980; Bechara et al. 1997; Loewenstein et al. 2001). People often base their judgment on emotional cues, if present (Slovic et al. 2002). These findings suggest that emotionally charged language may increase usage and perceived benefit. Finally, theoretical frameworks underlying behavior change interventions in chronic illness (e.g., cognitive behavioral therapy) generally suggest that internal events, such as self-efficacy and motivation, should be the primary target of intervention (Rosser et al. 2009). Bearden and Haws (2012) find that low self-control often underlies many consumer decisions. This result emphasizes the role of motivation in promoting decision-making that would serve the individual's long-term goals. For example, self-control bias leads consumers to think that their self-control is greater than it really is, and to trust themselves to eventually save enough for retirement. Yet, this bias will lead consumers to spend more money today, at the cost of saving for retirement in the future, while at the same time being fairly confident that this saving will occur.

All these principles pertaining to presentation of information, motivating users, and creating a sense of self-efficacy are also highly pertinent to financial decision-making. Further, lessons from a financial literacy program for students (Carlin and Robinson 2010) highlight the importance of including several criteria for knowledge: Students who received training tend to save more today, but their ability to make trade-offs between current costs and future benefits is somewhat impaired. As Kaenzig and Wüstenhagen (2010) show, consumer investment decisions for products and services with higher initial costs and lower operating costs are potentially subject to numerous cognitive biases, such as present-biased preferences or framing effects. Lynch et al. (2010) expand this to claim that consumers' financial illiteracy is apparent in major financial decisions involving time trade-offs, such as mortgages, retirement savings, and decumulation of savings in retirement.

Sharpe (2008, p. 328) points out that these tradeoffs also exist in health insurance, as: "Compared with those who have comprehensive health insurance, consumers with high deductible plans are more likely to economize on health care services. But, they are also more likely to delay or avoid necessary care." This suggests that a comprehensive scorecard approach can also be beneficial for investment and financial decisions in the health domain and in general.

The principles implemented in the scorecard also allow it to "nudge" the user toward making better decisions related to healthy lifestyles. Nudging, as defined by Thaler and Sunstein (2009, p. 6), is "alteration of people's behavior in a predictable way without forbidding any options or significantly changing economic incentives." Researchers also examine this approach and its ethical principles regarding health decisions (Blumenthal-Barby, Swindell, and Burroughs 2012). The scorecard's actionable language and presentation of information is meant to alter behavior so that users make more informed decisions about their health care and lifestyle choices to prevent chronic diseases. According to Thaler and Sunstein, many smokers, drinkers, and overeaters are willing to pay for decision aids to nudge them into making better decisions for their health. With a digital scorecard, this could be provided in a free and easy-to-use fashion.

A study on the effect of monetary incentives on weight loss programs tests theories of behavioral economics that indicate the potential effectiveness of a scorecard approach. Volpp et al. (2008) provide financial incentives for participants who achieve their weight loss goals, either consistently every time they weigh in on target or in a lottery system approach. Their study shows that incentive groups lose more weight on average than the control groups, and some key behavioral economic concepts emerge that pertain to the scorecard approach. Rapid feedback, as would be provided by the scorecard, fosters greater adherence to the weight loss program. The patient-centered scorecard gives users immediate feedback on their health status and ways to achieve better health.

Prior studies show that offering incentives to the participant rather than a physician is more likely to create behavior change. If users understand the many financial benefits of healthy lifestyles and improved health literacy, they will see the substantial financial incentives involved with adherence to the scorecard. However, Adams (2010) calls for more research on the long-term effects of behavioral economics and whether behavior change can be influenced in the long term. The appropriate use of the scorecard, on multiple occasions and in collaboration with a physician, can provide a nudge that can have lasting effects on health outcomes.

Although the main purpose of the Take Care scorecard is to improve health, it is also associated with other enduring benefits, perhaps most importantly to create a clear mental model of health. This involves a patient's set of concepts, ideas, beliefs, and values about what health is and what it means (Galt 2006), which even patients diagnosed with a chronic disease do not necessarily have. For example, about 60 percent of hypertensive patients do not know that exercise lowers blood pressure (Williams et al. 1998). Similarly, two out of three people with diabetes do not consider cardiovascular disease a significant risk factor (U.S. Department of Health and Human Services 2002).

Researchers recommend that preventive programs and public awareness messages educate patients about health indicators and their associated risks to minimize diabetes complications and healthcare costs (Okoro et al. 2004). The analogy to financial decision-making is clear—creating a mental model of good financial health is not a trivial task. Helping consumers understand that annual percentage rates (APR) and credit scores, as well as savings and retirement plans, are part of proper financial management, are important and worthy goals that a financial scorecard could accomplish.

Holtgrave and Weber (1993) compare two models of risk perception for both financial and health risk stimuli (such as radon gas exposure, and investing 80 percent of one's fortune in medical research). They find that a model inspired by Luce and Weber's Conjoint Expected Risk (CER) using dimensions of probability of gain, loss and status quo, and expected benefit and harm provide the best fit for most subjects and stimuli. The researchers presume that similar approaches underlie risky activities in health and finances. Incorporating a factor of dread related to health risks improved the explanatory power of their model. This attests to the proximity of health and financial judgments and to the potential benefit from cross-learning.

Preliminary Testing and Support for the Scorecard Idea

A pilot project at Carnegie Mellon University shows the true potential of a scorecard approach to health literacy and chronic disease prevention. Graduate students at Carnegie Mellon's Heinz College, School of Public Policy and Information Systems, conducted surveys of health literacy among college-educated students and designed and developed a prototype for an online scorecard (Bhavnani et al. 2011).

Surveys of over 200 Heinz College students, staff, and faculty assessed knowledge of BMI, blood pressure, blood sugar, cholesterol, smoking, exercise, and alcohol, both knowledge of the normal healthy range and awareness of a person's own value. In spite of high health literacy, only 11.9 percent of participants knew their blood sugar levels, and 22.7 percent knew the healthy range. Few participants (15.9 percent) knew their cholesterol levels, while 38.3 percent knew the normal range. All participants (100 percent) knew their values for the behavioral indicators—smoking, exercise, and alcohol intake—but only 36.6 percent knew the appropriate amount of exercise necessary for a healthy lifestyle, and 65.5 percent knew the healthy amount of alcohol intake. Most importantly, a majority (73.6 percent) of survey participants expressed interest in using a digital scorecard for regularly tracking their health status (Bhavnani et al. 2011). Exhibit 17.3 displays these results.

These numbers demonstrate a low level of health knowledge, even in educated populations. This highlights the potential for the scorecard to provide actionable knowledge, thereby hopefully reducing the prevalence of chronic diseases. The prototype website, called "Score Your Health," allowed users to input their information and calculate a comprehensive score showing which of the seven areas the user needed to improve. The low literacy levels coupled with high interest in a scorecard demonstrate the scorecard can prove to be a powerful tool in chronic disease prevention.

The survey also reveals some qualities of a health assessment tool that survey participants felt would most promote widespread use, and the scorecard would be able

EXHIBIT 17.3 Carnegie Mellon Survey Results of Personal Knowledge of Chronic Disease Indicators

Health Indicators	% Who Knew Their Own Value	% Who Knew the Normal Range
BMI	49.30	58.70
Blood pressure	59.70	54.70
Blood sugar	11.90	22.70
Cholesterol	15.90	38.30
Smoking	100.00	98.50
Exercise	100.00	36.60
Alcohol	100.00	65.50

Note: This exhibit shows that in a survey of student and faculty at Carnegie Mellon, people are unaware of their numbers involving their health.

to achieve all these qualities. Most respondents (77.2 percent) report that simplicity would be the feature most likely to make them use the application, and 59.1 percent note ease in understanding the tool (Bhavnani et al. 2011). Again, this suggests that any scorecard should use a format that promotes simplicity and comprehension, such as the short, action-oriented sentences and friendly formats proposed by Apfel et al. (2010).

To assess strengths and weaknesses of the simplified digital scorecard approach, Carnegie Mellon graduate students compared it with several similar health assessment tools (Bhavnani et al. 2011). The strengths of the scorecard, which all received the maximal ratings, include the ability to teach how to make healthy decisions, speed of use, detailed and actionable feedback, promoting learning after use, objectivity, and being easily understandable. Some weaknesses are credibility and ability to teach about a specific health risk (Bhavnani et al. 2011). With time and use, credibility of the scorecard can increase. Compared to the average values calculated for the five other health tools assessed at Carnegie Mellon, the scorecard approach appears to exceed existing tools in teaching the user how to make healthy decisions, tracking healthiness, promoting self-improvement, speed of use, giving actionable feedback, promoting learning while taking the quiz and after, and ease of understanding (Bhavnani et al. 2011). Exhibit 17.4 displays the comparison of the Take Care scorecard with the other instruments.

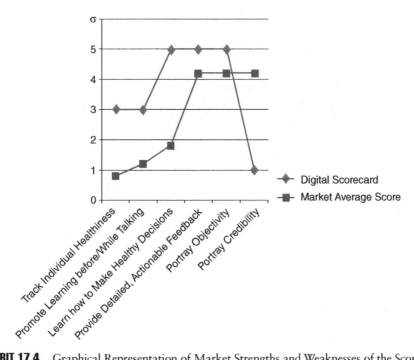

EXHIBIT 17.4   Graphical Representation of Market Strengths and Weaknesses of the Scorecard

Note: This exhibit shows that compared to other scorecards, the Take Care scorecard is better at tracking individual healthiness, promoting learning, teaching healthy decision-making, providing detailed and actionable feedback, and portraying objectivity.

LIMITATIONS

Scorecards may oversimplify health information and may be inappropriate for a minority of consumers (van Tol-Geerdink et al. 2006). However, Ratzan (2009) suggests that the benefits of greater ease of use and interpretability far outweigh the risk of oversimplification. Further, for consumers who want to fully understand the evidence underlying their score, supplementary material would be provided online, including graphical representations of the scores and access to evidence-based studies supporting the indicators presented similar to the format of the Cochrane Collaboration (Higgins and Green 2011).

IMPLICATIONS FOR FINANCIAL LITERACY

Health literacy and financial literacy are linked, as recently documented by a study of adults without dementia. Results agree with prior studies showing that poor health literacy results in lower overall health, but financial literacy also correlates with health status and behavior. Research shows positive correlations between numeric abilities and financial literacy, and health outcomes, defining better health status in terms of cognitive function, physical activity, and mental health (Bennett et al. 2012). This leads to the conclusion that higher rates of both health and financial literacy are necessary for improved health status.

In creating an Economic Stability Index (ESI), Hacker et al. (2012) include medical spending as a large consideration. According to Hacker et al. (2012, p. 5), the ESI measures the "degree to which individuals are protected against hardship-causing economic losses." The authors also note that medical-out-of-pocket spending is often a large risk for economic losses and one of the biggest worries of economic risk for Americans. Miron-Shatz (2009) also shows that finances are intertwined with health and well-being: Women who consider their finances when thinking about the future are less happy than those who do not spontaneously think about it. This may underlie the correlation between financial literacy and mental health status seen by Bennett et al. (2012). As Hacker et al. (2012, p. 12) note, the ESI is meant to help in defining precautionary savings as a "financial safety net." To calculate this safety net for health care, consumers would require improving their literacy—health and financial.

Sharpe (2008) calls for economists to help facilitate a better understanding of the health care market. Consumers cannot process health information and therefore sometimes go without health care. Sharpe (2008, p. 330) poses a question that is central to health literacy: "What changes in information delivery might help the consumer better understand and use highly technical and complex health information?" This chapter contends that a great need exists for improved health literacy and suggests using a scorecard approach as a tool to reduce chronic diseases and the economic burden of medical expenses. A similar need exists for financial literacy and a scorecard approach could help to fill this gap.

Currently, no standardized tool is widely used to measure financial literacy (Huston 2010). However, experts have created some simple tools such as Lusardi and Mitchell's (2005) use of three questions to assess financial literacy levels. In fact, a lack of agreement exists among studies for even a standard definition of financial literacy. As Huston notes, only eight (13 percent) studies of financial literacy in the past 10 years defined the term at all. Two of these used only financial knowledge as a definition, three referred to abilities, and two used both knowledge and ability in the definitions. Content areas of the studies of financial literacy could be divided into four categories: knowledge of money basics, borrowing, investing, and protecting resources. Most studies do not contain an indicator for whether the study participant is financially literate. A formalized definition and tool to assess financial literacy, as well as for education programs to improve the status of financial literacy in the public, are overdue. According to Way and Wong (2010) choice architecture, or nudging, can serve as a potentially successful tool for increasing both financial and health literacy. A scorecard approach to financial literacy can achieve all these goals.

Adopting a digital, standardized assessment tool for financial literacy can also serve educational purposes. For example, a website similar to the "Score Your Health" prototype can be created, asking simple financial literacy questions, rating the user's financial literacy level, explaining the questions answered incorrectly, and linking to resources that may help the user learn more about the topics questioned. Bases for creating the scorecard include trends found in recent financial literacy studies, the four content areas of financial literacy, and a standardized definition of financial literacy. The key to improving literacy levels is creating user-friendly tools that will encourage the participants to want to increase their scores. As Bertrand, Mullainathan, and Shafir (2006) suggest, future developments of the financial literacy scorecard should take into account specific populations' needs and decision-making considerations, including those at all income/wealth levels. In fact, other work (Bryan et al. 2012) shows that the beneficial association between literacy (both health and financial) and health care decision-making is stronger among those who are older, poorer, and at the lower ranges of cognitive ability. Because higher levels of health and financial literacy are associated with better decision-making (Hanoch et al. 2010), improvements in literacy could facilitate better decision-making and lead to improved quality of life in later years.

SUMMARY

This chapter proposes a succinct and actionable approach to overcoming health literacy barriers, thereby improving decision-making and ultimately preventing or curbing chronic disease and easing the medical and economic burden. A similar approach is proposed for improving financial decision-making, and, ultimately, outcomes. In the health domain, although patient participation is a key element in chronic disease prevention and improved outcomes, patients are often reluctant to participate.

The chapter presents a digital self-management tool for prevention and monitoring of chronic disease called the Take Care health scorecard. The scorecard captures overall health or preventable disease risk with a single number and a guideline with clear implications. It also promotes literacy by creating a clear mental model of health. In a pilot study, the majority of participants expressed interest in using a digital scorecard for regular monitoring of health status and most often rated simplicity and ease of use as the most important features of such a tool (Bhavnani et al. 2011).

In the financial domain, financial literacy is important to effective financial planning, including better investment choices and greater wealth accumulation. Yet, college graduates and others often do not understand basic financial concepts.

Way and Wong (2010) show that user-friendly tools encouraging participants to increase their scores lead to improved literacy. Moreover, both health and financial literacy share risk perception dimensions involving the probability of gain, loss, and status quo and expected benefit and harm (Holtgrave and Weber 1993). Additionally, financial literacy is correlated not only with health status and behavior but also with happiness. Thus, developing a scorecard to improve financial literacy may also lead to comprehensive well-being. This is a good example of how interventions at the micro level can have a lasting effect on economic outcomes.

DISCUSSION QUESTIONS

1. Despite being intuitively appealing, what are some objections to a health scorecard approach?
2. Who should apply a scorecard approach?
3. Discuss whether a scorecard approach can be appropriate for financial literacy or whether it is too simplistic.
4. What concepts should be included in a financial literacy scorecard?
5. How could a financial literacy scorecard best be used to better a population's understanding of financial concepts?

REFERENCES

Adams, Robert John. 2010. "Improving Health Outcomes with Better Patient Understanding and Education." *Risk Management and Healthcare Policy* 3:61, 61–72.

Adler, Linda, Farrokh Alemi, David G. Ansley, Patricia F. Brennan, Molly Joel Coye, David Gustafson, Joseph Henderson, Holly Jimison, Albert Mulley, John Noell, Kevin Patrick, Thomas C. Reeves, Thomas Robinson, and Victor Strecher. 1998. *Science Panel on Interactive Communication and Health Summary Statement*. Washington, DC: Office of Disease Prevention and Health Promotion, U.S. Department of Health and Human Services. Available at http://odphp.osophs.dhhs.gov/confrnce/partnr98/SciPICH.htm.

American College of Cardiology Foundation. 2011a. "Am I at Risk?" Available at www.cardiosmart.org/CardioSmart/AmIAtRisk.aspx.

American College of Cardiology Foundation. 2011b. "Learn about Heart Disease." Available at www.cardiosmart.org/heartdisease/cttbrowser.aspx?category=risk%20factors.

American Heart Association. 2011. "Life's Simple 7: Heart Health Factors." Available at http://mylifecheck.heart.org/Multitab.aspx?NavID=3.

Apfel, Franklin, Kara L. Jacobson, Ruth M. Parker, Julia Taylor, Tony Boyle, Joanna Groves, Jeremiah Mwangi, Scott Ratzan, and Carinne Allison. 2010. *Health Literacy: Action and Guide Part 2: Evidence and Case Studies*. Axbridge, UK: World Health Communication Associates Ltd. Available at www.whcaonline.org/uploads/publications/WHCAhealthLiteracy-28.3.2010.pdf.

Baker, David W., Michael S. Wolf, Joseph Fienglass, Jason A. Thompson, Julie A. Gazmararian, and Jenny Huang. 2007. "Health Literacy and Mortality among Elderly Persons." *Archive of Internal Medicine* 167:14, 1503–1509.

Barlow, Cate, Debbie Cooke, Kathleen Mulligan, Eric Beck, and Stanton Newman. 2010. "A Critical Review of Self-Management and Educational Interventions in Inflammatory Bowel Disease." *Gastroenterology Nursing* 33:1, 11–18.

Bearden, William O., and Kelly L. Haws. 2012. "How Low Spending Control Harms Consumers." *Journal of the Academy of Marketing Science* 40:1, 181–193.

Bechara, Antoine, Hanna Damasio, Daniel Tranel, and Antonio R. Damasio. 1997. "Deciding Advantageously before Knowing the Advantageous Strategy." *Science* 275:5304, 1293–1295.

Bennett, Jarred S., Patricia A. Boyle, Bryan D. James, and David A. Bennett. 2012. "Correlates of Health and Financial Literacy in Older Adults without Dementia." *BMC Geriatrics* 12 (June 12): 30–39. Available at www.biomedcentral.com/1471-2318/12/30.

Bertrand, Marianne, Sendhil Mullainathan, and Eldar Shafir. 2006. "Behavioral Economics and Marketing in Aiding Decision Making Among the Poor." *Journal of Public Policy & Marketing* 25:1, 8–23.

Bhavnani, Ashwin, Rebecca Tyrrell, Emily Allen, Won Dechpinya, Yun Gao, and Yasaman Torabi. 2011. "Design, Implementation, and Go-To Market Strategy for the Digital Health Scorecard: A Social Marketing Approach to Health Literacy." Unpublished manuscript, Carnegie Mellon University.

Blumenthal-Barby, Jennifer Swindell, and Hadley Burroughs. 2012. "Seeking Better Health Care Outcomes: The Ethics of Using the 'Nudge'." *American Journal of Bioethics* 12:2, 1–10.

Bryan, D. James, Patricia T. Boyle, Jarred S. Bennett, and David A. Bennett. 2012. "The Impact of Health and Financial Literacy on Decision Making in Community-Based Older Adults." *Gerontology* 58:6, 531–539.

Carlin, Bruce Ian, and David T. Robinson. 2010. *What Does Financial Literacy Training Teach Us?* National Bureau of Economic Research, No. w16721. Available at www.nber.org/papers/w16271.pdf?new_window=1.

Canoy, Dexter, and Iain Buchan. 2007. "Challenges in Obesity Epidemiology." *Obesity Reviews* 8:Supplement 1, 1–11.

Cleary, Patricia A., Trevor J. Orchard, Saul Genuth, Nathan D. Wong, Robert Detrano, Jye-Yu C. Backlund, Bernard Zinman, Alan Jacobson, Wanjie Sun, John M. Lachin, and David M. Nathan. 2006. "The Effect of Intensive Glycemic Treatment on Coronary Artery Calcification in Type 1 Diabetic Participants of the Diabetes Control and Complications Trial/Epidemiology of Diabetes Interventions and Complications (DCCT/EDIC) Study." *Diabetes* 55:12, 3556–3565.

Clark, Noreen M. 2003. "Management of Chronic Disease by Patients." *Annual Review of Public Health* 24 (1): 289–313.

Coleman, Mary Thoesen, and Karen S. Newton. 2005. "Supporting Self-Management in Patients with Chronic Illness." *American Family Physician* 72:8, 1503–1510.

Davis, Dave, Mike Evans Davis, Alex Jadad, Laure Perrier, Darlyne Rath, David Ryan, Gary Sibbald, Sharon Straus, Susan Rappolt, Maria Wowk, and Merrick Zwarenstein. 2003. "The Case for Knowledge Translation: Shortening the Journey from Evidence to Effect." *BMJ* 327:7405, 33–35.

Fox, Susannah, and Sydney Jones. 2009. *The Social Life of Health Information.* Washington, DC: Pew Internet and American Life Project. Available at www.pewinternet.org/~/media//Files/Reports/2009/PIP_Health_2009.pdf.

Galt, Kimberly A. 2006. *Developing Clinical Practice Skills for Pharmacists.* Bethesda, MD: American Society of Health-System Pharmacists.

Hacker, Jacob S., Gregory Huber, Austin Nichols, Philip Rehm, Mark Schlesinger, Craig Stuart, and Robert G. Valletta. 2012. "The Economic Security Index: A New Measure for Research and Policy Analysis." Working Paper 2012-21, Federal Reserve Bank of San Francisco. Available at www.frbsf.org/publications/economics/papers/2012/wp12-21bk.pdf.

Hanoch, Yaniv, Talya Miron-Shatz, Helen Cole, Mary Himmelstein, and Alex D. Federman. 2010. "Choice, Numeracy and Physicians-in-Training Performance: The Case of Medicare Part D." *Health Psychology* 29:4, 454–459.

Harvard Medical School. 2010. "American Ideal." *Harvard Heart Letter*, April. Available at https://www.health.harvard.edu/newsletters/Harvard_Heart_Letter/2010/April/american-ideal.

Higgins, Julian P. T., and Sally Green, eds. 2011. *Cochrane Handbook for Systematic Reviews of Interventions Version 5.1.0* [updated March 2011]. The Cochrane Collaboration. Available at www.cochrane-handbook.org.

Hill, Andrew T., Bonnie T. Meszaros, and Erin A. Yetter. 2012. "The Keys to Financial Success Curriculum: Impact on Personal Finance Behaviors." Working Paper, Federal Reserve Bank, Philadelphia. Available at www.aeaweb.org/aea/2012conference/program/retrieve .php?pdfid=608.

Holtgrave, David R., and Elke U. Weber. 1993. "Dimensions of Risk Perception for Financial and Health Risks." *Risk Analysis* 13:5, 553–558.

Huston, Sandra J. 2010. "Measuring Financial Literacy." *Journal of Consumer Affairs* 44:2, 296–316.

Institute of Medicine. 2001. "Improving the 21st-Century Health Care System." In Rona Briere, ed., *Crossing the Quality Chasm*, 61–88. Washington, DC: The National Academies Press.

Kaenzig, Joseph, and Rolf Wüstenhagen. 2010. "The Effect of Life Cycle Cost Information on Consumer Investment Decisions Regarding Eco-Innovation." *Journal of Industrial Ecology* 14:1, 121–136.

Lavizzo-Mourey, Risa. 2012. "We Must Focus on Preventing Disease If We Want Our Nation to Thrive." *The Atlantic*. Available at www.theatlantic.com/health/archive/2012/05/we-must-focus-on-preventing-disease-if-we-want-our-nation-to-thrive/257759/.

Loewenstein, George F., Elke U. Weber, Christopher K. Hsee, and Ned Welch. 2001. "Risk as Feelings." *Psychological Bulletin* 127:2, 267–286.

Lorig, Kate R., David S. Sobel, Anita L. Stewart, Byron William Brown, Jr., Albert Bandura, Philip Ritter, Virginia Gonzalez, Diana D. Laurent, and Halstead R. Holman. 1999. "Evidence Suggesting that a Chronic Disease Self-Management Program Can Improve Health Status While Reducing Hospitalization: A Randomized Trial." *Medical Care* 37:1, 5–14.

Lusardi, Annamaria, and Olivia S. Mitchell. 2005. "Financial Literacy and Planning: Implications for Retirement Wellbeing." University of Michigan Retirement Research Center.

Lynch, John G. Jr., Richard G. Netemeyer, Stephen A. Spiller, Stephen A., and Alessandra Zammit. 2010. "A Generalizable Scale of Propensity to Plan: The Long and the Short of Planning for Time and for Money." *Journal of Consumer Research* 37:1, 108–128.

Mandell, Lewis, and Linda Schmid Klein. 2009. "The Impact of Financial Literacy Education on Subsequent Financial Behavior." *Journal of Financial Counseling and Planning* 20:1, 15–24.

Mayo Clinic Staff. 2011. "5 Medication-Free Strategies to Help Prevent Heart Disease." *Mayo Foundation for Medical Education and Research (MFMER)*, January 12. Available at www.mayoclinic.com/health/heart-disease-prevention/WO00041/METHOD=print.

Miron–Shatz, Talya. 2009. "Am I Going to Be Happy and Financially Stable?": How American Women Feel When They Think about Financial Security." *Judgment and Decision Making* 4:1, 102–122.

Miron–Shatz, Talya, Yaniv Hanoch, Dana Graef, and Michal Sagi. 2009. "Presentation Format, Numeracy, and Emotional Reactions: The Case of Prenatal Screening Tests." *Journal of Health Communication* 14:5, 439–450.

Miron-Shatz, Talya, Ingrid Mühlhauser, Bruce Bower, Michael Diefenbach, Ben Goldacre, Richard S. W. Smith, David Spiegelhalter, and Odette Wegwarth. 2011. "Barriers to Health Information and Building Solutions." In Gerd Gigerenzer and J. A. Muir Gray, eds., *Better Doctors, Better Patients, Better Decisions: Envisioning Healthcare 2020*, Strüngmann Forum Report Volume 6, 191–214. Cambridge: MIT Press.

Miron-Shatz, Talya, and Scott Ratzan. 2011. "The Potential of an Online and Mobile Health Scorecard for Preventing Chronic Disease." *Journal of Health Communication* 16:2, 175–190.

Mozaffarian, Dariush, Aruna Kamineni, Mercedes Carnethon, Luc Djoussé, Kenneth J. Mukamal, and David Siscovick. 2009. "Lifestyle Risk Factors and New-Onset Diabetes Mellitus in Older Adults: The Cardiovascular Health Study." *Archive of Internal Medicine* 169:8, 798–807.

Murray, Elizabeth, Joanne Burns, Sharon See Tai, Rosalind Lai, and Irwin Nazareth. 2005. "Interactive Health Communication Applications for People with Chronic Disease." *Cochrane Database of Systematic Reviews* 4, CD004274.

National Institutes of Health. 2011. *Brain Basics: Preventing Stroke*. Bethesda, MD: Office of Communication and Public Liaison, National Institute of Neurological Disorders and Stroke. NIH Publication No. 11-3440b. Available at www.ninds.nih.gov/disorders/stroke/Brain_Basics-Preventing_Stroke_brochure.pdf.

Okoro, Catherine A., Ali H. Mokdad, Earl S. Ford, Barbara A. Bowman, Frank Vinicor, and Wayne H. Giles. 2004. "Are Persons with Diabetes Practicing Healthier Behaviors in the Year 2001? Results from the Behavioral Risk Factor Surveillance System." *Preventive Medicine* 38:2, 203–208.

Ratzan, Scott C. 2009. "Integrating Health Literacy into Primary and Secondary Prevention Strategies." *Institute of Medicine Workshop on Integrating Health Literacy into Primary and Secondary Prevention Strategies*, September 15. Washington, DC: Institute of Medicine. Available at www.iom.edu/~/media/Files/Activity%20Files/PublicHealth/HealthLiteracy/2009-SEP-15/02-Ratzan.pdf.

Ratzan, Scott C., and Ruth M. Parker. 2000. "Introduction." In *National Library of Medicine Current Bibliographies in Medicine: Health Literacy*. NLM Pub. No. CBM 2000-1. Bethesda, MD: National Institutes of Health, U.S. Dept. of Health and Human Services.

Rosser, Benjamin A., Kevin E. Vowles, Edmund Keogh, Christopher Eccleston, and Gail A. Mountain. 2009. "Technologically-Assisted Behavior Change: A Systematic Review of Studies of Novel Technologies for the Management of Chronic Illness." *Journal of Telemedicine and Telecare* 15:7, 327–338.

Sharpe, Deanna L. 2008. "Consumer Financial Issues in Health Care." In Jing Jian Xiao, ed., *Handbook of Consumer Financial Research*, 318–355. New York: Springer.

Slovic, Paul, Melissa Finucane, Ellen Peters, and Donald G. MacGregor. 2002. "The Affect Heuristic." In Thomas Gilovich, Dale Griffin, and Daniel Kahneman, eds., *Heuristics and Biases: The Psychology of Intuitive Judgment*, 397–420. Cambridge: Cambridge University Press.

Stewart, Anita L., Ron D. Hays, and John E. Ware, Jr. 1992. "Methods of Constructing Health Measures." In Anita L. Stewart and John E. Ware, Jr., eds., *Measuring Functioning and Well-Being: The Medical Outcomes Study Approach*, 67–85. Durham, NC: Duke University Press.

Thaler, Richard H., and Cass R. Sunstein. 2009. *Nudge: Improving Decisions about Health, Wealth, and Happiness*. New Haven, CT: Yale University Press.

U.S. Department of Health and Human Services. 2002. "HHS, American Diabetes Association Renew Campaign to Help People with Diabetes Know Their Cardiovascular Risks: New ADA Survey Shows Many Know Little about Risks of Heart Disease, Stroke." February 19. Available at http://archive.hhs.gov/news/press/2002pres/20020219.html.

Van Rooij, Maarten, Annamaria Lusardi, and Rob J. Alessie. 2011. "Financial Literacy, Retirement Planning, and Household Wealth." *The National Bureau of Economic Research*. Available at www.nber.org/papers/w17339.

Van Tol-Geerdink, Julia J., Peep F. M. Stalmeier, Emile N. J. T. van Lin, Erik C. Schimmel, Henk Huizenga, Wim A. J. van Daal, and Jan-Willem Leer. 2006. "Do Prostate Cancer Patients Want to Choose Their Own Radiation Treatment." *International Journal of Radiation Oncology · Biology · Physics* 66:4, 1105–1111.

Vernon, John A., Antonio Trujillo, Sara Rosenbaum, and Barbara DeBuono. 2007. "Low Health Literacy: Implications for National Health Care Policy." Washington, DC: George Washington University School of Public Health and Health Services.

Volpp, Kevin G., Leslie K. John, Andrea B. Troxel, Laurie Norton, Jennifer Fassbender, and George Loewenstein. 2008. "Financial Incentive–Based Approaches for Weight Loss." *JAMA: The Journal of the American Medical Association* 300:22, 2631–2637.

Wallsten, Thomas S., David V. Budescu, Rami Zwick, and Steven M. Kemp. 1993. "Preferences and Reasons for Communicating Probabilistic Information in Verbal or Numerical Terms." *Bulletin of the Psychonomic Society* 31:2, 135–138.

Way, Wendy L., and Nancy Wong. 2010. "Harnessing the Power of Technology to Enhance Financial Literacy Education and Personal Financial Well-Being: A Review of the Literature, Proposed Model, and Action Agenda." Working Paper 10-6, Center for Financial Security, University of Wisconsin, Madison.

White, Sheida. 2008. "Assessing the Nation's Health Literacy: Key Concepts and Findings of the National Assessment of Adult Literacy (NAAL)." AMA Foundation. Available at www.ama-assn.org/resources/doc/ama-foundation/hl_report_2008.pdf.

Williams, Mark V., David W. Baker, Ruth M. Parker, and Joanne R. Nurss. 1998. "Relationship of Functional Health Literacy to Patients' Knowledge of Their Chronic Disease: A Study of Patients with Hypertension and Diabetes." *Archives of Internal Medicine*, 158:2, 166–172.

Xu, Lisa, and Zia Bilal. 2012. *Financial Literacy around the World: An Overview of the Evidence with Practical Suggestions for the Way Forward.* World Bank Policy Research Working Paper No. 6107. Available at http://ssrn.com/abstract=2094887.

Yates, Dan, and Chris Ward. 2012. "Are Your Personal Financial Characteristics Healthy?" *Journal of Business & Economics Research* 10:4, 225–232.

Zajonc, Robert B. 1980. "Feeling and Thinking: Preferences Need No Inferences." *American Psychologist* 35:2, 151–175.

ABOUT THE AUTHORS

Talya Miron-Shatz is Founding Director of the Center for Medical Decision Making, Ono Academic College, and CEO of CureMyWay, a start-up company that creates software to support patients' decision making and healthy habit formation. She was a post-doctoral research fellow at Princeton University, and taught consumer behavior at the Wharton Business School, University of Pennsylvania. She examines how patients and health care professionals understand and convey risk information, and what makes people follow warnings and lifestyle regimens. Her research is widely published in peer reviewed journals including *Psychological Science*, *Health Psychology*, and *Emotion*. As part of her mission of translating academic knowledge into action, she consults pharmaceutical companies and related agencies, and writes about medical decision making for *Psychology Today*. Dr. Miron-Shatz received an MA in psychology and communications and a PhD in psychology from The Hebrew University.

Stephanie Gati is a recent graduate from Princeton University, with a degree in Ecology and Evolutionary Biology and a certificate in Global Health and Health Policy. Ms. Gati is a Fellow in the Princeton University Project 55 program at Aeras Global TB Vaccine Foundation in Rockville, Maryland. She is supporting teams performing clinical trials of six tuberculosis vaccine candidates in various African countries. She became interested in vaccine development after conducting her Princeton University senior thesis research on malnutrition and pneumococcal conjugate vaccine efficacy in rural populations in Kenya. During the summer of 2011, Ms. Gati was a Global Health Intern Johnson and Johnson in the Department of Government Affairs, working on initiatives to promote chronic disease prevention. Ms. Gati plans to attend medical school and become a public health physician.

ACKNOWLEDGMENT

The authors thank Glen Doniger and Joshua Zuckerman for their insightful contributions.

Investor Psychology

CHAPTER 18

Risk Perception and Risk Tolerance

Victor Ricciardi
Assistant Professor of Financial Management, Goucher College

Douglas Rice, CFP®
Assistant Professor of Business and Management,
Notre Dame de Namur University, Registered Investment Adviser,
and President, Institute for Financial Planning Education

INTRODUCTION

Risk is a topic area that has application in a wide variety of circumstances. This subject has diverse definitions, measurements, and explanations among individuals, organizations, and disciplines. Researchers have investigated the risk-taking behavior of individuals and groups at length within the decision sciences and business arena (Ricciardi 2008a, 2008b, 2010) and the fields of behavioral finance, financial psychology, and behavioral accounting (Ricciardi, 2004). The literature reveals that risk researchers from different disciplines offer various viewpoints in terms of how to define, explain, and assess risk.

In academic finance, the well-established and accepted viewpoint of risk is known as traditional finance (Ricciardi 2008a). A major aspect of traditional finance is the objective aspects of risk (e.g., standard deviation). Traditional finance focuses on the quantitative measure of risk. The foundation of this approach is the macro-level assessment of risk incorporating all investors within financial markets. The basis of the traditional finance viewpoint of risk is classical decision-making (also known as the *normative model*) and the premise of *rationality* (i.e., choosing the optimal alternative) in which an individual maximizes expected utility. A fundamental premise of this model is rationality in which people are risk averse and select the optimal choice over an investment with an equivalent expected value.

The main theory of traditional finance's view of risk is modern portfolio theory (MPT). MPT contends that rational investors apply diversification to optimize their portfolios and provides an approach for pricing a risky asset in this portfolio with the capital asset pricing model (CAPM). A fundamental premise of MPT is that a positive relationship exists between risk and return. The CAPM measures the link between a stock's movements and the volatility of the overall stock market. The model uses a stock's beta in tandem with the average investor's level of risk aversion to calculate the return that the individual requires on an individual stock. *Beta* is a measure of market risk in which the higher the beta, the more sensitive is the expected return on the stock to changes in the returns on the overall market.

Another important aspect of MPT is the risk tolerance of investors that considers how much risk an investor is willing to accept. Risk tolerance also has a direct relationship to an individual's asset allocation decision within a diversified investment portfolio and therefore has a profound influence on future wealth.

The purpose of this chapter is to provide a summary of the academic literature and the topics on risk perception and risk tolerance. The chapter has the following organization. The first section offers an alternative view to traditional finance by discussing the behavioral aspects of the risk perception espoused by behavioral finance along with a short discussion of the connection between risk perception and risk tolerance. Next, attention turns to an overview of risk tolerance and the major issues of the measurement of an individual's tolerance for risk. Then, the following two sections provide a discussion of some recent academic studies on the role of emotion in financial risk-taking behavior and then an examination of risk-taking behavior during the financial crisis of 2008. The next section presents some unresolved issues in the risk tolerance and perception domain. The last section summarizes the chapter.

RISK PERCEPTION

Risk perception is the subjective judgment process that investors employ when assessing risk and the degree of uncertainty. Risk perception incorporates various objective and subjective factors that affect how individuals make judgments about financial services and investment products. In terms of the objective factors of risk, Ricciardi (2008a) documents more than 150 financial and accounting proxy variables from the risk perception literature as potential risk indicators. The behavioral finance viewpoint also encompasses a subjective aspect of risk (e.g., the role of cognitive and emotional issues), and individual behavior plays a fundamental role in defining, evaluating, and explaining risk. Ricciardi (2004, 2008b) reports a broad list of more than 100 behavioral risk indicators in the behavioral finance literature and over 10 psychological risk attributes in the behavioral accounting literature.

The behavioral finance approach to risk is based on a different collection of topics than traditional finance. Risk perception is based on the descriptive model that explains how individuals actually make judgments and decisions in the real world. According to the descriptive approach, the explanation of how individuals act in this manner when assessing perceived risk is based on the assumptions of bounded rationality, satisficing, loss aversion, and prospect theory. *Bounded rationality* is the premise that an investor reduces the number of selections to a set of smaller abbreviated steps, even though this may oversimplify the final choice. Under these conditions of bounded rationality, individuals will choose the option they perceive as the satisfactory choice and this may not be the optimal choice (this is also known as *satisficing*). *Loss aversion* is based on the idea that investors assign more weight to losses than they do to gains. According to *prospect theory*, an individual evaluates an alternative of losses and gains based on an acceptable reference point (or anchor) in dollar terms related to the loss aversion concept. An emerging topic of examination by behavioral finance researchers concerns evaluating an inverse relationship between perceived risk and return. Ricciardi (2008b, 2010) provides a more extensive discussion of risk perception.

THE RELATIONSHIP BETWEEN RISK PERCEPTION AND RISK TOLERANCE

Although this topic of risk is very important, no general consensus exists on the definition of the various terms of risk including risk perception and risk tolerance (Roszkowski and Davey 2010). Therefore, this section provides some basic attributes associated with these two risk terms. *Risk perception* is the loss that an investor believes exists in purchasing a financial service or product from a particular company, whether a risk actually exists. The concept of perceived risk is an interdisciplinary and multidimensional process that depends on the particular situation, activity, or event (Ricciardi 2008a). Although Roszkowski and Davey (p. 43) define risk tolerance as the "amount of risk that an individual is willing to accept in the pursuit of some goal," Grable (2008, p. 4) describes risk tolerance as the "maximum amount of uncertainty someone is willing to accept when making a financial decision."

In terms of the link between risk perception and risk tolerance, Martinussen and Hunter (2009, p. 198) contend that the two concepts are "related and often confounded constructs," whereas Roszkowski and Davey (2010, p. 43) cite research studies that find these two topics "can independently contribute to risk-taking behavior." Littell, Tacchino, and Cordell (2003, p. 248) provide this practical perspective about these two risk concepts in which individuals "are often not fully aware of their true level of risk tolerance or of the factors that influence their perception of the riskiness of a situation."

AN OVERVIEW OF RISK TOLERANCE

This section provides a general discussion of risk tolerance including the definitional issues, the asset allocation decision, and the role of investment performance.

Definition of Risk Tolerance

A major problem within the risk tolerance literature is the lack of general agreement about the definition of this concept. The following discussion presents a wide variety of meanings and descriptions from governmental agencies, self-governing bodies, and risk experts.

Securities and Exchange Commission The Securities and Exchange Commission (SEC) (2004, p. 2) offers the following perspective on risk tolerance:

> *What are the best saving and investing products for you? The answer depends on when you will need the money, your goals, and if you will be able to sleep at night if you purchase a risky investment where you could lose your principal.*

In its recent guide to asset allocation, the Securities and Exchange Commission (2010, p. 1) includes an explanation of risk and defines risk tolerance as "your ability and willingness to lose some or all of your original investment in exchange for greater potential returns." From the perspective of professionals advising clients, the Financial Industry Regulatory Authority (FINRA) (2011) regulatory notice 11-25 specifically states that the agency does not define the term risk tolerance, but FINRA offers the 2010 SEC definition as a guideline.

This SEC definition adds some clarity but it fails to define the elements of the construct for the terms *ability* and *willingness*, or provide any guidance on how to measure these two terms. For instance, the word "ability" might include a strict standard of having an emergency savings account. If an investor does not have the ability or financial means to save for short-term emergencies, the argument could be made to delay starting a long-term investment fund for retirement. However, applying this strict interpretation in a regulatory framework is difficult and unreasonable because many individuals pursue investing activities without ample savings, investments, and insurance. A similar problem exists in applying the concept of willingness. For example, how does a practitioner assess how much a client is willing to lose when pursuing higher potential returns if the client does not understand the difference between a stock and a bond?

Other Governing Bodies   The International Organization for Standardization (ISO) (2005) defines risk tolerance as the degree of risk to which an individual is willing to accept a less favorable investment result in order to pursue a more favorable investment outcome. This definition has limitations because it fails to provide a clear measurement or application and omits the term ability, which presents further definitional ambiguity. According to Linciano and Soccorso (2012), the Financial Services Authority (FSA) (2011) and the European Securities and Markets Authority (ESMA) (2012) both publish guidelines regarding the need for firms to assess the client's preferences about risk taking, but without any guidance on how to do so.

Objective versus Subjective Meanings   The literature creates further uncertainty about the definition of risk tolerance. For example, Cordell (2002) contends that risk tolerance should be separated into risk capacity and risk attitude. *Risk capacity* is a more objective measure that includes age, income, and financial stability. By contrast, *risk attitude* is a more subjective measure that incorporates an investor's emotions. Rozkowski, Davey, and Grable (2005) acknowledge Cordell's perspective but focus the risk tolerance concept only on its subjective aspects. They note that the majority of clients and financial planners use risk tolerance in this manner. Both Cordell and Rozkowski et al. agree that the use of the risk tolerance term should be separate in terms of psychological issues and objective factors. This adheres to the SEC's use of the terminology for ability and willingness as distinct factors, although whether this was the agency's intention when it developed the definition of risk tolerance is unclear.

The Volatility Tolerance Approach   Some within the financial planning profession also view risk tolerance as a "volatility tolerance" approach. This fits into MPT with volatility being a proxy for risk. This approach attempts to address the issue of an investor selling in market downturns and attempts to identify the correct mix of assets to construct a portfolio that will be held given its historical volatility. This approach attempts to answer the question of "How much can the portfolio fall before the investor sells?" This method can be further enhanced by applying it with the slogan "of investors being able to sleep at night when markets become volatile" if the financial planner's business philosophy is to keep clients happy during market downturns. It also assumes that investors should maintain a "buy and hold" strategy throughout market fluctuations because eventually a *reversion to the mean* will occur (i.e., the premise that a financial security's low and high prices are temporary and the value of the instrument tends to return to its historical average return over time).

Although the volatility tolerance approach has merit, it also falls short of being robust. For example, investors who cannot tolerate a decline of more than a few percentage points in price will have to hold a large allocation in cash or secure debt leaving them exposed to both the risk of *inflation* (i.e., the probably that increases in the price of goods and services will undermine the value of an investment portfolio) and *shortfall risk* (i.e., the risk that an asset's actual return will be lower than the expected return or the investment return required to meet an individual's investment objectives). Similarly, those holding large debt allocations, especially long-term debt, due to low risk tolerance are exposed to *interest rate risk* (i.e., the probability an investment's market value will change due to a fluctuation in interest rates). For investors assuming a high risk tolerance, holding the investment solely based on the assumption of mean reversion, the number of years or the time horizon requirement for the asset classes to recover to their historical investment returns is unclear. A common practice with risk tolerance questionnaires is to inquire about losses over the past year, but most instruments fail to assess multiple losing years. For instance, the Japanese stock market decline from its peak in 1990 took more than two decades. Thus, based on this method, the volatility tolerance of some investors may not have been violated in any given year.

Asset Allocation Strategy

Another consideration is the application of these instruments between clients and financial planners in practice. A myriad of risk tolerance questionnaires exist that result in predetermined asset allocation strategy based on an individual's risk category (e.g., if a person is a risk seeker, risk neutral, or a conservative risk taker). The typical asset allocation is based on a diversification strategy across a percentage of equities, bonds, and cash. This may stem from previous definitions of risk tolerance dating back to Blume and Friend (1978). These authors contend that an accurate risk tolerance measurement attempts to identify an investor's appropriate asset allocation strategy with the goal of maximizing expected return in which an investor will tolerate a risky financial security and not sell too early. Under this definition, an investor's prescribed risk tolerance category has minimal value unless the financial planner develops an asset allocation strategy with the client in the context of a diversified investment portfolio.

The Securities and Exchange Commission (2010, p. 1) addresses asset allocation by stating, "The asset allocation that works best for you at any given point in your life will depend largely on your time horizon and your ability to tolerate risk." If a time horizon is added to the combination of the psychological (willingness) and objective capacity (ability) measures, then only one factor remains, which the SEC includes in the definition of risk tolerance in stating that risk is taken "in exchange for greater potential returns." That last component of the puzzle is determining how much return is needed to accomplish the investment goals of the client's portfolio.

The Role of Investment Performance

In a risk context, this determination of how much return is needed can be viewed as shortfall risk. An investor may have a low risk tolerance both psychologically and objectively as well as a short time frame but may still require a higher return than a conservative portfolio would provide. Thus, a need exists to balance the amount of risk against the need for a potential reward. Although financial planners may not consider shortfall risk during the investment process, such risk may influence investment performance. Thus, financial planners should include this concept in their discussions with clients.

MEASUREMENT OF RISK TOLERANCE

An important issue with risk tolerance questionnaires is the difficulty of measurement. Regardless of the reason, whether it is bias or a lack of a solid theoretical model, risk tolerance questionnaires vary widely. Rice (2005) identifies more than 130 different types and formats of risk questionnaires in his research study. A primary example of a typical risk tolerance question on a survey instrument is the Survey of Consumer Finances (SCF) that creates a single item self-assessment of a person's tolerance for risk. According to Grable and Schumm (2010, p. 118), the actual question on the SCF survey is as follows:

> *Which of the following statements on this page comes closest to the amount of financial risk that you are willing to take when you save or make investments?*
>
> *1. Take substantial financial risk expecting to earn substantial returns.*
> *2. Take above average financial risks expecting to earn above average returns.*
> *3. Take average financial risks expecting to earn average returns.*
> *4. Not willing to take any financial risks.*

As Grable and Schumm also note, this is one of the only risk tolerance questions on national surveys of consumers, and therefore its availability promotes an extensive use within the academic research literature.

Problems of Risk Tolerance Measurement

This section discusses the problems associated with the measurement of risk tolerance questionnaires and includes the following: the many types of risk tolerance questionnaires, the lack of uniformity between the risk tolerance profile versus the asset allocation recommendation, the development of an asset allocation choice for the respondent, and issues in advising clients related to the research findings based on demographic and socioeconomic factors.

Different Types of Questions, Questionnaires, and Scoring Methodology   Rice (2005) analyzes 131 risk questionnaires and finds large variances in both the risk tolerance questions and the scoring of the results. He analyzes the distribution of risk tolerance questions on these instruments. The main findings reveal a wide disbursement of surveys with 21 different categories of questions and an average of 6.48 different ways to ask a question in a given category. For example, the time horizon category includes 11 different question types. Although 35 percent of the questionnaires lack any reference to time horizon, the questionnaires still provide an asset allocation answer. Of the 65 percent of the questions having a question covering time horizon, 22 percent simply ask the investor's age without making a connection to the individual's financial objective. This implies that saving for a house a year from now and investing for retirement over the next 25 years should have the same risk tolerance and asset allocation. Only 47 percent of the questionnaires contained the more useful question "When will you use the money?"

Cochran (2002) contends that financial planners create and use their own risk tolerance questionnaires to assist their clients in developing a portfolio. The lack of a standard risk tolerance model or cumulative theory on which to base the development of questionnaires results in financial planners creating numerous surveys with some clearly better than others. Yook and Everett (2003), who report that the correlation of outcomes from six questionnaires varied from 0.3 to 0.8, contend this is not a consistent or uniform measurement of the same investor across different questionnaires.

Risk Tolerance Profile and Asset Allocation Recommendation Another consideration in Rice (2005) is the scoring methodology that produces a wide range of recommendations between the risk tolerance score and the asset allocation profile. For example, when the same self-described conservative (or risk averse) investor answers different questionnaires, the percentage of assets allocated to equities varies from 0 to 70 percent. When an investor who describes himself as an aggressive risk taker answers the same questionnaires, the allocation to bonds or cash or cash/bonds varies from 0 to 50 percent. So a risk conservative investor who wants to take little risk could hold up to 70 percent equities and an aggressive risk investor who wants to take considerable risk could own up to 50 percent bonds and cash. Clearly, each investment firm that creates its own risk tolerance questionnaire not only develops the actual questions but also the scoring system, which is based on the firm's own beliefs of what the results should mean. The Securities and Exchange Commission (2010, p. 6) provides the following warning about the risk tolerance scores and asset allocation recommendations from free online surveys offered by the financial services industry:

> *While the suggested asset allocations may be a useful starting point for determining an appropriate allocation for a particular goal, investors should keep in mind that the results may be biased towards financial products or services sold by companies or individuals maintaining the websites.*

Asset Allocation Option A more straightforward approach to determining the asset allocation would be to offer a set of asset allocation options to investors and let them choose the one they want. Rice (2005) reports that this approach is widely used with this one question being on 60 percent of the questionnaires studied. This evidence implies that investors are knowledgeable enough to consider all the relevant factors and make an informed decision. According to The Consumer Financial Literacy Survey developed by Harris Interactive Inc. (2012), 42 percent of respondents give themselves a C grade or worse on their knowledge of personal finance and only 19 percent assign themselves an A grade. The survey reveals that 80 percent of respondents state they would benefit from additional advice and answers to everyday questions from an investment professional. This evidence suggests that most investors do not think they are financially knowledgeable and would like some expert advice. Therefore, self-selection is implausible for most people.

Demographic and Socioeconomic Factors   The literature contains many findings about differences in risk tolerance across demographic and socioeconomic attributes. Roszkowski (2001) and Grable (2008) discuss the well-established findings on demographic and socioeconomic factors contained in the risk tolerance literature. For example, a comprehensive collection of experimental studies and survey-based endeavors on risk-taking behavior reveals the following evidence:

- **Gender:** Women tend to be less risk-taking (more conservative) than men.
- **Marital status:** Single individuals are more likely to make riskier decisions than married persons.
- **Age:** Younger people are inclined to be more risk-seeking than older individuals.
- **Education:** People with higher levels of education display a greater tendency to take risks.

Financial practitioners sometimes might be better off simply asking the SCF question to a client directly to determine what type of risk the individual wants to take rather than using stereotypes that may or may not be accurate. For example, financial planners often assume that risk tolerance decreases with age. However, Wang and Hanna (1997) show that when measuring risk tolerance by the ratio of risky assets to total wealth, risk tolerance increases with age.

THE ROLE OF EMOTION IN RISK PERCEPTION AND RISK TOLERANCE

An emerging topic in the risk perception and risk tolerance literature is the importance of emotions on investor decisions. Ricciardi (2008b) discusses 12 important factors that influence an individual's risk perception including worry and positive affect (emotions). For example, Ricciardi (2011) reports findings from a 2010 online survey with nearly 1,700 responses that a strong majority of investors associate the term "worry" with stocks (i.e., 70 percent of the sample) over bonds (i.e., 10 percent of the sample), while the remaining 20 percent did not own either asset class.

Finucane, Peters, and Slovic (2003) note the importance of understanding the differences among emotion, mood, and affect. An *emotion* is a state of consciousness linked to the arousal of feelings. A *mood* or *feeling* refers to any of the subjective responses, enjoyable or unpleasant, that an individual might experience from a specific situation. *Affect* is the emotional complex (i.e., negative or positive feelings) connected with an idea or mental state. This chapter, however, uses the terms interchangeably.

A Selective Review of Emotion and Risk

This section reviews research studies since 2008 on the relationship of emotion to risk-taking behavior, including how a positive or negative mood influences the decision-making process of investors, the role of seasonal depression, and the importance of trust.

Affect Infusion Model versus the Mood Maintenance Hypothesis   Grable and Roszkowski (2008) use a mail survey to examine whether evidence confirms how mood affects financial risk tolerance. The authors assess two different approaches: (1) the Affect Infusion Model (AIM), in which a positive (negative) mood increases (decreases) risk tolerance, and (2) the Mood Maintenance Hypothesis (MMH), in which a positive (negative) mood deceases (increases) risk tolerance. The authors measure whether a difference exists between individuals who are in a positive (happy) or not a positive mood when they complete a survey instrument. The study reports evidence supporting AIM, in which those who are 18 to 75 years old who are in a positive (happy) mood have a higher level of financial risk tolerance.

Lepori (2010) also conducts a study that examines risk taking by comparing the AIM and the MMH. The data analysis in this study assesses the influence of happy moods (measured by attendance at comedy movies over the weekend) in relation to an investment in risky financial securities (measured by the investment performance of the stock market in the United States on the subsequent Monday). The study's major finding is that stock market performance is lower on the Monday after the weekend attendance at comedy movies and this evidence supports the MMH in which people in a happy mood reveal a lower preference for risky assets (i.e., investors are more cautious toward risky securities).

Emotions, Risk, and the Investment Decision   This section examines studies on the influence of emotion and risk on how investors judge an investment product and the process they use to decide whether to buy or sell a security. Rubaltelli et al. (2010) examine how investors' emotional response to different types of mutual funds affects their decision to sell this financial asset. The respondents evaluate either a conventional mutual fund or socially responsible fund and disclose at what price they were willing to sell the mutual fund. The study finds that selling prices affect how investors feel about their mutual fund and this demonstrates a subjective aspect to risk. Rubaltelli et al. (p. 174) provide the following discussion of their results:

> *It is especially noteworthy that people with negative affective reactions toward their investments (both socially and nonsocially responsible ones) set the highest selling prices, since this result seems to show that only investors with initial negative expectations about an investment are prone to systematically counteract the disposition effect.... On the other hand,... people with positive reactions toward the nonsocially responsible fund were locked in by their initial impressions and were unable to sell the losing fund as quickly as people with negative feelings.*

Aspara and Tikkanen (2011) survey more than 400 individual investors from Northern Europe to determine how affective reactions about a company might be an additional motivation to invest in the firm's stock. Aspara and Tikkanen (p. 78) find that most individual investors have strong emotional responses that provide "extra motivation to invest in stocks, over and towards the company was, the stronger was his extra investment motivation." The authors attribute this strong positive relationship to the company stock to *self-affinity bias* (i.e., the stronger an individual's self-identification with a brand or a company, the more likely it is that this person will buy the company's product/service or invest in the firm's stock).

Wang, Keller, and Siegrist (2011) examine the perceived risk of 1,249 respondents from a German-language community of Switzerland about investment products. The study's main finding is participants perceive investments that are less complex (i.e., easier to understand) as less risky, which is mainly attributable to *familiarity bias* (i.e., individuals have a positive emotional response to assets about which they are familiar). For financial planners, Wang et al. (p. 18) offer this important observation: "The clients might overestimate the risk of a certain investment due to their lack of knowledge or underestimate the risk due to their overconfidence of the self-perceived knowledge. To fill the knowledge gap is important for effective risk communication."

Seasonal Depression and Risk-Taking Behavior Using a questionnaire from respondents at a North American university, Kramer and Weber (2012) examine the role of seasonal depression, risk-taking behavior, and financial decisions. The authors administer a unique multi stage research design to access risk aversion behavior and seasonal depression over different weather cycles (seasons). The study's main finding reveals that individuals who suffer from seasonal depression avoid financial risk taking throughout seasons with a reduction in daylight but are more willing to accept riskier financial choices in the spring and summer seasons.

Trust and Risk Perception Olsen (2012) investigates the role of trust as an emotional factor of individual risk perception and how this influences cumulative market risk premiums. Based on questionnaire data from 622 American Association of Individual Investors (AAII) respondents, findings document an inverse relationship between perceived risk and trust in a financial setting. Olsen (p. 311) further reveals that on an economic countrywide basis "ex-ante estimated common stock risk premiums and ex-post market interest rates vary inversely with national trust levels. In countries with greater interpersonal trust, risk premiums and interest rates are lower."

RISK-TAKING BEHAVIOR: THE INFLUENCE OF MARKET MOODS, BUSINESS CYCLES, AND ECONOMIC SHOCKS

The financial crisis of 2008 revealed the weakness of the United States financial system along with how investors react after a historic financial downturn. This section provides a discussion of studies published since 2009 that examine the role of emotions in financial markets and how the economic cycle or market crisis influences the risk-taking behavior of investors.

Economic Mood Studies before the Financial Crisis of 2008

Two recent studies using data before the financial crisis of 2008 reveal different findings on the influence of economic moods during business cycles versus times of economic shocks.

The Role of Business Cycles   Santacruz (2009) examines the role of risk tolerance of individual investors and economic mood during times of different market cycles. The study reveals that economic mood does not influence risk tolerance of investors. Therefore, the author contends that modifying an individual's risk tolerance profile is not vital to account for overall changes in market sentiment or the economic business cycle. However, Santacruz notes that a positive association between a person's risk tolerance and overall economic mood might result in herd behavior. This herd psychology by individual investors could lead to buying risky financial assets in bullish market cycles and selling them during market downturns, resulting in lower investment returns.

Influence of Economic Shocks   Malmendier and Nagel (2011) examine the influence of macroeconomic shocks on investor behavior and risk taking using data from the SCF for the period of 1960 to 2007. Investors who experience low investment performance in the stock market during their lifetime disclose a lower motivation or inclination for taking financial risk, are less likely to invest in stocks, allocate a lower percentage of their liquid assets to equities if they participate in the market, and are less enthusiastic toward future stock performance. For safer securities such as bonds, investors who previously had low returns in bonds during their lives are less likely to own bonds within their investment portfolio. Lastly, investor experience attributable to more recent investment returns has stronger effects on investor judgments and decisions especially among younger investors.

Studies of the Financial Crisis of 2008–2009

As Ricciardi (2010, p. 143–144) notes, a major cause of the financial crisis was that traditional finance "embraced the complex innovations and exotic instruments of financial risk management . . . which contributed to the September/October 2008 financial contagion." This historic event serves as an important inflection point that exposed the flaws in the assumptions and theories of the traditional finance school and contributed to the increased acceptance of the behavioral finance paradigm. This section provides the first phase of research studies that investigate the influence of this historic event. This small sample of studies documents a wide range of findings on the risk-taking behavior of investors.

The Role of Emotion   Several studies investigate the role of emotion and risk-taking behavior during the financial crisis of 2008–2009. Using a sample of participants in a university environment, Corter (2011) examines whether a person's risk tolerance and attitudes influence the responses to catastrophic episodes in financial markets. The study assesses the role of emotional, psychological, and financial factors of the market collapse that began in Fall 2008. The author finds that a person's investment risk tolerance (i.e., perceived risk) forecasts actual risk in the individual's portfolio and this serves as an indicator for losses in the value of the portfolio during the economic crisis. The findings reveal that a correlation between negative emotional responses and portfolio losses, based on an investor's risk tolerance, predicts self-reported adjustments in terms of investment strategy. According to Corter (p. 225), an individual's emotional response to "losses may be mitigated by higher levels of risk tolerance, yet higher levels of risk tolerance are associated with riskier portfolios, and . . . larger losses in a market downturn."

Davis and Madura (2012) evaluate winner (i.e., best performing stocks) and loser (i.e., worst performing stocks) portfolios attributed to the financial crisis between 2007 and 2008 to assess the specific attributes of both winner and loser stock investments. Based on a sample size of nearly 2,300 stocks, the worst performing portfolio posts a decline of nearly 90 percent whereas the best performing portfolio records a gain over 27 percent. As Davis and Madura (p. 81) comment, "smaller, value stocks with high-leverage significantly underperformed the market while investors shifted to larger, glamour stocks with high dividend yields." The authors contend the reasons for these findings are related to risk aversion, *regret avoidance* (i.e., individuals want to prevent situations that will result in experiencing any type of regret), and *projection bias* (i.e., the inclination to unconsciously believe that others share one's current judgments, ideals, or emotional states).

Burns, Peters, and Slovic (2012) examine the reaction to the financial crisis in order to evaluate the change in perceived risk throughout the crisis period. They undertook seven surveys between September 2008 and October 2009 in which at least 600 participants responded to each questionnaire and more than 400 individuals completed all seven questionnaires. This longitudinal survey of the general public examines risk perceptions and negative emotions about the economic crisis. The findings show individuals' perceptions of risk seem to decline mainly during the early stage of the crisis and then start to stabilize. The most predictive factor of increases in risk perception among participants is the negative emotions about the crisis. Burns et al. attribute this finding to the *risk as feelings effect* (i.e., the idea that individuals make quick, intuitive decisions about risky situations based on their emotions).

Shim and Serido (2010) report the emotional reaction of college students in the aftermath of the financial crisis. In a survey based on 748 responses, Shim and Serido (p. 4) disclose the effects of the crisis on student personal finances:

> *While typical cost-cutting strategies rose moderately, risky coping strategies rose at an alarming rate: three times as many students (+169 percent) dropped classes, twice as many (+106 percent) took leaves of absence, and 78 percent postponed health care. We also saw a 26 percent rise in the use of one credit card to pay another.*

A Decline in Risk-Taking Behavior   Another group of research studies finds the desire for risk taking declined during or after the market downturn. Bricker et al. (2011) examine the role of the financial crisis on families using interview data from the SCF before and after the financial crisis. In general, the study reports a much more cautious change in financial behavior among families after the economic downturn in interviews from mid-2009 to early 2010. Families disclose a reduction in tolerance for taking financial risk, and a higher level of *precautionary savings* (i.e., a greater demand for safer cash equivalent securities along with a preference for reducing overall spending behavior in the household).

Based on an online survey of more than 2,500 respondents, Pan and Statman (2012) find that individuals with higher levels of risk tolerance are more likely to be overconfident, have higher levels of trust, and are inclined to maximization (e.g., the requirement for above average investment performance). In general, males are more risk tolerant than females, whereas females have a higher tendency for regret, lower amounts of overconfidence, and lower propensity for maximization than their male counterparts. The authors also find that higher past performance causes individuals to invest in the stock market, while lower past investment performance results in people not investing in the stock market. According to Pan and Statman (p. 61–62), individuals surveyed about their overall levels of risk tolerance reveal "following high past returns are likely to overestimate it [i.e., their level of risk tolerance], swayed by exuberance. Investors who are asked following low past returns are likely to underestimate it [i.e., their level of risk tolerance], swayed by fear." Investors who were risk tolerant in 2007 held portfolios heavily weighted in stocks, which resulted in them selling this perceived risky asset class during the financial crisis in 2008 and 2009.

Minimal Change in the Risk-Taking Activity in the Short Term Other studies document only minor or no change in risk-taking behavior related to the financial crisis in the short term but reveal that the long-term effects on risk-taking behavior of the financial crisis are still unknown. Roszkowski and Davey (2010) investigate the influence of the financial crisis on the risk perception and tolerance for risk among investors. Using risk tolerance questionnaire data gathered before and after the economic crisis, the authors find only a small decrease in risk tolerance among investors. However, many investors view investing as a much more risky activity as a result of the crisis.

Bateman et al. (2011) examine the influence of the 2008 economic crisis on the retirement savings behavior of individuals from Australia in terms of investment decisions and risk aversion. The influence of the financial crisis on low-income and young retirement savers results in a greater preference for investment choices with higher cash option (i.e., safer financial assets) whereas higher income and older retirement savers reveal an inclination for riskier investment securities. Bateman et al. (p. 201) report that the retirement saver's individual risk preference "shows a small increase in mean risk aversion between the relatively tranquil period of early 2007 and the crisis conditions of late 2008."

Gerrans, Faff, and Hartnett (2012) assess investor risk tolerance by evaluating changes in tolerance within the financial crisis. The findings disclose only a small change in financial risk tolerance and that risk tolerance is based on psychological factors excessively affected by current market performance. During the market downturn, risk tolerance among investors was fairly constant over the short-term changes in the market. Yet, these events may affect and alter a person's degree of risk tolerance more progressively over time.

An Increase in Risk-Taking Behavior Hoffmann, Post, and Pennings (2013) report risk-taking appetite increases during the crisis. The authors investigate how investor perceptions of individuals transform and influence trading activity and risk taking by comparing monthly survey data with matching trading accounts during the financial crisis. During the months with the largest declines of the financial crisis, individuals' tolerance for risk and expectation of returns both decrease, and their perception of risk increases. However, near the end of the crisis, the perceptions of investors start to improve. Investors do not reduce the amount of risk exposure in their portfolios and do not reallocate investment funds from riskier assets to cash items. Investors perceive the lower stock prices as a buying opportunity and maintain trading activity during the crisis.

UNRESOLVED ISSUES IN THE RISK DOMAIN

This section addresses some unanswered issues about risk tolerance and risk perception that financial planners and their clients should consider. These issues include risk misperceptions about stocks and bonds, changes in risk tolerance over time, lack of standardization with risk tolerance profiles and the asset allocation strategy, and the presence of heuristics during the decision-making process.

Risk Perception of Stocks versus Bonds

An unfortunate aspect of the development of risk tolerance questionnaires is the standard practice and risk perception of associating risk with stocks and safety with bonds. Risk tolerance questionnaires uniformly assign the highest risk to stocks, followed by bonds and cash. The asset allocation strategy ignores interest rate and inflation risks. If bond prices are at very high levels and interest rates are very low, bonds could be more risky than stocks when market conditions change. An increase in interest rates would cause the value of bonds to decline and the individual's investment portfolio to decrease in value. Because the standard premise is to categorize investors with low risk tolerance into bond portfolios, this supposedly safe asset class might have a detrimental effect on portfolio value. If inflation were to increase, owning cash would expose those risk conservative investors to real losses in purchasing power. Financial planners when advising clients about risk tolerance should incorporate an asset allocation recommendation that considers the change of economic market cycles that incorporates interest rates and inflation.

Risk Tolerance Might Change over Time

The measurement of a person's risk tolerance level might change over time based on historical market events. Hanna and Lindamood (2009) suggest that after controlling for household characteristics and expectations, the changes in risk tolerance are more consistent with reactions to stock market changes than the cause of stock market changes. The authors believe that risk tolerance may not be a stable measure related to risk aversion but more of an attitude reflecting expectations. According to Roszkowski and Davey (2010), financial advisors disclose that many of their clients sell investments in bear markets in which these investors were previously comfortable. Some experts might consider this a collapse in the client's risk tolerance. However, Roszkowski and Davey suggest an alternative explanation that clients simply did not understand the risks they were taking until the perceived risk became an actual risk. Separating risk tolerance from risk perception, the authors conclude that the economic circumstances of 2008 did not dramatically affect risk tolerance, but a change occurred in people's risk perception, as indicated by respondents' self-assessments.

Relationship between Risk Tolerance and Asset Allocation

Another detrimental aspect of risk tolerance assessment is the lack of a standard for treating different asset classes such as cash versus stocks in recommending an asset allocation strategy. For example, the results of a risk tolerance questionnaire might assess that an investor can tolerate a portfolio with 100 percent allocation to stocks. Therefore, the asset allocation strategy could suggest a 100 percent investment in a stock mutual fund. Risk tolerance measurement is based on the assumption of identifying the maximum amount of financial pain (or downside risk) an investor can withstand and then attempts to suggest an asset allocation that will most likely cause it.

The psychometric model is the most widely used approach that tests for both reliability and validity of the risk tolerance instrument. This model is a commercially available questionnaire in which the results place the investor into a risk tolerance scale alongside other investors (Rozkowski et al. 2005). A given investor is shown as more risk tolerant than some percentage of investors. This demonstrates the psychological aspects of risk tolerance in a similar way to intelligence quotient (IQ). Individuals have a risk tolerance that needs to be shown in a relative, not an absolute, way. No current method exists to accurately connect this result into an asset allocation strategy. For example, even if a given investor has greater risk tolerance than 60 percent of the population, this finding does not provide an equivalent asset allocation recommendation.

Heuristics Influence the Financial Advising Process

Another issue arises when financial planners omit information when advising clients. This is attributable to a cognitive process of decision-making in which a person uses *heuristics* (i.e., mental shortcuts) to process large amounts of information that can sometimes result in mental mistakes. Practitioners and clients commonly use these heuristic judgments to assess and predict financial risk tolerance (Roszkowski 2001). For example, practitioners may use a heuristic that females are less risk tolerant than males and suggest more conservative portfolios. However, every female investor does not fit this risk stereotype and using such a heuristic can be misleading. In fact, researchers suggest that the majority of these heuristics can lead to serious miscalculations, incorrect categorizations of investors, and bad financial advice (Grable 2000, 2008).

SUMMARY

Risk incorporates a wide range of definitions across different fields, especially psychology and finance. The behavioral finance viewpoint of risk is a multi-factor judgment and decision-making process that is situational in nature based on the attributes of the asset class or financial service. An important issue in behavioral finance involves risk perception and risk tolerance because the process of judging how a person assesses information involves evaluating financial alternatives, which influences the final investment decision. Furthermore, understanding that the evaluation and measurement of risk possess an aspect (subjective) based on emotional factors is essential. The financial planning profession is only now beginning to realize the generational influence of the financial crisis of 2008–2009 on the risk-taking behavior of investors.

An important objective for financial planners and clients is to develop a long-term strategy that not only considers an individual's degree of risk tolerance for the expected return needed to achieve investment objectives, but also incorporates the psychological risk attributes (i.e., perceived risk) and how the individual reacts to real risk (i.e., actual risk) related events. Because the optimal asset allocation will not always be available as demonstrated by the behavioral finance school, conflicts must be addressed. Practitioners and investors both desire a risk tolerance instrument that resolves this conflict. Unfortunately, none of the existing risk tolerance questionnaires can be fully relied on to address these important issues correctly for a given investor. Therefore, when faced with this issue, investors need to make their own decisions to either reduce their financial goals because they desire a lower risk and return relationship or consider incorporating higher levels of risk and return in their investment portfolios in order to accomplish these goals if the clients are comfortable with this approach.

DISCUSSION QUESTIONS

1. Provide an overview of the traditional finance versus the behavioral finance perspectives of risk.
2. Provide several definitions of risk perception and risk tolerance.
3. List some problems associated with risk tolerance questionnaires.
4. Discuss the influence of the financial crisis on the risk-taking behavior of investors.

REFERENCES

Aspara, Jaakko, and Henrikki Tikkanen. 2011. "Individuals' Affect-Based Motivations to Invest in Stocks: Beyond Expected Financial Returns and Risks." *Journal of Behavioral Finance* 12:4, 78–89.

Bateman, Hazel, Towhidul Islam, Jordan Louviere, Stephen Satchell, and Susan Thorp. 2011. "Retirement Investor Risk Tolerance in Tranquil and Crisis Periods: Experimental Survey Evidence." *Journal of Behavioral Finance* 12:4, 201–218.

Blume, Marshall E., and Irwin Friend. 1978. *The Changing Role of the Individual Investor. A Twentieth Century Fund Report.* New York: John Wiley & Sons.

Bricker, Jesse, Brian Bucks, Arthur Kennickell, Traci Mach, and Kevin Moore. 2011. "Surveying the Aftermath of the Storm: Changes in Family Finances from 2007 to 2009." Working Paper, Federal Reserve Board. Available at www.federalreserve.gov/pubs/feds/2011/201117/201117pap.pdf.

Burns, William J., Ellen Peters, and Paul Slovic. 2012. "Risk Perception and the Economic Crisis: A Longitudinal Study of the Trajectory of Perceived Risk." *Risk Analysis: An International Journal* 32:4, 659–677.

Cochran, Robert A. 2002. "Trends to Watch in 2003: Enduring Lessons from FPA's Success Forum." *Research Magazine*, December 1. Available at http://business.highbeam.com/4459/article-1G1-95386679/eight-financialplanning-trends-watch-2003-enduring.

Cordell, David M. 2002. "Risk Tolerance in Two Dimensions." *Journal of Financial Planning* 15:5, 30–35.

Corter, James E. 2011. "Does Investment Risk Tolerance Predict Emotional and Behavioral Reactions to Market Turmoil?" *International Journal of Behavioral Accounting and Finance* 2:3–4, 225–237.

Davis, Sean, and Jeff Madura. 2012. "How the Shift to Quality Distinguished Winners from Losers During the Financial Crisis." *Journal of Behavioral Finance* 13:2, 81–92.

European Securities and Markets Authority. 2012. "Guidelines on Certain Aspects of the MiFID Suitability Requirements." Available at www.esma.europa.eu/system/files/2012-387.pdf.

Financial Industry Regulatory Authority. 2011. "Regulatory Notice 11-25." Available at www.finra.org/web/groups/industry/@ip/@reg/@notice/documents/notices/p123701.pdf.

Financial Services Authority. 2011. "Assessing Suitability: Establishing the Risk a Customer Is Willing and Able to Take and Making a Suitable Investment Selection." Available at www.fsa.gov.uk/pubs/guidance/fg11_05.pdf.

Finucane, Melissa L., Ellen Peters, and Paul Slovic. 2003. "Judgment and Decision Making: The Dance of Affect and Reason." In Sandra L. Schneider and James Shanteau, eds., *Emerging Perspectives on Judgment and Decision Research*, 327–364. Cambridge, UK: Cambridge University Press.

Gerrans, Paul, Robert W. Faff, and Neil Hartnett. 2012. "Individual Financial Risk Tolerance and the Global Financial Crisis." Working Paper, 25th Australasian Finance and Banking Conference. Available at http://ssrn.com/abstract=1990811.

Grable, John E. 2000. "Financial Risk Tolerance and Additional Factors That Affect Risk Taking in Everyday Money Matters." *Journal of Business and Psychology* 14:4, 625–630.

Grable, John E. 2008. "Risk Tolerance." In Jing Jian Xiao, ed., *Handbook of Consumer Finance Research*, 3–19. New York: Springer.

Grable, John E., and Michael J. Roszkowski. 2008. "The Influence of Mood on the Willingness to Take Financial Risks." *Journal of Risk Research* 11:7, 905–923.

Grable, John E., and Walter Schumm. 2010. "An Estimate of the Reliability of the Survey of Consumer Finances Risk-Tolerance Question." *Journal of Personal Finance* 9:1, 117–131.

Hanna, Sherman D., and Suzanne Lindamood. 2009. "Risk Tolerance: Cause or Effect." Working Paper, Academy of Financial Services Conference. Available at www.academyfinancial.org/09Conference/09Proceedings/(1C)%20Hanna,%20Lindamood.pdf.

Harris Interactiv Inc. 2012. "The 2012 Consumer Financial Literacy Survey." Available at www.nfcc.org/newsroom/FinancialLiteracy/files2012/FLS2012FINALREPORT0402late.pdf.

Hoffmann, Arvid O. I., Thomas Post, and Joost M. E. Pennings. 2013. "Individual Investor Perceptions and Behavior during the Financial Crisis." *Journal of Banking & Finance* 37:1, 60–74.

International Organization for Standardization. 2005. "ISO 22222 Personal Financial Planning Standard." Available at www.iso.org/iso/catalogue_detail.htm?csnumber=43033.

Kramer, Lisa A., and J. Mark Weber. 2012. "This Is Your Portfolio on Winter: Seasonal Affective Disorder and Risk Aversion in Financial Decision Making." *Social Psychological and Personality Science* 3:2, 193–199.

Lepori, Gabriele. 2010. "Positive Mood, Risk Attitudes, and Investment Decisions: Field Evidence from Comedy Movie Attendance in the U.S." Working Paper, Copenhagen Business School. Available at http://ssrn.com/abstract=1690476.

Linciano, Nadia, and Paola Soccorso. 2012. "Assessing Investors' Risk Tolerance through a Questionnaire." Working Paper, CONSOB, Research Division, Economic Research Unit. Available at http://ssrn.com/abstract=2207958.

Littell, David A., Kenn B. Tacchino, and David M. Cordell. 2003. *Financial Decision Making at Retirement*. Bryn Mawr, PA: The American College.

Malmendier, Ulrike, and Stefan Nagel. 2011. "Depression Babies: Do Macroeconomic Experiences Affect Risk Taking?" *Quarterly Journal of Economics* 126:1, 373–416.

Martinussen, Monica, and David R. Hunter. 2009. *Aviation Psychology and Human Factors*. Boca Raton, FL: CRC Press

Olsen, Robert. 2012. "Trust: The Underappreciated Investment Risk Attribute." *Journal of Behavioral Finance* 13:4, 308–313.

Pan, Carrie H., and Meir Statman. 2012. "Questionnaires of Risk Tolerance, Regret, Overconfidence, and Other Investor Propensities." *Journal of Investment Consulting* 13:1, 54–63.

Ricciardi, Victor. 2004. "A Risk Perception Primer: A Narrative Research Review of the Risk Perception Literature in Behavioral Accounting and Behavioral Finance." Working Paper, Social Science Research Network. Available at http://ssrn.com/abstract=566802.

Ricciardi, Victor. 2008a. "Risk: Traditional Finance versus Behavioral Finance." In Frank J. Fabozzi, ed., *The Handbook of Finance, Volume 3: Valuation, Financial Modeling, and Quantitative Tools*, 11–38. Hoboken, NJ: John Wiley & Sons.

Ricciardi, Victor. 2008b. "The Psychology of Risk: The Behavioral Finance Perspective." In Frank J. Fabozzi, ed., *The Handbook of Finance, Volume 2: Investment Management and Financial Management*, 85–111. Hoboken, NJ: John Wiley & Sons.

Ricciardi, Victor. 2010. "The Psychology of Risk." In H. Kent Baker and John R. Nofsinger, eds., *Behavioral Finance: Investors, Corporations, and Markets*, 131–149. Hoboken, NJ: John Wiley & Sons.

Ricciardi, Victor. 2011. "The Financial Judgment and Decision Making Process of Women: The Role of Negative Feelings." Third Annual Meeting of the Academy of Behavioral Finance and Economics, September. Available at http://ssrn.com/abstract=1936669.

Rice, Douglas. 2005. "Variance in Risk Tolerance Measurement: Toward a Uniform Theory." Doctoral Dissertation, Golden Gate University.

Roszkowski, Michael J. 2001. "Risk Tolerance in Financial Decisions." In David M. Cordell, ed., *Fundamentals of Financial Planning*, 5th ed., 237–298. Bryn Mawr, PA: The American College.

Roszkowski, Michael J., and Geoff Davey. 2010. "Risk Perception and Risk Tolerance Changes Attributable to the 2008 Economic Crisis: A Subtle but Critical Difference." *Journal of Financial Service Professionals* 64:4, 42–53.

Roszkowski, Michael J., Geoff Davey, and John E. Grable. 2005. "Insights from Psychology and Psychometrics on Measuring Risk Tolerance." *Journal of Financial Planning* 18:4, 66–77.

Rubaltelli, Enrico, Giacomo Pasini, Rino Rumiati, Robert Olsen, and Paul Slovic. 2010. "The Influence of Affective Reactions on Investment Decisions." *Journal of Behavioral Finance* 11:3, 168–176.

Santacruz, Lujer. 2009. "Effect of General Economic Mood on Investor Risk Tolerance—Implications for Financial Planning." *JASSA: Finsia Journal of Applied Finance* 1, 35–42.

Securities and Exchange Commission. 2004. "Determine Your Risk Tolerance." Available at www.sec.gov/investor/pubs/roadmap/risk.htm.

Securities and Exchange Commission. 2010. "Beginners' Guide to Asset Allocation, Diversification, and Rebalancing." SEC Pub. No. 062 (2/10). Available at https://www.my-benefit-info.com/PDF/Beginners_Guide.pdf.

Shim, Soyeon, and Joyce Serido. 2010. "Arizona Pathways to Life Success for University Students. Wave 1.5 Economic Impact Study: Financial Well-Being, Coping Behaviors and Trust Among Young Adults." Research Report, University of Arizona. Available at http://www.cgsnet.org/ckfinder/userfiles/files/APlusWave1_5_Final.pdf.

Wang, Hui, and Sherman Hanna. 1997. "Does Risk Tolerance Decrease with Age?" *Financial Counseling and Planning*, 8:2, 27–31.

Wang, Mei, Carmen Keller, and Michael Siegrist. 2011. "The Less You Know, the More You Are Afraid of a Survey on Risk Perceptions of Investment Products." *Journal of Behavioral Finance* 12:1, 9–19.

Yook, Ken C., and Robert Everett. 2003. "Assessing Risk Tolerance: Questioning the Questionnaire Method." *Journal of Financial Planning* 16:8, 48–55.

ABOUT THE AUTHORS

Victor Ricciardi is Assistant Professor of Financial Management at Goucher College. He teaches courses in financial planning, investments, corporate finance, behavioral finance, and the psychology of money. He is the editor of several eJournals distributed by the Social Science Research Network (SSRN) at www.ssrn.com, including behavioral finance, financial history, behavioral economics, and behavioral accounting. He received a BBA in accounting and management from Hofstra University and an MBA in finance and Advanced Professional Certificate (APC) at the graduate level in economics from St. John's University. He also holds a Graduate Certificate in personal family financial planning from Kansas State University. He can be found on Twitter @victorricciardi.

Douglas Rice, CFP® is an Assistant Professor of Business and Management at Notre Dame de Namur University. He teaches courses in investments, financial planning, corporate finance, and government budgeting. He has a practice as a Registered Investment Advisor. He is the founder of the Institute for Financial Planning Education, a nonprofit organization that promotes financial literacy. He has published Create *Your Own Personal Financial Plan: A Step-By-Step Method to Organize, Plan, and Manage Your Personal Affairs* and has also developed the software for financialplangrader.com, an online method for individuals to create and grade their own personal financial plan. He has published in the *Journal of Banking and Finance*. He received a DBA with a concentration in finance from Golden Gate University.

CHAPTER 19

Emotions in the Financial Markets

Richard Fairchild
Senior Lecturer in Corporate Finance, School of Management, University of Bath

INTRODUCTION

Traditionally, research in finance has been based on the assumption of *homo economicus*—the rational choice model that assumes investors are completely rational, balanced, emotionless, self-interested maximizers of expected utility with stable preferences. The traditional approach also assumes that investors are a homogeneous group with identical information sets and expectations. This standard perspective resulted in the development of Markowitz' portfolio theory, the capital asset pricing model (CAPM), and the efficient market hypothesis (EMH), among others.

During the last 20 years, behavioral finance arose as a response to observed anomalies in the financial market, which were inconsistent with the traditional paradigm (Ricciardi and Simon 2000; Barberis and Thaler, 2002). Particularly, the EMH has come under increasing scrutiny amid growing evidence that market values often diverge dramatically from fundamentals and volatility is excessive. Furthermore, according to the EMH, stock prices follow a random walk. In the real world, financial markets exhibit patterns with short-run momentum and long-run reversals (De Bondt and Thaler 1985, 1987). This suggests that carefully devised trading strategies at times beat the market in contrast to the efficient market.

In contrast to the traditional *homo economicus* view, behavioral finance takes the real world homo sapiens view: Real-world investors and traders make decisions based on bounded rationality (i.e., rationality based on human values and personal preferences), satisficing (i.e., select satisfactory options rather than optimal ones), and emotion. Originally, behavioral finance focused on cognitive biases and heuristics, giving little attention to emotions. The focus of this chapter is to consider the role and effect of emotions in the financial markets.

The chapter is organized as follows. The next section briefly outlines the behavioral finance research into cognitive biases. This section introduces prospect theory, which is a key behavioral finance model. Prospect theory provides an alternative risk-return framework, compared to the standard expected-utility theory (EUT). The next two sections discuss the introduction of emotions into prospect theory, particularly pride and regret. Emotions are analyzed in more depth including how emotions can affect trading and prices in financial markets. The section continues by considering the research in emotional finance, which examines the effect of investors' unconscious emotions on stock market behavior, employing a Freudian psychoanalytical framework. The penultimate section extends the analysis to consider emotional corporate finance, which examines the effect of managerial unconscious emotions on corporate finance decisions. The final section summarizes the chapter.

BEHAVIORAL FINANCE AND PROSPECT THEORY

Standard or traditional finance is based on the idea that actors are fully rational, unemotional maximizers of expected utility. Furthermore, the CAPM and portfolio theory are based on the assumption that people are risk-averse. Kahneman and Tversky's (1979) prospect theory introduced the idea that people are risk-averse when facing gains in wealth, but risk-seeking when facing losses in wealth (also known as loss aversion). Exhibit 19.1 illustrates prospect theory, where an agent's "utility" (a measure used by economists to represent happiness) is drawn as a function of changes in wealth. The shape of this function is such that, in the domain of wealth gains (to the right of the origin), an agent is risk-averse (gains higher utility from sure wealth compared to a gamble), while, in the domain of losses (to the left of the origin), an agent prefers to gamble because this provides a higher expected utility compared to the case of a sure loss.

The kink near the origin represents loss-aversion, whereby losses loom larger than gains. That is, an agent becomes more distressed by losses compared to the happiness experienced from equivalent gains. Behavioral economists use prospect theory to explain the *disposition effect*, which is an empirically observed phenomenon in which investors sell winning shares too quickly (risk-averse in the positive domain)

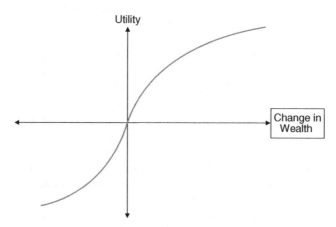

EXHIBIT 19.1   Prospect Theory

Note: This diagram demonstrates prospect theory as developed by Kahneman and Tversky (1979). It depicts utility as a function of changes in wealth. The function represents risk-aversion in the positive domain and risk-seeking in the negative domain. Incorporating emotions of pride (in the positive domain), and regret (in the negative domain) makes the investor more prone to the disposition effect (i.e., selling winners too quickly and holding losers too long).

and hold losing shares too long (risk-seeking in the negative domain). Mental framing of sunk losses may exacerbate this risk-seeking behavior in the negative domain. *Mental framing* refers to the way in which an agent mentally frames a problem. Here, mental framing refers to the phenomenon of an investor including a *sunk loss* that has already occurred in the investment. This increases an investor's risk-seeking propensity.

The original analysis of prospect theory (i.e., risk-averse in gains, risk-seeking in losses, combined with loss aversion and framing of sunk losses) focused on cognitive biases and paid limited attention to the effect of emotions. Beginning with the work of Bell (1982) and Loomes and Sugden (1982) on regret theory, scholars started to examine the effects of incorporating such emotions as regret, pride, joy, and elation with prospect theory.

Incorporating regret aversion has the effect of strengthening the disposition effect because it results in a greater tendency to hold losers too long, which is a phenomenon known as *entrapment*. According to psychologists, this happens because humans do not experience regret until they actually realize the loss. That is, until they sell their shares, the loss is merely a paper loss that can be put to the back of the mind. The anticipation of regret prevents the actor from realizing the loss. Hence, regret theory makes the important assumption that emotions can be anticipated. This matter is examined later when discussing unconscious emotions. In the positive domain of gains, scholars demonstrate that pride can strengthen the incentives to sell winners too quickly.

Summers and Duxbury (2012) investigate the effects of incorporating emotions into an experimental investment decision in order to ascertain whether cognition or emotional biases drive the disposition effect. In their experiment, the authors inform subjects that some shares that they own have now changed in price (the experiment incorporated both price increases and decreases), and ask them to consider whether to sell, hold, or buy more shares. In the first treatment, subjects learn that they inherited the shares from a relative. In the second treatment, they learn that they bought the shares. By considering these two treatments, the authors are able to consider the effects of positive and negative emotions of varying strengths on the disposition effect. Summers and Duxbury consider disappointment, regret, elation, and rejoicing as important emotions.

Specifically, Summers and Duxbury (2012) find that the disposition to hold on to losing shares is stronger for those subjects who originally bought them, compared to those who inherited them. This behavior is consistent with those who bought the shares experiencing the strong emotion of regret, compared to those who inherited the shares, who experienced the weaker emotion of disappointment. Similarly, when facing gains, those who originally bought the shares sold them more readily than those who inherited them. This is consistent with those who originally bought the shares experiencing the stronger emotion (rejoicing), compared to those who inherited the shares, who experienced the weaker emotion of elation.

In summary, this section introduces prospect theory, which can explain anomalous behavior in the financial markets such as the disposition effect. Kahneman and Tversky's (1979) original formulation of prospect theory focused on cognitive biases with little attention to emotions. Researchers later incorporated such emotions as regret and pride into prospect theory.

EMOTIONS

Emotions, affect, mood, and sentiment are distinct and different phenomena (Elster 1998; Ackert, Church, and Deaves 2003; Livet 2010). *Emotions* are transitory in nature and temporary and are aimed at an object, whereas the term *affect* relates to feelings. According to Ackert and Deaves (2010), psychologists generally agree that states such as happiness, sadness, anger, interest, contempt, disgust, pride, fear, surprise, and regret are emotions. *Mood* is a long-lasting effect that can last over several days, weeks, or months, and is not directed at anything specifically. Investor *sentiment* refers to a collective mood, usually relating to optimism or pessimism. Such sentiment may be periodic and cyclical (Baker and Wurgler 2007).

Elster (1998) identifies six features of emotions that differentiate them from other states. Ackert et al. (2003) apply these features to the particular case of a regretful investor. These features are as follows:

1. Emotions require c*ognitive antecedents* triggered by beliefs. An investor may regret an investment decision because he believes that he could avoid bad outcomes.
2. Emotions are *directed at an object*. The object of an emotion is typically the cognitive antecedent. For instance, a poorly performing investment is the object of a regretful investor.
3. Emotions involve *physiological arousal,* which refers to changes in hormonal conditions and the autonomous nervous system that accompanies emotions. A regretful investor may feel pangs or depression.
4. Emotions are accompanied by *physiological expressions*. These are observable expressions characterizing emotions such as facial expressions, posture, voice intonation, and outward appearance. A regretful investor may appear pale, with slumped shoulders.
5. Emotions have *valence*. That is, emotions can be placed on a scale with pleasure at one extreme and pain at the other. According to Ackert and Deaves (2010), valence, or the experience of pleasure versus pain, translates to happiness or unhappiness. A regretful investor is unhappy about a poor investment outcome.
6. Emotions result in a *tendency to act*. A regretful investor might act to avoid being exposed to similar investment opportunities.

A debate exists, particularly in the behavioral finance research, about whether emotions enhance or detract from decision-making. Some contend that emotions evolved to serve humans in a beneficial way. For example, emotions may have aided primitive man when confronting a bear in the woods, leading to the fight or flight decision (Ackert and Deaves 2010). Furthermore, for primitive man, such emotions may have been accompanied by pattern recognition (e.g., the slogan "if it looks like a bear, it probably is a bear"). Interestingly, many investors see patterns in financial charts where none may exist. Although emotion may have served our primitive ancestors well, emotions may be detrimental to effective action when the situation is complex. Thus, emotions may hinder effective financial decision-making.

EMOTIONS IN THE FINANCIAL MARKETS

A growing body of research examines the effect of moods, affect, and emotions on investor behavior in financial markets and the resulting effects on pricing. Dowling and Lucey (2005a, 2005b, 2005c) analyze the relationship among weather, moods, and equity prices globally and also specifically in Ireland and the United Kingdom. Other researchers find a correlation between occurrences unrelated to the financial markets, such as phases of the moon, sporting events, films, and market behavior, where the mediating variable may be mood or emotion. For example, if a nation performs well at an international sporting event, the resulting positive mood often results in an increase in stock market valuations, even though the fundamentals have not changed (Edmans, Garcia, and Norli 2007).

Another strand of research analyzes the effect of mood and emotions on investors' risk tolerance and risk-taking behavior. Debate surrounds two competing models of behavior: the affect infusion model and the mood maintenance model. The *affect infusion model* contends that a positive (negative) mood will increase (decrease) risk tolerance such that investors are willing to take more (less) risk. The *mood maintenance model* maintains that a good mood will lead to greater caution (i.e., investors want to maintain their good mood and therefore eschew risky situations). Grable and Roszkowski (2008) discuss this debate and provide evidence favoring the affect infusion model.

Stock markets may underreact to news over the short term, while over-reacting in the long run. Barberis, Schleifer, and Vishny (1998), and Daniel, Hirschleifer, and Subramanyam (1998) set forth theoretical behavioral models that attempt to explain this pattern. For example, Barberis et al. develop a model in which investor sentiment affects behavior. In their model, investors are subject to two biases—*conservatism* (a bias whereby investors react very slowly to new information) and *representativeness* (whereby investors have too much faith in recent market events representing longer-term patterns)—resulting in situations of overreaction (i.e., prices move too excessively) and under-reaction (i.e., prices react too slowly) to news. Daniel et al. develop a model in which overconfidence leads to over- and under-reaction. Both models consider the representative investor and do not consider how emotions and moods may transmit across investors, infecting the overall market. The next section further considers these models.

A debate exists as to whether emotions detract from investors' financial decision-making (Lerner and Keltner 2001; Lo, Repin, and Steenbarger 2005; Fenton-O'Creevy et al. 2011), or whether emotions may actually enhance investor performance (Ackert et al. 2003; Seo and Barrett, 2007). Emotions may result in prices diverging extensively from fundamentals either in terms of under- or over-valuation resulting from over- and under-reaction to news. Furthermore, the affect-infusion model demonstrates that investors may take excessive risk when in a positive mood. As a counter argument, Ackert et al. (2003) contend that emotions could have a positive effect on investors' decision-making. They cite neuro-biological studies such as Damasio (1994) and LeDoux (1996) indicating emotions can improve decision-making. According to Ackert et al., investors are often faced with overwhelming information about investment opportunities, and are required to act quickly. Deliberate, rational calculation may result in investor paralysis. In this situation, emotions may enhance decision-making by driving investors to action.

Thus, emotions can assist in making optimal decisions. Despite this debate, the evidence supplied in the remainder of this chapter suggests that, on balance, emotions hinder investors' effective decision-making.

Emotions, Social Moods, and Herding

Two distinct strands of theoretical and empirical research exist on herding behavior in the financial markets: rational and irrational herding (Hirshleifer and Teoh 2003). In rational herding models, investors rationally follow other investors' decisions, as investors' actions reveal private information to other investors. In irrational herding models, investors follow the herd due to cognitive or emotional biases. Most relevant to this chapter are the emotional herding models developed by Qin (2012), who considers the effect of regret in herding, and Salzman and Trifan (2005), who consider the coexistence of rational and emotional investors in a herding model.

In Qin (2012), investors observe other investors' buy-or-sell decisions and then decide whether to invest. By doing so, investors trade off the expected utility of their investment return and the expected disutility of regret. Qin demonstrates that an increase in price volatility can cause some investors to ignore their private information and exit the market. Furthermore, extremely high or low stock prices can result in a marketwide cascade.

Boswijk, Hommes, and Manzan (2007) develop a dynamic asset pricing model with heterogeneous, boundedly rational agents. Although the fundamental value of the risky asset is publicly available to all investors, they have different beliefs about the persistence of deviations of stock prices from their fundamental values. Although these authors do not specifically consider emotions, they do identify that heterogeneous investor types can affect herding and stock market behavior. Salzman and Trifan (2005), who also consider this idea, develop a model in which rational and emotional investors coexist and fight for market capital. The authors show that, under certain conditions, emotional traders may dominate the market by having a much more developed adaptive mechanism than their rational peers.

Paving the Way toward Emotional Finance

This section examines conceptual approaches that consider how investor emotions may result in herding behavior in the financial markets. This work serves as forerunners to the emotional finance paradigm, which is discussed later in this chapter.

Nofsinger (2003) develops a conceptual model analyzing the effects of social mood on herding behavior in the financial markets. He emphasizes that human interaction is equally as important as economic fundamentals. Nofsinger contends that both the general social mood and the general level of optimism/pessimism in society affect financial decision makers and stock market behavior. Furthermore, he suggests that the emotions of most financial decision makers are affected simultaneously. This creates correlated biases in financial decision-making across society linking behavior among investors, consumers, and corporate managers. Hence, Nofsinger's theory of social moods can explain herding behavior by individual investors, customers, and financial managers.

Interestingly, Nofsinger (2003) considers a sequence of events in which the social mood of all participants (e.g., investors, consumers, and corporate managers) interacts to affect the level of the stock market. He notes that communication is an important facet of human interaction because it spreads information and also has the power to persuade. Nofsinger refers to the herding model developed by Hong, Kubik, and Stein (2002), which considers social and nonsocial investors. The authors find that social investors are more likely to participate in the stock market and to develop a social multiplier effect.

Redhead (2008) considers the effect of economic, financial, psychological, and sociological factors on the behavior of the financial markets, particularly in the context of the high-tech bubble and crash of the late 1990s and early 2000s. He develops a conceptual framework in which all these drivers interact to create bubbles and crashes as well as excessive stock market volatility. His approach shares many features with the emotional finance approach reviewed later in this chapter. Particularly, he notes that Internet stocks achieved celebrity status, fueled by media hype. This drove investors' emotional attachment, and resulted in their prices greatly exceeding their fundamental values.

Thus far, this chapter has focused on research that considers the effect of conscious emotions in the financial markets. These are emotions of which an investor is aware and is able to anticipate. For example, regret aversion in which investors are unwilling to sell shares at a loss as they are aware that they will feel regret after selling partially drives the disposition. While holding the shares, investors only face a paper loss and can postpone the pain of regret. Hence, they consciously anticipate future feelings of regret, which induces them to hold losing shares too long.

As noted later, the emotional finance paradigm focuses on unconscious emotions. Prechter (2001) discusses the effect of unconscious emotions on herding behavior in the financial markets with particular attention to neuroeconomics (neurofinance). He maintains that human herding behavior results from impulsive mental activity, originating in the basal ganglia and limbic system. Furthermore, when the situation becomes highly emotionally charged, investors may be pushed toward irrational activity by the limbic system.

As Prechter (2001) notes, this emotionally driven herding behavior is irrational and detracts from financial decision-making. He suggests that a negative feedback loop can occur, whereby stress increases impulsive mental activity in financial situations, which results in failure and in turn increases stress.

The next section discusses a new research paradigm: emotional finance. This area of research analyzes the effects of unconscious emotions on investor behavior employing a Freudian psychoanalytical framework.

EMOTIONAL FINANCE AND UNCONSCIOUS EMOTIONS

In their seminal and groundbreaking work, Taffler and Tuckett (2005), Tuckett and Taffler (2008), and Eshraghi and Taffler (2009) institute a major paradigm shift by introducing a new field of research, namely *emotional finance*. This develops the research in behavioral finance by analyzing the effect of unconscious, infantile emotions on investors' decisions. Particularly, Taffler and Tuckett use Freud's (1911, 1916) theory of the "phantastic object," which Klein (1975) further develops, in order to explain investor behavior around stock market bubbles and crashes.

Taffler and Tuckett (2005) develop their theory from interviews with 52 fund managers in the United States and Europe. All fund managers have at least 10 years' experience in managing funds and most of them manage more than $1 billion in funds. As Tuckett and Taffler (2012, p. 83) note, "Everyday financial markets generate emotions. . . . Investment activity inevitably engages feelings and creates emotional conflict." Tuckett and Taffler's (2012, p. 83) interviews reveal the following.

> *The ways in which our fund managers talked about their investments, their lack of trust in their information sources and management, and their fears about losing their jobs if they performed badly, made clear that they are well aware of the emotional context in which they operate. In fact, the term "emotion" itself was volunteered freely in the interviews. Words expressing such feelings as love, hate, hope, fear, worry, disappointment, and trust similarly abound in the interviews.*

Emotional Finance: Core Concepts

Tuckett and Taffler (2012) identify the following core concepts of emotional finance: (1) unconscious conflict, (2) other relationships, (3) unconscious phantasies, (4) phantastic objects, (5) states of mind (divided and integrated states), and group feel. This chapter focuses only unconscious conflict, phantastic objects, and states of mind.

Unconscious Conflict   According to Tuckett and Taffler (2012), Freudian psychoanalysis reveals that unconscious conflict exists, as thoughts generate two types of feeling: pleasurable (exciting) or unpleasurable (painful, anxiety-generating, or loss provoking). Subjectively painful emotion conflicts are commonplace because many situations generate both pleasurable and unpleasurable feelings. Freud (1911, 1916) contends that people deal with these painful feelings by adopting three main defense mechanisms.

- *Splitting.* Mentally separating the good and bad feelings, with the latter being repressed and rendered unconscious.
- *Projection.* Unconsciously attributing unwanted feelings to others.
- *Denial.* Disavowal or repudiation of external reality about which the person does not want to know.

Phantastic Objects and States of Mind   According to Tuckett and Taffler (2008, p. 395), psychoanalytical theory defines a phantastic object as "a mental representation of something (or someone) which in an imagined scene fulfils the protagonist's deepest desires to have exactly what she wants, when she wants it." Furthermore, in the emotional finance psychoanalytical framework, people develop these deep-seated emotions in their childhood and they remain in their adult unconscious. Indeed, Eshraghi and Taffler, 2009, p. 5) quote Klein (1975) by stating: "Infantile feelings and phantasies leave, as it were, their imprints on the mind, imprints that do not fade away but get stored up, remain active, and exert a continuous and powerful influence on the emotional and intellectual life of the individual."

Furthermore, Eshraghi and Taffler (2009, p. 5–6) assert that "individuals are more susceptible to the phantastic object when a particular sense of reality blocks their thinking. . . . People make decisions in one of two basic oscillating states of mind, namely the depressive (D) state and the paranoid-schizoid (PS) state." Basically, in the D state, people see things as they really are, both good and bad. In the PS state of mind, they deal with psychic pain by mentally splitting the good from the bad.

According to the theory of the phantastic object, individuals transform an object into a phantasy. That is, they unconsciously assign a magical, exceptionally exciting, and highly desirable image to an object. Later, when reality sets in (the D state), conscious emotions of anger and blame dominate, combined with a hatred of reality. In relation to the financial markets, an innovation is required that captures the public imagination, such as tulips (tulip mania), mysterious investments (South-Sea Bubble and twenty-first century hedge funds), and Internet stocks (the late 1990s Internet bubble).

Anatomy of Stock Market Bubbles and Crashes

Emotional finance represents a considerable step forward in research into financial market behavior because it provides a unified framework for considering the evolution and trajectory of stock market bubbles and crashes. As Taffler and Tuckett (2005) note, the initial impetus is a mysterious, magical innovation, such as Internet stocks or hedge funds, that creates the phantastic object. Investors enter the paranoid-schizoid (PS) phase where they view these investments as infallible and certain to succeed. A mental splitting process occurs, in which the pain (i.e., the risk associated with the investment) is split from the pleasure (i.e., the excitement of the investment), and the risk is buried deep in the unconscious. Investors thus fall in love with these investments and value them for their qualities, such as excitement, over and above their financial rewards. Furthermore, at this stage, experts' views, such as financial analysts, academics, and even the press, are sacrosanct. Therefore, in the PS phase, mass buying of the stocks occurs and creates an irrational bubble. Because investors have fallen in love with the phantastic object and value it much beyond its financial rewards, they are willing to pay "silly money" for their investments, way above fundamental values.

However, at a critical tipping point, nagging doubts emerge. On entering the depressive (D) phase, reality (the painful risk) floods the conscious, and investors are overwhelmed with feelings of hate for the investment. In the D phase, they now revile those whom they viewed as experts in the PS phase. Thus, investors look for scapegoats and blame these experts. Panic occurs and results in mass selling. Therefore, the bubble bursts and the market crashes.

Emotional finance provides a framework that can explain consistently repeated episodes in history where financial markets have rapidly inflated toward an irrationally high peak (boom), followed by a sudden very rapid massive fall (the bubble bursting and the market crashing). For example, Tuckett and Taffler (2008) apply the framework to the Internet dot-com bubble, which occurred between 1995 and 2000. In the 18 months between October 1, 1998 and March 9, 2000, the Dow Jones Internet Index multiplied six times. In the next month, it halved in value and by the end of 2002 stood at only 8 percent of its high. Bellotti, Taffler, and Tian (2010), who examine the Chinese stock market bubble, find that between June 2005 and

October 2007, when the market peaked, the Chinese stock market increased fivefold and then fell dramatically, losing 70 percent of its value over the following year.

In the hedge fund bubble, hedge fund assets under management grew at the rate of 25 percent per year from 1990 to June 2008, peaking at almost $2 trillion. In the following six months, assets under management collapsed by almost a third. According to Eshraghi and Taffler (2009), investors may have viewed hedge funds as phantastic objects and viewed such funds as infallible and immensely valuable. Upon reflection, investors feel cheated and the once dominant desire for the phantastic object turns to anger and blame.

As Dow (2010) notes, Taffler and Tuckett's (2005) emotional finance approach does not attempt to model behavior in any deterministic way. If investors hold knowledge with uncertainty, they will switch from euphoric market behavior to panic as the potential of the bubble breaking gains force and the structure of the financial system becomes more fragile. Yet, investors cannot predict the nature and timing of events that provoke the onset of panic.

Tuckett and Taffler's (2008) framework provides a good ex post analysis of bubbles and crashes that can be used to fit any episode in history. However, as Dow (2010) maintains, it is not a forward-looking framework that can be used to predict the exact trajectory and timing of emotions and financial market behavior. The next section considers Fairchild's (2009) work on emotional corporate finance, which provides the first steps toward a formal, modeling approach.

EMOTIONAL CORPORATE FINANCE—A FORMAL MODEL

Understanding the effects of psychological biases on financial decision-making is enhanced by extending behavioral finance to behavioral corporate finance (Baker, Ruback, and Wurgler 2004; Fairchild 2007) because this subtopic examines the role of investors and managers. Behavioral finance considers the effects of investor's psychological biases, irrationality, and emotions on investor behavior and financial market outcomes. Behavioral corporate finance also considers the influence of managerial psychological biases, irrationality, and emotions on managerial behavior and corporate finance decision-making such as corporate investment appraisal, capital structure, and dividend policy. This extends the classical model of standard corporate finance.

Fairchild (2009) introduces emotional corporate finance (ECF), as a development of emotional finance. As emotional finance considers the effect of unconscious emotions and phantasies on investor behavior in the financial markets, ECF extends the analysis to also consider the effect of managerial unconscious emotions and phantasies on corporate finance decision-making. Fairchild's analysis focuses on investment appraisal. He develops a formal model that analyzes the effects of managerial phantasy (combined with investor phantasy) on the initial investment appraisal decision surrounding a new project, and subsequent managerial effort, which affects project performance.

The model analyzes a self-interested corporate manager who is considering a new investment opportunity requiring an initial investment that take place over two periods, with each period requiring managerial effort. The manager first decides whether to take the project (the investment appraisal decision), and, if he accepts the project, the manager then exerts effort in each of the two stages in developing the project toward a successful outcome. Hence, moral hazard exists in the form of potential effort-shirking.

The model develops Tuckett and Taffler's (2008) emotional finance theory as follows. The manager (together with the investors) initially (unconsciously) views the project as a phantastic object, with characteristics over and above its financial performance such as excitement and euphoria. At this stage, the manager and the investors view the project as infallible. Because the manager is sure the project will succeed, he splits off the risk of failure and buries it in his unconscious. This is the paranoid-schizoid phase in the Freudian psychoanalytical framework. This phase continues as long as the project appears to be successful. However, if the project has a failure at some point in its life, reality floods the manager's consciousness, and he enters the depressive stage. The manager's euphoria is destroyed and he switches to hating the project. Further, he now understands the risk of failure as part of the decision-making process.

This work has parallels with Tuckett and Taffler's (2008) emotional finance theory. First, the project is similar to a financial investment for investors. The manager's initial euphoria affects his investment appraisal decision. Similarly, in Tuckett and Taffler's conceptual analysis, initial euphoria affects the investor's decision to invest in Internet stocks or hedge funds. However, by considering emotional corporate finance, Fairchild (2009) extends their work by demonstrating that the manager's euphoria can affect the performance of the project because it affects the manager's effort level. In Tuckett and Taffler's analysis, investors' euphoria affects their investment decision, but investors cannot affect the performance of their investments. A second development is that Fairchild presents a formal model of ECF.

Fairchild (2009) formally models the effects of phantasy as follows. The manager unconsciously views the project as a phantastic object. At t_0, the manager views the project as infallible. That is, he believes that it will succeed for certain in both periods. The manager continues in his phantasy as long as the project continues to succeed. Furthermore, at this stage, the outside investors share the manager's phantasy. Therefore, the market value in t_0 exceeds fundamental value. At $t_{0.25}$, the investors switch from loving to hating the project, and therefore the project value crashes in the financial market. At $t_{0.25}$, the investors' hatred is eliminated, and the project value bounces back up.

If the manager accepts and invests in the project, then, at t_1, he exerts his first (stage 1) effort level. The manager's effort level affects the outcome of the project as follows. The project succeeds or fails with equal probability. In the case of success, project income is increasing with the manager's effort level. In the case of failure, the project achieves zero income. Exerting effort is costly for the manager. Hence, one can derive an optimal level of effort that maximizes the manager's payoff. Luck affects a project's success or failure with equal probabilities but the manager's skill and effort affect the outcome only in the case of success.

When considering his expected payoff, the manager inflates the success income by the phantasy parameter. At the first stage, the manager believes that the project is infallible. At t_2, the project achieves its first stage outcome (success or failure). If it succeeds, managerial phantasy carries over to the second stage of the project. The manager continues to believe that the project will succeed for sure. If the project fails at the first stage, managerial phantasy is destroyed and the manager switches to project hatred. Reality now floods the managerial consciousness and the manager realizes that the project will succeed or fail with equal probability.

Now, the manager is required to exert a second level of effort at the second stage. The first-stage project outcome crucially affects the manager's second stage effort level because the first stage outcome affects the manager's love or hate for the project, and the manager's belief that the project is infallible, or can fail. Fairchild (2009) notes that, if the project succeeds in the first stage, the manager's project phantasy is maintained throughout. Therefore, he exerts the same effort level in stage 1 and stage 2. If the project fails in stage 1, the manager switches from project phantasy to project hatred, and his effort level declines from t_1 to t_2. He now hates the project and also realizes that it will not succeed with certainty, and so he does not work as hard. Fairchild (2009) assumes that the assessment of the project then moves back to t_0 to consider the manager's initial investment appraisal decision. The author demonstrates that phantasy may induce the manager to invest in a value-reducing project as he mistakenly believes it to be infallible and gets unconscious pleasure from it, over and above its monetary value.

A further implication of Fairchild's (2009) analysis is that phantasy may result in high volatility of managerial emotions as the manager switches from project love to hate. In turn, this results in high volatility of managerial effort and project performance. Fairchild compares the results of his model with a benchmark case (based on standard corporate finance and classical decision theory), where the manager and investor are fully rational, unemotional, and optimizers. His key results are as follows:

- In the standard finance, which is the fully rational case, the manager exerts identical effort levels in t_1 and t_2.
- The manager exerts higher t_1 effort level in the phantasy case than in the unemotional, completely rational case.
- If the project succeeds at the end of t_1, the manager's phantasy is maintained, and he exerts the same effort level in t_2. Therefore, this t_2 effort level is higher than in the standard finance camp (tenets of classical decision theory).
- If the project fails at the end of t_1, the manager's phantasy switches to project hatred and he exerts lower effort in t_2. The t_2 effort level under phantasy hatred is lower than in the standard finance case.

These results demonstrate that managerial effort is more volatile in the phantasy case than in the fully rational, emotionless case due to the volatility of the manager's emotions. Now consider how this leads to higher volatility of project values in the phantasy case, compared to the standard corporate finance assumptions. Following t_1 success, the value of the firm in the phantasy case is higher than in the tenets according to standard corporate finance for two reasons: The manager continues to enjoy project phantasy and continues to believe that the project will succeed for certain. Following success in t_1, the manager exerts greater effort in the phantasy case than in the fully rational, emotionless case. Thus, in the case where the project succeeds at t_1, managerial phantasy and emotions actually enhance firm value. Effectively, project phantasy is desirable while the project is still winning. In contrast, in the case in which the project fails at t_1, firm value is lower in the emotional case due to the manager's switch from phantasy to hatred and his reduced effort level.

In the situation where the project succeeds in both periods, firm value is higher under the project phantasy scenario based on emotional corporate finance than in the fully rational setting based on standard corporate finance. Furthermore, if the project succeeds in the first period and fails in the second period, then firm value is higher under phantasy. If the project fails in the first and second periods, firm value is lower under phantasy. In the fully rational case, firm value is identical, whether the project succeeds then fails, or fails then succeeds. This is not true in the phantasy case; the order of success and failure affects firm value.

In summary, firm value is more volatile in the phantasy case compared to the fully rational, emotionless case due to the volatility of managerial emotions. Following project success in t_1, firm value is higher in the phantasy case than in the rational case, due to managerial euphoria. Following project failure in t_1, firm value is lower in the phantasy case than in the rational case due to managerial hatred of the project.

Exhibit 19.2 presents these results. The thin solid lines represent the fully rational, emotionless case and the thick dotted lines represent the emotional case. This exhibit shows the following:

- At t_0 firm value is lower in the rational case than the phantasy case.
- At $t_{0.25}$ firm value is higher in the rational case than in the phantasy case because the emotional investors overreact with hatred.
- At $t_{0.50}$ firm value is higher again in the emotional case, as emotional investor hatred is eliminated and the firm value bounces back up.
- From $t_{0.50}$ to date t_2, managerial project phantasy is value-enhancing while the project is succeeding, but managerial phantasy is value-reducing when the project starts failing.

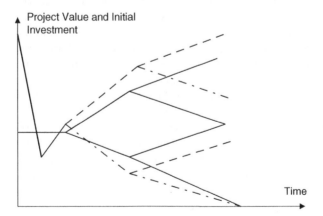

EXHIBIT 19.2 Formal Model of Emotional Finance

Note: This diagram depicts the formal emotional corporate finance model outlined in the chapter. The thin solid lines represent the fully rational, emotionless case and the thick dotted lines represent the emotional case. Thus, unconscious emotions can result in greater volatility of project values.

Managerial phantasy results in greater volatility of firm value compared to the rational, emotionless case because firm values are higher under success in the phantasy case than in the rational case, and lower under failure in the phantasy case than in than the rational case.

In summary, the model and the numerical example demonstrate that a project may initially be overvalued due to a manager's and investor's phantasy. When reality kicks in, the market may overreact negatively due to investors switching from phantasy to hatred. Later, as the hatred works its way out of the system, the project's value may bounce back up to its fundamental value. This fundamental value may incorporate the manager's phantasy, which encourages him to work hard to create value. This is the case while the project is succeeding. However, when the project begins to fail, the manager may turn against the project, switching from phantasy to hatred, thereby reducing his effort level.

Hence, phantasy can have negative consequences by inflating project values and may cause the manager to invest in ultimately value-reducing projects. However, phantasy has an upside, in that it increases managerial commitment to and effort in a project. While the project is performing well, phantasy may enhance value. However, when the project's fortunes take a downturn, the switch from phantasy to hatred may be very damaging to project value.

SUMMARY

This chapter examined the effects of investor emotions on financial market behavior. It started by considering early research that took into account the effect of investors' conscious emotions. Next, the chapter examined a new paradigm shift to emotional finance, which focuses on the effect of investors' unconscious emotions on financial market behavior. It uses a Freudian psychoanalytical framework to understand how unconscious emotions can result in stock market bubbles and crashes. Next, the chapter reviewed Fairchild's (2009) development of emotional corporate finance, which recognizes that corporate managers may view projects as phantastic objects.

Fairchild's analysis provides a basis for future research. First, he takes investors' and managers' phantasy parameters as exogenously given. Future researchers should develop a theoretical framework that endogenizes the formation of unconscious emotions, phantasies, and hatred of financial investments (in the case of investors) and projects (in the case of managers). Hermalin and Isen's (1999) formal model of emotion formation may prove fruitful. Second, in Fairchild's (2009) model, investors' and managers' phantasies occur independently (e.g., the model makes the assumption that investors face reality before the manager does). A richer model would consider the interaction of managers' and investors' phantasy. Third, researchers should consider the interaction between conscious and unconscious biases. A useful approach would be to consider the relationship between phantasy and overconfidence. Such an analysis would strengthen the relationship between behavioral corporate finance and emotional corporate finance.

Besides developing a theoretical analysis of emotional corporate finance, a challenge for future researchers would be to test this approach empirically. Researchers could extend the behavioral corporate finance approach, which employs various empirical techniques. When using a quantitative approach, the problem is to find a measure of unobservable managerial behavioral characteristics such as managerial overconfidence. Malmendier and Tate (2002, 2005) and Malmendier, Tate, and Yan (2005) examine the relationship between capital structure and managerial overconfidence. They use two proxies for overconfidence. First, they examine a managerial action (i.e., the early or delayed exercise of stock options) as a potential indicator of overconfidence. Second, they use an indirect measure (i.e., a press statement about the manager and his behavior) in an attempt to measure overconfidence. Future researchers in emotional corporate finance may attempt to use similar measures for managerial phantasy. Emotional corporate finance represents a development, building on Taffler and Tuckett's (2005) work in emotional finance, provides a challenging agenda for future theoretical and empirical research, and offers an alternative to standard corporate finance.

DISCUSSION QUESTIONS

1. Discuss whether emotions enhance or detract from investor decision-making.
2. Discuss the disposition effect and how emotions influence the disposition effect.
3. Discuss whether herding behavior in the financial markets is rational.
4. Discuss how the analysis of emotions differs between behavioral finance and emotional emotional finance.
5. Discuss how the emotional finance framework can be used to help explain financial market bubbles and crashes.
6. Explain how emotions might affect managerial behavior in an emotional finance framework.

REFERENCES

Ackert, Lucy F., Bryan Church, and Richard Deaves. 2003. "Emotion and Financial Markets." *Federal Reserve Bank of Atlanta Economic Review* 88:2, 33–41.

Ackert, Lucy F., and Richard Deaves. 2010. *Behavioral Finance: Psychology, Decision-Making, and Markets.* Mason, Ohio: South-Western Cengage Learning.

Baker, Malcolm P., Richard S. Ruback, and Jeffrey A. Wurgler. 2004. "Behavioral Corporate Finance: A Survey." Working Paper, Social Science Research Network. Available at http://papers.ssrn.com/sol3/papers.cfm?abstract_id=602902.

Baker, Malcolm P., and Jeffrey A. Wurgler. 2007. "Investor Sentiment in the Stock Market." *Journal of Economic Perspectives* 21:2, 129–152.

Barberis, Nicholas, Andrei Schleifer, and Robert Vishny. 1998. "A Model of Investor Sentiment." *Journal of Financial Economics* 49:3, 307–343.

Barberis, Nicholas, and Richard Thaler. 2002. "A Survey of Behavioral Finance." Working Paper, Social Science Research Network. Available at http://papers.ssrn.com/sol3/papers.cfm?abstract_id=327880.

Bell, David E. 1982. "Regret in Decision-Making under Uncertainty." *Operations Research* 32:5, 961–981.

Bellotti, Xijuan A., Richard Taffler, and Lin Tian. 2010. "Understanding the Chinese Stock Market Bubble: The Role of Emotion." Working Paper, Middlesex Business School, London.

Boswijk, H. Peter, C. H. Hommes, and Sebastiano Manzan. 2007. "Behavioral Heterogeneity in Stock Prices." *Journal of Economic Dynamics and Control* 31:6; 1938–1970.

Damasio, Antonio R. 1994. *Descartes' Error: Emotion, Reason, and the Human Brain.* New York: Putnam.

Daniel, Kent, David Hirschleifer, and Avanidhar Subramanyam. 1998. "A Theory of Overconfidence, Self-Attribution, and Security Market Under- and Over-reaction." *Journal of Business* 53:6, 1839–1886.

De Bondt, Werner, and Richard Thaler. 1985. "Does the Stock Market Overreact?" *Journal of Finance* 49:3, 793–805.

De Bondt, Werner, and Richard Thaler. 1987. "Further Evidence on Investor Overreaction and Stock Market Seasonality." *Journal of Finance* 42:3, 557–581.

Dow, Sheila. 2010. "The Psychology of the Financial Markets: Keynes, Minsky and Emotional Finance." In Dimitri B. Papadimitriou and L. Randall Wray, eds., *The Elgar Companion to Hyman Minsky*, 246-260. Cheltenham: Edward Elgar.

Dowling, Michael, and Brian M. Lucey. 2005a. "Are Weather Induced Moods Priced in Global Equity Markets?" Working Paper, School of Business Studies, University of Dublin.

Dowling, Michael, and Brian M. Lucey. 2005b. "Mood and UK Equity Pricing." Working Paper, School of Business Studies, University of Dublin.

Dowling, Michael, and Brian M. Lucey. 2005c. "Weather, Biorhythms, Beliefs and Stock Returns—Some Preliminary Irish Evidence." *International Review of Financial Analysis* 14:3, 337–355.

Edmans, Alex, Diego Garcia, and Oyvind Norli. 2007. "Sports Sentiment and Stock Returns." *Journal of Finance* 62:4, 1967–1998.

Elster, John. 1998. "Emotions and Economic Theory." *Journal of Economic Literature* 36:1, 47–74.

Eshraghi, Arman, and Richard Taffler. 2009. "Hedge Funds as Phantastic Objects." Paper Presentation, 13th Financial Reporting and Business Communications Conference, Cardiff Business School, July.

Fairchild, Richard. 2007. "Behavioral Corporate Finance: Existing Research and Future Directions." Working Paper, School of Management, University of Bath.

Fairchild, Richard. 2009. "From Behavioral to Emotional Corporate Finance: A New Research Direction." Working Paper, Social Science Research Network. Available at http://papers.ssrn.com/sol3/papers.cfm?abstract_id=1473742.

Fenton-O'Creevy, Mark, Gareth Davies, Jeffrey Todd Lins, Daniel Richards, Shalini Vohra, and Kristina Schaaf. 2011. "Emotion Regulation and Trader Performance." Conference Paper, 15th Conference of the European Association of Work and Organizational Psychology, Maastricht. Available at www.xdelia.org/wp-content/uploads/emotion_regulation_and_trader_performance.pdf.

Freud, Sigmund. 1911. "Formulations Regarding Two Principals of Mental Functioning." *The Standard Edition of the Complete Psychological Works of Sigmund Freud, vol XII.* London: Hogarth.

Freud, Sigmund. 1916. "Introductory Lectures on Psychoanalysis." *The Standard Edition of the Complete Psychological Works of Sigmund Freud, vol XVI.* London: Hogarth.

Grable, John E., and Michael J. Roszkowski. 2008. "The Influence of Mood on the Willingness to Take Financial Risks." *Journal of Risk Research* 11:7, 905–923.

Hermalin, Benjamin E., and Alice M. Isen. 1999. "The Effect of Affect on Economic and Strategic Decision Making." Working Paper, Social Science Research Network. Available at http://papers.ssrn.com/sol3/papers.cfm?abstract_id=200295.

Hirshleifer, David, and Siew Hong Teoh. 2003. "Herd Behavior and Cascading in Capital Markets: A Review and Synthesis." *European Financial Management* 9:1, 25–66.

Hong, Harrison, Jeffrey D. Kubik, and Jeremy C. Stein. 2002. "Social Interaction and Stock Market Participation." *Journal of Finance* 59:1, 137–162.

Kahneman, Daniel, and Amos Tversky. 1979. "Prospect Theory: An Analysis of Decision under Risk." *Econometrica* 47:2, 263–292.

Klein, Melanie. 1975. *Love, Guilt and Reparation, and Other Works: 1921–1945.* London: Karnac Books.

Lerner, Jennifer S., and Dacher Keltner. 2001. "Fear, Anger, and Risk." *Journal of Personality and Social Psychology* 81:1, 146–159.

LeDoux, Joseph. 1996. *The Emotional Brain: The Mysterious Underpinnings of Emotional Life.* New York: Simon and Schuster.

Livet, Pierre. 2010. "Rational Choice, Neuroeconomy, and Mixed Emotions." *Philosophical Transactions of the Royal Society* 365:1538, 259–269.

Lo, Andrew W., Dmitry V. Repin, and Brett N. Steenbarger. 2005. "Fear and Greed in Financial Markets: A Clinical Study of Day Traders." *American Economic Review* 95:2, 352–359.

Loomes, Graham, and Robert Sugden. 1982. "Regret Theory: An Alternative Theory of Rational Choice under Uncertainty." *Economic Journal* 92:368, 805–824.

Malmendier, Ulrike, and Geoffrey Tate. 2002. "CEO Overconfidence and Corporate Investment." Working Paper, Social Science Research Network. Available at http://papers.ssrn.com/sol3/papers.cfm?abstract_id=354387.

Malmendier, Ulrike, and Geoffrey Tate. 2005. "Does Overconfidence Affect Corporate Investment? CEO Overconfidence Measures Revisited." *European Financial Management* 11:5, 649–659.

Malmendier, Ulrike, Geoffrey Tate, and Jonathan Yan. 2005. "Corporate Finance Policies with Overconfident Managers." Working Paper, Social Science Research Network. Available at http://papers.ssrn.com/sol3/papers.cfm?abstract_id=895843.

Nofsinger, John. 2003. "Social Mood and Financial Economics." Working Paper, Washington State University.

Prechter, Robert. 2001. "Unconscious Herding Behavior as the Psychological Basis of Financial Market Trends and Patterns." *Journal of Psychology and Financial Markets* 2:3, 120–125.

Qin, Jie. 2012. "To Trade or Not to Trade: A Model of Regret and Investment." Working Paper, APEA, Seattle.

Redhead, Keith. 2008. "A Behavioral Model of the Dot.Com Bubble and Crash." Applied Research Working Paper Series, Coventry University.

Ricciardi, Victor, and Helen K. Simon. 2000. "What Is Behavioral Finance?" *Business, Education and Technology Journal* 2:2, 1–9.

Salzman, Diego A., and Emanuela Trifan. 2005. "Emotions, Bayesian Inference, and Financial Decision Making." Working Paper, Social Science Research Network. Available at http://papers.ssrn.com/sol3/papers.cfm?abstract_id=878278.

Seo, Myeong-Gu, and Lisa Feldman Barrett. 2007. "Being Emotional During Decision Making—Good or Bad? An Empirical Investigation." *Academy of Management Journal* 50:4, 923–940.

Summers, Barbara, and Darren Duxbury. 2012. "Decision-Dependent Emotions and Behavioral Anomalies." *Organizational Behavior and Human Decision Processes* 118:2, 226–238.

Taffler, Richard, and David Tuckett. 2005. "A Psychoanalytical Interpretation of Dot.com Stock Valuations." Working Paper, Social Science Research Network. Available at http://papers.ssrn.com/sol3/papers.cfm?abstract_id=676635.

Tuckett, David, and Richard Taffler. 2008. "Phantastic Objects and the Financial Market's Sense of Reality: A Psychoanalytical Contribution to the Understanding of Stock Market Instability." *International Journal of Psychoanalysis* 89:2, 389–412.

Tuckett, David, and Richard Taffler. 2012. *Fund Management: An Emotional Finance Perspective.* Charlottesville, VA: CFA Institute Research Foundation.

ABOUT THE AUTHOR

Richard Fairchild is Senior Lecturer in Corporate Finance in the School of Management, University of Bath, United Kingdom. After obtaining his undergraduate degree in economics, Professor Fairchild worked in the aerospace industry for several years, focusing on project finance, before returning to academia to obtain his master's degree in economics and PhD in corporate finance. His academic research focuses on behavioral and emotional corporate finance. He advises financial institutions on behavioral issues. Professor Fairchild is editor-in-chief for the *International Journal of Behavioral Accounting and Finance*, and is a book series editor for the Routledge Research Series on Behavioural Economics and Finance.

CHAPTER 20

Human Psychology and Market Seasonality

Lisa A. Kramer
Associate Professor of Finance, University of Toronto

INTRODUCTION

Classical economics and traditional finance rest partly on the premise that individuals make decisions unencumbered by emotions. Of course, the assumed goal of economic agents is to maximize utility, which can equally be thought of as happiness. Happiness is clearly an emotional state, yet many economists and financial academics seem to prefer not to think of happiness in terms of emotions, and the lexicon associated with feelings is typically deemed to be irrelevant in the realm of standard economic and financial analysis. Traditional economics and finance has no room for sadness, excitement, or any other mood-related characteristics that most people would admit affect their daily lives to some extent.

If people experience their emotions randomly over time and/or across individuals, then ignoring the impact of their emotions on economic quantities could be prudent. Similarly, if emotions affect decisions but those effects do not amount to anything in aggregate when considering financial markets or the economy broadly, then quantitative analyses need not take account of emotions or other features of human psychology. If, in contrast, mood affects individuals' economic and financial decisions, and if the sum effects of those decisions fail to net to zero across individuals or at the macroeconomic level, then conventional economic analysis faces major challenges. This chapter provides evidence that human psychology has important implications on decisions at the individual level and outcomes at the macro level, commonly known as micro and macro behavioral finance. More specifically, this chapter analyzes the extent to which synchronicity in the psychological experiences of many members of a population may lead to widespread seasonal patterns in financial markets.

To the extent compelling evidence exists that human emotions have an impact on individual investors' financial decisions, this clearly has important implications for investors making portfolio management decisions, financial professionals who provide advice to individuals, and the personal finance industry in general. These implications apply irrespective of whether individual-level behavioral tendencies have widespread implications at the overall market level. If, however, compelling evidence exists that marketwide regularities arise as a consequence of emotion-influenced decisions of individuals, then the implications are even broader-reaching, applying not only to individual investors, financial advisors, and professionals who work in the personal finance industry, but also to hedge fund and mutual fund managers, other large financial institutions, financial regulators, and the academics who conduct research on financial economics.

MOODS, EMOTIONS, AND SENTIMENT

In the parlance of psychologists, moods and emotions are distinct concepts. Emotions are affective states that tend to be fleeting and transitory, such as a momentary burst of anger experienced by a motorist or the sense of joy experienced by a parent watching an offspring's school play. Moods, in contrast, are a much more persistent affective state, including depression that can last for months or even years at a time and the joyful honeymoon phase experienced by newlyweds. Sentiment, which is a term more commonly used by economists, encompasses both mood and emotion. For simplicity, this chapter uses all three terms interchangeably, though the reader is advised to keep in mind the distinction between mood and emotion that exists more broadly.

WEATHER, MOOD, AND MARKETS

Richard Roll, a noted finance professor, may be the first researcher to suggest that the weather might influence financial markets. His insights came a decade before the start of a major surge in the academic literature studying the connection between emotions and markets. Roll (1984) finds that temperature surprises in Florida significantly influence the futures market price for orange juice. One can imagine nonpsychological reasons for a connection between weather and orange juice futures prices. For instance, freezing temperatures in Florida can markedly affect the orange crop, and such events could conceivably have rational price implications, especially when the temperature extremes are unanticipated. Roll finds evidence, however, of a persistent impact of temperature shocks on prices that seems to suggest some degree of market inefficiency. Nonetheless, his arguments make no reference to human psychology, instead leaving the connection between weather and price changes as an unexplained phenomenon.

Saunders (1993) provides the next important step exploring a link between the weather and markets. He studies U.S. stock index returns for the Dow Jones Industrial Average as well as both the value-weighted and equal-weighted New York Stock Exchange and American Stock Exchange indices and finds they are significantly related to the local weather in New York City. Aside from commenting that both clinical and experimental research show that weather has significant effects on human behavior and noting that the weather likely influences the mood of traders and other workers, he does not attempt to specify a formal path through which weather-induced mood might affect markets.

Hirshleifer and Shumway (2003) build on the work of Saunders (1993), revisiting the relationship between stock returns and the weather in the city of a market's exchange in 26 countries. They devise a novel measure for weather, considering surprises relative to seasonal average weather effects instead of surprises relative to recent weather forecasts issued 36, 24, and 12 hours in advance as studied by Roll (1984) or raw observed weather effects as utilized by Saunders (1993). Based on their measure, Hirshleifer and Shumway find that daily deviation from seasonally normal cloudiness is negatively related to stock return indexes. That is, the cloudier the weather is in the city of the exchange (relative to seasonal weather norms), the more negative is the impact on returns for that exchange. The authors ascribe this finding to the psychological phenomenon known as *misattribution bias*. The idea is that when one is in a bad mood, she is more likely to focus on negative information, or symmetrically, when one is in a good mood, she tends to focus on positive information. Further, people frequently misattribute their state of mind to the incorrect source, which can have spillover effects on decisions. The example Hirshleifer and Shumway cite is that people are often happier on sunny days than on cloudy days, which in turn can influence choices a person makes during the day, including financial choices. The misattribution bias can be attenuated if people are asked about the weather, perhaps because the question prompts them to recognize the direct connection between their mood and the weather. Hirshleifer and Shumway also cite evidence that sunshine and sunlight are linked with positive mood. They hypothesize that if people are in a good (bad) mood due to the weather, they may be more (less) inclined to buy stock, especially given the effects of misattribution bias.

Further exploring the importance of weather for financial markets, Cao and Wei (2005) perform an in-depth study of nine stock return indices across eight countries and find a negative correlation between temperature and stock returns. They conclude their findings are consistent with research in psychology that relates various temperatures to apathy and/or aggression. Their results are maintained after controlling for other known market regularities and performing various robustness checks.

DAYLIGHT, MOOD, AND MARKETS

A stream of studies has emerged exploring the link between seasonality in daylight, seasonality in mood, seasonality in financial risk tolerance, and seasonality in market returns. Before considering the empirical findings themselves, considering the underlying literatures in medicine and psychology is useful.

Weather, Daylight, and Mood

Weather is separate from but not independent of daylight. The time between sunrise and sunset defines daylight. While sunshine is a stochastic weather feature that may or may not be observed during daylight hours (depending on the amount of cloud cover), daylight itself is deterministic and perfectly predictable by date and latitude, following a cycle akin to a sine wave.

Humans and other animals experience circadian rhythms that vary with daylight, both at a high frequency (e.g., over the 24-hour cycle of a day) and at a low frequency (e.g., over the course of the year). Over the span of day, humans have sleep/wake cycles that are cued by daylight. During the year, people experience seasonal variation in mood that medical researchers and psychologists have extensively studied. Perhaps the best known form of seasonal mood variation in humans is seasonal affective disorder (SAD), a seasonal form of depression commonly known as winter blues. Individuals suffering from seasonal depression experience a range of symptoms—one of the most problematic of which is a dampened mood.

Studies suggest the basis for seasonal depression is physiological, with leading theories suggesting the condition is related to disruption in functions related to neurotransmitters and hormones such as serotonin. For example, Westrin and Lam (2007) discuss the etiology of SAD. Various researchers including Molin et al. (1996) and Young et al. (1997) consider a range of environmental factors, such as temperature, cloud cover, rainfall, humidity, and length of day. They find the amount of time between sunrise and sunset is the strongest cause of seasonal depression. Interestingly, authors including Watson (2000) and Keller et al. (2005) find no significant correlation between a range of weather variables and *transient* mood (i.e., mood fluctuations of short duration, in contrast to the persistent mood dampening associated with seasonal depression).

As catalogued by Kamstra, Kramer, and Levi (2012a), major challenges arise to estimating the prevalence of seasonal depression in populations, and especially in making comparisons across populations, in part because different researchers use different diagnostic criteria and sample selection methods. Nonetheless, studies suggest that between 1 and 10 percent of the U.S. population suffers from severe seasonal depression. Studies by Mersch (2001) and Thompson, Thompson, and Smith (2004) find estimates of the percentage of the population affected can vary considerably depending on latitude as well as sample selection and diagnostic criteria. Accordingly, different estimates invariably emerge from different studies. For example, Rosen et al. (1990) find 2 percent of the population in Florida and 10 percent of the population in New Hampshire suffer from SAD. Furthermore, severe seasonal depression appears to be the extreme of a continuum along which most or possibly all humans experience some degree of seasonal depression. For instance, Mersch et al. (1999, p. 1020) state "mood fluctuations over the seasons are not only present in SAD, but are—with smaller amplitude—also present in normal subjects as well." Further, Harmatz et al. (2000) find that even among individuals who do not meet the diagnostic criteria for SAD, depression varies significantly across the seasons and peaks in fall/winter, especially for women.

Clinical studies by researchers including Young et al. (1997) and Lam (1998) suggest that among North Americans who suffer from SAD, the onset of symptoms can begin in summer for a tiny subset of individuals, but most people begin suffering around the time of autumn equinox, when daylight is changing most rapidly. A small fraction of individuals begins recovering immediately after winter solstice, with the peak point of recovery occurring around spring equinox when daylight is increasing most quickly. As for locations outside of North America, researchers including Lam (1998) and Magnusson (2000) indicate that SAD appears to be more prevalent in countries located at higher latitudes, and Rosenthal et al. (1984) report that symptoms are milder closer to the equator. The timing of symptom onset and recovery appears to be similar across countries.

Mood and Financial Risk Aversion

An important element of the connection between mood and financial markets is the research finding that has been established between depression and risk aversion.

Several studies show that depressed people are more averse to risk. For instance Carton, Jouvent, Bungener, and Widlöcher (1992) and Carton, Morand, Bungenera, and Jouvent (1995) find depressed individuals score significantly more highly on standard risk aversion questionnaires than non-depressed individuals. Zuckerman, Buchsbaum, and Murphy (1980), Zuckerman (1984), and Horvath and Zuckerman (1993) provide further evidence of the connection between depression and risk aversion. Turning to the financial domain, Wong and Carducci (1991) and Harlow and Brown (1990) show that standard measures of risk aversion extend to risk of a specifically financial nature. Several other studies including Sciortino, Huston, and Spencer (1987), Harlow and Brown (1990), and Smoski et al. (2008) demonstrate an association between dampened mood and increased aversion to risk specifically of a financial nature.

Seasonality in Mood, Seasonality in Risk Aversion, and Seasonality in Markets

Given the apparent prevalence and synchronicity with which the seasons affect the moods of individuals, a natural question is whether seasonality in mood translates into seasonality in financial decisions and aggregate financial markets. A set of studies conducted over the past decade seeks to explore that question, as discussed in the next sections.

Stock Returns   Kamstra, Kramer, and Levi (2003) hypothesize that seasonality in depression is associated with large seasonal variation in the return to holding risky stocks in markets around the world. According to their hypothesis, if diminished length of day in the autumn causes investors' risk aversion to increase, those investors become less inclined to hold risky stocks. This would have an immediate negative influence on stock prices and returns. The price pressure would continue until investors sell sufficient quantities of their risky holdings to ensure their revised portfolios are consistent with their now higher risk aversion, or until the now higher expected return to holding risky stock sufficiently compensates them for their heightened distaste for risk. Following winter solstice, as the length of day starts to increase, investors would begin recovering from their depression and would become more willing to hold risky assets, at which time stock prices and returns would be positively influenced.

Kamstra et al. (2003) test this hypothesis using daily stock index returns and daylight data for nine international markets. They find significant seasonal variation in returns, and their attempt to identify the source of the seasonal variation rests on two factors. First, the fact that the prevalence and intensity of depression increase with latitude implies seasonal variation in returns ought to increase with latitude. Second, the fact that seasons are six months out of phase in the southern hemisphere suggests the seasonality in returns should be offset by six months in southern hemisphere markets. Thus, the authors consider stock markets at various latitudes in the northern hemisphere, ranging from Japan at 36°N to Sweden at 59°N. In the southern hemisphere, they consider South Africa, New Zealand, and Australia, all of which are located between 26°S and 37°S. After controlling for standard stock return regularities, they find significant evidence of seasonal variation in returns consistent with seasonally varying investor risk aversion that arises due to seasonal depression. The patterns are more prominent in stock markets at extreme latitudes, such as Sweden, where the seasonal fluctuations in daylight are more extreme. Furthermore, both the seasonal patterns and the seasons are six months out of sync in southern hemisphere markets such as Australia.

Other authors consider broader sets of countries. For example, Dowling and Lucey (2008) find similar results based on data from 37 countries. Further, Kamstra et al. (2012a) report similar evidence based on 36 countries' stock return indices, studying the series individually and clustered into groups based on latitude and hemisphere, and employing various different econometric methods and modeling approaches.

Time-Varying Price of Risk Garrett, Kamstra, and Kramer (2005) further examine the hypothesized relationship between seasonal depression and seasonal stock returns, exploring time-varying risk aversion in an equilibrium asset pricing model context and allowing the price of risk to vary through the seasons. Using daily and monthly data for six countries in both the northern and southern hemispheres, they find evidence consistent with the seasonal depression hypothesis. Specifically, the authors find that a conditional capital asset pricing model (CAPM), which allows the price of risk to vary seasonally (coincident with the timing documented in clinical studies of individuals who suffer from SAD), fully explains observed seasonal variation in returns. Stated differently, they find the price of risk varies seasonally.

Treasury Security Returns Kamstra, Kramer, and Levi (2012b) consider the other side of the risk coin. Whereas Kamstra et al. (2003) study seasonality in the rate of return to risky stocks, Kamstra et al. (2012b) examine seasonality in returns to safe securities. Their argument is that if seasonality in investor mood and investor risk aversion is associated with investors disfavoring risky stocks during some seasons, then investors ought to symmetrically favor safe securities during those same seasons. The study uses monthly returns to U.S. Treasury securities, arguably the safest securities available to investors worldwide, and a range of maturities spanning the medium-to-long term. The authors omit the shorter end of the maturity spectrum from their tabulated analysis due to the fact that the Federal Reserve Board aims explicitly to remove seasonal fluctuation in interest rates in the short-term Treasury securities. Nonetheless, they document similar evidence for all Treasury maturities in an earlier version of their manuscript.

Overall, Kamstra et al. (2012b) find statistically significant evidence of economically large seasonal differences in returns to U.S. Treasury securities. This is consistent with seasonal depression and seasonal risk aversion having an influence on investors' preference for safe securities. The authors find the seasonal variation in Treasury security returns does not appear to be driven by any of a wide range of alternate explanations, including macroeconomic cyclicality, various standard measures of investor sentiment, cross-market hedging between equity and Treasury securities, seasonality in the Treasury debt supply, seasonality in the Federal Open Market Committee meeting cycle, and seasonal variation in risk.

Mutual Fund Flows Kamstra, Kramer, Levi, and Wermers (2012) consider whether seasonal depression and seasonal variation in investor risk tolerance are associated with seasonal variation in the flow of funds into and out of mutual funds. If seasonal depression causes seasonal reallocation between safe and risky asset classes, this should show up in flows. They analyze net flow and net exchange data for risky and safe categories of mutual funds in Canada and the United States and for risky mutual funds in Australia. The authors find significant flows out of risky mutual fund categories and into safe categories in the fall, when daylight is diminishing. Further, their evidence shows that these patterns reverse when daylight is becoming more abundant. The patterns for risky mutual fund categories are offset by six months in Australia, as are the seasons. These results hold after controlling for other known regularities in mutual fund flows, and the findings withstand many robustness checks. A novelty of this paper relative to several other studies that consider the link between seasonal depression, seasonal risk aversion, and financial market seasonality is the fact that it considers quantities (by way of flows of funds) instead of prices.

Preference Parameters in an Asset Pricing Model Kamstra, Kramer, Levi, and Wang (2012) seek to determine whether a reasonable set of preference parameters exists that accounts for the empirically observed seasonal variation in equity returns and Treasury security returns. They consider an asset pricing model in which the representative agent has Epstein and Zin (1989) recursive preferences, with risk aversion and the elasticity of intertemporal substitution (EIS) both varying by season. Calibrating to consumption data, the model is able to match the magnitudes of equity and Treasury returns observed in U.S. markets across the seasons. Importantly, they find that it is essential to allow for seasonal variation in both risk aversion and EIS in order to closely match to the characteristics of observed returns. Allowing variation in only one or the other is insufficient.

Analyst Earnings Forecasts Dolvin, Pyles, and Wu (2009) explore the possibility that the widespread prevalence of seasonal depression has implications for the earnings forecasts issued by financial analysts in the United States. They find analysts are typically optimistic, similar to the finding of several other studies, and the optimism decreases during the months when seasonal depression is commonly observed. Further, the authors find stronger seasonal effects for analysts located in more northern states, consistent with the finding that seasonal mood effects are stronger at higher latitudes. Lo and Wu (2010) find similar results with respect to less optimistic analyst forecasts during periods when individuals experience seasonal depression.

Initial Public Offering Returns Dolvin and Pyles (2007) consider the possibility that seasonality in investor depression and investor risk aversion affect initial public offering (IPO) prices in the United States. They consider more than 4,000 issues of which just under half occurred during the fall and winter. Their results show significantly more IPO underpricing in the fall and winter seasons compared to the rest of the year. The authors recommend that for firms with flexibility in the timing of their public offerings, avoiding the times of the year during which people experience seasonal depression may be financially advantageous.

Real Estate Prices and Real Estate Investment Trust Returns Kaplanski and Levy (2012) study real estate price data from the United States, the United Kingdom, and Australia. They find prices follow a sinusoidal pattern over the course of the year on average during their 20-year sample and in most individual years of their sample. The authors also find greater seasonality at higher latitudes. Overall, their findings are consistent with the notion that individuals experience mood changes that spill over into the real estate market. Kaplanski and Levy explore a range of alternative explanations and find the SAD hypothesis dominates.

Perceived Market Risk In a study using data on the implied volatility of S&P 500 index options (i.e., the VIX), Kaplanski and Levy (2009) explore the possibility that SAD may lead to changes in investors' perception of risk. Commonly denoted the "fear index," the VIX is typically interpreted as a measure of the perceived volatility of stock returns over the next 30 days. Stock volatility is naturally determined largely by economic fundamentals, but may also be driven by changes in investor sentiment. Hence, variation in the VIX could come from either source. The authors decompose the VIX into one part that is explained by fundamentals and another part by sentiment. They find the sentiment-driven component of the VIX is significantly correlated with hours of daylight, which is consistent with the notion that seasonal depression helps to drive investors' perception of market risk. Notably, the authors do not find a significant relationship between hours of daylight and actual risk. Given their findings with respect to seasonality in financial risk perception, Kaplanski and Levy speculate that people's perceptions of the risks associated with other important life events may vary seasonally, including marriage and elective surgical procedures.

Bid-Ask Spreads DeGennaro, Kamstra, and Kramer (2008) study bid-ask spreads for U.S. stocks and find additional results consistent with the notion that seasonal depression and seasonal risk aversion influence financial markets. After controlling for several regularities known to influence spreads, they find the spreads quoted by an individual dealer are significantly wider during seasons when people are more risk-averse due to seasonal depression. This finding aligns with theory introduced by Stoll (1978) and Ho and Stoll (1981, 1983) that suggests greater dealer risk aversion leads to wider spreads. DeGennaro et al. contend that the interaction between seasonal variations in the width of spreads and previously documented seasonal variation in equity returns leads to a counterintuitive outcome for inside spreads. That is, during the seasons when individuals are more risk averse and quoted spreads are wider, inside spreads (i.e., the difference between the best bid and ask prices across all dealers) are narrower. These findings are robust to various tests and specification changes.

Individual-Level Analysis Most of the papers just described examine the connections between seasonality in mood, seasonality in risk aversion, and seasonality in markets by employing aggregate financial market data exclusively, and not data about individual-level decisions. Kramer and Weber (2012) are an exception in that they consider data from surveys and experiments conducted at the individual level. This enables them to examine whether individuals experience seasonally varying mood, seasonally varying risk aversion, and/or seasonally varying financial choices. The study participants include more than 300 faculty and staff at a large North American university, all of whom responded to questions at each of three points in time over the course of a year. The participants completed several questionnaires that clinicians use, including some that screen for current bouts of depression and others that diagnose whether one is prone to suffer from SAD in general. The researchers measured financial risk aversion by having participants take part in an incentive-compatible exercise. Participants received $20 in compensation for participating in the study and each had an opportunity to "invest" all, some, or none of those funds after the study ended. The investment, titled the Safe Asset Versus Risky (SAVR) task, mimics an actual financial investment by incorporating higher expected compensation for bearing risk. Those who preferred to take maximal risk could choose to invest all of their $20; in so doing they faced 50:50 odds of losing the entire $20 or receiving $42. Those who preferred not to take risk could choose to invest none of their $20, in which case they kept the entire amount. Those who chose to take intermediate levels of risk could allocate portions of their $20 (in 10 percent increments) between the safe and risky alternatives.

The outcome of the study reveals that individuals who are predisposed to experience seasonal depression (i.e., those who suffer from SAD) exhibit significantly greater levels of depression in the fall/winter than in the summer, and they are significantly less willing to take financial risk in the fall/winter than in the summer. Furthermore, individuals who suffer from SAD are significantly more depressed and less willing to take financial risk in the winter than are individuals who do not suffer from SAD.

The timing of this particular study overlapped with the financial crisis of 2008–2009, which complicated the analysis to some extent, with non SAD sufferers becoming more averse to financial risk as the financial crisis deepened. This suggests that a promising line of inquiry may exist into the combined interactions among seasons, the business cycle, and financial risk aversion.

DAYLIGHT SAVING TIME CHANGES, MOOD, AND MARKETS

Humans' sleep habits have a profound impact on their state of mind, and on their performance in the workplace. Kamstra, Kramer, and Levi (2001) highlight some catastrophic events from history that have been linked to humans' sleep imbalances, including the nuclear accident at Chernobyl, the Exxon Valdez oil spill, and the narrowly averted nuclear disaster at Three Mile Island. They also point to evidence from the psychology literature that documents an increase in car accident rates arising immediately after changes in sleep patterns that accompany daylight saving time changes, whether an hour of sleep is lost or gained. Building on these findings, the authors explore whether the changes in sleep patterns that accompany daylight saving time changes are associated with a systematic impact on stock market returns, perhaps through the anxiety that often accompanies sleep pattern disruption.

Kamstra et al. (2001) examine daily stock index returns from Canada, the United States, Germany, and the United Kingdom, and find significantly negative returns on the trading day that immediately follows the time change, both in the spring and in the fall. This finding is consistent with the possibility that investors become more averse to financial risk when their routine sleep habits are disturbed by the daylight saving time change.

Kamstra, Kramer, and Levi (2002) explore the data more deeply and rule out the possibility that a few negative outliers drive the effect. Instead, they find that the entire distribution of returns is shifted more toward negative values on the trading day immediately following daylight saving time changes relative to other trading days that immediately follow a weekend. They also comment on the possibility that the disruptions most individuals experience in their sleep patterns on weekends relative to weekdays, not just daylight saving time change weekends, may help explain the more general Monday effect, whereby stock returns on Mondays are more negative on average relative to other trading days.

ELATION, DEFLATION, AND MARKETS

Researchers have examined numerous ways in which events that are widely covered by the popular press or entertainment experiences that synchronize large numbers of individuals may affect financial markets. Among these are sporting events, catastrophes such as hurricanes, plane crashes, and terrorist attacks, shared experiences watching popular films, and the dissemination of sentiment through social networking websites.

Sporting Events and Marketwide Effects

Several papers study the possibility that the sentiment emerging from the outcome of major international sporting events may spill over into financial markets. Edmans, García, and Norli (2007) study international soccer, cricket, rugby, and basketball games. Their soccer sample includes international soccer matches, including World Cup tournaments, for 39 countries over 30 years, for a total of over 1,100 matches. They find economically large and statistically significant market declines after losses for a particular country. The effect is strongest for soccer matches, particularly important soccer matches, but it is evident for the other sporting events as well. The authors do not find a corresponding positive impact on markets following a country's win in an international sporting event. For the loss effect, the impact is greatest among small stocks. At the index level, the effect amounts to a one-day abnormal return of −49 basis points on average.

Edmans et al. (2007) maintain that a mood variable must satisfy three criteria in order to be plausibly linked to asset returns. First, the variable must have a strong and unambiguous impact on human mood. Second, the variable must impact a large fraction of the population and hence investors. Third, some degree of synchronicity or correlation must exist across individuals in terms of the mood impact. With respect to the context of sporting events in particular, the authors point to evidence from the psychology literature that suggests sporting fans respond asymmetrically to wins versus losses, which may help explain why they find significant marketwide effects following losses but not wins.

Kaplanski and Levy (2010a) explore the possibility of developing a profitable trading strategy based on the impact of sports-related sentiment on financial markets, particularly exploiting the asymmetric effect of wins versus losses and the fact that local market returns can spill over to influence aggregate U.S. market returns. The authors find a negative abnormal return in total U.S. equity markets. They note that investors can incorporate this regularity into an investment strategy in at least two different ways: (1) reduce an individual's exposure to U.S. equities during the period when the World Cup is being held, and (2) seek negative exposure to U.S. equities during the World Cup period by short selling. With the availability of exchange-traded funds with negative beta relative to the S&P 500, investors can implement the short-selling strategy at relatively low cost, though it comes with obvious risk because factors other than sports-related sentiment can lead to unexpected movements in returns.

Disasters and Marketwide Effects

Several studies examine the impact of catastrophes such as terrorist attacks, aviation accidents, and natural disasters on financial markets, in particular stock markets.

Terrorist Attacks Some papers studying terrorist attacks find the negative abnormal returns that occur during the period following the terrorist attack are roughly commensurate with the magnitude of property losses and anticipated future earnings losses (Carter and Simkins 2004; Karolyi and Martell 2010). According to Karolyi (2006, p. 15), the possibility remains that part of the share price reaction following terrorist attacks may reflect "some kind of psychological overreaction." Consistent with this line of reasoning, Becker and Rubenstein (2004) explore an asset pricing model that allows for fear of terror to affect investor behavior. Their model is novel in that it distinguishes between investor risk aversion and investor fear.

Aviation Accidents Papers studying the market reaction to fatal plane crashes provide mixed findings. For instance, Barrett et al. (1987) study a set of 78 fatal airline crashes and find a negative impact on airline stock returns that is significant for only one day after the accident. They conclude this finding is consistent with the efficient markets hypothesis in that there is no evidence of overreaction or underreaction. In contrast, a study of aviation accidents by Kaplanski and Levy (2010b) compares the magnitude of the abnormal negative returns associated with airline disasters with the magnitude of the economic losses associated with the crash. The authors find the temporary impact on airline prices is more than 60 times larger than the economic losses, which they conclude is consistent with the notion that increased investor anxiety following the disaster leads to a reduction in willingness to hold risky stocks which in turn affects returns. Kaplanski and Levy find stock returns recover a couple of days later, once investor anxiety presumably dissipates.

Natural Disasters To date, the behavioral finance literature has not focused much attention on the possibility that investor behavior may lead to an association between natural disasters and stock market returns. An exception is a study by Shan and Gong (2012) who exploit a natural experiment arising from an earthquake in China. Following the earthquake, firms with headquarters near the earthquake's epicenter experienced significantly lower stock returns than other firms. Further, they find the magnitude of economic losses and changes in systematic risk cannot account for the difference. This finding suggests human sentiment may play a role.

Some evidence from the insurance literature suggests devoting additional resources to investigating the possible connection between natural disasters and market returns may be worthwhile. For example, Lazarus and Narayanan (1996) study the impact of large hurricanes, such as Hurricane Andrew, on the stock price of insurance firms. While two potentially opposing effects influence firm values, one through the increase in cash outflows to fund insurance claims and the other through the increase in expected firm cash inflows due to higher future premiums, on balance the authors find a significant negative return to insurance firms that had policyholders who suffered losses. Lazarus and Narayanan do not investigate whether the magnitude of the stock impact is on par with the expected net losses to the firms and are thus agnostic on the question of overreaction/underreaction. Nevertheless, the possibility remains that human psychology plays a role in this context because the authors find evidence that insurance companies without exposure in hurricane-affected states experience negative returns at the time of the disaster, which implies the presence of industrywide contagion effects.

Entertainment, Social Media, and Marketwide Effects

Researchers have recently begun to explore the degree to which forms of entertainment such as motion pictures or social networking websites might play a role in financial markets.

Comedy Movie Attendance   As discussed, prior research suggests environmental factors such as daylight exposure and weather may affect investors and consequently financial markets. Lepori (2010) explores a completely different environmental factor: comedy movie attendance. His study starts with the observation that investors typically perform the bulk of their investment planning over the same period of time when they typically see movies: over the weekend. He incorporates findings from psychology studies showing that viewing film clips, whether happy or sad, influence individuals' moods. His overall finding is that stock returns are lower on the Monday immediately following high attendance at comedy movies, which he claims is consistent with the mood maintenance hypothesis (Isen and Patrick 1983), whereby individuals in a good mood are more likely to be cautious. Perhaps future research will seek to reconcile this finding with the seemingly contradictory evidence from other environmental studies suggesting an association between negative mood states such as depression and negative daily stock returns.

Social Media: Facebook and Twitter   Recent studies have turned to the task of using information gleaned from social networking websites to predict movements in financial markets. For example, Karabulut (2011) studies a measure constructed by Facebook Inc. called Gross National Happiness (GNH) and finds changes in GNH are positively correlated with the next day's U.S. stock index return. Further, Mao, Counts, and Bollen (2011) find evidence that sentiment data extracted from Twitter posts may be better able to predict financial market movements than standard consumer sentiment indices and macroeconomic data. These findings imply that financial market speculators may be able to exploit human sentiment in real time.

SUMMARY

Over the past decade in particular, a surge of research has explored the ways in which human emotion may affect both decision-making at the individual level and aggregate financial markets. While much evidence supports the claim that emotions and markets are intricately related, researchers should continue to explore reasonable alternative hypotheses. A feature of social science research is that definitively proving a particular human psychological characteristic is causatively related to a particular observed marketwide phenomenon may be impossible. Nevertheless, financial researchers should explore plausible alternative hypotheses besides appealing behavioral explanations. To the extent that many existing studies attempt to comprehensively explore both rational and behavioral explanations for what appear to be anomalous patterns in financial markets, convincing support exists for the view that emotions play a role in markets. Future research in this area promises to be worthy of additional attention.

DISCUSSION QUESTIONS

1. Provide an example of an economic mechanism through which a particular human emotion can affect financial markets. That is, describe in economic terms how a particular emotion may lead to a particular outcome in financial markets.
2. Discuss whether correlation between an environmental factor (such as cloud cover) and stock market index returns implies causation and indicate the implications of your response for behavioral finance researchers.
3. Identify three financial market regularities that are consistent with mood impacting markets.
4. Compare and contrast the traditional economics paradigm with the behavioral finance paradigm concerning the possibility that emotion or mood can affect humans' decisions.

REFERENCES

Angbazo, Lazarus A., and Ranga Narayanan. 1996. Catastrophic Shocks in the Property-Liability Insurance Industry: Evidence on Regulatory and Contagion Effects. *Journal of Risk and Insurance* 63:4, 619–637.

Barrett, W. Brian, Andrea J. Heuson, Robert W. Kolb, and Gabriele H. Schropp. 1987. "The Adjustment of Stock Prices to Completely Unanticipated Events." *Financial Review* 22:4 345–354.

Becker, Gary S., and Yona Rubenstein. 2004. "Fear and the Response to Terrorism: An Economic Analysis." Working Paper, University of Chicago.

Cao, Melanie, and Jason Wei. 2005. "Stock Market Returns: A Note on the Temperature Anomaly." *Journal of Banking and Finance* 29:6, 1559–1573.

Carter, David A., and Betty J. Simkins. 2004. "The Market's Reaction to Unexpected, Catastrophic Events: The Case of Airline Stock Returns and the September 11th Attacks." *Quarterly Review of Economics and Finance* 44:4, 539–558.

Carton, S., R. Jouvent, C. Bungener, and D. Widlöcher. 1992. "Sensation Seeking and Depressive Mood." *Personality and Individual Differences* 13:7, 843–849.

Carton, Solange, Pauline Morand, Catherine Bungenera, and Roland Jouvent. 1995. "Sensation-Seeking and Emotional Disturbances in Depression: Relationships and Evolution." *Journal of Affective Disorders* 13:3, 219–225.

DeGennaro, Ramon P., Mark J. Kamstra, and Lisa A. Kramer. 2008. "Does Risk Aversion Vary During the Year? Evidence from Bid-Ask Spreads." Working Paper, University of Toronto.

Dolvin, Steven D., and Mark K. Pyles. 2007. "Seasonal Affective Disorder and the Pricing of IPOs." *Review of Accounting and Finance* 6:2, 214–228.

Dolvin, Steven D., Mark K. Pyles, and Qun Wu. 2009. "Analysts Get SAD Too: The Effect of Seasonal Affective Disorder on Analysts' Earnings Estimates." *Journal of Behavioral Finance* 10:4, 214–225.

Dowling, Michael, and Brian M. Lucey. 2008. "Robust Global Mood Influences in Equity Pricing." *Journal of Multinational Financial Management* 18:2, 145–164.

Edmans, Alex, Diego García, and Øyvind Norli. 2007. "Sports Sentiment and Stock Returns." *Journal of Finance* 62:4, 1967–1998.

Epstein, Larry G., and Stanley E. Zin. 1989. "Substitution, Risk Aversion, and the Temporal Behavior of Consumption and Asset Returns: A Theoretical Framework." *Econometrica* 57:4, 937–969.

Garrett, Ian, Mark Kamstra, and Lisa Kramer. 2005. "Winter Blues and Time Variation in the Price of Risk." *Journal of Empirical Finance* 12:2, 291–316.

Harlow, W. V., and Keith C. Brown. 1990. "Understanding and Assessing Financial Risk Tolerance: A Biological Perspective." *Financial Analysts Journal* 6:6, 50–80.

Harmatz, Morton C., Arnold D. Well, Christopher E. Overtree, Kathleen Y. Kawamura, Milagros Rosal, and Ira S. Ockene. 2000. "Seasonal Variation of Depression and Other Moods: A Longitudinal Approach." *Journal of Biological Rhythms* 15:4, 344–350.

Hirshleifer, David, and Tyler Shumway. 2003. "Good Day Sunshine: Stock Returns and the Weather." *Journal of Finance* 58:3, 1009–1032.

Ho, Thomas S. Y., and Hans R. Stoll. 1981. "Optimal Dealer Pricing under Transactions and Return Uncertainty." *Journal of Financial Economics* 9:1, 47–73.

Ho, Thomas S. Y., and Hans R. Stoll. 1983. "The Dynamics of Dealer Markets under Competition." *Journal of Finance* 38:4, 1053–1074.

Horvath, Paula, and Marvin Zuckerman. 1993. "Sensation Seeking, Risk Appraisal, and Risky Behavior." *Personality and Individual Differences* 14:1, 41–52.

Isen, Alice M., and Robert Patrick. 1983. "The Effect of Positive Feelings on Risk Taking: When the Chips Are Down." *Organizational and Human Behavior* 31:2, 194–202.

Kamstra, Mark J., Lisa A. Kramer, and Maurice D. Levi. 2001. "Losing Sleep at the Market: The Daylight Saving Anomaly." *American Economic Review* 90:4, 1005–1011.

Kamstra, Mark J., Lisa A. Kramer, and Maurice D. Levi. 2002. "Losing Sleep at the Market: The Daylight Saving Anomaly: Reply." *American Economic Review* 92:4, 1257–1263.

Kamstra, Mark J., Lisa A. Kramer, and Maurice D. Levi. 2003. "Winter Blues: A SAD Stock Market Cycle." *American Economic Review* 93:1, 324–343.

Kamstra, Mark J., Lisa A. Kramer, and Maurice D. Levi. 2012a. "A Careful Re-Examination of Seasonality in International Stock Markets: Comment on Sentiment and Stock Returns." *Journal of Banking and Finance* 36:4, 934–956.

Kamstra, Mark J., Lisa A. Kramer, and Maurice D. Levi. 2012b. "Seasonal Variation in Treasury Returns." Working Paper, Schulich School of Business, York University.

Kamstra, Mark J., Lisa A. Kramer, Maurice D. Levi, and Tan Wang. 2012. "Seasonal Varying Preferences: Theoretical Foundations for an Empirical Regularity." Working Paper, Sauder School of Business, University of British Columbia.

Kamstra, Mark J., Lisa A. Kramer, Maurice D. Levi, and Russ Wermers. 2012. "Seasonal Asset Allocation: Evidence from Mutual Fund Flows." Working Paper, Smith School of Business, University of Maryland.

Kaplanski, Guy, and Haim Levy, 2009. "Seasonality in Perceived Risk: A Sentiment Effect." Working Paper, Hebrew University of Jerusalem.

Kaplanski, Guy, and Haim Levy. 2010a. "Exploitable Predictable Irrationality: The FIFA World Cup Effect on the U.S. Stock Market." *Journal of Financial and Quantitative Analysis* 45:2, 535–553.

Kaplanski, Guy, and Haim Levy. 2010b. "Sentiment and Stock Prices: The Case of Aviation Disasters." *Journal of Financial Economics* 95:2, 174–201.

Kaplanski, Guy, and Haim Levy. 2012. "Real Estate Prices: An International Study of Seasonality's Sentiment Effect." *Journal of Empirical Finance* 19:1, 123–146.

Karabulut, Yigitcan. 2011. "Can Facebook Predict Stock Market Activity?" Working Paper, Goethe University.

Karolyi, G. Andrew. 2006. "Shock Markets: What Do We Know about Terrorist and the Financial Markets?" *Canadian Investment Review*, Summer, 9–15.

Karolyi, G. Andrew, and Rodolfo Martell. 2010. "Terrorism and the Stock Market." *International Review of Applied Finance Issues and Economics* 2:2, 285–314.

Keller, Matthew C., Barbara L. Fredrickson, Oscar Ybarra, Stéphane Côté, Kareem Johnson, Joe Mikels, Anne Conway, and Tor Wager. 2005. "A Warm Heart and a Clear Head." *Psychological Science* 16:9, 724–731.

Kramer, Lisa A., and J. Mark Weber. 2012. "This Is Your Portfolio on Winter: Seasonal Affective Disorder and Risk Aversion in Financial Decision Making." *Social Psychological and Personality Science* 3:2, 193–199.

Lam, Raymond W. 1998. "Seasonal Affective Disorder: Diagnosis and Management." *Primary Care Psychiatry* 4:2, 63–74.

Lepori, Gabriele. 2010. "Positive Mood, Risk Attitudes, and Investment Decisions: Field Evidence from Comedy Movie Attendance in the U.S." Working Paper, Copenhagen Business School.

Lo, Kin, and Serena Shuo Wu. 2010. "The Impact of Seasonal Affective Disorder on Financial Analysts and Equity Market Returns." Working Paper, Sauder School of Business, University of British Columbia.

Magnusson, A. 2000. "An Overview of Epidemiological Studies on Seasonal Affective Disorder." *Acta Psychiatrica Scandinavica* 101:3, 176–184.

Mao, Huina, Scott Counts, and Johan Bollen. 2011. "Computational Economic and Finance Gauges: Polls, Search, & Twitter." Working Paper, Indiana University–Bloomington.

Mersch, P. 2001. "Prevalence from Population Surveys." In T. Partonen and A. Magnusson, eds., *Seasonal Affective Disorder: Practice and Research*, 121–140. Oxford: Oxford University Press.

Mersch, Peter Paul A., Hermine M. Middendorp, Antoinette L. Bouhuys, Domian G. M. Beersma, and Rutger H. van den Hoofdakker. 1999. "The Prevalence of Seasonal Affective Disorder in the Netherlands: A Prospective and Retrospective Study of Seasonal Mood Variation in the General Population." *Biological Psychiatry* 45:8, 1013–1022.

Molin, Jeanne, Erling Mellerup, Tom Bolwig, Thomas Scheike, and Henrik Dam. 1996. "The Influence of Climate on Development of Winter Depression." *Journal of Affective Disorders* 37:2–3, 151–155.

Roll, Richard. 1984. "Orange Juice and Weather." *American Economic Review* 74:5, 861–880.

Rosen, Leora N., Steven D. Targum, Michael Terman, Michael J. Bryant, Howard Hoffman, Siegfried F. Kasper, Joelle R. Hamovit, John P. Docherty, Betty Welch, and Norman E. Rosenthal. 1990. "Prevalence of Seasonal Affective Disorder at Four Latitudes." *Psychiatry Research* 31:2, 131–144.

Rosenthal, Norman E., David A. Sack, J. Christian Gillin, Alfred J. Lewy, Frederick K. Goodwin, Yolande Davenport, Peter S. Mueller, David A. Newsome, and Thomas A. Wehr. 1984. "Seasonal Affective Disorder: A Description of the Syndrome and Preliminary Findings with Light Therapy." *Archives of General Psychiatry* 41:1, 72–80.

Saunders, Edward M. 1993. "Stock Prices and Wall Street Weather." *American Economic Review* 83:5, 1337–1345.

Sciortino, John J., John H. Huston, and Roger W. Spencer. 1987. "Perceived Risk and the Precautionary Demand for Money." *Journal of Economic Psychology* 8:3, 339–346.

Shan, Liwei, and Stephen X. Gong. 2012. "Investor Sentiment and Stock Returns: Wenchuan Earthquake." *Finance Research Letters* 9:1, 36–47.

Smoski, Moria J., Thomas R. Lynch, M. Zachary Rosenthal, Jennifer S. Cheavens, Alexander L. Chapman, and Ranga R. Krishnan. 2008. "Decision-Making and Risk Aversion among Depressive Adults." *Journal of Behavior Therapy* 39:4, 567–576.

Stoll, Hans R. 1978. "The Supply of Dealer Services in Securities Markets." *Journal of Finance* 33:4, 1133–1151.

Thompson, Chris, Susan Thompson, and Rachel Smith. 2004. "Prevalence of Seasonal Affective Disorder in Primary Care: A Comparison of the Seasonal Health Questionnaire and the Seasonal Pattern Assessment Questionnaire." *Journal of Affective Disorders* 78:3, 219–226.

Watson, David. 2000. *Mood and Temperament.* New York: Guilford Press.

Westrin, Asa, and Raymond W. Lam. 2007. "Seasonal Affective Disorder: A Clinical Update." *Annals of Clinical Psychiatry* 19:4, 239–246.

Wong, Alan, and Bernardo J. Carducci. 1991. "Sensation Seeking and Financial Risk Taking in Everyday Money Matters." *Journal of Business and Psychology* 5:4, 525–530.

Young, Michael A., Patricia M. Meaden, Louis F. Fogg, Eva A. Cherin, and Charmane I. Eastman. 1997. "Which Environmental Variables Are Related to the Onset of Seasonal Affective Disorder?" *Journal of Abnormal Psychology* 106:4, 554–562.

Zuckerman, Marvin. 1984. "Sensation Seeking: A Comparative Approach to a Human Trait." *Behavioral and Brain Sciences* 7:3, 413–471.

Zuckerman, Marvin, Monte S. Buchsbaum, and Dennis L. Murphy. 1980. "Sensation Seeking and Its Biological Correlates." *Psychological Bulletin* 88:1, 187–214.

ABOUT THE AUTHORR

Lisa A. Kramer is an Associate Professor of Finance at the University of Toronto. She teaches undergraduate, master's, and PhD courses on behavioral finance. Her research interests include investments, capital market seasonality, human decisions, and emotions. Her research, which has been published in outlets including the *American Economic Review, Social Psychological and Personality Science*, and *Journal of Financial and Quantitative Analysis*, has been covered by media outlets including the *Wall Street Journal, Washington Post*, and *BusinessWeek*. She can be found on Twitter at @LisaKramer. Professor Kramer holds a BBA from Simon Fraser University and a PhD from the University of British Columbia.

CHAPTER 21

Neurofinance

Richard L. Peterson
Managing Director, MarketPsych LLC

INTRODUCTION

Behavioral finance studies describe market price anomalies and individual decision biases. Unfortunately, such descriptions of behavior have not proven amenable to generalization or predictive modeling. Neurofinance research illuminates the fundamental mechanisms that underlie how individual biases, irrational behavior, and collective buying and selling decisions emerge. Using research tools and techniques borrowed from the field of neuroscience, scientists are gaining the necessary insights to build comprehensive economic models of human economic behavior and decision-making.

Just as the field of economics provides a foundation for traditional finance, neuroeconomics research is informative of neurofinance. Neurofinance is not a separate field so much as a set of experimental techniques and tools that practitioners in many other fields adopt to investigate questions of central interest. *Neurofinance experimentation* is defined by the use of the scientific method to identify drivers and modifiers of choice behavior. Experimental apparatuses including neuroimaging and behavioral monitoring equipment are frequent tools of choice in such research. The use of neuroscientific research tools allows economists to look at biological drivers of decision-making. In particular, many economists are interested in investigating the origins of the nonoptimal decision-making. Issues addressed by neurofinance research include: (1) financial risk taking (both excessive and aversive); (2) expectation formation; (3) valuation; (4) information presentation and updating such as framing, reference points, and affective loading; (5) probability assessments under conditions of risk, uncertainty, and ambiguity; and (6) cooperation, competition, herding, and social influences on choice.

This chapter describes the progress researchers have made in contributing to our understanding of financial risk taking (including concepts of utility, emotional priming, probability assessments, and reference points) and social influences on choice (including moral concepts such as reciprocity, cooperation, trust, and revenge). As such, the remainder of the chapter consists of four sections: neuroscience primer, research methods, decisions and biases, and summary and conclusions.

Neurofinance studies of human behavior under conditions of risk and reward have identified significant neural correlates with behavior in areas of the brain that are involved in motivation, emotion, self-reflection, and strategy. Understanding the methods of neurofinance researchers first involves reviewing basic neuroanatomy and physiology.

NEUROSCIENCE PRIMER

The human brain is the product of millions of years of evolution. It is designed to efficiently and effectively interpret information, compete in a social hierarchy, and direct activity toward achieving goals while avoiding danger. The human brain evolved to optimally interface with a Stone Age world where dangers and opportunities were largely immediate, and social interactions were limited to other members of a hereditary clan. The Stone Age human brain is not optimized for managing many of the informational and relationship complexities of modern economic decision-making. Thus, many of the biases identified in behavioral finance may be traced back to the brain's evolutionary development.

There are many levels of function in the brain, from the actions of individual molecules to broad communications between lobes. At a molecular level, neural activity is driven by neurochemicals, small electrical currents, genetic (protein) transcription, and epigenetic cellular milieu. On the anatomical level, neural circuits cross brain regions and give rise to complex thoughts and behaviors. These are building blocks of a neurological understanding of the brain.

In the neuroeconomic academic literature, findings of interest reference significant statistical correlations between subject biology (e.g., genetic endowment, neural activations, and personality traits) and behavior (e.g., stated preferences, buying and selling decisions, and behavior). To researchers, changes in neurophysiology (e.g., fluctuations in blood flow, electrical activity, neurotransmitter activity, and cellular metabolism) and aberrations in neuroanatomy (e.g., brain structures, hormone levels, and neurotransmitter receptors) are of interest in their relation to financial and strategic decision-making. Understanding the findings of neurofinance researchers first requires an appreciation of basic neurobiology.

The Triune Brain

The brain can be conceptualized as having three major anatomical divisions. Each division is like the layer of an onion, with complex processes such as analytical decision-making in the outer layer, motivations and drives arising from the middle layer, and life-sustaining physiological processes originating in the innermost core. This conceptual schema is termed the "Triune" brain (MacLean 1990).

The cortex is the brain's logistical center. It is the director of executive function and motor control. The part of the cortex called the prefrontal cortex is of most interest to this chapter. The prefrontal cortex is involved in abstract thinking, planning, calculation, learning, and strategic decision-making (Prabhakaran, Rypma, and Gabrieli 2001). One part of the cortex, called the insular cortex, is evolutionarily distinct from the neocortex. When using the word "cortex," this chapter broadly refers to the neocortex and the prefrontal cortex, but excludes the insular cortex.

The brain's limbic system is the emotional driver of the brain. The limbic system is the source of primitive motivations and emotions including fear and excitement.

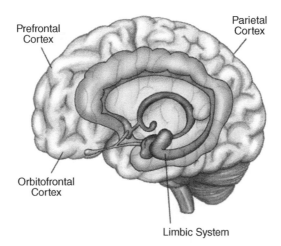

EXHIBIT 21.1 A Depiction of the Whole Brain

Note: The limbic system is situated underneath the cortex. The prefrontal cortex lies behind the forehead. The orbitofrontal cortex (OFC) is located behind the eyes and above the sinuses. The parietal cortex is situated at the posterior of the brain.

Exhibit 21.1 displays both the cortex and the limbic system. The third division of the brain is called the midbrain (also known as "the reptilian brain"). The midbrain manages the body's basic physiological processes, including respiration and heart rate, and it will not be discussed further in this chapter.

Traversing the three layers of the brain are neuronal pathways that deliver, integrate, and process information. Since the time of Aristotle, scientists and philosophers have loosely hypothesized the existence of two major brain functions that are fundamental to almost all human behavior: the *reward approach* (pleasure seeking) and the *loss avoidance* (pain avoidance) systems (Spencer 1880). These two motivational systems can be activated or deactivated independently. When humans face potential financial gains or losses, one or both of these systems may be used in the process of decision-making. This chapter presents a review of empirical evidence of the direct link between brain activation specific to these two systems: affective (emotional and feeling) states and financial decision-making.

The Reward System

Perceiving a potential reward in the environment sets the brain's approach system into action. Overall, the reward system coordinates the search for, evaluation of, and motivated pursuit of potential rewards. The neurons that carry information in the reward system transmit signals primarily via the neurotransmitter dopamine. The reward system lies along one of the five major dopamine pathways in the brain, the meso-limbic pathway as shown in Exhibit 21.2, which extends from the base of the brain, through the nucleus accumbens (NAcc) in the ventral striatum of the limbic system to the gray matter of the frontal lobes (MPFC) and the Anterior Cingulate Gyrus (ACC) (Bozarth 1994).

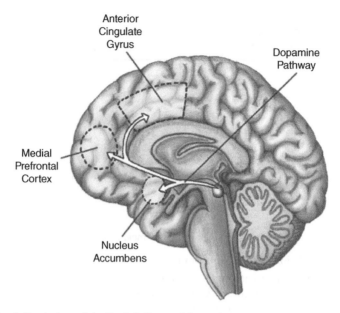

EXHIBIT 21.2 A Depiction of the Brain's Reward System

Note: The dopamine tract underlying the reward system extends from the midbrain through several structures key for reward valuation and motivation.

Dopamine was historically called the "pleasure" chemical of the brain. More recently, researchers have found dopamine to play a role in attention, mood, learning, motivation, and reward valuation and pursuit (among other functions). People who are electrically stimulated in brain regions with high concentrations of dopamine terminals report intense feelings of well-being (Heath 1964). Illicit drug use activates the dopaminergic pathways of the reward system. Dopamine activity in the reward system appears to correlate with subjective reports of positive affect (Knutson, Adams, Fong, and Hommer 2001).

On the one hand, hypoactivation or desensitization of the reward system results in a propensity to feel apathetic, have low energy, and engage in compensatory excitement and novelty-seeking behaviors such as pathological gambling and compulsive shopping. On the other hand, short-term gains energize dopamine flow in the reward circuit.

Loss Avoidance

A second fundamental motivational circuit governs loss avoidance. The loss avoidance system is activated when the brain recognizes potential threats or dangers in one's environment. Anxiety, fear, and panic are emotions that arise from the loss avoidance system, and pessimistic and worried thoughts are the cognitive sequelae of loss system activation.

The brain's avoidance system is less defined than the reward system. It runs through several regions of the brain's limbic system, in particular, the amygdala and the anterior insula. Its activity is mediated by serotonin and norepinephrine (among other neurotransmitters) and can be modulated with antidepressant medication such as selective serotonin reuptake inhibitors (SSRIs). Acute activations of the loss avoidance system lead to the subjective experience and physiological signs of anxiety (Bechara, Damasio, and Damasio 2000).

Activation of the brain's loss system results in stress, anxiety, disgust, pain, and even panic. The behavioral bias of loss aversion is fueled by fears of disappointment and regret, and appears to arise from amygdala activation (DeMartino, Kumaran, Holt, and Dolan 2009). The anterior insula is an area of the primitive cortex that governs the experiences of disgust, pain, and loss (Wright, He, Shapira, Goodman, and Liu 2004). Anterior insula activation precedes excessive risk aversion in one investment experiment. The physical and mental effects of stress are generated by hormonal and chemical pathways in the loss avoidance system.

Loss avoidance system activation affects the entire body through bloodstream hormone and neurotransmitter release. The perception of a threat activates the hypothalamus-pituitary-adrenal axis (HPA axis), which results in stress hormone and epinephrine (adrenaline) secretion into the bloodstream. The body's sympathetic nervous system (SNS) prepares the whole body for the fight or flight response to danger with nerve signals transmitted to every major organ system. When under threat and experiencing fear, signs of SNS activation include trembling, perspiration, rapid heart rate, shallow breathing, and pupillary dilation. The SNS is also responsible for the physical signs and symptoms of panic. As discussed later in the chapter, the experience of market volatility raises cortisol (a stress hormone) levels in traders (Coates and Herbert 2008).

Chronic activation of the loss avoidance system is indicated by the personality trait of neuroticism (Flory, Manuck, Matthews, and Muldoon 2004). Neuroticism is characterized by risk aversion. The prevalence of neuroticism has been weakly associated with the short form (s-allele) of the serotonin transporter gene, which leads to a decrease in serotonin sensitivity (Arnold, Zai, and Richter 2004).

The brain's insula is involved in the anticipation of aversive affective and noxious physical stimuli (Simmons, Matthews, Stein, and Paulus 2004) and in selective disgust processing (Wright et al. 2004). Paulus et al. (2003) show that insula activation is related to risk-averse decision-making; they report that insula activation is significantly stronger when subjects selected a risky response versus selecting a safe response in an experimental task. Second, the researchers find that the degree of insula activation is related to the probability of selecting a safe response following a punished response. Third, the degree of insula activation is related to the subjects' degree of harm avoidance and neuroticism as measured by personality questionnaires.

Because the reward and loss systems influence thought and lie beneath awareness, they often direct behavior automatically through subtle (and overt) emotional influences on judgment, thinking, and behavior. Fortunately, investigators have many tools for assessing the health of the brain's reward and loss avoidance systems.

RESEARCH METHODS

Researchers use a variety of sophisticated tools to understand how the brain works. Neuroimaging is the most widely used technology for understanding decision-making among neurofinance researchers. Most of the neuroimaging studies cited in this chapter use functional magnetic resonance imaging (fMRI). Using fMRI allows researchers to visualize changes in oxygenated blood flow, which serves as a proxy for brain metabolism. fMRI can yield resolution of brain voxels as small as $1 \times 1 \times 1$ millimeters over time intervals of one second. Positron emission tomography (PET), which is an alternative neuroimaging technique to fMRI, has a larger spatial resolution of approximately $3 \times 3 \times 3$ millimeters and can detect changes in glucose metabolism and blood flow only when a radioactive tracer has been injected into the subject. Other less widely used imaging techniques include magnetic resonance spectroscopy (MRS) and optical tomography (a brain activity monitoring technique using infrared light). Since the mid-1990s, fMRI has become the most common neuroimaging technique due to its low invasiveness, lack of radiation exposure, and relatively wide availability.

Other investigative technologies include behavioral measures, subjective reports, psychological tests, and electrophysiology. Electrophysiology involves measurements of heart rate, blood pressure, galvanic skin response (sweating), and other physical variables, many of which are indicators of reactive brain activation in limbic and midbrain regions. Pupillary eye measurements allow researchers to directly monitor the activity of the sympathetic nervous system (SNS). The SNS is involved in the fight or flight panic response.

Electromyograghs (EMGs) measure electrical activity during muscle contraction. When EMGs are used on facial muscles, very subtle states of happiness and concern can be measured. For example, analysts who are excited about an investment idea may have greater activation of their *zygomatic* facial muscles when they talk about that investment. The zygomatic muscles control smiling. The frontalis muscle on the forehead is activated by concern, revealed in a furrowed brow, and may be more active in traders during stressful market volatility.

In the 1970s and 1980s, many decision-making researchers used electroencephalograms (EEGs) for experimentation. An EEG is a test used to detect fluctuations in the electrical activity of the surface of the brain's cortex. EEGs are often used clinically to diagnose seizures. Some psychotherapists use EEGs for emotional biofeedback (so-called neurofeedback).

Single-neuron recording techniques are very invasive and are performed primarily on monkeys and rats. Such techniques have allowed researchers to model the activity of tiny neuronal bundles, including those used while computing the expected value of various decision options (Glimcher 2003). Genetic sequencing technologies such as the polymerase chain reaction (PCR) have revealed that genes correlate with prominent personality and behavioral traits, including financial risk taking. Assays of blood, saliva, and cerebrospinal fluid allow researchers to measure hormones (such as those mediating trust, aggression, and the stress response) and neurotransmitters (including those involved in impulsiveness), although using current techniques saliva can only be used to measure stress hormones and for gene collection.

A research technique most often used by neurologists is the study of patients with specific brain lesions. This technique caught the interest of behavioral economists in the mid-1990s. Small brain lesions secondary to focused strokes or tumors can cause isolated impairments. These impairments can provide much information about the function of specific brain regions.

Manipulations of diet (including dietary restrictions such as branched amino acids to lower endogenous tryptophan levels) and administration of exogenous chemicals such as medications, foods, vitamins, hormones, and intoxicants (benzo-diazepines, amphetamines, cocaine, tetrahydrocannabinol (THC), and alcohol) sig-nificantly affect decision-making through known neural mechanisms.

Neurofinance researchers widely use standard psychological research tools. These tools include report surveys, behavioral observation (most neurofinance experiments attempt to correlate behavioral observation with neural or hormonal activity), personality testing such as the NEO, and specific psychometric instruments including affect, depression, anxiety, psychoticism, impulsivity, and intuition rating scales.

Monitoring individual states of arousal is layered voice analysis (LVA), which can measure stress in the voice. Textual analysis of one's stated preferences or affects may also be a useful technique in measuring and quantifying attitudes, beliefs, and affect states.

Neurofinance experiments often attempt to draw conclusions about the decision-making process, typically via correlations of observed brain activation or hormone levels with behavioral outcomes. To address the criticism that "correlation is not causation," many neurofinance researchers are working on behavioral prediction, and many of the studies cited in this chapter focus on such prediction.

Neurofinance research relies on experimental designs that elicit value-based decision-making. Money is a useful experimental tool because it can be used as both an incentive and a punishment, and it is scalable and universally valued. Besides money, many experiments use consumer products as performance incentives. In pro-spective studies, the actual spending, purchasing, borrowing, and portfolio activities of subjects can be monitored in order to investigate long-term outcomes.

Psychological states such as anticipation, deliberation, learning, updating, and calculation can be measured and observed using neuroimaging techniques such as fMRI. In most cases, neurofinance researchers' key findings are established by iden-tifying population (group) effects, key individual differences in decision-making, and via manipulation of the information and frame of a decision task.

THE NEUROSCIENCE OF FINANCIAL DECISION-MAKING

Biological factors can influence financial decision-making. This section reviews both the exogenous influencers and the endogenous processes influencing financial decision-making.

Medications and Drugs of Abuse Alter Financial Risk Taking

If decision-making is dependent to some extent on the brain's underlying neuro-chemical milieu, then dietary changes, medications and illicit drugs, exercise, and other techniques shown to alter the brain's neurochemical activity could alter decision-making. Researchers have performed numerous studies with medications, which are standardized in dosage and relatively simple to administer and monitor.

Researchers have identified medications that directly alter risk/return percep-tions in behavioral experiments. This should not be surprising when considering that anxiety disorders, which are treated by many pharmaceuticals, are disorders of risk perception. Rogers, Lancaster, Wakeley, and Bhagwagar (2004) report that a common high blood pressure medication in the beta blocker family decreased experimental subjects' ability to perceive potential financial losses during a risky task.

Researchers also demonstrate that drugs of abuse affect financial decisions. For example, Lane, Cherek, Tscheremissine, Lieving, and Pietras (2005) designed an experiment in which subjects were given a choice between a certain but low-value positive expected value option ($0.01) or a zero expected value option with high return variability (the risky option). THC intoxicated subjects preferred the risky option significantly more than control subjects who had been administered a placebo. If they lost money after selecting the risky option, THC intoxicated subjects were significantly more likely to persist with the risky selection, while controls were more likely to move to the positive expected value option. Lane et al. (2004) report a similar preference and persistence with the risky option in alcohol intoxicated subjects as compared to controls.

Many members of the benzodiazepine class of medications are Food and Drug Administration (FDA)-approved for treatment of anxiety disorders. Anxiety disorders are characterized by excessive increases in risk perception and correlated decreases in risk taking. In experimental environments, benzodiazepine administration is associated with a dose-dependent increase in financial risk taking (Lane, Cherek, and Nouvion 2008). Deakin et al. (2004) show that a dose of the benzodiazepine diazepam (Valium) increased the number of points wagered in a risk-taking task only in those trials with the lowest odds of winning but the highest potential payoff. Lane, Tcheremissine, Lieving, Nouvion, and Cherek (2005) report that administration of the benzodiazepine alprazolam (Xanax) produced increased selection of a risky option under laboratory conditions. Interestingly, the strength of a subject's risk-seeking personality traits may be predictive of acute drug effects on risk-taking behavior. The studies cited here illustrate that common chemical compounds can alter an individual's propensity toward risky choice.

Financial Risk Taking and the Reward and Loss Avoidance Systems

Kuhnen and Knutson (2005) demonstrate the roles of the reward and loss avoidance systems in portfolio choices and investment errors. The goals of their study are twofold: (1) to determine whether anticipatory brain activity in the NAcc and anterior insula would differentially predict risk-seeking versus risk-averse choices, and (2) to examine whether activation in these regions would influence both suboptimal and optimal choices. Their evidence shows that while NAcc activation preceded both risky choices and risk-seeking mistakes, anterior insula activation preceded both riskless choices and risk aversion mistakes. These findings are consistent with the hypothesis that NAcc activation represents gain prediction (Knutson et al. 2001), while anterior insula activation represents loss prediction (Paulus et al. 2003). Therefore, the results indicate that beyond contributing to rational choice, anticipatory neural activation may also promote irrational choice. Thus, financial decision-making may require a delicate balance—recruitment of distinct anticipatory mechanisms may be necessary for taking or avoiding risks, but excessive activation of one mechanism or the other may lead to mistakes.

Overall, these findings suggest that two distinct neural mechanisms involving the NAcc and the anterior insula drive risk-seeking choices (e.g., gambling at a casino) and risk-averse choices (e.g., buying insurance). The findings are consistent with the notion that activation in the NAcc and the anterior insula, respectively, index positive and negative anticipatory affective states, and that activating one of these two regions can lead to a shift in risk preferences. This may explain why casinos surround their guests with reward cues (i.e., inexpensive food, free liquor, surprise gifts, and potential jackpot prizes)—anticipation of rewards activates the NAcc, which may lead to an increase in the likelihood of individuals switching from risk-averse to risk-seeking behavior.

Researchers find that positively exciting environmental cues can increase financial risk-taking. Risk taking is increased following activation of the subject's NAcc via priming with external pictures or video clips. Seeing a sexy picture activates the NAcc and makes subjects more likely to take a lower expected value gamble (Knutson, Wimmer, Kuhnen 2008). Furthermore, having experienced a recent "win" in an investment simulation makes subjects more likely to take an "irrational" risk (Kuhnen and Knutson 2005). In an experimental bubble, viewing an exciting video clip before trading begins increases the amplitude of the price bubble (Odean, Lin, and Andrade 2012). Knutson , Wimmer, Rick (2008) identify two clear predictors of purchasing. Activation of the NAcc demonstrated "liking" of consumer products, which predicted buying. Additionally, perceiving that a consumer item is cheap or on sale leads to activation of the MPFC, which predicts buying behavior (Knutson et al. 2007).

The Genetics of Financial Decision-Making

In the financial markets, researchers have found genetic markers that predispose individuals to higher levels of risky financial decision-making. In a genetic study by Kuhnen and Chiao (2009), subjects who have the DRD4 gene 7-repeat allele take 25 percent more risk in an investment task, while those with two copies of the short serotonin transporter gene (5-HTTLPR s/s) take 28 percent less risk.

In contrast to Kuhnen and Chiao's (2009) findings, Frydman et al. (2010) do not identify differences in risk taking across DRD4 allele and 5-HTT polymorphism carriers. The authors do, however, find a significant relationship with the MAOA-L gene. The MAOA gene produces an enzyme involved in catabolism of dopamine, norepinephrine, and serotonin. The abnormal variant MAOA-L is more active. Behavioral traits associated with this gene include impulsive risk taking and aggression. Those with this gene take more financial risks, but with higher expected utility. For these reasons, the gene has been nicknamed "The Warrior Gene." As Frydman et al. (p. 1) note, "Our computational choice model, rooted in established decision theory, showed that MAOA-L carriers exhibited such behavior because they are able to make better financial decisions under risk, and not because they are more impulsive."

Neurofinance researchers such as Mohr, Li, and Heekeren (2010) also find alterations in risk taking over the life span, with age-related changes in financial risk taking. For example, as a presumed result of the biological change that accompanies early life experiences and changes in dopaminergic and serontonergic transmission over the life span, the saving and investment patterns of people who came of age during traumatic economic events (e.g., the Great Depression or periods of low stock returns) are different from those who did not (Malmendier and Nagel 2009). Evidence also suggests that adolescents exhibit a different neural reaction to financial advice than adults (Engelmann, Moore, Capra, and Berns 2012). Researchers using the Swedish Twin Registry find that 25 percent of the individual variation in investment risk taking is due to genetic factors (Cesarini et al. 2010). This genetic variation in behavior also applies to investment style choices including such specific investment products as ethical/sustainable investment products.

Disposition Effect

Several neurofinance researchers investigate the tenets of prospect theory, with examinations of the neural correlates of loss aversion, reference point setting, the endowment effect, the disposition effect, and the repurchase effect. Neurofinance researchers find that some investors are more susceptible to the disposition effect (taking excessive risk in the realm of losses) and that this increased susceptibility can be traced to specific neural activations. Personality studies identify individuals with high neuroticism scores as having more reactive anterior insulas in the context of experiencing losses. When using personality testing and neuroimaging in tandem, the accuracy of predicting which individuals will exhibit risk seeking in the realm of losses may increase.

Neuroscientists in London designed an experiment that uses framing to elicit the neural process underlying loss aversion. In an fMRI study at University College London, Benedetto De Martino recruited 20 men and women to undergo three 17-minute brain scans. At the start of each trial, the subjects received English pounds worth about $95. The researchers then asked them to make a choice between receiving a certain outcome (a gain or a loss) and taking a gamble. The gamble they could accept was a simple 50–50 bet in which they wagered a predefined amount of their money. The gamble's expected value was equivalent to that of the certain option, so there was no financial reason subjects should show a preference for either the certain outcome or the gamble (De Martino et al. 2006).

When the researchers framed the choice as a decision between "keeping" a certain amount of money and gambling, most participants chose to "keep" their money. For example, when told they would keep 40 percent of the starting sum if they chose not to gamble (as in "Keep $38"), the volunteers typically played it safe, choosing to take the 50–50 gamble only 43 percent of the time. When told they would lose 60 percent of their initial pot if they did not gamble, they took the risk 62 percent of the time, even though the gambles always had the same expected value as the certain option. Interestingly, De Martino et al.'s (2006) results provide evidence that loss aversion is induced by the language used to frame a risky choice.

The subjects had the odds explained to them in detail before the experiment, and they knew that the probabilities in each situation were identical. Nonetheless, the language altered their decisions: "Keep $38" put them in a gain frame, and "Lose $38" induced a loss frame. When succumbing to loss aversion, the subjects' amygdalas (stimulated by danger) activated vigorously. When participants resisted the framing effect, the orbitofrontal cortex (involved in integrating emotion and reason) and the anterior cingulate cortex (responsible for sorting out internal conflicts) both activated. Four of the study participants acknowledged inconsistencies in their decision-making, choosing according to the frame rather than the odds. In explaining their actions, they said, "I know, I just couldn't help myself," according to De Martino (Vergano 2006, p. D4).

In a subsequent fMRI study, De Martino et al. (2009) demonstrate that two distinct neural circuits activated in response to expected value computation (reference point-independent values). They also find that a reference point (in this case ownership, as seen in the endowment effect) distorted the value computation. Their results show that activity in the orbitofrontal cortex and dorsal striatum tracked parameters such as expected value. In contrast, activity in the ventral striatum (the ventral striatum contains the NAcc) indexed the degree to which stated prices were distorted with respect to a reference point.

The *disposition effect*—the tendency to be risk averse in the domain of gains (sell winners too soon) and to be risk seeking in the domain of losses (hold losers too long)—is a behavioral bias thought to result from the framing effect. A study on the disposition effect by Brooks, Capra, and Berns (2012) identifies that neural activity in the ventral striatum may represent a psychological mechanism for the disposition effect in the domain of losses. In particular, the authors find that when an asset undergoing random walk price action falls below the purchase price, individuals who show attenuated ventral striatum activation during price upticks—only when the price is below the purchase price—also demonstrate a greater disposition effect. In explanation, Brooks et al. (p. 1) assert, "for some individuals, the disposition effect is likely driven by a belief that the asset will eventually return to the purchase price. . . ." This belief that the asset price will rise back to the purchase price accounts for the diminished reaction in the ventral striatum—the price rise was expected.

Knutson, Wimmer, Rick (2008) identify the right anterior insula as the brain structure whose activation is most predictive of the endowment effect as shown in Exhibit 21.3. When an individual experiences the potential pain of losing an endowed item (via selling the item) more acutely as seen in their greater activation of the right anterior insula, then they are more likely to exhibit the endowment effect by demanding a much higher sale price.

As would be expected if a human brain evolved from those of other primates, capuchin monkeys are susceptible to loss aversion and the endowment effect

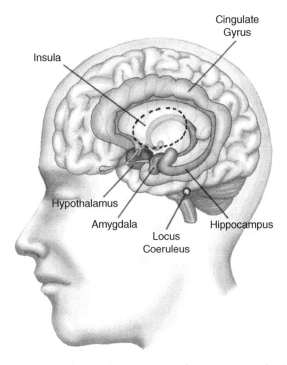

EXHIBIT 21.3 An Illustration of Several Structures in the Brain's Loss Avoidance System

Note: The loss avoidance system is distributed throughout several brain structures. These underlying structures are involved in detecting, processing, learning about, and responding to potential threats.

(Chen, Lakshminarayanan, and Santos 2006). Furthermore, loss aversion is not age-dependent. Human children, while unable to express gambles in terms of expected value, also demonstrate loss aversion, with no age-diminishing influence through college (Harbaugh, Krause, and Vesterlund 2002).

In a series of detailed experiments comprising both behavioral and neural data collection, Cary Frydman and colleagues at the California Institute of Technology identify drivers of the repurchase effect among traders. The *repurchase effect* refers to a tendency for traders to buy stocks they previously owned that have declined in value and avoid buying stocks they previously owned that have gone up in value. Of the 28 experimental traders in Frydman's study, all exhibit the repurchase effect (Frydman 2012).

Neural evidence reported by Frydman suggests that a regret signal—a counterfactual comparison—in the brain's ventral striatum (which contains the NAcc) drives the repurchase effect. Frydman finds that individuals with a high propensity to sell stocks with capital gains appear to have a low propensity to repurchase stocks with strong recent performance. Using a neural proxy for regret, he then identifies that this regret signal is encoded in the left ventral striatum. Frydman (p. 79) concludes that "experienced regret is a mediating factor of the inaction inertia effect," in which traders do not act to buy rising stocks they previously owned due to regret-fueled inertia. Those traders who have a stronger regret signal are predisposed to the repurchase effect—buying stocks they previously owned that have dropped, but not buying the same stocks if they have risen from the sale price.

Intertemporal Choice and Impulsivity

In experiments, most subjects discount future rewards, pursuing smaller sooner rewards rather than waiting for larger later ones, Thus, they sacrifice a rate of return on their money far greater than any they could earn via an average investment. The fact that most individuals "leave money on the table" by seeking rewards immediately rather than waiting has prompted inquiry from neurofinance researchers into the mechanisms by which such discounting occurs (also known as *hyperbolic discounting*).

Samuel McClure, a neuroscientist at Princeton University, performed a brain-imaging experiment with colleagues on volunteers engaged in a time discounting task. He gave subjects several decision pairs and asked them to state their preferences between them. For example, they could choose between an Amazon.com gift certificate worth $20.28 today and one worth $23.32 in one month. In a longer-term example, researchers asked subjects to, for example, choose between $30 in two weeks and $40 in six weeks (McClure et al. 2004).

McClure et al. (2004) find that time discounting results from the combined influence of two neural systems. Limbic regions drive choices in favor of immediately available rewards. The frontal and parietal cortices are recruited for all choices. These two systems are separately implicated in emotional and cognitive brain processes, and a competition appears between the two systems during discounting-type decisions, with higher limbic activation indicating a greater likelihood that immediate gratification will be pursued.

McClure et al. (2004) also find that when experimental subjects choose larger delayed rewards, cortical areas such as the lateral and prefrontal cortex show activity enhancement. These brain regions are associated with higher-level cognitive functions including planning and numerical calculation. McClure's theory is supported by a finding that in prisoners the cortical regions activated by delayed gratification are thinned. This may explain why their decisions are more often shortsighted than others (Yang et al. 2005). According to McClure et al. (p. 506), "Our results help to explain why many factors other than temporal proximity, such as the sight or smell or touch of a desired object, are associated with impulsive behavior. If limbic activation drives impatient behavior, it follows that any factor that produces such activation may have effects similar to that of immediacy." According to McClure et al., immediacy in time may be only one of many factors that, by producing limbic activation, engenders impatience and impulsive action.

Researchers find that temporal discounting may be a result of dual competing valuation mechanisms in the brain. In one circuit, the reward system values the magnitude of potential gains, while in the other network, the dorsolateral prefrontal cortex and other structures deactivate in response to the delay that must be experienced (Ballard and Knutson 2009).

The delay of a potential reward introduces uncertainty. Uncertainty decreases financial risk taking, especially when it is associated with ambiguity in payout probability or outcome magnitude, and the difference between uncertain versus ambiguous financial risks can be seen and tracked in neural activation patterns (Hsu et al. 2005).

Beyond impatience for financial rewards, a study of dieting finds that gastronomic impulse control appears to be based in circuitry shared with financial prudence. Self-control appears to be biologically modulated by a value signal encoded in the ventromedial prefrontal cortex (vmPFC). Exercising self-control involves the modulation of that value signal by the dorsolateral prefrontal cortex (DLPFC) (Hare, Camerer, and Rangel 2009). Unfortunately, like a muscle that becomes tired from overwork, practicing self-control depletes cognitive resources for future self-control. During periods of high cognitive load—multitasking or complex problem solving—external support prevents common errors. Neuroscientists find that financial advice reduces the cognitive load of individuals in an investing task (Engelmann et al. 2009). For this reason, individuals may seek financial advice afterward despite little evidence of financial benefit. The benefit of financial advice is in freeing up cognitive and emotional energy so that it may be expended elsewhere. In the case of selecting retirement savings accounts with varying penalties, individuals who are aware of their own weak self-control voluntarily increase punishments if they break their own savings agreement. Presumably they take this irrational action to prevent making choices they will later regret.

Emotions and Testosterone in the Trading Pit

Several researchers gather neuroecononomic data directly from traders. Lo and Repin (2002) take psychophysiological measurements from 10 traders during real-time intraday trading and find that traders experience physiological reactions during periods of market volatility. The study also shows that less experienced traders have significantly greater physiological reactivity to market volatility than their more experienced colleagues. Lo and Repin (p. 332) conclude, "Contrary to the common belief that emotions have no place in rational financial decision-making processes, physiological variables associated with the autonomic nervous system are highly correlated with market events even for highly experienced professional traders."

Coates and Herbert (2008) sample, under real working conditions, endogenous steroids from a group of male traders in the City of London. They report that a trader's testosterone level at 11 A.M. correlates with trading profitability over the remainder of the day. They also find that a trader's cortisol rises with both the variance of his trading results and the volatility of the market. Their results suggest that higher testosterone may contribute to economic return for traders, whereas cortisol appears to increase under conditions of increased risk perception. The authors postulate that testosterone and cortisol, because they are known to have cognitive and behavioral effects, may shift risk preferences and even affect a trader's ability to engage in rational choice as market conditions change.

Building on evidence that prenatal (in-utero) exposure to sex hormones (specifically androgens) affects future behavior, Coates, Gurnell, and Rustichini (2009) perform a follow-up study on the second-to-fourth digit length ratio (2D:4D), where a relatively longer fourth finger indicates higher prenatal androgen exposure. In a group of male traders engaged in what is variously called "noise" or "high-frequency" trading, the authors find that 2D:4D predicts the traders' long-term profitability as well as the number of years they remain in the business. 2D:4D also predicts the sensitivity of their profitability to increases both in circulating testosterone and in market volatility. In terms of profitability, the top one-third of the traders in terms of 2D:4D are 11 times more profitable than the bottom third.

The authors conclude that prenatal androgens increase risk preferences and promote more rapid visuomotor scanning and physical reflexes. The success and longevity of traders exposed to high levels of prenatal androgens further suggests that financial markets may select for biological traits rather than rational expectations.

The results of these studies suggest that hormonal exposure, whether in-utero or in real time as a result of market events, apparently affects profitability and risk taking. This hormonal evidence contributes to understanding neuroimaging data. Testosterone may increase dopamine secretion, such as that seen in fMRI experiments cited here, thus leading to increased financial risk taking through a neural mechanism.

Gender Differences in Neurology and Financial Behavior

While studies show that testosterone and cortisol levels affect financial decision-making in male traders, researchers have not directly studied the relationship between female trader biology and performance. However, the menstrual cycle appears to change how women deal with risky situations. While men may be more hormonally reactive to specific external events and competitive pressures, women have an internal hormonal cycle that significantly alters their risk taking and emotional state independent of external events. Phases of the menstrual cycle correlate with different risk taking in some studies, but not all studies on this topic have congruent findings. The risk-taking differences that occur over the female menstrual cycle appear due to hormone-modulated neural activity in the brain (Dreher et al. 2007).

THE IMPLICATIONS OF NEUROFINANCE RESEARCH FOR PRACTITIONERS

Currently no evidence-based decision tool based on neurofinance research is available to improve individual investment decision-making. Numerous technical limitations constrain the real-world application of tools such as fMRI and facial EMG for trader decision-making. Genetic studies, which may provide valuable insight into risk management style, remain controversial and demonstrate disparate findings. Electrophysiologic monitoring devices, some of which have been commercialized for traders, have not yet been empirically shown to increase trader performance. Psychopharmaceutical interventions such as psychostimulants (e.g., amphetamine derivatives) and hormone augmentation (e.g., testosterone) have numerous side effects and no clear benefits for the average financial decision maker.

As Lo and Repin (2002) and Coates and Herbert (2008) demonstrate, professionals are physiologically reactive and release stress hormones (cortisol) in response to market volatility, which changes cognition and in some cases increases biased decision-making. Many decision makers find the development of an analytic process and the presence of a human coach to improve their decision-making and financial outcomes. Several behavioral interventions to moderate innate affective responses are presented in Exhibit 21.4. Additionally, several cognitive practices reduce the deleterious cognitive effects of reactive hormones including reframing, self-awareness, and reappraisal, all of which are discussed in this section and outlined in Exhibit 21.5.

Meditation, peaceful reflection, and contemplation are disciplines used for millennia to manage reactive mental states via self-awareness. Evidence supports the value of self-awareness in improving trader performance. For example, Biais et al. (2002, p. 3) find that "highly self-monitoring" traders perform better than their peers in an experimental market. While noticing affect states is important, avoiding placing any value judgment on them is crucial. Many of the most successful practitioners in the financial industry, including Ray Dalio, chief executive officer (CEO) of Bridgewater Associates, the largest hedge fund in the United States, and Bill Gross,

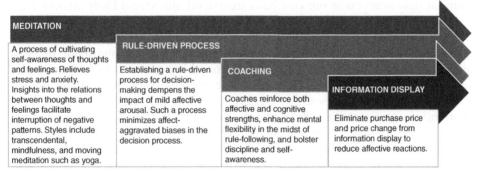

EXHIBIT 21.4 An Outline of Behavioral Strategies to Manage Affective Reactions and Improve Financial Decision-Making

Note: Successful financial practitioners use strategies such as meditation, establishing a rule-driven process, using a coach, and altering information display to reduce emotional (affective) arousal and resulting misjudgments.

CEO of PIMCO, the largest fixed income fund in the world, use daily meditative practices to cultivate self-awareness. Dalio practices transcendental meditation, and Gross practices Ashtanga yoga. Financial practitioners may practice noticing the thoughts, feelings, and attitudes that underlie their decision-making and notice the deleterious patterns in their behavior. Once these patterns are conscious, people can make plans for avoiding or eliminating their impact.

Many hedge funds use performance coaches with clinical psychology and psychiatry training who can respond dynamically to trader needs with clinical affective and cognitive interventions across circumstances. For example, Steve Cohen, billionaire CEO of SAC Capital—one of the consistently most successful hedge funds in the world—employed Ari Kiev, M.D. (now deceased) as an in-house performance coach for himself and his portfolio managers for over 15 years. Paul Tudor Jones, CEO of Tudor Investment Corporation, employs clinical and academic psychologist Brett Steenbarger, PhD, who specializes in trader psychology and short-term therapies, to coach Tudor portfolio managers and traders. Many other examples of such in-house coaches in the financial industry are available.

Many successful financial practitioners such as Dalio systematize as much of their decision-making process as possible. Dalio and Bridgewater are well-known for their Principles, a collection of written ethos that employees are expected to model. Dalio's firm follows simple macroeconomic investment rules that are designed to preempt decision biases from adversely influencing analyst judgment and portfolio manager decision-making. Such rule-following approaches provide distance between the decision maker and the decision outcome, thus reducing the negative impact of losses on judgment biases.

How information about investment returns is displayed significantly affects trading behavior, presumably through its impact on affect and arousal and the subsequent exacerbation of cognitive biases. Fortunately, the display of information can be optimized to reduce biased trading (Frydman 2012). Displaying the original purchase price of a stock and its recent change in value increased the repurchase bias in an experimental market. Frydman (p. 111) offers the following prescription in contrast to current regulatory policy: "If regulators stipulate that brokerage houses decrease the saliency of the capital gain by removing the cost basis from the regular financial statements (as in our cost basis treatment), this would likely attenuate the disposition effect, and could increase individual investor trading performance."

In addition to the previously discussed behavioral strategies to improve affect management, several cognitive interventions are available for improving decision quality, as seen in Exhibit 21.5. A decision journal is a common tool for recording and reviewing feedback about decision-making patterns over time. As in meditation, a decision journal improves self-awareness by making the individual conscious the relationships among feelings, thoughts, and behaviors. The challenge with a journal is maintaining a nonjudgmental perspective on past losses and gains because reviewing past losses itself can create an adverse response. For this reason, a journal is best utilized after establishing a meditation practice, when one can reframe losses as positive feedback for learning.

Neuroscientific evidence supports the practice of reframing realized financial losses as intellectual gains. George Soros is one of the most celebrated traders in market history, and he finds that reframing results from a "Belief in Fallibility." Soros (1995) explains that to others being wrong is a source of shame. But for Soros,

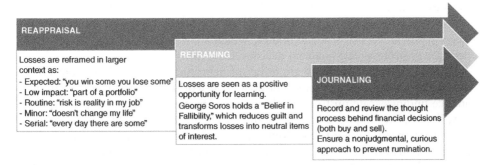

EXHIBIT 21.5   An Outline of Cognitive Strategies for Strengthening Financial Decision-Making

Note: Research shows that cognitive strategies including reappraisal, reframing, and decision journaling can reduce financial decision biases.

recognizing his mistakes is a source of pride. Soros explains that realizing that imperfect understanding is the human condition leads to no shame in being wrong, only in failing to correct our mistakes.

Researchers find that cognitive "reappraisal" reduces the impact of loss aversion on decision-making (Sokol-Hessner et al. 2009). *Reappraisal* refers to taking a perspective of a situation along several dimensions. Consider that in an experimental condition, researchers randomly ask subjects to think of their individual investments under the following conditions: (1) as part of a portfolio, (2) as one of many in a series, (3) as part of a routine job, (4) as expecting that losses are going to happen ("you win some and you lose some"), and (5) as not having direct consequences for their lives. In aggregate these cognitive reappraisals reduce both physiological reactions to losses (measured via galvanic skin response) and subsequent loss-averse behavior. According to Sokol-Hessner et al. (p. 1), "'perspective-taking,' uniquely reduced both behavioral loss aversion and arousal to losses relative to gains, largely by influencing arousal to losses."

SUMMARY

While biological predispositions affect the human mind, neurofinance is an emerging discipline whose key findings need replication and comprehensive modeling. Examples of biologically mediated influences on financial decision-making discussed in this chapter include medications, drugs of abuse, hormones, dietary restrictions, dietary additions, expert financial advice, massage, recent events (gains and losses), early life events, and framing decision options.

Important critiques of neurofinance address the lack of experimental replication of many early findings. Neurofinance studies are often expensive. Many researchers push the boundaries of existing decision science rather than replicating the studies of colleagues.

Another criticism focuses on sample sizes and composition. Because fMRI and other techniques are expensive and research funds can be difficult to procure for novel research, many fMRI studies use small samples of 20 or less. The subjects in these studies are typically students. Given observed differences in the biological substrates of decision-making over the life span, results found with young samples may not be confirmed for older individuals. Additionally, researchers draw most subjects from university student bodies, which may not reflect the learning and experience of professional financial decision makers.

Another concern is the ultimate utility of neurofinance research. Findings from very specific studies may not represent noisy real-world decision-making. Can neurofinance findings scale up to? Can the research results be used to improve public policy, financial trading, product marketing, and education? Some express concern that neurofinance thinking is too "reductionistic." The criticism goes that neurofinance researchers try to explain and model human behavior based on small pieces of data and anatomical findings, without taking into account the entire complex person, complete with conflicts, contradictions, and mixed motives.

As this chapter explains, neurofinance comprises an interdisciplinary approach to the question of how behavioral and cognitive biases influence investor behavior. Recent neurofinance research is deciphering how the environment of financial decision makers and the context of their work can be modified to optimize financial decision-making. Many of the most successful financial practitioners in history, including George Soros, Ray Dalio, Bill Gross, and Steve A. Cohen evolved decision strategies that strengthen decision vulnerabilities now identified as such in neurofinance research.

DISCUSSION QUESTIONS

1. As compared to classic studies in behavioral finance, how does neurofinance achieve additional explanatory power over nonoptimal financial decision-making?
2. Biologically speaking, what are some brain structures and chemicals that influence financial decision-making?
3. What techniques, supported by neurofinance, do successful financial practitioners use to improve their performance?
4. Identify the major criticisms of neurofinance research.

REFERENCES

Arnold, Paul D., Gwyneth Zai, and Margaret A. Richter. 2004. "Genetics and Anxiety Disorders." *Current Psychiatry Reports* 6:4, 243–254.

Ballard, Kacey, and Brian Knutson. 2009. "Dissociable Neural Representations of Future Reward Magnitude and Delay during Temporal Discounting." *NeuroImage* 45:1, 143–150.

Bechara, Antoine, Hannah Damasio, and Antonio R. Damasio. 2000. "Emotion, Decision Making and the Orbitofrontal Cortex." *Cerebral Cortex* 10:3, 295–307.

Biais, Bruno, Denis Hilton, Karine Mazurier, and Sébastien Pouge. 2002. "Psychological Traits and Trading Strategies." Working Paper, Centre for Economic Policy Research. Available at http://papers.ssrn.com/sol3/papers.cfm?abstract_id=302026.

Bozarth, Michael A. 1994. "Pleasure Systems in the Brain." In David M. Warburton, ed., *Pleasure: The Politics and the Reality*, 5–14. New York: John Wiley & Sons.

Brooks, Andrew M., Monica C. Capra, and Gregory S. Berns. 2012. "Neural Insensitivity to Upticks in Value Is Associated with the Disposition Effect." *Neuroimage*, 59:4, 4086–4093.

Cesarini, David, Magnus Johannesson, Paul Lichtenstein, Örjan Sandewall, and Björn Wallace. 2010. "Genetic Variation in Financial Decision-Making." *Journal of Finance* 65:5, 1725–1754.

Chen, M. Keith, Venkat Lakshminarayanan, and Laurie R. Santos. 2006. "How Basic Are Behavioral Biases? Evidence from Capuchin Monkey Trading Behavior." *Journal of Political Economy* 114:3, 517–537.

Coates John M., Mark Gurnell, and Aldo Rustichini. 2009. "Second-to-Fourth Digit Ratio Predicts Success among High-frequency Financial Traders." *Proceedings of the National Academy of Sciences* 106:2, 623–628.

Coates, John M., and Joe Herbert. 2008. "Endogenous Steroids and Financial Risk-Taking on a London Trading Floor." *Proceedings of the National Academy of Sciences* 105:16, 6167–6172.

Deakin Julia B., Michael Aitken, Jonathon Dowson, Trevor Robbins, and Barbara Sahakian. 2004. "Diazepam Produces Disinhibitory Cognitive Effects in Male Volunteers." *Psychopharmacology* 173:1–2, 88–97.

De Martino, Benedetto, Dharshan Kumaran, Beatrice Holt, and Raymond J. Dolan. 2009. "The Neurobiology of Reference-Dependent Value Computation." *Journal of Neuroscience* 29:12, 3833–3842.

De Martino, Benedetto, Dharshan Kumaran, Ben Seymour, and Raymond J. Dolan. 2006. "Biases and Rational Decision-Making in the Human Brain." *Science* 313:5787, 684–687.

Dreher, Jean-Claude, Peter J. Schmidt, Philip Kohn, Daniella Furman, David Rubinow, and Karen Faith Berman. 2007. "Menstrual Cycle Phase Modulates Reward-Related Neural Function in Women." *Proceedings of the National Academy of Sciences* 104:7, 2465–2470.

Engelmann, Jan B., C. Monica Capra, Charles Noussair, and Gregory S. Berns. 2009. "Expert Financial Advice Neurobiologically 'Offloads' Financial Decision-Making under Risk." *PLoS ONE* 4:3, e4957.

Engelmann, Jan B., Sara Moore, C. Monica Capra, and Gregory S. Berns. 2012. "Differential Neurobiological Effects of Expert Advice on Risky Choice in Adolescents and Adults." *SCAN* 7:5, 557–567.

Flory, Janine D., Stephen B. Manuck, Karen A. Matthews, and Matthew F. Muldoon. 2004. "Serotonergic Function in the Central Nervous System Is Associated with Daily Ratings of Positive Mood." *Psychiatry Research* 129:1, 11–19.

Frydman, Cary. 2012. "Essays in Neurofinance." Doctoral Dissertation. California Institute of Technology, Pasadena, CA. Available at http://thesis.library.caltech.edu/7076/.

Frydman, Cary, Colin Camerer, Peter Bossaerts, and Antonio Rangel. 2010. "MAOA-L Carriers Are Better at Making Optimal Financial Decisions under Risk." *Proceedings of the Royal Society B.* 278:1714, 2053–2059.

Glimcher, Paul W. 2003. *Decisions, Uncertainty, and the Brain: The Science of Neuroeconomics.* Cambridge, MA: MIT Press.

Harbaugh, William, Kate Krause, and Lise Vesterlund. 2002. "Prospect Theory in Choice and Pricing Tasks." Working Paper, Economics Department, University of Oregon.

Hare, Todd A., Colin F. Camerer, and Antonio Rangel. 2009. "Self-Control in Decision-Making Involves Modulation of the vmPFC Valuation System." *Science* 324:5927, 646–648.

Heath, Robert Galbraith. 1964. "Pleasure Response of Human Subjects to Direct Stimulation of the Brain: Physiologic and Psychodynamic Considerations." In Robert Galbraith Heath, ed., *The Role of Pleasure in Human Behavior*, 219–243. New York: Hoeber.

Hsu, Ming, Meghana Bhatt, Ralph Adolphs, Daniel Tranel, and Colin F. Camerer. 2005. "Neural Systems Responding to Degrees of Uncertainty in Human Decision-Making." *Science* 310:5754, 1680–1683.

Knutson, Brian, Christopher Adams, Grace W. Fong, and Daniel Hommer. 2001. "Anticipation of Increasing Monetary Reward Selectively Recruits Nucleus Accumbens." *Journal of Neuroscience* 21:RC159, 1–5.

Knutson, Brian, Grace Fong, Christopher S. Adams, and Daniel Hommer. 2001. "Dissociation of Reward Anticipation versus Outcome with Event-related FMRI." *NeuroReport* 12:174, 3683–3687.

Knutson, Brian, Scott Rick, G. Elliott Wimmer, Drazen Prelec, and George Loewenstein. 2007. "Neural Predictors of Purchases." *Neuron* 53:1, 147–157.

Knutson, Brian, G. Elliott Wimmer, Camelia M. Kuhnen, and Piotr Winkielman. 2008. "Nucleus Accumbens Activation Mediates the Influence of Reward Cues on Financial Risk Taking." *NeuroReport* 19:5, 509–513.

Knutson, Brian, G. Elliott Wimmer, Scott Rick, Nick G. Hollon, Drazen Prelec, and George Loewenstein. 2008. "Neural Antecedents of the Endowment Effect." *Neuron* 58:5, 814–822.

Kuhnen, Camelia M., and Joan Y. Chiao. 2009. "Genetic Determinants of Financial Risk Taking." *PLoS ONE* 4:2, e4362. Available at doi:10.1371/journal.pone.0004362.

Kuhnen, Camelia M., and Brian Knutson. 2005. "The Neural Basis of Financial Risk-Taking." *Neuron* 47:5, 763–770.

Lane, Scott D., Don R. Cherek, Cynthia J. Pietras, and Oleg V. Tcheremissine. 2004. "Alcohol Effects on Human Risk Taking." *Psychopharmacology* 172:1, 68–77.

Lane, Scott D., Don R. Cherek, and Sylvain Nouvion. 2008. "Modulation of Human Risky Decision Making by Flunitrazepam." *Psychopharmacology (Berl)* 196:2, 177–188.

Lane, Scott D., Don R. Cherek, Oleg V. Tcheremissine, Lori M. Lieving, and Cynthia J. Pietras. 2005. "Acute Marijuana Effects on Human Risk Taking." *Neuropsychopharmacology* 30:4, 800–809.

Lane, Scott D., Oleg V. Tcheremissine, Lori M. Lieving, Sylvain Nouvion, and Don R. Cherek. 2005. "Acute Effects of Alprazolam on Risky Decision Making in Humans." *Psychopharmacology* 181:2, 364–373.

Lo, Andrew, and Dmitry Repin. 2002. "The Psychophysiology of Real-Time Financial Risk Processing." *Journal of Cognitive Neuroscience* 14:3, 323–339.

MacLean, Paul D. 1990. *The Triune Brain in Evolution: Role in Paleocerebral Functions.* New York: Plenum Press.

Malmendier, Ulrike, and Stefan Nagel. 2009. "Depression Babies: Do Macroeconomic Experiences Affect Risk-Taking?" NBER Working Paper Series, Volume 14813. Available at http://ssrn.com/abstract=1369049.

McClure, Sam M., David I. Laibson, George Loewenstein, and Jonathan D. Cohen. 2004. "Separate Neural Systems Value Immediate and Delayed Monetary Rewards." *Science* 306:5695, 503–507.

Mohr, Peter N. C., Shu-Chen Li, and Hauke R. Heekeren. 2010. "Neuroeconomics and Aging: Neuromodulation of Economic Decision Making in Old Age." *Neuroscience & Biobehavioral Reviews* 34:5, 678–688.

Odean, Terrance, Shengle Lin, and Eduardo Andrade. 2012. "Bubbling with Excitement: An Experiment." Available at http://ssrn.com/abstract=2024549 or http://dx.doi.org/10.2139/ssrn.2024549.

Paulus, Martin P., Corianne Rogalsky, Alan Simmons, Justin S Feinstein, and Murray B. Stein. 2003. "Increased Activation in the Right Insula during Risk-Taking Decision Making Is Related to Harm Avoidance and Neuroticism." *NeuroImage* 19:4, 1439–1448.

Prabhakaran, Vivek, Bart Rypma, and John Gabrieli. 2001. "Neural Substrates of Mathematical Reasoning: A Functional Magnetic Resonance Imaging Study of Neocortical Activation during Performance of the Necessary Arithmetic Operations Test." *Neuropsychology* 15:1, 115–127.

Rogers, R. D., M. Lancaster, J. Wakeley, and Z. Bhagwagar. 2004. "Effects of Beta-adrenoceptor Blockade on Components of Human Decision-Making." *Psychopharmacology* 172:2, 157–164.

Simmons, Alan, Scott C. Matthews, Murray B. Stein, and Martin P. Paulus. 2004. "Anticipation of Emotionally Aversive Visual Stimuli Activates Right Insula." *Neuroreport* 15:14, 2261–2265.

Sokol-Hessner, Peter, Ming Hsu, Nina G Curleya, Mauricio R. Delgado, Colin F. Camerer, and Elizabeth F. Phelps. 2009. "Thinking Like a Trader Selectively Reduces Individuals' Loss Aversion." *Proceedings of the National Academy of Sciences* 106:13, 5035–5040.

Soros, George. 1995. *Soros on Soros*. New York: John Wiley & Sons.

Spencer, Herbert. 1880. *Principles of Psychology*. New York: Appleton Press.

Vergano, Dan. 2006. "Study: Ask with Care: Emotion Rules the Brain's Decisions." *USA Today*, August 7, D4.

Wright, Paul, G. He, Nathan A. Shapira, Wayne K. Goodman, and Yijun Liu. 2004. "Disgust and the Insula: fMRI Responses to Pictures of Mutilation and Contamination." *Neuroreport* 15:15, 2347–2351.

Yang, Yaling, Adrian Raine, Todd Lencz, Susan Bihrle, Lori LaCasse, and Patrick Colletti. 2005. "Volume Reduction in Prefrontal Gray Matter in Unsuccessful Criminal Psychopaths." *Biological Psychiatry* 57:10, 1103–1108.

ABOUT THE AUTHOR

Richard L. Peterson, MD, works at the intersection of psychology and financial markets, both as a portfolio manager and a consultant. He is the CEO of the MarketPsych Group, which offers behavioral training and consulting, sentiment data and investment research, and asset management services (www.marketpsych. com). Dr. Peterson's financial psychology research has been published in leading academic journals and textbooks and profiled in the financial media including CNBC, NPR, and the BBC. His book, *Inside the Investor's Brain* (John Wiley & Sons, 2007), was praised as "outstanding" and a "seminal text" by *Barrons* magazine. Dr. Peterson earned *cum laude* degrees in electrical engineering (BS), arts (BA), and medicine (MD) from the University of Texas. He performed postgraduate neuroeconomics research at Stanford University and is Board-certified in psychiatry. He lives in the New York area with his family.

CHAPTER 22

Diversification and
Asset Allocation Puzzles

Dimitris Georgarakos
Assistant Professor, Goethe University Frankfurt,
Senior Economist, DG-Research, European Central Bank,
Research Fellow, Center for Financial Studies

INTRODUCTION

Asset allocation and portfolio diversification decisions have recently received considerable attention from academics, financial practitioners, and policy makers. A debate centers on the investment decisions that households make. Empirical studies that examine these decisions, using either household survey data representative to the entire population or administrative data from various sources, often conclude that the observed behavior differs from what theoretical models predict.

This chapter describes empirical regularities documented by existing research that often deviate from standard theoretical models of optimal behavior. Campbell (2006) and Guiso and Sodini (2012) provide extensive reviews of the growing household finance literature. The chapter examines three major issues. The first issue regards the limited stock market participation that is well documented in numerous studies across various countries. Researchers have put forth various explanations for the so-called household stock market participation puzzle. These include fixed costs that such participation entails, a lack of financial literacy, poor cultural traits, and certain behavioral biases. In the context of stock investing, the chapter also examines why investors exit markets and portfolio allocations over time and across countries. The latter can provide insights for the portfolio decisions of households that face different institutions and market conditions.

The second issue concerns the extent of portfolio diversification. While financial practitioners often emphasize the benefits of portfolio diversification, many households tend to form poorly diversified portfolios, which lead to exposure to idiosyncratic portfolio risk. This issue involves various empirical challenges that researchers attempt to overcome by using data from different sources. The chapter emphasizes one aspect of poor portfolio diversification involving the strong preference of professional investors and households toward local or domestic securities. This tendency to underinvest in foreign securities that goes against the notion of international diversification is called the home equity bias puzzle.

The third main issue discussed refers to portfolio trading activity, in particular how trading activity relates to investor characteristics and stock market indices. The chapter presents some common biases in trading behavior (e.g., investors' propensity to realize gains early and sell losses late and the capital gain lock-in effect in taxable securities) and discusses trading patterns across certain types of assets.

The existing empirical literature notes two seemingly conflicting aspects of trading behavior. On the one hand, brokerage account owners tend to trade frequently, suffering in some cases net losses due to high transaction costs that excess trading entails. On the other hand, the vast majority of participants in individual retirement accounts (IRAs) choose to reallocate assets infrequently and exhibit considerable portfolio inertia over long periods in time. The former group typically consists of very affluent investors who feel quite confident trading securities. An examination of the population at large shows that the majority of households exhibit considerable inertia in trading securities. The chapter concludes with a brief discussion of the implications of the aforementioned three issues for household well-being and the economy in general.

HOUSEHOLD STOCK MARKET PARTICIPATION

Standard finance theory models predict that all investors should optimally allocate at least a small amount of their liquid assets in stocks. This is the case because investors who do not hold stocks have (locally) risk-neutral preferences, while stocks offer a positive equity premium over risk-free assets (Arrow 1971).

In contrast to standard theoretical predictions, various studies using micro survey data from different countries document that the majority of households do not participate in the stock market (Guiso, Haliassos, and Jappelli 2002). This is the case not only for directly owned publicly traded securities, but also for indirect forms of stock investing such as through mutual funds and IRAs. This empirical regularity is often termed the *household stock market participation puzzle* and it can be seen as a manifestation of the equity premium puzzle (Mehra and Prescott 1985).

Fixed Entry Costs, Background Risks, and Household Characteristics

The existence of fixed participation costs is the most compelling explanation for household limited stock ownership. Such costs may regard a one-time participation fee and may reoccur due to continuous participation. Apart from explicit brokerage and monetary fees, these costs may also involve non-tangible costs perceived by investors, costs of time, and costs of processing financial information, as well as costs of picking and monitoring advisors.

Various computational studies that calibrate portfolio choices over the life cycle with background income risk and liquidity constraints, derive zero stockholdings for certain ranges of cash on hand (i.e., liquid wealth and non-capital income) when assuming a fixed participation cost (Haliassos and Bertaut 1995; Cocco, Gomes, and Maenhout 2005). Others attempt to derive empirical estimates for such fixed entry costs (Vissing-Jørgensen 2002).

Factors that would lower the amount of stock investing the household would undertake if it had access to the stock market also serve to reduce the probability that it would pay any given fixed cost to participate in the stock market. More specifically, theory predicts that households with more cash on hand should have a higher demand for stocks and thus a higher probability of stock market participation. Studies document a significant influence of income and wealth on stock ownership, as Bertaut and Starr-McCluer (2002) show for the United States and Guiso and Jappelli (2002) show for Italy.

Further, theory predicts that increased exposure to undiversifiable background risk should reduce exposure to avoidable risks, even if the two risks are independent (Gollier and Pratt 1996). That is, because households with a higher background risk should reduce their exposure to stocks, they are less likely to pay the stock market participation fee.

One typical example of background risk is income risk. Household income is subject to transitory and/or permanent shocks. Background income risk tends to increase effective risk aversion, inducing households in turn to reduce their exposure to stock market risk (e.g., Viceira 2001). Guiso, Jappelli, and Terlizzese (1996) use Italian survey data with information on households' expectations about future labor and pension income levels. They find that, other things being equal, those with a higher uncertainty about their future earnings are less likely to invest in risky assets.

Another form of background risk is entrepreneurial risk, which is relevant for households that hold a substantial fraction of their wealth in their own business. Heaton and Lucas (2000) show that entrepreneurial risk should reduce stock investing even if it is uncorrelated with the returns of publicly traded securities. Health-related risks represent an additional source of background risk that grows in importance over time due to the demographic transition. Edwards (2008) and Yogo (2009) show that unexpected medical expenditures induce households to invest in safer assets. Rosen and Wu (2004), using data from the U.S. Health and Retirement Study (HRS), document a strong negative association between reported health problems and household stock holdings.

Better educated households typically face a steeper labor income profile over the life cycle, while their earnings are subject to lower uncertainty (Laibson, Repetto, and Tobacman 2003). This fact alone would induce more educated households to save less, given a lower incentive to accumulate for future shocks. However, those who are more educated typically process financial information more efficiently, thus facing lower participation costs. Empirical studies such as Bertaut and Starr-McCluer (2002) document significant effects of education on stock ownership that are net of income and accumulated wealth.

Alternative Explanations for Limited Stock Market Participation

Recent empirical studies identify certain factors that are likely to affect stock investing by amplifying fixed participation costs. For example, Hong, Kubik, and Stein (2004) provide evidence that sociability, as measured by frequency of contact with neighbors and church-going, fosters stock market participation. This is the case because word-of-mouth information sharing can lower information costs. Bogan (2008) shows that stockholding is more widespread among frequent Internet users because they have easier access to financial information.

Another factor relating to limited stock market participation involves a lack of financial literacy. According to Bernheim (1998), many households are unaware of basic financial concepts and often base their savings behavior on simple rules of thumb. Nevertheless, households face a rich set of asset choices that often involve complex, risky, and information-intensive financial instruments. At the same time, governments tend to shift responsibility of retirement financing away from Social Security and to households that face the additional challenge of securing adequate resources for retirement.

Lusardi and Mitchell (2007) report widespread financial illiteracy and associate it with poor preparation for retirement. Van Rooij, Lusardi, and Alessie (2011) ask a series of questions in the Dutch National Bank Household Survey (DNBHS) in order to measure respondents' financial literacy regarding basic and more advanced economic concepts. The former group of questions concerns basic economic knowledge (e.g., inflation, time value of money, and interest compounding) while the latter asks for differences between stocks and bonds, the essentials of portfolio diversification, and the relationship between interest rates and bond prices. Despite many respondents being aware of basic economic concepts, relatively few manage to answer correctly the more advanced financial literacy questions. The authors find a strong positive association between (advanced) financial literacy and stock market participation that is net of education and household resources. Stango and Zinman (2011) show that those unable to correctly calculate interest rates out of a payment sequence tend to accumulate lower wealth amounts.

Recent studies emphasize the role of cognitive abilities for investing in information-intensive assets such as stocks. Using data from the Survey of Health, Aging, and Retirement in Europe (SHARE), Christelis, Jappelli, and Padula (2010) find that respondents with lower cognitive capacity (i.e., reduced ability to recall words correctly out of a list that is read to them by the interviewer) are less likely to own stocks. Grinblatt, Keloharju, and Linnainmaa (2011), use Finish microdata from various sources, and link them with the IQ scores that Finish males accomplished during their mandatory military service. The authors find that a higher IQ contributes to stock ownership and to forming a better diversified portfolio, while its effect is also present among the wealthy.

Recent literature also focuses on factors such as lack of trust that can deter stock market participation, particularly so for well-to-do households. The issue of trust has important implications for the client (individual investor) and the expert (financial advisor) relationship throughout the financial planning process. Researchers typically measure trust using surveys that ask respondents to indicate (e.g., on a 1-to-10 scale) how much they trust other people in general. Guiso, Sapienza, and Zingales (2008) document a positive association between trust and stock investing. That is, in countries with a higher fraction of the population reporting high trust in others, stock ownership rates are higher. According to the authors, prospective investors who do not trust others perceive a higher probability of being cheated, which discourages them from stock investing.

According to Georgarakos and Pasini (2011), households with below median net wealth in Sweden, Denmark, and Switzerland exhibit twice as high stock ownership rates compared to their counterparts with more than median net wealth in Italy, Spain, and Austria. The authors find that regional variation in trust can be a key factor for such disparities in stockholding in Europe.

Two additional behavioral issues that influence stock market participation are knowledge about financial assets and investor expectations. Guiso and Jappelli (2005) point to asset ignorance as a factor that can inhibit participation in financial markets. They document that a non-trivial fraction of Italian households are unaware of the existence of stocks, mutual funds, and managed accounts as potential investment options. Another factor that can influence stockholding is the expectations that households form about stock market prospects. For example, Hudomiet, Kézdi and Willis (2009) and Hurd, van Rooij, and Winter (2011) use survey data from the United States and the Netherlands, respectively, that record household expectations about stock market returns. They find that households with more optimistic views about stock market prospects are more likely to invest in stocks.

Finally, limited stock market participation may also be the outcome of deviations from the standard expected utility framework. For example, according to prospect theory (Kahneman and Tversky 1979) agents are loss averse (i.e., they strongly prefer avoiding losses to making gains) and are often subject to narrow framing (i.e., do not consider the entire context of their portfolio when making a decision). Barberis, Huang, and Thaler (2006) find that individuals who are loss averse and suffer from narrow framing do not participate in the stock market even in the absence of fixed participation costs. Because loss aversion and narrow framing imply higher risk aversion, investors who contemplate making a small investment in stocks are less likely to participate.

Stock Market Exits

The presence of recurring costs that continuous participation entails can induce exits from the stock market. Certain factors that imply low demand for stocks (e.g., low resources, aging, and retirement) can also induce households to exit when their desired level of stock investing is insufficient to justify such recurring participation costs. Nevertheless, a household should take into account that such continuous participation costs and associated trading fees are typically lower than the potential costs needed to reenter at some period in the future.

Bertaut (1998) examines transitions out of the stock market. Using panel data from the 1983 and 1986 waves of the U.S. Survey of Consumer Finances (SCF), she finds that the relatively less wealthy, less educated, and more risk-averse stockholders in 1983 have a higher probability of leaving the stock market by 1986.

More recently, Bilias, Georgarakos, and Haliassos (2010) using repeated waves of the Panel Study of Income Dynamics (PSID), estimate the conditional probability of stock market exit in a given year and find that exits are mainly linked to limited resources and low education. They contend that the 2001 downswing encouraged households that did not participate in earlier years to stay out of the market rather than those who did participate to get out of the market.

CHANGES IN HOUSEHOLD PORTFOLIOS ACROSS TIME

According to statistics from repeated waves of the SCF, household ownership of stocks in any form (i.e., stocks held directly or indirectly through mutual funds or IRAs) increased from 32 percent in 1989 to 52 percent in 2001.

As Exhibit 22.1 shows, the prevalence of each of these three stockholding modes has not changed at an equal pace over the past two decades. Apparently, most of the expansion of the stockholder pool over the 1990s can be linked to the increased stock

EXHIBIT 22.1   Ownership Rates of Total Stocks and by Stockholding Mode

Year	Total Stocks	Stocks Held Directly	Mutual Funds	Stocks in Mutual Funds	IRAs	Stocks in IRAs
1989	31.8%	16.9%	10.8%	6.0%	38.3%	19.7%
1992	36.7	17.0	14.0	8.4	41.0	26.0
1995	40.4	15.2	15.3	11.3	46.5	30.3
1998	48.9	19.2	19.5	15.2	50.8	39.2
2001	51.9	21.3	21.1	16.7	54.0	43.4
2004	48.6	20.7	17.9	14.3	52.1	39.6
2007	51.2	17.9	14.0	10.8	54.6	44.1

Note: This exhibit shows percentage ownership rates of stocks and of different forms of stock-holding between 1989 and 2007. Calculations are based on weighted statistics that have been corrected for multiple imputations.
Source: Data come from several waves of the U.S. Survey of Consumer Finances.

ownership through IRAs. However, direct ownership of publicly traded securities and ownership through mutual funds has changed little over the past two decades.

Most empirical studies that examine stock market participation do not distinguish among stockholding modes. Nevertheless, such a distinction can be instructive given the differences in riskiness, management requirements, and liquidity that underline each stockholding mode. Direct stockholding is typically risky due to limited diversification, is management intensive, and is fairly liquid. Mutual funds are less liquid, but tend to be well-diversified and managed by professionals rather than individual investors. Retirement accounts, on the other hand, are typically tax-deferred and well diversified but quite illiquid.

Participation costs are also likely to differ across these modes. Directly held stocks are subject to brokerage fees and require both constant monitoring of the market and considerable information about firm characteristics. Mutual funds are also subject to fees, and require performance monitoring and informed choices among a complex menu of alternative funds. Yet, these funds delegate responsibility for asset allocation to professionals. While investment in retirement accounts is tax deferred, investment in stocks directly and through mutual funds is on an after-tax basis and dividends and capital gains are taxable.

Christelis, Georgarakos, and Haliassos (2011) distinguish among investments in different stockholding modes. They find that owners of IRAs are more likely to invest in other forms of stockholding (i.e., directly and through mutual funds). Nevertheless, this propensity is mainly due to the characteristics that led them to initially own IRAs rather than to any informational or other advantages gained through IRA ownership.

DIFFERENCES IN HOUSEHOLD PORTFOLIOS ACROSS COUNTRIES

While studies examine portfolio allocations within various countries, much less research focuses on international comparisons in household assets and liabilities. This is mainly due to the limited comparability and lack of harmonization of surveys on household finances that take place in different countries. Nevertheless, understanding what drives differences in household finances and portfolio allocations across countries can be of high policy relevance.

More recent surveys in different countries that share a common questionnaire design offer harmonized data. One such example is surveys that interview households comprised of individuals 50 years of age and above. The first U.S. HRS, which was conducted in 1992, served as a model for the English Longitudinal Study on Ageing (ELSA) conducted in England and for SHARE (originally conducted across 11 continental European countries but now expanded to 20 countries). Moreover, researchers have designed comparable surveys in China, Japan, Korea, and India.

Christelis, Georgarakos, and Haliassos (2013) recently used such harmonized data from HRS, SHARE, and ELSA to perform a large-scale international comparison in household portfolios across 13 countries. They document a significant heterogeneity in ownership and holdings of stocks, private businesses, homes, and mortgages across countries. The authors attribute most of this heterogeneity to differences in economic environments that households of similar characteristics living in different countries face.

For example, as Exhibit 22.2 shows, ownership of stocks (directly or indirectly held through mutual funds and retirement accounts), is greatest in Sweden, Denmark, and the United States. Stock ownership is smallest in Austria, Italy, Spain, and Greece. Homeownership is highest in Spain and Greece and lowest in Germany, the Netherlands, Switzerland, and Austria. The highest rates of business ownership are observed in Sweden and Switzerland, with the United States and Denmark a short distance behind them. Austria and England have the lowest rates of business ownership.

EXHIBIT 22.2   Differences in Asset Ownership across Countries

	Stock	Own Business	Home
United States	49.7%	9.8%	77.3%
Sweden	70.8	12.9	68.9
Denmark	56.1	9.6	69.2
Germany	25.4	6.5	51.2
Netherlands	24.9	6.9	55.2
Belgium	37.7	5.5	80.0
France	43.0	6.0	72.2
Switzerland	36.3	10.9	54.8
Austria	10.2	4.1	56.7
Italy	10.4	6.5	75.1
Spain	12.8	6.7	86.9
Greece	10.6	6.6	84.3
England	39.4	2.5	76.1

Note: This exhibit shows percentage ownership rates for three major asset categories (i.e., directly and indirectly held stocks, own business, and main home) across various countries for the population aged 50 and above. Calculations are based on weighted statistics from the 2004 wave of the following surveys: HRS for the United States, ELSA for the United Kingdom, and SHARE for 11 continental European countries.

The Federal Reserve started collecting nationally representative survey data with details on household assets and liabilities during the early 1980s in order to inform monetary policy and regulatory decisions. Collecting such data now extends to the euro area under the administration of the European Central Bank. The Household Finance and Consumption Survey (HFCS) is expected to shed light on wealth holdings and debts of European households facing different institutions and socioeconomic conditions.

PORTFOLIO DIVERSIFICATION

The benefits from portfolio diversification are well understood in finance since the seminal work of Markowitz (1952). Financial practitioners often emphasize these benefits. Whether households hold diversified portfolios is a topical issue that has important welfare and policy implications. Nevertheless, addressing this issue empirically is difficult without having sufficient data to provide a detailed picture of households' portfolio diversification.

More specifically, survey data representing the entire population do not typically provide details on the stocks in which households have invested. Recording the precise portfolio composition can be particularly problematic for indirect forms of stockholding, such as stocks held through mutual funds and retirement accounts. Thus, using these data to deduce the precise structure of portfolios as well as the covariance properties across different asset categories is impossible.

In an early study, Blume and Friend (1978) use representative population data from the 1962 Survey of Financial Characteristics of Consumers, conducted by the Federal Reserve, to assess portfolio diversification of direct stockholders. They find that the majority of direct stockholders hold stocks from just one or two different companies. Nevertheless, Blume and Friend cannot fully assess the breadth of these portfolios because the data do not offer information on mutual funds.

Kelly (1995) uses data from the 1983 wave of the SCF. She finds that direct stock owners do not typically own stocks from different companies. Yet, between households that own and do not own mutual funds, they hold a similar number of different stocks. Kelly concludes that limited diversification is still quite evident when considering indirect forms of stockholding such as through mutual funds, defined contribution plans, and IRAs.

Various studies use administrative data to assess portfolio diversification. These data come either from large brokerage providers (Odean 1998; Goetzman and Kumar 2008) or private pension plans (Madrian and Shea 2001; Agnew, Balduzzi, and Sundén 2003; Choi et al. 2004). While administrative data offer a precise picture of the portfolio structure held under a single provider, they do not take into account other financial assets that are likely to be held in different institutions or the real wealth owned by households.

A study by Calvet, Campbell, and Sodini (2007) overcomes some of the aforementioned limitations present in survey and administrative data. They use unique data from wealth tax registries that record individual wealth holdings (e.g., stocks, bonds, mutual funds, savings accounts, and real estate) and are representative of the entire Swedish population. Because their data set contains information on each asset in the individual portfolio, they can assess portfolio diversification.

Consistent with evidence from other countries, Calvet et al. (2007) find that relatively few households own stocks directly. Yet, of those households owning stock directly, the vast majority also invest in mutual funds. Because their data allow assessing the riskiness of each individual portfolio, the authors show that *idiosyncratic risk* (i.e., risk that can be eliminated by diversification) is higher for those who have invested mostly in stocks directly, relative to those who have invested a greater amount in mutual funds. For most Swedish households, investing in mutual funds not only reduces idiosyncratic portfolio risk but also contributes to forming well-diversified portfolios through international diversification. The authors also show that more educated and wealthier households tend to hold more diversified portfolios.

Underdiversification can entail substantial welfare losses especially for households allocating a large fraction of their wealth to risky assets. Nevertheless, when families hold most of the household wealth in safe assets, underdiversification has only limited implications for household welfare. Calvet et al. (2007) find that such welfare losses are limited among the Swedish households either because they hold well-diversified portfolios or because those who are exposed to idiosyncratic risk tend to invest a lower fraction of their wealth in risky assets.

Another indication of limited portfolio diversification can be the propensity of households to concentrate their investments in domestic securities. Statistics on investments of individuals and institutions across many countries clearly show that they only allocate a small amount of funds to foreign equities. French and Poterba (1991) are the first to document the home equity bias puzzle, which is inconsistent with the notion of diversification and the predictions of standard portfolio models such as the international capital asset pricing model (ICAPM) (Baele, Pungulescu, and Ter Horst 2007). In the case of stocks, the foregone benefits from international diversification can be substantial even after adjusting for exchange rate risk and border restrictions (Lewis 1999).

Although many studies use macro data to examine international asset diversification of institutional investors, relatively few use micro data to examine household investment in domestic and foreign assets. Bailey, Kumar, and Ng (2008) use administrative data from a brokerage firm and find that investing experience, asset accumulation, and some behavioral biases can contribute to forming internationally diversified portfolios. Karlsson and Nordén (2007) study the foreign investments of a nationally representative sample of Swedish households through their pension accounts. Their findings show that low job security, low economic resources, and low education are all associated with home-biased portfolios.

Using the SCF to examine determinants of households' decision to invest in foreign stocks and bonds, Kyrychenko and Shum (2009) find that financial sophistication and pessimistic expectations about the prospect of the U.S. economy induce ownership of foreign stocks and bonds. Christelis and Georgarakos (2013) use data from the same source and estimate a more complex model to estimate direct investment in stocks, bonds, and liquid accounts and their foreign counterparts. They document the existence of significant entry costs in the form of resources and information requirements that affect household investment in foreign stocks and are above any costs associated with stock market participation.

Researchers link investors' propensity to overweight their portfolios with domestic securities to some behavioral considerations. For example, investors tend to be more optimistic about domestic rather than foreign market prospects (Strong and Xu 2003). Graham, Campbell, and Huang (2005) show that investors who feel more competent about foreign investing (i.e., they report that they are aware of the associated risks and benefits) are more likely to hold internationally diversified portfolios. Some studies using data on the investment choices of professional money managers show a preference for investing in local securities and find that these investments typically earn abnormal returns (Choe, Kho, and Stulz 1999; Coval and Moskowitz 1999; Hau 2001).

Tax considerations are also likely to affect portfolio allocation across different asset categories. Garlappi and Huang (2006) present a model of optimal allocation of stocks between taxable and tax-deferred accounts. Bergstresser and Poterba (2004) examine empirically such asset allocations between taxable (e.g. direct stocks, mutual funds, and fixed income assets) and tax-deferred accounts (e.g., IRAs) in the United States. They find that investors hold a significant fraction of equities in tax-deferred retirement accounts, but also that households can reduce their tax burden by relocating money from fixed income assets to their tax-deferred accounts.

Lastly, households often face the challenge of allocating resources not only across different assets but also across time. In particular, households entering retirement need adequate resources to finance consumption over the remaining lifetime. Models of rational behavior prescribe that these households should hold life annuities in order to eliminate life span uncertainty and secure a constant income stream until death. Despite these benefits, only a few households choose to annuitize their retirement assets—a regularity that is often termed the *annuity puzzle* or the *annuitization puzzle* (Benartzi, Previtero, and Thaler 2011). Recent studies relate this puzzle to investors' inability to understand the benefits of a complex financial product such as annuities (Hu and Scott 2007; Browning, Finke, and Huston 2012).

HOUSEHOLD STOCK TRADING BEHAVIOR

Household stock trading behavior can have important implications for both the well-being of households and stock market prices and financial stability. Milgrom and Stokey (1982) derive zero optimal trading assuming rational expectations. By contrast, Grossman and Stiglitz (1980) predict optimal trading up to the point that investors equate the marginal costs and marginal benefits of trading. In a standard Merton (1969) model, investors should optimally adjust risky portfolio shares in response to wealth changes and the arrival of new information. Thus, in this context, portfolio rebalancing should occur frequently, while, as discussed later, empirical studies document widespread inertia.

To account for this empirical regularity, recent literature has augmented the Merton (1969) model with observation costs (e.g., portfolio and stock market monitoring costs in the case of household investing). Interestingly, the optimal portfolio adjustments implied by observation costs differ from those derived under standard fixed costs (Alvarez, Guiso, and Lippi 2012). According to the model in Abel, Eberly, and Panageas (2013), observation costs imply some optimal time-dependent adjustments, instead of state-dependent adjustments implied by models that introduce fixed entry costs (Duffie and Sun 1990). Alvarez et al. develop a model that features both observational and trading costs and considers consumption on durables. They find that such a model appropriately matches the trading frequency of a typical investor with small observation costs and larger transaction costs.

Some recent studies also link stock trading to certain deviations from rational investor behavior. As discussed later, overconfidence can induce investors to engage in excess trading, lowering realized returns net of transaction costs.

Empirical Studies Using Administrative Data

Tax considerations are likely to influence household trading. More specifically, if accumulated capital gains are taxed at realization, households are likely to be less prone to sell stocks that have increased in price to avoid paying the associated capital gains tax, and are more inclined to sell stocks that have decreased in price.

Yet, some behavioral biases prompt the opposite portfolio behavior from that induced by the aforementioned tax considerations. In particular, investors often appear reluctant to admit losses and to dispose of assets that have declined in price, but are keen to sell appreciated assets too early. This bias is called the disposition effect (Shefrin and Statman 1985; Odean 1998). Odean finds strong evidence for a disposition effect over most security transactions with the only exception being transactions that take place in December. Because December is the last month that investors can claim tax reductions on capital gains, they consider selling depreciated stocks an attractive option.

Although most existing studies on trading behavior use administrative data sets that provide information on stock transactions, the empirical evidence conflicts. Studies examining trading activity through brokerage accounts report excessive trading but those investigating transactions in IRAs document considerable trading inertia.

Barber and Odean (2000) use data from a large U.S. discount broker that provides trading services for common stocks without financial advice between 1991 and 1996. A typical household in their sample turns over 75 percent of its portfolio annually. That is, households engage in trading stocks excessively, possibly due to overconfidence (Odean 1999). Such extensive trading entails substantial transaction fees and often results in net stock portfolio returns substantially below the market. Based on this evidence, Barber and Odean conclude that trading can be hazardous to investor wealth.

Barber and Odean (2001) document that men trade 45 percent more than women and earn annual risk-adjusted net returns that are 1.4 percent less than those earned by women. Using data from the same source, Ivković, Poterba, and Weisbenner (2005) distinguish between trading on taxable and tax-deferred accounts. They document a lock-in effect for stocks with capital gains held in taxable accounts relative to those held in tax-deferred accounts, mainly for large stock transactions. For smaller transactions, the authors find evidence for a disposition effect in both types of accounts and especially at short investment periods.

Grinblatt and Keloharju (2001) use data from the central register of shareholdings in the Finnish Central Securities Depository that offers information on transactions made by all individual and institutional stockholders. The authors estimate a series of binary regressions to examine the determinants of buying and selling securities over a two-year period. They find evidence that investors are reluctant to realize losses and engage in tax-loss selling activity. Their results also show that past returns and historical price patterns affect trading.

Choi, Laibson, and Metrick (2002) compare trading patterns in 401(k) plans between participants with and without Internet trading access. They find that 18 months after the introduction of online Internet trading, trading frequency doubles but turnover rises by half. The estimated effects from Internet access are particularly strong for young, male, and wealthier participants. Ameriks and Zeldes (2004) use panel quarterly data on tax-deferred retirement account balances and contributions held by TIAA-CREF. Owners of such accounts are typically full-time employees at U.S. institutions of higher education and research. Although the authors mainly focus on examining age, cohort, and time effects on portfolio composition, they also report evidence on considerable trading inertia. They find that between 1987 and 1996, almost half of the participants in their sample made no changes to the share of stocks in either their retirement accumulation or in their flow contributions, despite the trivial cost of making such changes.

Agnew et al. (2003) examine a panel of nearly 7,000 401(k) retirement accounts from April 1994 to August 1998 and find very limited portfolio rebalancing. More than 87 percent of their observations of the annual number of trades in their panel is zero and only 7 percent exceeds one.

Mitchell et al. (2006) use data from a large administrative source that records 1.2 million workers in over 1,500 plans. They find evidence for profound inertia characterizing participants in 401(k) plans. More specifically, 80 percent of participants initiate no trades, while another 11 percent trade only once in a two-year period. Even among those few who trade, portfolio turnover rates are one-third of the typical turnover rate of professional fund managers.

Huberman and Sengmueller (2002) study the dynamics of investment in company stock within 401(k) plans by employees working in that company. They use aggregate (plan-level) data, constructed from filings to the Securities and Exchange Commission (SEC), on a panel of 153 plans over a maximum period of eight years. The authors find that high past returns attract more investments, while bad past returns do not result in a reduction in plan holdings of company stock. Given that they use aggregate data without any information on participant characteristics, Huberman and Segmueller cannot assess the role of individual attributes.

Studies also link choices of participants in 401(k) plans to the investment options available in each plan. Benartzi and Thaler (2001) find evidence that the menu design of a plan can lead participants to adopt some naïve diversification strategy such as allocating into stocks based on the proportion of stock funds in the plan. Elton, Gruber, and Blake (2006) maintain that some 401(k) investment menus prevent participants from choosing well-diversified portfolios. Iyengar, Jiang, and Huberman (2004) note that participants may suffer from choice overload, where complicated investment menus tend to discourage participation in the plan.

Finally, recent studies find evidence for learning through past trading experiences. According to Nicolosi, Peng, and Zhu (2013) experienced investors improve their portfolio performance. Yet, Barber et al. (2011) report that day traders are more likely to quit after experiencing continuous losses.

Empirical Studies Using Household Survey Data

Compared to survey data, administrative data have certain advantages. For example, such data do not suffer from measurement error and they allow estimating account-specific measures of performance. On the other hand, administrative data tend to involve selected samples (e.g., brokerage account owners are typically wealthy households that are eager to trade stocks frequently) and focus on one aspect of stock investing (e.g., directly held stocks from a single broker).

Souleles (1999) uses survey data representative of the U.S. population to examine portfolio trades. In particular, he studies determinants of the size of securities purchases, combining data from the Consumer Expenditure Survey (CEX) and the Michigan consumer sentiment surveys. Souleles finds that household-specific hedging motives have independent predictive power for the size of securities purchases above and beyond the information in returns, with marginal effects estimated to be bigger than those of returns.

Gouskova, Juster, and Stafford (2004) use PSID data from 1994 and 1999 and compare the relevance of wealth and income for stock market participation. They find an increased role for income and wealth variables in 1999 and evidence that lower mortgage payments contributed to purchasing stocks during that period.

Brunnermeier and Nagel (2008) study whether wealth fluctuations induce changes in risk aversion by looking at portfolio shares conditional on participation and using survey data from PSID and CEX. They find that wealth changes do not induce households to increase their portfolio share in risky assets, conditional on participation, but capital gains and losses do have an impact, with capital gains continuing to affect portfolio shares even after five years. Both findings are consistent with inactivity in trading stocks.

Bilias et al. (2010) use U.S. survey data from the SCF and the PSID to examine stock trading activity. Their evidence shows that households with brokerage accounts exhibit a high trading frequency, which is consistent with the literature that uses data from brokers. Moreover, trading frequency through brokerage accounts appears sensitive to stock index movements. Nevertheless, one should take into account that only a minority (i.e., less than one out of five) of U.S. households has a brokerage account over the 1989 to 2004 period examined, while the bulk of the population exhibits considerable trading inertia that is partially linked to household characteristics but less so to index movements.

This evidence helps to reconcile the conflicting findings of earlier studies for the excess trading through brokerage accounts and the systematic inertia in reallocations of funds invested in retirement accounts. The vast majority of households seems to exhibit considerable inertia and does not trade over long periods in time. Nevertheless, a relatively small group consisting of wealthy brokerage account owners tend to engage in excess trading that may result in net losses due to high transaction costs. Bilias et al. (2010) also show that among the few households owning brokerage accounts, the fraction of the wealth invested through them represents only a small fraction of their total financial wealth (i.e., less than 10 percent on average). Thus, to the extent that trading in brokerage accounts triggers volatility, overtrading may be relevant for asset pricing, but it is unlikely to be of major importance for household welfare.

SUMMARY

This chapter has discussed three key features of asset investing—participation in stock markets, portfolio diversification, and asset trading behavior—and presents the findings of various studies dealing with these features from different perspectives. As discussed, limited stock market participation is evident, at least until recently, in many countries. Assessing portfolio diversification is empirically challenging. Although many households do not seem to hold diversified portfolios, the welfare losses may not be substantial, given the relatively low participation in financial markets. The chapter also discussed trading behavior and the contrast between portfolio inertia over a substantial segment of the population and excess trading activity for wealthy investors with brokerage accounts. Empirical studies highlight a key role of household socioeconomic characteristics: less wealthy, uneducated, and less financially sophisticated households are more prone not to participate in stock markets, to hold less diversified portfolios, and to exhibit considerable trading inertia.

The three features of asset investing and the associated puzzling behavior of investors have implications both for household well-being and for the economy in general. Households must make investment choices from a menu of information-intensive and complex financial instruments. Governments tend to shift responsibility for retirement financing away from Social Security and toward households. Thus, households face increasingly demanding portfolio management requirements and must make informed financial decisions in order to cope with unexpected shocks and with the challenges of the old age.

Household asset allocations can also have wider repercussions, ranging from aggregate consumption and gross domestic product (GDP) to price stability in the relevant markets. Before the recent financial crisis, many U.S. households, especially among those with members approaching retirement, did not reduce their risk exposure in their retirement plans. According to recent evidence, households have adjusted their consumption in response to financial wealth losses that they experienced during the great recession (Christelis, Georgarakos, and Jappelli 2012).

To the extent that investor biases can be traced to the household characteristics such as low education and lack of sophistication, room exists for programs that aim to promote financial literacy. Additionally, appropriate default options in various retirement plans could direct households toward riskier or less risky portfolios, according to policy objectives. While the existing literature has helped improve understanding of how to make asset allocation and diversification decisions, more research is needed as new and more complete data become available.

DISCUSSION QUESTIONS

1. Explain why many households do not participate in the stock market.
2. Discuss how household participation in the stock market changed over time.
3. Explain whether households from different countries tend to hold similar portfolios.
4. Explain why households do not hold diversified portfolios.
5. Discuss how frequently households trade securities.

REFERENCES

Abel, Andrew B., Janice C. Eberly, and Stavros Panageas. 2013. "Optimal Inattention to the Stock Market with Information Costs and Transactions Costs." *Econometrica* 81:4, 1455–1481.
Agnew, Julie, Pierluigi Balduzzi, and Annika Sundén. 2003. "Portfolio Choice and Trading in a Large 401(k) Plan." *American Economic Review* 93:1, 193–215.

Alvarez, Fernando E., Luigi Guiso, and Francesco Lippi. 2012. "Durable Consumption and Asset Management with Transaction and Observation Costs." *American Economic Review* 102:5, 2272–2300.

Ameriks, John, and Stephen Zeldes. 2004. "How Do Household Portfolio Shares Vary with Age?" Working Paper, Columbia University.

Arrow, Kenneth. 1971. *Essays in the Theory of Risk Bearing.* Amsterdam: North Holland.

Baele, Lieven, Crina Pungulescu, and Jenke Ter Horst. 2007. "Model Uncertainty, Financial Market Integration and the Home Bias Puzzle." *Journal of International Money and Finance* 26:4, 606–630.

Bailey, Warren, Alok Kumar, and David Ng. 2008. "Foreign Investments of U.S. Individual Investors: Causes and Consequences." *Management Science* 54:3, 443–459.

Barber, Brad M., Yi-Tsung Lee, Yu-Jane Liu, and Terrance Odean. 2011. "Do Day Traders Rationally Learn about Their Ability." Working Paper, Berkeley University.

Barber, Brad M., and Terrance Odean. 2000. "Trading Is Hazardous to Your Wealth: The Common Stock Investment Performance of Individual Investors." *Journal of Finance* 55:2, 773–806.

Barber, Brad M., and Terrance Odean. 2001. "Boys Will Be Boys: Gender, Overconfidence and Common Stock Investment." *Quarterly Journal of Economics* 116:1, 261–292.

Barberis, Nicholas, Ming Huang, and Richard Thaler. 2006. "Individual Preferences, Monetary Gambles and Stock Market Participation: A Case for Narrow Framing." *American Economic Review* 96:4, 1069–1090.

Benartzi, Shlomo, Alessandro Previtero, and Richard H. Thaler. 2011. "Annuitization Puzzles." *Journal of Economic Perspectives* 25:4, 143–164.

Benartzi, Shlomo, and Richard H. Thaler. 2001. "Naive Diversification Strategies in Defined Contribution Saving Plans." *American Economic Review* 91:1, 79–98.

Bergstresser, Daniel B., and James Poterba. 2004. "Asset Allocation and Asset Location: Household Evidence from the Survey of Consumer Finances." *Journal of Public Economics* 88:9, 1893–1915.

Bernheim, Douglas. 1998. "Financial Illiteracy, Education and Retirement Saving." In Olivia Mitchell and Sylvester Schieber, eds., *Living with Defined Contribution Pensions*, 38–68. Philadelphia, PA: University of Pennsylvania Press.

Bertaut, Carol. 1998. "Stockholding Behavior of U.S. Households: Evidence from the 1983–1989 Survey of Consumer Finances." *Review of Economics and Statistics* 80:2, 263–275.

Bertaut, Carol, and Martha Starr-McCluer. 2002. "Household Portfolios in the United States." In Luigi Guiso, Michael Haliassos, and Tullio Jappelli, eds., *Household Portfolios*, 181–217. Cambridge, MA: MIT Press.

Bilias, Yannis, Dimitris Georgarakos, and Michael Haliassos. 2010. "Portfolio Inertia and Stock Market Fluctuations." *Journal of Money, Credit, and Banking* 42:4, 715–742.

Blume, Marshall E., and Irwin Friend. 1978. *The Changing Role of the Individual Investor: A Twentieth Century Fund Report.* New York: John Wiley & Sons.

Bogan, Vicky. 2008. "Stock Market Participation and the Internet." *Journal of Financial and Quantitative Analysis* 43:1, 191–212.

Browning, Chris, Michael S. Finke, and Sandra J. Huston. 2012. "Rational Choice with Complex Products: Consumer Valuation of Annuities." *Journal of Financial Counseling and Planning,* 23:2, 32–45.

Brunnermeier, Markus K., and Stefan Nagel. 2008. "Do Wealth Fluctuations Generate Time-varying Risk Aversion? Micro-Evidence from Individuals' Asset Allocation." *American Economic Review* 98:3, 713–736.

Calvet, Laurent E., John Y. Campbell, and Paolo Sodini. 2007. "Down or Out: Assessing the Welfare Costs of Household Investment Mistakes." *Journal of Political Economy* 115:5, 707–747.

Campbell, John Y. 2006. "Household Finance." *Journal of Finance* 61:4, 1553–1604.

Choe, Hyuk, Bong-Chan Kho, and René M. Stulz. 1999. "Do Foreign Investors Destabilize Stock Markets? The Korean Experience in 1997." *Journal of Financial Economics* 54:2, 227–264.

Choi, James J., David Laibson, Brigitte Madrian, and Andrew Metrick. 2004. "For Better or for Worse: Default Effects and 401(k) Savings Behavior." In David Wise, ed., *Perspectives on the Economics of Aging*, 81–125. Chicago: University of Chicago Press.

Choi, James J., David Laibson, and Andrew Metrick. 2002. "How Does the Internet Affect Trading? Evidence from Investor Behavior in 401(k) Plans." *Journal of Financial Economics* 64:3, 397–421.

Christelis, Dimitris, and Dimitris Georgarakos. 2013. "Investing at Home and Abroad: Different Costs, Different People?" *Journal of Banking and Finance* 37:6, 2069–2086.

Christelis, Dimitris, Dimitris Georgarakos, and Michael Haliassos. 2011. "Stockholding: Participation, Location, and Spillovers." *Journal of Banking and Finance* 35:8, 1918–1930.

Christelis, Dimitris, Dimitris Georgarakos, and Michael Haliassos. 2013. "Differences in Portfolios across Countries: Economic Environment versus Household Characteristics." *Review of Economics and Statistics* 95:1, 220–236.

Christelis, Dimitris, Dimitris Georgarakos, and Tullio Jappelli. 2012. "Wealth Shocks, Unemployment Shocks and Consumption in the Wake of the Great Recession." Netspar Discussion Paper No. 03/2012-010.

Christelis, Dimitris, Tullio Jappelli, and Mario Padula. 2010. "Cognitive Abilities and Portfolio Choice." *European Economic Review* 54:1, 18–39.

Cocco, Joao, Francisco J. Gomes, and Pascal J. Maenhout. 2005. "Consumption and Portfolio Choice over the Life-Cycle." *Review of Financial Studies* 18:2, 491–533.

Coval, Joshua D., and Tobias J. Moskowitz. 1999. "Home Bias at Home: Local Equity Preference in Domestic Portfolios." *Journal of Finance* 54:6, 2045–2073.

Duffie, Darrell, and Tong-sheng Sun. 1990. "Transactions Costs and Portfolio Choice in a Discrete-Continuous-Time Setting." *Journal of Economic Dynamics and Control* 14:1, 35–51.

Edwards, Ryan D. 2008. "Health Risk and Portfolio Choice." *Journal of Business and Economic Statistics* 26:1, 472–485.

Elton, Edwin J., Martin Gruber, and Christopher Blake. 2006. "The Adequacy of Investment Choices Offered by 401(k) Plans." *Journal of Public* Economics 90:6, 1299–1314.

French, Kenneth, and James Poterba. 1991. "Investor Diversification and International Equity Markets." *American Economic Review, Papers and Proceedings* 81:2, 222–226.

Garlappi, Lorenzo, and Jennifer Huang. 2006. "Are Stocks Desirable in Tax-Deferred Accounts?" *Journal of Public Economics* 90:12, 2257–2283.

Georgarakos, Dimitris, and Giacomo Pasini. 2011. "Trust, Sociability, and Stock Market Participation." *Review of Finance* 15:4, 693–725.

Goetzman, William, and Alok Kumar. 2008. "Why Do Individual Investors Hold Under-Diversified Portfolios?" *Review of Finance* 12:3, 433–463.

Gollier, Christian, and John W. Pratt. 1996. "Weak Proper Risk Aversion and the Tempering Effect of Background Risk." *Econometrica* 64:5, 1109–1123.

Gouskova, Elena, Thomas Juster, and Frank Stafford. 2004. "Exploring the Changing Nature of U.S. Stock Market Participation, 1994–1999." Working Paper, University of Michigan.

Graham, John R., Campbell R. Harvey, and Hai Huang. 2005. "Investor Competence, Trading Frequency, and Home Bias." NBER Working Paper No. 11426.

Grinblatt, Mark, and Matti Keloharju. 2001. "How Distance, Language, and Culture Influence Stockholdings and Trades." *Journal of Finance* 56:3, 1053–1073.

Grinblatt, Mark, Matti Keloharju, and Juhani Linnainmaa. 2011. "IQ and Stock Market Participation." *Journal of Finance* 66:6, 2121–2164.

Grossman, Sanford J., and Joseph E. Stiglitz. 1980. "On the Impossibility of Informationally Efficient Markets." *American Economic Review* 70:3, 393–408.

Guiso, Luigi, Michael Haliassos, and Tullio Jappelli, eds. 2002. *Household Portfolios.* Cambridge, MA: MIT Press.

Guiso, Luigi, and Tullio Jappelli. 2002. "Household Portfolios in Italy." In Luigi Guiso, Michael Haliassos, and Tullio Jappelli, eds., *Household Portfolios,* 251–289. Cambridge, MA: MIT Press.

Guiso, Luigi, and Tullio Jappelli. 2005. "Awareness and Stock Market Participation." *Review of Finance* 9:4, 537–567.

Guiso, Luigi, Tullio Jappelli, and Daniele Terlizzese. 1996. "Income Risk, Borrowing Constraints and Portfolio Choice." *American Economic Review* 86:1, 158–172.

Guiso, Luigi, Paola Sapienza, and Luigi Zingales. 2008. "Trusting the Stock Market." *Journal of Finance* 63:6, 2557–2600.

Guiso, Luigi, and Paolo Sodini. 2012. "Household Finance: An Emerging Field." CEPR Discussion Paper No. 8934.

Haliassos, Michael, and Carol Bertaut. 1995. "Why Do So Few Hold Stocks?" *Economic Journal* 105:432, 1110–1129.

Hau, Harald. 2001. "Location Matters: An Examination of Trading Profits." *Journal of Finance* 56:5, 1959–1983.

Heaton, John, and Deborah Lucas. 2000. "Portfolio Choice in the Presence of Background Risk." *Economic Journal* 110:460, 1–26.

Hong, Harrison G., Jeffrey D. Kubik, and Jeremy C. Stein. 2004. "Social Interaction and Stock Market Participation." *Journal of Finance* 59:1, 137–163.

Hu, Wei-Yin, and Jason S. Scott. 2007. "Behavioral Obstacles in the Annuity Market." *Financial Analysts Journal* 63:6, 71–82.

Huberman, Gur, and Paul Segmueller. 2002. "Company Stock in 401(k) Plans." Working Paper, Columbia Business School.

Hudomiet, Péter, Gábor Kézdi, and Robert J. Willis. 2009. "Stock Market Expectations and Portfolio Choice of American Households." *Journal of Applied Econometrics* 26:3, 393–415.

Hurd, Michael, Maarten van Rooij, and Joachim K. Winter. 2011. "Stock Market Expectations of Dutch Households." *Journal of Applied Econometrics* 26:3, 416–436.

Ivković, Zoran, James Poterba, and Scott Weisbenner. 2005. "Tax Loss Trading by Individual Investors." *American Economic Review* 95:5, 1605–1630.

Iyengar, Sheena, Wei Jiang, and Gur Huberman. 2004. "How Much Choice Is Too Much? Contributions to 401(k) Retirement Plans." In Olivia Mitchell and Stephen Utkus, eds., *Pension Design and Structure: New Lessons from Behavioral Finance,* 83–95. Oxford: Oxford University Press.

Kahneman, Daniel, and Amos Tversky. 1979. "Prospect Theory: An Analysis of Choice under Risk." *Econometrica* 47:2, 263–291.

Karlsson, Anders, and Lars Nordén. 2007. "Home Sweet Home: Home Bias and International Diversification among Individual Investors." *Journal of Banking and Finance* 35:9, 317–333.

Kelly, Morgan. 1995. "All Their Eggs in One Basket: Portfolio Diversification of US Households." *Journal of Economic Behavior and Organization* 27:1, 87–96.

Kyrychenko, Vlad, and Pauline Shum. 2009. "Who Holds Foreign Stocks and Bonds?" *Financial Services Review* 18:1, 1–21.

Laibson, David, Andreas Repetto, and Jeremy Tobacman. 2003. "A Debt Puzzle." In Philippe Aghion, Roman Frydman, Joseph Stiglitz, and Michael Woodford, eds., *Knowledge, Information, and Expectations in Modern Economics: In Honor of Edmund S. Phelps,* 228–266. Princeton, NJ: Princeton University Press.

Lewis, Karen K. 1999. "Trying to Explain Home Bias in Equities and Consumption." *Journal of Economic Literature* 37:2, 571–608.

Lusardi, Annamaria, and Olivia S. Mitchell. 2007. "Baby Boomer Retirement Security: The Roles of Planning, Financial Literacy, and Housing Wealth." *Journal of Monetary Economics* 54:1, 205–224.

Madrian, Brigitte, and Dennis Shea. 2001. "The Power of Suggestion: Inertia in 401(k) Participation and Savings Behavior." *Quarterly Journal of Economics* 116:4, 1149–1187.

Markowitz, Harry. 1952. "Portfolio Selection." *Journal of Finance* 7:1, 77–91.

Mehra, Rajnish, and Edward C. Prescott. 1985. "The Equity Premium: A Puzzle." *Journal of Monetary Economics* 15:2, 145–161.

Merton, Robert C. 1969. "Lifetime Portfolio Selection under Uncertainty: The Continuous-Time Case." *Review of Economics and Statistics* 51:3, 247–257.

Milgrom, Paul, and Nancy Stokey. 1982. "Information, Trade, and Common Knowledge." *Journal of Economic Theory* 26:1, 17–27.

Mitchell, Olivia S., Gary R. Mottola, Stephen P. Utkus, and Takeshi Yamaguchi. 2006. "The Inattentive Participant: Portfolio Trading Behavior in 401(k) Plans." Working Paper No. 2006–115, University of Michigan.

Nicolosi, Gina, Liang Peng, and Ning Zhu. 2013. "Do Individual Investors Learn from Their Trade Experience?" *Journal of Financial Markets*, forthcoming.

Odean, Terrence. 1998. "Are Investors Reluctant to Realize Their Losses?" *Journal of Finance* 53:5, 1775–1798.

Odean, Terrence. 1999. "Do Investors Trade Too Much?" *American Economic Review* 89:5, 1279–1298.

Rosen, Harvey, and Stephen Wu. 2004. "Portfolio Choice and Health Status." *Journal of Financial Economics* 72:3, 457–484.

Shefrin, Hersh, and Meir Statman. 1985. "The Disposition to Sell Winners Too Early and Ride Losers Too Long: Theory and Evidence." *Journal of Finance* 40:3, 777–790.

Souleles, Nicholas. 1999. "Household Securities Purchases, Transactions Costs, and Hedging Motives." Rodney L. White Center for Financial Research Working Paper No. 24–99.

Stango, Victor, and Jonathan Zinman. 2011. "Fuzzy Math, Disclosure Regulation, and Market Outcomes: Evidence from Truth-in-Lending Reform." *Review of Financial Studies* 24:2, 506–534.

Strong, Norman, and Xinzhong Xu. 2003. "Understanding the Equity Home Bias: Evidence from Survey Data." *Review of Economics and Statistics* 85:2, 307–312.

Van Rooij, Maarten, Annamaria Lusardi, and Rob Alessie. 2011. "Financial Literacy and Stock Market Participation." *Journal of Financial Economics* 101:2, 449–472.

Viceira, Luis. 2001. "Optimal Portfolio Choice for Long-Horizon Investors with Non-Tradable Labor Income." *Journal of Finance* 56:2, 433–470.

Vissing-Jørgensen, Annette. 2002. "Towards an Explanation of Household Portfolio Choice Heterogeneity: Nonfinancial Income and Participation Cost Structures." NBER Working Paper No. 8884.

Yogo, Motohiro. 2009. "Portfolio Choice in Retirement: Health Risk and the Demand for Annuities, Housing, and Risky Assets." NBER Working Paper No. 15307.

ABOUT THE AUTHOR

Dimitris Georgarakos is an Assistant Professor in Finance at Goethe University, Frankfurt and works part-time as Senior Economist in the Directorate General-Research in the European Central Bank (ECB). He is also a research fellow at the Center for Financial Studies (CFS) in Frankfurt and has held a previous position as a lecturer in economics at Queen Mary, University of London. His research has appeared in such peer-reviewed journals as the *Review of Economics and Statistics*, *Journal of Money, Credit and Banking*, *Review of Finance*, and *Journal of Banking and Finance*. He obtained an MSc in economics and finance from the University of York and a PhD in economics from the University of Essex.

CHAPTER 23

Behavioral Portfolio Theory and Investment Management

Erick W. Rengifo
Associate Professor of Economics, Fordham University
Rossen Trendafilov
Assistant Professor of Economics, Truman State University
Emanuela Trifan
Quantitative Analyst, Bayerngas Energy

INTRODUCTION

The goal of this chapter is to provide a survey of the most important development in behavioral portfolio theory. The chapter has the following organization. The first section examines prospect theory (PT) and compares it to expected utility theory (EUT). It extends the concept of loss aversion to myopic loss aversion. The second section introduces safety-first portfolio theory as a precursor to the SP/A theory, which is discussed in third section. The evaluation of the risky outcomes is based on the need for security (fear) and potential (hope) as well as a given aspiration level. This section concludes by comparing SP/A theory and PT.

Next, behavioral portfolio theory (BPT) is presented as a combination of some main ideas from SP/A theory and PT. Two major specifications of BPT are described and compared to conventional portfolio theory. One considers a single mental account and the other considers multiple mental accounts.

The last section introduces the behavioral asset pricing model (BAPM). The consumption preferences are classified as utilitarian and value-expressive preferences. BAPM is compared to CAPM and the three-factor model. The chapter finishes with two discussions on the impact of value expressive preferences and perceived risk on the expected returns.

PROSPECT THEORY AND EXPECTED UTILITY THEORY

Prospect theory (PT) (Kahneman and Tversky 1979) and its extension called cumulative prospect theory (CPT) (Tversky and Kahneman 1992) constitute cornerstones of behavioral finance. CPT exhibits additional features, such as using cumulative instead of separable decision weights; the coverage of decision problems under both risk and uncertainty and with any number of outcomes; the formulation of distinct weighting functions for gains and losses; and the introduction of diminishing sensitivity and loss aversion.

PT rebuts the basic principles of the expected utility theory (EUT), which is the major approach regarding decision-making under risk in neoclassical economics. The need to change the traditional framework resulted from observations that real decision situations deviated from theoretically prescribed behaviors.

Proponents of EUT assume that investors can process all information at their disposal and form unbiased judgments. Thus, the assumption is that investors can assess their expected utilities as a linear combination of final states, weighted by the probabilities of the corresponding events with these outcomes. These probabilities are mostly updated by means of the Bayes rule, which states how probabilities can be revised based on new information, and must be well-known to the investors. The utility function is taken to be unique for all possible outcomes. Moreover, investors exhibit consistent preferences and risk-averse behaviors, so that the utility function is concave in wealth.

Experiments and empirical observations reveal different effects that violate the basic normative axioms imposed by EUT on human preferences and choices. Tversky and Kahneman (1992) summarize these as framing effects, nonlinear preferences, source dependence, risk seeking, and loss aversion.

PT attempts to incorporate these psychological aspects in the decision-making process that are considered to rely on the individual perception of reality. In essence, PT was not intended to be a normative theory based on axioms as EUT, but rather a descriptive approach attempting to capture empirically observed behaviors. PT assumes that decisions are rarely based on final states (or outcomes), but on subjectively perceived changes in welfare generated by these outcomes. Decision makers form perceptions relative to a subjective reference point, so that they can distinguish between gains and losses. Wakker and Tversky (1993) and Chateauneuf and Wakker (1999) provide axiomatizations of CPT for decisions under uncertainty and risk.

According to Kahneman and Tversky (1979), the human choice process develops in two stages. The first stage refers to editing of choice alternatives (prospects) and entails a mental representation of them. It implies different operations, such as coding, combination of probabilities of prospects with identical outcomes, segregation of the risk-free component from the risky one, cancellation of components or of outcome-probability pairs that are common among prospects, simplification of prospects (e.g., by probability or outcome rounding), and detection of dominance where the dominated alternatives are rejected. The sequence of these editing operations influences the final edited prospect, hence the preferences order. This phenomenon is also known as the *framing of the problem*.

The second stage consists of evaluating the edited prospects and the final choice, which is the prospect with the highest ascribed value. The evaluation phase implies the assessment of an overall value of each choice alternative, denoted as *prospective value*. Formally, it represents the weighted sum of the values subjectively assigned by each individual to the possible outcomes, where outcomes are separately treated as gains (henceforth denoted by a symbol +) or losses (denoted by −). According to Tversky and Kahneman (1992), the prospective value V of outcome i, where $i = 1 \ldots n$, yields

$$V_i = V_i^+ + V_i^- = \sum_{x_i} \pi_i^+ v(x_i^+) + \sum_{x_i} -\pi_i^- v(x_i^-) \tag{23.1}$$

where v stands for the value function and π for the decision weights. Finally, x_i denotes the possible outcomes $i = 1 \ldots n$ and x^+ (x^-) indicates the domain of gains (losses).

The subjective value of outcomes is encompassed by the so-called value function, which exhibits several particular features. First, it addresses the perceptional segmentation into two domains with different evolutions. These domains correspond to gains and losses so that the value function is asymmetric. The delimitation of the loss and gain domains takes place with respect to a subjective reference point. Formally, the value function is a function of two variables: the reference point and the magnitude of changes with respect to this reference. CPT considers the reference point to be fixed. Schmidt (2003) develops an extended axiomatization for variable references that accounts for the derivation of both the value function and the decision weights. Davies (2005) extends the notation in Schmidt in order to allow for the independence of the reference point and hence of the initial endowment and thus provides a basis for the unification of the frameworks for risky and risk-free choices.

The value function exhibits diminishing sensitivity in both domains (i.e., its variation decreases with the magnitude of gains and losses, respectively). Additionally, as people appear to be more reluctant to incur losses compared to gains of the same size—a property denoted as *loss aversion*, the value function presents a kink at the origin. Consequently, the value function has to be zero at the reference point, steeper for losses than for gains, as well as concave in the domain of gains and convex in the domain of losses. In sum, the value function is S-shaped. Norsworthy et al. (2004) find empirical evidence on the U.S. market for reference dependence, asymmetric valuation of gains and losses, and diminishing sensitivity.

The CPT of Tversky and Kahneman (1992) formulates the value function v of an individual (investor) k. Often their formulation is normalized to the form of

$$v(x_i) = \begin{cases} x_i^\alpha, & for\, x_i \geq 0 \\ -\lambda(-x_i)^\beta, & for\, x_i < 0 \end{cases} \tag{23.2}$$

where x_i denotes the possible outcomes. In addition, $0 < \alpha, \beta \leq 1$ are specific parameters describing risk aversion and, λ is known as the loss aversion coefficient. The specific parameters of the value function are estimated in Tversky and Kahneman to be $\alpha = \beta = 0.88$ and $\lambda = 2.25$. The result that $\alpha, \beta < 1$ confirms the diminishing sensitivity of the value function in both domains. Further estimates of the curvature parameters are computed in Wu and Gonzales (1996) both for their own data set ($\alpha = 0.52$) and for the data set in Camerer and Ho (1994) ($\alpha = 0.37$). The estimation of λ conforms to median responses obtained in an experiment concerning two-outcome prospects with monetary outcomes and numerical probabilities conducted in Tversky and Kahneman. Exhibit 23.1 illustrates the corresponding course.

According to PT, the outcomes that enter the prospective value may not be weighted by their simple probabilities as in the traditional EUT, but by the subjectively perceived counterparts of these probabilities. The latter are denoted as (cumulative) probability weighting functions (or decision weights) and represent complex, nonlinear functions of probabilities. This idea originates in the findings of various psychological experiments showing that individuals manifest the tendency to overweight (underweight) small (moderate to large) probabilities. Formally, the weighting functions are

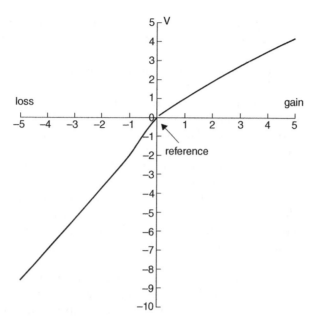

EXHIBIT 23.1   The PT-Value Function

Note: The exhibit shows the PT-value function for $\lambda = 2.25$, $\alpha = \beta = 0.88$. The value function is concave in the gains domain, convex in the loss domain, and has a kink at the reference point, which is at the origin.

designed to be increasing in probability and to exhibit diminishing sensitivity (i.e., steeper evolution) at the endpoints of the probability scale (i.e., in 0 and 1). This yields the specific inverted S-shape (concave for small and convex for large probabilities). Also, the decision weights are mostly subcertain (i.e., add up to a value less than 1). Prelec (1998) proposes further qualitatively similar formulations.

Loss Aversion

As previously discussed, one of the main innovations of PT is to introduce the notion of loss aversion as a common feature of decision-making under uncertainty. This concept stands for the empirically observed asymmetric impact of losses and gains on behavior. In other words, the decrease in utility generated due to the marginal loss is higher in absolute value than the increase from a marginal gain of the same size. As Hastie and Dawes (2001) note, losses are more painful than the pleasure of an equivalent gain.

In general, loss aversion is modeled in parallel with risk aversion. According to Rabin (2000a, 2000b), this is necessary as EUT cannot properly describe the risk aversion over modest stakes. Two main reasons favor this assertion and became the main points in which PT disagrees from EUT. First, an investor's risk attitude cannot be fully described by means of a sole parameter, which is risk aversion. This idea that a need exists for more than one parameter underlies in PT the formulation of the value function, which is based on two parameters describing risk aversion (α, β) and a loss aversion coefficient (λ). Second, preferences are not necessarily linearly dependent on the outcome probabilities, an idea that has fostered the introduction of the probability weighting functions.

Köbberling and Wakker (2005) consider loss aversion as a natural component of the risk attitude. It can be clearly delimited from two further components, namely the utility (expressed by the value function) and the probability weighting (reflected in the decision weights). Being related to the kink of the value function at the origin, loss aversion can be measured by the ratio of the left and right derivatives of the value function at the reference point. This ratio corresponds to the coefficient λ of the PT-value function in Equation 23.2 and is referred to as the *index of loss aversion*. For linear specifications of the value function, the index of loss aversion is identical to the loss aversion coefficient λ.

The literature provides various estimations of the coefficient of loss aversion λ. Tversky and Kahneman (1992) provide one of the first estimates based on an experimental sample of untrained students and under the assumption of a power value function amounting to λ = 2.25. Moreover, Benartzi and Thaler (1995) assess the parameter λ of a piecewise linear value function to be 2.77. The estimations rely on Monte Carlo replications of real market data of stocks, bonds, and Treasury bills between 1926 and 1990. In the context of an original procedure designed to test for loss aversion, Schmidt and Traub (2002) obtain λ = 1.43 from experimental data. The same estimate amounts to 2.87 when considering merely loss-averse choices. The subjects (students) are assumed to perceive choice alternatives according to CPT (i.e., with the specific value function and nonlinear decision weights). Schmidt and Traub conclude that loss aversion may be due to the extent rather than to the occurrence of loss-averse choices. In the considered sample, women appear to perform more and higher loss-averse choices compared to men. Furthermore, the loss aversion coefficient obtained by Berkelaar, Kouwenberg, and Post (2004) amounts to 2.50 for a piecewise concave power utility function with a kink at the reference point. For the same utility function but as a result of simultaneous generalized method of moments (GMM) estimation of both the loss aversion parameter λ and the risk aversion parameter γ, they derive λ = 2.711. Contrary to the previously mentioned studies that draw back on numerical estimation, Berkelaar et al. derive closed-form solutions for the optimal portfolio of the representative loss-averse agent in a discrete one-period equilibrium setting.

Myopic Loss Aversion

The literature extends the concept of loss aversion in order to (better) accommodate with empirically observed anomalies such as the *equity premium puzzle*. This puzzle refers to the abnormally higher historical returns of stocks over government bonds, which implies a suspiciously high level of risk aversion among investors. One popular extension introduced in Benartzi and Thaler (1995), which is called *myopic loss aversion* (mLA), relies on the joint effect of loss aversion and narrow framing. *Loss aversion* refers to the increased discomfort generated by losses compared to the pleasure of making gains of the same size. Introduced by Thaler (1980), *mental accounting* denotes the perception of current and future financial outcomes in mentally distinct partitions to which different levels of utility are assessed. Due to the presence of loss aversion, the aggregation of these different accounts over outcomes and over time is dynamic.

Narrow framing represents an aspect of mental accounting that accounts for the tendency to evaluate performance more frequently. This tendency results from the excessive attention paid to financial prospects. According to Kahneman and Lovallo (1993), the isolated evaluation of single risky prospects prevents the reduction of risk obtained by pooling different risk sources.

Thaler et al. (1997) define *myopic investors* as traders who narrowly frame both decisions and outcomes. The former type of narrow framing manifests with respect to short-term choices and the latter one concerns frequent evaluations of performance. For example, regarding the criticism that EUT cannot give a clear account of the risk-averse behavior with respect to small risks, Rabin and Thaler (2001) emphasize that this behavior precisely originates in the excessive focus on small risks due to their isolated consideration. Also, Thaler et al. design an experimental setting that allows performing separate tests on loss aversion and myopia. The results of their tests confirm these two phenomena as well as the role of loss aversion versus risk aversion. Gneezy and Potters (1997) directly test mLA on a group of students whose evaluation horizon (i.e., degree of myopia) is manipulated through the supplied feedback information.

Gneezy, Kapteyn, and Potters (2003) extend their study to a competitive (experimental) setting where agents face each other by trading units of one risky asset during several successive auctions. The results reinforce the existence of mLA and point out a positive impact on prices. Haigh and List (2005) adapt the setting in Gneezy and Potters (1997) in order to accommodate for the behavior of real players in financial markets. Their combined lab-field experiment compares the behavior of professional futures and option traders at the Chicago Board Exchange with the one of undergraduate student subjects. Apparently, professional traders suffer from mLA to an even greater extent than college students.

However, these empirical tests investigate mLA by isolating it from other decisional elements of potential importance. Research replicating some of the empirical studies heretofore mentioned reach different conclusions in this regard. Langer and Weber (2001) demonstrate theoretically and provide empirical evidence for the fact that the interaction of different PT factors such as loss aversion, diminishing sensitivity, and nonlinear probability weights can entail situations when myopia causes an increase of the willingness to invest. Blavatskyy and Pogrebna (2005) note that the nonlinear perception of probabilities manifests simultaneously but contrary to loss aversion and can even reverse the effect of the latter when probability distortions are sufficiently pronounced. Also, Fellner and Sutter (2005) conclude that mLA depends not only on the feedback frequency, but also on the length of the investment horizon. However, an experimental test meant to disentangle between feedback frequency and investment flexibility conducted by Bellemare, Krause, Kröger, and Zhang (2005) conflicts with these findings indicating that mLA can be attributed to the feedback frequency as assumed in earlier empirical tests.

SAFETY-FIRST PORTFOLIO THEORY

The safety-first framework aims to minimize the probability of ruin. An investor is ruined when his terminal wealth becomes smaller than a predetermined subsistence level (i.e., minimum level). Roy (1952) focuses on the case with no risk-free security and a low subsistence level. In the special case when all portfolio return distributions are constrained to be normal, minimizing the probability of ruin is equivalent to minimizing the number of standard deviations in which the subsistence level lies below the mean returns. In the case that the returns are not normally distributed, Roy relies on Chebyshev's inequality to support that the same minimization solution applies. An implication is that all optimal safety-first portfolios lie on the mean-variance frontier. However, Shefrin and Statman (2000) contend that the optimal safety-first portfolios are not mean-variance efficient.

According to Elton and Gruber (1995), two generalizations of the safety-first portfolio are available. Kataoka (1963) developed the first one, which eliminates Roy's notion of a predetermined subsistence level. Telser (1955) developed the second generalization, which considers both a fixed subsistence level and a ruin probability. In Telser's model, a portfolio is considered safe if the probability of ruin does not exceed a certain level. Arzac and Bawa (1977) extend Telser's model by allowing the probability of ruin to vary.

SP/A THEORY

Lopes (1987) proposed SP/A theory, which Lopes and Oden (1999) further developed. SP/A theory is a general framework rather than a specific theory of portfolio choice. This theory can also be regarded as an extension of the Arzac (1974) version of the safety-first portfolio model. As Shefrin (2008) notes, SP/A theory is a psychologically-based theory of choice among risky alternatives.

SP/A theory integrates two logically and psychologically separate criteria: SP and A. In SP/A theory, Lopes (1987) defines **S** as standing for security, where security is what motivates risk-averse people in their behavior. **P** means potential and risk-seeking people are motivated by the desire for potential. **A** stands for the aspiration level. It is a situational variable that represents the opportunities at hand such as "What can I get?" and the constraints imposed by the environment such as "What do I need?"

Shefrin and Statman (2000) show that SP/A theory shares features with the safety-first portfolio model. Lopes' idea of "security" is similar to "safety" in the safety-first model in the sense that it formulates the same general concern about avoiding low levels of wealth. This has the effect of reducing the degree to which the investor chooses zero consumption and zero wealth in states where he might experience losses. The idea of aspiration level can be related to a reference point in CPT, and generalizes the safety-first concept of reaching a specific target value. Potential relates to a general desire to reach high levels of wealth.

According to Shefrin (2008), SP/A theory has greater explanatory power for how people make choices than prospect theory. Consequently, SP/A theory is a better choice for a framework upon which to build both behavioral portfolio theory and behavioral asset pricing theory. Shefrin notes that even Kahneman proposed that SP/A theory might provide a better approach to explaining why behavioral portfolios tend to combine very safe and very risky assets.

Lopes (1987) explains that tensions occur in two places in her theory. One involves the trade-off between security and potential. In a financial context, this means that if the investor wants security, he will pay for it by accepting lower returns and vice versa. Security/potential defines a dispositional variable, meaning the investors choose between avoiding bad outcomes and approaching good ones. The second type of tension occurs as different situations create different patterns of agreement and disagreement between the motivation for security or potential and the immediate needs and opportunities influencing the aspiration level.

Security and Potential

Lopes (1987, 1990, 1995) and Lopes and Oden (1999) use a linear utility function and capture the attitude toward risk using a weighing function. In SP/A theory, the objective function is a weighted sum of wealth increments, similar to the expected value of wealth. As Lopes states, security motivation (fear) operates by weighing the probabilities of the worst outcomes in a lottery more heavily than the best outcomes. Thus, people would respond as if they are using a downward-biased value for the expected wealth if they were unusually pessimistic. In the same fashion, potential motivation (hope) results in overweighting the probability of the best outcomes relative to the worst outcomes. In this case, people would respond by using an upward-biased estimate for expected wealth if they were unusually optimistic.

Formally, the SP/A framework represents fear and hope through a transformed probability distribution function, a method introduced by Quiggen (1982, 1993) and Yaari (1987). According to Lopes (1987, 1990, 1995), every agent possesses fear and hope (the motivation for security and potential) and fear and hope modify the weighting function. When the function is convex, it represents the emotion of fear through the overweighting of probabilities associated with the most unfavorable outcomes. In the concave case, the function represents the emotion of hope. In SP/A theory, the final shape of the weighting function is a combination of the representative functions describing fear and hope. Lopes describes this specific shape, which is concave to the left and convex to the right, as "cautious optimism." As Gonzalez and Wu (1999) show, the function used by Lopes has the same general inverse S shape as the PT weighting function used by Tversky and Kahneman (1992). Gonzalez and Wu also contend that the two functions represent different psychological processes. Lopes' function reflects the motivation for security and potential and Tversky and Kahneman's function reflects psychophysics.

In the framework proposed by Lopes (1987, 1990, 1995) and Lopes and Oden (1999), fear affects the attitude toward a risky outcome through a reweighting of the probabilities. Specifically, Lopes computes expected wealth $E(W)$ using

$$h_s(D) = D^{1+q_s} \qquad (23.3)$$

where D is the probability of the investor to receive an increment in wealth W; h_s is the transformation function; q_s is a non-negative parameter describing the strength of fear (need for security); and the subscript s stands for security. Hope operates like fear, but it induces higher weighting of lower probabilities, which are associated with higher outcomes. The counterpart of $h_s(D)$ is

$$h_p(D) = 1 - (1-D)^{1+q_p} \qquad (23.4)$$

where h_p is the transformation function and q_p is the nonnegative parameter describing the strength of hope (need for potential) and the subscript p stands for potential. The shape of the transformation function is a convex combination of h_s and h_p, reflecting the relative strength of each. Specifically, the transformation function $h(D)$ has the form

$$h(D) = \delta h_s(D) + (1 - \delta)h_p(D) \qquad (23.5)$$

where δ lies between 0 and 1 and describes the strength of fear relative to hope.

SP/A theory provides a parsimonious behaviorally-based framework for portfolio selection. In particular, it easily lends itself to an asset pricing framework that combines behavioral beliefs and behavioral preferences. A key feature of SP/A-based behavioral portfolio theory is bipolarity in that investors form portfolios that combine very safe securities with very risky securities.

In SP/A theory, the investor substitutes the expected wealth $E(W)$ with the expected value of wealth $E_n(W)$, replacing the probability attached to the ith event with the difference

$$h(D_{i+1}) - h(D_i) \qquad (23.6)$$

Aspiration

According to Lopes (1987), the aspiration level in any given situation can have at least three different origins: (1) the direct evaluation of what is safe or reasonable to expect, (2) the direct contextual influence of the alternative choices that exist, and (3) outside influences. Lopes and Oden (1999) explain that the **A** criterion functions on the basis of stochastic control in which the agents are assumed to evaluate the attractiveness of lotteries by $D(A)$, which is the probability that a given lottery will yield an outcome at or above some aspiration level α.

Evaluation

According to Lopes (1987, 1990, 1995), risky outcomes are evaluated in terms of $E_n(W)$ and $D(A)$. $E_n(W)$ is the expected value of W based on the decision weights from the transformation function $h(D)$, which represents the security and potential motivations (SP component). $D(A)$ is the probability that the payoff will be α or higher. These two variables are similar to the augments in the safety-first model.

To demonstrate the intuition behind making choices in the SP/A framework, Lopes (1987) gives the following example concerning the way farmers make choices about the crops they plant. The subsistence farmer can choose between food crops and cash crops. The food crops have low but stable prices, while the cash crops have more variable prices but higher expected return. According to Lopes, farmers follow a simple rule: They plant food crops to the point where their subsistence needs are met and then allocate the remainder of their land to cash crops. She suggests that farmers gamble on cash crops because they aspire to escape poverty.

This agricultural example has two aspiration levels: One is subsistence and the other is some level above subsistence. The fear of falling below subsistence motivates the allocation to food crops. This is the same approach adopted by the safety-first theory. The aspiration of alleviating poverty motivates planting the rest of the land with cash crops. The farmer's problem is similar to Friedman and Savage's (1948) observation that people simultaneously purchase insurance and lottery tickets.

Lopes (1987) explains that although fear intensifies risk aversion, risk taking can be intensified either by hope or necessity. Traditional finance theory suggests that economic agents are not supposed to take risk unless they can afford it. However, as Kunreuther and Wright (1979) show, sometimes the poorest farmers devote the same share of land to cash crops as the richest farmers. In a similar fashion, Bowman (1982) notes that companies that undergo economic difficulties often engage in a riskier behavior than economically stable companies. In both cases, the source of the riskier behavior is arguably nested in necessity. If insufficient safety exists even when safety is the main goal, then the riskier choice might be the only choice.

Comparison of SP/S Theory with Cumulative Prospect Theory

According to Shefrin (2008), PT and SP/A share many features in common. The weighting function in both features an inverse S-shape. Further the reference point in CPT can be associated with the aspiration point in SP/A. Additionally, SP/A similarly defines outcomes in terms of gains and losses and is consistent with the framing effects of CPT.

However, the psychological base of the two theories is different. In CPT, the inverse S-shape of the weighting function is interpreted in terms of psychophysics. In SP/A, the inverse S-shape of the weighting function represents a conflict between security and potential. CPT relies on probability weighting to explain risk-averse choice in the loss domain: Small probabilities are over weighted, thereby offsetting the effect of convexity in the utility function. SP/A theory relies on the aspiration point and associated probability threshold. Similar arguments apply to the gains domain.

The two theories model the attitude to risk in different ways. In CPT, attitude to risk is represented by the shape of the utility function. In SP/A theory, utility is linear and attitude to risk is captured by the weighting function. In contrast to CPT, the utility function in SP/A has no kink, and therefore does not change from strict convexity to strict concavity at the kink. In CPT, the degree of curvature to the utility function is mild in both the gain and the loss domain. Although Lopes and Oden (1999) develop SP/A using a linear utility function, they indicate that utility functions exhibit mild concavity in practice.

BEHAVIORAL PORTFOLIO THEORY

Shefrin and Statman (2000) combine some of the main ideas from SP/A theory and prospect theory into a new framework, which they call *behavioral portfolio theory* (BPT). BPT features an efficient frontier in a similar way as traditional finance theory that relies on mean-variance analysis. The authors examine both the BPT efficient frontier with the mean-variance efficient frontier and demonstrate that the two frontiers generally do not lead to the same results. The reason is that the investors who employ the mean-variance frontier simply choose their portfolios with respect to the expected returns (mean) and the risk (measured by the variance). In the case of BPT, investors choose portfolios on the basis of expected wealth, need for security and potential, aspiration levels, and the probability of achieving given aspiration levels. Further, the optimal portfolios chosen by the BPT investors are different from those selected under the capital asset pricing model (CAPM). Another difference is that in the CAPM, investors allocate their funds between the market portfolio and the risk-free security but in the BPT framework, investors choose the optimal portfolios that are similar to combinations of lottery tickets and bonds.

Shefrin and Statman (2000) develop two specifications of BPT. One considers a single mental account (BPT-SA) and the other considers multiple mental accounts (BPT-MA). Under BPT-SA, the agents consolidate all their portfolios in one mental account by considering covariances. In the BPT-MA specification, the investors separate their portfolios in different mental accounts and do not consider the covariances between these mental accounts. The next section provides more detail about each of these BPT specifications.

BPT-SA

Similar to the mean-variance investors, the BPT-SA agents consider the portfolio as a whole but the optimization criteria differ. The mean-variance efficient frontier is in (μ, σ) space where μ stands for mean and σ stands for standard deviation. The mean-variance frontier is obtained by maximizing μ for fixed σ. In BPT-SA, the efficient frontier is in $(E_n(W), Pr(W \le A))$ space, where the first component is related to the SP and the second one is related to A. Therefore, the BPT-SA frontier is obtained by maximizing $E_n(W)$ for fixed $Pr(W \le A)$. Shefrin and Statman (2000) provide detailed solutions with linear utility function and the CRRA utility function.

BPT-MA

In Shefrin and Statman (2000), mental accounting is the characteristic that separates BPT-SA and BPT-MA. BPT-SA investors integrate their portfolios by considering the covariances. BPT-MA investors overlook covariances and segregate their portfolios into separate mental account layers. Mental accounting is a characteristic of prospect theory. Shefrin and Statman (1985) suggest that the original purchase price serves as a reference point in investment decisions. They use prospect theory to explain why investors sell winners too early and hold losers too long. Tversky and Kahneman (1986) demonstrate that the decision process for the investors becomes complicated and difficult due to covariance and other properties of joint probability distributions. Investors simplify their choices by using mental accounts.

Sometimes investors can be characterized only by a low or high aspiration level. However, investors generally combine both because they want to avoid poverty and to have a chance to become rich. Such portfolios combining low and high aspiration levels can be represented by different mental account layers. The investors allocate some of their wealth in a lower layer, the goal of which is to avoid poverty. They also allocate some of their wealth in a higher layer designed to gain riches. Statman (2010) notes that investors might behave as if they are risk-averse in the lower layer (need for security), while they behave as if they love risk in the upside potential layer. These investors are motivated by aspirations, not attitudes toward risk.

Shefrin (2008) contends that an agent who has multiple mental accounts will be characterized with individual utility function for each individual account and an overall utility function that depends on the individual ones. The agent has to allocate wealth among the separate mental accounts in order to maximize overall utility. The accounts are not integrated and the agents overlook the covariances, which may lead the agent to borrow for leverage in the high aspiration account and lend in the lower aspiration account. Further, the investor might have a short position for a given security in one layer and a long position for the same security in a different layer.

Evidence from experiments and practice suggests that investors overlook covariances. Using an experiment, Kroll, Levy, and Rapoport (1988) demonstrate that if subjects are given the expected returns and the variance-covariance matrix for a number of securities, they ignore covariances when constructing their portfolios.

Jorion (1994) offers similar evidence from practice by observing institutional investors. In the allocation of funds, investors often put securities in one mental account and currencies in another. They separate the management of securities from the management of currencies and the structure they create is inherently suboptimal because it ignores covariances between securities and currencies.

BEHAVIORAL ASSET PRICING MODEL

Shefrin and Statman (1994) present behavioral capital asset pricing theory as an alternative to the CAPM. The behavioral asset pricing model (BAPM) as described by in Shefrin and Statman (1994), Statman (1999, 2010), and Statman, Fisher, and Anginer (2008) has two groups of economic agents. One group consists of information traders who behave according to the CAPM, exhibit no cognitive errors, and have mean-variance preferences. The second group represents noise traders, who do not conform to the CAPM, exhibit cognitive errors, and do not have strict mean-variance preferences.

As Statman (1999, 2010) indicates, the preferences for consumption in behavioral finance can be divided into two groups: utilitarian and value-expressive. From an investment point of view, utilitarian preferences are referred to as "fundamental" and the value-expressive preferences are known as "sentiment." Rational agents restrict their choice by utilitarian preferences. In investment contexts these are preferences for high return and low risk. However, rationality is hard to extend to value-expressive preferences such as the display of social responsibility in a socially responsible mutual fund, the display of wealth in a hedge fund, or the excitement of an initial public offering (IPO).

THE BAPM, CAPM, AND THREE-FACTOR MODEL

In the BAPM the expected returns depend on behavioral betas that are relative to the efficient mean-variance portfolio. Because noise traders affect market prices, the efficient mean-variance portfolio is not the market portfolio. For example, if noise traders like growth stocks, this might increase the prices of growth stocks relative to value stocks. In such case, the BAPM efficient mean-variance portfolio, in contrast to the market portfolio, will tilt toward value stocks.

Estimating betas in the BAPM and the CAPM contexts presents several difficulties. Although the current academic literature provides the construction principles of the market portfolio, it cannot be precisely constructed in practice. For that reason, researchers create proxies for the true market portfolio using stock indices such as the S&P 500. In the case of the BAPM beta, the problem of using a proxy is even more aggravated because the BAPM-efficient portfolio changes over time.

Fama and French (1992) formulate an extension to the CAPM that attempts to enrich its structure. Their three-factor model adds market capitalization and book-to-market ratio to beta as variables that affect expected returns. As Statman (2010) notes, a main difference between the three-factor model and the BAPM is in interpreting these variables. In traditional (standard) finance, market capitalization and book-to-market ratios are measures of risk. Because researchers consider small-cap stocks and stocks with high book-to-market ratios as risky, such stocks have high expected returns. However, from the prism of the BAPM, capitalization and book-to-market ratio represent reflections of affect or admiration (an emotion) and representativeness (a cognitive bias). This type of rendition of the three-factor model induces investors to identify desirable stocks (good stocks) as stocks of "good" companies and undesirable stocks (bad stocks) as the stocks of "bad" companies. Small-cap stocks and stocks with high book-to-market ratios are stocks of "bad" companies. Interestingly, banks' stocks in 2008 exhibited such characteristics. These companies generate negative affect (or emotion), inducing investors to avoid them in their portfolios and thus push stock prices down and expected returns up.

In an informal way, the CAPM, three-factor model, and BAPM can be represented and compared in the following way.

The CAPM

Expected return of a stock = f (market factor) (23.7)

The three-factor model

Expected return of a stock = f (market factor, book-to-market factor, market cap factor) (23.8)

The BAPM

Expected return of a stock = f (market factor, book-to-market factor, market cap factor, momentum, affect factor, social responsibility factor, status factor, etc.) (23.9)

Expected Returns and Value Expressive Preferences

Statman (2010) contends that investors prefer assets characterized by low volatility in prices and earnings. Further, investors also like stocks with characteristics such as large capitalization, high price-to-book ratios, and high price-to-earnings ratios. Thus, investors price stocks with likable features higher leading to lower expected returns. For example, large-cap stocks have low expected returns. In the BAPM, stocks with desirable characteristics also have low expected returns (Shefrin and Statman, 1994; Statman, 1999).

The existence of information traders who conform to the CAPM framework and noise traders who conform to the behavioral framework complicates the path from preferences to portfolio choice as described by Shefrin and Statman (1994) and Pontiff (2006). If most investors are noise traders who believe that good stocks are stocks of good companies (companies with positive affect), then these stocks will be priced higher and the information traders who behave rationally will be aware of that. Further, the information traders will try to exploit noise traders' beliefs by buying the stocks of "bad" companies (companies with high negative affect) because these companies are undervalued due to the emotional choice of the noise traders who stay away from them.

Statman et al. (2008) explain that if the arbitrage of the informed traders offsets the effects of the noise traders on the stock prices and returns, the value expressive preferences in the form of affect have no role in the asset pricing model. In the case of incomplete arbitrage, however, value expressive preferences do play a role in the asset pricing model.

According to Statman (2010), no perfect (risk free) arbitrage is possible in that case because if information traders have reliable but imperfect information, such traders would like to act on this information and increase "bad" stocks in their portfolios relative to others. However, as they allocate additional funds to these specific stocks, their portfolios become riskier. The increase in risk leads information traders to limit the amount devoted to those stocks and in this way limits the effect on price and the returns.

Statman et al. (2008) provide further evidence that affect, which has value expressive characteristics, underlies the market-capitalization and book-to-market factors of the three-factor models. They illustrate a BAPM in which expected returns are high when stocks are risky and also when negative affect is high. In summary, expected returns depend not only on utilitarian characteristics but also on value expressive characteristics that investors could value.

Expected Returns and Perceived Risk

A main implication of traditional financial analysis is that higher risk should be rewarded with higher return, which is based on the assumption of risk aversion. However, Ricciardi (2008) provides a survey of the literature that shows conflicting findings on that topic. Indeed, some studies, including Fama and French (1992, 1993) and Strong and Xu (1997), suggest that no relationship exists between risk and return. Others such as Haugen (1999) and Easley, Hvidkjaer, and O'Hara (2002) report an inverse relationship between risk and return, where higher risk is associated with lower return.

The issue of an inverse relationship between risk and return is also known as *Bowman's paradox*, where companies undertake higher risk while expecting lower returns. Bowman (1982) reports that companies suffering economic difficulties often engage in riskier behavior. He further demonstrates that as the level of economic difficulty increases, companies earn a lower rate of return and take more risk. Bowman proposes that prospect theory can explain the negative relationship between risk and return. Lopes (1987) provides the SP/A view of the same behavior. Ricciardi (2008) provides further discussion on this topic.

SUMMARY

This chapter details the latest advances in behavioral portfolio theory. Starting with prospect theory, the chapter develops several key ideas such as loss aversion and mental accounting and introduces different behaviorally based portfolio models. The chapter continues with safety-first portfolio theory, evolves to the SP/A model, and then compares SP/A to prospect theory. Next, the chapter introduces the BAPM, which combines some main ideas from SP/A theory and PT into a new framework. Finally, a discussion introduces how value expressive preferences and perceived risk shape expected returns. The chapter emphasizes the inability of traditional finance theory and EUT to correctly represent the multifaceted behavior of the players on the financial stage. Instead, the chapter points to a resolution in the rich and flexible frameworks of behavioral portfolio theory.

DISCUSSION QUESTIONS

1. Describe loss aversion and myopic loss aversion.
2. Explain the main differences between CPT and SP/A.
3. Discuss whether the efficient mean-variance portfolio frontier and the BPT efficient portfolio frontier lead to the same results.
4. Identify the main differences between the three-factor model and the BAPM.

REFERENCES

Arzac, Enrique R. 1974. "Utility Analysis of Chance-Constrained Portfolio Selection." *Journal of Financial and Quantitative Analysis* 9:6, 993–1007.

Arzac, Enrique R., and Vijay S. Bawa. 1977. "Portfolio Choice and Equilibrium in Capital Markets with Safety-First Investors." *Journal of Financial Economics* 4:3, 277–288.

Bellemare, Charles, Michaela Krause, Sabine Kröger, and Chendi Zhang. 2005. "Myopic Loss Aversion: Information Feedback vs. Investment Flexibility." *Economic Letters* 87:3, 319–324.

Benartzi, Shlomo, and Richard Thaler. 1995. "Myopic Loss Aversion and the Equity Premium Puzzle." *Quarterly Journal of Economics* 1:110, 73–92.

Berkelaar, Arjan, Roy Kouwenberg, and Thierry Post. 2004. "Optimal Portfolio Choice under Loss Aversion." *Review of Economics and Statistics* 86:4, 973–987.

Blavatskyy, Pavlo, and Gana Pogrebna. 2005. "Myopic Loss Aversion Revisited: The Effect of Probability Distortions in Choice under Risk." Working Paper No. 249, University of Zurich.

Bowman, Edward H. 1982. "Risk Seeking by Troubled Firms." *Sloan Management Review* 23:4, 33–42.

Camerer, Colin F., and Teck-Hua Ho. 1994. "Violations of the Betweenness Axiom and Non-linearity in Probability." *Journal of Risk and Uncertainty* 88:2, 167–196.

Chateauneuf, Alain Jacques, and Peter Wakker. 1999. "An Axiomatization of Cumulative Prospect Theory for Decision Under Risk." *Journal of Risk and Uncertainty* 18:2, 137–145.

Davies, Greg B. 2005. *"Dynamic Reference Points: Investors as Consumers of Uncertainty."* Working Paper, University College, London.

Easley, David, Soeren Hvidkjaer, and Maureen O'Hara. 2002. "Is Information Risk a Determinant of Assest Returns?" *Journal of Finance* 57:5, 2185–2221.

Elton, Edwin J., and Martin J. Gruber. 1995. *Modern Portfolio Theory and Investment Analysis*. New York: John Wiley & Sons.

Fama, Eugene F., and Kenneth R. French. 1992. "The Cross-Section of Expected Stock Returns." *Journal of Finance* 47:2, 427–465.

Fama, Eugene F., and Kenneth R. French. 1993. "Common Risk Factors in the Returns on Stocks and Bonds." *Journal of Financial Econometrics* 33:1, 3–56.

Fellner, Gerlinde, and Matthias Sutter. 2005. "Causes, Consequences, and Cures for Myopic Loss Aversion—An Experimental Investigation." Working Paper, Vienna University of Economics.

Friedman, Milton, and L. J. Savage. 1948. "The Utility Analysis of Choices Involving Risk." *Journal of Political Economy* 56:4, 279–304.

Gneezy, Uri, Arie Kapteyn, and Jan Potters. 2003. "Evaluation Periods and Asset Prices in a Market Experiment." *Journal of Finance* 58:2, 821–837.

Gneezy, Uri, and Jan Potters. 1997. "An Experiment on Risk Taking and Evaluation Periods." *Quarterly Journal of Economics* 102:2, 631–645.

Gonzalez, Richard, and George Wu. 1999. "On the Shape of the Probability Weighting Function." *Cognitive Psychology* 38:1, 129–166.

Haigh, Michael S., and John A. List. 2005. "Do Professional Traders Exhibit Myopic Loss Aversion? An Experimental Analysis." *Journal of Finance* 60:1, 523–534.

Hastie, Reid, and Robyn M. Dawes. 2001. *Rational Choice in an Uncertain World: The Psychology of Judgment and Decision Making*, 2nd ed. Thousand Oaks, CA: Sage.

Haugen, Robert A. 1999. *The New Finance: The Case Against Efficient Markets*. Upper Saddle River, NJ: Prentice Hall.

Jorion, Philippe. 1994. "Mean-Variance Analysis of Currency Overlays." *Financial Analysis Journal* 50:3, 48–56.

Kahneman, Daniel, and Amos Tversky. 1979. "Prospect Theory: An Analysis of Decision." *Econometrica* 2:47, 263–291.

Kahneman, Daniel, and Dan Lovallo. 1993. "Timid Choices and Bold Forecasts—A Cognitive Perspective on Risk Taking." *Management Science* 39:1, 17–31.

Kataoka, Shinji. 1963. "A Stochastic Programming Model." *Econometrica* 31:1/2, 181–196.

Köbberling, Veronika, and Peter P. Wakker. 2005. "An Index of Loss Aversion." *Journal of Economic Theory* 122:1, 119–131.

Kroll, Yoram, Haim Levy, and Ammon Rapoport. 1988. "Experimental Tests of the Separation Theorem and the Capital Asset Pricing Model." *American Economic Review* 78:3, 500–518.

Kunreuther, Howard, and Gavin Wright. 1979. "Safety First, Gambling, and the Subsistence Farmer." In James A. Roumasset, Jean-Marc Bousard, and Inderjit Singh, eds., *Risk, Uncertainty and Agricultural Development*, 213–228. New York: Agricultural Development Council.

Langer, Thomas, and Martin Weber. 2001. "Prospect Theory, Mental Accounting, and Differences in Aggregated and Segregated Evaluation of Lottery Portfolios." *Management Science* 47:5, 716–733.

Lopes, Lola L. 1987. "Between Hope and Fear: The Psychology of Risk." *Advances in Experimental Social Psychology* 20, 255–295.

Lopes, Lola L. 1990. "Re-Modeling Risk Aversion: A Comparison of Bernoullian and Rank Dependent Value Approaches." In George M. von Furstenberg, ed., *Acting under Uncertainty: Multidiscipliniray Conceptions*, 267–299. Boston, MA: Kluwer Academic Publishers.

Lopes, Lola L. 1995. "Algebra and Process in the Modeling of Risky Choice." In Jerome Musemeyer, Reid Hastie, and Douglas Medin, eds., *Decision Making from a Cognitive Perspective*, 177–220. San Diego, CA: Academic Press.

Lopes, Lola L., and Gregg C. Oden. 1999. "The Role of Aspiration Level in Risk Choice: A Comparison of Cumulative Prospect Theory and SP/A Theory." *Journal of Mathematical Psychology* 43:2, 286–313.

Norsworthy, John R., Rifat Gorener, Richard E. Schuler, Irvin W. Morgan Jr., and Ding Li. 2004. *"Expected Utility, Prospect Theory, and Asset Pricing."* Working Paper, Rensselaer Polytechnic Institute Financial Technology.

Pontiff, Jeffrey. 2006. "Costly Arbitrage and the Myth of Idiosyncratic Risk." *Journal of Accounting and Economics* 42:1–2, 35–52.

Prelec, Drazen. 1998. "The Probability Weighting Function." *Econometrica* 66:3, 497–528.

Rabin, Matthew. 2000a. "Diminishing Marginal Utility of Wealth Cannot Explain Risk Aversion." In Daniel Kahneman and Amos Tversky, eds., *Choices, Values, and Frames*, 202–208. Cambridge: Cambridge University Press.

Rabin, Matthew. 2000b. "Risk Aversion and Expected-Utility Theory: A Calibration Theorem." *Econometrica* 68:5, 1281–1292.

Rabin, Matthew, and Richard H. Thaler. 2001. "Anomalies: Risk Aversion." *Journal of Economic Perspectives* 15:1, 219–232.

Ricciardi, Victor. 2008. "Risk: Traditional Finance versus Behavioral Finance." In Frank J. Fabozzi, ed., *Handbook of Finance: Volume 3: Valuation, Financial Modeleing, and Quantitative Tools*, 11–38. Hoboken, NJ: John Willey & Sons, Inc.

Roy, Arthur D. 1952. "Safety-First and the Holding of Assets." *Econometrica* 20:3, 431–449.

Schmidt, Ulrich. 2003. "Reference Dependence in Cumulative Prospect Theory." *Journal of Mathematical Psychology* 25:2, 122–131.

Schmidt, Ulrich, and Stefan Traub. 2002. "An Experimental Test of Loss Aversion." *Journal of Risk and Uncertainty* 25:3, 233–249.

Shefrin, Hersh. 2008. *A Behavioral Approach to Asset Pricing*, 2nd ed. San Diego, CA: Academic Press.

Shefrin, Hersh, and Meir Statman. 1985. "The Disposition to Sell Winners Too Early and Ride Losers Too Long: Theory and Evidence." *Journal of Finance* 40:3, 777–790.

Shefrin, Hersh, and Meir Statman. 1994. "Behavioral Capital Asset Pricing Theory." *Journal of Financial and Quantitative Analysis* 29:3, 323–349.

Shefrin, Hersh, and Meir Statman. 2000. "Behavioral Portfolio Theory." *Journal of Financial and Quantitative Analysis* 35:2, 127–151.

Statman, Meir. 1999. "Behavioral Finance: Past Battles and Future Engagements." *Financial Analysts Journal* 55:6, 18–27.

Statman, Meir. 2010. "What Is Behavioral Finance?" In Arnold. S. Wood, ed., *Behavioral Finance and Investment Management*, 1–12. Charlottesville, VA: Research Foundation Publications.

Statman, Meir, Keneth L. Fisher, and Deniz Anginer. 2008. "Affect in a Behavioral Asset-Pricing Model." *Financial Analysts Journal* 64:2, 20–28.

Strong, Norman, and Xinzhong G. Xu. 1997. "Explaining the Cross-Section of UK Expected Stock Returns." *British Accounting Review* 29:1, 1–23.

Telser, Lester G. 1955. "Safety First and Hedging." *Review of Economic Studies* 23:1, 1–16.

Thaler, Richard H. 1980. "Toward a Positive Theory of Consumer Choice." *Journal of Economic Behavior and Organization* 1:1, 39–60.

Thaler, Richard H., Amos Tversky, Daniel Kahneman, and Alan Schwartz. 1997. "The Effect of Myopia and Loss Aversion on Risk Taking." *Quarterly Journal of Economics* 112:2, 647–661.

Tversky, Amos, and Daniel Kahneman. 1986. "Rational Choice and the Framing of Decisions." *Journal of Business* 59:4, 251–278.

Tversky, Amos, and Daniel Kahneman. 1992. "Advances in Prospect Theory: Cumulative Representation of Uncertainty." *Journal of Risk and Uncertainty* 5:4, 297–323.

Wakker, Peter, and Amos Tversky. 1993. "An Axiomatization of Cumulative Prospect Theory." *Journal of Risk and Uncertainty* 7:7, 147–176.

Wu, George, and Richard Gonzales. 1996. "Curvature of the Probability Weighting Function." *Management Science*, 42:12, 1676–1690.

Yaari, Menahem E. 1987. "The Dual Theory of Choice Under Risk." *Econometrica* 55:1, 95–115.

ABOUT THE AUTHORS

Erick W. Rengifo is an Associate Professor in the Economics Department at Fordham University. He is a founder of Spes Nova Inc, a nonprofit corporation whose main goals are to provide funding to microenterprises, assist in market creation, and provide insurance products for the working poor around the world. He is also the founder and director of the Center for International Policy Studies. Professor Rengifo is an active scholar with interests in behavioral finance, risk management, insurance, microfinance, micro-insurance, and econometrics. He is a private consultant in the fields of microfinance, micro-insurance, algorithmic trading, investments, and risk management. Professor Rengifo holds a PhD in economics with a concentration in finance and econometrics from Catholic University of Louvain-Belgium.

Rossen Trendafilov is Assistant Professor of Economics in the Economics Department at Truman State University, where he teaches macroeconomics and financial economics. He maintains active academic research in the fields of financial economics, behavioral finance, financial econometrics, market microstructure, algorithmic trading, data mining, Fourier series analysis, wavelet analysis, and fractal analysis. Professor Trendafilov consults on portfolio selection, trading strategies, algorithmic trading, and econometric modeling. He was a member of a hedge fund administration and also worked as a junior auditor and private consultant in Bulgaria. Professor Trendafilov holds a PhD in economics from Fordham University with a concentration in finance and market microstructure.

Emanuela Trifan is Quantitative Analyst at Bayerngas Energy GmbH Munich, Germany. Dr. Trifan works in the fields of commodities price determination and forecast, portfolio optimization, risk management, and price database management. She has held research associate positions in Goethe University Frankfurt am Main, Darmstadt University of Technology, and University "Politehnica" Bucharest, where while pursuing an active research agenda, she taught multiple courses in finance, mathematics, and econometrics. Dr. Trifan holds a PhD in economics with a focus on behavioral economics from Darmstadt University of Technology, Germany and also holds a degree in industrial engineering from University "Politehnica" Bucharest.

CHAPTER 24

Post-Crisis Investor Behavior: Experience Matters

Joseph V. Rizzi
President, Macro Strategies, LLC

INTRODUCTION

The initial impact of the financial crisis of 2008 on investors was substantial. A panic induced a shift away from risky assets (e.g., common stocks) toward safer, more liquid investments (e.g., government bonds). The recovering economy and improved financial markets may trigger a return to pre-crisis risk appetite and investments. Nonetheless, current investor behavior suggests otherwise, especially for certain age groups (Zick, Mayer, and Giaubitz 2012).

A disagreement exists about the longer-term impact of the financial crisis on investor expectations, especially investor willingness to invest in the stock market. Traditional finance theory suggests investor experiences are irrelevant. All that matters are asset market fundamentals. Furthermore, investor risk tolerances are stable. Behavioral finance and recent evidence imply otherwise (Malmendier and Nagel 2011). Macroeconomic experiences can affect investors' expectations and willingness to invest in the stock market as risk tolerances are time varying.

Nonetheless, questions remain, such as whether investors weigh all experiences equally and whether they give greater weight to recent experiences or early formative experiences. The answer to these questions has important implications for asset allocation decisions, the equity risk premium, and longer term investor behavior.

This chapter begins with a behavioral finance framework and then discusses why experiences matter and to whom they matter most. It includes a review of the collective memory hypothesis on generation Y (i.e., individuals aged 18 to 34). As the chapter explains, both individual and group experiences influence risk taking. This can move asset prices away from fundamentals. Next, the chapter examines evidence and implications. Finally, the chapter offers tentative conclusions and possible future directions about this rapidly evolving field of behavioral finance. The financial crisis is likely to have a persistent impact on the risk tolerance and perceptions of young adults, which in turn could affect asset allocations and the market price of risk.

BEHAVIORAL FINANCE FRAMEWORK

Risk can be classified along two dimensions. The first concerns high-frequency events with relatively clear cause-and-effect relationships. Other risks, such as market crashes, occur infrequently. Consequently, the cause-and-effect relationship is unclear. The second dimension is impact severity. No matter how remote, investors should not ignore high-impact events because they can threaten their ability to pay off debt, contribute money to investment funds, and fund future lifestyle changes such as retirement. Exhibit 24.1 reflects the dual dimensions of a risk map involving frequency and impact severity.

Cyclical risks are low-frequency-high-impact events characterized by their negative skew and fat-tailed loss distributions. Investors incurring such risk can expect mainly small positive events but are subject to a few cases of extreme loss. Consequently, these risks are difficult to understand because of two factors. First, insufficient data are available to determine meaningful probability distributions. In this case, the statistics are descriptive, not predictive (Knight 1921). Second, and perhaps more important, infrequency clouds hazard perception, which concerns the degree of seriousness attached to an event. Risk estimates become anchored on recent events. Overemphasis on recent events can also produce disaster myopia during a market crisis as instruments are priced as if another crisis will occur. These facts lead to risk mispricing and the procyclical nature of risk appetite, which is amplified by leveraging and deleveraging.

Traditional finance uses quantitative risk-management models based on portfolio and option pricing theory that provides a framework on how investors should act. These traditional finance models build on expected utility theory (EUT), which

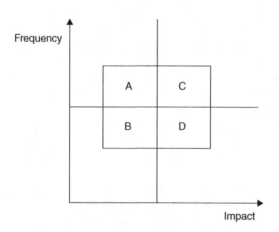

A: High frequency/low impact events: reflected in risk pricing.
B: Low frequency/low impact events: treated as a cost of business.
C: High frequency/high impact events: managed though control.
D: Low frequency/high impact events: frequently ignored.

EXHIBIT 24.1 Risk Map

Note: This exhibit illustrates the dual aspects of risk—frequency and impact severity. Quadrants A, B, C, and D indicate the likely responses to different combinations of frequency (high or low) and impact (high or low).

views investors as expected utility maximizers (Friedman and Savage 1948). Empirical support of EUT is mixed with numerous reported anomalies including holding losers too long, selling winners too soon, engaging in excess trading, and herding (Ellsberg 1961).

An alternative prospect theory developed by Tversky and Kahneman (1992) can explain these facts. Instead of being expected utility (E(U)) maximizers, prospect theory views investors as expected regret (E(r)) minimizers focusing more on losses than gains. EUT focuses on wealth changes. The value function in prospect theory is based on gains or losses relative to a reference point, usually par or the original purchase price. Exhibit 24.2 reflects the risk-averse behavior of investors by giving extra emphasis to the downside of uncertain events. The value function is convex in the loss domain but concave for gains. This exhibit indicates that people's choices reflect risk taking when their decision involves losses, but risk aversion for gains.

Behavioral finance examines how investors gather, interpret, and process information. Specifically, behavioral finance concentrates on perception and cognitive bias and recognizes that models can influence behavior and shape decisions. These biases can corrupt the decision process, leading to suboptimal results as emotions override self-control.

Market signals are complex and include both information and noise (Silver 2012). Information concerns facts affecting fundamental values. As Black (1986) notes, noise is a random blip erroneously interpreted as a signal. Investors have developed shortcuts, rules of thumb, or heuristics to process market signals. These belief-based heuristics incorporate biases or cognitive constraints, which are now investigated.

Regret

Risk is forward-looking and involves exposure to the consequences of uncertain events. Regret, however, is backward-looking and focuses on responsibility for what people could have done but did not do. Regret underlies several biases. For example,

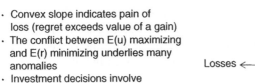
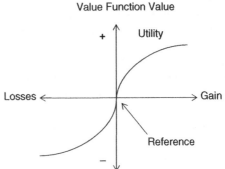

EXHIBIT 24.2 Investors Minimize Expected Regret

Note: This exhibit illustrates the value function of Kahneman and Tversky's (1979) prospect theory, which replaces the utility function of expected utility theory.

people try to minimize regret by seeking confirming data, suppressing conflicting information, and taking comfort that others made the same decision. Consequently, regret can inhibit learning from past experiences.

Sunk costs are one type of regret bias. *Sunk-cost bias* involves avoiding loss recognition despite evidence the loss has already occurred and a further loss is likely. Examples include the reluctance to sell impaired or underperforming assets at reduced prices. Usually, decision makers defend reluctance based on the market price being too low. Most investors, however, reject the logical alternative of acquiring additional exposure at the market price to exploit the alleged underpricing; thus, illustrating in this instance that price is of secondary importance relative to regret.

Panic conditions, such as those that occurred in 2008 and 2009, are also based on a combination of regret and herding. In a crisis, the reference is pessimism and people actively seek bad news to confirm their beliefs. Thus, to minimize regret, they follow the herd to avoid being left behind and engage in panic selling. This further depresses prices, leading to continued forced selling and the creation of a positive feedback loop as occurred in the fourth quarter of 2008.

Another regret-related bias is the *house money effect* in which investors take on increased risk when investing profits. Investors are willing to assume greater risks when they are up in a bull market and less risk in a bear market. They perceive regret to be less when the risk of winnings is involved rather than risk of initial capital. This procyclical phenomenon leads to "buy high and sell low" behavior.

This illustrates the reflexivity or feedback principle (Soros 1994) whereby markets affect psychology and psychology affects markets. Positive feedback is self-amplifying, while negative feedback is self-corrective. For example, collateral values rise during a bull market. This increases access to lower priced funding and liquidity, which fuels further gains.

Overconfidence

Overconfidence occurs when people exaggerate their predictive skills and ignore the impact of chance or outside circumstances. This behavior results in underestimating outcome variability in which self-attribution and hindsight reinforce overconfidence. *Self-attribution* involves internalizing success while externalizing failure. Investors take credit for results during an economic boom but blame their subsequent losses on unforeseen market circumstances. The direction of overconfidence is usually positive, reflecting a related optimism bias. *Hindsight* involves selective recall of confirming information to overestimate one's ability to predict the correct outcome, which inhibits learning. Disappointments and surprises typically follow long periods of overconfidence.

Industry experts are especially prone to overconfidence based on knowledge and control illusions. People often confuse knowledge with familiarity. A number of industry experts, including the former Fed chairman Alan Greenspan, who missed the collapse of the housing and structured credit bottom reflects this mistaken use of familiarity as knowledge. Recently released 2007 Federal Reserve meeting notes indicate a similar miss by Greenspan's successor, Ben Bernanke, who misread the seriousness of the crisis unfolding in late 2007. This misinterpretation is partly due to misguided overreliance on traditional finance quantitative models without understanding their limitations. Key model limitations include the following:

- **Homogeneous populations**. Statistical models require large homogeneous populations with a long history of observations. People tend to extrapolate limited observations leading to the gambler's fallacy. As Shefrin (2000, p. 18) notes, "Gambler's fallacy arises because people misinterpret the law of averages, technically known as the 'law of larger numbers.' They think the law of large numbers applies to small samples as well as to large samples."
- **Statistical loss distribution**. Loss distributions for credit are skewed, with unexpected event losses hidden in the distribution's fat tails. Models tend to be blinded by the mean and underestimate extreme events.
- **Historical basis**. History is a guide to the future, not the answer. In fact, the essence of risk is that more things can happen than did happen. The past represents but one possible outcome from an event sequence and is not an independent observation. History becomes less relevant as markets and underwriting practices change. This was especially true for mortgage default models that ignored the impact of securitization of mortgage originator underwriting practices, thereby missing the regime change.
- **Uncertainty**. Decisions involve elements of both risk (known unknowns) and uncertainty (unknown unknowns). Financial models adequately contemplate the former but inadequately deal with the latter. Because managing uncertainty requires judgment, not calculation, it is prone to bias. The *illusion of control* reflects the unfounded belief in one's ability to influence or structure around uncertain events. Risk is shunned when people believe they cannot escape its consequences due to their inability to control it. Fear increases risk aversion because it causes a reduced sense of control. This reflects a pessimistic overestimate of costs while underestimating gains. Pessimism is heightened by anchoring when someone gives disproportionate weight to the first information received. Time-delayed consequences magnify overconfidence as individuals weigh short-term performance at a higher level than longer-term consequences. These occur whenever short-term benefits clash with long-term effects.

Statistical Bias

Statistical bias involves confusing beliefs for probability and skill for chance. Economics is a social science based on human behavior. As Sharpe (2007) notes, prices are not determined by random number machines but come from trades by real people. Feedback loops, prices, trades, and people complicate statistical modeling.

Investors find accepting change difficult and are frequently fooled by randomness. A manifestation is the *representative bias*, whereby people see patterns in random events. They interpret short-term success as "hot hands" by a skilled investor and cannot distinguish results based on luck versus skill. Thus, the "lucky fool" is rewarded and encouraged until luck turns and losses are incurred (Taleb 2004).

Another statistical error before the financial crisis in 2008 is *extrapolation bias*. This occurs when people assume current events or trends continue into the foreseeable future independent of historical experience, sample size or mean reversion. Perhaps, the most dangerous statistical bias is *disaster myopia*, which occurs whenever people underestimate low-frequency but high-impact events. Because the subjective probability of an event depends partly on recent experience, people consider expectations of low-frequency events, such as a market or firm collapse, as having a very small chance of happening. They ignore these types of events or deem them impossible, particularly when recent occurrences are lacking. This causes a false sense of security because people tend to underestimate the risk of unlikely events that are neither impossible nor remote. In fact, unlikely events are likely to occur because so many unlikely events can occur (Bak 1996). Thus, the longer the time period, the higher is the likelihood of a black swan event occurring (Taleb 2007). Such an event involves high profile and hard to predict rare events beyond the realm of normal expectations.

Herding

The previous discussion concerned individual psychological aspects of risk decision-making. Social aspects to decision-making occur when others influence someone's decisions as reflected in herding and groupthink.

Herding occurs when a group of individuals mimics the decisions of others. Through herding, individuals avoid falling behind and looking bad if they pursue an alternative action. Herding is based on the social pressure to conform and reflects safety by hiding in the crowd. In doing so, someone can blame any failing on the collective action and maintain his reputation. Even though a person recognizes market risk, following the crowd has its own reward. Herding reduces regret by rationalizing that you did no worse than your peers. It constrains envy during an upswing and panic during a down market.

A related effect is an informational cascade. A *cascade* is a series of self-reinforcing signals obtained from the direct observation of others. Individuals perceive these signals as information, even though they may be reacting to noise. This is referred to as a *positive feedback loop* or *momentum investing*, which can produce short-term self-fulfilling prophecies.

Herding amplifies credit cycle effects as decisions become more uniform. The cycle begins with a credit expansion leading to an asset price increase. Investors rush to avoid being left behind and use rising asset values to support even more credit. This explains why bankers continued risk practices even though they feared such practices were unsustainable and would lead to a crisis. Eventually, an event occurs, such as a move by the central bank, triggering an asset price decline. This causes losses, a decline in credit availability, and an exit of investors, which in turn strains market liquidity.

Sentiment Risk

The aggregate investor error based on biases is *sentiment risk*, which is a belief about fundamentals not supported by facts. Risk aversion is a component of sentiment risk, which can be either optimistic or pessimistic and is time varying, as reflected in Exhibit 24.3, which highlights the dynamic nature of asset prices over time relative to their value.

Sentiment risk is zero in an efficient market. Markets in the short term can be micro efficient for individual instruments, but macro inefficient for the market as a whole. Thus, markets are prone to over- and under-valuations. Arbitrage limits,

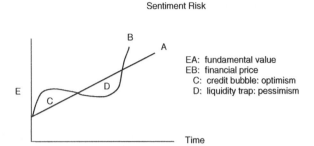

EXHIBIT 24.3   Sentiment Risk

Note: This exhibit illustrates the divergence of price from fundamental (intrinsic) value. Price is driven by behavioral factors but value is based on fundamentals.

such as liquidity traps, prevent exploiting misevaluation. *Liquidity traps* occur when institutions hoard cash as a behavior toward increased market uncertainty. Arbitragers are unable to obtain sufficient funding to correct market price divergences from underlying cash flow fundamentals. Additionally, during the short term, the direction of the inefficiency is likely to widen due to momentum and herding behavior (Shefrin 2008). Most investors ignore sentiment risk, which causes losses when sentiment changes. Exhibit 24.4 reflects investor responses based on the interplay of sentiment and market valuation. Investor responses are not constant but they are state-specific.

As Exhibit 24.4 shows, during a late-stage boom or bust with high sentiment levels, in Quadrant A, behavioral finance risk factors dominate and quantitative traditional risk measures are unreliable. This situation reflects irrational exuberance where momentum and herding driven by high liquidity levels principally drive prices. Fundamentals rule as in B and C. As Debels (2006) notes, prices may diverge from fundamentals but arbitragers quickly eliminate such differences. Quadrant D represents irrational despondency found in market value bottoms where fear replaces greed. Investors are guided by selective memories and information, and influenced by the actions of others. Consequently, they can confuse preferences with predictions. The next section now turns to an application of behavioral finance principles to determine the financial crisis's impact on investor behavior.

		Sentiment	
		High	Low
Market Valuation	Boom	A	B
	Bust	D	C

EXHIBIT 24.4   Investor Responses to Different Market States

Note: This exhibit demonstrates that as valuation increases in the boom stage and reinforces positive investor sentiment but unwinds in the bust stage.

HISTORY DEPENDENT RISK TOLERANCE: THE COLLECTIVE MEMORY HYPOTHESIS

The same historical events can have a dissimilar impact on different age groups. This is reflected in a differing willingness to take risk among generations.

Experience Matters

According to traditional finance theory, rational expectations assume individuals act in their own best interest and use all available information. Thus, the basis of asset prices is fundamentals, not experience. The traditional finance school also assumes that risk preferences are stable. Passive base rate knowledge both cancels out and swamps experiences. Consider, however, that individual experience, through feedback about outcomes of previous actions and observing market outcomes, can trump historical facts, especially for certain groups. According to Mitchell (1927), Pigou observed this when he noted that the error of optimism dies in a crisis, but gives rise to the error of pessimism. The way people behave depends not only on economic factors but also on historical, political, cultural, and psychological factors. In fact, as Friedman and Schwartz (1963) suggest, a financial crisis is as much a social phenomenon as an economic event. The contraction after the 1929 stock market crash shattered beliefs in a new era. The contraction installed an exaggerated fear of continued instability, the anger of stagnation, and the possibility of recurrent unemployment. Basically, people expect to see what they have already seen.

This is similar to Keynesian dampening (i.e., a reduction of confidence) of "animal spirits" to assume risk caused by economic downturns. In other words, animal spirits reflect investor confidence to undertake risk (Akerloff and Shiller 2009). This helps explain why investor asset allocations have changed since the financial crisis. The change can have important financial stability implications (Deutsche Bundesbank 2005). Quantitative measures of risk appetite indicate that risk appetite is at a modern low (Credit Suisse 2013). This affects the relative valuation of safe versus riskier assets based on a fear of black swan events.

Recent salient events also have a more profound effect on young adults, which can last for a lengthy period of time. Consider the risk tolerance diagram in Exhibit 24.5. *Risk tolerance* is the degree of return variability an investor is comfortable assuming. Traditional socioeconomic factors such as age, wealth, and income explain only a small portion of risk tolerance. History dependent collective group experiences may explain the difference. As Exhibit 24.5 shows, individual risk tolerances are affected by more than traditional socioeconomic factors.

Recent events strongly influence young individuals with short life histories or minimal financial experience or knowledge. This is also known as *recency bias* in which investors remember and overly weight recent events or experiences as part of the decision-making process. They are more likely to be influenced by socioeconomic factors such as wealth and income. Early successes, whether by luck or skill, encourage overconfidence. Conversely, early disappointments can cause pessimism. Essentially, events shape beliefs that function as ideas around which an individual's life is organized, thereby becoming an unconscious template (Kiev 2002).

Exhibit 24.6 shows a way of thinking about the process. As the potential consequence become more painful, investors reduce risk exposure by moving down the

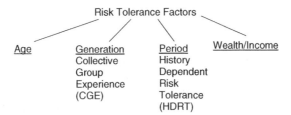

EXHIBIT 24.5 Risk Tolerance and Socioeconomic Factors

Note: Adding age group categories and period factors provides greater explanatory power to the traditional age, wealth, and income characteristics.

capital market line (CML). Younger investors were insufficiently prepared for the financial crisis related losses due to insufficient wealth buffers. Thus, the impact of the crisis was more severe for them. Job losses and reduced discretionary income caused some younger individuals to move back into their parents' homes. This, in turn, triggered a precautionary response of reduced risk tolerance.

Changes in risk tolerance can not only trigger movements along the CML, but also cause shifts in the slope of the CML itself. Increased risk aversion following a crisis causes a steeper slope. Decreased risk aversion such as occurred during the 2003–2007 boom flattened the slope.

Severe events triggering experiences beyond an individual's risk tolerance are likely to trigger leftward movements along the CML. Many younger investors suffered losses during the crisis. Consequently, they scaled back their investment allocations to equities. Perversely, this causes them to endanger future retirement goals by sacrificing returns by underinvesting in risky assets.

Investors overweight personal experiences compared to rational Bayesian learning in which they give equal weight to experience and passive knowledge. This is consistent with the reinforced learning hypothesis whereby investors reduce actions given past unfavorable outcomes and lose sight of the bigger picture. Additional support from anchoring and availability biases supporting extrapolation is also possible. *Behavioral memory biases* and the *availability heuristic*, which refers to

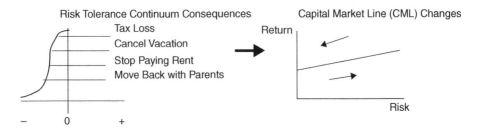

EXHIBIT 24.6 Impact of Risk Tolerance on Capital Market Line (CML) Positions

Note: The left section highlights the increasingly painful personal consequences of moving farther out in the negative or left tail of the probability distribution. This reduces risk tolerance and triggers a leftward move by investors on the capital market line (CML) contained in the right section of the exhibit.

overweighting evidence that is easy to recall, lead to overweighting strong, vivid, and recent events like the financial crisis (Ilmanen 2011). The result is investor preferences from a shared environmental shock, such as the financial crisis, are likely to be similar. In fact, Spence (2011) notes that investor preferences can be seen as composed of two factors. The first is stable risk aversion as suggested by neoclassical finance (i.e., assumed by traditional finance theory). The second is an unstable risk aversion component tied to an emotional assessment of market shocks during which feedback loops contingent on human behavior influence markets (Silver 2012). Shifting risk tolerance becomes a primary determinant of market tipping points with leverage acting to amplify results.

Exhibit 24.7 shows a stylized model of risk tolerance changes (Rosenberg 2012). This exhibit reflects not only the level of risk tolerance, but also its change. The length and persistence of the change can last for decades. According to Ilmanen (2011), depression related pessimism slowly eroded, only ending in the 1960s. An interesting question is whether the change is an emotional reaction to the crisis (higher risk aversion) or a rational adjustment to increased risk. In any event, this effect is likely to dissipate slowly as it takes many observations to relearn about equity tail risk, which includes more extreme downside events than normally expected.

The financial crisis of 2008–2009 offers the opportunity to determine the experience impact on investor stock market risk tolerance. The evidence suggests younger generation Y investors have been most affected. They have experienced a decade of flat and extremely volatile stock market returns, which has resulted in reduced confidence in the stock market. The times that people live through substantially affect investment behavior. People learn from example and direct experience because limits exist to the adequacy of passive knowledge (Gladwell 2005). Experience is clearly different from knowledge, and that difference, while not permanent, is persistent.

Malmendier and Nagel (2011) test this result by taking 40 years of household survey data to determine asset allocations, risk tolerance, and stock market participation levels. A challenge for their study is to control for omitted factors that could be correlated with macroeconomic shocks. They carefully control for traditional sociometric factors such as age, wealth, and income. The results indicate that investors experiencing low stock market returns during critical periods in their

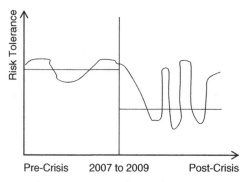

EXHIBIT 24.7 Stylized Model of Post-Crisis Risk Tolerance

Note: This exhibit illustrates the magnitude of the change in post-crisis risk tolerance. During the post-crisis period, risk tolerance became more variable than during the pre-crisis period.

lives are more risk averse, less likely to participate in the stock market, and more likely to maintain a lower portion of their wealth in stocks than other investor groups. These results are similar to their previous study on the impact of inflation experiences on asset allocation decisions (Malmendier and Nagel 2012). The result is that personal equity market experiences influence investor decisions and allocations across birth cohorts. Bad market experiences and poor returns increase risk aversion and decrease stock market participation. Malmendier and Nagel find that a 1 percent decrease in experienced returns produces a 50 basis point decline in expected future returns. Thus, experiences affect investment expectations and decisions. As a follow-up, they are researching how much of the experience effect is due to changes in investor preferences as opposed to beliefs to further refine the analysis (LaPlante 2011).

Nagel (2012) believes younger investors are more sensitive to recent negative returns than older investors because they have a limited life history. Consequently, younger investors are more prone to alter behavior based on recent results than older investors who have decades of prior experience. The net result is a new normal for younger investors involving more prudence and a lower asset allocation to stocks. Hoffman, Post, and Pennings (2011) offer counter evidence while Guiso, Sapienzo, and Zingales (2011) and Opperee (2011) offer supporting evidence. As Davies (2012) notes, younger investors may be suffering from myopic loss aversion. The current stressful investing environment may be compressing their time horizon and distorting their risk perception consistent with myopic loss aversion.

Alternatively, Malmendier and Nagel (2011) believe experience effects could represent an attempt by investors to learn from their lifetime experience instead of all available historical data. In any event, the financial crisis may have created an entire lost generation of younger, more risk-averse investors. Another example of lingering memories influencing asset prices and investor behavior is the elevated bond risk premium that followed the great inflation of 1969 to 1982 (Malmendier and Nagel 2012).

Generational memory is consistent with the life course approach to financial planning, which suggests risk and investment behavior are a function of the economic environment of the times. The competing rigid life cycle approach focuses primarily on age. The key is that individuals in different generations experience macroeconomic events at different stages of their lives. Thus, the impact of these events can differ (Schuman and Corning 2012).

Evidence Supporting Higher Dependent Risk Tolerance

Sociology provides support for the Malmendier and Nagel (2011) history dependent risk attitude. Schuman and Corning (2012) find that national and world events experienced early in life are more likely to be remembered and shape future attitudes and actions. Traditionally, behavioral finance is psychology based and deals with individual or micro effects. Using sociology allows focusing more on macro market effects. It distinguishes the effects of general lifetime experiences from those occurring in the critical period of young adulthood due to the primary effect (Mannheim 1952). Critical period experiences are more likely to affect future attitudes, actions, and risk tolerance. The critical period from the ages of 17 to the early 30s corresponds to generation Y. This effect is likely to persist in that group as a form of generational memory (Petroski 2007). The effect will fade from collective memory as those who experienced it retire and new events occur affecting different generations. New events, such as another recession, can bring these effects back into the forefront.

Following Fama's (1970) efficient markets hypothesis analysis, the three forms of behavioral finance are as follows:

1. **Weak form**. While some agents are not fully rational, arbitrage can quickly eliminate discrepancies from fundamentals.
2. **Semistrong form**. Asset prices can diverge for long periods from fundamentals for some but not all markets.
3. **Strong form**. Sentiment primarily drives asset prices.

Malmendier and Nagel (2011) and related literature support the semistrong form of behavioral finance.

Additional evidence supporting the three forms includes:

- The *equity risk premium* (i.e., this additional return compensates individuals for taking on the higher risk of the stock market compared to a risk-free asset such as a U.S. Treasury bill) after falling for several years has begun to increase. The equity risk premium serves as a barometer of investor pessimism. The increased premium is larger than can be explained by wealth changes and is difficult to justify absent behavioral based risk aversion.
- Stock market volume is down despite equity levels returning to pre-crisis levels.
- S&P trading volume in 2012 is about 50 percent of the trading volume in 2008.
- Cash hoarding for firms and individuals is at record levels.

Individual investors are withdrawing funds from equity investment funds despite a rebounding market. In fact, 2012 had the largest sell-off from equity mutual funds since the crisis year of 2008 despite a double digit stock market return (Credit Suisse 2013). Investors have withdrawn more than $900 billion from U.S. equity funds since 2000. The share of wealth invested in equity has declined from more than 50 percent in 2000 to the current level of 37 percent, while the share of wealth invested in fixed income has grown. Some equity mutual fund outflows have converted to exchange traded funds (ETFs). These conversions are, however, much smaller than the mutual fund outflows (Bianco 2012).

Although the financial crisis has ended, investors have a heightened fear of its return. The irony is that the Federal Reserve's low rate policy objective was to push investors into riskier assets. This has been offset by declining investor risk tolerance. Consequently, investors are holding more low risk assets such as cash and bonds. Individual investor risk decisions will filter through to their investment advisors via changing allocations. This, unfortunately, can adversely affect their long-term wealth due to an exaggerated sensitivity to losses (Nelson 2012).

Investor Implications of the Generational Memory Hypothesis

The implications of the generational memory hypothesis (GMH) are likely to be substantial and long-lasting as generation Y moves through its investment life cycle,

EXHIBIT 24.8 Generational Memory Hypothesis (GMH) Implications

	Neoclassical	GMH
Impact of history on different generations	Same	Different
Investor impact	Minor	Substantial
Persistence	Short	Long
Cyclicality	No	Procylical
Asset price determinants	Fundamentals	Sentiment
Equity risk premium	Unchanged	Increase
Equity participation rate	Unchanged	Decrease
Risk tolerance on affected generation	Unchanged	Decrease
Weight of experiences compared to knowledge	Equal	Higher

Note: This exhibit contrasts neoclassical and GMH investor behavior on various dimensions.

which will last years. This belief is supported by the long recovery period following a financial crisis (Reinhart and Rogoff 2009).

Exhibit 24.8 provides a summary of the implications of the GMH as compared to neoclassical theory. This figure shows a long-term impact on younger generation investor risk decisions. This impact is likely to increase the equity risk premium (Cogley and Sargent 2008).

The major impact of the financial crisis will center on the price of risk and in adjusting to revised investor risk to tolerance levels (Klement and Miranda 2012). Currently, this impact is reflected in weak initial public offerings (IPOs) and merger volumes despite a recovering stock market. Asset prices and performance depend not only on cash flows but also on the changing price of risk. In turn, behavioral factors strongly influence the price of risk.

The financial crisis of 2008–2009 with its 50 percent drop in stock market value is seared into the collective investor memory—especially generation Y investors. Investors are more focused on reacting to macro developments than asset fundamentals. The shift from return on capital to return of capital underlies the move away from equities into perceived lower risk fixed income by certain investor groups (Klement and Miranda 2012). Consequently, spreads between bonds and equities are expected to widen despite Federal Reserve efforts to keep real rates near zero. This has affected the relative price of equity compared to the cost of debt. The 2012 ratio of the cost of equity to debt is approaching three times, which is almost twice its historical average.

Eventually, prices converge to fundamental value unless a changing price of risk, which tends to be countercyclical, affects the feedback between behavioral and fundamentals. Exhibit 24.9 reflects this relationship. The weighting between behavioral and fundamental factors, such as cash flow, risk and timing, changes based on market conditions. The feedback between these factors complicates the analysis. For example, irrational pessimism can depress asset values, which further reinforces pessimism.

The adaptive market hypothesis (Lo 2004) reflects the interplay between behavioral and fundamental factors. Individuals adapt to changing environmental

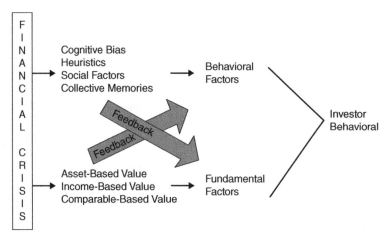

EXHIBIT 24.9 Feedback between Behavioral and Fundamental Factors

Note: This exhibit illustrates that investor behavior is determined by more than just fundamentals. Behavioral factors, including collective memories, also influence behavior.

Source: Adapted from Suto and Toshino (2004).

conditions such as the financial crisis using simple heuristics (i.e., mental shortcuts). This leads to an unstable risk-reward relationship as the price of risk changes. This means the equity risk premium is time varying. Also, the performance of investment strategies depends on market environments. Recent financial economics theory supports these findings (Ilmanen 2011). The key to performance is to adapt to changing market conditions. A major market change caused by the financial crisis is the alteration of the investor population. Many investors had never experienced a financial crisis and suffered large losses, and thus have exited the market. Consequently, a different group of investors with different preferences and risk tolerance populate the post-crisis market. The decline of equity asset allocations reflects this shift.

SUMMARY

According to Marks (2011), experience is what someone receives when he does not get what he wanted. Experiences, especially large unsettling ones, incurred during the financial crisis matter as investors base future expectations on experiences as well as fundamental factors. Malmendier and Nagel's (2011) generational-based collective memories hypothesis suggests the investor impact, while not permanent, is likely to be long term as memories only gradually decay after a major event such as the recent financial crisis. The greatest impact of this crisis is likely to be on generation Y due to the primary effect. Individuals who are 40 or older tend to be less responsive to negative economic shocks (Giuliano and Spiimbergo 2009).

Experience-based risk tolerances are time varying. The self-reinforcing price impact will trigger pro-cyclical waves of optimism and pessimism, which affect perception and the overall price of risk as reflected in the equity risk premium and asset allocation decisions. Investor behavior has shifted away from equities toward fixed income investments, which investors perceive as having lower tail risk. Behavioral memory biases have distorted generational probability assessments and the impact on their long-term portfolio returns is substantial. All data are not the same. Whether investors lived through the recent financial crisis matters, especially for certain investor groups. The financial crisis may have created generation Y great recession babies. The financial climate in which people grow up has a lifelong impact on their risk, investment perceptions, and behavior.

DISCUSSION QUESTIONS

1. Explain the collective memory hypothesis and discuss the evidence that supports it.
2. Discuss the impact of the recent financial crisis on investor behavior.
3. Differentiate between collective memories and traditional financial economics.
4. What general conclusions can be drawn from research on experience?

REFERENCES

Akerloff, George A., and Robert J. Shiller. 2009. *Animal Spirits: How Human Psychology Drives the Economy, and Why It Matters for Global Capitalism.* Princeton, NJ: Princeton University Press.

Bak, Per. 1996. *How Nature Works.* New York: Springer.

Bianco, James. 2012. "Mutual Fund Flows vs. ETF Flows." *The Big Picture.* Available at www .ritholtz.com/blog/2012/08/mutual-fund-flows-vs-etf-flows/.

Black, Fisher. 1986. "Presidential Address: Noise." *Journal of Finance* 4:3, 529–544.

Cogley, Timothy, and Thomas Sargent. 2008. "The Market Place of Risk and the Equity Premium: A Legacy of the Great Depression." *Journal of Monetary Economics* 55:3, 454–476.

Credit Suisse. 2013. "The State of Risk Appetite." *Market Focus*, January 17, 1–12. Available at https://www.credit-suisse.com/investment_banking/doc/market_focus.pdf.

Davies, Greg B. 2012. "Behavioralizing Finance." *Barclays Wealth*, March.

Debels, Thierry. 2006. *Behavioral Finance.* Leonberg, Germany: Garant.

Deutsche Bundesbank. 2005. "Risk Appetite in a Dynamic Financial Environment." *Monthly Report*, October.

Ellsberg, David. 1961. "Risk Ambiguity and the Savage Axioms." *Quarterly Journal of Economics* 75:4, 643–669.

Fama, Eugene. 1970. "Efficient Capital Markets: A Review of Theory and Empirical Work." *Journal of Finance* 25:2, 383–417.

Friedman, Milton, and Leonard Savage. 1948. "Utility Analysis of Choices Involving Risk." *Journal of Political Economy* 56:4, 279–334.

Friedman, Milton, and Anna Jacobson Schwartz. 1963. *A Monetary History of the United States—1967–1960.* Princeton, NJ: Princeton University Press.

Giuliano, Paola, and Antonio Spiimbergo, 2009. "Growing Up in a Recession: Beliefs and the Macroeconomy." Discussion Paper No. 4365, IZA, Bonn, Germany.

Gladwell, Malcolm. 2005. *Blink: The Power of Thinking without Thinking.* New York: Little Brown.

Guiso, Luigi, Paola Sapienzo, and Luigi Zingales. 2011. "Time Varying Risk Aversion." Available at www.Kellogg.Northwestern.edu/faculty/sapienza/htm/risk_aversion.pdf.

Hoffman, Arvid, Thomas Post, and Joost Pennings. 2011. "How Severe Was the Impact of the Financial Crisis on Individual Investor Perception and Behavior." Netspar Discussion Paper.

Ilmanen, Antti. 2011. *Expected Returns: An Investor's Guide to Harvesting Market Rewards.* Hoboken, NJ: John Wiley & Sons.

Kahneman, Daniel, and Amos Tversky. 1979. "Prospect Theory: An Analysis of Decision under Risk." *Econometrica* 47:2, 263–291.

Kiev, Ari. 2002. *The Psychology of Risk.* Hoboken, NJ: John Wiley & Sons.

Klement, Joachim, and Robin Miranda. 2012. "Kicking the Habit: How Experience Determines Financial Risk Preferences." *Journal of Wealth Management* 15:2, 10–25.

Knight, Frank. 1921. *Risk, Uncertainty and Profit.* Boston: Houghton Mifflin.

LaPlante, Alice. 2011. "Depression Babies: How Our Economic Experiences Affect Investment Behavior." Available at www.gsb.Stanford.edu/news/research/nagel.depression.

Lo, Andrew. 2004. "Reconciling Efficient Markets and Behavioral Finance: The Adaptive Markets Hypothesis." Available at http//ssrn.com/sol3/papers.cfm?abstract_id=728864.

Manneheim, Karl. 1952. "The Problem of Generations." *Essays on the Sociology of Knowledge.* London: Routledge.

Malmendier, Ulrike, and Stefan Nagel. 2011. "Depression Babies: Do Macroeconomic Experiences Affect Risk Taking?" *Quarterly Journal of Economics* 126:1, 373–416.

Malmendier, Ulrike, and Stefan Nagel. 2012. "Learning from Inflation Experiences." Working Paper, Stanford University and University of California–Berkeley.

Marks, Howard. 2011. *The Most Important Thing.* New York: Columbia University Press.

Mitchell, Wesley. 1927. *Business Cycles: The Problem and Its Setting.* New York: National Bureau of Economic Research.

Nagel, Stefan. 2012. "Macroeconomic Experiences and Expectations: A Perspective of the Great Recession." Paper Prepared for Academic Consultants Meeting of the Board of Governors of the Federal Reserve System, May 14.

Nelson, Christina. 2012. "Daniel Kahneman on the Psychology of Your Clients . . . Oh, And Your Own Mental Hiccups." *Journal of Financial Planning,* October, 16–19. Available at www.fpanet.org/docs/assets/FE63370E-0915-AAB1-594F476148F5EFA0/10Q.pdf

Opperee, Erick. 2011. "Long-Term Investors and Their Asset Allocation: Where Are They Now." *International Monetary Fund Report,* September, 1–48. Available at www.imf.org/External/Pubs/FT/GFSR/2011/02/pdf/ch2.pdf.

Petroski, Henry. 2007. *Success through Failure.* Princeton, NJ: Princeton, University Press.

Reinhart, Carmen, and Kenneth Rogoff. 2009. *This Time Is Different: Eight Centuries of Financial Folly.* Princeton, NJ: Princeton University Press.

Rosenberg, Michael R. 2012. "Bloomberg's Financial Condition Watch: Overview." July 25, 3–9. Available at www.bloombergbriefs.com/files/blp_072512_211710.pdf.

Schuman, Howard, and Amy Corning. 2012. "Generational Memory and the Critical Period." *Public Opinion Quarterly* 76:1, 1–31.

Sharpe, William. 2007. *Investors and Markets.* Princeton, NJ: Princeton University Press.

Shefrin, Hersh. 2000. *Beyond Greed and Fear.* Boston, MA: Harvard Business School Press.

Shefrin, Hersh. 2008. *Ending the Management Illusion.* New York: McGraw-Hill.

Silver, Nate. 2012. *The Signal and the Noise.* New York: Penguin.

Soros, George. 1994. *The Alchemy of Finance: Reading the Mind of the Market.* Hoboken, NJ: John Wiley & Sons.

Spence, Michael. 2011. *The Next Convergence.* New York: Farrar, Strauss, and Giroux.

Suto, Masahi, and Megumi Toshino. 2004. "Cognitive Biases of Japanese Institutional Investors: Consistency with Behavioral Finance." Working Paper, Institute of Finance, Waeseda University.

Taleb, Nassim. 2004. *Fooled by Randomness.* New York: Texere.

Taleb, Nassim. 2007. *The Black Swan: The Impact of the Highly Improbable.* New York: Random House.

Tversky, Amos, and Daniel Kahneman. 1992. "Advances in Prospect Theory: Cumulative Representation of Uncertainty." *Journal of Risk and Uncertainty* 5:4, 297–323.

Zick, Cathleen P., Robert N. Mayer, and Karl Giaubitz. 2012. "The Kids Are All Right: Generational Differences in Response to the Great Recession." *Journal of Financial Counseling and Planning* 23:1, 3–16.

ABOUT THE AUTHOR

Joseph V. Rizzi is President of Macro Strategies, LLC, which specializes in providing financial and risk solutions. He has 30 years of financial experience as a banker both in the United Sates and Holland with ABN AMRO Bank in Structured Products and Risk Management and as a senior investment strategist at CapGen Financial, which focuses on community bank investments. Mr. Rizzi has written extensively on financial matters and is coauthor of Mergerprof, a blog focusing on mergers and acquisitions and other corporate finance topics. He has served as adjunct instructor at several universities and given presentations to numerous professional organizations around the world. Mr. Rizzi has a BSC from DePaul University, an MBA from the University of Chicago, and a JD from the University of Notre Dame.

Trading and Investing Psychology and Strategies

Five

The Psychology of Trading and Investing

Julia Pitters
Assistant Professor of Psychology, Webster University, Vienna
Thomas Oberlechner
Chief Science Officer, iMATCHATIVE

INTRODUCTION

Then up he got with a light heart, free from all his troubles, and walked on until he reached his mother's house, and told her how very easy the road to good luck was.

Grimm and Grimm (2012, p. 12)

This quote from a Grimm fairy tale describes the experience of Hans in Luck after he had traded a piece of gold the size of his head for a horse, the horse for a cow, the cow for a pig, the pig for a goose, and the goose for a grindstone that finally fell into the water. This series of transactions shows how trading behavior may objectively be unsuccessful but subjectively still be rewarding and valuable. The traditional finance approach, which is based on rational expectations and profit maximization, fails to provide an explanation for this behavior because it is not economically rational. However, not only in fairy tales but also in real world markets seemingly irrational trading decisions take place, as the recent financial crises have amply demonstrated around the globe.

New approaches are needed to describe, explain, and predict trading and investing decisions. These approaches should not only take into account the dynamics between different market forces and human actors but also consider the plethora of nonrational aspects that occur when humans form decisions. This chapter explores the role of psychology in trading and investment decisions in financial markets.

The tension between traditional finance and the psychological perspectives of these markets reflects the difference between the outcome-based outside appearance and the inner decision-making dynamics of financial markets. The normative model of traditional finance suggests how market participants should behave and assumes that participants process information fully rationally. By contrast, the descriptive approach of decision making used in psychology explains how market participants actually form their decisions both in experimental situations and real-life markets.

This latter approach demonstrates how humans fail to be rational when making decisions in the markets (Katona 1975; Shapira 1986; Frey 1990; Jagric et al. 2010).

Psychologists emphasize that all trading decisions represent a form of human behavior. Comparable to decision outcomes in other walks of life, market outcomes also are the result of affective, cognitive, and social processes. Instead of presenting market behavior in abstract models, psychologists search for accurate descriptions of how people actually make decisions and how participants have limitations processing information rationally (Slovic 1986; Zeckhauser, Patel, and Hendricks 1991). The research methodologies for achieving these descriptions are based on making observations, asking study participants to choose between preformulated investment scenarios, analyzing the introspection of decision makers, and conducting representative surveys and experiments in controlled laboratory settings. The combination of these empirical methods leads to valid descriptive insights about trading and investing decision making.

To introduce the psychological factors discussed and to understand the complex dynamics of trading in markets, consider the following example of a simple purchase in a fruit market. A tourist wants to buy a specific product such as a pineapple that is offered in the market. For her purchase, she is looking for the best balance between quality and price. In the market, she faces many retailers who sell pineapples. One of the many psychological factors that come into play in her decision making is her personality by considering questions including:

- Is she easy to please or a perfectionist?
- Does she like to trade and communicate with the sellers?
- Is she convincing?
  Her purchase decision may further depend on her mood and emotions.
- Is she tired or is she in a good mood? Both may enable sellers to convince her to buy their product.
- Is she angry or depressed and thus more critical?
- Further, does she like the seller because she finds him sympathetic and wants to support him or does she dislike him?

Various cognitive aspects will also influence what she considers rational, including:

- Does she know all the facts about what makes a good quality pineapple?
- Is she informed about changing price levels?
- Does she have experience buying pineapples?
- What are the influences on her decision time pressure, the selective availability of information, her "anchoring" to the first suggested price she hears, and her implicit notion of what pineapples should cost?
  Moreover, social norms and cultural differences influence her decision, such as:
- Does she consider fairness considerations when trading?
- Which ethical principles and ideals does she follow? Does she know about the cultural norms?

Finally, rumors and the impact of media shape her judgment, including:

- Has she learned in a biased travel guide about the best pineapples in town?
- Has she heard from other tourists what they would pay?

As the example of the pineapple purchaser shows, psychological variables on the individual, social, and macro level influence financial decision-making processes. Exhibit 25.1 provides an overview of the psychological variables such as personality, affect, cognition, norms, and news discussed in the remainder of this chapter.

PERSONALITY VARIABLES

On the dispositional level of individual market participants, the question arises about how much the nature of their personality influences trading processes. Books about financial markets such as Carew and Slatyer (1989) often contend that personality is essential for becoming a good dealer and education cannot compensate for it. Accordingly, many practicing traders believe that their success is rooted in an individual's personality traits and characteristics. According to these market practitioners, good traders are rare and specific traits play the key role in their trading performance (Oberlechner 2004). Thus, numerous personality tests for traders are available that promise profits based on their ability to identify the ideal trading personality. Some of these tests are based on Carl Jung's theory of personality and the widely known Myers Briggs Type Indicator, which posits that trading success may depend on the individual's level of introversion versus extroverson, sensation versus intuition, thinking versus feeling, and judgment versus perception (Tharp 2012).

Oberlechner's (2004) comprehensive survey among European foreign exchange traders allows a deeper analysis of the question of what the best traders

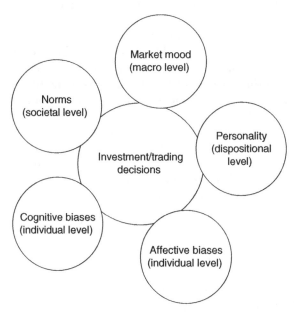

EXHIBIT 25.1   An Overview of Psychological Factors on the Dispositional, Individual, Societal, and Macro Level that Shape Investment and Trading Decisions

Note: This exhibit provides an overview of the psychological variables such as personality, affect, cognition, norms, and news that influence investment and trading decisions.

have in common. The survey established an initial list of potentially important characteristics for successful trading based on opinions and informal feedback of foreign exchange traders and other trading experts. This led to 25 personality-related traits, personal skills, and cognitive abilities. Then, hundreds of professional traders evaluated the importance of these characteristics and added any additional characteristics that they considered important for successful traders. Factor analysis of all the submitted answers reveals that traders based their ratings on the following eight comprehensive personality-related factors that define successful traders:

1. *Disciplined cooperation.* In market environments defined by sudden market swings and high degrees of unpredictability, trading discipline may be the only aspect that individual traders can actually control. Disciplined cooperation consists of three distinct components. First, it involves a strong motivational component that reinforces other success factors. Second, disciplined cooperation involves adhering to stop-loss order limits (i.e., selling a security when it reaches a certain predefined price) and avoiding such risk-taking biases as overconfidence and the illusion of control (Goldberg and Nitzsch 2001). Third, it involves cooperation with others in the trading team and in one's trading institution. For example, this is shown in traders who are disciplined in their reporting of trading losses and receive timely support from their colleagues and supervisors.

2. *Tackling decisions.* The factor called tackling describes traders' readiness for assertive and proactive decision making in a risky environment. Electronic dealing and matching systems make possible the buying and selling of hundreds of millions of dollars in the foreign exchange market in split seconds (Luca 2000). Thus, one main aspect of a tackling approach toward trading decision making is a trader's willingness to forge ahead by taking a risk. Moreover, because trading in a hectic market environment requires high degrees of concentration for extended periods of time, the ability to remain focused and to cope with stress are other important aspects of this tackling attitude toward one's trading decisions (Kahn and Cooper 1993, 1996).

3. *Market meaning making.* This factor represents individual traders' ability to quickly define a "view" of the market based on their personal judgment. Because the market is changing, this factor requires experience and intuition when rapidly anticipating possible market developments.

4. *Emotional stability.* This factor allows traders to focus on their strategy and to stay focused in difficult market environments.

5. *Information processing.* This factor combines both the ability to process information quickly and simultaneously and to have analytical thinking skills.

6. *Interested integrity.* This component is related to the characteristics curiosity and integrity.

7. *Autonomous organization.* This factor is associated with defining traders' ability to independently organize the work process of trading and to maintain a positive attitude toward it.

8. *Information handling.* This factor addresses how traders collect, handle, and pass on information to others, including the processing of information by mathematical means or using computers.

Although all eight personality-related factors are important for a successful trader, traders perceive the first five factors as comparatively more important. Detailed analyses of traders' ratings reveal a strong consensus on the importance of these eight factors. Interestingly, demographic aspects such as the traders' family status, age, and gender do not influence how respondents perceive the importance of the success factors.

Hedge fund manager Lex van Dam, a former Goldman Sachs trader who is known for his participation in the BBC series *Million Dollar Traders*, conducted a telling experiment on whether someone can be trained to become a good trader. Van Dam gave eight novices about $1 million of his money with the assignment to trade in the stock market for a period of two months. At the beginning of the experiment, the novices received two weeks of training. Although the experiment took place during an extremely turbulent trading period in financial history, the novices outperformed professional traders. Van Dam (2012) concludes that by learning a few fundamentals even those without professional backgrounds or knowledge can become successful traders.

Because female traders conduct only 5 percent of trading activity worldwide (Coates 2012), a question is whether women make better traders than men. In general, evidence does not show that gender differences account for successful trading but may affect the previously defined personality factors. For instance, although men are generally more risk-seeking (factor 2), they also show the tendency to be more overconfident (factor 1) (Barber and Odean 2001).

Oberlechner, Pitters, and Baillie (2010) investigate the levels of confidence among spectators of an international sports event in their ability to correctly predict the outcomes of games and to generate positive returns in an online trading contest. The study finds that when women are confident of their predictions and their ability to make betting profits, they base their belief that they would succeed on luck. By contrast, men base their confidence in their predictions and profits on subjectively perceived expertise and skills. This phenomenon is relevant to predictions in financial markets. Traders and other market participants regularly overestimate the accuracy of their predictions and their trading skills. The following section discusses overconfidence in trading behavior as a widespread affective individual bias among investors.

AFFECT AND COGNITION

The majority of economic approaches to financial markets relies on a cognitive understanding of decision making and views feelings as irrational. Because such approaches perceive feelings as harming the interests of market participants striving for profits, they do not assume that feeling have any (lasting) influence on the market level (Pieters and Van Raaij 1988).

In contrast, a psychological approach acknowledges the importance of affect to market participants and may even consider affect to be essential for market decisions. Here affect refers to an overall term for emotions, feelings, and mood, but many authors differentiate between affect and emotion (Shouse 2005).

Affect

Affective reactions have the power to influence trading decisions in multiple ways. Psychological research shows that information and stimuli that are compatible with a person's mood are learned better than stimuli that are incompatible with current mood (Bower 1981; Forgas and Bower 1988). Likewise, moods influence the kind of material that one can retrieve from memory. If a person is happy, he can recall positive stimuli more easily, and if a person is sad, he can remember negative stimuli (Bower and Forgas 2000). The same principle of mood-congruent information processing applies to expectations of the future. For example, such peripheral cues from the environment as the weather can influence peoples' mood and their subsequent evaluation of life satisfaction (Schwarz and Clore 1988). According to the mood maintenance hypothesis (Isen and Simmonds 1978), people tend to maintain positive mood states and positive mood is associated with reduced information processing and less critical thinking. Applying the hypothesis to financial markets, Kliger and Kudryavtsev (2013) investigate the role of mood in investors' reactions to revisions in analyst recommendations. They find that negative stock price reactions to recommended downgrades are significantly stronger during periods in which daylight is increasing than during periods in which daylight is decreasing.

Distinguishing between decision-making effects, which can be attributed to pure affective and cognitive reactions, is difficult because affect and cognition interact. However, for a clearer arrangement, the chapter presents them separately.

Status Quo Tendency and the Endowment Effect   The *status quo tendency* explains a phenomenon that observers note among traders who pursue a losing strategy even when the strategy has already caused losses for an extended period. This tendency is especially visible in general trading styles and preferences. Traders often base their approach on their previous trading experience. This is known as *anchoring bias* in which traders use a past decision as a reference point. They are unlikely to change this approach even after following an unsuccessful strategy (Oberlechner 2004). Strategies used by taxpayers also reflect the tendency of following an initial (unsuccessful) behavior (Kastlunger, Kirchler, Mittone, and Pitters 2009).

An especially strong form of the status quo tendency occurs when decisional escalations in trading decisions take place. When this situation occurs, affective processes tempt traders not only to keep their losing positions but also to expand them. This phenomenon of "throwing good money after bad money" is also known as the *sunk cost effect* (Arkes and Blumer 1985).

Closely related to the status quo bias is the *endowment effect,* which states that individuals value a good more when they already possess it than they are willing to pay in order to get it. In a well-known study, Kahneman, Knetsch, and Thaler (1990) give participants a mug and the chance to sell or trade it for an equally priced alternative good. The authors find that people's psychological threshold to accept a price for a mug they already own is about twice as high as the price they are willing to pay for the same mug in order to possess it. However, this endowment effect is not a stable entity. Using an experimental setting, Paolacci, Burson, and Rick (2011) show that participants could be trained to reduce the endowment effect.

From the perspective of economic utility maximization, the status quo tendency and endowment effect are irrational and lead to decisions that are clearly biased. Instead of focusing on future outcomes and objective investment returns, these two effects are based on subjective reasoning and experience.

Psychologically, three reasons explain the affective and psychological dynamics involved in these effects. First, sticking to one's decisions once they are made is often based on emotional commitment (Etzioni 1988). Once people are emotionally invested in their beliefs, they may have difficulty changing them based only on information or other cognitive measures (Berelson and Steiner 1964). Second, regret theory postulates that people base their decisions on the likelihood of how much unpleasant regret they expect to experience (Bell 1982; Loomes and Sugden 1982). Because people do not like to feel regret, they attempt to estimate the extent of possible regret involved in each decision choice, compare the choices based on the amount of anticipated regret, and then decide in favor of the option that minimizes their expected regret. Third, decision makers seek to reduce their cognitive dissonance, a process first described by Festinger (1957). *Cognitive dissonance* is a feeling of unease that is generated by a discrepancy between actual behavior and individual beliefs that leads decision makers to find a way to reduce this emotional burden.

To summarize, the status quo bias and the endowment effect explain the psychological tendency of market participants to preserve and even reinforce an initial trading strategy instead of changing it in light of new and better information. The next section discusses overconfidence, which is one of the psychological keys to traders' difficulties when considering relevant information and experience.

Overconfidence When people are asked for self-evaluations of their health, driving skills, education, or workplace, most rate themselves as more successful than average (Dunning, Heath, and Suls 2004; Horswill, Waylen, and Tofield 2004). Behavioral economists now acknowledge the importance of this feature among economic agents in financial settings, often referring to it as "overconfidence bias" (Barber and Odean 2001; Larrick, Burson, and Soll 2007).

Of all possible arenas of human overconfidence, finance and investments are particularly important. When people overestimate their own financial abilities, this may affect their investment decision making and the consequences of these decisions. Overconfidence in financial investment abilities may lead to substantial losses, as suggested by many private and business insolvencies in Europe or debt overloads in the United States (Creditreform 2012). High failure rates and low average returns suggest that overconfidence tempts too many people to enter markets as entrepreneurs (Koellinger, Minniti, and Schade 2006). Overconfident capital investment in property by U.S. banks may be the source of the subprime crisis of 2008.

Overconfidence is not characteristic of all areas of human experience and not all people are overconfident. For example, people tend to overestimate their own abilities when solving simple tasks but usually underestimate their skills when confronted with difficult tasks (Moore and Cain 2007). Psychologists observe that overconfidence is usually present in those areas of experience where people feel competent. For example, Dunning (2005) finds that 94 percent of college professors regard themselves as more competent than other professors. Likewise, financial experts often overestimate their investing skills and therefore take high risks in their decisions. In a study of more than 400 North American professional foreign currency dealers, Oberlechner and Osler (2012) identify two different kinds of overconfidence. Dealers underestimate the uncertainty of forecasts and overestimate their own abilities. When asked how successful they rate themselves compared to other dealers, three quarters of the dealers rated themselves above average. The results of a Jordanian investor sample also show overconfidence about trading skills and investment decisions. Alrabadi, Al-Gharaibeh, and Zurigat (2011) report that overconfidence significantly increases based on the years of trading experience.

According to the rational choice assumption held by traditional finance proponents, overconfident attitudes and behavior are unreasonable and should be avoided by agents who pursue maximum profits. Again, the following question arises. If overconfidence is irrational and counterproductive from the viewpoint of traditional finance, what explains the widespread existence of overconfidence?

Psychological research provides several possible explanations for the overconfidence phenomenon. Part of this research focuses on what has been termed the "better-than-average effect" (Alicke and Govorun 2005; Larrick et al. 2007). Psychologists explain this disposition to overestimate one's own skills and abilities with a basic human need for self-esteem. From a clinical perspective, the bias to regard oneself unrealistically above average is psychologically healthy and a lack of it may be connected to low self-esteem (American Psychiatric Association 1994). In stark contrast to the traditional finance view that overconfidence is irrational, psychologists find that among the people experiencing an identical amount of positive and negative events, depressed people see the world more realistically while people who are not depressed use optimistic interpretations as a coping strategy (Seligman 1990; Wills 1997). As the theory of self-esteem suggests (Aronson, Wilson, and Akert 2010), people have a strong need to see themselves as good and competent. They develop a self-concept containing values and traits that need to be fulfilled in order to maintain their self-esteem (Pyszczynski, Solomon, Greenberg, and Stewart-Fouts 1995). Traits that are relevant for the self-concept thus need to be protected.

Terror Management and Investment   Starting with the observation that individuals try to maintain their self-esteem, Solomon, Greenberg, and Pyszczynski (1991, 2004) raise the central question of why people strive for self-esteem. They offer a psychological explanation inspired by Becker (1973) and his concept of denial of death. According to Becker, people have to cope with an uncomfortable situation and their knowledge that they will ultimately die. Employing a strategy that involves coping, orientation, and distraction, they attribute a deeper meaning to life by believing in defined values and by attempting to be valuable members of society. However, whenever they are reminded of their own death (which can experimentally be achieved by asking participants to write down thoughts that come to mind when they think of death), people are prone to defend their personal values by expressing even more extreme attitudes than usual, or by degrading any perceived opposition to their personal value system more harshly than usual.

A meta-analysis of more than 250 controlled experiments conducted in the field shows an effect between so-called mortality salience (MS) and an increase in defense of one's worldview and self-esteem (Burke, Martens, and Faucher 2010). Some studies show that MS also influences investment decisions. Psychologists report that MS generally increases materialism (Arndt, Solomon, Kasser and Sheldon 2004) and that MS on television increases the attraction of advertised products (Dar-Nimrod 2012). These psychological insights are striking and show that *terror management theory* (i.e., the social psychological field that studies the effects of mortality salience) provides a basis for further research on the psychology of trading and investment.

Empathy and Altruism Empathy is another important phenomenon that is missing in the traditional finance understanding of trading and investing. Making a purchase from a kind old woman with a small retail store after a shared smile (despite the fact that her products are overpriced and of poor quality) makes little sense from the viewpoint of economic rationality. Likewise, giving a generous tip to a waiter in a restaurant that will never be visited again may seem economically irrational. In contrast, psychologists readily acknowledge that the likelihood that people invest in specific goods, people, and companies depends on their level of empathy. From a social psychological perspective, the empathy-altruism theory offers an explanation (Batson 1991). According to this theory, altruistic behavior depends on the empathy experienced toward another person. If empathy is high, altruistic behavior is probable; if empathy is low, people will only support others when doing so is worthwhile financially.

Cognition

Even if traders prefer to make optimal decisions based on a price-value balance, they cannot always process all relevant information needed because they are easily distracted and influenced by available information.

Cognitive Biases Instead, traders unconsciously use so-called decision-making *heuristics* (i.e., rules of thumb that enable people to make decisions within a limited time frame). The concept of heuristics as human biases can be traced to Francis Bacon's list of idols. Bacon described how these phantoms of the human mind distract humans from reasonable decisions. For example, when Bacon defines the idols of the tribe as the human tendency to lazily generalize by exaggerating and disproportionately weighting available information instead of responding to the actual cases or elements that can be observed (Spedding 1861), his reasoning comes close to the modern formulation of the representativeness heuristic explained later in this section.

Although heuristics may have such profitable and functional aspects as speeding up and simplifying the decision-making process, they often lead to systematic and predictable mistakes (Tversky and Kahneman 1974). Thus, their use in trading decisions can lead to collective market outcomes that are at odds with rationality as defined by traditional finance.

According to the *representativeness heuristic*, market participants simply base their judgments on the apparent resemblance between two situations and neglect other important information such as statistical and historical base rates. The representativeness heuristic provides a convincing explanation for asset price overreactions due to new information (Luo 2012). Further, according to the *availability heuristic*, people judge the likelihood of an event simply based on the availability of information about the event. People judge events that are easily accessible (e.g., market events recently reported in the news) as more likely and more frequent than events that are more difficult to imagine (Tversky and Kahneman 1973).

Another example for a psychological heuristic is the anchoring and adjustment heuristic, which is based on a mental process of anchoring and adjusting information to available cues, no matter how unrealistic these cues are. Decision makers often use the anchoring and adjustment heuristic in the bargaining or negotiating process. For example, sellers usually start by suggesting a much higher price than the actual value of their product. Early anchors can influence even seasoned experts. For example, real estate agents may adjust their independent estimations of how much a property is worth in the direction of previously provided made-up listing prices (Northcraft and Neale 1987).

A final cognitive bias discussed here is *hindsight bias*, which is a decision-making phenomenon colloquially known as the "I knew it all along" effect. This bias describes people's tendency to express a priori subjective certainty about specific outcomes when asked a posteriori. In other words, once they know the answer to a certain question or the outcome of an uncertain development, people think that they knew it all along. The phenomenon is evident, for example, when people watch quiz shows and blame the contestants for their ignorance after the host reveals the correct answers. As this example shows, the effect may be harmless in daily life but it can be costly in financial settings. For example, hindsight bias may provide traders with a wrong sense of security when making their decisions, which can lead to excessive risk-taking behavior. Further, this bias may impede traders' learning from experience by distorting their memory of what actually was a bad trading decision with negative outcomes into a harmless or even successful experience (Calvillo 2012). Researchers show that this kind of hindsight bias affects economic expectations on Euro-related attitudes towards the currency (Hoelzl, Kirchler, and Rodler 2002).

Prospect Theory and Framing   Kahneman and Tversky's (1979) prospect theory provides a comprehensive psychological explanation for human decision making under uncertainty. While expected utility theory (EUT) assumes that people are generally risk-averse, prospect theory holds that a basic difference exists between situations involving gains and losses. When people make risky decisions in gain situations, they tend to be risk-averse; when the alternatives of a risky choice involve losses, people are risk-seeking. The S-shaped function of prospect theory entails a subjectively defined reference point that decides whether people perceive a decision in terms of possible gains or possible losses. For losses the curve is steeper, suggesting that losses loom larger than gains. As demonstrated by the concavity and convexity of the curve, people perceive the difference between the reference point and, say, $50 as stronger than the difference between $300 and $350.

Whether someone perceives a decision as involving losses or gains depends on subjective framing processes. Framing can be explained by looking at an event from different viewpoints, such as the same glass of water being seen as half full or as half empty. Researchers have successfully applied prospect theory to diverse fields of decision making. For instance, Pitters, Kirchler, and Witte (2007) show that an amount of money gained through a salary increase (i.e., gain framing) is less likely to be invested than when the same amount money is available due to a tax reduction (i.e., loss framing). Prospect theory also explains the widespread tendency of market participants to close winning trading positions too early and to let losing trading positions continue too long (Shefrin and Statman 1985).

Herding, Norms, and Ethics

Decision makers are influenced not only by perceptions on the individual level but also by information on a societal level. What other people do, think, or expect may have a further impact on trading and investment decisions.

Herding and Psychological Conformity   Whether people choose the restaurant that is most frequented by others, pay for a chair on a crowded section of the beach that is surrounded by empty beach and chairs, or find a place in the back of the lecture hall although many free seats are available in the front, herding or social proof is a common behavior (Cialdini et al. 1999).

In financial markets, herding behavior can be explained by *conformity*, which is a psychological phenomenon that exists even in small groups. As the Asch (1956) study demonstrates, participants adjust simple evaluations of the length of lines to the incorrect judgment of others in the group. Although the participants in Asch's experiment had the clearly defined task of matching the length of lines, subjects in the market consistently face the more ambiguous challenge of turning highly complex market information into trading decisions. In such ambiguous situations as financial markets, herding provides a helpful strategy of psychological orientation. The psychological tendency of human decision makers to overweigh readily available information may reinforce herding.

The herding process can explain many processes in financial markets such as extreme exchange rate volatility. Participants who imitate the behavior of others instead of processing market information independently endorse existing market trends (Scharfstein and Stein 1990). Kremer and Nautz (2013) offer new evidence on the causes and consequences of herding by institutional investors. Based on a comprehensive database of every transaction made by financial institutions in the German stock market, the authors show that institutions engage in herding behavior on a daily basis. Chinese and Indian stock markets also show evidence of herding behavior resulting from culturally different market conditions. In the Chinese market, herding is greater during a falling market with high trading volumes. In contrast, in India herding occurs mainly during upswings (Lao and Singh 2011).

New trading and information technologies may also fuel herding behavior in the financial markets. As these technologies provide participants with real-time market information and make virtually the same information available to all market participants, they enable participants to constantly adjust their own decision making to collective market behavior. According to Oberlechner (2004), the application of computer-aided trading decision systems enables large parts of the market to react simultaneously and similarly and thus intensify herding.

Social and Cultural Norms   Social norms defining how members of a group or collective should behave in a certain context influence trading behavior. Corporate trading governance as an ethical norm can provide a fair basis for trading and reduce unfair practices such as insider trading. Yet, breaking social norms can provide an individual trading advantage for individual traders' efforts to maximize their profits (Kumar and Page 2013).

Given the global dimension of trading in today's markets, understanding cultural norms may be a key to market success. For example, based on their shared past under the Habsburg Empire and the mutual cultural understanding created by this past, Austria benefits from its close trading relations with the Eastern European states. Moreover, a cross-cultural study by Weber and Hsee (1998) finds that participants from China are less risk averse, as measured by buying prices for risky financial options, than their American counterparts. The authors identify marked cultural differences in their perceptions of the extent of risk but show that the attitudes toward dealing with risk are equal. This finding may have a practical impact for cross-cultural negotiation and commerce. Kim and Wei (2002) find that foreign investors outside Korea are more likely to engage in positive feedback trading strategies and in herding than the branches/subsidiaries of foreign institutions in Korea or foreign individuals living in Korea.

Ethics   The topic of ethical investment is more relevant today than ever. An increasing number of investors choose goods, stocks, and entire portfolios based on whether these investments make an ethical contribution to society. These ethical attitudes can be conscious but they also can be implicit. As Pitters and Oberlechner (2011) show, when people are asked for their reasons for a specific evaluation or opinion, their reasoning usually contains a strong ethical component such as utilitarian thinking (i.e., efforts to maximize the benefit of all or of the majority of people) or deontological thinking (i.e., evoking rules and fairness principles). In the aftermath of the ethical dilemma posed by the financial crisis in 2009, these researchers ask experts (i.e., economic journalists) and the public whether they consider state interventions to rescue ailing companies as justified and to give the reason for their opinion. Pitters and Oberlechner interpret and classify the explanations provided according to their underlying ethical school of thought. Although the majority of experts tend to support state interventions and justify these interventions based on a utilitarian ethical perspective, most laypersons oppose state interventions and base their opinions on deontological reasoning. Such implicit ethical positions play an important role in trading and investment decisions (Oberlechner 2007). Ethics plays a leading role on various individual, organizational, and cultural levels of investment decision makers.

NEWS, RUMORS, AND MARKET MOOD

For their decision making, market participants use countless market information sources ranging from casual conversations with colleagues to economic reports of market analysts and global news services. Because of time and attention limitations, they cannot fully integrate the information of all these sources in an unbiased manner. Instead, they must choose and reduce available information, weigh the importance of news and news sources, and focus on some news while neglecting other choices. Because no explicit guidelines are available for how to choose and filter the best information, traders emphasize that each trader needs to develop a personal system of filtering news (Oberlechner 2004). Thus, the basis for their selections and biases is psychological rather than economic and rational.

Moreover, market participants usually cannot easily differentiate objectively between trustworthy and rumor-based information. *Rumors* are accusations that are passed along based on doubt rather than on evidence (Allport and Postman 1947; DiFonzo, Bordia, and Rosnow 1994). Rumors bear a close resemblance to news because they also explain meaningful events and similarly are perceived as positive or negative by the receiver. Rumors play a decisive role in news reporting on financial markets. For example, Osterberg and Wetmore-Humes (1993) compare daily press reports on U.S. central bank intervention with actual intervention data. Their evidence shows that interventions reported by the *Wall Street Journal* may not have occurred, whether reported as facts or pure rumors.

Because high levels of ambiguity generally characterize financial markets, they provide a fertile ground for rumors (Allport and Postman 1947; Rosnow 1991). Rumors play a particularly important role in forecasts of the future and contribute to a collectively experienced market mood that serves as a heuristic and influences investment decisions.

The overall mood of a country due to the economic situation, which can also be perceived as a macrosocial threat (Scheffer and Witte 2004) may affect the prescribed variables relevant for trading success. In the beginning of 2012, when the rating agency Standard & Poor's decided that countries such as France would lose their triple A credit rating, this decision influenced not only the economic situation of creditworthiness but also the national pride of a whole nation.

Based on a representative survey of the Austrian population, Oberlechner and Pitters (2010) investigate whether perceptions of general market mood as portrayed in the media are relevant to self-ratings of individual investment success. The authors hypothesize that investors use perceptions of market mood as information for attributions of personal investment success. Oberlechner and Pitters find that people living in urban areas perceive market mood as portrayed in the media as more negative than do those people living in rural areas. However, the more rural participants perceive the market mood as negative, the more successful they consider their personal investment skills. Thus, market mood serves as information to evaluate personal investment skills.

SUMMARY

This chapter summarizes the role of psychology in trading and investing and discusses selected studies that show how researchers have systematically observed and investigated psychological factors in market decisions. This discussion demonstrates the presence of many relevant psychological processes in trading and investing. On the individual level, while personality in general does not necessarily predict investment success, specific traits may be beneficial for successful trading and investing. Moreover, individual variables on the affective and cognitive levels such as mood, empathy, mortality salience, and cognitive heuristics can lead to irrational trading decisions. On a collective level, social norms and herding influence market behavior. Finally, market rumors and investment mood are important psychological influences on trading and investing on the macro level. Besides more traditional methods of studying the role of psychology in trading and investing, novel approaches advance our knowledge of what matters in financial decision making. For example, the analysis of metaphors used by decision makers helps in understanding trading attitudes, investing intentions, and subjective market conceptualizations (Oberlechner, Slunecko, and Kronberger 2004; Christiandl, Oberlechner, and Pitters 2013). Financial markets and their participants provide a rich setting for testing psychological theories and insights.

DISCUSSION QUESTIONS

1. Explain the difference between the descriptive psychological perspective to trading and investing and the traditional finance approach.

2. Identify five personality traits that professional traders have defined to determine investment success and discuss the role of gender differences.
3. Discuss why some traders cannot make rational decisions and the impact of affective and cognitive biases.
4. Outline which phenomena on a societal level influence trading and investing behavior.
5. Discuss aspects on a macro level that may influence investment decisions.

REFERENCES

Alicke, Mark D., and Olesya Govorun. 2005. "The Better-Than-Average Effect." In Mark D. Alicke, David A. Dunning, and Joachim I. Krueger, eds., *The Self in Social Judgment*, 85–106. New York: Psychology Press.

Allport, Gordon W., and Leo J. Postman. 1947. *The Psychology of Rumor*. New York: H. Holt and Company.

Alrabadi, Dima W., Mohammad A. Al-Gharaibeh, and Ziad M. Zurigat. 2011. "What Makes Investors Overconfident? Evidence from the Amman Stock Exchange." *European Journal of Economics, Finance and Administrative Sciences* 43:1, 28–34.

American Psychiatric Association. 1994. *Diagnostic and Statistical Manual of Mental Disorders*, 4th ed. Washington, DC: American Psychiatric Association.

Arkes, Hal R., and Catherine Blumer. 1985. "The Psychology of Sunk Cost." *Organizational Behavior & Human Decision Processes* 35:1, 124–140.

Arndt, Jamie, Solomon Sheldon, Tim Kasser, and Kennon M. Sheldon. 2004. "The Urge to Splurge: A Terror Management Account of Materialism and Consumer Behavior." *Journal of Consumer Psychology* 14:3, 198–212.

Aronson, Elliot, Timothy D. Wilson, and Robin M. Akert. 2010. *Social Psychology*. New York: Longman.

Asch, Solomon E. 1956. "Studies of Independence and Conformity: I. A Minority of One against a Unanimous Majority." *Psychological Monographs* 70:9, 1–70.

Barber, Brad M., and Terrance Odean. 2001. "Boys Will Be Boys: Gender, Overconfidence, and Common Stock Investment." *Quarterly Journal of Economics* 116:1, 261–292.

Batson, Charles D. 1991. *The Altruism Question: Toward a Social-Psychological Answer*. Hillsdale, NJ: Erlbaum.

Becker, Ernest. 1973. *The Denial of Death*. New York: Free Press.

Bell, David E. 1982. "Regret in Decision Making under Uncertainty." *Operations Research* 30:5, 961–981.

Berelson, Bernard, and Gary A. Steiner. 1964. *Human Behavior: An Inventory of Scientific Findings*. New York: Harcourt, Brace and World.

Bower, Gordon H. 1981. "Mood and Memory." *American Psychologist* 36:2, 129–148.

Bower, Gordon H., and Joseph P. Forgas. 2000. "Affect, Memory, and Social Cognition." In Erik Eich, John. F. Kihlstrom, Gordon H. Bower, Joseph P. Forgas, and Paula M. Niedenthal, eds., *Cognition and Emotion*, 87–157. New York: Oxford University Press.

Burke, Brian, Adolf Martens, and Erik H. Faucher. 2010. "Two Decades of Terror Management Theory: A Meta-Analysis of Mortality Salience Research." *Personality and Social Psychology Review* 14:2, 155–195.

Calvillo, Dustin P. 2012. "Working Memory and the Memory Distortion Component of Hindsight Bias." *Memory* 20:8, 891–898.

Carew, Edna, and Will Slatyer. 1989. *Forex: The Techniques of Foreign Exchange*. Sydney: Allen and Unwin.

Christiandl, Fabian, Thomas Oberlechner, and Julia Pitters. 2013. "Belastung oder Gelegenheit"—Eine Metaphernanalyse zur Wahrnehmung der Finanzkrise durch wirtschaftliche Laien." *Wirtschaftspsychologie*, forthcoming.

Cialdini, Robert B., Wilhelmina Wosinska, Daniel W. Barrett, Jonathan Butner, and Malgorzata Gornik-Durose. 1999. "Compliance with a Request in Two Cultures: The Differential Influence of Social Proof and Commitment/Consistency on Collectivists and Individualists." *Personality and Social Psychology Bulletin* 25:10, 1242–1253.

Coates, John. 2012. *The Hour between Dog and Wolf. Risk Taking, Gut Feeling and the Biology of Boom and Bust*. New York: Penguin Press.

Creditreform. 2012. "Insolvenzen in Europa." Available at www.creditreform.de.

Dar-Nimrod, Ilan. 2012. "Viewing Death on Television Increases the Appeal of Advertised Products." *Journal of Social Psychology* 152:2, 199–211.

DiFonzo, Nicholas, Prashant Bordia, and Ralph L. Rosnow. 1994. "Reining in Rumors." *Organizational Dynamics* 1:23, 47–62.

Dunning, David. 2005. *Self-Insight: Roadblocks and Detours on the Path of Knowing Thyself*. New York: Psychology Press.

Dunning, David, Chip Heath, and Jerry M. Suls. 2004. "Flawed Self-Assessment: Implications for Health, Education, and the Workplace." *Psychological Science in the Public Interest* 5:3, 69–106.

Etzioni, A. Amitai. 1988. "Normative-affective Factors: Toward a New Decision-Making Model." *Journal of Economic Psychology* 2:9, 125–150.

Festinger, Leon. 1957. *A Theory of Cognitive Dissonance*. Stanford, CA: Stanford University Press.

Forgas, Joseph P., and Gordon H. Bower. 1988. "Affect in Social Judgments." *Australian Journal of Psychology* 40:2, 125–145.

Frey, Bruno. 1990. *Economics as a Science of Human Behavior*. Dordrecht: Kluwer.

Goldberg, Joachim, and Rüdiger von Nitzsch. 2001. *Behavioral Finance*. New York: John Wiley & Sons.

Grimm, Jacob, and Wilhelm Grimm. 2012. *The Complete Grimm's Fairy Tales*. Seattle: CreateSpace.

Hoelzl, Erik, Erich Kirchler, and Christa Rodler. 2002. "Hindsight Bias in Economic Expectations: I Knew All Along What I Want to Hear." *Journal of Applied Psychology* 87:3, 437–443.

Horswill, Mark, Andrea E. Waylen, and Matthew I. Tofield. 2004. "Drivers' Ratings of Different Components of Their Own Driving Skill: A Greater Illusion of Superiority for Skills That Relate to Accident Involvement." *Journal of Applied Social Psychology* 34:1, 177–195.

Isen, Alice M., and Stanley Simmonds. 1978. "The Effect of Feeling Good on a Helping Task That Is Incompatible with Good Mood." *Social Psychology Quarterly* 41:4, 345–349.

Jagric, Timotej, Tanja Markovic-Hribernik, Sebastjan Strasek, and Vita Jagric. 2010. "The Power of Market Mood—Evidence from an Emerging Market." *Economic Modelling* 27:5, 959–967.

Kahn, Howard, and Cary L. Cooper. 1993. *Stress in the Dealing Room*. London: Routledge.

Kahn, Howard, and Cary L. Cooper. 1996. "How Foreign Exchange Dealers in the City of London Cope with Occupational Stress." *International Journal of Stress Management* 3:3, 137–145.

Kahneman, Daniel, Jack L. Knetsch, and Richard Thaler. 1990. "Experimental Test of the Endowment Effect and the Coase Theorem." *Journal of Political Economy* 5:1, 193–206.

Kahneman, Daniel, and Amos Tversky. 1979. "Prospect Theory: An Analysis of Decisions under Risk." *Econometrica* 47:2, 313–327.

Kastlunger, Barbara, Erich Kirchler, Luigi Mittone, and Julia Pitters. 2009. "Sequences of Audits, Tax Compliance and Tax Paying Strategies." *Journal of Economic Psychology* 30:3, 409–418.

Katona, George. 1975. *Psychological Economics*. New York: Elsevier Scientific Publishing Company.

Kim, Woochan, and Shang-Jin Wei. 2002. "Foreign Portfolio Investors Before and During a Crisis." *Journal of International Economics* 56:1, 77–96.

Kliger, Doron, and Andrey Kudryavtsev. 2013. "Out of the Blue: Mood Maintenance Hypothesis and Seasonal Effects on Investors' Reaction to News." *Quantitative Finance*, forthcoming.

Koellinger, Philipp, Maria Minitti, and Christian Schade. 2006. "I Think I Can, I Think I Can: Overconfidence and Entrepreneurial Behavior." *Journal of Economic Psychology* 28:4, 502–527.

Kremer, Stephanie, and Dieter Nautz. 2013. "Causes and Consequences of Short-Term Institutional Herding." *Journal of Banking and Finance* 37:5, 1676–1686.

Kumar, Alok, and Jeremy Page. 2013. "Deviations from Norms and Informed Trading." *Journal of Financial and Quantitative Analysis*, forthcoming.

Lao, Paulo, and Harminder Singh. 2011. "Herding Behavior in the Chinese and Indian Stock Markets." *Journal of Asian Economics* 22:6, 495–506.

Larrick, Richard, Katherine A. Burson, and Jack B. Soll. 2007. "Social Comparison and Confidence: When Thinking You Are Better Than Average Predicts Overconfidence (and When It Does Not)." *Organizational Behavior and Human Decision Processes* 102:1, 76–94.

Loomes, Graham, and Robert Sugden. 1982. "Regret Theory: An Alternative Theory of Rational Choice under Uncertainty." *Economic Journal* 92:368, 805–824.

Luca, Cornelius. 2000. *Trading in the Global Currency Markets*. New York: New York Institute of Finance.

Luo, Guo Y. 2012. "The Representativeness Heuristic and Asset Price Reaction to New Information." *Journal of Trading* 7:3, 40–51.

Moore, Don A., and Daylian M. Cain. 2007. "Overconfidence and Underconfidence: When and Why People Overestimate (and Underestimate) the Competition." *Organizational Behavior and Human Decision Processes* 103:2, 197–213.

Northcraft, Gregory B., and Margaret A. Neale. 1987. "Experts, Amateurs, and Real Estate: An Anchoring-and-Adjustment Perspective on Property Pricing Decisions." *Organizational Behavior and Human Decision Processes* 39:1, 84–97.

Oberlechner, Thomas. 2004. *The Psychology of the Foreign Exchange Market*. Chichester: John Wiley & Sons.

Oberlechner, Thomas. 2007. *The Psychology of Ethics in the Finance and Investment Industry*. Research monograph. Charlottesville, VA: The Research Foundation of the CFA Institute.

Oberlechner, Thomas, and Carol L. Osler. 2012. "Survival of Overconfidence in Currency Markets." *Journal of Financial and Quantitative Analysis* 47:1, 91–113.

Oberlechner, Thomas, and Julia Pitters. 2010. "Confidence in One's Own Investment Skills: A Survey of Demographic Differences, Luck Attribution, and the Influence of Perceived Market Mood." Paper presented at the 27th International Congress of Applied Psychology in Melbourne, Australia.

Oberlechner, Thomas, Julia Pitters, and Donald Baillie. 2010. "Anticipating Outcomes of Soccer Games: How Perceived Expertise, Topic Importance, and Luck Influence Spectators' Prediction Confidence." Paper presented at the 27th International Congress of Applied Psychology in Melbourne, Australia.

Oberlechner, Thomas, Thomas Slunecko, and Nicole Kronberger. 2004. "Understanding the Foreign Exchange Market through Metaphors." *British Journal of Social Psychology* 43:1, 133–156.

Osterberg, William P., and Rebecca Wetmore-Humes. 1993. "The Inaccuracy of Newspaper Reports of U.S. Foreign Exchange Intervention." *Economic Review (Federal Reserve Bank of Cleveland)* 4:29, 25–33.

Paolacci, Gabriele, Katherine Burson, and Scott Rick. 2011. "The Intermediate Alternative Effect: Considering a Small Tradeoff Increases Subsequent Willingness to Make Large Tradeoffs." *Journal of Consumer Psychology* 21:4, 384–392.

Pieters, Rik G. M., and Fred Van Raaij. 1988. "Functions and Management of Affect: Applications to Economic Behavior." *Journal of Economic Psychology* 9:2, 251–282.

Pitters, Julia, Erich Kirchler, and Erich H. Witte. 2007. "Steuersenkung Oder Gehaltserhöhung? Zur Psychologischen Wirkung Von Unterschiedlich Formuliertem Einkommenszuwachs Auf Die Konsumabsicht." *Wirtschaftspsychologie* 9:4, 61–67.

Pitters, Julia, and Thomas Oberlechner. 2011. "Die Finanzkrise und das Allgemeinwohl. Wie Werden Staatsinterventionen Ethisch Gerechtfertigt?" In Dominik Enste and Friedrich Schneider, eds., *Jahrbuch Schattenwirtschaft 2009/2010*, 97–124. Münster: LIT Verlag.

Pyszczynski, Thomas, Sheldon Solomon, Jeff Greenberg, and Michelle Stewart-Fouts. 1995. "The Liberating and Constraining Aspects of Self: Why the Freed Bird Finds a New Cage." In Annerieke Oosterwegel and Robert A. Wicklund, eds., *The Self in the European and North American Culture: Development and Processes*, 357–373. Dordrecht: Kluwer Academic Publishers.

Rosnow, Ralph. 1991. "Inside Rumor: A Personal Journey." *American Psychologist* 46:5, 484–496.

Scharfstein, David, S., and Jeremy C. Stein. 1990. "Herd Behavior and Investment." *American Economic Review* 80:3, 465–479.

Scheffer, Julia, and Erich H. Witte. 2004. "Der Einfluss von Makrosozialer Wirtschaftlicher Bedrohung auf die Leistungsfähigkeit." Hamburger Forschungsberichte, University of Hamburg.

Schwarz, Norbert, and Gerald L. Clore. 1988. "How Do I Feel about It? Informative Functions of Affective States." In Klaus Fiedler and Joseph Forgas, eds., *Affect, Cognition and Social Behavior*, 44–62. Toronto: Hogrefe.

Seligman, Martin E. P. 1990. *Learned Optimism.* New York: Knopf.

Shapira, Zur. 1986. "On the Implications of Behavioral Decision Making Theory to Economics." In Alan J. MacFadyen, and Heather W. MacFadyen, eds., *Economic Psychology: Intersections in Theory and Application*, 621–644. Amsterdam: North-Holland.

Shefrin, Hersh, and Meir Statman. 1985. "The Disposition to Sell Winners Too Early and Ride Losers Too Long." *Journal of Finance* 40:3, 777–790.

Shouse, Eric. 2005. "Feeling, Emotion, Affect." *M/C Journal* 8.6. Available at http://journal.media-culture.org.au/0512/03-shouse.php.

Slovic, Paul. 1986. "Psychological Study of Human Judgment: Implications for Investment Decision Making." In Hal R. Arkes and Kenneth R. Hammond, eds., *Judgment and Decision Making: An Interdisciplinary Reader*, 173–193. New York: Cambridge University Press.

Solomon, Sheldon, Jeff Greenberg, and Thomas Pyszczynski. 1991. "A Terror Management Theory of Social Behavior: The Psychological Functions of Self-Esteem and Cultural Worldviews." In Mark P. Zanna, ed., *Advances in Experimental Social Psychology* 24, 93–159. New York: Academic Press.

Solomon, Sheldon, Jeff Greenberg, and Thomas Pyszczynski. 2004. "The Cultural Animal: Twenty Years of Terror Management Theory and Research." In Jeff Greenberg, Sander L. Koole, and Thomas Pyszczynski, eds., *Handbook of Experimental Existential Psychology*, 13–34. New York: Guilford.

Spedding, James. 1861. *The Letters and the Life of Francis Bacon.* London: Longman, Green, Longman, and Roberts.

Tharp, Van. 2012. "Tharp Trader Test." Available at www.tharptradertest.com/default.aspx?question=1.

Tversky, Amos, and Daniel Kahneman. 1973. "Availability: A Heuristic for Judging Frequency and Probability." *Cognitive Psychology* 5:2, 207–232.

Tversky, Amos, and Daniel Kahneman. 1974. "Judgment under Uncertainty: Heuristics and Biases." *Science* 185:5157, 1124–1131.

Van Dam, Lex. 2012. *How to Make Money Trading*. London: Portico.

Weber, Elke, and Christopher Hsee. 1998. "Cross-Cultural Differences in Risk Perception, but Cross-Cultural Similarities in Attitudes towards Perceived Risk." *Management Science* 44:9, 1205–1217.

Wills, Thomas A. 1997. "Modes and Families of Coping: An Analysis of Social Comparison in the Structure of Other Cognitive and Behavioral Mechanisms." In Bram Buunk and Frederick X. Gibbons, eds., *Health Coping and Well Being—Perspectives from Social Comparison Theory*, 167–194. Mahwah, NJ: Erlbaum.

Zeckhauser, Richard, Jayendu Patel, and Darryll Hendricks. 1991. "Nonrational Actors and Financial Market Behavior." *Theory and Decision*, 31:2–3, 257–287.

ABOUT THE AUTHORS

Julia Pitters is Assistant Professor of Psychology at Webster University in Vienna, Austria, and also currently holds a guest professorship at Webster University Thailand. She is a guest lecturer at several other Austrian universities. Her major research interests are in the fields of tax psychology and financial decision making. Professor Pitters worked as consultant and project manager for a market and social research company and is now an associate partner of the independent consultancy Pitters Trendexpert. She studied psychology and sociology at the universities of Würzburg and Hamburg (Germany) and completed a PhD in economic psychology at the University of Vienna.

Thomas Oberlechner is Chief Science Officer at iMATCHATIVE, a San Francisco based company specializing in developing groundbreaking investment matching solutions through a combination of science, technology, and advanced analytics. He was Senior Research Professor and Psychology Department head at Webster University in Vienna, Austria, and visiting professor and researcher at Harvard University, Massachusetts Institute of Technology, University of Cologne, and other universities. His research on psychological factors of decision making in financial markets has led him into the trading floors of the world's leading banks and other market participants. Dr. Oberlechner has published in numerous academic and professional journals including the *British Journal of Social Psychology*, *Journal of Economic Psychology*, and *Journal of Financial and Quantitative Analysis*. He has also published a book (*The Psychology of the Foreign Exchange Market*) and a research monograph (*The Psychology of Ethics in the Finance and Investment Industry*). He attended the University of Vienna and Harvard University and holds a PhD in psychology and multiple master's degrees in psychology, counseling, consulting psychology, and law.

CHAPTER 26

The Surprising Real World of Traders' Psychology

Denise K. Shull
Principal, The ReThink Group Inc.
Ken Celiano
Contributing Author, Principal, Even-Keel Trading, and Trading Psychologist
Andrew Menaker
Contributing Author, Principal, Andrew Menaker LLC and Trading Psychologist

INTRODUCTION

People have speculated about the workings of their minds for centuries. As capitalism emerged and markets evolved to trade not only in commodities but in other financial securities, the questions and conundrums increased. How does a person make the best prediction decision when the irreducible question is what perception of value other market participants will have in the future. Known as Theory of Mind (ToM), the difficulty of predicting others' future value perceptions has led to innumerable variations on quantitatively based decisions. Yet, sophisticated and previously successful market interaction strategies, such as J.P. Morgan's now-infamous "2012 London Whale" (i.e., the nickname for a trader who successfully traded a complex strategy for an extended period of time before his positions were significantly large that other hedge funds were able to trade en masse against him), self-destruct on essentially a regular basis.

Recognizing both the remaining mysteries in human judgment and the incomplete resolution in probabilistic answers, some market participants have hired psychological consultants. For example, SAC Capital hired Dr. Ari Kiev, a psychiatrist who had coached Olympians, and he remained at SAC for nearly two decades. Around the globe, banks, hedge funds, and traders continue to hire psychological consultants from different theoretical persuasions to improve their performance.

Conventional trading psychology maxims state "control your emotions" and "plan the trade, trade the plan." Yet, the vast majority of professional and semiprofessional traders, in the privacy of a consulting relationship, report the near impossibility of both. Making connections between a multitude of brain and psychological science research now reveals why.

Most perception is unconscious. Decisions require affect or what is thought of as feelings and emotion. When detecting a problem of uncertainty, the brain virtually demands a judgment call. The latter makes exactly following a trading plan more an exercise in frustration than profitability. Furthermore, as a product of the brain, the mind now strongly appears to be socially constructed and body interdependent from birth if not before. In development, the brain acquires patterns of perception that turn into adult fractal-like subjective expectations and experiences. These previously misunderstood elements of decision-making about risk within uncertainty are now coming to be understood as at least, but in all likelihood, more relevant than the intellectual task of fundamental financial and probabilistic analyses.

Simultaneously, the work of the relatively new discipline of behavioral finance enjoys widespread interest. Known as the biases and heuristics literature, the research demonstrates what are believed to be intractable human tendencies to misperceive. Examples of heuristics (i.e., cognitive mental shortcuts) include the overweighting of recent experience and the unequal weighting of gains and losses. Advocates of behavioral finance admit, however, that this discipline lacks a unifying theory as to why these thinking mistakes occur. Looking inside the subjective experience of traders' numerous decisions provides a hypothesis.

Unconscious affective context, which at any given moment includes the trader's visceral and immediate and distant emotional experiences, mediates the full perception and judgment of risk and uncertainty. An embodied cognition arising from a combination of conscious intellectual work, unconscious interpretations, the interplay of testosterone and cortisol with brain and body structures such as the amygdala and the heart offers a rich data set to explore.

This chapter provides a brief overview of the related research plus real-world examples from trader performance consulting rooms to illustrate a seemingly truer version of not only trader psychology but also investing and risk psychology in general. The chapter is organized as follows. The first section reviews a wide cross section of related brain and psychological research. Within this review of the relevant literature, the touchstone of social context sets the stage for currently popular topics such as unconscious thought, the ways in which the body is much more involved in thinking than previously believed, the neurochemistry of risk perception and recent work on the value of emotional awareness in risk judgments. Next, the chapter contains two case studies of professional traders being coached by psychologists who work specifically with traders. These case studies demonstrate various elements covered in the recent research related to how the body and brain deal with trading decisions. A summary and conclusions wrap up the chapter.

WHAT SCIENCE REVEALS ABOUT HOW PEOPLE THINK

Human beings are neither their mind nor a "self" in isolation. Science provides evidence showing how the human brain and its perceptual inclinations occur as a result of and reflective of the social milieu in which it exists.

The Pivotal Reality of the Group

Neuroeconomists Huettel and Kranton (2012) could be stating the obvious when they write that social context can dramatically influence decisions. Yet, a transition from understanding man as an individual to one as a socially created operator has yet to be embraced. In fact, Hasson et al. (2012) recently wrote about "brain-to-brain coupling" and called for a change in perspective from the single brain model to a multibrain approach in cognitive research. Based on archeological research on the human processes for developing tools, Grove and Coward (2008, p. 387) note that it "is not the individual neuron, nor even necessarily the individual brain, but instead the socio-cognitive context in which brains develop and tools are manufactured and used."

Siegel (2012b) synthesizes how and why not only our tools but also our brains, perceptions, thoughts, and decisions depend on the social, unconscious, and affective context in which people find themselves. Highlighting the early stage of research on the influence of social context, Cozolino (2006, p. 3) states, "we are just beginning to understand that we have evolved as social creatures and that all of our biologies are interwoven."

Social Brains in Traditional Finance

In finance, the power of the social brain appears to extend first to the seemingly cognitive interpretation of the market. Bruguier, Quartz, and Bossaerts (2010) use brain imaging to reveal how market participants who rely more heavily on Theory of Mind (ToM)—or anticipating other people's thoughts and intentions—are better at correctly predicting the movement of stock prices. The authors also unexpectedly demonstrate a simultaneous lack of activity in brain areas associated with probabilistic thinking.

The groundbreaking nature of this ToM finding is reminiscent of the days when markets first began to be systematically and quantitatively analyzed. Nobel Laureate Harry Markowitz (1952) emphasizes a social factor in his classic work on modern portfolio theory (MPT). According to Markowitz, the first step in asset allocation is to determine what one believes and the second step is to follow the novel mathematical approach to investment choices set forth in this seminal paper. He emphasizes that his paper focuses on step two but cautions readers to avoid skipping explicit beliefs analysis. Beliefs evolve through social milieus. Parents, teachers, friends, and bosses all contribute to the beliefs on which any risk taker relies. People learn from others and the learning creates beliefs.

The Reality of the Unconscious

In the late 1800s, Freud posited the existence of an unconscious mind. Today, research supports the reality of cognitive and affective (feeling and emotion) unconscious brain processes. Evaluating the possibility of unrelated and presumably unconscious factors influencing market decisions, Lee and Schwarz (2012) find that being exposed to the smell of fish reduced by 24 percent the likelihood that an individual would subsequently invest money. They were evaluating the power of the metaphor "something smells fishy." Yet, Risen and Critcher (2011) find that visceral states, such as the likely feeling of disgust lingering from the fish, can implicitly color beliefs.

Dijksterhuis and Nordgren (2006) propose an "unconscious thought theory" and illustrate its importance in resolving complex questions. They find that unconscious thought produces more satisfying results than conscious thought. Summarizing the evolving perspectives on conscious versus unconscious, Bargh and

Morsella (2008, p. 73) find that research shows the presence of several independent unconscious behavioral guidance systems including perceptual, evaluative, and motivational.

Embodied Cognition in Risk and Uncertainty Judgment

Part of why or how unconscious thought may work appears to be that not all thought is based in the mind. Research reveals that our bodies play a large role in the inputs to and the outputs from the human brain. Reimann et al. (2012) list 42 separate studies connecting the body to traditionally perceived products of the mind. Hung and Labroo (2011) find that firming one's muscles resulted in the creation of additional willpower. Subjects demonstrate increased ability to tolerate pain and overcome food temptations among other willpower-related challenges. Siegel (2012a, p. 484–485) writes "that we continually evaluate, without awareness, the context of a situation for its inherent threats to survival and match the body's physiological state with social engagement, fight-flight-freeze, or shut-down behaviors."

Affect and Emotion as the Body-Brain Connection

Affect generally refers to the totality of the way someone feels at any given moment. This may include basic physical feelings such as being tired, a mood such as being irritable, and a specific emotion such as annoyance. Although no truly clear and agreed-on lines exist between affect and emotion, one can safely think of affect as a meteorological system and emotions as the heat or rain that can be observed as a specific result. Many authors, however, use the terms affect, mood, feelings, and emotions interchangeably.

Summarizing the then findings of neuroeconomics (also known as neurofinance), Camerer, Loewenstein, and Prelec (2005, p. 29) emphasize the new view on the critical role of affect and emotion by stating "It is not enough to 'know' what should be done, one must also 'feel' it." This statement relies partially on Bechara (2004) and evidence showing the absolute requirement for emotion in the ability to make any decision. Specifically, the embodied cognition (thinking with our bodies) summary from Reimann et al. (2012, p. 105) asks whether "emotions function as the bridge between bodily perceptions and downstream cognitive processing such as judgment and choice. . . ." Indeed, Naqvi, Shiv, and Bechara (2006) note the many critical connections between bodies, states of feelings, and decisions within uncertainty.

If emotion is a fundamental element of decisions, the issue becomes defining what emotion actually is. In fact, a disagreement over the basics exists. The theory of psychological constructionism is now challenging on various levels the arguably still reigning idea of "basic emotions" by Ekman (1992)—universal emotions of anger, fear, disgust, sadness, happiness, and surprise.

Barrett and Bliss-Moreau (2009), two of the main proponents of psychological constructionism, contend that emotions arise from the interaction of basic psychological ingredients not specific to a certain type of subjective feeling. They explain the psychological construction view of emotions using the analogy of recipes and baking. Using flour, butter, and chocolate says nothing about whether someone is making cookies or a cake. Fear to one person is not necessarily the same subjective experience, nor does it create the exact same blueprint in the body. Fear can be broken down into more elemental units.

Specifically missing from the basic emotions literature is what may be the most often felt unconscious or even semiconscious feeling in trading—regret. During meetings and workshops with clients, coaching experts report professional traders often say "but it may have come back or I was afraid to lose what I had gained." Colloquially, this is referred to as fear of missing out (FOMO), which appears to underscore the emotion of fear of future regret as described by Loomes and Sugden (1982) and discussed specifically in the context of auction markets by Filiz-Ozbay and Ozbay (2007).

In a meta-analysis where researchers attempt to review and relate all the work previously done on a particular question, Lindquist et al. (2012, p. 121) argue convincingly for the constructionist point of view.

> *Overall, we found little evidence that discrete emotion categories can be consistently and specifically localized to distinct brain regions. Instead, we found evidence that is consistent with a psychological constructionist approach to the mind: A set of interacting brain regions commonly involved in basic psychological operations of both an emotional and non-emotional nature are active during emotion experience and perception across a range of discrete emotion categories.*

Elements in Embodied Cognition and Psychological Constructionism

Despite reports of the discovery of a brain area responsible for one or another human ability, the research is not as far along as these reports imply (Anderson, Kinnison, and Pessoa 2013). Nevertheless, researchers are making progress at increasingly rapid rates. Recent findings identify four elements within a human that are particularly relevant to traders: brain structures, neurochemistry, heart rate, and vagal nerves.

Brain Structure

Until very recently, neuroscience viewed the brain structure called the amygdala as the locale and arbiter of all fear (LeDoux 2003). Cunnigham and Brosch (2012), however, find that instead of amygdala involvement equaling fear, the brain structure plays a broader role in evaluating the meaning of any stimuli. Furthermore, evidence by Feinstein et al. (2013) shows that with certain types of fears, the amygdala may not be required. Their work reveals a difference in how the brain processes fear resulting from verifiable external threats and fear resulting from internally generated perceived threats. This is a major finding in fear research.

Speaking to a potential physiological template of fear that may mediate a trader's unconscious and fractal like re-experience, Visser et al. (2013) find that how one acts out, or "does" fear subsequent to a particular experience (e.g., falling from a horse and then fearing horses), could be predicted by how the brain was firing at the time of the initial fear-creating event. This possibility becomes exceptionally relevant when examining how fractal or fractal-like perceptions could emerge from the brain years later.

Neurochemistry

In the realm of neurochemistry, Coates and Herbert (2008) find that a trader's morning testosterone level, a known contributor to the emotion of confidence, predicted that day's level of profit but that testosterone increased over time to the point of inducing excessive confidence and in turn, risk taking. Conversely, Stanton et al. (2011) find that both low and high testosterone individuals display less aversion to risk. Furthermore, Stanton, Mullette-Gillman, and Huettel (2011) find significant seasonal variations in testosterone, which appear opposite of the noted seasonal variation in market movements.

Coates and Herbert also find that cortisol, a hormone associated with stress and presumably anxiety and fear, rises with both the variance in a trader's profits and losses and with market volatility. This research points to what appear to be keys in a body-brain system of perceiving and reacting to market behavior and trading choices.

Heart Rate

Cortisol is a factor in heart rate. According to Appelhans and Luecken (2006, p. 229), "heart rate variability (HRV) analysis is emerging as an objective measure of regulated emotional responding (generating emotional responses of appropriate timing and magnitude)." Fenton-O'Creevy et al. (2012), who study traders and HRV, find that traders with more experience display relatively high rates of high-frequency HRV, which researchers associate with higher levels of confidence. The two upcoming cases both employ HRV biofeedback tools to aid in making traders aware of their unconscious affective contexts via the data from their heart rate.

Vagal Nerves

Associated with HRV is polyvagal theory proposed by Porges (1995). This theory posits the development of a more differentiated vagal nerve system. The *vagus nerve* is the primary nerve connecting the brain stem to the heart and all parts of the body. With a nod to the aforementioned social functioning of the brain, Porges (2009) maintains that a more evolutionarily recent connection between the face and heart provides a truer explanation of the biological systems mediating the connections between social interaction and brains, emotional response and heart rate.

The Complexity of Risk Decisions and Trading Psychology

Although science is making exponential progress in providing a truer understanding of humans, risk perception, and subsequent behavior, much research is still needed to understand the interaction of thinking, feeling, internal and "external" or known bodily states. Platt and Huettel (2008, p. 402) state that "only through explicit interdisciplinary, multi-methodological and theoretically integrative research will the current plethora of perspectives coalesce into a single descriptive, predictive theory of risk-sensitive decision-making under uncertainty." As an example of this kind of research, Todd, Cunningham, Anderson, and Thompson (2012) assert that the same feeling causes both the direction of attention and the resulting affect for having placed one's attention in a certain direction. Specifically, Todd et al. (p. 365) state that:

> *"affect-biased attention"—the predisposition to attend to certain categories of affectively salient stimuli over others—provides an important component of emotion regulation. Affect-biased attention regulates subsequent emotional responses by tuning one's filters for initial attention and subsequent processing. By reviewing parallel research in the fields of emotion regulation and affect-biased attention, as well as clinical and developmental research on individual differences in attentional biases, we provide convergent evidence that habitual affective filtering processes tuned and re-tuned over development and situation, modulate emotional responses to the world. Moreover, they do so in a manner that is proactive rather than reactive.*

For example, many traders rely heavily on complex quantitative analyses. Peters et al. (2006) conclude that affect itself creates greater use of numbers in decision-making. More recently, Peters (2012) finds that greater numeracy leads to fewer instances of framing bias but that those who are highly numerate also tend to overuse numbers.

According to Huettel, Song, and McCarthy (2005, p. 3304), how the brain responds to uncertainty depends on the particular demands of a task. That is, context matters. In fact, Hsu et al. (2005) posit a specific "warning" circuit that is called up when the brain perceives uncertainty. As "quants"' often note, the assumptions and the subsequent market regime determine whether a model—the standard mathematical representation of the market—works and, more importantly, for how long it works.

Psychoanalytic Ideas, Fractal Subjective Experience, and Trader Decisions

Bringing Freud into this discussion could cause alarm because people often recoil at just the simple mention of his name. However, the legendary trader George Soros (Institute for New Economic Thinking 2010) invested in research on a distinctly Freudian explanation known as *emotional finance*. Tuckett and Taffler (2008, p. 389) make their case for an explanation based in Freud's version of psychoanalytic theory:

> *Based on the evidence of historical accounts, supplemented by some interviewing, the authors suggest a psychoanalytic approach focusing on unconscious phantasy relationships, states of mind, and unconscious group functioning can explain some outstanding questions about financial bubbles which cannot be explained with mainstream economic theories.*

In an alternative adaptation of what were originally psychoanalytic concepts, Shull (2012) contends that the markets induce what were originally Freudian ideas of transference and repetition as defined by LaPlanche and Pontalis (2012). Based on interviews with hundreds of traders, Shull identifies traders' experiences to be the subjective equivalent of fractals in nature. Fractals in turn are a part of the bodies of work known as chaos theory or nonlinear dynamical systems.

Supportive of this concept, Luecken et al. (2006) propose a cognitive-affective model in which early relationships with mothers, fathers, and other family members create the development of later emotional and cognitive responses to environmental challenges that then influence the body's reactivity to events. Additional work on the possibility of fractal geometry applying to the brain comes from Dixon, Holden, Mirman, and Stephen (2012, p. 51) who note that:

> *Changes in cognitive performance exhibit a fractal (i.e., power-law) relationship between size and time scale. These fractal fluctuations reflect the flow of energy at all scales governing cognition. . . . The cognitive system exhibits not just a single power-law relationship between fluctuation size and time scale but actually exhibits many power-law relationships, whether over time or space. This change in fractal scaling, that is, multifractality, provides new insights into changes in energy flow through the cognitive system.*

The specifics of fractal geometry and nonlinear dynamical systems exist within the broader field of study known as complex systems. According to Pezard and Nandrino (2001), theoretical and experimental results from studying the application of chaos theory to psychopathology demonstrate the concepts to be more than just metaphorical.

Yet, the state of the theory when applied to human and trader psychology remains under development. As Wagenmakers, van der Mass, and Farrell (2012, p. 87) note:

> *After more than 15 years of study, [. . .] What the complex-systems approach has arguably failed to deliver are concrete insights about how people perceive, think, decide, and act. Without formal models that implement the proposed abstract concepts, the complex-systems approach to cognitive science runs the danger of becoming a philosophical exercise in futility. The complex-systems approach can be informative and innovative, but only if it is implemented as a formal model that allows concrete prediction, falsification, and comparison against more traditional approaches.*

This chapter and its case studies in particular offer factors for just such a model.

The Fear-Confidence Spectrum and the Value of Considered Articulation

Kircanski, Lieberman, and Craske (2012) find that simply articulating one's fears has a more positive impact on the ability to act in the face of fear than other common strategies including cognitive reappraisal (i.e., the usage of intellectual explanation to recharacterize a situation). In findings validating Lane's Levels of Emotional Awareness (LEAS) scale (Lane et al. 1990), Kircanski et al. also find that the more negative words the individual used the better his performance. In study of 101 active stock investors, Barrett (2007, p. 923) uses an investment simulation to examine emotion and the perception of investment choices:

> *Contrary to the popular belief that feelings are generally bad for decision making, we found that individuals who experienced more intense feelings achieved higher decision-making performance. Moreover, individuals who*

were better able to identify and distinguish among their current feelings achieved higher decision-making performance via their enhanced ability to control the possible biases induced by those feelings.

I NEED TO BE A HERO AGAIN

The following case demonstrates a primary strategy of developing self-awareness of unconscious affective context.

Trader W

Trader W manages a small hedge fund involving more than $10 million of assets under management. Several years ago he received the industry accolade of fund manager of the year. He subsequently closed that event-driven fund and opened a new fund using a "global macro" strategy. W is highly intelligent and analytical: "I was in the 99.9th percentile of SAT scores." He comes from a family of high achievers and his wife has a doctorate from an Ivy League university.

Struggling with performance in his new fund, W sought help. "My analysis is spot on, but I need help following through and executing trades based on it. Even if it's a high conviction idea and I am confident in it, I end up doing trades that are impulsive." "How can I control myself?" he asked. W explained the success of his previous fund as follows: "My analysis led me to the right market position. I was a hero to my investors and I need to be a hero again. I want to bask in the glory again."

W's new fund uses a discretionary approach requiring many more decisions about market entries and exits, whereas his previous event-driven fund required fewer decisions. W routinely held losers well beyond his predetermined stop-loss and averaged down on losing positions. Taking a loss frequently resulted in a sequence of impulsive trades. W stated, "I have a strong need to be right, being wrong is difficult to tolerate."

When asked to explain his need to be right, he replied, "It's as if loss is unacceptable to me; it's an existential threat; I'll do anything to avoid this existential threat." When asked to describe what the existential threat feels like, he was at a loss for words, saying only, "It's extreme."

Coaching focused on assisting W to direct his analytical ability inward. To avert the typical impulsive mistakes of adding to losers and "revenge" trading (i.e., the common occurrence of traders taking a losing trade and then engaging in a series of other trades originally believed to be likely to make the money back), he needed to develop awareness of why and how his emotional reactions seemed as if he needed to respond to an "existential threat." Deciphering these elements involved W revealing information about his feelings, both current and from memories, and examining repetitive feelings. This "emotions as information" approach makes conscious what has been unconscious and provides insight into the current underlying affect supporting the maladaptive behavior.

After several attempts at encouraging W to describe his emotional experience in greater detail, the initial presenting problem, "I'm having trouble executing on my analysis," took on an entirely new meaning. The question became, why does W react so strongly when the market does not conform to his analysis or expectations?

What emerged early was a person with a bright, analytical, and thoughtful mind conducting extensive market analyses who became repeatedly impulsive in the moments when prices did not immediately conform to his expectations. A losing trade or missing a market move induced doubling down (adding to losing positions) or revenge trading.

On several occasions after incurring outsized losses, W considered closing the fund. During these periods, W devoted even longer hours to research and, notably, increased the frequency and detail of market notes he e-mailed to clients. He explained: "If I can't perform well, at least I can show my clients that I have the right ideas and that I'm working hard for them, and maybe they won't abandon me." The latter behavior likely revealed a deeper nuance to validating himself and regaining hero status.

While growing up, W's family social milieu was one that highly prized achievement and status. As a result, W developed a mostly unconscious belief that being less than perfect or even not working hard enough would result in his not receiving approval or acceptance in his family. W logically feared that his clients would potentially abandon him as a result of his poor performance. However, the intensity of the fear can be directly associated with an underlying fear of abandonment by his family.

He rebuffed attempts to analyze the origin of his fear of abandonment. "I probably have a minor abandonment issue with my father but I don't want to talk about that." In one consult he resisted progress with: "Maybe it's true that understanding why I react so strongly to losses could help me to control myself, but I'm not sure I want to know the reason. What I want from you is a checklist, a series of steps I have to go through that will keep me on track in trade executions."

Despite knowing a checklist was not the answer to his situation, his coach nevertheless developed a checklist. W's fund had its most severe drawdown while using the checklist: "It's a great checklist, but apparently my need to be right is too overwhelming and I ignore the checklist when I need it most." Given that W had previously agreed that understanding his unconscious motivations could be instrumental to resolving his repetitive feelings and mistakes, his adamant desire for a checklist can be seen as an attempt to avoid the discomfort of facing an intense emotional need to be right.

The behavioral expression of his unconscious affect and belief system can be seen in W's attempts to not realize any losses. Perfectionism is not simply striving to be the best but it is also about the deep-seated belief that perfection will secure approval. This is a common example of how psychology appears to be fractal.

When W accepted the underpinnings around his strong emotional reaction to losses and his unusually strong need to be right ("it's an existential threat"), the coaching shifted toward strategies and processes designed to maintain this deepened self-awareness as a primary risk management tool. Besides the dialectical experience, the coach also used biofeedback to leverage the effort. As W maintained awareness of his need for validation, his trading improved.

As an example of how the social interaction of coaching becomes a platform for change, coaching increased in frequency at W's request. As the rapport deepened, the relationship itself served as a trigger for W's need to be right, often manifesting in frequent midsentence interruptions to challenge, point out something, or show that he was right. A psychoanalytic view deems this as *transference*—unconsciously invoking emotional patterns set up in the past as relevant in the present—as is his reaction to the market as a whole.

An opportunity arose where W secured a pitch meeting with a very large investor who seeded small hedge funds. Afterward, W was upset. "As soon as I left the meeting I realized I was too focused on showing how intelligent I am, not selling the fund." W had once again acted out the fractal-like unconscious affective needs. The experience became a pivot point and as a result, his trading improved and the investor invested in the fund six months later after reviewing W's improved performance.

Over 18 months W became more proficient at identifying his emotions as indicators of the previously unconscious affective context that had supported his unprofitable trading. This resulted in not only improved fund performance but also in reported improvements in other life arenas such as losing weight, better managing stress, and improving relationships. As of this writing, W's focus is on developing and trusting his unconscious pattern recognition and experiential learning, otherwise known as intuition.

THE HEART OF A QUANT

Another case is an example of accessing and influencing unconscious affective contexts via physiological tools supplemented with the social interaction of dialogue.

Trader Q

"I need the market to talk to me [. . .]. I need to know it, I need to just look at it and know which way it's going to move, the eyes, the legs, you know, I want to move the way the market goes; I'm trying to get that extrasensory perception." So began a three-year coaching relationship with Trader Q, who traded at a proprietary trading firm. He sought help for both his quantitative and discretionary trading.

Q was a PhD physicist with multiple additional academic credentials including a master's degree in financial engineering. Q wanted to increase his ability to access his intuition to improve his trading performance. This case highlights using interventions for increased psychophysical awareness designed to help Q to better execute his decisions confidently in the midst of financial market uncertainty.

Q was implicitly displaying the realization that the ability to envision the thoughts and feelings of others—a construct called Theory of Mind—could improve his performance. According to Q, the market is "an object with tons of people implementing something in that software; they are debating within themselves; probably their emotions are incorporated in that chart."

To achieve the enhanced perception that Q wanted depended on his ability to access the data existing in his neurobiology in a manner Porges (2009) has labeled "neuroception." This term means realizing an unconscious affective indicator of safety or danger can become conscious or known. Traders must continually assess the risk of loss in their positions. In what some emotion neuroscientists call "bottoms-up" affect, wins and losses unconsciously translate into virtual life or death situations.

These decisions correspond to Siegel's (2012a, p. 484–485) discussion of the evaluation of threats to survival versus positioning for social engagement: "We continually evaluate, without awareness, the context of a situation for its inherent threats to survival and match the body's physiological state with social engagement, fight-flight-freeze, or shut-down behaviors." The challenge within performance consulting is how to assist with creating neuroception and then to integrate insights from this embodied cognition with the analytical proficiency of the mind.

Despite his initial skepticism about the efficacy of performance coaching, which was born out of his past reliance on his intellect in navigating the world, Q realized that his data and quantitative models were insufficient to permit him to access the intuitive and emotional understanding of the markets that he desired. Q spent most of his early career working as a physicist and researcher in prodigious laboratories within Ivy League institutions. He was trained to analyze large data sets and identify relationships among hard to measure variables and to use statistical models to make sense of complex phenomena. Failing to find fulfillment in this profession, Q believed that trading offered the promise of independence from the drudgery of laboratory work and greater financial reward.

Q's personality tended toward anxiety, obsessive thinking, interpersonal insecurity, and a compulsive drive for control. He managed his anxiety through elaborate analysis that ironically tended to obscure the phenomena he was trying to understand. Spontaneity was lacking as deliberate routines were his strong, even debilitating, preference. When gripped with self-doubt, as was frequently his situation, he resorted to acquiring more intellectual knowledge, believing it would settle emotional turmoil. Nevertheless, no matter how many mathematical models he used to make sense of his world, they always seemed to produce a repetitious conclusion and feeling state: I'm not safe.

If safety was what Q was seeking, uncertainty was the incontrovertible reality of becoming a successful trader. The objective in coaching was to devise ways for him to increase his understanding of the financial markets in which he traded while simultaneously helping him understand his own embodied cognition and unconscious affective context occurring in reaction to the uncertainty he faced. Disappointing others and being perceived as not good enough emerged as a core theme that gripped and compromised Q's confidence. He referenced the "lack of faith from my father" as a powerful inhibitor and distracter throughout his life. Within the trading group where he worked, growing concerns about whether he was capable echoed his remembrances of his father's lack of faith and naturally added substantial stress. His lifelong solution to creating faith in turn materialized in a desperate desire to "get it right" through knowledge, precision, and detailed routines.

As part of the coaching process, the coach used a biometric tool to help Q acquire data about himself. These data, reflecting states in his body mediated through a combination of brain structures, hormones, and vagal nerves such as described in polyvagal theory, could be used to signal him as to the presence and level of unconscious affective states influencing his behavior.

The tool employed was a heart rate biofeedback technology called emWave from the company HeartMath. The software portion is based on heart rate variability (HRV) analysis, which assesses the presence of psychophysiological stress indications. The algorithmic nature of the tool appealed both to Q's analytical tendencies and to his computer programming background. That aspect enabled him to accept the coach's unfamiliar embodied cognition approach to achieving the understanding that Q sought.

Through deliberate practices of viewing the biofeedback, breathing changes, and dialogue concerning his affective states, Q increased his range of tolerance for volatility and uncertainty. Rather than being caught in either extremes of distress (low frequency HRV) or confidence (high frequency HRV), Q became more adept at adjusting to changing market volatility. Reducing tension in the body seemed to improve confidence in the mind. He no longer was unable to tolerate sudden shifts in market direction, but became more accepting and able to "go with the flow"—a version of his original request for the "market to talk to me."

Coaching sessions also dealt with issues in Q's personal life and family experiences. These experiences had translated in a fractal fashion to his trading performance. For example, Q's experience of feeling that his father did not have confidence in him fueled his lack of confidence in himself. In the course of coaching, he realized the parallel between that perceived lack of confidence and his tendency to rely on external sources—data, algorithms, intellectual knowledge—in his trading.

As often happens, due to the transfer of unconscious affective expectations to anyone in an authority position, Q also expressed inspiration from the coach's unexpected profession of confidence in his trading potential. This exemplifies how new social and emotional contexts seemingly can modify biologically based older states of feeling.

Over a three-year period, Q made noticeable progress. Historical barriers of risk aversion and lack of aggressive execution occurred less frequently. He was able to rely less on seeking additional data and more on his intuition and judgment in making market decisions.

SUMMARY

Traders W and Q both reveal the presence of unconscious affect and demonstrate its impact on their judgment, decisions, and behavior. W sees losing trades as an "existential" threat where instead of the reality of the empirical, objective threat of losing money, he worries deeply over a threat to his very existence. Clearly exceptional cognitive capacity alone fails to produce consistently successful trading. Other factors matter.

In what can only be called an unexpected development for Wall Street, the brain and psychological sciences are now elucidating how feelings and emotions actually work within perception, judgment, and behavior. Visceral body states contribute to what once were considered products of the intellect alone. If flexing muscles can increase willpower, what does being rational really involve? If smelling fish can quantitatively influence investing decisions, what are the elements constructing thinking itself?

The experience of these two traders validates emerging research insights of a social brain, unconscious affective context, and at least a fractal-like, if not literally fractal, dimension to human perception. In traders' descriptions of experiences in trading and earlier in life, consultants find matches of uncanny similarity. The initial experience—the feeling a child has in reaction to an authority figure—reoccurs in adult life in the seemingly completely unrelated situations of financial market participation.

The repetitive subjective experiences described demonstrate how what began in familial social situations extends to reactions to the social risk of markets and also to the human-to-human interaction of being coached. Their behaviors also demon-strate the application of regret theory where the fear of booking losses causes trading decisions—adding to losing trades, for example—that while designed to avoid future regret almost inevitably cause more regret.

In the realm of external context and social brains, Q's entry into psychological coaching illustrates an understanding of the need to tap into the natural human abil-ity to use Theory of Mind skills as demonstrated by Bruguier et al.'s (2010) study of trader intuition.

Adapting the work from embodied cognition and unconscious affective context has also led to other cases of improvements in performance in a major bank desk head in Asia, multiple former hedge fund managers in all career stages, and inde-pendent and proprietary firm traders. Becoming conscious of repetitive but previ-ously unconscious affective experiences, through dialogue and other tools, precedes positive changes in trader performance.

The next step in a complete view of trading and even investing psychology is de-signing research studies to deliver more empirical data. Documenting the real world should lead to reducing individual, bank, and global finance system risk.

DISCUSSION QUESTIONS

1. Identify the key new, emerging concepts involving perception, judgment, and risk decision-making under uncertainty.
2. Explain why Trader W insisted that a checklist would be the solution to behav-ioral risk management and why having a checklist was insufficient to change his behavior.
3. Why did the meeting with the large potential investor represent an important development in W's performance?
4. How did biofeedback assist Trader Q in becoming a more proficient trader?

REFERENCES

Anderson, Michael L., Josh Kinnison, and Luiz Pessoa. 2013. "Describing Functional Diversity of Brain Regions and Brain Networks." *NeuroImage* 73:0, 50–58.

Appelhans, Bradley M., and Linda J. Luecken. 2006. "Heart Rate Variability as an Index of Regulated Emotional Responding." *Review of General Psychology* 10:3, 229–240.

Bargh, John A., and Ezequiel Morsella. 2008. "The Unconscious Mind." *Perspectives on Psychological Science* 3:1, 73–79.

Barrett, Lisa Feldman. 2007. "Being Emotional During Decision Making—Good or Bad? An Empirical Investigation." *Academy of Management Journal* 50:4 923–940.

Barrett, Lisa Feldman, and Eliza Bliss-Moreau. 2009. "Affect as a Psychological Primitive." In Mark P. Zanna, ed., *Advances in Experimental Social Psychology* 41, 167–218.

Bechara, Antoine. 2004. "The Role of Emotion in Decision-Making: Evidence from Neuro-logical Patients with Orbitofrontal Damage." *Brain and Cognition* 55:1, 30–40.

Bruguier, Antoine J., Steven R. Quartz, and Peter Bossaerts. 2010. "Exploring the Nature of 'Trader Intuition'." *Journal of Finance* 65:5, 1703–1723.

Camerer, Colin, George Loewenstein, and Drazen Prelec. 2005. "Neuroeconomics: How Neuroscience Can Inform Economics." *Journal of Economic Literature* 43:1, 9–64.

Coates, John M., and Joe Herbert. 2008. "Endogenous Steroids and Financial Risk Taking on a London Trading Floor." *Proceedings of the National Academy of Sciences* 105:16, 6167–6172.

Cozolino, Louis. 2006. *The Neuroscience of Human Relationships: Attachment and the Developing Social Brain*. New York: W.W. Norton & Company.

Cunningham, William A., and Tobias Brosch. 2012. "Motivational Salience Amygdala Tuning from Traits, Needs, Values, and Goals." *Current Directions in Psychological Science* 21:1, 54–59.

Dijksterhuis, Ap, and Loran F. Nordgren. 2006. "A Theory of Unconscious Thought." *Perspectives on Psychological Science* 1:2, 95–109.

Dixon, James A., John G. Holden, Daniel Mirman, and Damian G. Stephen. 2012. "Multifractal Dynamics in the Emergence of Cognitive Structure." *Topics in Cognitive Science* 4:1, 51–62.

Ekman, Paul. 1992. "An Argument for Basic Emotions." *Cognition & Emotion* 6:3–4, 169–200.

Feinstein, Justin S., Colin Buzza, Rene Hurlemann, Robin L. Follmer, Nader S. Dahdaleh, William H. Coryell, Michael J. Welsh, Daniel Tranel, and John A. Wemmie. 2013. "Fear and Panic in Humans with Bilateral Amygdala Damage." *Nature Neuroscience* 16:3, 270–272.

Fenton-O'Creevy, Mark, Jeffrey Lins, Shalini Vohra, Daniel Richards, Gareth Davies, and Kristina Schaaff. 2012. "Emotion Regulation and Trader Expertise: Heart Rate Variability on the Trading Floor." *Journal of Neuroscience, Psychology and Economics* 5:4, 227–237.

Filiz-Ozbay, Emel, and Erkut Y. Ozbay. 2007. "Auctions with Anticipated Regret: Theory and Experiment." *American Economic Review* 97:4, 1407–1418.

Grove, Matt, and Fiona Coward. 2008. "From Individual Neurons to Social Brains." *Cambridge Archaeological Journal* 18:3, 387–400.

Hasson, Uri, Asif A. Ghazanfar, Bruno Galantucci, Simon Garrod, and Christian Keysers. 2012. "Brain-to-Brain Coupling: A Mechanism for Creating and Sharing a Social World." *Trends in Cognitive Sciences* 16:2, 114–121.

Hsu, Ming, Meghana Bhatt, Ralph Adolphs, Daniel Tranel, and Colin F. Camerer. 2005. "Neural Systems Responding to Degrees of Uncertainty in Human Decision-Making." *Science* 310:5754, 1680–1683.

Huettel, Scott A., and Rachel E. Kranton. 2012. "Identity Economics and the Brain: Uncovering the Mechanisms of Social Conflict." Philosophical Transactions of the Royal Society B: *Biological Sciences* 367:1589, 680–691.

Huettel, Scott A., Allen W. Song, and Gregory McCarthy. 2005. "Decisions under Uncertainty: Probabilistic Context Influences Activation of Prefrontal and Parietal Cortices." *Journal of Neuroscience* 25:13, 3304–3311.

Hung, Iris W., and Aparna A. Labroo. 2011. "From Firm Muscles to Firm Willpower: Understanding the Role of Embodied Cognition in Self-Regulation." *Journal of Consumer Research* 37:6, 1046–1064.

Institute for New Economic Thinking. 2010. Grant awarded to David Tuckett. Available at http://ineteconomics.org/press-release/grant-awarded-david-tuckett/.

Kircanski, Katharina, Matthew D. Lieberman, and Michelle G. Craske. 2012. "Feelings into Words: Contributions of Language to Exposure Therapy." *Psychological Science* 23:10, 1086–1091.

Lane, Richard D., Donald M. Quinlan, Gary E. Schwartz, Pamela A. Walker, and Sharon B. Zeitlin. 1990. "The Levels of Emotional Awareness Scale: A Cognitive-Developmental Measure of Emotion." *Journal of Personality Assessment* 55:1–2, 124–134.

LaPlanche, Jean, and Jean-Bertrand Pontalis. 2012. *The Language of Psychoanalysis*. London: Karnac Books.

LeDoux, Joseph. 2003. "The Emotional Brain, Fear, and the Amygdala." *Cellular and Molecular Neurobiology* 23:4, 727–738.

Lee, Spike W. S., and Norbert Schwarz. 2012. "Bidirectionality, Mediation, and Moderation of Metaphorical Effects: The Embodiment of Social Suspicion and Fishy Smells." *Journal of Personality and Social Psychology* 103:5, 737–749.

Lindquist, Kristen A., Tor D. Wager, Hedy Kober, Eliza Bliss-Moreau, and Lisa Feldman Barrett. 2012. "The Brain Basis of Emotion: A Meta-Analytic Review." *Behavioral and Brain Sciences* 35:03, 121–143.

Loomes, Graham, and Robert Sugden. 1982. "Regret Theory: An Alternative Theory of Rational Choice under Uncertainty." *Economic Journal* 92:368, 805–824.

Luecken, Linda J., Bradley M. Appelhans, Amy Kraft, and Ana Brown. 2006. "Never Far from Home: A Cognitive-Affective Model of the Impact of Early-Life Family Relationships on Physiological Stress Responses in Adulthood." *Journal of Social and Personal Relationships* 23:2, 189–203.

Markowitz, Harry. 1952. "Portfolio Selection." *Journal of Finance* 7:1, 77–91.

Naqvi, Nasir, Baba Shiv, and Antoine Bechara. 2006. "The Role of Emotion in Decision Making: A Cognitive Neuroscience Perspective." *Current Directions in Psychological Science* 15:5, 260–264.

Peters, Ellen. 2012. "Beyond Comprehension: The Role of Numeracy in Judgments and Decisions." *Current Directions in Psychological Science* 21:1, 31–35.

Peters, Ellen, Daniel Västfjäll, Paul Slovic, C. K. Mertz, Ketti Mazzocco, and Stephan Dickert. 2006. "Numeracy and Decision Making." *Psychological Science* 17:5, 407–413.

Pezard, Laurent, and Jean-Louis Nandrino. 2001. "Dynamic Paradigm in Psychopathology: 'Chaos Theory,' from Physics to Psychiatry." *L'Encephale* 27:3, 260–268.

Platt, Michael L., and Scott A. Huettel. 2008. "Risky Business: The Neuroeconomics of Decision Making under Uncertainty." *Nature Neuroscience* 11:4, 398–403.

Porges, Stephen W. 1995. "Orienting in a Defensive World: Mammalian Modifications of Our Evolutionary Heritage. A Polyvagal Theory." *Psychophysiology* 32:4, 301–318.

Porges, Stephen. 2009. "The Polyvagal Theory: New Insights into Adaptive Reactions of the Autonomic Nervous System." *Cleveland Clinic Journal of Medicine* 76:Supplement 2, S86–S90.

Reimann, Martin, Wilko Feye, Alan J. Malter, Joshua M. Ackerman, Raquel Castaño, Nitika Garg, Robert Kreuzbauer, Aparna A. Labroo, Angela Y. Lee, Maureen Morrin, Gergan Y. Nenkov, Jesper H. Nielsen, Maria Perez, Gratiana Pol, Jose Antonia Rosa, Carolyn Yoon, and Chen-Bo Zhong. 2012. "Embodiment in Judgment and Choice." *Journal of Neuroscience, Psychology, and Economics* 5:2, 104–123.

Risen, Jane L., and Clayton R. Critcher. 2011. "Visceral Fit: While in a Visceral State, Associated States of the World Seem More Likely." *Journal of Personality and Social Psychology* 100:5, 777–794.

Shull, Denise. 2012. *Market Mind Games: A Radical Psychology of Investing, Trading and Risk.* New York: McGraw-Hill.

Siegel, Daniel J. 2012a. *Pocket Guide to Interpersonal Neurobiology.* New York: W.W. Norton & Company.

Siegel, Daniel J. 2012b. *Developing Mind: How Relationships and the Brain Interact to Shape Who We Are.* New York: Guilford Press.

Stanton, Steven J., O'Dhaniel A. Mullette-Gillman, and Scott A. Huettel. 2011. "Seasonal Variation of Salivary Testosterone in Men, Normally Cycling Women, and Women Using Hormonal Contraceptives." *Physiology & Behavior* 104:5, 804–808.

Stanton, Steven J., O'Dhaniel A. Mullette-Gillman, R. Edward McLaurin, Cynthia M. Kuhn, Kevin S. LaBar, Michael L. Platt, and Scott A. Huettel. 2011. "Low- and High-Testosterone Individuals Exhibit Decreased Aversion to Economic Risk." *Psychological Science* 22:4, 447–453.

Todd, Rebecca M., William A. Cunningham, Adam K. Anderson, and Evan Thompson. 2012. "Affect-Biased Attention as Emotion Regulation." *Trends in Cognitive Sciences* 16:7, 365–372.

Tuckett, David, and Richard Taffler. 2008. "Phantastic Objects and the Financial Market's Sense of Reality: A Psychoanalytic Contribution to the Understanding of Stock Market Instability." *International Journal of Psychoanalysis* 89:2, 389–412.

Visser, Renee M., H. Steven Scholte, Tinka Beemsterboer, and Merel Kindt. 2013. "Neural Pattern Similarity Predicts Long-Term Fear Memory." *Nature Neuroscience Advance* 16, 388–390. Available at http://dx.doi.org/10.1038/nn.3345.

Wagenmakers, Eric-Jan, Han L. J. van der Maas, and Simon Farrell. 2012. "Abstract Concepts Require Concrete Models: Why Cognitive Scientists Have Not Yet Embraced Nonlinearly Coupled, Dynamical, Self-Organized Critical, Synergistic, Scale-Free, Exquisitely Context-Sensitive, Interaction-Dominant, Multifractal, Interdependent Brain-Body-Niche Systems." *Topics in Cognitive Science* 4:1, 87–93.

ABOUT THE AUTHORS

Denise K. Shull is the Principal of The ReThink Group. She belongs to several societies in the psychological and brain sciences. After succumbing to the lure of Wall Street where she traded and managed trading desks, she returned to the convergence of neuropsychology and risk decision-making. She authored *Market Mind Games*, which outlines a novel approach to overcoming unconscious biases in risk decision-making. She has appeared on CNBC and Bloomberg and been profiled by the *Financial Times*, *Wall Street Journal*, and *Bloomberg Businessweek*. She holds an MA from the University of Chicago in neuropsychology.

Ken Celiano is a major owner of Even Keel Trading, a niche coaching firm targeting professional traders and hedge fund managers. Dr. Celiano taught a course in trading psychology at Northwestern University, published several articles in trading magazines, and appeared in the media discussing his work using social interaction and biometric technology. He holds a doctorate in clinical health psychology from Illinois School of Professional Psychology.

Andrew Menaker is a private performance coach for traders and actively trades. He has provided psychological consultation for banks, hedge funds, and proprietary trading firms since 1995. He has been profiled by the *Wall Street Journal* and is a frequent speaker at industry events. Dr. Menaker was profiled in *Traders at Work— How the World's Most Successful Traders Make Their Living in the Markets*. He is a member of the American Psychological Association, Association for Psychological Science, and Society for Neuroeconomics. He has a master's degree in research psychology and a PhD in clinical psychology from the California School of Professional Psychology.

CHAPTER 27

Trading and Investment Strategies in Behavioral Finance

John M. Longo, CFA
Clinical Professor of Finance and Economics, Rutgers Business School—
Newark and New Brunswick, and Chief Investment Officer, The MDE Group, Inc.

INTRODUCTION

Behavioral finance was once on the fringe of academic finance, but now it clearly has wide acceptance with investment professionals and individual investors. Although behavioral finance is not a new concept, it has garnered increasing attention and respect in recent years. Keynes (1936) understood the role of investor psychology in markets when he indicated that "animal spirits" drove prices. According to Benjamin Graham (1973, p. xv), the father of value investing, "The investor's chief problem—and even his worst enemy—is likely to be himself." The ultimate imprimatur occurred in 2002, when Daniel Kahneman and Vernon Smith received the Nobel Memorial Prize in Economic Sciences for their work in behavioral finance and experimental economics. Thaler (1999), a leading scholar in the field, predicts that the term "behavioral finance" will be a redundant term, noting, "What other kind of finance is there?"

This chapter focuses on questions related to the practical analysis and understanding of behavioral finance. For example, what investment strategies associated with behavioral finance have been at least partially successful? What excess returns have these strategies historically generated? Are these strategies likely to continue to add value? How are investment funds attempting to capitalize on behavioral biases? What are some current and future trends in behavioral finance?

The remainder of this chapter has the following organization. The first section examines the distinction between trading and investment strategies. Next, the chapter analyzes how active versus passive strategies fit into a behavioral finance framework. The subsequent section documents evidence that average investors suffer from behavioral biases that negatively affect their performance. The chapter next analyzes a range of short-term trading approaches and then long-term investment oriented strategies grounded in behavioral finance. The next section discusses current and future trends in behavioral based strategies. Lastly, the chapter summarizes its findings and concludes.

DISTINCTION BETWEEN TRADING AND INVESTMENT STRATEGIES

From an analytical perspective, behavioral biases can occur within a short-term trading strategy or long-term investment time horizon. Graham and Dodd (1934, p. 16) distinguish between short-term speculation and long-term investment as follows: "An investment operation is one which, upon thorough analysis promises safety of principal and an adequate return. Operations not meeting the requirements are speculative."

Although Graham and Dodd's definition makes intuitive sense, it lacks clear points of demarcation from an organizational perspective. This chapter describes *investment strategies* as those with investment horizons generally greater than one year. For example, the *reversal effect* pioneered by DeBondt and Thaler (1985) where long-term winners (losers) subsequently underperform (outperform) is an example of an investment strategy according to Graham and Dodd's definition.

Conversely, *trading strategies* have investment horizons less than one year and as short as a millisecond. The *momentum effect*, popularized by Jegadeesh and Titman (1993), would fall under this definition of a trading strategy. The *momentum effect* is the tendency for rising equity prices to rise further and falling equity prices to keep falling. In general, trading strategies are more germane to the ultracompetitive hedge fund industry, while investment strategies are more suitable for the typical mutual fund, pension fund, or individual investors. Of course, exceptions exist, but the one-year investment horizon demarcation point provides some clarity from a testing perspective. Lastly, the tax authorities in many countries (e.g., Internal Revenue Service in the United States) distinguish between short- and long-term security holdings. The latter horizon in general is taxed at a 15 to 20 percent capital gains rate in the United States, while the former is taxed at higher rates at or near the investors' marginal tax bracket. A provision of the Obamacare legislation resulted in an additional 3.8 percent tax on investment income for wealthy individuals.

ACTIVE VERSUS PASSIVE INVESTMENT STRATEGIES AND BEHAVIORAL FINANCE

Behavioral finance adherents generally fall into the active management camp because they often believe that behavioral biases are systematic and exploitable in nature, at least from a social science perspective. In other words, the law of gravity or quantum mechanics in the physical sciences is likely to hold true almost 100 percent of the time. However, in the social sciences, a model that provides, for example, 55 percent accuracy is likely to add substantial value over the long term. A simple way of assessing the value in a model that has modest predictive ability, relative to one that is purely random, is to consider what would happen if someone won 55 percent of the time when betting on black in a game of roulette. Certainly, any individual spin of the roulette wheel may result in a loss, namely, red or green in this example. However, the individual makes enough of these small bets to have a very successful financial outcome over time.

Reviewing some simple arithmetic may be helpful in seeing the difficulty of outperforming a passive benchmark. Sharpe (1991) demonstrates that the average investor cannot outperform the average return on an investment when including transaction costs. That is, the person will underperform. Although professional fund managers (i.e., sharks, smart money, or informed investors) should be able to take advantage of retail investors (i.e., dumb money or uninformed investors), empirical evidence does not support this notion. In fact, the evidence typically shows that professional fund managers cannot consistently outperform a market index, such as the S&P 500, on a risk-adjusted basis. For example, Bodie, Kane, and Marcus (2010) show the performance of the average equity mutual fund versus the Wilshire 5000 equity index. Consistent with Sharpe's theoretical results, their results indicate that professional fund managers modestly underperform the benchmark.

Investors' risk tolerance may also affect their asset allocation strategies. For example, most investors do not make yearly adjustments to retirement accounts because they suffer from status quo bias (Kahneman, Knetsch, and Thaler 1991). *Status quo bias* refers to an irrational preference for the current state of affairs. The status quo or current investment posture is taken as a reference point. Any change from the initial reference point is perceived as a loss.

Several approaches may be beneficial to investors in order to overcome the status quo biases. The first approach is to use automatic rebalancing in a 401(k) plan, such as reverting to a 60 percent equity and 40 percent fixed income portfolio on January 1 of each year or a person's birthday. Active asset allocation is a second approach to overcoming the status quo bias because it forces active decision-making on the part of investors or their advisors. Lastly, a life cycle fund engages in active asset allocation, typically becoming more conservative as a specific target date approaches, such as a planned retirement date.

Yet, a glimmer of hope exists for advocates of active management. Several studies such as Malkiel (1995) and Bollen and Busse (2005) find modest evidence showing persistent performance. That is, winning (losing) managers, on balance, keep on winning (losing). For example, the investment performance of Warren Buffett, Peter Lynch, James Simons, George Soros, and other members of the proverbial investment hall of fame provide support for the persistence theory, while the overall distribution of outperformers remains consistent with market efficiency.

If markets are not fully efficient, active management may be a worthwhile activity for those willing to put substantial amounts of time and rigorous effort into the endeavor. However, any active manager should have a healthy respect for both the difficulty in outperforming an index on a risk-adjusted basis and in overcoming (broadly defined) transaction costs. Investors who lack a passion for the financial markets or access to highly knowledgeable and experienced financial advisors are likely best served with index funds. Vanguard and Dimensional Fund Advisors (DFA) have both built phenomenally successful businesses using index funds as their primary investment approach. This chapter is mainly designed for those who believe in active management and want to improve their investment performance by capitalizing on knowledge from behavioral finance.

Currently, many successful investment firms base their investment decisions on behavioral finance principles. For example, LSV Asset Management, a firm formed by three academic "stars" of behavioral finance research, has about $65 billion under management. The "Investment Philosophy" section of the LSV's website states, "The fundamental premise on which our investment philosophy is based is that superior long-term results can be achieved by systematically exploiting the judgmental biases and behavioral weaknesses that influence the decisions of many investors"

(LSV Asset Management 2013). Fuller and Thaler Asset Management have trademarked the term "The Behavioral Edge®" to succinctly describe their strategy. This firm's home page states, "Investors make mental mistakes that can cause stocks to be mispriced. Fuller & Thaler's objective is to use our understanding of human decision-making to find these mispriced stocks and earn superior returns" (Fuller and Thaler Asset Management 2013).

AVERAGE INVESTORS SUFFER FROM BEHAVIORAL BIASES

The old adage that a picture is worth a thousand words likely applies to Exhibit 27.1. The exhibit shows that the average investor in equity funds over the 15-year period from 1998 through 2012 averaged returns less than half those earned by the S&P 500 Index. Even after taking into account (actively managed fund) fees and transaction costs, the average investor clearly underperformed during this period. What is probably driving this result is the behavioral bias of "chasing" investment performance. That is, the typical investor buys what has done well recently and, on the downside, often sells near the market lows. Although the success of following momentum strategies is discussed throughout this chapter, investors are typically not nimble enough in their investment decisions to profit from the momentum anomaly. They often buy an asset after it has risen substantially in price, perhaps due to media attention given to these "star" investments. Inevitably, a loss occurs. If the loss is severe, a "capitulation" event often occurs, where the investor sells near a bottom.

The investment implications of the Exhibit 27.1 are perhaps twofold. A portfolio of index funds may best serve investors with long-term horizons so they do not succumb to the performance chasing bias. Investors using an active management approach should exercise extreme caution in their entry and exit points. In some instances, following a dollar cost averaging approach may be a better course of action. For the active trader, the momentum anomaly likely works in the short run—for

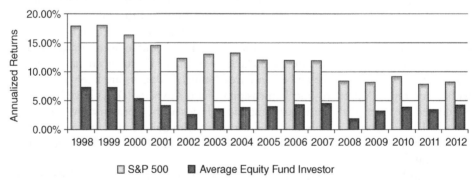

EXHIBIT 27.1   Long-Term Annualized Returns: S&P 500 Index versus the Average Equity Fund Investor

Note: This exhibit shows that the average investor in equity funds substantially underperforms the S&P 500 Index. The likely sources of this underperformance are investors chasing returns and buying near market tops and capitulating and selling near market bottoms.

Source: Dalbar, Inc. (2013). Reprinted with permission.

example, buy (short) what has worked well (poorly) recently, but be poised to exit the investment if the market cycle changes.

PROBLEMS WITH TRADITIONAL INVESTMENT STRATEGIES

Many widely accepted academic theories of traditional finance and practitioner investment strategies fall short of their promises when implemented over a full market cycle. This section examines several strategies, such as those based on Markowtz (1952, 1959) portfolio theory, the dividend discount model (DDM), hedge funds, and the endowment model, and discusses where each falls short of performance expectations in practice. The inability of these approaches to effectively describe financial reality creates an opening for behaviorally based investment strategies, which is the focus of the following section.

Problems with Markowitz Portfolio Theory

Markowitz (1952, 1959), who shared the 1990 Nobel Memorial Prize in Economic Sciences, provides one of the seminal contributions to finance. He was the first to explicitly measure portfolio risk and fully understood the impact of correlation on the risk of the portfolio, rather than merely the risk of the underlying securities. Markowitz also developed a quadratic program, a substantial mathematical achievement, to solve for what he termed as *efficient portfolios* (i.e., the investment opportunity set that maximizes return for a given level of risk or minimizes risk for a given level of return).

Although many still use Markowitz portfolio theory at the asset allocation level, its practicality has limitations at the individual stock selection level for most investor applications. First, the efficient frontier is unstable. In other words, a recommended portfolio for an investor today may differ markedly from a new optimization for the same investor at a later date. Financial advisors would lose credibility with their clients by recommending major portfolio adjustments on such a frequent basis. Second, the practical application of the Markowitz model, like nearly all models, is based on the quality of its inputs, such as the expected return and risk as measured by the standard deviation of each security. The most common methods for obtaining estimates all have flaws, such as the capital asset pricing model (CAPM), market model, arbitrage pricing theory (APT), and Fama-French three-factor model. Third, an important flaw with practical applications of the Markowitz model is that correlations often increase close to a perfect positive correlation (+1) during times of economic distress, thus eliminating the benefit of diversification, which is a central assumption of the model. Therefore, the investment principle of diversification often does not provide meaningful help precisely when investors need it most.

Problems with Dividend Discount Model

The *dividend discount model* (DDM) basically states that the price of a stock (or other asset) equals the present value of the future cash flows generated by the asset. Theoretically, its logic is unassailable. Investors know that "time is money" and that they should discount future cash flows back to the present. Yet, applying the model in the real world reveals its shortcomings. Although valuing an asset as the present value of future cash flows works well for bonds, it remains a challenging task for stocks that exist in perpetuity. How can an analyst reliably predict dividends or earnings for a firm out one year, let alone in perpetuity?

The DDM has three major forms: no growth, constant growth, and irregular growth. Let's look at the constant growth version of the model, often called the *Gordon constant growth model*, because of its wide use in finance textbooks and the Chartered Financial Analysts (CFA) program. Its equation is as follows:

$$P_0 = \frac{D_1}{(r-g)} \tag{27.1}$$

where P_0 is today's price estimate; D_1 is the estimate of next year's dividend (or free cash flow); r is the discount rate or cost of equity capital estimate; and g is the estimate of the terminal or constant growth rate of dividends (or free cash flow).

Assume that an investor can estimate each of the variables on the right-hand side of Equation 27.1 with a reasonable degree of precision. A simple numerical example illustrates some practical difficulties of the DDM, despite its theoretical elegance. Assume a base case that next year's dividend (or free cash flow) is $1 per share, the discount rate is 12 percent, and the constant growth rate is 3 percent. Investors often conduct a sensitivity analysis by varying the discount rate and growth rate. Varying the projected dividend next year is possible, but they make this adjustment less often.

Exhibit 27.2 shows the results for a range of discount rates and growth factors. Making relatively minor changes in the inputs results in a large variation in the price. Under the base case assumptions, the stock price is $11.11. Using a more optimistic scenario with a 10 percent discount rate and 5 percent growth rate results in a price of $20.00. This is a difference of 80 percent from the base case. Using a more pessimistic scenario of a 14 percent discount rate and a 1 percent growth rate results in a price of $7.69, representing a 31 percent drop from the base case. The range of

EXHIBIT 27.2   Sensitivity of the Dividend Discount Model

	DDM Value per Share		
	Discount Rate		
Growth Rate (%)	10%	12%	14%
1	$11.11	$9.09	$7.69
2	12.50	10.00	8.33
3	14.29	11.11	9.09
4	16.67	12.50	10.00
5	20.00	14.29	11.11

Note: The DDM is often of little use in practice due to its sensitivity to the inputs. Small changes in the growth and discount rates may result in large changes to the price target. Almost any price target may be justified with minor changes to the inputs to the DDM.

reasonable estimates (e.g., $7.69 to $20.00) is so wide it often makes the DDM of limited use to professional fund managers. In essence, an investor can justify almost any valuation by changing the inputs.

Although the DDM can add some value, especially for dividend-paying stocks in the mature stage of their life cycle, analysts and investors should be wary of using it as a primary valuation technique. The DDM may also provide a valuable reality check during anomalous periods of overreaction, on both the upside and downside, in the market. Using the DDM as a reality check against the prices of technology stocks during times such as the Internet bubble period of the late 1990s through early 2000 may have added substantial value. Almost any application of the DDM to technology stocks would have indicated huge overvaluation. For example, the stock price performance of Microstrategy, a business intelligence software maker, provides one dramatic example of the irrationality that occurred during this period. Microstrategy went from roughly $25 per share shortly after its initial public offering (IPO) in mid-1998 to a breathtaking $3,500 a share at the peak of the Internet bubble in March 2000. The stock ultimately crashed to $4 a share and rebounded to $108 in March 2013, still down almost 97 percent from its peak.

Problems with Hedge Funds and Endowment Model

In the 2000–2002 aftermath of the Internet bubble, hedge funds were highly popular in the investment world. *Hedge funds* are private investment vehicles sold to high net worth investors or institutions. The average hedge fund provided modestly positive returns during each of these calendar years, while most equity indexes plunged double digits and lost more than half their value on a peak-to-trough basis. Although hedge fund assets increased more than tenfold from 2000 to 2012, the illusion of hedge fund invincibility was dispelled in 2008 when the average hedge fund lost 23.25 percent, according to the Hedge Fund Research (HFRX) Index. A similar and somewhat more surprising breakdown occurred in 2011 when the HFRX Index lost 8.87 percent compared to modestly positive S&P 500 performance (Eder 2011).

In light of these disappointments, investment managers and their constituencies alike were dismayed to learn that many hedge funds—despite their name—had no material "hedge" or risk reduction features. More recently, the term "hedge fund" has evolved to refer simply to an investment within a partnership structure that has the ability to charge incentive fees. The last decade has not been a good one for hedge fund performance. Somewhat ironically, 2008 was the best year of relative performance for hedge funds over the last 10 years in comparison to the S&P 500. But for the full decade, hedge funds, as measured by the HFRX index, underperformed inflation according to an analysis performed by *The Economist* (2012). That analysis further shows that hedge funds underperformed a simple 60 percent/40 percent equity bond index during the same period by an astounding margin. That is, the equity bond index returned 90 percent while the HFRX Hedge Fund Index was up only 17 percent.

What hedge fund investors often overlook is that these vehicles must achieve huge gross returns in order to deliver merely adequate net returns to the client. This is an important issue in recent years in an environment of high correlations, low yields, and limited returns. To understand why this is the case, consider an investment in a typical hedge fund. To be conservative, assume that the underlying individual hedge fund charges fees of 1.5 percent of assets and 20 percent of profits. In fact,

EXHIBIT 27.3 Hedge Fund Gross versus Net Returns

Calculation of Net Return to Investor	%
Hypothetical gross return of fund	14.0
Hedge fund: transaction costs	–2.0
Hedge fund: base fee	–1.5
Hedge fund: expenses	–0.5
Hedge fund: incentive fee (20%)	–2.0
Net return to investor	8.0

Note: Hedge funds are burdened with high invest-ment fees and underlying expenses. In this example, a 14 percent gross return for the fund shrinks to an 8 percent net return for the investor.

many hedge funds charge 2 percent of assets plus 20 percent of profits. Also assume an annual expense ratio of 0.5 percent for the hedge fund partnership structure and that the individual hedge fund pays 2 percent in annual transaction costs.

Exhibit 27.3 shows that the net returns to an investor are startling. A seem-ingly impressive 14.0 percent gross return shrinks to a far more modest 8.0 percent net return after paying fees and expenses. A fund of funds structure may exacer-bate the problem because it may require that underlying managers produce nearly a 17.0 percent gross return to net 8 percent to the end investor. As the name suggests, a *fund of funds* is a hedge fund that holds positions in underlying individual hedge funds. This extra return is necessary to cover the additional layer of partnership expenses as well as a typical fee structure of 1 percent of assets plus 10 percent of the profits in a fund of funds structure.

The main lesson is not that hedge funds are expensive or have underperformed, but that they need to generate superior gross returns to deliver acceptable net returns to investors. This often causes hedge fund managers to stretch for returns, creating unrecognized and uncompensated risk as managers take above-market risks with investor capital to generate returns sufficient to cover their very substantial fees and underlying expenses. Additionally, limited hedge fund transparency often pre-vents investors from recognizing the added risk until they no longer have time to respond. Other hedge fund flaws also exact their toll. Lockup provisions, gates, or side pockets limit exit opportunities once added risk issues are uncovered. A *lockup provision* refers to the minimum holding period for a hedge fund, without incurring a substantial early exit fee. *Gates* on a hedge fund limit the ability to redeem from a hedge fund even after the lockup period expires. Gates are usually erected during times of substantial redemptions for a hedge fund. *Side pockets* refer to holdings in illiquid assets, such as private equity investments, that hedge fund investors hold after requesting redemption. Transparency not only plays a role in uncovering fraud or unacceptable risks, but it also helps investment managers better understand where a particular hedge fund fits within their portfolios.

A prodigy of the Markowitz model called the *endowment model*, popularized by David Swenson of Yale, added large positions in hedge funds, private equity, and other illiquid sophisticated investments in an attempt to enhance returns while reducing risk. The focus on leveraged, illiquid, and alternative investments differentiates the endowment model from a traditional mix (e.g., 60 percent and 40 percent) of equity and debt, respectively. Despite attractive long-term performance, the endowment model failed during the financial crisis of 2007–2008 with many of its adherents losing in excess of 25 percent of invested capital.

Endowment funds are investment funds set up by nonprofit institutions to help finance their activities and long-term strategic plans. The endowment funds of some of the most prestigious American universities experienced substantial losses during the recent financial crisis. For example, during the fiscal year 2009 (July 1, 2008 through June 30, 2009), endowment performance for the following institutions dropped dramatically: Harvard (–27.3 percent), Stanford (–25.9 percent), Yale (–24.9 percent), and Princeton (–22.7 percent). The typical investor cannot replicate the investment opportunity set afforded to Yale and other large endowments.

In short, problems with existing models used by institutional and some retail investors provide opportunities for behaviorally based strategies with the objective of profiting from the mistakes of the "crowd." Behavioral models are also likely to better explain how the markets work. The next section of this chapter focuses on these short-term strategies.

SHORT-TERM BEHAVIORALLY BASED TRADING STRATEGIES

The prior section established some of the problems with traditional financial theories and techniques used by practitioners. Fortunately, the behavioral finance literature provides some guidance into strategies that appear to consistently generate superior risk-adjusted returns. This section focuses on trading-oriented behavioral strategies that generally have a holding period of less than one year. These strategies are fallible and do not have the theoretical elegance of Markowitz portfolio theory or the CAPM, but are of practical value to professional investors. The behavioral finance literature suggests that these biases are unlikely to disappear quickly, raising the prospect of market-beating strategies.

Momentum

The success of momentum strategies is one of the most serious challenges to the efficient market hypothesis (EMH). The *EMH* states that security prices reflect all available information. Hence, consistently beating the market by devising an investment strategy that regularly delivers superior risk-adjusted returns is impossible. A common catchphrase among technical analysts for momentum is that "the trend is your friend." In other words, winning investments keep winning, while losing investments keep losing, at least in relation to a market index. Momentum can be measured in many ways, but its calculation typically examines the price of an asset relative to an index. The relative strength and moving average statistics are among the most common statistics used to measure momentum. These metrics are computed below:

$$\text{Relative strength} = (1 + R_x)/(1 + R_i) \qquad (27.2)$$

where R_x is the return of a stock or other asset over the specified time period and R_i is the return of an appropriate index or benchmark over the specified time period. Analysts sometimes normalize the relative strength figure into a relative strength index (RSI) with a value between 0 and 100. A number close to zero indicates that the security has experienced the worst performance versus its peers in the index over the specified time period, while a number closer to 100 signifies the best relative performance.

The short-term behavior of variables, such as stock prices, often shows a jagged, erratic pattern. Technicians often use a moving average to smooth out this volatile pattern in order to make judgments that do not flip-flop from buy to sell ratings too often. Moving averages can vary by length and they are typically analyzed in pairs. For example, a short-term trader may focus on the 5-day moving average relative to its 20-day moving average. Investors with longer horizons often focus on the 50-day moving average relative to the 200-day moving average. In both instances, if the shorter-term moving average is higher than the longer-term moving average, technical analysts generally view the investment as having relative strength. In this case, the relative strength is with respect to recent values of the investment, rather than performance versus an index.

$$\text{Moving average} = (P_1 + P_2 + \ldots + P_N)/N \tag{27.3}$$

where
  $P_1 =$ the closing price of the asset on period (e.g., day) 1
  $P_2 =$ the closing price of the asset on period (e.g., day) 2
  $P_N =$ the closing price of the asset on period (e.g., day) N
  $N =$ the number of observations.

The calculation in Equation 27.3 is a simple moving average or just a moving average. Technicians often compute variations of the simple moving average, such as an exponentially weighted moving average, to put more weight on recent price movements. Exhibit 27.4 shows the 50-day versus 200-day moving average for Google in late May, 2013. The chart is bullish because the short-term moving average is higher than the longer-term moving average, and therefore indicative of positive price momentum.

Jegadeesh and Titman (1993) find that the momentum earns abnormal returns of roughly 1 percent per month for periods up to 12 months, but that the effect is the strongest in the three- to six-month range. Momentum is likely to add value because this approach is based on the central tenets of behavioral finance. Investors often mimic the behavior of other investors. If an individual observes another making large profits buying Amazon.com stock, the individual may follow suit. Momentum may also add investment value due to the way news makes its way into stock prices. In some instances, investors provide news to reporters and therefore legally trade on news before it is published. Unfortunately, in some circumstances, investors illegally trade on insider information and leave "footprints" in the price action of security prices. Other investors may infer that this abnormal buying causes prices to increase or decrease further.

Margin calls may also play a role in momentum. A *margin call* is a demand by a brokerage firm to deposit cash or securities in a financial account to provide collateral

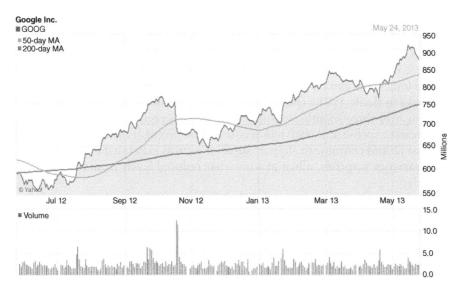

EXHIBIT 27.4   50-Day versus 200-Day Moving Average for Google

Note: This exhibit shows the 50-day versus the 200-day moving average for Google in late May, 2013. The chart is bullish because the short-term moving average is higher than the longer-term moving average, which indicates positive price momentum.

Source: Yahoo Finance. http://finance.yahoo.com/q/ta?s=GOOG&t=1y&l=on&z=l&q=l&p= m50%2Cm200&a=&c=/.

for recently experienced losses. A losing investment on the long side may result in the mandatory sale of securities, depressing prices further. Similarly, a losing investment on a short sale position may result in a "short squeeze" causing an additional increase in prices. A *short squeeze* is a request from a brokerage firm to an investor to cover a short sale position, which often results in a sharp increase in the price of the covered stock. Lastly, successful fund managers often receive cash inflows. In many instances they buy (short-sell) their existing holdings, pushing prices higher (lower).

Earnings Surprises

An *earnings surprise* is the difference between the reported earnings per share (EPS) (i.e., the actual EPS) and the consensus sell-side estimate (i.e., the estimated EPS), tracked by First Call, or another sell-side earnings aggregator. The surprise is positive if the reported EPS is greater than the consensus EPS estimate. Conversely, the surprise is negative if the company reports a number less than the consensus. Analysts often normalize the earnings surprise figure as a percentage, as shown below:

$$\text{Earnings surprise percent} = \text{Reported earnings number}/$$
$$\text{Consensus earnings number} - 1 \qquad (27.4)$$

Researchers often sort earnings surprises into deciles. For example, an early study by Rendleman, Jones, and Latané (1982) shows how stocks with the biggest earnings surprise in decile 10 outperform those in decile 9 and decile 8, and so forth. A "long only" strategy could simply purchase stocks in decile 10 and, according to the historical Rendleman et al. numbers, earn abnormal returns of roughly 8 percent in the three months after the earnings announcement. Hedge funds may have an interest in a long/short variant of the strategy, going long stocks in decile 10 and selling short stocks in decile 1. The spread between these deciles is roughly an astonishing 16 percent over three months, multiplied by any leverage used by the hedge fund, net of interest expense and transaction costs. More recent studies such as Jegadeesh and Livnat (2006) continue to support superior returns generated by firms reporting positive earnings surprises, albeit at somewhat reduced levels from the Rendleman et al. study.

Why do earnings surprises persist? Jegadeesh and Titman (1993) are likely the first researchers to document underreaction as a persistent bias. The *underreaction bias* suggests that for some firms, new information gradually makes its way into the current price of a security, rather than the instantaneous approach suggested by the EMH. Investors often perceive prior winning or "glamour," stocks as remaining market leaders for an extended period. Conversely, previous losing stocks, or "dogs," often need time for skeptical investors to believe that their prior disappointing performance has truly changed.

In contrast to the Jegadeesh and Titman (1993) approach on momentum in stock returns, Dreman and Berry (1995) discuss underreaction in the framework of analyst estimates and valuation metrics. In the context of earnings surprises, when news arises, investors are skeptical so they need time to accept that the news is real or sustainable. So, firms with positive earnings surprises get some benefit of good news. Conversely, the market penalizes firms with negative surprises, but perhaps not to the full extent that might be warranted. More elementary, buying and selling does not happen instantaneously. Some investors take time to process an earnings report and conduct appropriate follow-up research, thereby resulting in a delayed reaction. Lastly, good management knows how to use the slogan "under promise and over deliver." Perhaps the management of firms with negative earnings surprises has not mastered this technique or operates in more volatile businesses that are not subject to the same earnings clarity. Tversky and Kahneman (1981) find that *framing* (i.e., adjusting the way that firms present earnings to investors) can sometimes fool investors and therefore may be another explanatory factor behind the persistence of the earning surprise anomaly.

Form 13F Filings and Hedge Fund Herding

The Securities and Exchange Commission (SEC) requires that all institutional investment managers with more than $100 million in assets under management report a portion of their holdings on a quarterly basis via Form 13F. Unfortunately, a fund does not have to disclose all holdings. For example, funds do not have to disclose short sale and some derivative positions but they must disclose long positions in stocks and options. Form 13F filings provide important information on the holdings of the portfolio of top portfolio managers, such as those managed by billionaire hedge fund managers. Professional investors widely follow these filings and seek to piggyback on the research and strong connections of the "star" managers. Does mimicking some of the trades reported in 13F filings pay? In a word, "Yes."

For example, Brav, Jiang, Partnoy, and Thomas (2008) find abnormal returns of 7 percent per year for activist hedge funds using Form 13F data.

Put/Call Ratio and Other Investor Sentiment Indicators

The term *investor sentiment* is synonymous with the terms *feeling* and *emotion* of investors. Clearly, these terms differ from purely rational behavior or the EMH. Analysts have created and historically applied several sentiment indicators to the market as a whole, but some may also be applicable to individual equities. This section discusses some investor sentiment indicators and the behavioral logic related to why they may be of value to investors.

Some attribute the put/call ratio indicator to investing legend Martin Zweig, who was best known for "calling" the Crash of 1987. Unlike most technical indicators that tend to be trend-following, the put/call ratio is a contrarian metric. Puts (sell) options enable investors to profit from a decline in the price of an asset and call (buy) options enable them to profit from a rise in a stock or other asset. A high value of the put/call ratio tends to indicate that investors are excessively bearish, hence perhaps the market may trend upward. Historically, more traders tend to buy call options then put options because the market goes up over the long term, so a value greater than 1 for the put/call ratio is uncommon. Many technicians view a value of the ratio as greater than 0.6 as bullish for equities. A behavioral connection to the put/call ratio is one of overreaction, or having the pendulum of market psychology move too far in one direction of price.

Arms (1996) devised the trading index (TRIN), which is sometimes called the Arms Index after its creator. Technicians generally believe that when a stock rises (falls) on high volume it is good (bad) news. Volume is the strength of the signal. If many stocks rise on high volume, this suggests a bullish signal. Conversely, if many stocks decline on high volume, TRIN provides a bearish omen. Equation 27.5 shows the TRIN calculation.

$$\text{TRIN} = (\text{Advancing issues/Declining issues})/ \\ (\text{Advancing volume/Declining volume}) \qquad (27.5)$$

Because TRIN is a ratio of a ratio, its interpretation may be confusing. TRIN values less than 1 indicate bullish sentiment and strategy (i.e., many stocks are increasing on high relative volume to the decliners). Conversely, TRIN values greater than 1 are bearish. TRIN is consistent with the herding behavioral bias documented by Lakonishok, Shleifer, and Vishny (1992) as well as the euphoric (despair) feeling that often occurs in bull (bear) markets.

The *Barron's confidence index* is a ratio of the average yield-to-maturity of its best-grade bond list compared to the average yield-to-maturity of its intermediate grade bond list. Analysts often multiply this ratio by 100 to give a number more resembling that of a stock or index price. This index is roughly the equivalent of the ratio of AA or better bond yields to BBB bond yields. Because AAA bonds always sell at a lower yield to maturity than BBB bonds due to their lower credit risk, the index always trades at a value less than one. The Barron's confidence index examines the relative level of this ratio. Because values closer to one indicate a willingness to take on credit risk, they may be signs of an improving economy, a bullish stock market, and optimism bias. *Optimism bias* is the tendency to view one's own risk as less than that of others. Conversely, values well below one may indicate flight to quality or panic movements. Hence, low values would be bearish for stocks. Analysts consider index levels below 80 as bearish and values above 90 as bullish for stocks. In short, sentiment indicators attempt to measure the pulse or mood of the market and are therefore at the heart of behavioral biases of the market as a whole. The next section of this chapter focuses on long-term investment strategies.

LONG-TERM BEHAVIORALLY BASED INVESTMENT STRATEGIES

The behavioral finance literature documents several *long-term investment strategies* (i.e., those with holding periods greater than one year) that persistently generate superior risk-adjusted returns. This section focuses on several of these strategies, explaining their logic and the historical returns generated by the strategies. In the case of the Dogs of the Dow anomaly, an exchange traded fund (ETF) has been created to enable investors to simply and efficiently invest in the strategy.

Long-Term Price Reversals or Mean Reversion

The previous section discussed the shorter-term momentum effect in stock prices. That is, a strategy where winners (losers) kept winning (losing) for periods up to 18 months, but especially over a three-to-six month time frame. What about the momentum effect over the longer term? Researchers, such as DeBondt and Thaler (1985), find that over a three-to-five year period the reverse occurs. In others words, a basket of winners (losers) over the prior three to five years becomes losers (winners) over the next three to five years. DeBondt and Thaler report that the prior losers subsequently outperform the prior winners by 25 percent over a three-year period and with less risk.

Behavioral finance researchers view this finding as an *overreaction effect* in which investors tend to extrapolate trends over long periods. A basket of "star" stocks, despite the occasional IBM or Google, rarely can maintain its leadership position as a "hot stock" for an extended period. Some star stocks often attract intense competition or perhaps never deserved their star status. Conversely, a basket of stocks containing companies "left for dead" can often rebound despite some high profile stocks such as Enron, Kodak, and General Motors dropping dramatically.

Dogs of the Dow and Other Value Anomalies

Researchers such as Fama and French (1992) find that value stocks outperform growth stocks. However, investors suffer from behavioral bias that causes them to assume growth stocks have a better historical investment performance than value stocks most of the time. Of course, many ways are available to measure value, such as low price/ earnings (P/E), low price-to-book (or its reciprocal book-to-market), low price-to-cash flow, and high dividend yield. The focus on a specific valuation metric is how this anomaly differs from the (price) momentum and reversal effects discussed earlier. The Dogs of the Dow strategy provides an intuitive example of the strategy in action and its possibly related behavioral bias. It focuses on the 10 highest dividend yielding stocks among the 30 stocks in the Dow Jones Industrial Average (DJIA). The strategy received widespread attention after the publication of *Beating the Dow* by Michael O'Higgins (1991). O'Higgins finds that the "dogs" strategy outperformed the (full) DJIA by about 3 percentage points a year.

Why may this strategy add value? Clearly, it is tied to the value anomaly, but the strategy may also be a variant of the "too big to fail" theme that analysts typically apply to banks. Although some former Dow stocks such as Kodak and General Motors fail, the vast majority are large, well capitalized, international companies. Jack Welch, legendary former chief executive officer of General Electric (GE) once noted that GE would be number one or two in each industry where it competes. If not, GE will fix or exit the business. Combining these thoughts suggests that although blue chip Dow companies may suffer from missteps, they can typically recover and shareholders will ultimately reward these stocks. A hefty dividend, with the strategy yielding 3.6 percent in April 2013, can help boost returns, especially when reinvesting dividends. ALPS Sector Dividend Dogs ETF (SDOG), an exchange traded fund (ETF), started in mid-2012 in an attempt to mimic the strategy.

Accruals Anomaly

Differences exist between earnings and cash flow. The former is an accounting construct, which is easy to manage; the latter shows the inflows and outflows of cash and is more difficult to manipulate. The reported earnings number relies on management choices of inventory valuation (e.g., last-in-first-out (LIFO) versus first-in-first-out (FIFO)), allowance for doubtful accounts, accounts payable, accounts receivable, and so forth. A "red flag" exists if a persistent difference occurs between earnings and cash flow over time, after adjusting for expected items such as depreciation, amortization, and changes in working capital.

Sloan (1996), who first identified the accruals anomaly, constructs a long/short portfolio with the long (short) portfolio consisting of firms with the least (most) accruals. He finds abnormal returns of roughly 10 percent a year for his long/short portfolio. Sloan suggests that the results are due to overreaction and cognitive errors as a result of Wall Street's fixation on earnings. This anomaly may also be a framing issue because management can apparently fool investors, at least some of the time, by putting the best spin on reported earnings. Currently, several ETFs such as the Forensic Accounting ETF (FLAG) use accounting quality of earnings filters, such as accruals.

CURRENT AND FUTURE TRENDS IN BEHAVIORAL FINANCE STRATEGIES

Overwhelming evidence suggests that the markets sometimes deviate from rationality. The EMH is "dead" in terms of the view that security prices always reflect all available information. However, alpha or persistent outperformance remains elusive. *Alpha* is a portfolio's actual return minus its expected return. The expected return is usually given from an asset pricing model such as the CAPM. Analysts and investors often deem portfolio managers with positive historical alphas as being successful, while those providing negative alphas may have less than secure job prospects.

Why is obtaining alpha in an investment strategy challenging despite a growing list of market anomalies? This occurs because humans are neither consistently rational nor irrational. Furthermore, the publication and widespread dissemination of an anomaly likely diminishes its effectiveness going forward. Hence, financial economists are unlikely to develop a unified CAPM type model that will neatly and simultaneously explain in a straightforward equation(s) both rational and irrational behavior. Hong and Stein (1999) have made perhaps the most valiant effort thus far to reconcile the various behavioral finance biases, such as momentum, underreaction, and overreaction.

Yet, hope remains for those who believe in active management. Documenting behavioral finance errors is somewhat akin to mapping the human genome. The current state of the art of personalized medicine is not that one can completely avoid disease, but that it might be detected earlier, making treatment more effective. Similarly, investors aware of the myriad of behavioral biases may be unable to completely avoid mistakes. Avoiding behavioral biases should be the minimum goal for any investor. The best case for the behavioral finance astute investor is to capitalize on the mistakes of others.

At least two areas are available for fruitful research in behavioral finance. The first is to analyze the wave of "big data" that is exploding across the Internet. Big data includes things such as Twitter feeds, Web-browsing behavior, video search, retail sales analysis, and data obtained from analog semiconductor devices. Analysis of big data may enable researchers to uncover emerging trends and hot products. Obviously, such a "black box" output would have important implications for picking investments. Some hedge fund managers are analyzing satellite images and Twitter data, looking for an investment edge.

A second fruitful area for research is combining or disentangling behavioral anomalies. For example, this chapter discusses the overreaction bias across diverse areas such as momentum, accruals, and reversals. Once again, using a medical analogy, having a holistic view of how biases interact, rather than focusing on one specific item, is important.

SUMMARY

Behavioral finance now has broad approval among financial practitioners. However, many in academic finance still are proponents of the traditional finance school. Investment professionals and individual investors argue that securities markets are inefficient in the context of prices and do not always reflect all available information. Clearly, achieving a positive alpha for a portfolio remains elusive for most managers, but findings of behavioral finance may provide important clues. Indeed, successful asset management firms, such as LSV Asset Management and Fuller and Thaler Asset Management, are thriving with findings from the behavioral finance field as the foundation for their strategies.

Important anomalies including momentum, accruals, value, reversals, earnings surprises, and herding have their roots in behavioral finance. Combining several of these anomalies into an investment strategy is likely the future of active investment management. Unfortunately, a unified theory of behavioral finance is unlikely to fit into a nice, simple CAPM type equation. Investment analysts will become akin to doctors analyzing the vast complexity of the human genome. An individual may be susceptible to a specific disease based on his genetic makeup, but something, such as an environmental trigger, must activate it. Successful investment analysts will analyze not only the fundamental and technical aspects of securities but also the behavioral factors that ultimately influence their prices.

DISCUSSION QUESTIONS

1. Explain why momentum-based strategies may persistently generate excess returns.
2. Explain how behavioral finance may do a better job at explaining the existence and popping of asset pricing bubbles than the EMH.
3. Explain why no unified model of behavioral finance exists akin to the CAPM.
4. Using concepts from behavioral finance, discuss why many investors pursue active management despite most studies finding that index funds outperform the vast majority of active fund managers over time.
5. Make an analogy between the human genome and list of biases found in the behavioral finance literature. Discuss how analysts analyzing securities may be similar in some respects to doctors analyzing diseases.

REFERENCES

Arms, Richard W., Jr. 1996. *The Arms Index (Trin Index): An Introduction to Volume Analysis*. Columbia, MD: Marketplace Books.

Bodie, Zvi, Alex Kane, and Alan Marcus. 2010. *Investments*, 9th ed. New York: McGraw-Hill.

Bollen, Nicolas P., and Jeffrey A. Busse. 2005. "Short-Term Persistence in Mutual Fund Performance." *Review of Financial Studies* 18:2, 569–597.

Brav, Alon, Wei Jiang, Frank Partnoy, and Randall Thomas. 2008. "Hedge Fund Activism, Corporate Governance, and Firm Performance." *Journal of Finance* 63:4, 1729–1775.

Dalbar, Inc. 2013. "Quantitative Analysis of Investor Behavior 2013: The Asset Allocation Cure." Research Study, Dalbar, Inc. Available at www.qaib.com/public/default.aspx.

DeBondt, Werner F. M., and Richard H. Thaler. 1985. "Does the Stock Market Overreact?" *Journal of Finance* 40:3, 793–805.

Dreman, David N., and Michael A. Berry. 1995. "Overreaction, Underreaction, and the Low-P/E." *Financial Analysts Journal* 51:4, 21–30.

Eder, Steve. 2011. "Investors Disappointed with Hedge Funds, But Sticking with Them." *Wall Street Journal*. Available at http://blogs.wsj.com/deals/2011/11/11/investors-disappointed-with-hedge-funds-but-sticking-with-them/.

Fama, Eugene F., and Kenneth R. French. 1992. "The Cross-Section of Expected Stock Returns." *Journal of Finance* 47:2, 427–465.

Fuller and Thaler Asset Management. 2013. Available at www.fullerthaler.com.

Graham, Benjamin. 1973. *The Intelligent Investor*, 4th ed. New York: Harper & Row.

Graham, Benjamin, and David L. Dodd. 1934. *Security Analysis*. New York: Whittlesey House/McGraw Hill.

Hong, Harrison, and Jeremy C. Stein. 1999. "A Unified Theory of Underreaction, Momentum Trading and Overreaction in Asset Markets." *Journal of Finance* 54:6, 2143–2184.

Jegadeesh, Narasimhan, and Joshua Livnat. 2006. "Post-Earnings-Announcement Drift: The Role of Revenue Surprises." *Financial Analysts Journal* 62:2, 22–34.

Jegadeesh, Narasimhan, and Sheridan Titman. 1993. "Returns to Buying Winners and Selling Losers: Implications for Stock Market Efficiency." *Journal of Finance* 48:1, 65–91.

Kahneman, Daniel, Jack L. Knetsch, and Richard H. Thaler. 1991. "Anomalies: The Endowment Effect, Loss Aversion, and Status Quo Bias." *Journal of Economic Perspectives* 5:1, 193–206.

Keynes, John Maynard. 1936. *The General Theory of Employment, Interest and Money.* London: Macmillan.

Lakonishok, Josef, Andrei Shleifer, and Robert W. Vishny. 1992. "The Impact of Institutional Trading on Stock Prices." *Journal of Financial Economics* 32:1, 23–43.

LSV Asset Management. 2013. Available at www.lsvasset.com/about/about.html.

Malkiel, Burton G. 1995. "Returns from Investing in Equity Mutual Funds 1971–1991." *Journal of Finance* 50:2, 549–572.

Markowitz, Harry M. 1952. "Portfolio Selection." *Journal of Finance* 7:1, 77–91.

Markowitz, Harry M. 1959. *Portfolio Selection: Efficient Diversification of Investments.* New York: John Wiley & Sons.

O'Higgins, Michael B. 1991. *Beating the Dow: A High-Return, Low-Risk Method for Investing in the Dow Jones Industrial Stocks with as Little as $5,000.* New York: HarperCollins.

Rendleman, Richard J., Jr., Charles P. Jones, and Henry A. Latané. 1982. "Empirical Anomalies Based on Earnings' Yields and Market Values." *Journal of Financial Economics* 10:3, 269–287.

Sharpe, William F. 1991. "The Arithmetic of Active Management." *Financial Analysts' Journal* 47:1, 7–9.

Sloan, Richard G. 1996. "Do Stock Prices Fully Reflect Information in Accruals and Cash Flows about Future Earnings?" *Accounting Review* 71:2, 289–316.

Thaler, Richard H. 1999. "The End of Behavioral Finance." *Financial Analysts Journal* 55:6, 2–7.

The Economist. 2012. "Going Nowhere Fast: Hedge Funds Have Had Another Lousy Year, to Cap a Disappointing Decade." Available at www.economist.com/news/finance-and-economics/21568741-hedge-funds-have-had-another-lousy-year-cap-disappointing-decade-going.

Tversky, Amos, and Daniel Kahneman. 1981. "The Framing of Decisions and the Psychology of Choice." *Science* 211:4481, 453–458.

ABOUT THE AUTHOR

John M. Longo, CFA, is Clinical Professor of Finance and Economics at Rutgers Business School, and Chief Investment Officer and Chairman of the Investment Committee for The MDE Group. He is a member of the advisory board of The Bloomberg Institute, which is Bloomberg's educational subsidiary. Professor Longo has appeared on CNBC, Bloomberg TV, Bloomberg Radio, Fox Business, BBC World, The (Ron) Insana Quotient, and several other programs. He has been quoted in the *Wall Street Journal, Thomson Reuters, Dow Jones MarketWatch,* and dozens of other periodicals. Professor Longo is author/editor of *Hedge Fund Alpha: A Framework for Generating and Understanding Investment Performance.* He is a member of the editorial boards of the *Journal of Performance Measurement* and the *Journal of Financial Planning & Forecasting.* He holds BA, MBA, and PhD degrees from Rutgers University.

Special Investment Topics

Ethical and Socially Responsible Investing

Julia M. Puaschunder
Associate, Harvard University Faculty of Arts and Sciences,
Center for the Environment

INTRODUCTION

The 2008–2009 world financial crisis climaxed the societal demand for imbuing social responsibility in economic markets. Financial social responsibility (FSR) bridges the financial world with society in socially responsible investment (SRI), in which socially conscientious investors select securities foremost for social, environmental, and institutional ethicality aspects (Mohr, Webb, and Harris 2001; Beltratti 2003; Williams 2005). In the international arena, various SRI practices emerged concurrently. This chapter captures the nature, history, international practice, and future perspectives of FSR. Outlining international SRI customs and examining potential socio-psychological motives of financial social investors helps to draw conclusions about the future potential of SRI to avert emergent risks and imbue trust in the global economy in the aftermath of the world financial crisis. FSR can serve as a way to help prevent future economic downfalls and contribute to financial social global governance.

The remainder of the chapter is organized as follows. The next section covers SRI forms and investor motives of socially conscientious asset allocations followed by an outline of the history of FSR and performance correlates of SRI. The chapter then summarizes international differences of FSR as well as the institutional harmonization of FSR. The penultimate section examines SRI in the post 2008–2009 world financial crisis era with special attention to behavioral economics. The final section offers a summary and conclusions.

SOCIALLY RESPONSIBLE INVESTMENT

FSR integrates social concerns in financial investments (Soana 2011). Socially conscientious investors pursue financial goals while catalyzing positive change in screenings, shareholder advocacy, community investing, and social venture capital funding (Livesey 2002; Matten and Crane 2005; Puaschunder 2011c). Socially responsible screenings are double bottom line analyses of corporate economic performance and social responsibility. That is, socially conscientious investors consider corporate social responsibility (CSR) in financial decision-making and allocate financial resources based on the societal impacts of the funded entities.

Screenings watch corporate track records of societal impacts, environmental performance, human rights attribution, and fair workplace policies as well as health and safety standards. Positive screenings select corporations with sound social and environmental records that consider human rights and labor standards, equal opportunities, environmental protection, consumer safety, community concerns, and stakeholder relations. Negative screenings exclude corporations contributing to socially irresponsible activities such as addictive products and services (e.g., liquor, tobacco, and gambling), defense (e.g., weapons, firearms, and land mines), environmentally hazardous production (e.g., pollution and nuclear power), and humanitarian deficiencies (e.g., discrimination and human rights violations). Specialty screens target excessively high executive compensation, abortion, and animal testing. Post-hoc negative screenings remove investment capital from ethically questionable markets to attribute global governance goals (McWilliams and Siegel 2000; Broadhurst, Watson, and Marshall 2003). In political divestiture, socially responsible investors use their market power to pressure governments violating ethical and legal international standards (Starr 2008).

Screenings are often complemented by shareholder advocacy and activism—the active engagement of shareholders in corporate policy and managerial decision-making (Schueth 2003). Resolutions allow shareholders to request corporate board information and vote on corporate issues in shareholder meetings. The vast majority of shareholders exercise their voting rights by proxy granting third party voting rights on matters before the corporation (Little 2008). Active endowments integrate social responsibility in university planning through proxy voting. Shareholder dialogues influence corporate policies and practices without formal resolutions and investment withdrawals. Shareholder activism also comprises pro-social political lobbying, consumer boycotts, and corporate confrontations drawing public attention to corporate social conduct (Sparkes and Cowton 2004).

Community investing started in the 1970s with direct investments and investor set-asides for unserved and underserved low-income groups. Community development banks provide at-risk communities access to financial services—ranging from credit, equity, and banking products—to support housing, education, child care, and health care. Community development venture capital funds start-ups in undeveloped and underdeveloped regions (Schueth 2003). Related social venture capital supports social entrepreneurs to vitalize communities and foster positive societal change. Supplementary financial empowerment aims at financial education, mentoring, and assistance of underprivileged populations.

Today's FSR expressions are manifold and a growing diversity is forecast (Social Investment Forum Report 2006; Baker and Nofsinger 2012). SRI already embraces a variety of stakeholders motivated to integrate social considerations in their asset allocation styles. Bridging the financial world with society, SRI engages public and private economic (e.g., institutional and private investors), organizational (e.g., labor union representatives, banking executives, and fiduciaries) and societal (e.g., representatives of international organizations, non-governmental organizations (NGOs), public policy specialists, media representatives, and academics) stakeholders. The largest segment of screened accounts includes private and institutional portfolios managed by fiduciaries (e.g., private equity executives, fund managers, and investment managers), who are opinion leaders with the potential to advocate for SRI (Nilsson 2008). As information agents, banking executives advise clients about SRI and benefits of FSR.

Institutional investors range from public pension funds to small nonprofit organizations featuring corporations, state and municipal governments, religious organizations, hospitals and health care facilities, college and university endowments, foundations, and trade unions driving social and environmental endeavors. Public policy specialists regulate finance accountability and aid, adopting socially responsible market evaluation criteria. NGOs monitor corporate conduct and shareholder activism as SRI prerequisites (Mohr et al. 2001). Labor union representatives implement social responsibility in financial markets—foremost in the areas of human rights, labor conditions, and minority empowerment. The academic community, especially finance experts, behavioral economists, sociologists, and social psychologists, spearheaded SRI. Media representatives select and process information about socially responsible corporate conduct and FSR.

Apart from economic profitability calculus and strategic leadership advantages, investors choose SRI for efficiency and long-term competitive advantages coupled with altruistic and personal social responsibility values, entrepreneurial zest, and self-expression (Statman 2008; Cheah et al. 2011; Puaschunder 2011b). Utility derived from altruism, transparency, and social status prospects gained from ethicality are additional SRI drivers. Self-enhancement of future-oriented SRI options additionally supplements profit maximization goals (Puaschunder 2012).

HISTORICAL EMERGENCE

Social and ethical considerations in financial markets have a long tradition stemming from religious roots. In medieval times, Christianity imposed financial restrictions based on the Old Testament. The Catholic Church prohibited *usury*—loans with excessive or abusive interest rates—as early as 1139. Judaic writings praised ethical monetary conduct. Methodism urged avoiding "sinful" trade and profit-maximizing exploitation (Cuesta-Gonzalez and Valor-Martinez 2007). Since the seventeenth century, the Quaker Society of Friends eschewed the military and slave trade. The U.K. Methodist Church advocated for ethical corporate conduct. The Christian Pioneer Fund was first to officially exclude sin stocks after the world wars. Today, Islamic banking still restricts adult entertainment and gambling (Renneboog, Horst, and Zhang 2007).

The early beginnings of modern SRI are attributed to social responsibility concerns in the face of social, environmental, and political deficiencies and humanitarian crises (Williams 2005). In the post–World War II era, first financial social considerations ideas sparked in the wake of legislative compulsion, information disclosure, and governmental policies encouraging trustees' social responsibility (Solomon, Solomon, and Norton 2002; Sparkes and Cowton 2004). During the 1960s, stakeholder pressure and anti-Vietnam War movements alerted institutional investors to sell napalm-producing Dow Chemical shares. Civil rights campaigns and social justice initiatives opposed college endowments funding warfare. Minority empowerment, consumer rights activism, and environmentalism sensitized for financial social conscientiousness (Sparkes 2002; Renneboog et al. 2007). Since 1969, the Council on Economic Priorities has rated corporate social and environmental performance. After a Yale conference introduced FSR, university committees advised trustees on social investment. Subsequently, Methodist clergy created the PAX World Fund aimed at divestiture from Vietnam War supporters (Broadhurst et al. 2003). The Dreyfus Third Century Fund opened the following year to avoid sin stocks and improve social labor standards.

By the mid-1970s, a large number of governments had enacted shareholder rights to address corporate activities that caused social injury and many universities established committees to advise trustees on SRI and shareholder rights. The Investor Responsibility Research Center (IRRC) and the Interfaith Center on Corporate Responsibility (ICCR) were launched to promote shareholder advocacy and proxy resolutions around the same time (Social Investment Forum Report 2006). In 1972, activists criticized Harvard University for owning petroleum shares. The case of the Angolan repressive government provided a discussion of political divestiture (Alperson et al. 1991). In 1976, the Sullivan Principles fostered equal remuneration and workplace opportunities to empower minorities (Voorhes 1999).

During the 1980s, U.S. universities, investors, and churches, as well as city and state governments, practiced political divestiture to dismantle the South African apartheid regime (Schueth 2003; Soros 2008). Environmental catastrophes in Chernobyl and Bhopal and the Exxon Valdez oil spill perpetuated shareholder activism. With the desire to set standards for corporate social engagement and environmentally conscientious conduct, social investors started positive screenings in the beginning of the 1990s. The Domini 400 Social Index institutionalized ratings of Standard & Poor's (S&P) 500 corporations. The microfinance revolution and the cooperative banking system galvanized SRI (Brenner 2001).

Within recent decades FSR boomed in the wake of globalization and political trends strengthening the societal role of financial institutions. Political libertarianism implicitly shifted social responsibility onto the private sector. Deregulated liberalization attributed a rising share of global governance onto financial markets. Financial social considerations leveraged into an implicit fiduciary responsibility (Sparkes and Cowton 2004). As social global governance has increasingly entered financial markets since the turn of the century, a growing proportion of investment firms and governmental agencies have adopted a more socially conscientious investment philosophy (Sparkes 2002; McCann, Solomon, and Solomon 2003; Knoll 2008). Information disclosure on corporate social conduct in combination with benchmarking of corporate social engagement and governmental encouragement of trustees' social conscientiousness propelled SRI.

Institutional investors concurrently used their clout to influence corporate conduct and actively demanded corporate governance reforms to act on societal concerns. The advanced consideration of FSR by major institutional investors matured SRI from a niche market option that specialist retailers offered to a more mainstreamed asset allocation style (Mathieu 2000). SRI reached unprecedented diversity featuring a wide range of social engagement possibilities (Rosen, Sandler, and Shani 1991). As SRI gained prominence and broadened in size, scale, and scope, practitioners and academics started documenting state-of-the-art FSR practices. Business professionals reported and analysts monitored social, ethical, and environmental corporate performance. Social and environmental stock exchange rating agencies and certifications measured SRI impacts regarding economic profits and social impact.

Historical Investment Performance of SRI Funds versus Conventional Funds

Empirical investigations of the relationship between SRI and profitability offer no stringent, generalizable pattern (Hamilton, Hoje, and Statman 1993). While some evidence holds SRI outperforming the market (e.g., Kempf and Osthoff 2007; Huppé 2011), others show underperformance (e.g., Fowler and Hope 2007). Yet, some studies report no difference between SRI and conventional market indices (e.g., Abramson and Chung 2000; Boutin-Dufresne and Savaria 2004; Sjöström 2011).

During the 1990s, the Domini 400 Social Index consistently outperformed the S&P 500 (Harvey 2008). Data of the 100 Best Corporate Citizens corporations underlined the SRI ability to outperform the Standard & Poor's 500 Index (S&P 500) (Kotler and Lee 2005). Additionally, a pool of 277 corporations listed at the Toronto Stock Exchange exhibits a positive relationship among social responsibility, positive financial return, and low volatility from 1996 to 1999. Sector-specific investigations relate corporate environmental responsibility to higher risk-adjusted returns (Cohen, Fenn, and Konar 1997; Posnikoff 1997).

In contrast, evidence depicts stocks of 451 U.K. corporations with sound social performance as significantly underperfoming the market, while corporations with low corporate social performance considerably outperform the market (Statman 2005; Brammer, Williams, and Zinkin 2005). Within the Australian market, evidence shows that ethical funds display significant undervaluation from 2002 to 2005 (Jones et al. 2008). Studies by Ngassam (1992), Meznar, Nigh, and Kwok (1994), Wright and Ferris (1997), and McWilliams, Siegel, and Teoh (1999) report political divestiture to be associated with shareholder wealth losses.

Abramson and Chung (2000) as well as Boutin-Dufresne and Savaria (2004) report no difference in the financial performance or volatility rates of SRI compared to the rest of the market. In closing, whether SRI is associated with an increase or decrease in shareholder return and volatility is inconclusive (Hamilton et al. 1993; Berman et al. 1999).

The inconsistency of findings is attributed to manifold SRI expression forms and measurement deficiencies. Positively screened SRI funds are more likely to feature information technology (IT) and alternative energy industries that attract innovative venture capital providers. Positively screened SRI options tend to be more volatile, yet if successful, grant high profitability. As for excluding high-return, high-volatility industries such as petroleum, defense, and addictive substances, negatively screened options are more likely to underperform the market but at the same time are robust to overall market changes. Negative screening asset holders are more loyal to their choice in times of crises, which contributes to the stability of these funds (Bauer and Smeets 2012).

Data on the profitability of political divestiture indicate a potential first mover advantage for early divestiture. In a cost and benefit analysis, SRI implies short-term expenditures but grants long-term sustainable investment streams. In the short run, screened funds have higher expense ratios than unscreened ones. That is, social responsibility imposes an instantaneous "ethical penalty" of decreased immediate shareholder revenue (Mohr and Webb 2005; Tippet 2001). Yet, in the long run, SRI options offer higher stability as well as lower turnover and failure rates compared to general assets (Dhrymes 1998; Stone et al. 2001; Geczy, Stambaugh, and Levin 2003; Schröder

2003; Guenster et al. 2005; Weber, Mansfeld, and Schirrmann 2010). Being based on more elaborate decision-making processes, once investors make their socially responsible decision, they are more likely to stay with their choice (Little 2008). As a matter of fact, SRI options are less volatile and more robust during cyclical changes (Bollen and Cohen 2004).

Although the empirical evidence diverges on whether SRI funds outperform or underperform the market, cognitive decision-making errors (also known as *heuristics*) lead to a natural propensity to undervalue SRI funds' performance (Schröder 2007). The anchoring bias would assume that once investors perceive a negative performance of SRI funds, then overriding this prior perception is difficult, even if novel FSR performances improved. Representativeness errors lead people to overestimate the likelihood of familiar events to repeat and extrapolate from negative anchors. Psychological losses looming larger than gains may lead to SRI underperformance being perceived more negatively than outperforming SRI funds may be appreciated (Kahneman and Tversky 1972). A way to overcome decision-making biases is to evaluate alternatives concurrently instead of individually (Puaschunder and Schwarz 2012).

Most SRI studies do not consider externalities, which lowers the external validity of the results and calls for a more holistic examination of SRI in the international arena (McWilliams et al. 1999). Understanding international differences of SRI may help in developing a favorable framework to guide a successful SRI implementation.

INTERNATIONAL DIFFERENCES

SRI bridges the finance world with society (Schueth 2003). In the international arena, various SRI practices emerged concurrently as national rules and legal jurisdictions shaped corporate and financial social conduct (Steurer 2010). In recent decades, SRI grew qualitatively and quantitatively in the Western world due to historical incidents, legislative compulsion, and stakeholder pressure (Carroll 1979; Wolff 2002). Originally stemming from a small number of specialist ethical investment funds, SRI emerged into an investment philosophy adopted by a growing proportion of Western investment houses and governmental agencies reporting on social, ethical, and environmental corporate aspects around the globe (Mohr et al. 2001; Knoll 2008). Financial social conscientiousness increasingly became an element of fiduciary duty, particularly for long-term investors overseeing international portfolios (Social Investment Forum Report 2006).

FSR booms in the Western world and has primarily been adopted in Anglo-Saxon and Central Europe markets. While Anglo-Saxon countries such as the United States and the United Kingdom are prominent for private investments, European financial systems are renowned for governmental and institutional banking. Common law Anglo-Saxon countries (e.g., the United States, Canada, Australia, and the United Kingdom) are more politically liberal, featuring less institutionalized SRI (Matten and Moon 2004). Anglo-Saxon fiduciary responsibility focuses on return on investments, while Western European Roman law-dominated territories grant fiduciaries more leeway in considering the overall societal impact of the asset-issuing entities. Civil law countries (e.g., central European countries) tend to place greater emphasis on stakeholder participation in corporate governance (Reinhardt, Vietor, and Stavins 2008).

North America

Today, the United States features-in a landscape of highly dispersed share ownership-the broadest variety of SRI options and socially responsible perform-ance measurement indices. Having grown out of niche market options for value-led investors, SRI evolved in the United States due to disclosure of corporate social externalities and shareholder activism in the wake of sociopolitical concerns. The 1981-enacted American Social Investment Forum as a professional body for indi-vidual and institutional SRI constituents introduced SRI to the American market (Broadhurst et al. 2003). Since 2004 various corporate scandals led to legislation addressing disclosure of proxy votes (Little 2008). In numeric terms, shareholders and others proposed 348 resolutions on social and environmental issues in the United States, of which more than 50 percent reached a proxy vote in 2005 (Social Investment Forum Report 2006). In the same year, $2.5 trillion in assets were attributed as socially responsible funds, which accounted for 20.7 percent of all U.S. investments (Williams 2005).

In Canada, legal obligations require corporate directors and officers to act in the best interest of the entity without ignoring stakeholders (Borok 2003). In 1986, the Ethical Growth Fund officially introduced SRI in Canada (Williams 2005). Based on the U.S. model, the 2001 Canadian Institute of Chartered Accountants established disclosure guidelines backed by mandatory obligations (Sparkes and Cowton 2004). Since 2006 the Canadian Securities Administrators mandated mutual funds to pub-licly disclose their proxy voting policies and records. SRI is organized by the Social Investment Organization (SIO), renowned for surveys and conferences (Williams 2005). Community investing recently boomed in Canada (Social Investment Forum Report 2006).

Europe

Europe has a long history of incorporating corporate social conduct into institu-tional investments (Sutton 2004; Reinhardt et al. 2008). As European legislation emphasizes stakeholder participation in corporate governance, European corpo-rate boards often include employee representatives. Civil law countries tend to codify profit-sacrificing corporate behavior as cultural traditions value corporate social conscientiousness, while the more politically liberal United Kingdom per-mits corporate managers to engage in socially beneficial activities as long as this is in the shareholders' greater interests. Social democracies, such as France and German-speaking countries, legally back stakeholder interests (Roe 2000; Lynch-Fannon 2007; Reinhardt et al. 2008). German corporate law does not even explic-itly oblige the management to maximize shareholder value (Corfield 1998). While SRI booms in Northern and Central Europe, the movement is slower to take off in Southern Europe. Community investing is prominent in Latin countries such as Italy, France, and Spain.

Quantitatively, the growing European SRI market, excluding the Nordic region, recently comprised around 400 green, social, and ethical funds worth €1.138 billion (approximately U.S. $1.5 billion dollars) in 2008 accounting for 18 percent of the market share (European Social Investment Forum Report 2012). In 2006, the United Kingdom led the SRI movement with €8.0 billion (U.S. $10.5 billion) in total assets, followed by Germany (€6.7 billion, U.S. $8.8 billion), Austria (€5.3 billion, U.S. $6.9 billion),

France (€3.1 billion, U.S. $4.1 billion), Switzerland (€2.9 billion, U.S. $3.8 billion), Italy (€2.7 billion, U.S. $3.5 billion), and Sweden (€2.5 billion, U.S. $3.3 billion).

In the United Kingdom, which is the European SRI leader, first U.K. Victorian concerns about employment conditions sparked corporate social conduct (Sparkes 2002). The Mercury Provident established ethical finance in 1974, which was introduced to retail banking in 1992. In 1997, a group of university affiliates launched a campaign for ethical and environmental pension funds. Since 2000, sustainable and responsible investment policies require all occupational pension funds to formally adopt social, ethical, and environmental policies (Sparkes and Cowton 2004; Williams 2005). The U.K. government regulations pressured pension funds to declare the extent to which they consider environmental, social or ethical considerations in the selection, retention, and realization of investments (Sparkes 2002). Similar regulations have been passed in Germany and Sweden and are currently being considered by the European Parliament (Steurer 2010).

The Nordic European countries are renowned for a Scandinavian law framework. In 2007, the Belgian government enacted political divestiture by restricting Belgian investors' ability to in finance warfare. Sweden's 2000 Public Pension Fund Act required all Swedish national pension funds to report investments' environmental and social externalities (Steurer 2010). While the law leaves leeway to what extent funds have to comply, the rule fostered access to information and awareness for SRI. Additionally, a joint ethical council offers investment recommendations for stakeholders. As Steurer notes, the Dutch Green Funds Scheme provides information on SRI tax exemptions.

In Continental Europe, the French Pension Research Fund offers insurance plans in line with SRI principles. In German-speaking Roman law countries, SRI was propelled in the wake of peace movements and the 1970s green wave promoting environmental protection. The *Gemeinschafts* and *Ökobank* were the first SRI traders. Major influences are attributed to green parties, the 1991 Renewable Energy Act, information campaigns, and tax exemptions (Williams 2005).

The Pacific Rim

Australian corporate law requires corporate managers to make decisions in the best interest of the corporation, yet a statutory business judgment rule grants considerable discretion (Reinhardt et al. 2008). Australian direct share ownership fosters individual investors' SRI screenings. The first Australian ethical investment movement began in the early 1980s leading to the Australian Ethical Investment Trust in 1989 (Cummings 2000). The Ethical Investment Association (EIA) emerged throughout the 1990s to launch SRI benchmarking reports and a SRI symbol to approve socially responsible products. The Financial Service Reform Act of 2002 introduced financial disclosure statements followed by SRI disclosure guidelines (Williams 2005). From 2001 to 2004, SRI rose by more than 100 percent from AUS $10.5 to $21.5 billion (approximately U.S. $9.7 to $19.8 billion dollars), making SRI the fastest growing investment segment in Australia (Jones et al. 2008).

Emerging Markets

SRI drives international development in emerging markets foremost through community investing, microfinance, and enterprise development for social entrepreneurs

(Social Investment Forum Report 2006). Latin America (foremost Brazil) and South Africa are newly emerging and rapidly growing SRI markets. Asia is a promising growth market for SRI, reaching U.S. $2.7 billion in total SRI assets (Sparkes and Cowton 2004). Japan accounted for Asia's leading SRI market with more than 100 billion yen spread over 10 SRI funds. The 2011 crisis followed by a financial investment drain from Japan, however, may slow or even halt this trend. Hong Kong as Asia's additional SRI expansion market may take over the lead in Asia. More than 12 screened funds are available in the Islamic banking territories Malaysia, Taiwan, and Singapore.

Developing World

In the developing world, SRI practices vary across countries as laws and regulations are often not well enforced (Reinhardt et al. 2008). Oversight is challenged by a lack of accountability in SRI practices and nontransferable customs. This inadequate FSR standardization hampers the SRI adoption. Standardized SRI policies could help regulatory enforcement and monitoring to overcome principal-agent discrepancies, conflicts of interest, and corruption. To foster a general understanding of FSR and streamlined SRI conduct on a grand scale, international organizations have set out to harmonize FSR practices on the international level.

INSTITUTIONAL HARMONIZATION OF FSR

International organizations align various SRI practices by defining FSR standards and guiding the SRI implementation from a global governance perspective (Puaschunder 2010). Transnational entities play a pivotal role by institutionally supporting FSR and streamlining disparate SRI practices. The United Nations (UN) led the international public administration of FSR by creating the Principles for Responsible Investment (PRI) and the Responsible Investment in Emerging Markets Initiative. In January 2004, the UN invited a group of leading financial institutions to form a joint financial sector initiative under the guidance of the United Nations Global Compact's (UNGC) board to discuss financial investment banks and fiduciaries' social responsibility implementation.

Subsequently responding to rising SRI trends all over the world, the UNGC division and the UN Environment Programme (UNEP) Finance Initiative launched the Principles for Responsible Investment (PRI) in collaboration with the New York Stock Exchange (NYSE) in 2006. The PRI support socially responsible investors and harmonize financial social conscientiousness to create repeatable models for positive societal change within the investment community. Under the auspices of the UNGC and the UNEP Finance Initiative, the PRI invite institutional investors to consider SRI and mobilize chief executive officers of the world's largest pension funds to advance financial social considerations at the international level. Corporations joining the PRI have been reporting profits, efficiency, product innovation, and market segmentation advantages but also intangible reputational gains, improved employee morale, and consumer satisfaction.

In February 2008, the UN Conference on Trade and Development (UNCTAD) launched the Responsible Investment in Emerging Markets initiative at the Geneva

PRI office. This public-private partnership fosters transparency and disclosure for the integration of environmental, social, and corporate governance in emerging markets. The key constituents are stock exchange and financial analyst communities. Investment banks and fiduciaries are assisted in implementing social responsibility as a risk management tool (Ricciardi 2010). NGOs are invited to advance accountability.

The era of globalization puts a novel perspective on FSR as a market option to enhance global governance goals through financial market forces. In particular, the 2008–2009 financial turmoil began to portray FSR as an essential key for economic markets to function well and SRI as a financial market-stabilizing means.

SRI IN THE POST 2008–2009 WORLD FINANCIAL CRISIS ERA OF GLOBALIZATION

Caused by the neglect of social responsibility in global financial markets, the world economy has weakened since August 2008. The announcement of the recapitalization of the finance sector in October 2008 halted liberalization trends and perpetuated skepticism and mistrust in unregulated markets (Gangl et al. 2012). Since the outbreak of the crisis, the societal call for social responsibility in corporate and financial markets has reached unprecedented momentum. The revelation of corporate social misconduct and financial fraud steered consumers and investors to increasingly pay attention to social responsibility within market systems (Roberts 2010). Public and private leaders as well as academics searched for financial social conscientiousness-enhancing market structures to restore public trust in financial markets because of recent events such as corporate capital hoarding, liquidity traps, and the London Interbank Offered Rate (LIBOR) scandal (*The Economist* 2012; Tumpel-Gugerell 2009).

The current widespread acknowledgment of financial social conscientiousness as a vital economic market ingredient and the regulatory renaissance in the finance world are predicted to advance SRI (Duchac 2008). The heralded age of heterodox economic thinking climaxed the call for integrating social facets into mainstream economic models. SRI has become a prominent term in quasi-democratic bottom-up movements around the world (*The Economist* 2008). As for robustness to market fluctuations, SRI appears as a favorable market option in times of crises. Financial social conscientiousness also promises to help overcome emergent risks in the age of globalization.

Globalization led to an intricate set of interactive relationships among individuals, organizations, and states (Centeno and Tham 2012). Deepening nets of interactions challenge human foresight as faster transactions transmit positive and negative externalities. Perturbations arising from novel interdependencies impose dangers for mankind. Over time and in crowds, a single decision may no longer merely have limited local effects, but also global consequences (Centeno and Tham 2012; Summers and Pritchett 2012). In webs of unconscious decision-making fallibility, responsibility blurring over time can turn to hard-to-foresee risks for collectives (Bazerman and Moore 2008; Leonhardt, Keller, and Pechmann 2011; Centeno and Tham 2012). With growing globalization and a rising population as well as quickening of transfer speed, emergent risks developed into systemic problems (Okamoto 2009; Centeno and Tham 2012; Summers and Pritchett 2012).

The currently evolving emergent risk theory captures these insufficiently described shadows of the invisible hand in the era of globalization (Miller and Rosenfeld

2010; Centeno and Tham 2012). Building on behavioral economics research insights about fallible decision-making, emergent risk theory sets out to depict economic contagion of mutually dependent market actors. Emergent risk theory describes how individual decision-making fallibility can resonate in economic systems and impose systemic risks within markets over time and in crowds. In seeking to understand the leap from the individual decision maker failing to recognize unethical consequences down the road and the mass of individuals being unaware of the cumulative and potentially disastrous outcomes of their actions, emergent risk studies aim at alleviating unexpected dangers in the age of globalization (Centeno and Tham 2012).

Emergent risks are potential causes of the 2008–2009 world financial crisis. In the aftermath of the financial meltdown caused by unforeseeable effects of unethical decision-making, the demand for understanding of emergent risks follows the call for novel economic thinking. As prevailing economic theories have shed less attention on collective outcomes of economic choices over time in the pre–2008 financial crisis era, new economic thinking must widen the interdisciplinary lens to understand how to diminish emergent risks in globalized economic markets. As a potential remedy, FSR appears as emergent risk prevention to avert future socially irresponsible financial conduct. Introducing financial social conscientiousness as emergent risk mitigation within globalized economic markets lets SRI appear as a panacea to avert future financial crises and as a powerful means to stabilize financial markets.

Ingraining social conscientiousness in financial markets also promises to positively resonate in the industry. If investors increasingly become willing to pay for socially responsible assets, firms in general will be incentivized to adopt more socially responsible practices. In this scenario, investors will have to accept some degree of socially responsible contributions in response to rising socially conscientious market options. SRI thus holds the potential to lift entire market industries onto a more socially favorable level in the future. FSR also opens a window of opportunity for reestablishing stakeholders' trust in financial markets as a countercyclical means to overcome our current age of angst featuring corporate capital hoarding, liquidity traps, and mistrust in the finance community steered by the most recent LIBOR/Euribor scandal (Coen and Roberts 2012). Enhancing understanding of FSR may help avert emergent risks and thereby sustainably improve financial market stability in the global economy of this generation and the following.

SUMMARY

In recent decades, various SRI forms have emerged in the wake of investors' social conscientiousness being steered by socioeconomic crises. International differences of FSR have led to an institutional harmonization of FSR. In the aftermath of the 2008–2009 world financial crisis, the demand for ingraining ethicality in economic markets highlighted the importance for research on FSR. As recently weakened market economies are attributed to a missing well-rounded understanding of real-world financial market responsibility, describing SRI may help to resolve societal losses imbued in the novelty and complexity of FSR. Access to information on SRI will help inform asset managers and financial analysts about the link between CSR and SRI in order to drive financial institutions to consider environmental and social responsibility. Outlining SRI as a market choice with tangible and intangible investment advantages will aid financial advisors in incorporating environmental and social corporate governance in their portfolio allocation strategies. Advocating a successful rise of social responsibility within modern market economies is aimed at SRI becoming a mainstream feature of financial decision-making, which will lift entire market industries onto a more socially conscientious level while serving the greater goal of fostering positive societal change (Glac 2009).

Qualitative interviews on SRI with stakeholders could help to resolve societal losses imbued in the novelty of the phenomenon and aligning incoherent viewpoints on SRI. Deriving insight on stakeholder-specific success factors of FSR should allow for a reduction of socioeconomic losses due to the complexity of the novel phenomenon and help to effectively promote SRI to the finance community. Information on SRI success factors will encourage trustees to accept social responsibility as a state-of-the-art fiduciary obligation and supervisory boards to incorporate SRI criteria in financial management strategies. Financial analysts assessing market opportunities will help to integrate environmental and social criteria in the formulation of investment mandates. Multi-stakeholder analyses may attribute the newly defined role of public and private constituents in social contributions and search for the optimum balance of deregulated market systems and governmental control in providing FSR. Based on stakeholder-specific demands, governmental assistance could contribute to the implementation and administration of CSR and SRI with attention to private sector and civil demands.

Information about the stability and effectiveness of SRI during times of crisis could help in promoting the idea of FSR. SRI trend analyses with attention to stakeholder-specific views in the aftermath of the recent world financial crisis and socioeconomic success factors of FSR could innovatively be coupled with information on SRI as a window of opportunity in times of crises. Expert interviews could also take a unique snapshot of socioeconomic changes and societal moods implied by financial turmoil (Puaschunder 2011a). Collecting once-in-a-lifetime-available information on the social representations of financial social conscientiousness in post-crisis markets not only offers a unique historic snapshot of the prevailing economic climate but also helps understanding economic downturns' potential to drive ethicality in economic markets. Understanding the contents of social representations and emotionality arising from SRI perceptions in the aftermath of the world financial crisis will allow to guide future societal financial conscientiousness trends. Portraying the idea of SRI conduct as emergent risk prevention will allow finding favorable incentive structures and prescriptive public policies to enhance FSR as a market stability prerequisite and leverage SRI as a means to re-establish trust in financial markets.

While ingraining social conscientiousness in financial markets appears as a way to avert future economic crisis, behavioral economists may contribute their insights on the human natural laws of social responsibility to strengthen the idea of financial social conscientiousness (Puaschunder 2011b). Evolutionary psychologists may explore the emergence of ethicality in human beings by investigating what aspects of social responsibility are ingrained in human traits and which ones are nurtured by external factors. Financial market experiments may test microeconomic facets of investor behavior.

Organizational behavior scholars may add by attributing how goals can stipulate ethicality and validate the proposed socio-psychological SRI framework to distinguish moderators of investors' willingness to trade off financial profits for social gratification. Investigating socio-psychological motives of FSR could help retrieve recommendations on how to integrate social responsibility in financial markets and add information on SRI to leverage from a niche market solution to a state-of the-art financial practice. Behavioral ethics specialists may inform about accidental ethicality mishaps in order to overcome human ethicality bounds and alleviate potential financial-social decision-making predicaments (Bazerman and Moore 2008; Bazerman and Tenbrunsel 2011; Shu, Gino, and Bazerman 2011).

While micro-behavioral economists may in particular focus on human socially responsible cognition in the search for ethicality nudges, macro-economists may explain how individual social responsibility can shape collective market outcomes. Market assessments using event study methodology could investigate SRI supply and demand changes implied by the world financial crisis. Some view SRI as an emergent risk panacea and way to stabilize financial and economic markets in the post-financial crisis era. Acknowledging SRI's potential to bestow market actors with trust in the economy and understanding a crisis's opportunity to ingrain social responsibility in market operations follows the greater goals of fostering economic prosperity and societal progress.

DISCUSSION QUESTIONS

1. Identify and discuss potential implications and challenges of the 2008–2009 world financial crisis on FSR.
2. Identify several examples of ethical investing and SRI.
3. Discuss the performance of SRI funds relative to conventional mutual funds.
4. Identify where SRI is practiced and explain how.
5. Identify who attempts to harmonize SRI practices.

REFERENCES

Abramson, Lorne, and Dan Chung. 2000. "Socially Responsible Investing: Viable for Value Investors?" *Journal of Investing* 9:3, 73–81.

Alperson, Mayra, Alice T. Tepper-Marlin, Jonathan Schorsch, and Rosalyn Wil. 1991. *The Better World Investment Guide: One Hundred Companies Whose Policies You Should Know about before You Invest Your Money.* Council on Economic Priorities. New York: Prentice Hall.

Baker, H. Kent, and John R. Nofsinger, eds. 2012. *Socially Responsible Finance and Investing: Financial Institutions, Corporations, Investors, and Activists.* Hoboken, NJ: John Wiley & Sons.

Bauer, Rob, and Paul Smeets. 2012. "Social Preferences and Investor Loyalty." Working Paper, Social Science Research Network. Available at http://ssrn.com/abstract=2140856.

Bazerman, Max H., and Donald Moore. 2008. *Judgment in Managerial Decision Making.* Hoboken, NJ: John Wiley & Sons.

Bazerman, Max H., and Ann E. Tenbrunsel. 2011. *Blind Spots: Why We Fail to Do What's Right and What to Do About It.* Princeton: Princeton University Press.

Beltratti, Andrea. 2003. "Socially Responsible Investment in General Equilibrium. Economic Theory and Applications." Working Paper, Social Science Research Network. Available at http://papers.ssrn.com/sol3/papers.cfm?abstract_id=467240.

Berman, Shawn L., Andrew C. Wicks, Suresh Kotha, and Thomas Jones. 1999. "Does Stakeholder Orientation Matter? The Relationship between Stakeholder Management Models and Firm Financial Performance." *Academy of Management Journal* 42:5, 488–506.

Bollen, Nicolas P. B., and Mark A. Cohen. 2004. "Mutual Fund Attributes and Investor Behavior." Working Paper, Vanderbilt University.

Borok, Tuvia. 2003. "A Modern Approach to Redefining in the Best Interests of the Corporation." *Windsor Review of Legal and Social Issues* 15:3, 113–114.

Boutin-Dufresne, Francois, and Patrick Savaria. 2004. "Corporate Social Responsibility and Financial Risk." *Journal of Investing* 13:1, 57–66.

Brammer, Stephen, Geoffrey Williams, and John Zinkin. 2005. "Religion and Attitudes to Corporate Social Responsibility in a Large Cross-Country Sample." *Journal of Business Ethics* 71:3, 229–243.

Brenner, Reuven. 2001. *The Force of Finance: Triumph of the Capital Markets.* New York: Texere.

Broadhurst, Dominic, Janette Watson, and Jane Marshall. 2003. *Ethical and Socially Responsible Investment: A Reference Guide for Researchers.* München: Saur.

Carroll, Archie B. 1979. "A Three-Dimensional Model of Corporate Social Performance." *Academy of Management Review* 4:4, 497–505.

Centeno, Miguel A., and Alex Tham. 2012. "The Emergence of Risk in the Global System." Working Paper, Princeton University.

Cheah, Eng-Tuck, Dima Jamali, Jonnie E. V. Johnson, and Ming-Chien Sung. 2011. "Drivers of Corporate Social Responsibility Attitudes: The Demography of Socially Responsible Investors." *British Journal of Management* 22:2, 305–323.

Coen, David, and Alasdair S. Roberts. 2012. "The New Age of Uncertainty." *Governance* 25:1, 5–9.

Cohen, Mark, Scott A. Fenn, and Shameek Konar. 1997. "Environmental and Financial Performance: Are They Related?" Working Paper, Vanderbilt University.

Corfield, Andrea. 1998. "The Stakeholder Theory and Its Future in Australian Corporate Governance: A Preliminary Analysis." *Bond Law Review* 10:2, 213–232.

Cuesta-Gonzalez de la, Marta, and Carmen Valor-Martinez. 2007. "Fostering Corporate Social Responsibility through Public Initiative: From the EU to the Spanish Case." *Journal of Business Ethics* 55:3, 275–293.

Cummings, Laura A. 2000. "The Financial Performance of Ethical Investment Trusts: An Australian Perspective." *Journal of Business Ethics* 25:3, 167–177.

Dhrymes, Phoebus J. 1998. Socially Responsible Investment: Is it Profitable? *The Investment Research Guide to Socially Responsible Investing.* The Colloquium on Socially Responsible Investing. Available at www.columbia.edu/~pjd1/.

Duchac, Jonathan. 2008. "The Perfect Storm: A Look Inside the 2008 Financial Crisis." Presentation, Vienna University of Economics and Business, December 15.

European Social Investment Forum Report. 2012. September 5. Available at www.eurosif.org/.

Fowler, Stephen J., and Chris Hope. 2007. "A Critical Review of Sustainable Business Indices and Their Impact." *Journal of Business Ethics* 76:3, 243–252.

Gangl, Katharina, Barbara Kastlunger, Erich M. Kirchler, and Martin Voracek. 2012. "Confidence in the Economy in Times of Crisis: Social Representations of Experts and Laypeople." *Journal of Socio Economics* 41:5, 603–614.

Geczy, Christopher C., Robert F. Stambaugh, and David Levin. 2003. *Investing in Socially Responsible Mutual Funds.* Philadelphia: The Wharton School.

Glac, Katharina. 2009. "Understanding Socially Responsible Investing: The Effect of Decision Frames and Trade-off Options." *Journal of Business Ethics* 87:1, 41–55.

Guenster, Jeroen, Nadja Derwall, Rob Bauer, and Kees Koedijk. 2005. "The Economic Value of Corporate Eco-Efficiency." Working Paper, Erasmus University.

Hamilton, Sally, Jo Hoje, and Meir Statman. 1993. "Doing Well While Doing Good? The Investment Performance of Socially Responsible Mutual Funds." *Financial Analysts Journal* 49:6, 62–66.

Harvey, Campbell. 2008. "Campbell R. Harvey's Hypertextual Finance Glossary." Available at www.duke.edu/~charvey/Classes/wpg/bfglosa.htm.

Huppé, Gabriel A. 2011. "Alpha's Tale: The Economic Value of CSR." Principles for Responsible Investment Academic Conference, September. Available at http://ssrn.com/abstract=1969583.

Jones, Stewart, Sandra van der Laan, Geoff Frost, and Janice Loftus. 2008. "The Investment Performance of Socially Responsible Investment Funds in Australia." *Journal of Business Ethics* 80:2, 181–203.

Kahneman, Daniel, and Tversky, Amos. 1972. "Subjective Probability: A Judgment of Representativeness." In Daniel Kahneman, Paul Slovic, and Amos Tversky, eds., *Judgment under Uncertainty: Heuristics and Biases*, 32–47. Cambridge: Cambridge University Press.

Kempf, Alexander, and Peer Osthoff. 2007. "The Effect of Socially Responsible Investing on Portfolio Performance." *European Financial Management* 13:5, 908–922.

Knoll, Michael S. 2008. "Socially Responsible Investment and Modern Financial Markets." Working Paper, University of Pennsylvania Law School.

Kotler, Philip, and Nancy Lee. 2005. *Corporate Social Responsibility: Doing the Most Good for Your Company and Your Cause.* Hoboken, NJ: John Wiley & Sons.

Leonhardt, James M., Robin L. Keller, and Connie Pechmann. 2011. "Avoiding the Risk of Responsibility by Seeking Uncertainty: Responsibility Aversion and Preference for Indirect Agency when Choosing for Others." *Journal of Consumer Psychology* 21:4, 405–413.

Little, Kent. 2008. *Socially Responsible Investing: Put Your Money Where Your Values Are.* New York: Penguin.

Livesey, Sharon. 2002. "The Discourse of the Middle Ground: Citizen Shell Commits to Sustainable Development." *Management Communication Quarterly* 15:3, 313–349.

Lynch-Fannon, Irene. 2007. "The Corporate Social Responsibility Movement and Law's Empire: Is There a Conflict?" *Northern Ireland Legal Quarterly* 58:1, 1–22.

Mathieu, Eugenie. 2000. *Response of UK Pension Funds to the SRI Disclosure Regulation.* London: UK Social Investment Forum.

Matten, Dirk, and Andrew Crane. 2005. "Corporate Citizenship: Toward an Extended Theoretical Conceptualization." *Academy of Management Review* 30:1, 166–179.

Matten, Dirk, and Jeremy Moon. 2004. "'Implicit' and 'Explicit' CSR: A Conceptual Framework for Understanding CSR in Europe." 20th EGOS Colloquium, July 1–3, Ljubljana, Slovenia.

McCann, Leo, Aris Solomon, and Jili F. Solomon. 2003. "Explaining the Growth in U.K. Socially Responsible Investment." *Journal of General Management* 28:4, 15–36.

McWilliams, Abagail, and Donald Siegel. 2000. "Corporate Social Responsibility and Financial Performance: Correlation or Mis-Specification?" *Strategic Management Journal* 21:2, 603–609.

McWilliams, Abagail, Donald Siegel, and Siew H. Teoh. 1999. "Issues in the Use of the Event Study Methodology: A Critical Analysis of Corporate Social Responsibility Studies." *Organizational Research Methods* 2:4, 340–365.

Meznar, Martin B., Douglas Nigh, and Chuck C. Kwok. 1994. "Effect of Announcements of Withdrawal from South Africa on Stockholder Wealth." *Academy of Management Journal* 37:6, 1633–1648.

Miller, Geoffrey, and Gerald Rosenfeld. 2010. "Intellectual Hazard: How Conceptual Biases in Complex Organizations Contributed to the Crisis of 2008." *Harvard Journal of Law and Public Policy* 33:2, 807–840.

Mohr, Lois A., and Deborah J. Webb. 2005. "The Effects of Corporate Social Responsibility and Price on Consumer Responses." *Journal of Consumer Affairs* 39:1, 121–147.

Mohr, Lois A., Deborah J. Webb, and Katherine E. Harris. 2001. "Do Consumers Expect Companies to Be Socially Responsible? The Impact of Corporate Social Responsibility on Buying Behavior." *Journal of Consumer Affairs* 35:1, 45–72.

Ngassam, Chris. 1992. *An Examination of Stock Market Reactions to U.S. Corporate Divestitures in South Africa.* Newark, DE: University of Delaware.

Nilsson, Jonas. 2008. "Investment with a Conscience: Examining the Impact of Pro-Social Attitudes and Perceived Financial Performance on Socially Responsible Investment Behavior." *Journal of Business Ethics* 83:2, 307–325.

Okamoto, Karl S. 2009. "After the Bailout: Regulating Systemic Moral Hazard." *UCLA Law Review* 57:1, 183–236.

Posnikoff, Judith F. 1997. "Disinvestment from South Africa: They Did Well by Doing Good." *Contemporary Economic Policy* 15:1, 76–86.

Puaschunder, Julia M. 2010. "On Corporate and Financial Social Responsibility." Doctoral Thesis, University of Vienna, Faculty of Psychology.

Puaschunder, Julia M. 2011a. "Ethical Decision Making under Social Uncertainty: An Introduction of Überethicality." Library of Congress United States of America Copyright Office, Copyright Catalogue TXu001782130/2011-11-04.

Puaschunder, Julia M. 2011b. "Intergenerational Equity as a Natural Behavioral Law." Library of Congress United States of America Copyright Office, Copyright Catalogue TXu001743422/2011-03-08.

Puaschunder, Julia M. 2011c. "On the Emergence, Current State and Future Perspectives of Socially Responsible Investment." Weatherhead Center for International Affairs Working Paper, Harvard University. Available at www.wcfia.harvard.edu/node/6552.

Puaschunder, Julia M. 2012. "On Eternal Equity in the fin-de-millénaire." Manuscript in progress. Available at www.academia.edu/1957366/On_Eternal_Equity_in_the_fin-de-millenaire.

Puaschunder, Julia M., and Gary Schwarz. 2012. "How Joint Decision Making Curbs Hyperbolic Discounting but Blurs Social Responsibility in the Intergenerational Equity Public Policy Making Domain." *The Situationist*, Harvard University. Available at http://thesituationist.wordpress.com/2012/12/17/the-situation-of-intergenerational-equity/.

Reinhardt, Forest L., Richard H. Vietor, and Robert N. Stavins. 2008. "Corporate Social Responsibility through an Economic Lens." *Review of Environmental Economics and Policy* 2:2, 219–239.

Renneboog, Luc D. R., Jenke R. T. Horst, and Chendi Zhang. 2007. "Socially Responsible Investments: Methodology, Risk and Performance." Tilburg University Center for Economic Research Discussion Paper 2007–2031, Tilburg University.

Ricciardi, Victor. 2010. "The Psychology of Risk." In H. Kent Baker and John R. Nofsinger, eds. *Behavioral Finance: Investors, Corporations, and Markets*, 131–149. Hoboken, NJ: John Wiley & Sons.

Roberts, Alasdair S. 2010. *Disciplined Democracies: Global Capitalism and the New Architecture of Government*. Oxford: Oxford University Press.

Roe, Mark. 2000. "Political Preconditions to Separating Ownership from Corporate Control." *Stanford Law Review* 53:3, 539–586.

Rosen, Barry N., Dennis M. Sandler, and David Shani. 1991. "Social Issues and Socially Responsible Investment Behavior: Preliminary Empirical Investigation." *Journal of Consumer Affairs* 25:2, 221–234.

Schröder, Michael. 2003. "Socially Responsible Investments in Germany, Switzerland, and the United States." Centre for European Economic Research Discussion Paper 03-10.

Schröder, Michael. 2007. "Is There a Difference? The Performance Characteristics of SRI Equity Indices." *Journal of Business Finance & Accounting* 34:1–2, 331–348.

Schueth, Steve. 2003. "Socially Responsible Investing in the United States." *Journal of Business Ethics* 43:3, 189–194.

Shu, Lisa L., Francesca Gino, and Max H. Bazerman. 2011. "Dishonest Deer, Clear Conscience: Self Preservation through Moral Disengagement and Motivated Forgetting." *Personality and Social Psychology Bulletin* 37:4, 330–349.

Sjöström, Emma. 2011. "The Performance of Socially Responsible Investment: A Review of Scholarly Studies Published 2008–2010." Working Paper, Social Science Research Network. Available at http://ssrn.com/abstract=1948169.

Soana, Maria G. 2011. "The Relationship between Corporate Social Performance and Corporate Financial Performance in the Banking Sector." *Journal of Business Ethics* 104:1, 133–148.

Social Investment Forum Report. 2006. *Report on Socially Responsible Investing Trends in the United States*. Social Investment Forum Industry Research Program 10-Year Review. Available at http://ussif.org/pdf/research/Trends/2005%20Trends%20Report.pdf.

Solomon, Jili F., Aris Solomon, and Simon D. Norton. 2002. "Socially Responsible Investment in the UK: Drivers and Current Issues." *Journal of General Management* 27:3, 1–13.

Soros, George. 2008. *The New Paradigm for Financial Markets: The Credit Crisis of 2008 and What It Means*. New York: Public Affairs.

Sparkes, Richard. 2002. *Socially Responsible Investment: A Global Revolution*. Chichester: John Wiley & Sons.

Sparkes, Richard, and Chris J. Cowton. 2004. "The Maturing of Socially Responsible Investment: A Review of the Developing Link with Corporate Social Responsibility." *Journal of Business Ethics* 52:1, 45–57.

Starr, Martha A. 2008. "Socially Responsible Investment and Pro-Social Change." *Journal of Economic Issues* 42:1, 5173.

Statman, Meir. 2005. "Socially Responsible Indexes: Composition and Performance." Working Paper, Social Science Research Network. Available at http://ssrn.com/abstract=705344.

Statman, Meir. 2008. "Socially Responsible Investors and Their Advisors." *Journal of Investment Consulting*, 9:1, 15–26.

Steurer, Reinhard. 2010. "The Role of Governments in Corporate Social Responsibility: Characterizing Public Policies on CSR in Europe." *Policy Science* 43:1, 49–72.

Stone, Bernell K., John B. Guerard, Mustafa N. Gületkin, and Greg Adams. 2001. "Socially Responsible Investment Screening: Strong Evidence of No Significant Cost for Actively Managed Portfolios." Working Paper, FS Insight. Available at www.socialinvest.org/pdf/research/Moskowitz/2001%20Honorable%20Mention%20-%20Moskowitz.pdf.

Summers, Lawrence H., and Lant Pritchett. 2012. *Societies of the World: The Future of Globalization: Issues, Actors, and Decisions*. Cambridge: Harvard University Faculty of Arts and Sciences.

Sutton, Michele. 2004. "Between a Rock and a Judicial Hard Place: Corporate Social Responsibility Reporting and Potential Legal Liability under Kasky v. Nike." *University of Missouri-Kansas City School of Law Review* 72:3, 11–59.

The Economist. 2008. "Just Good Business." January 17. Available at www.economist.com/node/10491077.

The Economist. 2012. "The LIBOR Scandal: The Rotten Heart of Finance: A Scandal over Key Interest Rates Is about to Go Global," July 7. Available at www.economist.com/node/21558281.

Tippet, John. 2001. "Performance of Australia's Ethical Funds." *Australian Economic Review* 34:2, 170–178.

Tumpel-Gugerell, Gertrude. 2009. "Monetary Policy Challenges in the Light of the Current Financial Market Development." Notes to the speech delivered at the Vienna Alpbach Talks, June 15.

Voorhees, Nathalie. 1999. The US Divestment Movement: How Sanctions Work: Lessons from South Africa. New York: St. Martin's Press.

Weber, Olaf, Marco Mansfeld, and Eric Schirrmann. 2010. "The Financial Performance of SRI Funds between 2002 and 2009." Working Paper, Social Science Research Network. Available at http://ssrn.com/abstract=1630502.

Williams, Geoffrey. 2005. "Are Socially Responsible Investors Different from Conventional Investors? A Comparison across Six Countries." Working Paper, University of Bath.

Wolff, Martin. 2002. "Response to 'Confronting the Critics.'" *New Academy Review* 1:1, 230–237.

Wright, Peter, and Stephen Ferris. 1997. "Agency Conflict and Corporate Strategy: The Effect of Divestment on Corporate Value." *Strategic Management Journal* 18:1, 77–83.

ABOUT THE AUTHOR

Julia M. Puaschunder is an Associate of the Harvard University Faculty of Arts and Sciences Center for the Environment. As a behavioral economist, she launched research projects in Australia, Austria, Canada, China, Germany, Indonesia, Switzerland, and the United States. She conducted research for the Austrian Academy of Sciences, Austrian Federal Ministry of Science and Research, European Commission, Fulbright Commission, Max Kade Foundation, and the U.S. Department of Education. Professor Puaschunder was a scholar at The Australian National University, University of Munich, and The Open Society Institute & Soros Foundation. She delivered invited presentations at Harvard University and Princeton University. Recently, she joined the Harvard Law School Project on Law and Mind Sciences Board of Contributors. Professor Puaschunder holds an MPA from Syracuse University and MA, MBA, and two PhD degrees from the University of Vienna and the Vienna University of Economics and Business.

CHAPTER 29

Mutual Funds and Individual Investors: Advertising and Behavioral Issues

John A. Haslem
Professor Emeritus of Finance, Robert H. Smith
School of Business, University of Maryland

INTRODUCTION

The purpose of this chapter is to review interactions between mutual funds and individual investors in choosing equity mutual funds. Probably the largest question is why both sophisticated and unsophisticated investors persist in investing in actively managed funds that generally result in underperformance. Actively managed funds have a long history of spending money on advertising because they find that it results in increasing assets under management. Fund management companies realize that investors chase past performance in the mistaken belief that historical returns predict future investment performance. Funds further take advantage of investors by increasing advertising when past performance is high. Advertising encourages many investors to make fund choices because they are inexperienced, unaware, and have low financial literacy, including a lack of knowledge of both transparent and obscure fund commissions, expenses, and charges. Any persistence in high fund performance is also much more likely attributable to luck than to portfolio manager's expertise. The Securities and Exchange Commission (SEC) has also failed to prohibit performance advertising or to require it to be understandable.

The remaining sections provide a discussion of the following topics: (1) advertising and performance; (2) advertising, expenses, and flows; (3) advertising, emotions, and choice; (4) behavioral persuasion in advertising and choice; (5) education, financial knowledge, and choice; (6) emotions, behavior, and choice; (7) emotions, behavioral finance, and choice; (8) financial literacy and active management; (9) price and performance sensitivity and repricing; and (10) sentiment contrarian behavior and actual performance. The final section provides a brief summary and conclusions. Haslem (2003, 2010a) discusses funds in depth, including risk and performance.

ADVERTISING AND PERFORMANCE

Mutual funds use advertising because they have found that it works to increase assets under fund management and fund adviser (investment adviser) profits. In other words, this mutual fund business model is based on asset growth. Relatively fixed overhead is applied to a larger asset base resulting in higher levels of fees paid by mutual shareholders and more profits for the financial services industry (e.g., mutual fund companies and financial advisors).

The major driving force behind equity mutual fund advertising is recent fund performance. Funds have apparently learned from experience that past performance affects investor fund choices. Investors buy funds with attention-grabbing recent performance because they believe it will persist. Funds are rational, but misleading, when they advertise high past performance when possible. Funds have learned to exploit investors by advertising past performance, and investors lacking knowledge have widely followed them down the road.

The investor belief in chasing past fund performance is widely established and paints a disturbing picture of fund capabilities. Individual investors are generally unaware, unsophisticated, and have low financial literacy. Investors often lack specific knowledge of fund attributes crucial to generating superior returns. Such investors lack knowledge of opaque higher cost soft-dollar trades and "soft dollars" of research rebates to fund advisers, and revenue sharing payments with broker rebates of "adviser fall-out benefits" from "excess" payments. Even more disturbing, investors do not appear to be fully aware of transparent expense ratios and component management fees, 12b-1 fees, and other expense percentages of fund total net assets. Haslem (2008, 2010a, 2011a, 2012a, 2012b) discusses the importance of normative transparency of disclosure and transparent and opaque costs.

Investors are thus encouraged to take the easy path of selecting funds with high past performance, which is provided in overabundance through fund advertising. Even more sophisticated investors may use a similar approach and focus on past performance. Mutual funds advertise performance much more frequently when recent returns have been generally high and investors are optimistic or overconfident, but the opposite also occurs when recent returns are generally low and investors are pessimistic.

Mutual fund advertising increases investor purchases, which is the key for fund advisers. Fund advisers receive more dollars in expense ratios as asset size increases with board approved fee percentages of net total assets. Fund advisers focus on growth of fund assets and their profits generally prevail over shareholder fiduciary interests.

Investors need to know the facts about using past fund performance as a strategy. The results of using past performance as a predictor of future performance are often confused with portfolio manager skill. When past fund performance does persist, it is more likely a stroke of luck than stock-picking skill. In fact, Barras, Scaillet, and Wermers (2010) find only 2.2 percent of actively managed domestic funds significantly outperformed benchmarks over 31 years, and only 0.06 percent of the funds revealed actual manager skill rather than luck.

Standard & Poor's Soe and Luo (2012) also report using past performance as a strategy fails for 1,020 domestic actively managed mutual funds. For the five years ending March 2012, only about 5 percent of funds maintained top-half performance rankings over five consecutive 12-month periods, while 6 percent were predicted to repeat by chance alone. However, funds with the lowest rankings persisted in their performance.

Mutual fund families use selective advertising that features only the highest performing funds and investors act as if they are the only funds in play. With no mention of underperforming funds, investors attribute high performance to portfolio manager skill and presume it will persist. The role of luck in performance is not in evidence. Fund families are likely to have one or more funds with high performance at any given time simply due to luck.

The bottom line is that mutual fund performance advertising works to attract new investors. Advertising exploits the tendency of individual investors to pursue past performance and the findings overwhelmingly demonstrate that investors do not benefit because performance fails to persist in the future.

Mutual fund advertising negatively affects investors, because it:

- Promotes performance chasing behavior;
- Implies that past performance predicts future returns;
- Attracts investors through performance-enhanced advertising;
- Emphasizes performance when stock prices are high;
- Results in investors earning lower returns;
- Encourages and facilitates poor fund choices;
- Ignores expense ratios, front-end loads, and fees;
- Discourages investor portfolio rebalancing;
- Increases investor portfolio turnover, transaction costs, load fees, expenses, and capital gains taxes by chasing performance;
- Increases fund assets under management and fund adviser profits at the expense of investors.

One might think there is no regulation of mutual fund performance advertising, but the major problem is that federal statutes are inconsistent. The Securities Act of 1933 prohibits any false statement or omission of material facts in sales of securities. The SEC also explicitly regulates fund performance advertisements, including sales loads, and provides standards. The Securities Exchange Act of 1934 prohibits false statements of material facts in sales of securities. The Investment Company Act of 1940, which regulates the fund industry, also prohibits false statements of material facts and omission of facts that would make statements misleading. The Financial Industry Regulatory Authority (FINRA), the financial industry's self-regulating body, has adopted SEC-approved rules that prohibit false and misleading statements of material facts and omission of material facts.

The SEC has major responsibility for mutual fund regulation. Unfortunately for investors, the SEC has neither prohibited performance advertising nor required unambiguous advertising stating that use of high past performance to predict future performance is a failed strategy. Palmiter and Taha (2011) discuss these regulatory issues.

ADVERTISING, EXPENSES, AND FLOWS

Investors appear to respond differently to advertising and fund related expenses. For example, Barber, Odean, and Zheng (2005, p. 2095) argue that "the purchase decisions of mutual fund investors are influenced by salient, attention-grabbing information. ... They buy funds that attract their attention through exceptional performance, marketing, or advertising." Yet, investors respond differently to separate categories of mutual fund expenses. A significant negative relationship exists between front-end loads and fund flows, but no overall relationship exists between operating expenses and fund flows. Operating expenses include 12b-1 fees for marketing and advertising used to attract cash flows.

The importance of advertising is identified by separating mutual fund operating expenses into two parts: 12b-1 fees and all other operating expenses. When this is done, Barber et al. (2005) find that 12b-1 fees alone are positively related to fund flows, which indicate the importance of advertising to investor purchases. This is true for all sample funds, large funds, and older funds. The result is that investors are more likely to buy funds with higher marketing expenses, but less likely to buy funds with higher overall operating expenses.

A possible reason for the importance of advertising in investor choice of mutual fund selection might be investor search costs. Barber et al. (2005, p. 2114) state:

> *Perhaps investors find it extremely costly to search for mutual funds. Thus, rather, than incur the hassle of finding a fund, they merely invest in funds that come to their attention through advertising. In short, these investors knowingly sacrifice performance . . . to reduce the hassle of picking a mutual fund.*

Haslem (2009) discusses advertising and investor learning.

One footnote to the analysis of mutual fund advertising relates to front-end loads. Investors have grown sensitive to front-end loads more quickly than to operating expenses because front-end loads are more transparent to investors. The result is a consistent negative relationship between front-end loads and fund flows that is stronger than between operating expenses and flows. Barber et al. (2005, p. 2117) conclude this discussion by noting "[M]utual fund advertising does work. On average, any negative effect of expense fees on fund flows is more than offset when that money is spent on marketing: non-marketing expenses, however, reduce fund flows."

ADVERTISING, EMOTIONS, AND CHOICE

Data on portfolio choices provided from Sweden's public pension system find that mutual fund advertising influences participant fund choices. Advertising data are provided from nearly 24,000 advertisements and over 20,000 commercials. A study by Cronqvist (2006) analyzes the role of mutual fund advertising and its impact on investor fund choices. The vast majority of investors are familiar with fund advertising in print media and on television, but print advertising is more informative. Fund advertising is higher when fund returns are higher, but funds that advertise more do not earn higher post-advertising excess returns (i.e., annual returns net of category returns). Haslem (2010b) discusses advertising and investor choice.

The influence of the advertising content is normally consistent with the behavioral ("as is"), rather than the rational model of persuasion. The behavioral model finds that investor fund choices are characterized by cognition and emotion, and investor attitudes can change without cognition. Even slight investor exposure to fund advertising can elicit positive emotion, even if direct information is not provided. However, investors can also be overexposed to advertising that limits its effectiveness.

Analysis provides four major findings. First, only a small fraction of mutual fund advertising provides direct information of fund attributes relevant for rational investors, such as expense ratios. Second, funds that advertise more do not provide higher post-advertising excess returns and do not signal higher-skilled portfolio managers. Third, advertising influences fund choices even if little or no direct information is provided. Fourth, advertising motivates investors to select funds with higher fees and risks, which may be explained by active management investing in risky "hot" sectors and "home bias" (i.e., preference given to local securities) in selecting investments. The results are lower current fund net asset values (NAVs) per share and investor returns.

A significant positive relationship exists between mutual fund advertising and investor fund choices. However, why does fund advertising influence investors—is it direct information, signals of higher quality, or simply investor exposure? Haslem (2010c) discusses why advertising works.

Direct Information

Advertising, as the "direct information" hypothesis states, reflects the traditional information role of advertising. Direct information reduces search costs by enabling inspection of rational attributes, such as fund fees. Cronqvist (2006) finds the content of fund advertising is classified as: (1) "fee cues," which provide fee messages; (2) "performance cues," which provide Morningstar or other ratings, fund returns, or fund return comparisons; and (3) "other cues," which provide all other advertising. Fee cues represent 8 percent of fund advertising dollars, performance cues 30 percent, and other advertising cues 62 percent.

Little support exists for the direct information hypothesis. Only a small percentage of fund advertising appears directly informative of fund fees. Less than 1 percent of all advertising allows investors to compare fund expense ratios. Fund advertising is not an important information source for investors rationally seeking funds with lower fees.

Quality Signaling

Advertising as the "quality signaling" hypothesis is tested by analyzing whether mutual funds that advertise more are associated with higher post advertising abnormal returns, relative to a Morningstar category. Total advertising is the measure of the strength of the quality signal. However, evidence does not support this hypothesis. Cronqvist (2006) only finds evidence of a small negative-positive association between fund advertising and abnormal returns.

Mutual fund advertising predicts little of the variation in post-advertising abnormal returns, but cues may exist for which quality signaling may apply. No evidence indicates that higher advertising signals abnormal returns by better managers with little experience, better managers of specialized assets, better funds with little media coverage, or better foreign funds.

No way may be available to ensure a positive relationship between fund manager quality (through repeat business) and advertising. If no mechanism ensures that low quality funds do not get repeat business, then advertising cannot be used as a quality signal in the fund industry.

Investor Choices

Although mutual fund advertising provides little information, does it influence investor choices? The answer appears to be "yes" based on a significant positive relationship between fund advertising and investor fund share purchases, but with some overexposure in evidence. Funds that advertise may also differ on characteristics that investors view as important. Funds that advertise more include local funds, larger funds, funds with more recent media coverage, and funds with higher recent returns. The effect of fund advertising is large and at least as large as the effect of fund size, media coverage, or past performance, but less than the home (local) fund bias. However, the assertion that more fund advertising causes investors to invest more is difficult to substantiate.

Other Advertising

While performance advertising is the most important type of advertising, other advertising also plays a role. Performance advertising and past performance both have positive effects on investor inflows. This finding is consistent with the disproportionate amounts of investor cash flows to funds that performed well in the recent past. The significant positive interaction between performance advertising and past performance suggests funds use this type of advertising to sell what investors care about—past performance. Other types of mutual fund advertising also have positive effects on investor cash inflows, but with about one half the effectiveness of performance advertising. A five-star Morningstar rating is a case in point because this is considered an excellent ranking within the financial services industry for an individual mutual fund.

Advertising Returns

Mutual fund advertising has both direct and indirect returns. Personal finance magazines are more likely to recommend funds that advertise. More and better magazine recommendations are important determinants of investor cash inflows. Estimates show that over five or so years fund fees from this advertising exceed its cost. However, limitations exist to the optimal amounts funds should spend on advertising. Marginal returns to advertising decrease from investor overexposure.

Advertising, Returns, and Risk

Although a weak negative relationship exists between mutual fund advertising and post-advertising fund abnormal returns, whether funds that advertise underperform funds that do not advertise is unclear. Mutual funds that advertise may want to avoid price competition with respect to expense ratios. Funds use product differentiation for this purpose, which may even be based on a rationally unimportant fund characteristic. Investors have been known to pay higher expense ratios for meaningless differentiation that provides no direct information.

Even so, this type of advertising may be effective in attracting investor attention and may motivate them to consider mutual funds with higher expense ratios. The relationship between advertising and expense ratios may reflect that these funds bundle investor advice services with higher expenses. In any case, a positive relationship exists between fund advertising and expense ratios.

The risk characteristics of mutual funds that advertise may be economically significant. Funds that advertise are less likely to be index funds and more likely to invest in hot sectors and local securities.

Cronqvist (2006, p. 1) concludes the discussion as follows:

> [O]nly a small fraction of fund advertising is directly informative about characteristics relevant for rational investors, such as fund fees. Higher quantities of advertising do not signal ex ante higher unobservable fund manager ability, because funds that advertise more are not associated with higher post-advertising excess returns. Fund advertising is shown to affect investors' choices, although it provides little information. . . . Finally, advertising is found to steer people towards portfolios with higher fees and more risk, through higher exposure to equities, more active management, more "hot" sectors, and more home bias.

BEHAVIORAL PERSUASION IN ADVERTISING AND CHOICE

Persuasion is communication of information designed to get customers to accept certain ideas. Communication content is designed to increase its effectiveness as persuasion. In financial advertising, persuasion is communication content designed to influence investor choices. Traditional and behavioral models differ in explaining how investors process communication content.

Mullainathan and Shleifer (2006) compare the traditional economic and behavioral models in financial advertising. The traditional economic model uses financial information designed to change/update rational investor beliefs. The behavioral model uses factual or spurious financial information designed to match prevailing investor beliefs. The authors compare the two models using the content of financial advertising in *Money* and *Businessweek* over a decade. The evidence shows that information content is generally consistent with the behavioral model.

Traditional versus Behavioral Models

Mullainathan and Shleifer (2006) discuss two types of models—traditional models and behavioral models—relating to advertising content. The traditional model makes several predictions about the content of advertising. For example, this model predicts that advertising content provides not only product choices and fees but also risk and return data. Another prediction is that the advertising does not present current returns if they do not persist. If the advertising provides returns, they are relative to enabling investors to assess portfolio manager quality. Haslem (2011b) discusses advertising, behavior, and investor choice.

Behavioral models provide different predictions about advertising content. For instance, such models predict that advertising content provides investor cognitive and emotional responses but often omits relevant data designed for rational responses. Advertising may include incomplete, misleading, and even irrelevant information, convey information consistent with prevailing investor beliefs but omit that which is not, and encourages speculation more than contrarian investing.

The behavioral approach to persuasion models the world as a system of connected associations that represent investor experience and beliefs. Persuasive advertising content must be connected to these beliefs to be successful. For example, the Marlboro Man is an advertising icon based on the behavioral model. The advertisement's persuasion content was tremendously successful in tapping into male self-images of masculinity, independence, and freedom, all of which were embodied in the picture (no words) of a handsome mature cowboy smoking on a horse. This icon models behavioral associative thinking rather than simply providing information.

The behavioral model makes other predictions about mutual fund advertising content. For instance, this model predicts that the advertising content includes fund returns and ratings when past market returns are high, and omits them when returns are low. The presentation of current returns depends on past market returns, not past fund returns. Finally, the advertising focuses on growth when the market is rising and protection when the market is falling.

Mullainathan and Shleifer (2006, p. 24) conclude the discussion as follows:

[W]e provide evidence supportive of the behavioral model of persuasion. Over the course of the internet bubble, advertisers tapped into the growth system of beliefs when stock prices were rising, and into the protection system when prices were falling. Evidence on both the use of fund returns in ads and the choice of products being promoted is consistent with the view that firms supply messages which investors are disposed to interpret favorably at the moment. At a minimum, financial institutions encourage speculation rather than contrarian behavior through their persuasion strategies. But, there is also a broader point. . . . Competitive markets in information deliver what consumers want.

EDUCATION, FINANCIAL KNOWLEDGE, AND CHOICE

Wilcox (2003) examines how investors choose mutual funds in a particular category. In particular, Wilcox obtains data from 50 current mutual fund investors based on 20 choice tasks. The investor demographics are diverse. The study attributes are limited to information in prospectuses and shareholder annual reports. The findings of the study reveal that investors pay considerable attention to past fund performance and overweight front-end loads relative to expense ratios when assessing overall fund expense structures. Investors with greater knowledge of basic finance are less likely to make reasonable fund choices.

Mutual fund advisers understand they need effective marketing, but they have only limited understanding of how investors make fund choices. Thousands of funds and numerous external information sources are available to assist investors in making choices. With the large growth in individual and defined contribution retirement plans, investors are now much more engaged in making fund decisions.

Past Performance

Attributes of mutual fund past performance are more important to investors than fund fees. The most important past performance attributes are 1-year and 10-year past returns. Investors pay most attention to fund attributes that are cognitively accessible, and they ignore attributes that are difficult to assess (Wilcox 2003).

As discussed, Wilcox (2003) finds past fund performance has little or no ability to predict performance persistence. Finding persistence in risk-adjusted fund performance is very difficult. Even sophisticated portfolios of actively managed funds find outperforming passive index funds difficult. Investors with short investment horizons pay more attention to past fund performance than investors with longer horizons.

Fund Fees

Costs of a particular mutual fund provide investors with more information about expected future total returns relative to other funds. The ability or inability of portfolio managers to provide superior performance affects gross returns on fund assets. Skilled portfolio managers are likely to outperform other funds in the same category, and underperform if portfolio managers are unskilled.

Mutual fund fees reduce net returns on fund assets. Portfolio manager skill is not important to long-run relative fund performance. In fact, asset selection skill probably does not exist in the popular use of the term, and the fund's relative return is best described as random. The record on fund fees is absolutely clear—investors should pay great attention to fund fees when making fund choices.

Investor Decisions

As previously noted, mutual fund investors not only give much attention to past performance but also overweight front-end loads relative to management fees in the decision process. A strong popular perception exists that individuals who possess the following attributes are better investors if they (1) are wealthier, (2) are more highly educated, (3) are men, (4) hold more types of funds, (5) are more knowledgeable about basic finance, and (6) have long investment horizons. The analysis predicts how fund attribute weights change across investor profiles. Baker and Haslem (1973, 1974a, 1974b) and Baker, Hargrove, and Haslem (1977) analyze investor attributes and risk and return preferences.

In fact, highly educated, wealthier, and male investors are less successful in making mutual fund choices, and give less emphasis to expense ratios. As Wilcox (2003, p. 658) concludes, "highly educated consumers and those who demonstrated greater knowledge of basic finance made poorer, not better, decisions than did their less financially savvy counterparts." Wealthy and highly educated investors overweight front-end loads relative to expense ratios, and are more biased in assessing fee structures. These types of investors also give more weight to past fund performance. Investors with basic financial knowledge are more biased in evaluating fee structures and give more attention to short-term performance.

The types of mutual funds investors hold do not affect their preferences. Investors with longer investment horizons pay less attention to past performance. No evidence indicates investors give more attention to expense ratios than front-end loads. This would not be the case if investors had a better understanding of expenses. Branded funds (well-known and respected funds) also provide more confidence to long-term investors. Finally, the results cast doubt on the investment abilities of what are commonly known as savvy investors. Investor knowledge of finance contributes little to more profitable fund choices. As Wilcox (2003, p. 658) concludes, "highly educated consumers and those who demonstrated greater knowledge of basic finance made poorer, not better, decisions than did their less financially savvy counterparts."

Management Implications

Mutual fund investors are becoming more averse to front-end loads and therefore funds need to find other revenue sources. Investors with greater knowledge of basic finance are especially averse to loads, and those with lower levels of knowledge are less averse to front-end loads. Investors with greater knowledge of basic finance are likely to avoid load funds, and therefore funds might find offering no-load funds to them desirable. Knowledge of investor profiles is important to fund choices of distribution channels. Haslem (2013b) discusses fund distribution.

SEC mutual fund disclosure requirements are inadequate to improve investor fund choices. Disclosure should state that past fund performance does not predict future performance, provide complete disclosure of fund fees, and explain the importance of small differences in fund fees on investor returns over time.

EMOTIONS, BEHAVIOR, AND CHOICE

Kuhnen and Knutson (2011) find emotions play a role in decision-making under risk and the process of investing itself produces strong emotional responses. *Affect* refers to feelings or emotions that change investor choices by modifying risk preferences and/or beliefs and provides a framework for explaining deviations from rational choices due to behavioral biases. Affect, whether from exogenous manipulations or endogenously by prior actions, is important for risk taking.

Positive emotional states induce investors to take more risk and to be more confident in evaluating investment options. However, negative emotions have the opposite effect. Investors update beliefs consistent with the motive of maintaining positive affect and avoiding negative affect by taking into account new information at odds with prior choices. Market characteristics, economic policies, or organizational design that influence decisions and outcomes affect emotional brain circuits.

Two areas of the brain in particular are engaged in decision-making under risk: the *nucleus accumbens* and *anterior ansula*. The nucleus accumbens processes information about gains and motivates investors toward potentially rewarding cues. Activation in this structure is associated with positive arousal. The anterior insula processes information about losses and motivates investors to avoid aversive cues. Activation in this structure is associated with negative arousal.

Activation of these two areas of the brain also helps predict whether investors will choose risky or less risky investments. Higher activation in the nucleus accumbens increases the likelihood of switching to risky assets. Conversely, activation in the anterior insula increases the likelihood of switching to less risky assets. In sum, investor emotions matter in decision-making under risk, whether due to exogenous factors or results of prior decisions. Excitement (positive arousal) and anxiety (negative arousal) affect risk preferences and the ways investors learn.

The first goal is to determine whether changes in emotion affect financial choices by altering risk preferences or beliefs. These changes arise from outside or within the activity of investing. The second goal is to construct a framework that changes investor choices by modifying risk preferences and/or beliefs and explains deviations in rational choices due to behavioral biases. This framework is based on the impact of the limbic system on decision-making.

Analysis conducted by Kuhnen and Knutson (2011) involves participation of selected university students in a research trial. The trial includes 90 equity securities and low-risk bonds. The trial requires participants to update their beliefs about the distribution of returns of a risky security. The results find that exogenous and endogenous cues affect risk-taking behavior. Affect-inducing stimuli (given investor beliefs) change risk preferences. Negative affect causes higher risk aversion and positive affect causes more risk seeking.

Affect and Beliefs

Student subject investors in the study by Kuhnen and Knutson (2011) choose beliefs that match prior choices and thereby avoid the negative affect of admitting mistakes. This is not the confirmation bias, where investors consult information sources that help confirm their beliefs. The results here refer to errors in the process of rejecting incorrect hypotheses. Investors undervalue or reject information that disagrees with past choices.

Kuhnen and Knutson (2011, p. 623) conclude as follows:

> *In an investment selection task that requires subjects to update their beliefs about the return distribution of a risk asset, we find that events associated with positive and arousing emotions such as excitement lead to riskier choices, while those associated with negative and arousing emotions such as anxiety lead to more risk averse choices. Moreover, affect influences the belief formation process. Positive arousal increases the subjects' confidence in their ability to evaluate the risky investments they are faced with. Beliefs about these investments are updated in a way that is consistent with the self-preservation motive of maintaining positive affect and avoiding negative affect. Specifically, subjects do not fully incorporate news that contradict their prior choices, and form incorrect posterior beliefs.*

EMOTIONS, BEHAVIORAL FINANCE, AND CHOICE

Research in psychology and neurology has important implications for economics and finance. According to Sapra and Zak (2009), *neurofinance* focuses on financial markets and the gaps between rational efficient markets and market reality—behavioral finance. The focus on financial markets includes the predictability of asset returns, liquidity, and bubbles and crashes. The "rational man" of rational expectations theory accurately estimates probabilities of future outcomes and makes optimal decisions that maximize utility. The rational man is unemotional, with a constant degree of risk aversion and cognitive ability in making complex decisions.

Neuroeconomics blends behavioral psychology, neurology, and economics—behavioral economics. Findings in behavioral economics are inconsistent with predictions of rational choice. Behavioral theories take a normative view based on empirical observation of investor-revealed preferences and choices. Behaviorists find that decision-making is driven by affect—emotional responses to stimuli that are often driven by autonomic mechanisms beyond human consciousness.

Sapra and Zak (2009, p. 31) support the behavioral model of financial markets:

> [S]*tock markets are reflections of human behavior, not that of Homo economicus. If humans are rational in the traditional sense, then markets naturally will reflect such rationality through purely efficient pricing. However, we know that humans are rarely fully rational; we are characterized by biases and internal conflicts, resulting in decision making often at odds with that of rational man. As a result, the prices of financial assets reflect real human behavior, and thus can indeed become depressed. So long as prices are determined by aggregate human decisions, they will convey fundamental valuation, but also fear, paranoia, exhilaration and euphoria as well. Markets do indeed reflect the human psyche, but the human psyche is imperfect.*

Shiller (2006, p. 1–2), however, discusses neoclassical finance and behavioral finance as two "distinct revolutions," which he summarizes as follows:

> *The first was the neoclassical revolution in finance that began with the capital asset pricing model and efficient markets theory around the 1960s, and with the intertemporal capital asset pricing model and arbitrage-based option-pricing theory in the 1970s. The second was the behavioral revolution in finance which began in the 1980s with questions about the sources of volatility in financial markets, with the discovery of numerous anomalies, and with attempts to incorporate into financial theory Kahneman and Tversky's 1979 prospect theory, and other theories from psychologists.*
>
> *The two revolutions came at different times and largely from different people, and so it may naturally be assumed that the two approaches are incompatible. Those who are most impressed with the neoclassical finance sometimes seem to regard behavioral finance as an uprising of the heathens. In fact, however, the two revolutions in finance have always been intertwined, and some of the most important applications of their insights will require the use of both approaches.*

FINANCIAL LITERACY AND ACTIVE MANAGEMENT

As Muller and Weber (2010) note, the lack of investor financial sophistication might explain the strong growth in actively managed equity mutual funds. Some 85 percent of fund assets are actively managed. However, even the most sophisticated investors overwhelmingly invest in actively managed funds. The "smart money effect" argues that superior selection abilities provide a reason to invest in actively managed funds. However, there is only weak evidence of superior fund selection abilities among financially literate investors. Thus, the lack of financially literate investors cannot explain the growth in actively managed funds. Haslem (2010b) discusses overconfident sophisticated investors.

In general, mutual fund investors appear unaware of mutual fund risks and returns, especially for actively managed funds. Financial knowledge among investors appears limited among most investors and financial literacy is likely the key to understanding fund investing. Unsophisticated investors appear unaware that investing in actively managed funds is a failed strategy and therefore they often depend on fund advertising to make fund choices.

Muller and Weber (2010) analyze whether higher levels of financial literacy coincide with improved fund selections and whether literacy affects the tendency to invest in actively managed funds rather than lower-cost index funds. They use data from an online sample of 3,000 German mutual fund investors in the analysis. The participants have a wide range of financial literacy. Participant self-assessed financial knowledge is significantly and positively related to financial literacy test scores.

Financial Literacy Associations

Mutual fund investors who are highly financially literate have numerous attributes and implications: (1) They engage in some passive (index) investing, but primarily invest in actively managed funds; (2) they have lower future performance (alphas); (3) they engage in choices unrelated to performance differences; (4) they have lower risk-adjusted returns; (5) they have lower front-end loads; (6) they are less likely to misjudge risk; (7) they engage in choices unrelated to management fees; (8) they have more accurate estimates of fund fees; (9) they engage in choices unrelated to growth in actively managed funds; (10) they are overconfident in their ability to identify outperforming funds; (11) they do not choose funds with higher performance and significantly lower fees; (12) they make choices that may reflect portfolio concentration, excess trading, and home bias; (13) they are less likely to choose traditional broker channels; and (14) they choose brokers who are less likely to sell actively managed funds.

Literacy and Active versus Passive Funds

Mutual fund investors with high financial literacy favor actively managed funds. These investors are aware of lower cost exchange traded funds (ETFs) and index funds, but they do not invest in them. They are confident in their fund selection skills and overwhelmingly choose actively managed funds. Haslem, Baker, and Smith (2006, 2008) discuss the performance of index and actively managed funds.

Smart Money Effect

Muller and Weber (2010) discuss the smart money effect whereby investors with high financial literacy: (1) invest in higher performing actively managed mutual funds; (2) fail to choose higher performing funds that outperform the market; (3) engage in fund choices that, except for the first year, do not significantly differ in performance and decline over time; (4) have small short-lived selection skills; (5) choose funds by chasing fund performance; and (6) are overconfident in their ability to select higher performing funds. They find that the smart money investor spends "dumb money" in choosing actively managed funds.

Financial Literacy and Expenses

Muller and Webber (2010) find mutual fund investors with high financial literacy make numerous choices with respect to loads and expenses. They: (1) are more likely to purchase funds with lower loads; (2) are more likely to purchase index funds: (3) are more likely to receive load discounts on large purchases; (4) make more precise estimates of management fees; (4) do not choose low-cost funds; (5) make choices unrelated to future performance; (6) are less likely to use more costly broker distribution; and (7) are more likely to select lower-cost funds online.

Financial Literacy and Returns

As Muller and Webber (2010) note, mutual fund investors with higher financial literacy and incorrect performance perceptions have: (1) unrealistic perceptions of portfolio manager ability to generate high returns with low risks (inverse relationship between risk and return); (2) overly optimistic memories of past fund performance; and (3) biased views of past performance that impede investors learning how to choose higher performing funds.

Muller and Weber (2010, p. 142) find the following:

> The results suggest that financial literacy in not related to mutual fund selection skill [and] . . . any fund selection skills among sophisticated respondents are minor and short-lived at best. . . . Overconfidence is a possible explanation for why even sophisticated participants mostly select active funds. There is a strong positive relation between financial literacy and better-than-average thinking [self-assessed investment skills]. Hence, . . . investors with higher financial literacy scores believe themselves to be better than average in their mutual fund choices. Apparently they are not.

Haslem (2010b) describes highly financially literate mutual fund investors as "The Wizards of Overconfidence," while investors with low financial literacy depend on funds described as "The Wizards of Advertising."

PRICE AND PERFORMANCE SENSITIVITY AND REPRICING

Navone (2012) finds a negative relationship between mutual fund past performance (service quality) and expense ratios (price). Performance-sensitive investors hold high quality funds and performance-insensitive investors hold low quality funds. The negative relationship between past performance and expense ratios arises from a rational policy where investment-insensitive investors are charged higher prices. Haslem (2013c) discusses pricing in imperfect fund markets.

Mutual fund investors apparently do not consider expense ratios as a component of net returns. The investment process indicates that investors consider past performance and expenses separately. The importance investors assign to each component varies according to gender, income, and education. Moreover, if search costs and information availability affect how investors react to past performance, an even stronger impact has to be expected on investor sensitivity to expenses, which are more difficult to find than past performance. Haslem, Baker, and Smith (2007) discuss fund performance relative to expenses.

Navone (2012) states mutual fund pricing decisions are analyzed as a strategic investor response to expenses measured in conjunction with investor sensitivity to past performance. The two sensitivities differ in time series and cross-section, and several major differences are found.

While investor performance sensitivity increases monotonically with past performance, price sensitivity does not. Investor price sensitivity increases with past performance in the lower portion of the fund performance ranking, but decreases in the upper portion. For funds in the lower portion of the ranking, investor flows become more sensitive to past performance and also to expense ratios. However, for funds in the upper portion, an increase in investor performance sensitivity is met by a decline in the sensitivity of investor flows to expenses known as the "distraction effect." When funds do well, investors appear to forget about expenses, as if distracted by perceived management ability and relative expected returns.

Search costs and mutual fund visibility affect investor performance and expense sensitivity differently. Investor flows of funds with lower search costs (larger and older funds and major fund management companies) are, *ceteris paribus*, less sensitive to past performance and more sensitive to expenses. This difference is explained by greater availability of information on past fund performance. Investors appear to rely heavily on easy to find data when search costs are high and on hard to come by data only for highly visible funds.

Navone (2012) finds investor flow sensitivities differ for past mutual fund performance and expenses. As found in specialized information providers, fund expenses steadily increased from 1986 to 2006, which indicates an increasing relevance in the decision process. Analysis of changes in mutual fund expense ratios (repricing decisions) in response to changes in investor sensitivity to performance and expenses shows funds strategically time their repricing decisions to optimize the effect on investor flows. As Navone notes, a decline in expected sensitivity of investor flows to past performance and expenses is associated with higher subsequent changes in expense ratios, even after controlling for changes in fund size that could result in a diminished effect of fund fixed costs. The opportunistic nature of this repricing behavior is confirmed by the fact that it appears to be stronger for funds with lower Morningstar Stewardship Grades. Haslem (2013a) discusses Morningstar ratings and grades.

Mutual fund flows cannot be fully explained by investor sensitivity to performance. While performance sensitivity increases with past fund performance, sensitivity to expense ratios does not. Investors who buy funds with high past performance appear distracted and pay little attention to prices. Investor price sensitivity increases with fund visibility, while performance sensitivity declines. Although no visible trend occurs in investor performance sensitivity, price sensitivity has increased with more availability of information for retail investors.

Navone (2012, p. 1302) concludes the discussion as follows:

> [I]nvestment companies strategically time their repricing decisions in order
> to exploit time variations in price and performance sensitivities: Increases
> in expense ratios are positively correlated with decreases in the expected

sensitivity of investment flows to both performance and prices. The opportunistic nature of this behavior is confirmed by the fact that the repricing policies of mutual funds with high-quality governance are less aggressive.

SENTIMENT CONTRARIAN BEHAVIOR AND ACTUAL PERFORMANCE

According to Massa and Yadav (2012), behavioral finance shows that sentiment affects stock prices. In the absence of arbitrage that corrects mispriced stocks, a broad wave of sentiment is predicted to have cross-sectional affects that vary across stocks. When investor sentiment is high, the prices of high-sentiment stocks (i.e., high sentiment loadings) are inflated and subsequent returns are lower. When sentiment is low, prices of high-sentiment stocks are lower than they should be and returns are higher. However, the effect of sentiment is not symmetrical. That is, while high sentiment stocks have higher returns after periods of low sentiment, they underperform relatively more after periods of high sentiment. This behavior provides fund managers with the opportunity to increase performance by investing primarily in low sentiment stocks, which is so-called sentiment contrarian behavior (SCB).

Consistent loading on low-sentiment stocks should greatly outperform when market sentiment is high and does not differ significantly when market sentiment is low. This strategy would be more efficient if the mutual fund manager could identify the degree of sentiment loading (high or low) on stocks and predict the degree of market sentiment. Fund managers are likely to be able to do this as fund inflows provide information to determine which stocks (high sentiment stocks) are more sensitive to market sentiment.

However, sentiment is also a source of risk that is priced in cross-sectional stock returns. That being the case, a sentiment strategy implies a high loading of risk that mutual fund managers can exploit. Does this strategy provide high gross-of-sentiment risk performance? The performance hypothesis states active and informed fund managers use sentiment strategies to generate higher performance for investors. Massa and Yadav's (2012) camouflage hypothesis states fund managers load up on sentiment risk and provide higher returns hidden as performance. Sentiment risk is related to the overall mood of investors in the market, which means investors are less aware of or less sensitive to the risk. Investors react positively to higher returns generated by the sentiment strategy even if they are only compensation for higher risk.

Massa and Yadav (2012) find that sample stocks are not consistently either high- or low-sentiment, but alternate smoothly and predictably. Stocks in the top quintile of positive loading on sentiment have a 61 percent probability of remaining in the top quintile for the next 12 months. The authors find each fund's loading on sentiment by aggregating its holdings and then ranking funds by how negatively they load on sentiment. Once they identify funds by the SCB, they use the information to explain fund performance.

The findings reflect a strong positive relationship between mutual fund SCB and performance. High (first quintile) SCB funds outperform low (fifth quintile) SCB funds, even controlling for standard risk factors and fund characteristics. High SCB funds outperform low SCB funds by 36 basis points (bps) in raw returns per month, 31 bps in four-factor alphas using excess returns, and 19 bps in four-factor alphas using net-of-style adjusted returns. These results are confirmed in multivariate analysis that controls for fund and family characteristics using numerous performance measures. High SCB funds have higher alphas than low SCB funds in the following 12 months.

Massa and Yadav's (2012) study offers several related findings: (1) SCB performance is not related to portfolio liquidity; (2) SCB is not the outcome of passive or conventional strategies; (3) SCB is negatively related to R^2 and these funds follow more idiosyncratic strategies; (4) high SCB funds time the level of market sentiment and invest in low sentiment stocks when market sentiment is high; and (5) loadings on sentiment betas are insignificant when market sentiment is low and become very significant when sentiment is high.

The authors test sentiment risk to determine whether SCB funds generate higher performance (performance hypothesis) or just higher risk (camouflage hypothesis). In the first case, higher SCB produces higher net-of-standard-risk performance. However, SCB may be the result of a deliberate loading on a different risk: sentiment risk. Therefore, Massa and Yadav (2012) determine whether the higher returns of high SCB funds are due to performance or represent compensation for the risk of investing in low sentiment beta stocks when market sentiment is high. The results show that high SCB funds do not outperform low SCB funds if the nonlinear loading on sentiment risk is controlled. That is, the effect of sentiment loading on performance is nonlinear in sentiment, and once controlled no cross-sectional difference in returns occurs across different SCB funds.

For the SCB strategy to be successful, the market cannot recognize sentiment risk and compensates sentiment risk as a type of performance. Massa and Yadav (2012) test this condition by relating fund flows to performance, and reporting performance net of four-factor alphas and that performance representing sentiment risk. Analysis of the convex relationship of performance to flows separately identifies the portion due to sentiment exposure and permits assessment of whether investors perceive it as performance or risk exposure. The evidence shows that investors react to sentiment exposure as if it were simply performance. Investors react in a nonlinear way in which higher sentiment exposure is interpreted as higher performance that leads to more fund inflows. The flow-performance sensitivity that corresponds to SCB-generated performance is approximately one half the performance of the five-factor alpha model. This evidence supports for the camouflage hypothesis.

The findings also provide evidence of (1) fund risk-taking behavior in the presence of investors with scarce information ability; (2) mutual fund manager portfolio "window dressing"; (3) more performance persistence in large fund families due to unequal resource allocation; (4) a link between sentiment strategies and family affiliation due to detailed information about sentiment and its use in marketing; (5) why fund managers do not take advantage of sentiment by arbitraging away the abnormal profits it creates; and (6) structural/organizational factors preventing fund managers from taking advantage of information from investor trades to increase performance, which reduces potential agency conflict.

Overall Findings

Massa and Yadav (2012) test two hypotheses to determine whether mutual funds exploit market sentiment. The first hypothesis states active and more informed fund managers engage in sentiment strategies to provide higher performance, net of risk.

The camouflage strategy states mutual funds load up on sentiment risk to provide higher risk returns disguised as performance. Sentiment risk is related to the mood of the market, but investors are less aware of this risk.

Massa and Yadav's (2012) findings show that high SCB mutual funds outperform low SCB, funds, even after controlling for standard risk measures and fund characteristics. The SCB effect is large and stronger when first of the month market sentiment is high. The effect is also persistent and unrelated to portfolio illiquidity. The SCB-performance relationship is partly due to a passive negative loading on the market. Mutual funds with higher SCB are more informed and use more idiosyncratic strategies, not conventional or passive, that follow from deliberate active choices. High SCB mutual funds load negatively on sentiment when market sentiment is high, betting on reversal. These funds time the level of market sentiment and invest in low sentiment beta stocks when market sentiment is high.

Do SCB mutual funds generate higher performance or just higher risk (camouflage hypothesis)? Does the higher return of high SCB funds represent real performance or just compensation for the risk of investing in low sentiment beta stocks when market sentiment is high? High SCB funds do not outperform low SCB funds if the nonlinear loading on sentiment risk is controlled.

This strategy is successful because the market does not recognize the existence of sentiment risk and compensates sentiment-risk taking as a kind of performance. This result is shown by relating fund flows to performance and separately reporting performance net of four-factor alphas and the part of performance due to sentiment risk.

Massa and Yadav (2012, p. 26) conclude the discussion as follows:

> These findings show that some fund managers cleverly exploit the sentiment risk in the market to load up investors with risk exploiting investors' inability to identify sentiment risk. . . . This strategy is successful because the market does not recognize the existence of a sentiment risk and remunerates sentiment-risk taking as a sort of performance.

SUMMARY

This chapter reviews important interactions between mutual funds and individual investors in choosing equity mutual funds. It answers several questions related to this subject that have yet to be completely resolved, but which reflect sound findings toward this goal. Actively managed funds spend large amounts on advertising because they find that it works in increasing assets under management. Advertising affects investor choices because investors are often unsophisticated and uninformed, with low financial literacy. Many investors focus on past fund performance on the mistaken assumption that high past returns predict future returns. Persistence in high fund performance results more frequently from luck than from skillful portfolio managers. Investors often choose funds that attract their attention with high performance, but also by advertising and marketing. Any negative effect of expenses on fund flows is more than offset by spending the money on marketing.

A combination of cognition and emotions determines investor fund choices. Advertising can affect these choices by arousing positive emotions that make investor attitudes toward funds more positive even if it provides little direct information.

Advertising motivates investors toward funds with higher expenses and more risk. Persuasion is advertising communication designed to influence investor fund choices. This advertising is based on the behavioral model that applies factual or spurious financial information designed to match prevailing investor beliefs—investors get what they want. Highly educated investors who are more wealthy males make poorer fund choices. Such investors give less attention to fund expenses and overweight front-end loads, are more biased in assessing fee structures, and give more weight to past fund performance. Investor knowledge of finance contributes little to making more profitable fund choices.

Affect refers to investor responses to emotional stimuli that change fund choices by modifying risk preferences or beliefs. Affect provides a framework for explaining deviations from rational choices due to behavioral biases. Positive emotions cause investors to be more confident and take on more risk. Negative emotions have the opposite effect. Investors update beliefs to maintain positive affect and to avoid negative affect by taking account of new information at odds with prior choices.

Neurofinance focuses on the gap between the rationality of efficient markets (standard finance) and market reality (behavioral finance). Behavioral finance finds that autonomic responses beyond human consciousness often drive investor decisions. Investors with high financial literacy are confident in their fund selection skills and primarily choose actively managed funds. The smart money effect states these investors select high performing actively managed funds. However, these investors do not select higher performing funds, but rather are overconfident in their abilities and pursue past fund performance.

Fund flows cannot be fully explained by investor sensitivity to performance. While investor sensitivity to performance increases with past fund performance, sensitivity to prices (expense ratios) does not. Investors who buy funds with high past performance appear "distracted" and pay little attention to prices. Investor sensitivity to prices increases with fund visibility, while investor sensitivity to performance declines. Funds strategically time repricing decisions to exploit time variations in investor sensitivity to prices and performance. A decline in expected sensitivity of investor flows to both past fund performance and prices is associated with subsequent fund increases in prices.

Behavioral finance indicates that investor sentiment affects stock prices but its cross-sectional affect varies. If investor sentiment is high, prices of high-sentiment stocks (high sentiment loadings) are inflated and subsequent returns are lower. If sentiment is low, prices of high-sentiment stocks are lower than they should be and subsequent returns are higher. Stocks with high sentiment have higher returns following periods of low sentiment, and they underperform relatively more after periods of high sentiment. This so-called sentiment contrarian behavior provides fund managers with the opportunity to increase performance by investing primarily in low sentiment stocks.

Sentiment is also a source of risk that is priced in cross-sectional stock returns. In this case, a sentiment strategy implies a high loading of risk that can be exploited by mutual fund managers. The camouflage hypothesis holds that fund managers load up on sentiment risk and provide higher risk returns hidden as performance. Sentiment risk is related to overall investor mood in the market, which means investors are less aware or less sensitive to the risk. Investors react positively to the higher returns of sentiment strategy even if they are only compensated for higher risk.

DISCUSSION QUESTIONS

1. What is behavioral persuasion in advertising designed to do?
2. Explain why affect refers to investor emotions that change fund choices.
3. Explain the focus of behavioral finance.
4. Explain why financial literacy is likely key to understanding investing.
5. Explain why fund pricing decisions are a strategic response to investor sensitivity to expenses in conjunction with their sensitivity to past performance.
6. Why do mutual funds follow a "camouflage strategy" that loads up on sentiment risk that investors interpret as real performance?

REFERENCES

Baker, H. Kent, and John A. Haslem. 1973. "Information Needs of Individual Investors." *Journal of Accountancy* 136:November, 64–69.

Baker, H. Kent, and John A. Haslem. 1974a. "The Impact of Investor Socio-Economic Characteristics on Risk and Return Preferences." *Journal of Business Research* 2:4, 469–476.

Baker, H. Kent, and John A. Haslem. 1974b. "Toward the Development of Client-Specified Valuation Models." *Journal of Finance* 29:4, 1255–1263.

Baker, H. Kent, Michael B. Hargrove, and John A. Haslem. 1977. "An Empirical Analysis of the Risk and Return Preferences of Individual Investors." *Journal of Financial and Quantitative Analysis* 12:3, 377–389.

Barber, Brad R., Terrance Odean, and Lu Zheng. 2005. "Out of Sight, Out of Mind: The Effects of Expenses on Mutual Fund Flows." *Journal of Business* 78:6, 2095–2119.

Barras, Laurent, Olivier Scaillet, and Russ Wermers. 2010. "False Discoveries in Mutual Fund Performance: Measuring Luck in Estimated Alphas." *Journal of Finance* 65:1, 179–216.

Cronqvist, Henrik. 2006. "Advertising and Portfolio Choice." Working Paper, Social Science Research Network. Available at http://ssrn.com/abstract=920693.

Haslem, John A. 2003. *Mutual Funds: Risk and Performance Analysis for Decision Making.* Oxford, UK: Blackwell Publishing.

Haslem, John A. 2008. "An Idea Whose Time Has Come." *Journal of Indexes* 11:3, 42–45, 47.

Haslem, John A. 2009. "Investor Learning and Mutual Fund Advertising and Distribution Fees." *Journal of Investing* 18:4, 53–56.

Haslem, John A., ed. 2010a. *Mutual Funds: Portfolio Structures, Analysis, Management, and Stewardship.* Hoboken, NJ: John Wiley & Sons.

Haslem, John A. 2010b. "Mutual Funds and Investor Choice." *Journal of Indexes* 16:6, 42–44, 58.

Haslem, John A. 2010c. "Why Does Mutual Fund Advertising Work? Some Complementary Evidence." *Journal of Index Investing* 1:1, 55–60.

Haslem, John A. 2011a. "Issues in Mutual Fund Soft-Dollar Trades." *Journal of Index Investing* 2:2, 76–85.

Haslem, John A. 2011b. "Mutual Funds: Advertising, Behavioral Models, and Investor Choice." *Journal of Index Investing* 1:4, 12–17.

Haslem, John A. 2012a. "Issues in Mutual Fund Revenue Sharing Payments." *Journal of Index Investing* 3:1, 52–57.

Haslem, John A. 2012b. "Mutual Fund Total Cost Construct." *Journal of Index Investing* 3:3, 27–33.

Haslem, John A. 2013a. "Identifying Stewardship Mutual Funds for Individual Investors." *Journal of Investing* 22:1, 104–111.

Haslem, John A. 2013b. "Issues in Mutual Fund Distribution." Working Paper, Social Science Research Network. Available at http://ssrn.com/abstract=2070112.

Haslem, John A. 2013c. "Mutual Fund Markets are Imperfectly Competitive." *Journal of Index Investing* 4:1, 32–42.

Haslem, John A., H. Kent Baker, and David M. Smith. 2006. "Are Retail S&P 500 Index Funds a Financial Commodity? Insights for Investors." *Financial Services Review* 15:2, 99–116.

Haslem, John A., H. Kent Baker, and David M. Smith. 2007. "Identification and Performance of Equity Mutual Funds with High Management Fees and Expense Ratios." *Journal of Investing* 16:2, 32–51.

Haslem, John A., H. Kent Baker, and David M. Smith. 2008. "Performance and Characteristics of Actively Managed Retail Equity Mutual Funds with Diverse Expense Ratios." *Financial Services Review* 17:1, 49–68.

Kuhnen, Camelia M., and Brian Knutson. 2011. "The Influence of Affect on Beliefs, Preferences and Financial Decisions." *Journal of Financial and Quantitative Analysis* 46:3, 605–626.

Massa, Massimo, and Vijay Yadav. 2012. "Do Mutual Funds Play Sentiment?" Working Paper, Social Science Research Network. Available at http://ssrn.com/abstract=2023642.

Mullainathan, Sendhil, and Andrei Shleifer. 2006. "Persuasion in Finance." Working Paper, Social Science Research Network. Available at http://ssrn.com/abstract=864686.

Muller, Sebastian, and Martin Weber. 2010. "Financial Literacy and Mutual Fund Investments: Who Buys Actively Managed Funds?" *Schmalenbach Business Review* 62:April, 125–153.

Navone, Marco. 2012. "Investors' Distraction and Strategic Repricing Decisions." *Journal of Banking and Finance* 36:5, 1291–1303.

Palmiter, Alan R., and Ahmed E. Taha. 2011. "Mutual Fund Performance Advertising: Inherently and Materially Misleading?" *Georgia Law Review* 46:2, 1–48.

Sapra, Steven G., and Paul J. Zak. 2009. "Neurofinance: Bridging Psychology, Neurology, and Investor Behavior." Working Paper, Social Science Research Network. Available at http://ssrn.com/abstract=1323051.

Shiller, Robert J. 2006. "Tools for Financial Revolution: Neoclassical versus Behavioral Finance." *Financial Review* 41:1, 1–8.

Soe, Aye, and Frank Luo. 2012. "Does Past Performance Persist?" *S&P Indexes, S&P Persistence Scorecard*. Working Paper, Social Science Research Network. Available at http://ssrn.com/abstract=2079822.

Wilcox, Ronald T. 2003. "Bargain Hunting or Star Gazing? Investors' Preferences for Stock Mutual Funds." *Journal of Business* 76:4, 645–663.

ABOUT THE AUTHOR

John A. Haslem is Professor Emeritus of Finance in the Robert H. Smith School of Business at the University of Maryland. He served as a founding academic affairs dean and founding chair of the finance department. He was awarded the Panhellenic Association's "Outstanding Teacher Award" for his first of a kind mutual funds course. Professor Haslem studied at Duke University, Harvard University, and the University of North Carolina, and taught at the University of North Carolina and University of Wisconsin. His research has appeared in the *Journal of Finance, Journal of Business, Journal of Financial and Quantitative Analysis, Journal of Money, Credit and Banking, Journal of Business Research*, and *Financial Analysts Journal* among others. He has contributed to six books including *Mutual Funds: Risk and Performance Analysis for Decision Making* and *Mutual Funds: Portfolio Structures: Analysis, Management, and Stewardship*. Professor Haslem has served as a consultant to the U.S. Department of Justice, NASA Goddard Space Flight Center, law firms, investors, and corporations.

CHAPTER 30

Real Estate Investment Decision-Making in Behavioral Finance

Eli Beracha
Assistant Professor of Real Estate and Finance, University of Wyoming
Hilla Skiba
Assistant Professor of Finance, University of Wyoming

INTRODUCTION

The real estate market shares several psychological biases with traditional financial markets. Combining these behavioral biases with severe limits to arbitrage that include the illiquid aspects of the market, high transaction costs, and short sale restrictions often magnify the effect of cognitive and emotional issues on real estate valuations. As a result, real estate prices in the short and medium run often diverge from their fundamental values and market price adjustments are gradual. This is particularly noticeable in the residential real estate market where most participants are inexperienced, unsophisticated investors and driven by financial, emotional, and personal motives.

Irrational behavior of real estate market participants was partly a driving force behind the residential real estate boom and bust cycle that occurred during the first decade of this millennium. Because this cycle has had severe negative effects on both the United States and the global economy, it serves as a reminder of the widespread economic consequences that aggregated irrationality by real estate market participants can cause.

This chapter focuses on established psychological attributes in residential and commercial real estate and in real estate investment trusts (REITs) and has the following organization. The first section discusses the importance of the real estate market and the links between this market and the overall economy and financial markets. The next section discusses specific limitations to arbitrage (e.g., illiquidity, uniqueness of the properties, and short sale constraints) and then reviews common micro-level biases that influence individual decision-making including overconfidence, slow reaction to information, mental accounting, familiarity, anchoring, loss aversion, and ownership bias. This section also discusses how these behavioral tendencies manifest themselves specifically in real estate markets. The third section reviews why macro-level biases largely drive the documented phenomena in the real estate markets. These three market-related phenomena are momentum in real estate returns, real estate bubbles, and the real estate price overreactions. Specifically, this section discusses the recent bubble and correction that took place between 2000 and 2012. The final section offers a summary and conclusions.

THE REAL ESTATE MARKET AND THE GENERAL ECONOMY

The value of the primary residence represents the largest component of the net worth for most U.S. homeowners and those in most of the developed countries around the world. Regardless of whether an increase in housing wealth increases utility, home values affects many households' financial decisions. For example, homeowners who witness a rapid price appreciation in the value of their home are likely to feel better about their financial situation and spend their disposable income more freely than they otherwise would (Campbell and Cocco 2005). Because consumer spending is a major driver of gross domestic product (GDP) growth, in aggregation, the performance of the housing market has a material effect on the growth of GDP around the world. For example, Case, Quigley, and Shiller (2005) show that the effect of housing wealth on consumer spending is greater than the effect of wealth created by the stock market. They partially attribute this to the public perception that housing wealth is more permanent relative to stock market wealth.

The effect of the real estate market on the U.S. economy became even more pronounced as recent innovations in the financial markets introduced products, such as the home equity line of credit (HELOC) and low cost refinancing that allow homeowners to access their home equity more quickly and cheaply. With these products (combined with careless actions by some financial institutions), homeowners can easily convert increases in the value of their residence into spendable cash by borrowing money against the value of their home. As a result, during the housing boom of the early 2000s, many homeowners in states such as California, Florida, and Nevada could borrow and spend large amounts of money. Moreover, because the general consensus during that period was that housing prices could not decrease, homeowners believed that they could continuously borrow money that they would never have to pay back as long as their houses appreciated faster than the rate of interest. These unsustainable housing market conditions propelled a surge in consumer spending that supported a seemingly healthy U.S. GDP growth.

Just as rapid appreciation of the value of homes infused spending in the United States, the sharp decline in home prices that started in 2007 triggered a substantial decrease in spending that was a main driver of the "Great Recession." The decrease in spending resulted from the wealth destruction caused by lower home valuations combined with the reintroduction of borrowing constraints to many American households as home equity disappeared in many homes across the United States. Although states experiencing a more rapid decline in home values were affected to a larger extent, the impact of declining home values was widespread.

REAL ESTATE MARKET AND FINANCIAL MARKET

Many individuals have a direct financial exposure to the real estate market (mainly through their home) and to the traditional financial markets. This implies that the expected performance and volatility of one market may influence individuals' investment behavior and their decisions with respect to asset allocation. Cocco (2005) finds a generally negative relationship between households' investments in housing and their investments in financial markets. This is particularly true for younger and poorer households with limited total financial wealth. Cocco also maintains that homeowners seek a degree of total level of risk exposure for their financial nest egg. As a result, higher volatility in home prices causes homeowners to invest a smaller portion of their wealth in the stock market, which some view as riskier than the housing market.

The initial down payment that homeowners make when they purchase their home also affects their attitude toward the risk associated with the real estate portion of their portfolio. Homeowners who purchase their home with little or no money down do not have "skin in the game" because in most cases they are not liable for any negative equity that may result from a reduction in the value of their home (Ben-David 2012). In these cases, homeowners face an asymmetric outcome where they would benefit from an appreciation in their home value, but will not suffer when their home depreciates. Rational participants who face a "heads I win, tails you lose" scenario are likely to make larger and riskier bets than they otherwise would. During the early 2000s, lenders only required little or no down payment from potential homeowners and this arguably helped to facilitate a greater appetite for real estate risk exposure.

Prices of both financial and real assets should reflect general strong economic growth. Evidence also shows a feedback loop between the performance of financial assets and the housing market at the local level. Anderson and Beracha (2012) illustrate that the performance of companies' stocks headquartered in a particular city have a material effect on home values located in the same city. The effect is most noticeable for homes located in the more expensive areas of the city, which are likely to be the areas where executives (those that may have the most exposure to financial markets) choose to reside.

INEFFICIENCIES AND THE REAL ESTATE MARKETS

According to Ritter (2003) the two building blocks of behavioral finance are (1) limits to arbitrage and (2) cognitive psychology. Limits to arbitrage refer to the difficulty of buying or selling a financial asset and this may make arbitraging misvaluations difficult. Evidence indicates that due to both behavioral biases and limits to arbitrage, traditional financial markets, such as the stock market, are not fully efficient. Examples of large misvaluations include historic events such as the Japanese stock price bubble in the 1980s, the October 1987 market crash, and the technology bubble of 1999–2000. Because the real estate market is especially prone to both limits to arbitrage and behavioral biases, it displays a greater level of price inefficiencies compared to the stock market. Several authors find that the real estate market historically has not been efficient and that investors can earn abnormal returns in the long run. For example, Coyne, Goulet, and Picconi (1980) document consistent outperformance of real estate over stocks and bonds on a risk-adjusted basis. Several authors, including Case and Shiller (1989, 1990) also report predictability in the home prices.

The following sections discuss how the real estate market displays the two building blocks of behavioral finance—limits to arbitrage and psychological biases—and review the related real state literature.

Limits to Arbitrage

The real estate market exhibits severe limits to arbitrage including illiquidity of the asset, high transaction costs, uniqueness and indivisibility, and severe constraints to short sales. This section reviews the specific characteristics of the real estate market that limit arbitrage.

Illiquidity and High Transaction Costs   Under normal market conditions, residential real estate is on the market for weeks or even months before a seller accepts an offer. Commercial real estate properties, particularly those with unique characteristics, are available for even longer before they sell. Because the seller often hires a professional agent to help market the property, the cost of real estate transactions that the seller incurs is substantial. For example, commissions of 5 to 6 percent of the sell price for residential homes and 2 to 3 percent on larger commercial properties are the general rule rather than the exception. Other monetary expenses such as packing and relocation costs as well as nonmonetary burdens such as hassle and effort can also be substantial.

Due to this long and expensive process, even if a particular real estate owner is aware of the fact that her property is overvalued, she will be reluctant to sell it and move to the sidelines until market prices return to equilibrium. As a result, real estate prices that deviate from equilibrium will take a long time to correct. The illiquidity of the real estate market also affects sellers' decisions about whether to accept an offer that is somewhat below their perceived value of the property. Sellers cannot directly observe the tradable value of their property and do not know when the next offer will come. Therefore, waiting for a higher offer may be a long and costly process that causes some sellers to accept a seemingly low offer.

Uniqueness and Indivisibility   Unlike the stock or the bond market where homogeneity exists, no two real estate properties are identical. This implies that in order for the real estate market to be efficient, millions of unique properties need to be fairly priced, accounting for each property's specific features, characteristics, and condition. Because the seller initially prices each property (the asking price) rather than the collective market forces, this introduces each seller's personal biases about the property. Such biases could be based on personal attachment to the property or the seller's preferences for real estate characteristics. These factors also contribute to price clustering (e.g., sellers price more properties at $200,000 than at their fair value of $198,357), which introduces price inefficiencies. Finally, because buyers typically cannot acquire a portion of a property, those who are looking for a property in a particular price range will not bid on a more expensive property even if they strongly believe that it represents a good market value. The same concept also applies for buyers with a high price range who by luck or skill identify undervalued properties priced well below their price range.

Short Sale Constraints   When real estate prices deviate from their fundamental values, market participants have difficulty forcing prices back to equilibrium. This is because short selling in the real estate market is not feasible. Similarly, simultaneous buying and selling of similar properties in different markets in order to benefit from price imprecision is expensive and nearly impossible to execute. Due to these short sale constraints, even if some real estate market participants realize that prices deviate from fundaments in a large way, their ability to benefit from the situation is limited. This increases the likelihood that prices will stay in disequilibrium for extended periods as pessimistic investors choose not to participate in the market. While real estate futures on a few housing markets are currently available for trading on the Chicago Board Options Exchange (CBOE), these futures are still subject to a very thin market and therefore cannot effectively address the real estate short sale constraint.

Psychological Biases

This section reviews common micro-level biases that influence individual decision-making specifically in real estate transactions. These biases include overconfidence, slow reaction to information, mental accounting, familiarity, anchoring, loss aversion, and ownership bias. The section also gives examples of behavioral biases in real estate markets.

Inexperienced Participants and Overconfidence   The majority of the participants in the residential real estate market and even a large portion of commercial real estate investors are novice or unsophisticated investors. This implies that most real estate participants have limited experience and lack knowledge about buying and selling real estate. Worzala, Sirmans, and Zietz (2000) survey pension fund and large insurance companies' fund managers on their risk/return assumptions about different investment alternatives including REITs. The survey results show that both types of investors assume a low risk/high expected return for familiar asset classes. Both investor classes are also less familiar with real estate investment and assign high risk/low expected return.

Behavioral finance documents that experience and overconfidence are negatively related so that the more experience investors gain, the less subject to overconfidence bias they become (Gervais and Odean 2001). More experienced investors can understand their own abilities better, whereas inexperienced participants often suffer from overconfidence and overly weight their own (limited) past experience rather than a larger and more inclusive sample. As Gervais and Odean show, inexperienced participants are also more inclined to make unwise investment decisions and to attribute their success to skill and their failure to bad luck. The authors also show that individual investors are more overconfident in their abilities compared with institutional investors. In an experimental study, Bloomfield, Libby, and Nelson (1999) show that less informed investors are more overconfident compared with their more informed counterparts.

In the context of real estate, an inexperienced individual who, for example, has recently sold her property for a large nominal profit compared with the purchase price, is likely to display a high level of confidence when searching for her next real estate property. As a result, she is likely to overpay for that property or reject an attractive potential investment opportunity. As previously discussed, experienced institutional investors in the real estate market, especially for residential real estate, are largely absent. Consequently, the pool of buyers and sellers is more likely to suffer from overconfidence than the pool of investors in the stock market.

Wang et al. (2000) study overconfidence in real estate markets from the perspective of builders. They find that overconfidence is related to overbuilding during bull markets and general volatility in some Asian real estate markets. The unique characteristic of many Asian real estate markets is that builders can sell units in developments before completion. The authors use this pre-sale market as a private signal to the developer that may fuel overconfidence and overbuilding.

Conservatism Bias and Slow Reaction to Information Because real estate sellers and buyers typically do not adjust their reservation price based on the constant arrival of new economic data, they are subject to conservatism bias. Conservatism bias leads investors to underweight new information and to be slow to change their beliefs about an asset. For example, when the Federal Reserve announces an unexpected change of the discount rate or when the number of jobs created in the market during a particular period is different than anticipated, real estate participants do not modify their asking or reservation prices instantaneously. While new economic data eventually will have an effect on real estate transactions, the effect is often slow and gradual, unlike the immediate effect that similar information has on stock and bond prices. This phenomenon allows real estate participants who are aware of the eventual effect of current economic data to take advantage of the current prices that are yet to reflect this new information.

Mental Accounting Behavioral studies such as Thaler (1985, 1999) document that investors tend to consider their assets separately rather than jointly and fail to see interactions between different asset classes. Financial economists often consider real estate and stock market investment and labor income as separate investment decisions. Mental accounting can lead to heavily locally biased portfolios, where labor income, stock market wealth, and real estate are all heavily dependent on local factors. Similarly, mental accounting may alter investors' decisions about whether to sell or buy a particular asset included in their portfolio, regardless of the expected performance of any or all other assets. Mental accounting is especially prevalent with regard to real estate because real estate often represents a large share of the wealth and many also attach a subjective and sentimental value to this portion of their portfolio.

Information and Familiarity Many investors in the traditional financial markets have access to all publicly available information on a particular stock or bond. Due to recent technological advances, such information is easily and timely accessible via the Internet regardless of the investor's physical location. Consequently, all stock and bond investors can simultaneously evaluate the same information and act accordingly. Yet, even with such information transparency, investors still tend to invest more in securities based in their own country or region (local or home asset bias) and in securities that they are more familiar with (familiarity bias) (French and Poterba 1991; Coval and Moskowitz 1999; Huberman 2001).

In the real estate market, some relevant information about a particular property is publicly unavailable and much of this information is not readily accessible via the Internet. For example, a local real estate agent or a curious neighbor may know more about a particular property that is placed on the market before this information becomes public. Even when the details on a particular property are available via the web, other critical information about the property may not be. How desirable is the neighborhood in which the property is located? What is the quality of the schools surrounding the property? What are the recent dynamics and trends of the housing market in the area? How well has the property been maintained? These are only a few questions that are difficult to answer from a distance and therefore may only be available to local real estate participants. The difficulty of accessing real estate information from a distance only magnifies the already substantial local and familiarity biases that real estate participants display because most of them are reluctant to purchase a property in a distant and unfamiliar location regardless of the opportunities presented by that location. Different local tax and ownership rules as well as the inherently large expenditure that is associated with each single real estate transaction also contribute to investors' real estate local bias.

Garmaise and Moskowitz (2004) study the role of asymmetric information in the real estate markets and document that information barriers are major determinants of buyers' behavior. Market participants solve information barriers by purchasing nearby properties. Uninformed buyers also tend to focus on properties that are easier to value and have longer histories.

False Reference Points, Anchoring, and Money Illusion Similar to other financial assets, when real estate owners consider selling their property, some irrelevant false reference points may influence their reservation price. For example, these false reference points may include the price they paid for the property, the price their neighboring property previously sold for, or the outstanding balance on their mortgage. Not only are these reference points often irrelevant, but sellers also tend to think about these values in nominal terms and not adjust them for inflation (Stephens and Tyran 2012). This kind of behavior, which the literature refers to as the "money illusion," further reduces the relevance of the typical reference points, especially during periods of high inflation.

Northcraft and Neale (1987) study the anchoring heuristic in a group of students and real estate agents. These researchers ask subjects to make pricing decisions about real estate properties. Consistent with Slovic and Lichtenstein (1971) and Tversky and Kahneman's (1974) seminal work on the anchoring heuristic, Northcraft and Neale predict that an arbitrarily chosen anchor would influence value estimates of real estate prices and that estimates would be insufficiently adjusted away from the reference point. According to the authors, anchoring is relevant to a bargaining setting such as the market for residential real estate, where the fair market value of the property is not objectively determinable and buyers and sellers use a bidding process to arrive at the actual selling price. In their experiment, they find that the initial asking price of a house, which was manipulated among the subjects to be either near or far to the true value of the property, served as an anchor in the buying process, when all the other information about the property and neighborhood was held constant. Also, manipulated listing prices significantly influence the informed real estate professionals in the study.

Lambson, McQueen, and Slade (2004) also document that anchoring bias plays a role in buyers' willingness to pay a premium for a property. First, the authors document that out-of-state buyers (less informed investors) pay a premium for real estate. The higher prices are partially due to higher search costs, but can also be partially explained by anchoring effects. They study investors in the Phoenix real estate market and find that the buyers are influenced by prices of real estate in their home markets that serve as anchors in the decision-making process. Investors from home states that have overall higher price levels in real estate may shorten their search in the out-of-state market and are willing to pay higher prices on the same property compared to the informed local buyers.

Finally, Black and Diaz (1996) and Diaz (2009) document that potential home-buyers often use the property's asking price to estimate its value and that previous estimates by other experts influence the real estate appraisal process. In these studies, the researchers provide participants with different asking prices or appraisal values. These references points greatly influence the opinion of the participants about the property value regardless of their accuracy or relevancy.

Disposition Effect and Loss Aversion Researchers have applied the concept of loss aversion to real estate markets to explain several observed phenomena, including low transaction volumes during trough periods and seller behavior in general. The *disposition effect* and more specifically loss aversion refer to the unwillingness of investors to realize losses, and what at least partially causes investors to hold on to their losing assets for too long. Loss aversion partly explains the documented strong positive correlation between prices of homes and sales volume. According to Genesove and Mayer (2001), sales volume can fall to one half from real estate peak to trough. Also, Stein (1995) documents positive correlation between volume and price level in the United States.

Genesove and Mayer (2001) apply a loss aversion story to the Boston condominium market from 1990 to 1997, during a period of an upswing and a downswing in the prices of the condominiums. According to prospect theory, a seller who is facing a loss is expected to set a higher reservation price than a seller facing an equal size gain on his home. Sellers, whose units' expected selling price has fallen below the original purchase price, set the asking price of their unit higher than others in a magnitude of 25 to 35 percent above the fair market value. The authors also find that owner-occupants suffer from loss aversion more than investors. Consequently, brokers in real estate markets avoid taking on clients who are facing large losses on their homes because of these sellers' unrealistic expectations about the target selling prices.

Seiler et al. (2008) study regret aversion and false reference points in the context of real estate markets. The authors use a survey method to study subjects who evaluate their experience in a real estate transaction on a home that appreciated in price over the study period. They give some subjects hindsight information that the home price peaked at a higher price than the current price. The subjects rate their experience significantly lower when they know that they could have made more money compared to when they did not know the high value of the property, even though the return is exactly the same. The authors also document that demographic differences are significant in regret aversion. Women tend to suffer more regret aversion and U.S. investors are more sensitive to regret aversion than their Asian counterparts. In a related study, Seiler and Seiler (2010) document that in severe market downturns, investors cope with losses in the form of false reference points, which in the long run will cause greater realized regret.

Ownership Bias Theoretically, the decision about whether to buy or rent a home should be purely based on a financial cash flow analysis. According to that theory, an individual looking for a house would compare the present value of future rent payment on a particular property to the present value of all costs associated with purchasing a similar property. The individual should choose the option with the lower present value or be indifferent between buying and renting if the present value of each of these options is similar.

However, in reality the financial comparison between buying and renting is very complex and includes many subjective projections on future events that can substantially affect the decision. Most individuals are unable to fairly compare the financial expected benefits from buying and renting. Behavioral and nonmonetary factors can also influence them when making that decision. Homeownership in the United States is often referred to as the American dream. Purchasing a house can be an emotional event determining where a family will reside for the foreseeable future. Many view homeownership as wealth enhancing, a source of civic pride, and a way to improve self-esteem, prevent crime, and create child development and positive educational outcomes, among other benefits. As a result, about two thirds of U.S. households who own their primary residence are willing to pay a premium for owning rather than renting their residence.

Beracha and Johnson (2012) conduct a comprehensive comparison between buying and renting. Their results reveal that, on average, renting a residence is associated with a monetary benefit over buying one. This monetary benefit appears during the majority of the 32 years included in the analysis and across different locations. While the monetary benefit from renting is counterintuitive to the general population that views homeownership as wealth enhancing, it is consistent with the notion that homeownership is associated with a financial price premium. On average, from a purely monetary perspective, residential real estate appreciated about 2 percent too slow each year in order to justify buying over renting. This implies that, if rational and aware of the cost of ownership, homeowners are willing to pay 2 percent of their home value each year for the nonmonetary benefits associated with homeownership mentioned earlier. Moreover, a cross-sectional examination of the homeownership premium suggests that homeowners are paying the highest premium over renters in areas that experienced the highest price appreciation in the past. This behavior indicates that homeowners are projecting higher future price appreciation for the already most expensive and least affordable areas rather than more rational expectations of a general reversion to the mean.

OBSERVED INEFFICIENCIES IN REAL ESTATE MARKETS

This section reviews three macro-level phenomena in real estate markets that are largely driven by the micro-level behavioral factors already discussed in the previous section. These three phenomena are momentum in returns to real estate, real estate market bubbles, and overreaction of real estate prices. Some maintain that the global financial crisis and the Great Recession that began in 2007 was largely a result of spillover from the real estate market collapse (Shiller 2008). Therefore, understanding the behavioral biases that affect the broad real estate market becomes ever more important.

Momentum in Returns to Real Estate

The financial literature widely documents momentum in asset prices. *Momentum* can be defined as the positive autocorrelation in prices from the previous period to the next, so that last period's winners tend to be the winners of the present period. Researchers find that momentum in real estate relates to many different factors. Some of these factors include illiquidity (Jegadeesh and Titman 2001), high information asymmetry and turnover (Zhang 2006), and short sale constraints (Ali and Trombley 2006). In comparison to stocks, all the factors that relate to momentum are present in the real estate markets and most of them impose stronger constraints on efficiency.

In addition to limits to arbitrage, researchers also document behavioral biases relating to momentum in asset prices. These behavioral factors include investor overconfidence and self-attribution biases (i.e., investors attribute success to their own skill and failures to bad luck), documented in stocks by Daniel, Hirschleifer, and Subrahmanyam (1998) and Chui, Titman, and Wei (2010) among others. As discussed in the previous section on inefficiencies in real estate markets, a unique characteristic of this market is the level of inexperience displayed by the majority of the buyers and sellers.

The market for residential real estate is far from efficient. Rather, it displays high levels of momentum and price predictability from one quarter to the next. Case and Shiller (1989) are the first to point out high levels of autocorrelation in housing prices. They examine housing prices in four major U.S. cities and show that prices tend to follow a similar trend for at least one full year. Beracha and Skiba (2011) extend the analysis to cover all U.S. metropolitan areas. They document that housing momentum is not only statistically significant but also economically meaningful. The authors show that using a simple momentum strategy, based on previous real estate winners and losers, yields nearly 9 percent annually over a 26-year period. The momentum in housing prices is particularly high in the more volatile U.S. real estate markets, mainly in the Northeast and West regions, which are often characterized by an inelastic supply of land. The statistical and economic significance of the autocorrelation in housing price changes is present for seven calendar quarters, on average, which is much longer than the positive autocorrelation in stocks, which remains significant for less than 12 months (Jegadeesh and Titman 1993).

Researchers also document a momentum effect in REITs. Chui, Titman, and Wei (2003) and Brounen (2008) find high levels of positive autocorrelation in U.S. REITs. However, because REITs are in many ways similar to and traded like stocks, the price momentum that they exhibit is less material compared with the momentum in actual residential and commercial real estate markets.

Real Estate Bubbles

Behavioral biases are often present in asset pricing bubbles. This section discusses the real estate market bubble in the United States during the first decade on the new millennium and how behavioral biases relate to the severe overvaluation of houses.

Exhibit 30.1 displays the housing price index in real terms from 1890 to 2012. Despite a few periods of major price decreases (e.g., during the Great Depression) and increases (after World War II), the real cumulative home price appreciation during the 110 years spanning 1890 to 1999 was practically zero. Then, during the 7-year period beginning in the year 2000, home prices rose sharply and roughly doubled in real terms.

Shiller (2007) discusses the boom in housing prices in the 2000s and the consequences of these high prices to the future housing prices and the economy. As early

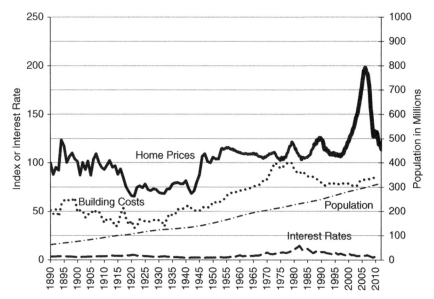

EXHIBIT 30.1 Home Prices in the United States: 1890 to 2012

Note: The exhibit shows home price index in the United States from 1890 to 2012 in real terms with a base value of 100. The exhibit also shows the U.S. population in millions, building costs in real terms, and the nominal interest rate. All data are in annual terms.

Source: Schiller (2005). Printed with permission. Available at http://www.irrationalexubernce.com.

as in 2005, Shiller points out that fundamentals such as rents or construction costs could not explain the price appreciation. Two commonly used metrics to valuate home prices are home prices relative to income or rent. Exhibit 30.2 illustrates that the ratio of median house price to per-capita income reached nearly an all-time high in 2005. Similarly, Exhibit 30.3 shows that the rent-to-price ratio also dipped to its lowest level at that time. These two ratios relative to historic norms suggest that the housing market was overpriced at that time.

Shiller (2007) attributes the rapid increase in the value of residential real estate during that period to behavioral and psychological factors. He contends that a feedback mechanism or a "social epidemic" that viewed housing as an investment opportunity because of extravagant expectations about the future fueled the unsustainable changes in home prices. The smooth and continuous increase in home prices during the bubble period is consistent with the momentum phenomenon and with the notion that real estate price deviation from fundamentals can last for years.

Piazzesi and Schneider (2009) offer more support for psychological drivers of the real estate bubble. They use survey-based analysis to study households' beliefs during the boom period. The authors first document a large heterogeneity in households' views about housing and the economy. Their cluster analysis reveals that a small "momentum cluster" was largely responsible for the increase in the prices far above their fundamental levels. Although the momentum cluster was small, its size was unprecedented in the real estate market and kept growing until the peak of the boom. Thus, the small number of extremely optimistic investors was largely responsible for the high prices without owning a large share of the housing stock.

EXHIBIT 30.2   Home Price to Income per Capita in the United States: 1975 to 2012

Note: The exhibit illustrates the ratio of median house price to per-capita income in the United States from 1975 to 2012. Both the median home price and per-capita income are quarterly values. A high home price to per-capita income ratio indicates less affordable home prices.

Source: The author's calculations are based on data from the Bureau of Economic Analysis, the U.S. Census, and the Federal Housing Finance agency.

EXHIBIT 30.3   Rent to Price Ratio in the United States: 1975 to 2012

Note: This exhibit shows average rent to average home price ratio in the United States from 1975 to 2012. Both the average rent and average home price data are quarterly values. A low rent to price ratio indicates high home price levels.

Source: Davis, Lehnert, and Martin (2008) provide estimates until 2007. Data are extrapolated until 2012 using using rent data from the Bureau of Labor Statistics and the home price index from the Federal Housing Finance agency.

In their two part analysis, Piazzesi and Schneider (2009) document that the first part of the boom (2002 and 2003) was largely due to the view that the time to buy real estate was good because of favorable credit conditions. During the second phase of the boom (2004 to 2006), the overall enthusiasm about housing was declining. However, the number of extremely optimistic investors increased from 10 percent to 20 percent.

Piazzesi and Schneider (2009) also point out two important distinctions between the stock market and the housing market. Stock market prices may rise above their fundamentals when pessimistic investors are not allowed to short (Miller 1977) and optimists own all the available supply of the security. Unlike the stock market, optimists in the housing market cannot buy all the housing supply and drive prices high because they own 100 percent of the asset. However, in the housing market, the recorded prices only reflect transactions that have actually taken place, which represent a small fraction of the market. Thus, unlike in more active markets, the optimists can have a large effect on prices without owning a large share of the overall market.

Barberis (2011) discusses psychological biases that may have led to the housing bubble and the consequent financial crisis of 2007–2008. He suggests that the real estate bubble may have formed because of several behavioral biases. Barberis contends that investors have a tendency to extrapolate past outcomes too far into the future, where the extrapolation itself is motivated by representativeness. Representativeness heuristic refers to individuals' tendency to categorize a situation or its likelihood based on past experiences. Daniel et al. (1998) propose that the real estate bubble may have formed because of investors' overconfidence and that people overestimated the precision of their forecasts. When investors gather information about an asset, they give too much weight to positive information about the asset because of overconfidence.

Barberis (2011) also notes that the effect of playing with "house money" could have helped fuel the housing overpricing. After gains, people become less risk averse and become less concerned about future losses, and the buying behavior will drive prices even higher. According to Barberis, representativeness bias may have had most to do with the housing bubble, so that people over-extrapolate the past outcomes when estimating the future. Given that the broad U.S. housing market had never experienced a sharp and lasting nominal price decline since the Great Depression, past outcomes certainly did not help to hinder the growth.

In addition to the households, rating agencies and suppliers of loans to the subprime borrowers also fueled the real estate bubble. The rating agencies were overconfident in giving high ratings to the subprime securities and underestimated probabilities of defaults. Similarly to households, representativeness bias may have caused lenders and rating agencies to extrapolate past outcomes, fueled by the notion that housing prices never fall.

The banks' balance sheets of subprime securities also contributed to the crisis. Barberis (2011) uses behavioral biases to explain why banks were caught holding these assets and why rating agencies were giving AAA ratings to risky securities. Although some may argue that banks' risk taking and bad incentives were to blame, Barberis offers an alternative explanation. He asserts that a reasonable explanation of banks' behavior may have included *cognitive dissonance* (i.e., the mental conflict that occurs when new information conflicts with previously held beliefs), so that bankers may have manipulated their own beliefs to hold on to a positive self-image and the idea that the job they were doing was valuable to the society, instead of risky and hazardous.

Overreaction in Real Estate Prices

Seminal work by De Bondt and Thaler (1985, 1987) in behavioral finance documents that investors overreact to dramatic news events and as a result past losers tend to outperform past winners and past winners tend to underperform past losers in the long run (in case of stocks in 36-month windows). Overreaction to negative news by real estate market participants during the market downturn in 2007 to 2009 also drove home prices below their fundamental values.

As Exhibit 30.1 shows, the housing market experienced an unprecedented price decline beginning in 2006 and only began showing some signs of stabilization in 2012. This continuous five-year decline was sharp enough to fully erase the real housing price gains that took place during the bubble period. The smooth and consistent nature of the price decline is also consistent with the housing price momentum phenomenon. This period was a mirror image of the early 2000s, when the momentum in real estate prices drove prices far above their fundamentals during the bull market. During that period a feeling of extreme optimism dominated the market and positive feedback traders were willing to pay higher and higher premiums on their homes. During the bear market the situation reversed. Many buyers suffered great losses and exited the market completely. Pessimism replaced the feeling of optimism and a fear-fueled negative momentum drove prices below their fundamental values. Potential buyers were afraid of a continuous downward trend in home prices and sat on the sidelines. During that time, many homeowners used the price for which they purchased their house or the value of their house at the peak of the housing market as a false reference point. Thus, homeowners who did not have to sell their houses refused to so at fair market prices.

Barberis (2011), among other scholars, points out that loss aversion may have driven the large declines in prices after the bubble burst. Evidence shows that real estate market participants suffer from loss aversion, and that loss aversion especially determines seller behavior in the housing market (Lane, Seiler, and Seiler, 2011). Loss aversion also explains why houses tend to remain unsold on the market for long periods during a bust period. This can partially explain both the overreaction in home prices and the slow rebound period from extreme drops in such prices.

Lane et al. (2011) suggest other behavioral explanations to the slow rebound in home prices during the bust periods. They document that behavioral biases have a large impact on homeowners' unwillingness to list their properties for sale, when they are "underwater" (i.e., the loan amount on the home is greater than the fair market value of the home). The most important behavioral bias is *familiarity bias*, which in this case represents the unrealistic thought that owners' current property presents the best return potential. The status quo bias or inertia, which sellers also exhibit, causes them to stay in their current homes simply because they already own them and may explain some unwillingness to sell.

Finally, mental accounting can be linked to the periods of overreaction in the housing markets. Seiler, Seiler, and Lane (2012) document that mental accounting affects loss aversion. When subjects of their study move away from holding real estate in isolation toward holding real estate as a part of their portfolio, they tend to be more willing to sell their real estate for a loss. On the other hand, when investors consider real estate in isolation, they are less likely to recognize their losses.

Exhibits 30.2 and 30.3 show that the historical ratio of median house price to per-capita income and price-to-rent ratios reached their all-time highs in 2005. It also shows that after the 2007–2012 market correction, both the price to per-capita income ratio and the price-to-rent ratios are at their all-time lows in 2012. The all-time low levels of these two important ratios indicate that the market sharply over-reacted after the peak of the bull market.

Beracha, Skiba, and Hirschey (2012) study the overreaction in the U.S. housing market. They document that the overreaction from 2007 to 2011, similar to the market bubble, is regional in nature. The authors also find areas that experienced the most severe overvaluation during the bubble often exhibit the most obvious under-valuation at the end of the bust.

SUMMARY

Research shows that the real estate market, especially the market for residential real estate, is inefficient. Many market participants are inexperienced, novice investors who are driven by psychological biases. When the unsophisticated investor base is combined with severe limits to arbitrage, misvaluations often occur and price corrections take a long time to occur. Real estate prices tend to be predictable for many quarters and the real estate market is prone to overvaluations that are followed by sharp corrections. Given that the real estate market is a substantial part of the economy and an important determinant of consumer confidence and spending, understanding the underlying motives of buyers and sellers in the markets becomes especially important.

Many common cognitive biases and emotional factors documented in this market drive prices above their fundamental values during bull markets and below fundamentals during bear markets. During bull markets, investor overconfidence, self-attribution bias, and ownership bias drive prices higher. During bear markets, loss aversion, false reference points and anchoring, status quo bias, and familiarity bias drive prices below their true values.

Irrational behavior by real estate market participants partly drove the residential real estate boom and bust cycle that took place during the first decade of this millennium. This boom and bust cycle has had severely negative effects on the United States as well as the global economy and shows the widespread economic consequences of irrationality by real estate market participants.

DISCUSSION QUESTIONS

1. Discuss why limits to arbitrage are severe in the real estate market.
2. Explain why real estate market participants are likely to be overconfident and how overconfidence can lead to overvaluations.

3. What other psychological biases besides overconfidence influence real estate market participants' decision-making?
4. Which behavioral biases likely drove the overreaction in real estate prices that took place from 2007 to 2012?

REFERENCES

Ali, Ashiq, and Mark A. Trombley. 2006. "Short Sales Constraints and Momentum in Stock Returns." *Journal of Business Finance and Accounting* 33:2–4, 587–615.

Anderson, Christopher W., and Eli Beracha. 2012. "Frothy Housing Markets and Local Stock-Price Movements." *Journal of Real Estate Finance and Economics* 45:2, 326–346.

Barberis, Nicholas C. 2011. "Psychology and the Financial Crisis of 2007-2008." Working Paper, Yale University.

Ben-David, Itzhak. 2012. "High Leverage and Willingness to Pay: Evidence from the Residential Housing Market." Working Paper, Fisher College of Business.

Beracha, Eli, Hilla Skiba, and Mark Hirschey. 2012. "The Ship Appears to Be Turning." *Journal of Housing Research* 21:2, 261–280.

Beracha, Eli, and Ken Johnson. 2012. "Lessons from Over 30 Years of Buy versus Rent Decisions: Is the American Dream Always Wise?" *Real Estate Economics* 40:2, 217–247.

Beracha, Eli, and Hilla Skiba. 2011. "Momentum in Residential Real Estate." *Journal of Real Estate Finance and Economics* 43:3, 299–320.

Black, Roy T., and Julian Diaz III. 1996. "The Use of Information versus Asking Price in the Real Property Negotiation Process." *Journal of Property Research* 13:4, 287–297.

Bloomfield, Robert J., Robert Libby, and Mark W. Nelson. 1999. "Confidence and the Welfare of Less-Informed Investors." *Accounting, Organizations and Society* 24:8, 623–647.

Brounen, Dirk. 2008. "The Boom and Gloom of Real Estate Markets." Working Paper, Erasmus University Rotterdam.

Campbell, John Y., and João F. Cocco. 2005. "How Do House Prices Affect Consumption? Evidence from Micro Data." NBER Working Paper No. 11534.

Case, Karl E., and Robert J. Shiller. 1989. "The Efficiency of the Market for Single-Family Homes." *American Economic Review* 79:1, 125–137.

Case, Karl E., and Robert J. Shiller. 1990. "Forecasting Prices and Excess Returns in the Housing Market." *Real Estate Economics* 18:3, 253–273.

Case, Karl E., John M. Quigley, and Robert J. Shiller. 2005. "Comparing Wealth Effects: The Stock Market versus the Housing Market." *Advances in Macroeconomic* 5:1, 1–32.

Chui, Andy C. W., Sheridan Titman, and K. C. J. Wei. 2003. "Intra-Industry Momentum: The Case of REITs." *Journal of Financial Markets* 6:3, 363–387.

Chui, Andy C. W., Sheridan Titman, and K. C. J. Wei. 2010. "Individualism and Momentum around the World." *Journal of Finance* 65:1, 361–392.

Cocco, João F. 2005. "Portfolio Choice in the Presence of Housing." *Review of Financial Studies* 18:2, 535–567.

Coval, Joshua D., and Tobias J. Moskowitz. 1999. "Home Bias at Home: Local Equity Preference in Domestic Portfolios." *Journal of Finance* 54:6, 2045–2073.

Coyne, Thomas J., Waldemar M. Goulet, and Mario J. Picconi. 1980. "Residential versus Financial Assets." *Journal of Portfolio Management* 7:1, 20–24.

Daniel, Kent, David Hirshleifer, and Avanidhar Subrahmanyam. 1998. "Investor Psychology and Security Market Under- and Overreactions." *Journal of Finance* 53:6, 1839–1886.

Davis, Morris, A., Andreas Lehnert, and Robert F. Martin. 2008. "The Rent-Price Ratio for the Aggregate Stock of Owner-Occupied Housing." *Review of Income and Wealth* 54:2, 279–284.

De Bondt, Werner F. M., and Richard Thaler. 1985. "Does the Stock Market Overreact?" *Journal of Finance* 40:3, 793–805.

De Bondt, Werner F. M., and Richard Thaler. 1987. "Further Evidence on Investor Overreaction and Stock Market Seasonality." *Journal of Finance* 42:3, 793–805.

Diaz, Julian III. 2009. "An Investigation into the Impact of Previous Expert Value Estimates of Appraisal Judgment." *Journal of Real Estate Research* 13:1, 57–66.

French, Kenneth R., and James M. Poterba. 1991. "Investor Diversification and International Equity Markets." *American Economic Review* 81:2, 222–226.

Garmaise, Mark J., and Tobias J. Moskowitz. 2004. "Confronting Information Asymmetries: Evidence from Real Estate Markets." *Review of Financial Studies* 17:2, 405–437.

Genesove, David, and Christopher Mayer. 2001. "Loss Aversion and Seller Behavior: Evidence from the Housing Market." *Quarterly Journal of Economics* 116:4, 1233–1260.

Gervais, Simon, and Terrance Odean. 2001. "Learning to Be Overconfident." *Review of Financial Studies* 14:1, 1–27.

Huberman, Gur. 2001. "Familiarity Breeds Investment." *Review of Financial Studies* 14:3, 659–680.

Jegadeesh, Narasimhan, and Sheridan Titman. 1993. "Returns to Buying Winners and Selling Losers: Implications for Stock Market Efficiency." *Journal of Finance* 48:1, 65–91.

Jegadeesh, Narasimhan, and Sheridan Titman. 2001. "Profitability of Momentum Strategies: An Evaluation of Alternative Explanations." *Journal of Finance* 56:2, 699–720.

Lambson, Val E., Grant R. McQueen, and Barrett A. Slade. 2004. "Do Out-of-State Buyers Pay More for Real Estate? An Examination of Anchoring-Induced Bias and Search Costs." *Real Estate Economics* 32:1, 86–126.

Lane, Mark A., Michael J. Seiler, and Vicky L. Seiler. 2011. "Identifying Behavioral Explanations for a Subset of the Real Estate Shadow Market." *Journal of Housing Research* 20:2, 191–210.

Miller, Edward M. 1977. "Risk, Uncertainty, and Divergence of Opinion." *Journal of Finance* 32:4, 1151–1168.

Northcraft, Gregory B., and Margaret A. Neale. 1987. "Experts, Amateurs, and Real Estate: An Anchoring-and-Adjustment Perspective on Property Pricing Decisions." *Organizational Behavior and Human Decision Process* 39:1, 84–97.

Piazzesi, Monika, and Martin Schneider. 2009. "Momentum Traders in the Housing Market: Survey Evidence and a Search Model." *American Economic Review* 99:2, 406–411.

Ritter, Jay R. 2003. "Behavioral Finance." *Pacific-Basin Finance Journal* 11:4, 429–437.

Seiler, Michael J., and Vicky L. Seiler. 2010. "Mitigating Investor Risk-Seeking Behavior in a Down Real Estate Market." *Journal of Behavioral Finance* 11:3, 161–167.

Seiler, Michael J., Vicky L. Seiler, and Mark A. Lane. 2012. "Mental Accounting and False Reference Points in Real Estate Investment Decision Making." *Journal of Behavioral Finance* 13:1, 17–26.

Seiler, Michael J., Vicky L. Seiler, Stefan Traub, and David M. Harrison. 2008. "Regret Aversion and False Reference Points in Residential Real Estate." *Journal of Real Estate Research* 30:4, 461–474.

Shiller, Robert J. 2005. "Irrational Exuberance," 2nd ed. Princeton, NJ: Princeton University Press.

Shiller, Robert J. 2007. "Understanding Recent Trends in House Prices and Home Ownership." NBER Working Paper 13553.

Shiller, Robert J. 2008. *The Subprime Solution: How Today's Global Financial Crisis Happened, and What to Do about It.* Princeton, NJ: Princeton University Press.

Slovic, Paul, and Sarah Lichtenstein. 1971. "Comparison of Bayesian and Regression Approaches to the Study of Information Processing in Judgment." *Organizational Behavior and Human Decision Process* 6:6, 649–744.

Stein, Jeremy C. 1995. "Prices and Trading Volume in the Housing Market: A Model with Down-Payment Constraints." *Quarterly Journal of Economics* 110:2, 379–406.

Stephens, Thomas A., and Jean-Robert Tyran. 2012. "'At Least I Didn't Lose Money' Nominal Loss Aversion Shapes Evaluations of Housing Transactions." University of Copenhagen Discussion Paper, No. 12–14.

Thaler, Richard H. 1985. "Mental Accounting and Consumer Choice." *Marketing Science* 4:3, 199–214.

Thaler, Richard H. 1999. "Mental Accounting Matters." *Journal of Behavioral Decision Making* 12:3, 183–206.

Tversky, Amos, and Daniel Kahneman. 1974. "Judgment under Uncertainty: Heuristics and Biases." *Science, New Series* 185:4157, 1124–1131.

Wang, Ko, Yuqing Zhou, Su Han Chan, and K. W. Chau. 2000. "Over-Confidence and Cycles in Real Estate Markets: Cases in Hong Kong and Asia." *International Real Estate Review* 3:1, 93–108.

Worzala, Elaine, G. Stacy Sirmans, and Emily N. Zietz. 2000. "Risk and Return Perceptions of Institutional Investors." *Journal of Real Estate Portfolio Management* 6:2, 153–166.

Zhang, X. Frank. 2006. "Information Uncertainty and Stock Returns." *Journal of Finance* 61:1, 105–137.

ABOUT THE AUTHORS

Eli Beracha is an Assistant Professor at the College of Business at the University of Wyoming. He teaches real estate finance, investments, and corporate finance at the undergraduate and MBA levels. Professor Beracha conducts empirical research in the areas of real estate and finance and he is the editor of the *Journal of Real Estate Practice and Education*. He has published in such journals as *Real Estate Economics, Journal of Real Estate Finance and Economics, Journal of Real Estate Research, Financial Analysts Journal*, and *Journal of Financial Research*. Professor Beracha is also the recipient of a several prestigious awards such as the 2012 ARES "Best Housing Research Paper Award" and the 2009 "Red Pen Award" from the *Journal of Housing Research*. In addition to his scholarly work, he has more than 12 years of practical experience in the area of real estate investments. Professor Beracha received his PhD in finance from the University of Kansas.

Hilla Skiba is an Assistant Professor at the College of Business at the University of Wyoming. She teaches behavioral finance, international finance, investments, and corporate finance at the undergraduate and master levels. Her research interests are mainly in the areas of international finance, institutional investor performance, and real estate finance. Specifically, her work deals with cultural influences on financial decision-making, underdiversification and performance, and the behavior of real estate market participants. Her work has been published in journals such as *Journal of Real Estate Finance and Economics, Journal of Banking and Finance, Journal of Corporate Finance*, and *Journal of Housing Research*. Her research has earned several awards including the best paper award at the Midwestern Finance Association and a finalist for the best paper award at the Financial Management Association. Professor Skiba received her PhD in finance from the University of Kansas.

Answers to Discussion Questions

CHAPTER 2 TRADITIONAL AND BEHAVIORAL FINANCE

1. Describe the primary differences in the measurement of risk between the utility function used in expected utility theory by traditional finance and the value function posited by prospect theory in behavioral finance.

   The value function in prospect theory reflects three important properties that distinguish it from the traditional utility function. First, value is measured in terms of changes in wealth from a reference point whereas a utility function measures value based on the level of wealth. Second, the value function is convex for losses reflecting risk taking and concave for gains reflecting risk aversion whereas an individual's utility function evaluates risk aversion, risk neutrality, or risk loving. Third, the value function is steeper for losses than for gains due to loss aversion.

2. What is the difference between risk aversion and loss aversion?

   Risk aversion refers to the preferences of a person who would prefer the expected value of a gamble to the gamble itself. Loss aversion refers to the finding that people view a gain as adding less to utility than a loss of equal size takes away from it.

3. What does modern portfolio theory (i.e., traditional finance) say about how an investor should form an optimal stock portfolio?

   The investor should identify the optimal portfolio, which is the market basket. Next, the investor decides how much risk he is willing to take. If more risk averse, the investor would put a larger proportion of assets into a risk-free security and the balance into the market portfolio.

4. How does Simon's concept of satisficing differ from the traditional finance approach in which investors maximize expected utility?

   Satisficers make choices that satisfy their most important needs. In the traditional approach, people consider all available alternatives and pick the one that maximizes utility.

5. Describe a heuristic that can be used in decision-making and whether it is ecologically rational.

   Responses to this question will vary. An example is ecologically rational if it is a rule of thumb that leads to good decisions because of the structure of information. For example, if small stocks typically outperform large stocks and an investor makes selections based only on size, picking small stocks is ecologically rational.

CHAPTER 3 BEHAVIORAL ECONOMICS, THINKING PROCESS, DECISION-MAKING, AND INVESTMENT BEHAVIOR

1. Highlight key differences between the two major approaches to behavioral economics for investment behavior.

   The two major approaches to behavioral economics for investment behavior are the errors and biases approach and the bounded rationality approach. The errors and biases approach to behavioral economics pioneered by Kahneman and Tversky (1979) uses neoclassical decision-making benchmarks to measure the efficiency of decision-making processes and outcomes. Some contend that humans are prone to errors in decision-making because of limitations to their processing capabilities and to how emotions bias their decisions. This generates decision outcomes that are suboptimal from both the decision maker's and society's perspective. Behaving more neoclassically would mean acting in an emotionally detached and highly calculating manner. In the bounded rationality approach pioneered by Simon (1955, 1978, 1987), neoclassical decision-making tools typically achieve inefficient and ineffective outcomes given processing capabilities of the human brain and the decision-making environment. People develop decision-making shortcuts or heuristics that often include emotions and intuitions in their decision-making toolbox. These typically result in the best possible decision outcomes. However, the possibility for error and room for improvement in decision-making processes and environment still exist.

2. Identify some issues about financial market outcomes that behavioral economics attempts to address and explain.

   The evidence of the outcomes of investor behavior is not easily reconciled with the predictions of traditional economics and finance. For example, investor behavior often does not generate outcomes that are efficient, which produces suboptimal economic returns and market prices that often deviate from their fundamental values exemplified by bubbles and busts. This is contrary to an important facet of the efficient market hypothesis showing strong evidence that the returns of active market traders or investors are typically below those generated by passive investors. This finding suggests that active (more neoclassical) decision-making strategies, using modern knowledge technology, including sophisticated data gathering and analyses typically do not beat less calculating behavior that relies on decision-making shortcuts or heuristics. Therefore, what many scholars view as more rational behavior often generates subpar economic and financial outcomes.

3. Compare the errors and biases approach to the origins of financial crises with the bounded rationality approach.

The errors and biases approach focuses on systematic errors and biases in decision-making that are psychologically rooted, whereas the bounded rationality approach focuses on the decision-making environment. From the perspective of the errors and biases approach, changing the decision-making environment can do little to affect inbred cognitive illusions that can fuel financial crises. The latter can be a fundamental cause of errors in decision-making that can cause financial crises. For example, deregulation that reduces the cost to decision makers of making risky decisions incentivizes overly risky behavior and can generate financial bubbles. This is also called moral hazard. Given a predisposition toward overconfidence and overoptimism by many investors, an appropriately designed decision-making environment could minimize the extent of socially suboptimal economic decisions. Overconfidence and overoptimism need not generate severe booms and consequent busts. Also, an improved state of information can reduce the probability and extent of financial crises. Misleading information and information that is difficult to understand or locate can contribute to errors in decision-making, given the incentive environment, even in the absence of relevant cognitive biases.

4. Identify the critical differences between conventional risk and Knightian uncertainty and the importance of these differences for understanding investor behavior.

   Conventional risk assumes that risk is probabilistic and calculable. The ability to estimate the probability of an event such as a financial outcome is an essential assumption of traditional finance, but this is not the only type of risk. Behavioral finance pays attention to risk that is not calculable with any degree of certainty. A large variance surrounds this type of risk, which is called Knightian uncertainty. Once risk is not easily calculable, decision makers resort to shortcuts such as gut feeling (animal spirits), the opinion of others, and past experience to make decisions. These heuristics can generate better investment decisions than trying to estimate risk when such estimates are highly imprecise.

5. Discuss the concept of overconfidence and how this relates to investment failure and possible errors in investor decisions.

   Investors who are overconfident believe that they can affect outcomes to a greater extent than they actually can. When this occurs they will invest in projects or overinvest because of overconfidence bias. Overconfidence translates into investors believing that they can generate a 50 percent rate of return when the evidence suggests no more than a 10 percent rate of return. A huge gap exists between what one believes can be and what most probably will be achieved. Overconfident investors underestimate the risk of their investment and take greater risk than is wise. One source of overconfidence is ignoring *sentiment-based risk*, which is risk derived from decision makers acting on emotional considerations. Investors sometimes ignore evidence that contracts their evaluation of risks and outcomes. For example, many successful entrepreneurs bet against existing evidence that indicates they were doomed to fail. Overconfidence typically relates to average prospects of success and failure and risks and is not typically tailored to the specific characteristic of individual investors. Yet, not all people are overconfident.

CHAPTER 4 FINANCIAL LITERACY AND EDUCATION

1. Discuss the various facets that the term financial literacy has been used to describe and which is most appropriate from a human capital perspective and useful from a research perspective.

The academic literature uses the terms financial literacy and financial knowledge interchangeably. Hung, Parker, and Yoong (2009) and Huston (2010) contend that financial knowledge is a part of, but not equivalent to, financial literacy. Financial literacy is a form of human capital that is specific to personal finances. Financial literacy includes knowledge and skills in the areas of money basics, borrowing, investing, and resource protection. Because financial literacy is a form of human capital, it represents an individual's potential to make appropriate financial decisions, but does not necessarily imply that the individual uses that human capital to make decisions. Some definitions of financial literacy include behavioral outcomes. This is neither appropriate in terms of human capital theory nor particularly useful from a research standpoint. Financial literacy is a concept separate from financial decisions and financial behaviors. Some use financial literacy to mean financial education. Financial education is a process designed to enhance a person's financial literacy, but does imply that a person is financially literate.

2. Discuss the main methods used to measure financial literacy in the academic literature and describe which method is most appropriate.

Academic studies measure financial literacy in many ways. A widely used measure is a three-item instrument developed by Lusardi and Mitchell (2007a, 2007b, 2008, 2009). However, many researchers question this method because the instrument lacks breadth of content and relies primarily on measuring numeracy rather than the human capital specific to personal finance. Knoll and Houts (2012) focus on measuring financial knowledge using item response theory. They use existing financial literacy items to create a financial knowledge scale consisting of 20 items covering the four main areas of personal finance: money basics, borrowing, investing, and protection. The main drawbacks of this approach include the lack of attention to financial skill, the use of items that are available rather than constructed specifically for the purpose of measuring financial literacy, and the disproportionate representation of the personal finance content, which may or may not be appropriate.

Another method proposed to measure financial literacy is the Financial Literacy Assessment Test (FLAT). The purpose of this instrument is to capture the human capital—both knowledge and skills—specifically related to personal finance. The 20 items contained in the instrument are equally distributed among the four areas of personal finance and include an accompanying scoring grid designed to aid in interpreting financial literacy scores to determine whether a person is financially literate.

3. Distinguish between financial literacy and numeracy and discuss the empirical evidence related to the relationship between numerical ability and decision-making quality.

Numeracy refers to the ability to accurately calculate mathematical problems. This ability may reduce the time cost and increase the quality of decisions that require knowledge of percentages, the ability to compare a value today with a compounded value in the future and to understand the impact of inflation on nominal dollar values over time. Consumers with greater numeracy skills are better prepared for retirement (Banks, O'Dea, and Oldfield 2010), invest in higher quality portfolios (von Gaudecker 2011), have a greater understanding of credit card terms (Soll, Keeney, and Larrick 2013), and are better able to make comparisons of credit values over time (Stango and Zinman 2011). Gustman, Steinmeier, and Tabatabai (2012), however, find evidence that mathematical ability is related to other household characteristics that may drive positive financial behaviors and is not an independent predictor of pension knowledge. When financial literacy and numeracy measures are combined, van Rooij, Lusardi, and Alessie (2011) find that financial literacy significantly affects stock ownership but numeracy does not. Although numerical ability and positive decision-making quality are correlated, the pathway from numeracy to behavior is not well understood.

4. Discuss the role of motivation in financial literacy.

When the consequences of financial decisions are greater, consumers are more motivated to invest time and effort to increase financial literacy. When women have greater responsibility for making financial decisions (e.g., following the death of a spouse or a divorce), their financial literacy scores increase (Hsu 2011). Subjects with larger pensions are more likely to have higher knowledge of pension characteristics independent of income and numeracy (Gustman, Steinmeier, and Tabatabai 2012). Younger employees with more to gain from better retirement decisions are more likely to seek financial education (Clark, Morrill, and Allen 2012), as are those who place a greater value on future consumption (Meier and Sprenger 2007). These findings suggest that public provision of financial education will be most effective at the point of sale and to consumers who believe they have the most to gain from making better decisions.

CHAPTER 5 HOUSEHOLD INVESTMENT DECISIONS

1. Identify two assumptions that traditional financial models make about individual investment behavior and discuss their impact.

Traditional financial models generally assume that all people make perfectly rational decisions and no financial market frictions exist. Because these assumptions are not always valid, traditional financial models may not fully and accurately reflect actual household investment decision-making behavior. For example, household market participation is generally much lower than predicted by financial models.

2. List three types of market frictions and discuss how they can affect investment behavior.

Three primary market frictions that affect investment behavior are transaction costs, information costs, and taxes. Transaction costs and information costs make investments more costly and thus serve to decrease individual and household participation in financial markets. Taxes have differing effects on individual and household investment behavior. Tax-advantaged investment vehicles generally become more attractive to investors as their income increases. Tax considerations also influence the realization of gains and losses in household portfolios.

3. Discuss how family structure influences household investment decision-making behavior.

Many aspects of family structure affect household financial decision-making behavior. The number of children a couple has, the average spacing between siblings, and the timing of births within a marriage affect family savings. Rapid child-bearing early in marriage inhibits asset growth and these effects persist over a couple's lifetime. Evidence also shows that young children depress savings for young families but increase savings for marriages of duration greater than five years. A child presence in the household is associated with a higher risk tolerance for the highest income households but is generally associated with a lower risk tolerance. Having only female children increases the probability of holding stock (risky assets) for married respondents and having only male children increases the probability of holding stock for single females. A family shock with respect to marital status also affects household savings and portfolio choice. Further, overconfidence affects male trading and investment behavior but marriage ameliorates this behavioral bias.

4. Discuss how mental health issues affect household investment decision-making behavior.

Generally, households affected by mental illness decrease their investments in risky assets. Mental health problems that limit cognitive abilities such as numeracy, verbal fluency, and memory abilities also contribute to a lack of participation in financial markets. Traumatic life experiences can decrease the probability of individuals holding risky assets. Further, mental health problems decrease the probability of households holding voluntary contribution pension accounts.

CHAPTER 6 PERSONALITY TRAITS

1. Describe the characteristics of each of the Big Five personality traits.

Higher Extraversion is associated with a greater desire for sensation seeking and excitement. Higher Agreeableness is related to greater understanding of the motivations of others and unselfish tendencies. Higher Conscientious is associated with great strength of purpose and honesty. Neuroticism is linked to negative feelings about oneself and emotional instability. Openness to Experience is characterized by the desire to seek out new opportunities and information.

2. What personality traits are associated with risk taking? How do these traits relate to risk-taking propensities?

Studies suggest important roles for Extraversion, Neuroticism, and Conscientiousness. Extraverts may crave the excitement brought about by higher exposure to risk. For such investors, risk is emotionally arousing. Neurotic investors may avoid risk as adverse outcomes might worsen the negative feelings about oneself that neuroticism brings. Conscientiousness might lead to more considered decision-making and thus reduce risk-taking propensities.

3. What is the biological basis of the gender differences in decision-making and risk taking?

Males consistently exhibit a greater preference for risk than females. Chemistry plays an important role in explaining this difference. Men have greater levels of testosterone than women. Biological gender is easy to measure and facilitates convenient sample formation. Including personality traits in studies of behavior enables accounting for many differences naively ascribed to biological gender.

4. Discuss how understanding a person's personality could help improve decision-making quality.

Self-knowledge may lead to an understanding of what motivates an individual's thoughts and actions. Those who can reflect on these motivations may be able to consciously overcome economically suboptimal dispositions. Such conscious action is difficult because personality is, to some extent, hardwired into a person's biology. Conscious thought to overcome the personality-driven dispositions requires considerable effort.

CHAPTER 7 DEMOGRAPHIC AND SOCIOECONOMIC FACTORS OF INVESTORS

1. What do Barber and Odean (2001) theorize is a key factor in explaining the difference in investor behavior across gender? What evidence do they provide to support their argument?

Barber and Odean (2001) theorize that overconfidence leads men to invest more aggressively than women. They contend that overconfidence in one's valuations of securities increases trading activity. As evidence, they show that men trade 45 percent more than women, which also leads to a greater reduction in returns.

2. Discuss the importance of marital status in determining how aggressively men invest. What are some of the outstanding issues with this research?

As Sunden and Surette (1998) show, marriage generally does not lead to greater risk aversion because marital status affects men and women differently. Married men are more risk-averse than single men but this is not the case for married women. Papke (1998) does not find a significant difference in investor behavior across gender. A selection bias still exists when comparing married men with single men and married women with single women that these studies fail to consider.

3. With respect to intergeneration transfers of financial knowledge, what evidence shows differences across racial groups?

   Hurst, Luoh, and Stafford (1998) find that African Americans have historically been less likely to hold financial assets and use traditional banking services. Chetiji and Stafford (1999) find a strong connection between the financial behaviors of parents and their children. When considering parental stock holdings, the effects previously attributable to race diminish.

4. Discuss the role of income on investor behavior. How does it match up against the life cycle theory?

   Hinz, McCarthy, and Turner (1997) find that higher incomes lead to more aggressive investing. This corresponds with the life cycle theory stating that investment risk should reflect the expected value of the future income stream. Higher levels of income, all else being equal, should lead to higher levels of investor risk. Jagannathan and Kocherlakota (1996) also show that investor risk increases with income but decreases with age and wealth.

CHAPTER 8 THE EFFECT OF RELIGION ON FINANCIAL AND INVESTING DECISIONS

1. Discuss whether empirical studies show dependence between religion and the political economy.

   Several empirical studies show positive dependence between religion and economic factors. For instance, McCleary and Barro (2006) use several proxies, such as belief in heaven and hell, to show whether a positive dependence exists. In their empirical design, the authors use the variable "religion" as exogenous and endogenous. In contrast, some authors support the positive dependence interpretations. For example, Eum (2011) shows that McCleary and Barro's evidence does not hold true for different periods. He suggests that religious variables do not have a significant, constant influence on economic growth.

2. Explain why economists sometimes use religion to explain financial and investment decisions.

   The success of economic and financial theories rests on the relevance of the variables researchers use to explain the phenomena they observe. This set sometimes includes political and social-related variables. Researchers added religion into their empirical frameworks to better understand its role in driving various aspects such as the investors' psychological behavior and their risk attitudes.

3. Discuss the impact of religion on individual behavior.

Religion has a central function in people's lives because it provides psychological insurance regarding uncertainly and risk. Religion also plays a crucial role in influencing an individual's beliefs and behavior. Religion can influence individual personal traits such as risk aversion. Moreover, attending a particular form of religious education, choosing specific neighborhoods in which to live, and practicing regular religious rituals can shape how one lives and acts.

Religion presents a moral values system and enables social groups to distinguish appropriate and inappropriate attitudes. Ample evidence suggests that religion promotes ethical behavior and moral values involving trust, loyalty, generosity, honesty, cooperation, integrity, hard work, and thrift. Religion also triggers a high sensitivity toward the prosocial reputation within the community group.

Evolutionary theory highlights the importance of local social and religious norms on an individual's preference. Thus, religion is likely to influence investment decisions.

4. Discuss the role of religion in influencing personal financial attitudes.

Economists, including behavioral ones, are often reluctant to incorporate religion into their analyses. Thus, the relationship of how religion influences personal financial behavior is not well understood. Recent studies examine how religious beliefs affect the investment decision process based on one's risk perception. Empirical surveys reveal that religious orientation dictates individual risk choice. Specifically, Protestants and Catholics exhibit an aversion to pure risk, but express an opposite attitude toward speculative risk (e.g., gambling). While Protestants and Muslims are extremely reluctant to gamble, Catholics have a higher propensity to engage in gambling, which impairs their portfolio's performance.

Religion affects an investor's psychological state by encouraging entrepreneurial activity (self-employment) and stimulates the tendency to invest. Religion influences investors' tendency to be friendlier, happier, and more satisfied with their lives than others. A person's religious leanings can distort the distribution of stock returns.

5. Explain how religious attitudes affect firm behavior.

Religion not only plays a central role in economic development and investor decision-making but also presents a key feature in understanding firm behavior. Religion interferes with firm policies in different ways. Research shows that religion interferes with managerial behavior in terms of excessive risk aversion. Thus, managers align their investment choices with low levels of risky investments triggering lower long-term growth for the firm. Religion mitigates managerial misbehavior and curbs intentional misreporting.

Religious affiliation affects a firm's capital structure choice. Capital structure decisions differ substantially between firms located in highly Protestant versus highly Catholic areas. Religion also constitutes a prevalent monitoring tool for firm governance by curbing managerial opportunism to realize personal gain. Finally, evidence shows that firms headquartered in highly religious areas exhibit lower equity financing costs and spur corporate governance.

6. Discuss how religion interferes with the interplay between financial and investing decisions.

Religion can interfere with the structure and design of the financial instruments that firms use with their contractual parties. For instance, the three monotheistic religions—Judaism, Christianity, and Islam—in addition to Buddhism and Hinduism forbid using interest in designing financial instruments. Accordingly, using standard debt contracts involving interest is forbidden.

CHAPTER 9 MONEY AND HAPPINESS: IMPLICATIONS FOR INVESTOR BEHAVIOR

1. Discuss whether money can buy happiness.

If money is defined as personal income and happiness is defined by life satisfaction, money can buy happiness to some degree. Research findings indicate that income and happiness correlate strongly from the low-to middle-income level but the positive association becomes weaker when income increases from the middle to high level. Research also shows that pursuing material goals decreases happiness and spending for others and meaningful social causes increases happiness. Consumers who are seeking a happy life may consider these research findings when making personal financial decisions.

2. What is the Easterlin Paradox?

The Easterlin Paradox refers to the notion that economic growth measured by per capita gross domestic product (GDP) is not associated with happiness measured by life satisfaction over time. This paradox has economic importance, especially in many developing countries such as China. If economic growth is not associated with happiness, why should countries focus on economic development? Although some economists claim to have solved the paradox, others believe the paradox is unsolved and requires more comprehensive research. Researchers propose several explanations for this paradox. For example, one possible explanation involves social comparison. People who compare their incomes with their peers are likely to feel dissatisfied if the degree of their income increase is lower than that of their peers. Another possibility is the adaptation effect. When income increases, people are temporarily happy but the happiness eventually fades. Some researchers also believe data sources and country specifics contribute to this paradox.

3. Identify the similarities and differences of the effects of inflation and unemployment on happiness.

Evidence shows that both inflation and unemployment have negative effects on happiness when measured by life satisfaction. The negative effect of unemployment is greater than that of inflation. For consumers, experiencing unemployment is more painful than suffering inflation. These findings have important implications for economic policy makers when they face situations that they need to control for inflation or the unemployment rate.

4. Discuss whether happier people make more money.

Research findings indicate that people who report a higher level of life satisfaction do better financially. Researchers speculate that happier people may have other psychological characteristics that are desirable in labor markets, such as cheerfulness and optimism. Also, happier people may be healthier, have more social networks, and possess higher self-esteem. All these factors may be important for success at work. Researchers also find differences between extremely happy people and moderately happy people in terms of life outcomes. Extremely happy people do better in close relationships and volunteer work while moderately happy people are more successful in earning higher income, attaining a higher level of education, and participating in politics.

5. What can practitioners in the investment industry learn from research findings on money and happiness?

Although research evidence on money and happiness provides some clues for practitioners in the investment industry, the following observations are largely speculative. Investment professionals may experience a lower level of daily happiness than people who are not in the investment industry because the former work long hours under much pressure. They may also have lower levels of life satisfaction due to their highly demanding work. Yet, the selection of this career path and job fit with personal abilities and personalities could help offset the lower than average happiness level. If investment professionals are highly motivated to work hard, they may consider long hours and high pressure as prerequisites for success on their jobs. Investment professionals could live a meaningful life if they engage in socially responsible investing and sacrifice monetary benefits when they face moral dilemmas at work. To live a happier life while remaining in the investment industry, they may adjust their working hours to allow more quality time with their family and friends. They could also be more selective in their investment options and make positive contributions to the economy.

CHAPTER 10 MOTIVATION AND SATISFACTION

1. What are the strengths and weaknesses of the classical economic approach?

The classical economic approach has both strengths and weaknesses. The strengths are that it is highly quantitative and objective. Consumer preferences are stated in numerical form, often through dollars expended. Disputing conclusions that are based on impartially arrived-at numbers with the amount of pleasure equated with the amount of dollars expended is difficult. A major weakness of the classical approach is that consumer preferences and satisfaction are based on both dollars and time expended on enjoyable activities. Moreover, the entire process assumes that people act rationally in machinelike fashion. Individuals often have more than one goal and their goals may conflict. Classical economic theory indicates how people should act but the field of behavioral finance looks at how they actually perform.

2. Explain the advantages and disadvantages of Maslow's hierarchy of needs approach.

Maslow's hierarchy of needs approach has both advantages and disadvantages. The advantages are that people broadly appear to climb the hierarchical ladder. The hierarchy is easy for people to understand and embrace. The popularity of the hierarchy over a long period attests to its influence. Its disadvantages include having values that are not universal, or even the same for people within one country, and can depend on interest and income status. Further, individuals may address more than one need at any one time and measuring these needs can be subjective.

3. Discuss Thaler and Shefrin's major contributions to behavioral finance.

Thaler and Shefrin criticize orthodox economics as being too structured and also outline the weaknesses of Modigliani's (1980) life cycle theory. They make a case for laboratory experimentation and discuss the conflict between spending today and saving for the future. Thaler and Shefrin use the multiple selves approach, which conflicts with the one choice approach in classical economics. They discuss the idea of self-control bias, which is not part of orthodox economics, and suggest ways of achieving it through limiting choice and respecting "mental accounting." The behavioral aspects modify but do not replace Modigliani's approach.

4. Discuss whether self-actualization should be everyone's goal.

Self-actualization is a growth goal, not a deficiency goal. In other words, one can view physiological needs, safety needs, belongingness and love needs, and self-esteem needs as factors that people who have not reached that level lack, while self-actualization is a higher broadening need. Some view self-actualization as aspirational, with humanists saying that all people should strive to better themselves. Others believe that a focus on materialistic pursuits retards individual growth. Interviewing typical individuals might uncover a satisfaction with buying goods and stopping below this highest level need. Some assume that the self-esteem stage is a sufficiently high step to achieve. The fact that different disciplines and theories of motivation reach alternative conclusions should not be puzzling. In summary, self-actualization is probably not everyone's goal.

5. Discuss whether life planning is a legitimate area for financial planners to offer clients.

Life planning is a relatively new alternative for personal financial planners, and debate surrounds this issue. Its goal can be to help clients supplement material goals with something more. If planners are not qualified to render personal judgments, they could restrict their advice to financial matters. If planners engage in a close personal relationship with clients, the client should feel comfortable discussing almost any topic. Life planning often has a strong financial component. In summary, some planners may want to engage in life planning as a specialty but this is something that is unsuitable for every planner.

6. Identify and discuss the contributions of motivation and satisfaction within behavioral and personal finance.

Motivation propels people to take certain actions. Satisfaction is the outcome, whether it is relatively positive or negative. Negative satisfaction is dissatisfaction. In contrast to classical economic theory, motivation under behavioral finance is more multidimensional. Besides monetary rewards, others include feelings of accomplishment, a concern about others, and a potential conflict between individual goals and those of the family. Satisfaction can range widely in degrees of intensity and stability. However, by restricting the term to *life satisfaction*, people limit themselves to feelings that are more important and more lasting (i.e., they are not as subject to strong fluctuations in results).

Viewing personal finance as traditional money finance limits the contribution of motivation and satisfaction. Money becomes the focal point of everyone's efforts. Behavioral finance enhances the role of motivation and satisfaction within personal finance. It indicates that people must look beyond money to many other variables to identify what makes people act the way they do. The nature of those motivational variables involves differing interpretations from behavioral life cycle theory to humanism ranging from a literal interpretation of Maslow's rigid hierarchical structure to a more amorphous humanistic rejection of money values. The traditional and behavioral approaches are integrated in life planning.

In sum, motivation and the desire for satisfaction, whether the ultimate end or simply pleasure in achievement, provide the underpinning for most financial theories. However, both factors have an enhanced role in those approaches beyond traditional money finance.

CHAPTER 11 POLICY-BASED FINANCIAL PLANNING: DECISION RULES FOR A CHANGING WORLD

1. In the context of financial planning, define the term "policy" and identify the characteristics of good policy.

A *policy* is a principle or rule to guide decisions and achieve rational outcomes. In the context of financial planning, a good policy has several characteristics. One characteristic is that it delivers new answers in light of changing circumstances. A good policy is also broad enough to encompass any changing circumstances and consistently returns a clear, unambiguous answer.

2. A client says, "I believe education is critically important to a successful life so I would like to pay for my grandson's college education." This statement encompasses a belief and a goal. Write an example of a policy for this client.

The following are sample policies for this client.

- We will segregate assets equal to four times the current in-state tuition for Massachusetts.
- We will purchase the prepaid tuition plan for the state in which our grandson lives (this first part is not a policy, but rather an action plan), and segregate assets from our regular portfolio equal to the estimated room and board for a state university.
- We will save 25 percent of every bonus or other windfall that we receive until we have accumulated sufficient funds to pay the state-estimated cost of tuition, room, board, and books for the state university.
- We will reimburse our grandson for tuition for every semester in which he attains a B average or better.

3. Explain how financial planning policies incorporate a client's values and beliefs.

During the discovery process, the financial planner learns about the client's values and beliefs. In the course of the financial planning process, the planner identifies goals that when appropriately established reflect values and beliefs, and also makes and eventually implements recommendations. If circumstances change, both planners and clients often have difficulty remembering the beliefs and values behind the goals and recommendations. The design of policies attempts to incorporate values and beliefs. An action item, such as save $400 a month toward next year's family vacation, is very clear. However, when another goal arrives, such as buying a new car, remembering that the client believes in minimizing debt (i.e., has a preference for minimizing downside risk) other than for the purchase of appreciating assets can be difficult. A policy stating "save for the purchase of non-appreciating assets over a 12- to 24-month period" would clearly show how the client should save for the car purchase and what the person could afford to pay for a car at the end of that period.

4. Discuss how the process of developing financial planning policies helps lead to a client embracing the ongoing and changing recommended action items.

The development of financial planning policies is an interactive and collaborative process that ultimately results in statements reflecting the client's values and beliefs. A structured process for gathering information about these values and beliefs leads to a higher level of client trust and relationship commitment. Evidence indicates that the policy-driven mode of financial planning is the only statistically significant predictor of client trust and relationship commitment. In turn, trust and commitment are associated with qualities predictive of a successful financial planning engagement, including higher client satisfaction and retention, and a greater propensity to reveal personal and financial information and to implement planning recommendations. Because financial planning is a high credence service, clients are going to evaluate the service by the "how" of the service. Policy-based financial planning incorporates methods and communication that contribute to clients positively evaluating the how of the process and service.

CHAPTER 12 FINANCIAL COUNSELING AND COACHING

1. When and where did financial counseling develop as a field of study and practice?

   Financial counseling has its roots primarily in the home economics movement that began in the mid-to-late 1800s. The term "home economics" is a fair description of the early studies conducted to determine how resources (e.g., time, money, talent, and labor) were managed at the household level. Some economists began to apply principles of economics to study consumer and household consumption and decision-making in relation to the allocation of scarce resources, labor, household composition, transportation, fertility, and health. Researchers and land-grant university extension specialists took steps to organize studies and training dedicated to establishing financial counseling as a field of study and practice. Family and consumer economists have maintained an interest in applying economic principles to develop normative strategies to help people function within the broader economic environment. Yet, establishing family resource management within the context of family economic theory gave financial counseling a true academic home.

2. Identify and briefly explain the four approaches that financial counselors commonly use when engaging with clients.

   The four major approaches to financial counseling include: (1) resource acquisition, (2) family resource management, (3) psychological, and (4) systems. The resource acquisition perspective focuses on helping clients gain access to private and public resources. The family resource management viewpoint helps clients gain the skills and resources necessary to engage in behavioral change. The psychological perspective views financial issues as a symptom of other underlying problems that need to be addressed through psychotherapy. The premise of the systems perspective is the notion that behavioral change occurs most readily when addressing financial questions at a family, rather than an individual, level.

3. Describe the differences among financial counseling, financial coaching, financial therapy, financial planning, and life planning.
   - Financial counseling is the professional field of assisting clients to obtain economic well-being and security. It uses skills, information, and other resources to assist clients in changing behavior in financial management, consumption, and lifestyle in order to obtain and maintain economic security. Financial counselors provide guidance in ways to achieve baseline levels of financial health without regard to wealth accumulation. Others view financial counseling as a short-term educative process concerned with helping people to help themselves by applying financial information, education, and guidance

to specific situations. It typically involves helping people clarify issues, explore options, assess alternatives, make decisions, develop strategies, and plan courses of action.

- Financial coaching helps others set goals and develop strengths to meet and surpass goals and also provides ongoing feedback and guidance.
- Financial therapy is the integration of cognitive, emotional, behavioral, relational, and economic aspects that promote financial health.
- Financial planning is the process of reviewing a wide variety of topics related to a client's financial affairs such as insurance, tax, retirement, estate, investments, and special needs. Few planners get involved with helping clients create a spending plan (i.e., budget), negotiate with creditors, or change spending behaviors. Financial planners help clients manage their cash flow and net worth position in order to create wealth over the life span as a way to fund tangible financial goals.
- Life planning is a process of helping people focus on the true values and motivations in their lives, determine their goals and objectives, and use these values, motivations, goals, and objectives to guide the planning process and to provide a framework for making choices and decisions in life that has financial and non-financial implications or consequences.

4. Go to www.youtube.com/watch?v=wEfQ4nOz6s8&feature=youtube and watch the video in order answer the following questions.
    - What kind of help did this couple receive from Housing and Credit Counseling, Inc. (HCCI) as it relates to this chapter?

Although the couple qualified to file for bankruptcy, the couple chose to use a debt repayment plan to help them repay all their credit card debt. The financial counseling they received taught them new skills and helped to change their spending behavior in order to repay all their debt and begin saving for a vacation.

- How was the help the couple received from HCCI beneficial?

The couple was able to repay their debt, which helped relieve stress and anxiety.

- If financial counseling services were unavailable for this couple, where could they have sought help?

If a financial counseling service agency was unavailable in their area, they could have sought help from a financial service practitioner who offers pro bono financial counseling, a mental health professional who specializes in financial issues, or self-help resources. In some communities, churches and certain non-profit agencies provide basic financial education classes and even offer individual counseling. Unfortunately, if a financial counseling agency such as HCCI is not in the community, finding financial help that is skilled in addressing their in-depth, complex financial situation could be difficult. This is due to the reality that financial planners typically do not conduct financial counseling and most mental health workers do not have the necessary financial expertise to help the couple pay down their debt rather than file for bankruptcy.

5. How can the fields of financial counseling and coaching increase their credibility and quality of services?

Few empirical studies document the effectiveness of financial counseling and financial coaching in general or the usefulness of specific practice management models specifically. Those seeking financial counseling and financial coaching services receive services that tend to be inconsistent from one counselor/coach to the next with no evidence to support whether the approach the counselor/coach is using actually works in any context. Thus, the fields of financial counseling and coaching can increase their credibility and quality of services by providing a theoretical orientation and empirical evidence to support behavioral change outcomes. Also, more established fields in these two areas would present college-educated students with additional career opportunities after graduation and would be able to provide these services more widely to the general public. The current lack of such a theoretical orientation and empirical evidence continues to hinder the potential growth and impact of financial counseling and financial coaching as helping professions.

CHAPTER 13 FINANCIAL THERAPY: DE-BIASING AND CLIENT BEHAVIORS

1. Describe the primary differences among the concepts and practice of financial planning, financial counseling, and financial therapy.

In professional practice, financial planning typically targets high-income or affluent individuals and families. Most financial planners focus on investment management, tax planning, and retirement planning. Compared to financial planners, financial counselors usually have greater expertise in credit/debt management and cash flow management and serve low-and middle-income families. Professionals practicing financial therapy usually tend to focus on working with clients to help them understand their past financial decisions and behaviors, change their future financial behaviors, and communicate more effectively about personal finances with their family members. The practice of all three involves improving the financial well-being of families.

2. Explain the need for a new field of financial therapy.

Research from the fields of behavioral finance/economics and neuroeconomics shows that individuals are subject to cognitive and emotional biases that may lead to suboptimal financial decisions. Research also indicates that personal finances can have detrimental effects on individuals' stress level and interpersonal relationships. Unfortunately, most financial and mental health professionals do not receive education and training specific to the other's field of study. Financial therapy interventions are needed to improve individuals' suboptimal way of thinking about money and negative financial behaviors.

3. Describe the four models of professional collaboration in providing financial therapy services.

The four models of professional collaboration in providing financial therapy services are the referral framework, parallel framework, consultative framework, and integrative framework.

- The *referral framework* is the least collaborative method. It involves identifying when a client could benefit from a financial planning or therapy intervention and simply making the necessary referral to another professional.
- The *parallel framework* involves the financial planner and therapist both working with the same client at different times but communicating about interventions and the client's progress toward common goals.
- The *consultative framework* involves the therapist or planner inviting the other practitioners to join occasional meetings as needed to help address a specific concern or issue.
- The *integrative framework* entails the client and two practitioners working together to address both financial and relational issues through integrative and systemic collaboration.

4. Discuss whether clear evidence exists as to which theoretical or conceptual approach to financial therapy is likely to be most effective.

Researchers have not tested most theoretical and conceptual approaches to financial therapy. Without empirical support, knowing which approach is most effective is difficult. Different approaches may be more effective depending on the presenting client issues and the skill set of the financial therapist.

5. Describe two opportunities for future research in the field of financial therapy.

Future research in the field of financial therapy should:

- Examine how cultural and historical contexts as well as religion affect the financial well-being of individuals, couples, and families.
- Investigate how people form attitudes toward money and maladaptive money behaviors.
- Test the effectiveness of financial therapy interventions.
- Test models of professional collaborations used to provide financial therapy.
- Develop theory-based assessment tools and techniques.

CHAPTER 14 TRANSPERSONAL ECONOMICS

1. What influence does Freud's pleasure principle exert over the U.S. economy?

Currently, American business practices support the claim made by Austrian psychiatrist Victor Frankl, a founder of transpersonal psychology, that barring a transcendent life purpose humans will grasp for pleasure and avoid pain. According to the American Psychological Association (2011), the fastest rising health and environmental problems stem from overconsumption rather than scarcity of resources. Much overconsumption satisfies immediate sensory needs at the expense of longer-term objectives such as ensuring Earth's habitability.

2. How does mindfulness practice assist in rational decision-making?

Studies on meditation reveal that pathways in the prefrontal cortex are strengthened through mindfulness practice (Siegel 2007). The prefrontal cortex is the brain region responsible for planning and rationality. Similar to building muscle, more meditation leads to stronger pathways and heightened impulse control.

3. Discuss the costs and benefits of allowing other life forms into the Eco.

Permitting other creatures into the Eco would entail a major restructuring of the West's economy. With fewer beings available for exploitation, fewer ways would be available to meet economic objectives. New technologies and substitutions would need to be developed to fill the gap left behind. Human examples of broadening the Eco include women's suffrage and civil rights. The most obvious benefit of giving reverence to other life forms would be environmental sustainability. Less tangible benefits include deeper appreciation, connection, and communion with other life forms.

4. Despite occupational constraints brought by an open Eco, Jains are exceptionally prosperous. What are some possible reasons for this prosperity?

Jains are prosperous for several reasons. By supporting the monks and nuns engaged in religious work, Jain laity consider their commercial success as a holy duty. Another reason Jain householders regard financial wealth as a necessity is the belief that the five vows are easier to follow in times of abundance. Finally, Jains prefer to run an economic surplus and to be net givers to society, rather than drains on society's resources. Jains have concentrated in the merchant, banking, and moneylending businesses. They flock to the cities where they can engage in these commercial activities without compromising the doctrine of ahimsa. As a result of their honesty in business, they also attract the trade of non-Jains. As shown by Jain Irrigation Systems, sustainability is an integral part of any business endeavor where long-term service is privileged over short-term exploitation.

5. Identify the four emergent qualities of transpersonal CFPs and discuss how they affect their practices.

The four emergent qualities revealed by the CFPs in Snow's (2009) study are: integrity, a holistic client approach, open-mindedness, and inner spiritual guidance. Ironically, even though income was not the primary motivation, rather a natural by-product for the transpersonal CFPs, these practitioners enjoy higher client retention rates resulting in a more predictable income stream. Transpersonal CFPs also report higher job satisfaction and authentic relationships with their clients. These practices create an upward spiral of mutually beneficial relationships between clients and professionals.

CHAPTER 15 ADVISING THE BEHAVIORAL INVESTOR: LESSONS FROM THE REAL WORLD

1. Provide several examples of ways in which investors are their own worst enemies.

Investors jeopardize their long-term investment goals through numerous cognitive and emotional biases. Examples of these include failing to rebalance portfolios, including 401(k) and other retirement accounts; focusing too much on the income that their portfolio generates without giving due consideration to the riskiness of high-yielding assets; and failing to take inflation sufficiently into account when investing. Investors sometimes fail to integrate tax management adequately into their investment portfolios.

2. Explain why investors underperform the actual funds and asset classes in which they are invested.

Investors tend to underperform fund and market returns for several behavioral reasons. First, they attempt to time the market, which generally results in poor performance. Second, investors often sell when markets are falling and buy when markets are rising. Third, they chase hot funds, assuming that strong performance of actively managed funds will persist. Finally, their excessive trading activity reduces returns by increasing losses to taxes and results in higher trading costs.

3. Discuss the meaning of suboptimal investing, provide some examples of suboptimal strategies, and explain why suboptimal may actually be right for some investors.

Suboptimal investing refers to investing that may be less than ideal from the standpoint of modern portfolio theory. Examples of suboptimal investment strategies include dollar-cost averaging instead of lump-sum investing and using variable annuities to replace equity allocations in a portfolio. Such suboptimal strategies, tailored to an individual investor's circumstances, may ultimately provide a better investing experience for an investor by providing more peace of mind and keeping the investor in risky assets for the long term.

4. Discuss how investment advisors can help their "behavioral" clients.

Advisors should understand investor psychology and strive to understand each client's investment experience and risk tolerance. This may require asking questions such as "How would you react if your retirement portfolio declined in value by 40 percent in a market crash?" Instead of stating opinions or acting as if one can predict the future, advisors can show research to clients relevant to their situations. Finally, an effective way to communicate with clients is to relate experiences with other clients who have faced similar life events such as divorce or the loss of a loved one.

5. Indicate some strategies that investors could employ to profit from investor behavior.

Investor behavior is often predictable. Investors may adjust exposure to assets such as equities according to the sentiment of market participants. In other words, investors may adopt contrarian strategies when looking at indicators of investor sentiment such as mutual fund flows and the VIX index of implied volatility. Additionally, investors may embrace a long-term investing strategy of tilting portfolios toward risk factors such as momentum and small-cap and value stocks that have historically rewarded investors with returns in excess of the market's average.

CHAPTER 16 RETIREMENT PLANNING: CONTRIBUTIONS FROM THE FIELD OF BEHAVIORAL FINANCE AND ECONOMICS

1. List and explain some challenges and risks that are unique to the retirement problem.

   Two types of challenges that affect one's retirement saving and planning are behavioral and financial in nature. Behavioral challenges inhibit people from participating and staying in an available retirement plan. Here, the result is having an insufficient amount of funds for retirement. Biases, heuristics, framing, and self-control are among the behavioral factors. Financial challenges include poor asset selection and poor management of funds, among others. Some risks associated with the retirement problem include inflation, institutional/fund insolvency, and investment performance.

2. Referring to the Life Cycle Needs by Age Group Model in Exhibit 16.1, identify where you are on the life cycle and the major life events that you should be planning for in the next five years. Indicate whether you are on track to be able to fund these requirements to the desired level and simultaneously meet your saving objectives for your anticipated retirement date.

   The answer to this question depends on the individual. For example, a person who is 45 would be referring to the following typical major financial decisions at this point in her life cycle: assisting with higher education for children, investing, updating retirement plans, and developing estate plans. The evaluation should consist of comparing how a combination of current savings and the specific plans in place to accumulate future wealth cover these requirements. If a deficiency occurs, what obstacles have contributed to a current or prospective shortfall? Has hyperbolic discounting over-weighted the desire of current consumption and delayed rational savings actions? Has procrastination/status quo bias been a force in delaying systematic rational actions to save more? In sum, are you on track for reserving funds for important events in life on the near term and accumulating wealth for your retirement? What role, if any, have emotions and overconfidence played in avoiding serious retirement planning? Has estate planning incorporated the reality of the natural decline in the quality of financial decision-making after reaching the mid-fifties?

3. Identify several ways to make better decisions about retirement.

- Avoid common behavioral pitfalls such as procrastination, overconfidence, confirmation bias, and home bias as explained in the chapter. Sacrificing present income for future use during retirement is not easy. Yet, envisioning what the picture may look like by not saving enough for retirement makes the decision to save easier.
- Use realistic assumptions about discount rates, life expectancy after retirement, and similar inputs.
- Set aside enough funds each period for investment toward retirement and make sure not to draw down from such savings unless needed for emergencies.

4. Discuss how considering some aspects of trust may help in making better decisions about retirement.

Considering the following aspects of trust may help in making better retirement decisions. First, individuals need to be aware that public trust in markets and financial institutions can be broken at any time. For example, the 2008 great recession resulted in a sizable loss in the value of retirement savings accounts. Such an event highlights the importance of being creative in finding dependable and safer places to invest funds. For example, one possibility would be to invest a portion of funds in alternative assets, including commodities, which are not as exposed to market sentiments as traditional asset classes such as stocks and bonds. Second, individuals need to consider the impact of an abuse of public trust in markets and institutions by dishonest market makers and/or market participants on the different stages on retirement planning. Such awareness may enable exerting even more diligence and care in what and where individuals invest their retirement savings.

CHAPTER 17 KNOWING YOUR NUMBERS: A SCORECARD APPROACH TO IMPROVED MEDICAL AND FINANCIAL OUTCOMES

1. Despite being intuitively appealing, what are some objections to a health scorecard approach?

One of the main criticisms of the scorecard is that it may be an over-simplified approach to chronic disease prevention. The card features indicators reflecting what is considered healthy for the general population. However, after this prototype is generated and in use, further versions can be created and tailored to specific populations. Additionally, another objection is the possibility of a high fallout rate for long-term use, and the question of whether short-term use will be effective in creating changes in health. Yet, even after one use, the tool may be able to educate the user and provide a first step toward a healthy lifestyle.

2. Who should apply a scorecard approach?

Several major stakeholders can drive this approach. Organizations such as the Red Cross are interested in the Take Care Scorecard, to be used by volunteer health care professionals, as a means of quickly evaluating patients' health and targeting interventions to those who are in the greatest need. Governments can also use the scorecard to track the health status of towns, cities, and states, thereby monitoring and targeting public health initiatives for the needs of the population.

3. Discuss whether a scorecard approach is appropriate for financial literacy or whether it is too simplistic.

Like a health literacy scorecard, a financial literacy scorecard can be an important indicator of a person's strengths and weaknesses, and can help to pinpoint the areas in need of further education programs. While a financial scorecard is a simplified approach, when incorporated with other interventions and programs, it can be a powerful tool. Further, individuals who feel inadequate for dealing with financial issues may find the short, user-friendly card less intimidating than lengthier, more thorough materials. The pilot project of the Take Care Scorecard shows that users value the simplicity of the scorecard approach. Additional studies show that even minimal training in personal finance topics may make a difference in outcomes.

4. What concepts should be included in a financial literacy scorecard?

Similar to previous scorecards developed by Lusardi and Mitchell (2005), a financial literacy scorecard should test for understanding of basic concepts, such as inflation, compound interest, risk diversification, and stock risk. Another term to include in the scorecard is annual percentage rate (APR), which is relevant to any credit card. Including APR in the scorecard may help familiarize users with this term, give them a range of what interest rates are or are not acceptable, and perhaps prompt them to further inquire about them.

5. How could a financial literacy scorecard best be used to better a population's understanding of financial concepts?

Once the core concepts to be included in the financial literacy scorecard are defined, it can be a useful tool for educational and monitoring purposes. School systems can add it to their curricula, such as in home economics or personal finance courses. Banks and other financial institutions can post it on their websites for broad distribution. Human resources departments can provide the scorecard to employees, and colleges can use it as material for students to learn financial lessons for life.

CHAPTER 18 RISK PERCEPTION AND RISK TOLERANCE

1. Provide an overview of the traditional finance versus the behavioral finance perspectives of risk.

An important aspect of the traditional finance view is the objective aspects of risk. For example, MPT, the CAPM, and beta are all based on quantitative factors.

The positive relationship between risk and return is a fundamental premise because most investors exhibit risk aversion (i.e., individuals have a fondness for less risk rather than more risk) and make judgments based on perfect rationality (i.e., choosing the optimal outcome). As a result, investors expect a premium for experiencing additional risk.

The behavioral finance perspective of risk is based on both the objective factors (e.g., standard deviation and beta) and subjective issues (e.g., heuristics and emotions) in evaluating risk for a specific financial product or service. A major tenet is the concept of loss aversion in which people assign more weight to losses than they do to gains, and select the satisfactory option although this may not be the optimal choice. An emerging research topic in behavioral finance is the idea of an inverse (negative) relationship between perceived risk and expected return.

2. Provide several definitions of risk perception and risk tolerance.

Risk perception is the subjective decision-making process that people employ when evaluating risk and the degree of uncertainty. Risk perception includes an assortment of quantitative and qualitative factors that influence how investors make choices about financial services and products. A basic definition of risk tolerance is the degree of risk that an investor is willing to accept in the pursuit of an investment objective. However, the research literature documents a wide range of meanings for risk tolerance by various governing bodies such as the SEC and risk experts. For example, the SEC defines risk tolerance as the capacity and willingness to lose a portion or most of one's initial investment in exchange for potentially higher investment returns. International Organization for Standardization (2005) defines risk tolerance as the amount of risk in which a person is willing to encounter a less favorable investment outcome in order to pursue a more favorable investment result. Roszkowski and Davey (2010) define risk tolerance as the degree of risk that an investor is willing to allow in the pursuit of a financial objective. Grable (2008) views risk tolerance as the maximum amount of loss or uncertainty an individual is willing to accept when assessing an investment.

3. List some problems associated with risk tolerance questionnaires.

Some major problems with risk tolerance questionnaires are the lack of conformity for a number of important issues including a basic definition, a standardized theory or academic model, and measurement inconsistencies. Rice (2005) evaluates the characteristics of more than 130 risk questionnaires and identifies additional problems including the large availability of different types of questionnaires along with the wide variability in the format of the actual questions.

4. Discuss the influence of the financial crisis on the risk-taking behavior of investors.

Risk researchers are only now starting to examine and assess the potential long-term influences of the financial crisis of 2008–2009 on investor risk tolerance and perception. The few research studies of the recent economic crisis provide a mixture of different findings. A major concern among the financial planning profession and policy makers is the long-term effects on some investors who are likely to remember this traumatic event during their entire lifetime. This might result in investors being overweighted in bonds and underinvested in stocks because they might have a lower amount of risk tolerance combined with an increasing level of risk perception for equities.

CHAPTER 19 EMOTIONS IN THE FINANCIAL MARKETS

1. Discuss whether emotions enhance or detract from investor decision-making.

The finance literature contains a debate about whether emotions enhance or detract from investor decision-making. For example, Ackert and Deaves (2010) contend that emotions evolved to serve humans in beneficial ways. Emotions may have been particularly useful for our ancestors when confronted with danger (e.g., when facing a bear in the woods), leading to the impulsive fight or flight decision. Ackert and Deaves (2010) relate this primitive emotional instinct to modern-day trading in financial markets, where investors often need to make quick decisions in the face of overwhelming and complex information and extreme time pressures. Some contend that emotions provide the impetus for investors to act.

However, other scholars such as Lerner and Keltner (2001), Lo, Repin, and Steenbarger (2005), and Fenton-O'Creevy et al. (2011) contend that emotions detract from efficient financial decision-making, particularly in complex situations. For example, the affect-infusion model may result in investors taking excessive risk when in a positive mood. Investor anxiety may result in paralysis, inaction, and insufficient risk taking.

Emotions and moods may affect both decision-making and prices in financial markets. For example, emotions and moods could lead investors to react to events unrelated to corporate performance such as sporting events, weather, even phases of the moon. Emotions could also lead to investor over- and underreaction to news and in inefficient herding behavior in the financial markets. Despite this debate, the overall evidence suggests that, on balance, emotions hinder investors in making effective decisions.

2. Discuss the disposition effect and how emotions influence the disposition effect.

The disposition effect describes the empirically observed tendency for investors to sell winning financial securities too quickly and to hold losing investments too long. A prospect theory framework can help justify this behavior. Prospect theory maintains that agents, such as investors, are risk-averse in the positive domain (i.e., when making gains), but are risk-seeking in the negative domain (i.e., when evaluating losses). This explains the disposition effect: Risk-averse investors sell quickly in order to obtain the sure gain, rather than gamble. Yet, in the negative domain, they become risk-seeking by holding losing securities too long in order to gamble, rather than taking the sure loss.

Originally, both prospect theory and the disposition effect were based on preferences and cognition and paid little attention to the effect of emotions. Later, scholars maintained that considering emotions could strengthen the disposition effect. Regret theory (Bell 1982; Loomes and Sugden 1982) suggests anticipated regret strengthens people's risk-seeking behavior in the face of losses. Pride-seeking behavior also strengthens the motivation to sell quickly when making a gain. Summers and Duxbury (2012) provide experimental evidence that pride and regret strengthen the disposition effect.

3. Discuss whether herding behavior in the financial markets is rational.

The finance literature contains a debate about whether herding behavior in the financial markets is rational or irrational. In fact, two classes of herding models exist relating to rational and irrational herding. Rational behavior serves as the basis for the original herding models. The idea is that investors decide sequentially whether to invest or not based on private signals. Sequential decisions to invest reveal private information to all other investors. Hence, if sufficient agents invest, it is rational for subsequent investors to ignore their private signals and invest.

In irrational herding models, investors follow the herd due to cognitive or emotional biases. In Qin's (2012) herding model, the emotion of regret drives investors to exit the market in the face of increased price volatility. This can result in a marketwide cascade, particularly when stock prices are extremely high or low.

In Boswijk, Hommes, and Manzan's (2007) dynamic asset pricing model, heterogeneous investors have different beliefs about the persistence of deviations of stock prices from their fundamental values. This can drive herding. Salzman and Trifan (2005), who also consider this idea, develop a model in which rational and emotional investors coexist and fight for market capital. The authors show that under certain conditions, emotional traders may dominate the market by having a much more developed adaptive mechanism than their rational peers.

Nofsinger (2003) considers the effects of social mood on herding behavior in the financial markets. Redhead (2008) considers the effect of economic, financial, psychological, and sociological factors on the behavior of the financial markets, particularly in the context of the high-tech bubble and crash of the late 1990s and early 2000s. Prechter (2001) discusses the effect of unconscious emotions on herding behavior in the financial markets with particular attention to neuroeconomics. He notes that this emotionally driven herding behavior is irrational. Prechter suggests that a negative feedback loop can occur whereby stress increases impulsive mental activity in financial situations, which results in failure and in turn increases stress. Interestingly, Prechter (p. 120) states that "the interaction of many minds in a collective setting produces super-organic behavior that is patterned according to the survival related functions of the primitive portions of the brain. . . . Patterns of herding behavior will remain immutable."

4. Discuss how the analysis of emotions differs between behavioral finance and emotional finance.

In the behavioral finance framework, scholars focus on conscious emotions. For example, the basis of regret aversion is the idea that investors are aware of regret and can fully anticipate that they would experience regret when selling a losing share. Emotional finance represents a paradigm shift by focusing on unconscious, infantile emotions in a Freudian psychoanalytical framework.

5. Discuss how the emotional finance framework can be used to help explain financial market bubbles and crashes.

Emotional finance provides a unified, Freudian psychoanalytical framework that can explain many of the preceding financial market bubbles and crashes such as the tulip mania, U.S. railroad stocks, Internet stocks, and hedge funds. Emotional finance particularly relates stock market trajectory to investors' unconscious emotional trajectory.

In the emotional finance framework, the emotional roller coaster proceeds as follows. An initial mysterious, magical innovation such as Internet stocks draws the attention of the investing public. This innovation becomes a "phantastic object." In the first stage, investors enter the paranoid-schizoid (PS) phase. They view these investments as infallible and certain to succeed. A mental splitting process occurs where the pain (i.e., the risk associated with the investment) is split from the pleasure (i.e., the excitement of the investment), and the risk is buried deep in the unconscious. Investors fall in love with these investments and value them for their qualities, such as excitement, over and above their financial rewards. Furthermore, investors hold the views of experts, such as financial analysts, academics, and even the press, as sacrosanct. Therefore, in the PS phase, mass buying of the stocks occurs and creates an irrational bubble. Because investors fall in love with the phantastic object and value it much beyond its financial rewards, they are willing to pay "silly money" for their investments, way above fundamental values.

However, at a critical tipping point, nagging doubts emerge. On entering the depressive (D) phase, reality (the painful risk) floods the conscious, and investors are overwhelmed with feelings of hate for the investment. In the D phase, they now revile those whom they viewed as experts in the PS phase. Thus, investors look for scapegoats and blame these experts. Panic occurs, resulting in mass selling. Therefore, the bubble bursts and the market crashes.

6. Explain how emotions might affect managerial behavior in an emotional finance framework.

As emotional finance considers the effect of unconscious emotions and phantasies on investor behavior in the financial markets, emotional corporate finance extends the analysis to consider the effect of managerial unconscious emotions and phantasies on corporate finance decision-making such as investment appraisal, capital structure, and dividend policy. Fairchild's (2009) existing formal modeling framework focuses on investment appraisal. According to Fairchild, just as investors may fall in love with a magical new financial investment opportunity (e.g., high-tech stocks or hedge funds) that they consider to be infallible and mystical, corporate managers may feel the same about new investment projects.

Hence, the managers' emotional trajectory toward the project may be considered using the same framework that Taffler and Tuckett (2005) applied to investors.

CHAPTER 20 HUMAN PSYCHOLOGY AND MARKET SEASONALITY

1. Provide an example of an economic mechanism through which a particular human emotion can affect financial markets. That is, describe in economic terms how a particular emotion may lead to a particular outcome in financial markets.

   Many possible answers are available for this question. For example, research shows that depressed individuals are more averse to financial risk. If a large proportion of investors simultaneously experience increased risk aversion, their willingness to hold risky stock may fall. The result could be increased stock-selling pressure, which would lead directly to a drop in daily stock returns. Alternatively, stock returns could drop even without trades if risk-averse investors simply demand higher returns for holding risky stock in light of their mood.

2. Discuss whether correlation between an environmental factor (such as cloud cover) and stock market index returns implies causation and indicate the implications of your response for behavioral finance researchers.

   Correlation does not imply causation. Hence, behavioral finance researchers need to explore alternative explanations, including rational explanations, before concluding that the evidence is consistent with the possibility that human psychology causes a particular marketwide phenomenon. A feature of social science research is that definitively proving causation can be difficult if not impossible.

3. Identify three financial market regularities that are consistent with mood impacting markets.

   Many financial market regularities may be consistent with mood impacting markets. For example, negative daily returns are correlated with cloudy days in the city of the market, which is consistent with investor misattribution bias. Negative sentiment associated with losses in international sporting events is associated with economically large downturns in that country's stock exchange. Following aviation disasters, negative abnormal returns on aviation stocks are larger than the associated economic losses, which is consistent with investor overreaction.

4. Compare and contrast the traditional economics paradigm with the behavioral finance paradigm concerning the possibility that emotion or mood can affect humans' decisions.

   Classical economics assumes individuals maximize utility. Although most economists broadly consider utility to be a measure of overall happiness, they usually measure utility only on the basis of quantities that relate to wealth and variability in wealth. The traditional economics paradigm does not leave room for the possibility that emotions or mood affect humans' decisions. That is, traditional economics has no role for emotions such as sadness, excitement, or glee to enter into decisions. The newer paradigm of behavioral finance, however, considers the possibility that such characteristics may affect how people make decisions.

CHAPTER 21 NEUROFINANCE

1. As compared to classic studies in behavioral finance, how does neurofinance achieve explanatory power over non-optimal financial decision-making?

   Neurofinance researchers use research tools including neuroimaging, hormone assays, and genetic tests that identify the biological substrates of observed behavior. In particular, many researchers use predictive studies of decision-making, which achieve causative explanatory power (versus correlative analyses). As a result of understanding the biological drivers of suboptimal financial behavior, researchers and others have developed interventions that accommodate or alter the underlying neurobiology of financial decision makers.

2. Biologically speaking, what are some brain structures and chemicals that influence financial decision-making?

   The primary neural motivation systems are the reward approach system, which governs reward valuation and opportunity pursuit, and the loss avoidance system, which motivates threat detection and avoidance. Neurochemicals such as dopamine (excitatory) and serotonin (anxiolytic) can influence financial decision-making. Medications including benzodiazepines and beta blockers and drugs of abuse such as marijuana and alcohol also alter financial risk taking.

3. What techniques, supported by neurofinance, do successful financial practitioners use to improve their performance?

   Neurofinance provides insights into risk-taking behavior, biases, and ideal display of profit/loss information. Self-awareness of thoughts, feelings, life events, and behaviors around the times of best and worse decisions is improved through a meditative practice and keeping a decision journal. Coaches are helpful for reducing short–term arousal and facilitating reframing. Reframing is a cognitive technique by which losses are reframed as positive opportunities to learn. Reappraisal is comprised of a collection of cognitive techniques that expand perspective, thus reducing short-term stress and the biases that are exacerbated by such stress. Adopting a rule-driven process helps decision makers avoid many situations of uncertainty by allowing them to offload responsibility into their rules (rules should be broad and time-tested to avoid overfitting). Information about the profit and loss of positions should not be displayed relative to the purchase price or the entry price.

4. Identify the major criticisms of neurofinance research.

Critics of neurofinance often point to small sample sizes, lack of replication, noisy data (especially in fMRI experimentation), and reductionism in the explanations that result from piecing together disparate research threads.

CHAPTER 22 DIVERSIFICATION AND ASSET ALLOCATION PUZZLES

1. Explain why many households do not participate in the stock market.

Evidence shows that many households do not invest in stocks either directly or indirectly (e.g., through mutual funds or retirement accounts). The most compelling explanation for the limited household participation in the stock market is the existence of fixed participation costs. Such costs include not only brokerage and other pecuniary fees, but also the costs of time required to collect information about mutual funds and monitor investment performance. Other factors can either augment such participation costs or play an independent role in discouraging investors from owning stocks. These factors include low cognitive skills, low financial literacy, limited participation in social activities, ignorance about financial assets, and lack of trust.

2. Discuss how household participation in the stock market changed over time.

Survey data keep track of household asset choices over long periods in time. According to repeated waves from the U.S. Survey of Consumer Finances, the stockholder base expanded during the 1990s. This expansion took place mainly through household investment in stock IRAs. Smaller changes in stock investing occur through mutual funds and brokerage accounts across time.

3. Explain whether households from different countries tend to hold similar portfolios.

The recent availability of survey data from different countries with harmonized information on asset holdings and debts allows large-scale international comparisons in household portfolios. These comparisons show that households in different countries tend to form very heterogeneous portfolios. That is, considerable heterogeneity exists in ownership rates of and amounts invested in stocks, houses, other real estate, and businesses across countries. Recent research finds evidence that this is mainly due to differences in economic environments that households of similar characteristics living in different countries face. The availability of new internationally comparable survey data may help researchers identify factors that drive these differences.

4. Explain why households do not hold diversified portfolios.

Despite the benefits of portfolio diversification being well understood in finance, many households do not hold diversified portfolios. Although limited portfolio diversification is more evident among less educated and less financially sophisticated investors, it is also present in the portfolios of the wealthy. One common case of limited portfolio diversification is the propensity of many investors to concentrate their investments in domestic securities (the so-called home equity bias). Studies show that investors tend to be more optimistic about the prospects of domestic securities but they need to assume additional information and pecuniary costs in order to invest in foreign assets.

5. Discuss how frequently households trade securities.

The vast majority of households exhibit considerable trading inertia. Studies show that most of the households who own IRAs adjust only infrequently the composition of their asset holdings. Researchers link this inertia to investor characteristics such as low resources and education. Yet, a small fraction of investors, mainly consisting of brokerage account owners, trade securities frequently and sometimes experience net losses due to high transaction costs. This selected sample of wealthy investors and their investments through brokerage accounts represents only a small fraction of their total wealth.

CHAPTER 23 BEHAVIORAL PORTFOLIO THEORY AND INVESTMENT MANAGEMENT

1. Describe loss aversion and myopic loss aversion.

People appear to be more reluctant to incur losses compared to gains of the same size—this is known as *loss aversion*. Conforming to the loss aversion, the value function exhibits diminishing sensitivity in both gains and losses domains (i.e., its variation decreases with the magnitude of gains and losses, respectively). A popular extension called *myopic loss aversion* (mLA) relies on the joint effect of loss aversion and narrow framing. The narrow framing represents an aspect of mental accounting that accounts for the tendency to evaluate performance more frequently. This tendency results from the excessive attention paid to financial prospects.

2. Explain the main differences between CPT and SP/A.

The psychological basis of the CPT and SP/A differs. In CPT, the inverse S-shape of the weighting function is interpreted in terms of psychophysics. In SP/A, the inverse S-shape of the weighting function represents a conflict between security and potential. CPT relies on probability weighting to explain risk-averse choice in the loss domain. CPT overweights small probabilities, thereby offsetting the effect of convexity in the utility function. SP/A theory relies on the aspiration point and associated probability threshold. Similar arguments apply to the gains domain.

    The two theories model the attitude toward risk in different ways. In CPT, attitude toward risk is represented by the shape of the utility function. In SP/A theory, utility is linear and the weighting function captures attitude toward risk. In contrast to CPT, the utility function in SP/A has no kink and does not change from strict convexity to strict concavity. In CPT, the degree of curvature to the utility function is mild in both the gain and the loss domains. Although Lopes and Oden (1999) develop SP/A using a linear utility function, they indicate that utility functions exhibit mild concavity in practice.

3. Discuss whether the efficient mean-variance portfolio frontier and the BPT efficient portfolio frontier lead to the same results.

Shefrin and Statman (2000) examine both the BPT efficient frontier and the mean-variance efficient frontier and demonstrate that they generally do not lead to the same results. The reason is that the investors using the mean-variance frontier simply choose their portfolios with respect to the expected returns (mean) and the risk (measured by the variance). In the case of PBT, investors choose portfolios based on expected wealth, need for security and potential, aspiration levels, and the probability of achieving given aspiration levels. Further, in the case of multiple mental accounts (BPT-MA), investors overlook covariances and segregate their portfolios into separate mental account layers. Thus, the optimal portfolios that BPT investors choose differ from those selected under the CAPM.

4. Identify the main differences between the three-factor model and the BAPM.

One major difference between the three-factor model and the BAPM is interpreting the variables. In the context of traditional finance, market capitalization and book-to-market ratios are interpreted as measures of risk. Small-cap stocks and stocks with high book-to-market ratios are considered risky, with high expected returns. However, in the BAPM, capitalization and book-to-market ratios are interpreted as reflections of affect, which is an emotion, and representativeness, which is a cognitive bias. This type of rendition of the three-factor model leads investors to identifying desirable stocks.

CHAPTER 24 POST-CRISIS INVESTOR BEHAVIOR: EXPERIENCE MATTERS

1. Explain the collective memory hypothesis and discuss the evidence that supports it.

The collective memory hypothesis suggests time varying history matters for risk tolerance as the experience of a collective economic shock changes investor behavior. Essentially, investors weight experience over historical passive information. Various researchers provide support for this hypothesis including Malmendier and Nagel (2011, 2012), Nagel (2012), and Schuman and Corning (2012).

2. Discuss the impact of the recent financial crisis on investor behavior.

Although not permanent, the expected long-term impact on risk tolerance is likely to be persistent and negative. The impact, especially on generation

Y (ages 18 to 34), will shift to increased prudence at the expense of return. Equity allocations are likely to decrease while fixed income will increase, which in turn will increase the price of risk reflected in the equity risk premium.

3. Differentiate between collective memories and traditional financial economics.

According to the collective memories hypothesis, historical experiences affect risk tolerance. For example, investor experience affects the equity risk premium. Experiences influence critical period generations more than others and also influence investors' asset allocations. Behavioral experiences, not just fundamental factors, affect asset prices. Additionally, traditional financial economics assumes stable risk tolerance.

4. What general conclusions can be drawn from research on experience?

Information alone is insufficient to change attitudes. Experience is necessary. Experience has the greatest impact on younger individuals given that their beliefs are still flexible and can be changed by experience. History matters because it shapes beliefs and future actions. The likely impact of having lived through the financial crisis on investors, especially younger investors, is a reduction in risk tolerance. This is reflected in their asset allocation decisions, such as in the long-term reduction in generation Y equity allocations. This may increase the equity risk premium and the cost of equity, thereby affecting investments in the real economy.

CHAPTER 25 THE PSYCHOLOGY OF TRADING AND INVESTING

1. Explain the difference between the descriptive psychological perspective to trading and investing and the traditional finance approach.

The normative model of traditional finance is based on how individuals should behave and assumes that participants process information fully and rationally. By contrast, the descriptive approach of decision-making used in psychology explains how market participants form their decisions and how their decisions are systematically biased.

2. Identify five personality traits that professional traders have defined to determine investment success and discuss the role of gender differences.

The five most important personality variables of professional traders are: (1) disciplined cooperation, (2) tackling decisions, (3) market meaning making, (4) emotional stability, and (5) information processing. Although general investment success cannot be attributed to gender differences, evidence shows that men are more risk-seeking and overconfident than women.

3. Discuss why some traders cannot make rational decisions and the impact of affective and cognitive biases.

Some traders may be unable to make rational decisions because they require objective and complete information and cannot treat such information in an unbiased way. Phenomena including the status quo tendency, endowment effect, overconfidence, empathy or even mortality salience may affectively influence decision-making processes. Traders may also base their judgment on heuristics (rules of thumb) and behave differently in gain or loss situations. Here, affect and cognition closely interact.

4. Outline which phenomena on a societal level influence trading and investing behavior.

Herding processes can explain many processes in financial markets such as extreme exchange rate volatility. Participants who imitate the behavior of others instead of processing market information independently endorse existing market trends. Further, social and ethical norms that define how market participants should behave may shape investment behavior.

5. Discuss aspects on a macro level that may influence investment decisions.

Traders face a plethora of market information from diverse news sources and need to develop their own system of filtering such information. Often, the basis for their selection is psychological rather than economic or rational. Rumors provide a powerful source of information and can lead decision makers away from trustworthy information. Traders can use the general market mood (e.g., produced through a national financial crisis) to judge their own personal investment success.

CHAPTER 26 THE SURPRISING REAL WORLD OF TRADERS' PSYCHOLOGY

1. Identify the key new, emerging concepts involving perception, judgment, and risk decision-making under uncertainty.

Cognition or thinking emerges from a combination of the body, the brain, and what people experience as emotions. Bodily and visceral changes can change perception. Flexing muscles, for example, can increase a feeling of willpower. Feeling or affective states unconsciously color perceptions and therefore traders' decisions. Repetitive interpretations and behavior during trading may be fractal in that the subjective experience during trading reveals essentially a reenactment of assumptions learned earlier in life.

2. Explain why Trader W insisted that a checklist would be the solution to behavioral risk management and why having a checklist was insufficient to change his behavior.

Although W initially agreed that understanding the unconscious affective context supporting his unwanted trading behaviors could lead to better decisions and improved performance, he initially resisted attempts to analyze his emotions.

This was partly due to his limited ability to identify and differentiate his emotions (e.g., only being able to say, "It's extreme") in his attempt to clarify what facing a loss feels like. The checklist provided an intellectual tool that he expected he could achieve perfection on, somewhat like a quiz. The checklist did not work because it did not address the source of his impulsive trading decisions.

3. Why did the meeting with the large potential investor represent an important development in W's performance?

The meeting dynamics played directly into W's need for personal validation. His performance in the meeting was his behavioral expression of his need to be seen as perfect and a potential hero. For W, these desires reveal a partially unconscious and probably fractal belief that being perfect will secure acceptance and approval.

4. How did biofeedback assist Trader Q in becoming a more proficient trader?

By displaying the physiological signs of anxiety and fear on a chart similar to data displays Q used, HRV information informed him of when he was becoming particularly fearful. With this information, he could employ breathing techniques to alter his physiological state that in turn created a different subjective and possibly even unconscious affective experience. In practicality, this translates into a feeling of confidence and safety, which in turn supports more objective perceptions and reduces trading decisions that previously were mostly expressions of fear.

CHAPTER 27 TRADING AND INVESTMENT STRATEGIES IN BEHAVIORAL FINANCE

1. Explain why momentum-based strategies may persistently generate excess returns.

Momentum is consistent with the overreaction bias in the behavioral finance literature. Investors often mimic what other investors are doing. Momentum may also add value due to the way news makes its way into stock prices. In some instances, investors bring news to the attention of reporters and therefore legally trade on news before it is published. In other instances, investors illegally trade on inside information and leave "footprints" in the price action of security prices. Other investors may note this abnormal buying and push prices up or down further. Margin calls may also play a role in momentum. A losing investment on the long side may result in the forced sale of securities and further depress prices. Similarly, a losing investment on a short sale position may result in a short squeeze, causing a further rise in prices. Lastly, successful fund managers often receive cash inflows. In many instances they buy (short sell) their existing holdings and push prices higher (lower).

2. Explain how behavioral finance may do a better job at explaining the existence and popping of asset pricing bubbles than the EMH.

The EMH does not permit market bubbles. The strong form of the EMH states that security prices reflect all available information. According to behavioral finance, irrational pricing may periodically persist in securities prices. Recent examples of market bubbles over the past two decades include the Internet stock bubble and the real estate bubble. Microstrategy was one example from the Internet bubble. Microstrategy went from roughly $25 per share shortly after its IPO in mid-1998 to $3,500 a share at the peak of the Internet bubble in March of 2000. It ultimately crashed to $4 a share and rebounded to $108 in March 2013. Behavioral finance can easily explain these dramatic movements, while the EMH has to go through contortions to argue that Microstrategy's stock moved in a rational manner.

3. Explain why no unified model of behavioral finance exists akin to the CAPM.

According to the CAPM, which is an outgrowth of Markowitz portfolio theory, investors are rational mean-variance maximizers. The behavioral finance literature documents many instances in which investors deviate from this behavior. For example, well-known biases in this literature include overreaction, underreaction, and momentum. The chapter discusses several investment anomalies including momentum, earnings surprises, and accruals. These variables are not part of the CAPM. Because investors have many biases, which they do not consistently follow, and do not always behave rationally, developing a single unified model would be extremely difficult.

4. Using concepts from behavioral finance, discuss why many investors pursue active management despite most studies finding that index funds outperform the vast majority of active fund managers over time.

Many investors believe that behavioral biases exist in the aggregate, but that they do not apply them. Investors of this mindset, who lack superior financial skills, may be subject to the optimism and overconfidence biases. The rewards for active investing are potentially great. This equivalent of a lottery ticket may entice investors to pursue active strategies even in the absence of true investment talent.

Conversely, some investors possess superior investment talent. Famous investors such as Warren Buffett and George Soros have consistently earned superior returns over long periods of time and their success gives optimism to other active investors. Successful asset management firms, such as LSV Asset Management and Fuller and Thaler, rely on principles from behavioral finance. Hence, investors who are highly knowledgeable of the behavioral finance literature may be able to outperform index funds if they can develop and successfully apply behaviorally based investment strategies.

5. Make an analogy between the human genome and list of biases found in the behavioral finance literature. Discuss how analysts analyzing securities may be similar in some respects to doctors analyzing diseases.

Doctors must diagnose patients based on incomplete information such as vital signs, blood tests, and personal genomes. An individual may be susceptible to a specific disease based on his genetic makeup, but something, such as an environmental trigger, must activate it. Investment analysts also must make decisions, such as determining whether to buy, sell, and hold an asset and setting set portfolio weights, based on incomplete information. Behavioral biases are similar to environmental factors that may cause prices to deviate from purely rational values. Successful investment analysts may be able to analyze the fundamental and technical aspects of securities as well as the behavioral factors that ultimately influence their prices.

CHAPTER 28 ETHICAL AND SOCIALLY RESPONSIBLE INVESTING

1. Identify and discuss potential implications and challenges of the 2008–2009 world financial crisis on FSR.

The 2008–2009 world financial crisis highlighted the importance of social responsibility for the functioning of market economies. In the aftermath of the 2008–2009 financial turmoil, FSR appears as an essential component for the well-functioning of economic markets and SRI as a means to avert future financial crises. To better understand social responsibility as an economic market prerequisite, future research may capture socio-psychological motives of FSR. Understanding SRI may help to resolve societal losses imbued in the novelty and complexity of FSR. Access to information on SRI will help inform asset managers and financial analysts about the link between CSR and SRI in order to aid financial institutions in considering environmental and social responsibility. Outlining SRI as a market choice with tangible and intangible investment advantages may lead financial advisers to incorporate environmental and social corporate governance in their portfolio allocation strategies. Advocating a successful rise of social responsibility within modern market economies is aimed at SRI becoming a mainstream feature of financial decision-making. This may entire market industries onto a more socially conscientious level while serving the greater goal of fostering positive societal change.

2. Identify several examples of ethical investing and SRI.

Screenings serve as a means of examining the corporate economic performance and social responsibility of corporations. Screenings emphasize corporations with sound social and environmental records that pay attention to human rights and labor standards, equal opportunities, environmental protection, consumer safety, community concerns, and stakeholder relations. Screenings exclude corporations contributing to socially irresponsible activities such as addictive products and services, defense, environmentally hazardous production, and humanitarian deficiencies. Political divestiture removes assets from politically incorrect governments violating ethical and legal international standards. Shareholder advocacy and activism is the active engagement of shareholders in corporate policy and managerial decision-making. investing features direct investments and investor set-asides for unserved and underserved low-income groups.

3. Discuss the performance of SRI funds relative to conventional mutual funds.

Empirical investigations of the relationship between SRI and profitability offer no stringent pattern because some studies find SRI outperforming the market, others underperforming the market, and some report no difference between SRI and conventional market indices. The inconsistent findings are attributed to manifold SRI expression forms. Positively screened SRI options tend to be more volatile, yet if successful, grant high profitability. Negatively screened options are more likely to underperform the market but also more robust to overall market changes. Political divestiture appears to hold a first mover advantage for early divestiture. Overall, SRI implies short-term expenditures, but grants long-term sustainable investment streams. Cognitive decision-making errors, such as anchoring and representativeness biases, may lead to a natural propensity to undervalue SRI funds' performance. Due to loss aversion, negative SRI performance may stay more vividly in investors' memories.

4. Identify where SRI is practiced and explain how.

SRI is practiced throughout the international arena. In the Western world, SRI has primarily been adopted in Central Europe and Anglo-Saxon markets. While Anglo-Saxon countries, such as the United States and the United Kingdom, are prominent for private investments, European financial systems are renowned for governmental and institutional banking. Common law Anglo-Saxon countries including the United States, Canada, Australia, and the United Kingdom are more liberal in institutionalizing SRI. Anglo-Saxon fiduciary responsibility focuses on return on investment, while western European Roman law-dominated territories grant fiduciaries more leeway in considering the overall societal impact of the asset-issuing entities. Civil law countries such as central European countries are prone to emphasize stakeholder participation in corporate governance.

Today, the United States features the broadest variety of SRI options and socially responsible performance measurement indices. In Canada, legal obligations require corporate directors and officers to act in the best interest of the entity with attention to stakeholders. Incorporating corporate social conduct in institutional investments is prominent in Europe. Australian corporate law requires corporate managers to make decisions in the best interest of the corporation. In emerging markets, SRI drives international development through community investing, microfinance, and enterprise development through social entrepreneurs. In the developing world, SRI varies across countries and corporate laws are often not well-enforced.

5. Identify who attempts to harmonize SRI practices.

International organizations harmonize differing SRI practices throughout the world. International organizations align SRI practices by defining FSR standards and guiding the SRI implementation from a global governance perspective. Transnational entities play a pivotal role in institutionally supporting FSR and streamlining disparate SRI practices. The United Nations (UN) leads the international public administration of financial social responsibility with its Principles for Responsible Investment (PRI) and the Responsible Investment in Emerging Markets Initiative. Subsequently responding to rising SRI trends all over the world, the UNGC division and the UN Environment Programme (UNEP) Finance Initiative launched the Principles for Responsible Investment (PRI) in collaboration with the New York Stock Exchange (NYSE). The UN Conference on Trade and Development (UNCTAD) founded the Responsible Investment in Emerging Markets initiative at the Geneva PRI office in order to promote transparency and disclosure for the integration of environmental, social, and corporate governance in emerging markets.

CHAPTER 29 MUTUAL FUNDS AND INDIVIDUAL INVESTORS: ADVERTISING AND BEHAVIORAL ISSUES

1. What is behavioral persuasion in advertising designed to do?

   Behavioral persuasion in fund advertising is designed to influence investor choices by tapping into their current beliefs. For example, Wilcox (2003) notes highly educated, wealthier, and male investors are less successful in making fund choices than are less sophisticated investors, and give less emphasis to expense ratios.

2. Explain why affect refers to investor emotions that change fund choices.

   Positive emotions lead to riskier and more confident choices and negative emotions lead to more risk-averse choices. Current beliefs are updated to maintain positive affect and to avoid negative affect, and new information is rejected that disagrees with past fund choices.

3. Explain the focus of behavioral finance.

   Behavioral finance focuses on financial markets and gaps between market efficiency and market reality. Behavioral theories are based on investor revealed preferences and choices that are rarely fully rational.

4. Explain why financial literacy is likely key to understanding investing.

   Unsophisticated investors depend on fund advertising and invest in actively managed funds, which is a failed strategy. Financially literate investors tend to be overconfident in their own abilities and believe they make better fund choices. However, most of the time this does not result in higher investment returns.

5. Explain why fund pricing decisions are a strategic response to investor sensitivity to expenses in conjunction with their sensitivity to past performance.

   Investor performance sensitivity increases with past performance but price sensitivity does not. Price sensitivity increases with past performance for lower performing funds but decreases for higher performing funds. For lower performing funds, investor flows become more sensitive to past performance and to prices. For higher performing funds, an increase in investor performance sensitivity is joined by a decrease in investor flow sensitivity to expenses. The latter investors are distracted by prospective fund performance and ignore expenses.

6. Why do mutual funds follow a "camouflage strategy" that loads up on sentiment risk that investors interpret as real performance?

This "sentiment contrarian behavior" (SCB) is related to performance and is a deliberate fund choice. Funds reduce sentiment risk when market sentiment is high anticipating a market decline. This strategy does not provide investors with abnormal returns net of sentiment risk. Funds with high SCB do not outperform after controlling for the nonlinear loading on sentiment risk. Investor flows increase because the market does not recognize sentiment risk and compensates this risk as a "sort of performance."

CHAPTER 30 REAL ESTATE INVESTMENT DECISION-MAKING IN BEHAVIORAL FINANCE

1. Discuss why limits to arbitrage are severe in the real estate market.

Limits to arbitrage are severe in the real estate market because transaction costs are very high and the market is characterized by extremely illiquid assets that are rarely bought and sold. Real estate properties are also unique and indivisible. Finally, short selling is not feasible in most real estate assets.

2. Explain why real estate market participants are likely to be overconfident and how overconfidence can lead to overvaluations.

The majority of the participants in the residential real estate market and even a large portion of commercial real estate investors are not professional investors. This implies that most real estate participants have limited experience with buying and selling real estate. Several studies in behavioral finance document that experience and overconfidence are negatively related, so that the more experience the investors gain, the less subject to overconfidence bias they become. This is because the more experienced investors can better understand their own abilities, whereas inexperienced participants often suffer from overconfidence and place large weight on their own (limited) past experience rather than on a larger and more inclusive sample. An inexperienced individual who recently sold her property for a large nominal profit, compared with the purchase price, is likely to display a high level of confidence when searching for her next real estate property. As a result, she is likely to overpay for that property, which in aggregate can lead to overvaluation.

3. What other psychological biases besides overconfidence influence real estate market participants' decision-making?

The real estate market reflects many psychological biases besides overconfidence that influence decision-making by market participants, including:

Mental accounting. Mental accounting is especially prevalent in real estate because it often represents a large share of someone's wealth. Also, many real estate owners attach a subjective and sentimental value to this portion of their portfolio.

Familiarity bias. The difficulty of accessing real estate from a distance only magnifies the already substantial local and familiarity bias that real estate participants display. This is because most are reluctant to purchase a property in a distant and unfamiliar location regardless of the opportunities presented by that location.

False reference point. When real estate owners consider selling their property, an irrelevant false reference point often influences their reservation price. Such false reference points include the price they paid for the property, the price of a previously sold neighboring property, or the outstanding balance on their mortgage.

Loss aversion. Loss aversion or the disposition effect partly explains the documented strong positive correlation between housing prices and sales volume. Homeowners facing a loss are often reluctant to sell properties whose current market prices are less than what they initially paid.

Ownership bias. Ownership bias suggests that homeowners are willing to pay a high premium for owning rather than renting a home. Homeowners pay the highest premium over renters in areas that experienced the highest price appreciation in the past. This behavior indicates that homeowners are projecting higher future price appreciation for the already most expensive and least affordable areas rather than more rational expectations of a general reversion to the mean.

4. Which behavioral biases likely drove the overreaction in real estate prices that took place from 2007 to 2012?

During the bear market, many buyers suffered great losses and exited the market completely. The feeling of pessimism and a fear-fueled negative momentum drove prices arguably far below their fundamental values. A possible explanation for this overreaction is that many homeowners used the price for which they purchased their house or the value of their house at the peak of the housing market as a false reference point. Thus, homeowners who did not have to sell their houses refused to do so at fair market prices. Loss aversion combined with a false reference point of the market peak values likely caused prices to fall below fundamental values. Also, mental accounting can be linked to the periods of overreaction in the housing markets. Homeowners who move away from holding real estate in isolation toward holding real estate as a part of their portfolio tend to be more willing to sell their real estate for a loss. Conversely, when individuals view real estate in isolation, they are less likely to recognize their losses.

Index

Printed and bound by CPI Group (UK) Ltd, Croydon, CR0 4YY

23/04/2025

14660928-0003